Stalin's
Daughter

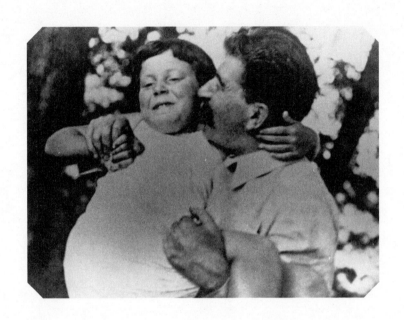

Stalin's Daughter

The Extraordinary and Tumultuous
Life of Svetlana Alliluyeva

Rosemary Sullivan

HARPER

An Imprint of HarperCollins*Publishers*

HarperCollins books may be purchased for educational, business, or sales pro-
motional use. For information, please e-mail the Special Markets Department
at SPsales@harpercollins.com.

FIRST EDITION

*Frontispiece: Eight-year-old Svetlana with her father, Joseph Stalin, on vacation in
Sochi.*

Library of Congress Cataloging-in-Publication Data

Sullivan, Rosemary.

Stalin's daughter : the extraordinary and tumultuous life of Svetlana Alliluyeva
/ Rosemary Sullivan. — First edition.

pages cm

Includes bibliographical references.

ISBN 978-0-06-220610-7

1. Allilueva, Svetlana, 1926–2011. 2. Children of heads of state—Soviet
Union—Biography. 3. Stalin, Joseph, 1879–1953—Family. 4. Stalin, Joseph,
1879–1953—Influence. 5. Soviet Union—History—1925–1953—Biography.
6. Immigrants—United States—Biography. 7. Defectors—United States—
Biography. I. Title.

DK275.A4S85 2015

947.084'2092—dc23

[B] 2014045982

15 16 17 18 19   OV/RRD   10 9 8 7 6 5 4 3 2 1

For my mother,
Leanore Marjorie Guthrie Sullivan

Contents

PART TWO: The Soviet Reality

—————

PART THREE: Flight to America

—————

PART FOUR: Learning to Live in the West

—————

Djugashvili Family Tree

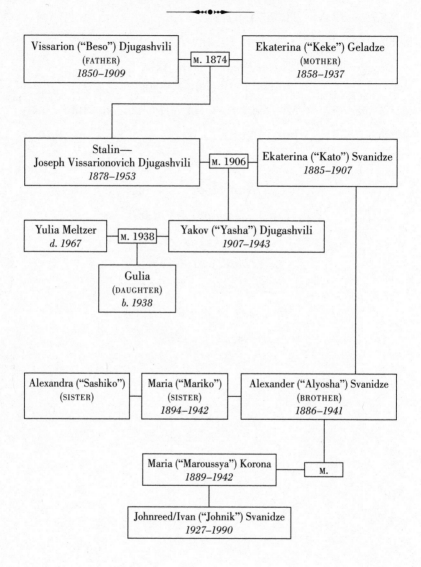

ALLILUYEV FAMILY TREE

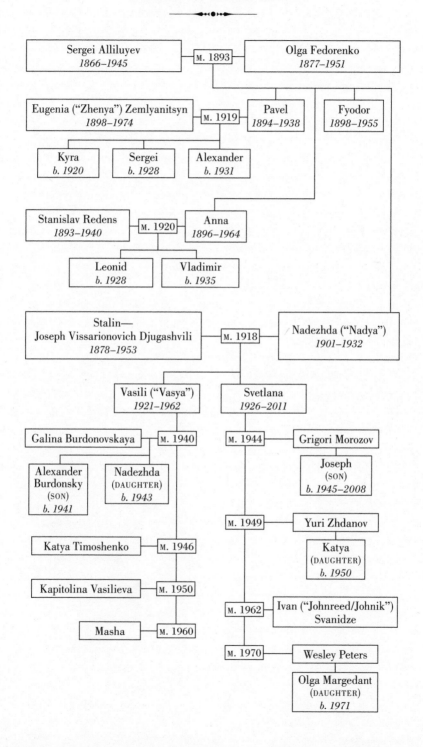

Preface

What would it mean to be born Stalin's daughter, to carry the weight of that name for a lifetime and never be free of it? In the USSR, Stalin was mythic. He was the *vozhd*, the supreme leader who built the Soviet Union into a superpower and won the war against the Nazis. To his millions of Soviet victims, however, he was the man responsible for the Terror and the infamous Gulag. In the West, he was widely demonized as one of the world's most brutal dictators. Try as she might, Svetlana Alliluyeva could never escape Stalin's shadow. As she lamented, "Wherever I go, whether to Australia or some island, I will always be the political prisoner of my father's name."[1]

In the USSR, her life was unimaginably painful. Her mother, Nadezhda Alliluyeva, committed suicide when Svetlana was only six and a half. In the purges of the Great Terror in the late 1930s, Stalin did not spare his family. Her beloved Aunt Maria and Uncle Alexander Svanidze, the brother and sister-in-law of Stalin's first wife, were arrested and executed as enemies of the people; their son Johnik, her childhood playmate, disappeared. Uncle Stanislav Redens, the husband of her mother's sister Anna, was executed. Uncle Pavel, her mother's brother, died of a heart attack brought on by shock. When she'd just turned seventeen, her father sentenced her first love, Aleksei Kapler, to the Gulag for ten years. The Nazis killed her half brother Yakov in a prisoner-of-war camp in 1943. In 1947 and 1948, during the wave of repression known as the Anti-Cosmopolitan Campaign, her mother's sister Anna and Pavel's widow, Zhenya, were sentenced to seven years in solitary confinement. Zhenya's daughter Kyra was imprisoned and then exiled.

After her father's death in 1953, the tragedies continued. Her elder brother, Vasili, was arrested and eventually died of alcoholism in 1962. Her literary friends in the mid-1960s were sent to forced-labor camps. When she finally found peace in a loving relationship with a man named Brajesh Singh, she was officially refused the right to marry him before he died, though she was given official permission to carry his ashes back to India.

In the middle of her life, at the age of forty-one, Svetlana Alliluyeva decided, impulsively, to defect. On the evening of March 6, 1967, she walked into the American Embassy in New Delhi requesting asylum. This was both an escape from her past and a search for the freedom denied to her in the Soviet Union, where she claimed that she was treated like government property. The American State Department initially refused her entry into the United States on the grounds that her defection would destabilize relations with the Soviets. She waited in Switzerland as diplomats searched for a country to take her.

When she was finally allowed into the United States on a tourist visa, Americans greeted her as the most famous defector ever to leave the USSR. She was soon the *millionaire* defector—*Twenty Letters to a Friend*, the memoir she had written in 1963 and carried out of the Soviet Union, was bought for an advance payment of $1.5 million. But she did not understand the concept of money; she gave away much of it and soon lost the rest to the manipulations of Olgivanna Wright, the widow of Frank Lloyd Wright, who lured her into marriage with Wesley Peters, the head architect of Wright's Taliesin Foundation. At the age of forty-five, Alliluyeva gave birth to Olga Peters. Her daughter was a consolation. She had abandoned her twenty-one-year-old son, Joseph, and sixteen-year-old daughter, Katya, when she fled the Soviet Union. KGB intrigues prevented her from contacting them for the next fifteen years.

Her laconic humor helped. She could say, "I don't any longer have the pleasant illusion that I can be free of the label 'Stalin's daughter.' . . . You can't regret your fate, though I do regret my mother didn't marry a carpenter."[2] She spent most of her forty-four years in the West as a nomad, moving over thirty times, even briefly defecting back to the Soviet Union.

She was called unstable. The historian Robert Tucker remarked that "despite everything, she was, in some sense, like her father."[3] And yet it's astonishing how *little* she resembled her father. She did not believe in violence. She had a risk taker's resilience, a commitment to life, and an unexpected optimism, even though her life spanned the brutalities of the twentieth century in the most heartrending of ways, giving her a knowledge of the dark side of human experience, which few people are ever forced to confront. Caught between two worlds in the Cold War power struggles between East and West, she was served well by neither side. She had to slowly learn how the West functioned. The process of her education is fascinating and often sad.

Alliluyeva had as much trouble explaining her father as anyone else did. Her attitude toward Stalin was paradoxical. She unequivocally rejected his crimes, yet he was the father who, in her childhood memory, was loving—until he wasn't. She sought, with only partial success, to understand what motivated his brutal policies. "I don't believe he ever suffered any pangs of conscience; I don't think he ever experienced them. But he was not happy, either, having reached the ultimate in his desires by killing many, crushing others, and being admired by some."[4]

However, she warned that to dismiss him as simply monstrous would be a grave error. The question is what happens to a human being in his private life and within a particular political system that dictates such a history. She always insisted that her father never acted alone. He had thousands of accomplices.

Svetlana Alliluyeva imagined that in the West she could construct a private life as a writer and find someone with whom she could share it. Despite valiant efforts, she believed she had failed, though others are not so sure. It's astonishing that she survived at all.

Stalin's Daughter

━━━

The Defection

At 7:00 p.m. on March 6, 1967, a taxi drew up to the open gates of the American Embassy on Shantipath Avenue in New Delhi. Watched carefully by the Indian police guard, it proceeded slowly up the circular drive. The passenger in the backseat looked out at the large circular reflecting pool, serene in the fading light. A few ducks and geese still floated among the jets of water rising from its surface. The embassy's exterior walls were constructed of pierced concrete blocks, which gave the building a light, airy look. The woman noted how different this was from the stolid institutional Soviet Embassy she had just left. So this was America.

Svetlana Alliluyeva climbed the wide steps and stared at the American eagle embedded in the glass doors. All the important decisions of her life had been taken precipitately. Once she crossed this threshold, she knew that her old life would be irrevocably lost to her. She had no doubt that the wrath of the Kremlin would soon fall on her head. She felt defiant. She felt terrified. She'd made the most important decision of her life; she'd escaped, but into what she had no idea. She did not hesitate. Clutching her small suitcase in one hand, she rang the bell.

Danny Wall, the marine guard on desk duty, opened the door. He looked down at the small woman standing before him. She was middle-aged, neatly dressed, nondescript. He was about to tell her the embassy was closed when she handed him her passport. He blanched. He locked the door behind her and led her to a small adjacent room. He then phoned Robert Rayle, the second secretary of the embassy, who was in charge of walk-ins—defectors. Rayle had been out, but when he returned the call minutes later, Wall gave him the secret code indicating the embassy had a Soviet defector, the last thing Rayle was expecting on a quiet Monday evening in the Indian capital.

When Rayle arrived at the embassy at 7:25, he was pointed to a room where a woman sat talking with Consul George Huey. She turned to Rayle as he entered, and almost the first thing she said to him was: "Well, you probably won't believe this, but I'm Stalin's daughter."[1]

Rayle looked at the demure, attractive woman with copper hair and pale blue eyes who stared steadily back at him. She did not fit his image of Stalin's daughter, though what that image was, he could not have said. She handed him her Soviet passport. At a quick glance, he saw the name: Citizeness Svetlana Iosifovna Alliluyeva. Iosifovna was the correct patronymic, meaning "daughter of Joseph." He went through the possibilities. She could be a Soviet plant; she could be a counteragent; she could be crazy. George Huey asked, nonplussed, "So you say your father was Stalin? *The* Stalin?"[2]

As the officer in charge of walk-ins from the Soviet bloc, Rayle was responsible for confirming her authenticity. After a brief interview, he excused himself and went to the embassy communications center, where he cabled headquarters in Washington, demanding all files on Svetlana Iosifovna Alliluyeva. The answer came back one hour later: "No traces." Headquarters knew nothing at all about her—there were no CIA files, no FBI files, no State Department files. The US government didn't even know Stalin *had* a daughter.[3]

While he waited for a response from Washington, Rayle interrogated Svetlana. How did she come to be in India? She claimed that she had left the USSR on December 19 on a ceremonial mission. The Soviet government had given her special permission to travel to India to scatter the ashes of her "husband," Brajesh Singh, on the Ganges in his village— Kalakankar, Uttar Pradesh—as Hindu tradition dictated. She added bitterly that because Singh was a foreigner, Aleksei Kosygin, chairman of the Council of Ministers, had personally refused her request to marry him, but after Singh's death, she was permitted to carry his ashes to India. In the three months she'd spent here, she'd fallen in love with the country and asked to be allowed to stay. Her request was denied. "The Kremlin considers me state property," she said with disgust. "I am Stalin's daughter!" She told Rayle that, under Soviet pressure, the Indian government had refused to extend her visa. She was fed up with being treated like a "national relic." She would not go back to the USSR. She looked firmly at Rayle and said that she had come to the American Embassy to ask the US government for political asylum.[4]

So far, Rayle could conclude only that this utterly calm woman believed what she was saying. He immediately understood the political implications if her story was true. If she really was Stalin's daughter, she was Soviet *royalty*. Her defection would be a deep psychological blow to the Soviet government, and it would make every effort to get her back. The American Embassy would find itself in the midst of a political maelstrom.[5]

Rayle remained suspicious. He asked her why her name wasn't Stalina or Djugashvili, her father's surname. She explained that in 1957 she had changed her name from Stalina to Alliluyeva, the maiden name of her mother, Nadezhda, as was the right of every Soviet citizen.

He then asked where she had been staying. "At the Soviet

Embassy guesthouse," she replied, only several hundred yards away. How had she managed to slip away from the Soviet Embassy without being noticed? he asked. "They are having a huge reception for a visiting Soviet military delegation and the rest of them are celebrating International Women's Day," she replied. He then asked her how much time she had before her absence at the guesthouse would be noticed. She might have about four hours, she explained, since everyone would be drunk. Even now she was expected at the home of T. N. Kaul, the former Indian ambassador to the USSR. She said in sudden panic: "I really have to call his daughter, Preeti, to let her know I'm not coming."[6]

For Rayle this was a small test. He replied, "OK, let me dial the number for you." He searched for the number, dialed, and handed her the phone. He listened as she explained to T. N. Kaul and to his daughter that she had a headache and wasn't going to make it for dinner. She said her affectionate good-byes to both.[7]

Then she passed Rayle a battered sheaf of paper. It was a Russian manuscript titled *Twenty Letters to a Friend* and bearing her name as author. She explained that it was a personal memoir about growing up inside the Kremlin. Ambassador Kaul, whom she and Brajesh Singh had befriended in Moscow, had carried the manuscript safely out of the USSR a year ago January. As soon as she'd arrived in New Delhi, he returned it to her. This was astonishing: Stalin's daughter had written a book. What might it reveal about her father? Rayle asked if he could make a copy of it, and she assented.

Following his advice as to the wording, she then wrote out a formal request for political asylum in the United States and signed the document. When Rayle warned her that, at this point, he could not definitely promise her asylum, Svetlana demonstrated her political shrewdness. She replied that "if the

United States could not or would not help her, she did not believe that any other country represented in India would be willing to do so." She was determined not to return to the USSR, and her only alternative would be to tell her story "fully and frankly" to the press in the hope that she could rally public support in India and the United States.[8] The refusal to protect Stalin's daughter would not play well back home. Svetlana understood how political manipulation worked. She'd had a lifetime of lessons.

Rayle led Svetlana to a room on the second floor, handed her a cup of tea and some aspirins for the splitting headache she'd developed, and suggested she write a declaration—a brief biography and an explanation of why she was defecting. At this point, he excused himself again, saying he had to consult his superiors.

The US ambassador, Chester Bowles, was ill in bed that night, so Rayle walked the ten minutes to his home in the company of the CIA station chief. Ambassador Bowles would later admit that he had not wanted to meet Svetlana personally on the chance that she was simply a nutcase. With Bowles's special assistant Richard Celeste in attendance, the men discussed the crisis. Rayle and his superiors realized there was not going to be enough time to determine Svetlana's bona fides in New Delhi before the Soviets discovered she was missing. Bowles believed that the Soviet Union had so much leverage on the government of India, which it was supplying with military equipment, that if it found out Svetlana was at the US Embassy, Indian forces would demand her expulsion. The embassy would have to get her out of India.

At 9:40 p.m., a second flash cable was sent to headquarters in Washington with a more detailed report,[9] stating that Svetlana had four hours before the Soviet Embassy noted her absence. The message concluded, "Unless advised to the contrary we will try to get Svetlana on Qantas Flight 751 to Rome leaving Delhi at 1945Zulu (1:15 AM local time)." Eleven minutes later, Washington acknowledged receipt of the cable.[10]

The men discussed their options. They could refuse Svetlana help and tell her to return to her embassy, where it was unlikely her absence had been noticed. But she'd made it clear she would go to the international press with the story. They could keep her in Roosevelt House or in the chancery, inform the Indians that she'd asked for asylum in the United States, and await a court decision. The problem with this option was that the Indian government might take Svetlana back by force. The embassy could try to spirit her out of India covertly. None of these were good options.

The deciding factor was that Svetlana had her Soviet passport in her possession. This was unprecedented. The passports of Soviet citizens traveling abroad were always confiscated and returned to them only as they boarded their flights home. That afternoon the Soviet ambassador to India, I. A. Benediktov, had held a farewell luncheon for Svetlana. It was a grim affair. He was furious with her because she had delayed her departure from India long past the one month authorized by her Russian visa, and Moscow was now demanding her return. She was compromising his career. She would be getting on that flight back to Moscow on March 8.

"Well, if I must leave," she'd said, "where's my passport?" Benediktov had snarled to his aide: "Give it to her."[11] Here Svetlana showed she truly was Stalin's daughter. When she demanded something, she was not to be refused. Benediktov had made a huge mistake that he would pay for later. For the Soviets, Svetlana was the most significant defector ever to leave the USSR.

Sitting in his sickbed, Chester Bowles made a decision. With her Indian papers in order and her Russian passport,

Svetlana could openly and legally leave India. He ordered a US B-2 tourist visa stamped in her passport. It would have to be renewed after six months. He asked Bob Rayle if he would take her out of India. Rayle agreed. The men returned to the embassy.[12]

It was 11:15 p.m. As they prepared to leave for the airport, Rayle turned to Svetlana. "Do you fully understand what you are doing? You are burning all your bridges." He asked her to think this over carefully. She replied that she had already had a lot of time to think. He handed her $1,500 from the embassy's discretionary funds to facilitate her arrival in the United States.

She was led down a long corridor to an elevator that descended to the embassy garage. Clutching her small suitcase, which contained her manuscript and a few items of clothing, she climbed into a car. A young marine sergeant and the embassy Soviet affairs specialist, Roger Kirk, recently back from Moscow, climbed in beside her. They smiled. It was electrifying to be sitting next to Stalin's daughter. She wondered, "Why did Americans smile so often? Was it out of politeness or because of a gay disposition?" Whatever it was, she, who had never been "spoiled with smiles," found it pleasant![13]

Rayle phoned his wife, Ramona, to ask her to pack his bags for a trip of several days and to meet him at Palam airport in one hour. He did not tell her where he was going. He then went to the Qantas Airlines office and bought two first-class open tickets to the United States, with a stopover in Rome. He soon joined the other Americans at the airport—by now there were at least ten embassy staff members milling about in the relatively deserted terminal, but only two sat with Svetlana.[14]

Svetlana easily passed through Indian customs and immigration and, in five minutes, with a valid Indian exit visa and her US visitor's visa, joined Rayle in the international departure lounge. When Rayle asked her if she was nervous, she replied, "Not at all," and grinned. Her reaction was in character. Svetlana was at heart a gambler. Throughout her life she would make a monumental decision entirely on impulse, and then ride the consequences with an almost giddy abandon. She always said her favorite story by Dostoyevsky was *The Gambler*.

Though outwardly cool, Rayle himself was deeply anxious. He was convinced that, as soon as they discovered her missing, the Soviets would definitely insist that she be handed over. If she was discovered at the airport, the Indian police would arrest her, and there would be nothing he could do. He felt the consequences for her would be grave.[15] Execution would have been the old Stalinist style, but her father had been dead fourteen years. Still, the current Soviet government took a hard line on defectors, and imprisonment was always a possibility. When the classical dancer Rudolf Nureyev defected in 1961, he was sentenced in absentia to seven years' hard labor. In Rayle's mind must also have been the recent trials of the writers Andrei Sinyavsky and Yuli Daniel. In 1966 they'd been sentenced to labor camps for their "anti-Soviet" writings, and they were still languishing there. The Kremlin would not risk a public trial of Svetlana, but she might disappear into the dark reaches of some psychiatric institution. Svetlana, too, must have had this in mind. Sinyavsky was an intimate friend. At least she knew that, were she apprehended, she would never be allowed out of the Soviet Union again.

The Qantas flight to Rome landed punctually, but Rayle's relief soon turned to dread as he heard the announcement that the flight would be delayed. The plane had developed mechanical difficulties. The two sat in the departure lounge waiting as minutes turned to hours. Rayle looked at Svetlana. She, too, had begun to be agitated. To cope with the mounting tension, Rayle got up periodically to check the arrivals desks. He knew that the regular Aeroflot flight from Moscow arrived at 5:00

a.m. and a large delegation from the Soviet Embassy always came to greet the diplomatic couriers and the various dignitaries arriving or departing. Members of the Aeroflot staff were already beginning to open their booth. Finally, the departure for Rome was announced. At 2:45 a.m. the Qantas flight for Rome was airborne at last.[16]

As they were in midair, a cable about the *defector* arrived at the American Embassy in New Delhi. In Washington Donald Jameson, who served as CIA liaison officer to the State Department, had informed Deputy Undersecretary of State Foy Kohler of the situation. Kohler's reaction was stunning—he exploded: "Tell them to throw that woman out of the embassy. Don't give her any help at all."[17] Kohler had recently served as American ambassador to the USSR and believed that he had personally initiated a thaw in relations with the Soviets. He didn't want the defection of Stalin's daughter, especially coinciding with the fiftieth anniversary of the Russian Revolution, muddying the waters. When the embassy staff read the flash cable rejecting Svetlana's appeal for asylum, they replied, "You're too late. They've gone. They're on their way to Rome."[18]

The staff failed to check the status of the Qantas flight. Had they discovered that Svetlana and Rayle were sitting for almost two hours in the airport lounge and could have been recalled, Svetlana would have been driven back to the embassy and "kicked out." The whole course of her life would have gone very differently. But Svetlana's life always seemed to dangle on a thread, and chance or fate sent her one way rather than another. She would come to call herself a gypsy. Stalin's daughter, always living in the shadow of her father's name, would never find a safe place to land.

PART ONE

—

The

Kremlin
Years

Chapter 1

———

That Place of Sunshine

Family group, c. 1930. *Standing, from left:* Mariko and Maria Svanidze, Stalin's sisters-in-law from his first marriage. *Seated in center, from left:* Alexandra Andreevna Bychkova (Svetlana's nanny), Nathalie Konstantinova (governess), and Svetlana's maternal aunt Anna Redens. *Front row, from left:* Svetlana and her brother, Vasili, with Nikolai Bukharin's daughter sitting on his knee. *Standing on right:* Sergei Alliluyev, Svetlana's maternal grandfather.

O ver her lifetime, Svetlana often would take out the photographs from her early childhood and muse over them, experiencing that lovely, brutal nostalgia of photos trapping time. Her mother had always been the one with the camera taking the pictures. Everyone at the family gatherings was so young and alive, so simple and ebullient, wearing a picnic face. The first six and a half years of her life, until her mother's death in 1932, were, in Svetlana's mind, the years of sun. She would speak of "that place of sunshine I call my childhood."[1]

Who can live without personal retrospect? We will always glance back to our childhood, for we are shaped deep in our core by the impress of our parents, and we will always wonder how that molding determined us. Svetlana willfully believed in her happy childhood, even as she gradually understood that it was secured by untold bloodshed. What was it about this strange childhood that she would always turn to it for solace?

Svetlana grew up in the Kremlin, the citadel of the tsars, a walled fortress on the edge of the Moskva River, almost a small autonomous village but with imposing towers, cathedrals, and palaces centered on Cathedral Square with massive gates opening onto Red Square and the city beyond. One might think this royal fortress was impossibly grand, but when she was born there in 1926, the second child of Joseph and Nadezhda ("Nadya") Stalin, the Russian Revolution was only nine years old. The public would always see her as the princess in the Kremlin, but her father's Bolshevik discipline dictated a relatively modest life.

The Stalins lived in the old Poteshny Palace, a three-story building erected in 1652. It was known as the Amusement Palace and served as a theater for comic performances until, in the nineteenth century, it housed the offices of the Okhrana, the tsar's secret police. The Poteshny retained its elegant theatrical chandeliers and carpeted staircase, up which the Stalins climbed to their gloomy, high-ceilinged apartment on the second floor.

Svetlana remembered that apartment: "There was [a room] for the governess, and a dining room large enough to have a grand piano in it. . . . In addition there was a library, Nadya's room, and Stalin's tiny bedroom in which stood a table with telephones."[2] There were two rooms for the children (she shared hers with her nanny), a kitchen, the housekeeper's room, and two bathrooms. Wood-burning stoves heated all the rooms. As she described it, "it was homely, with bourgeois furniture." Families of other Bolshevik leaders lived across the lane in the Horse Guards building and casually dropped by.

In keeping with the ideology of the Party, there was no private property. Everything belonged to the state, down to the wineglasses and silverware, which meant, in the end, that everything was up for grabs. In the early days, even Party members had ration cards for food, but their use was hypothetical. In a country where the populace was starving, there was always enough food for the intimate soirees when the Party magnates gathered in one another's apartments. All the leaders were assigned one of the country dachas abandoned by the rich upper classes who had fled in the early days of the Revolution.

When Svetlana was born, on February 28, she entered an already crowded household. Her brother Vasili had been born five years earlier, on March 21, 1921. The story went around that Nadya, demonstrating Bolshevik austerity and an iron will, had walked to the hospital after dinner to deliver her son. Once the ordeal was over, she phoned home to congratulate Stalin.[3] Svetlana's half brother Yakov Djugashvili, the child of Stalin's first marriage, had also joined the household in 1921. Yakov was nineteen years older than Svetlana and would become her champion until his brutal death in a Nazi POW camp.

Family life had a Chekhovian quality, with relatives wandering into and out of the Kremlin apartment. There were two branches of the family: the Alliluyevs and the Svanidzes. Nadya's own family constantly visited. By now the large clan included Nadya's parents, Olga and Sergei Alliluyev; her brothers, Fyodor and Pavel; Pavel's wife, Eugenia ("Zhenya"); her sister, Anna; and Anna's husband, Stanislav Redens. All the family members would come to play tragic parts in the Stalin narrative.

The Svanidze branch arrived from Georgia in 1921, shadows out of Stalin's past. In 1906, when the Georgian-born Joseph Stalin was still just a local agitator fomenting revolution under the code name Soso, he married the sister of a school friend and fellow underground revolutionary, Alexander ("Alyosha") Svanidze. In those prerevolutionary days, when the triumph of the Bolsheviks seemed impossibly distant, Svanidze's three sisters ran an haute couture fashion house in Tiflis (Tbilisi), called Atelier Hervieu. The waiting room was always full of counts, generals, and police officers. While the sisters fitted the dress of a general's wife in one room, the revolutionaries discussed their plans for sabotage next door and hid their secret documents inside the stylish mannequins.[4]

The youngest sister, the exquisitely lovely Ekaterina Svanidze, whom everyone called Kato, fell in love with the mysterious and witty Comrade Soso. By then he was head of the Bolshevik faction in Tiflis, and it was no surprise that the tsar's secret police often came calling. Kato was pregnant within months of their marriage and gave birth to Yakov in March 1907. She contracted typhus shortly afterward. The family reported that Kato, just twenty-two, died in Soso's arms on November 22, 1907. At the funeral, a distraught Soso threw himself into the grave with the coffin, and then he disappeared for two months.[5]

Stalin's first wife, Ekaterina "Kato" Svanidze, who died in 1907.

Looking back, Stalin would tell his daughter, Svetlana, that Kato "was very sweet and beautiful: she melted my heart"[6]— but not quite enough, it seemed, for him to assume responsibility for their infant son. He abandoned Yakov to the care of his mother-in-law and the Svanidze sisters. One of the few contacts that the family had with Stalin was a letter from Siberia during one of his pre-Revolution exiles, asking them to send him wine and jam.[7]

On a visit to Georgia in 1921, the Svanidze family encouraged Stalin to bring his fourteen-year-old son back with him to Moscow. Stalin's brother-in-law, Alyosha Svanidze, who'd been so close to Stalin in his early revolutionary days, also came, bringing along his sisters, Mariko and Sashiko, thus joining the Kremlin elite. A Europeanized Georgian, Alyosha had studied in Germany and was something of a dandy. His beautiful, flamboyant wife, Maria, from a wealthy Jewish family, who had sung in the Tiflis opera before her marriage, came with him. It would have been much safer for them had they all stayed in Georgia.

Artyom Sergeev, Nadya and Stalin's adopted son, occasionally visited. His father had been killed in 1921 while testing a new high-speed train powered by an airplane engine. Though Artyom's mother was still alive, Stalin adopted the boy, in keeping with the Bolshevik custom of assuming the care of orphans of Party members. Artyom became the bosom buddy of Svetlana's brother Vasili.[8]

The only person who was always absent from these family gatherings was Stalin's mother, Ekaterina, affectionately known as Keke. Nadya would write her mother-in-law encouraging letters: "Things here seem to be all right, we're very well. The children are growing up. . . . Altogether we have terribly little free time, Joseph and I. . . . Still, I'm not complaining and so far, I'm coping with it all quite successfully."[9]

Though she had visited the Kremlin once to meet Nadya, Stalin's widowed mother refused to abandon her beloved Georgia. She lived in the old Viceroy's Palace in Tiflis, where she chose to occupy a room on the ground floor next to the servants' quarters, while the top floors were reserved for social functions.

To Svetlana, who seems to have met her only once in Georgia, her paternal grandmother, Keke, was a stranger and therefore rarely a part of her family mythology. Svetlana knew the stories: that her grandfather Vissarion "Beso" Djugashvili had been a cobbler who, in his drunken rages, had beaten his son brutally until Keke finally kicked him out. Keke had scraped together the money to send Joseph to the Gori Church School and then on to the Tiflis Seminary, intending him to become a priest. Svetlana always said that the notorious brutality of the Orthodox priests, who punished their students with solitary confinement for days in dungeonlike cells, had shaped her father's penchant for cruelty.

Stalin's mother, Ekaterina "Keke" Djugashvili, who refused to leave her native Georgia to visit Moscow.

As an adult, Svetlana would only sparingly comment on her father to friends, but one of the things she did say was that the only person her father ever feared was his mother.[10] But such was the mystification in which her father cloaked himself that even his daughter did not know his real birth date. Stalin was actually born on December 6, 1878, a year earlier than he claimed.[11] In keeping with his habit of inventing much of his own biography, Stalin chose December 21, 1879, as his official birthday. The family always celebrated on this day.

This, then, was Svetlana's intimate family. She maintained that at the center of it all was her mother, Nadya, who died when Svetlana was six and a half. What does a child remember of her mother at such an age? By her sudden disappearance, Nadya became a key to understanding Svetlana's emotional life. The photograph Svetlana most loved was the one of her mother holding her when she was an infant. It was proof that her mother loved her.

Svetlana couldn't remember her mother's face, but she could remember the smell of her Chanel perfume, which Nadya wore despite Stalin's disapproval. Her mother would come into her room to say good night, would touch her, then touch her pillow, and she would fall asleep engulfed in perfume.[12] But she could barely remember her mother kissing her or stroking her hair. Her mother was a strict disciplinarian. Hearing from Vasili, her tattletale older brother, that she'd been naughty, Nadya wrote to her daughter from her vacation in Sochi:

Hello, Svetlanochka!

I had a letter from Vasya [Vasili] saying that my little girl is carrying on and being terribly naughty. I hate getting letters like that. . . . When Mama went away, her little girl made a great many promises, but now it turns out she isn't keeping them. Please write and let me know whether you've decided to be good or not. You decide. You're a big girl and are able to think for yourself. Are you reading anything in Russian? I'm waiting to hear from you.

Your Mama[13]

This letter, written when Svetlana was four or five, was the only letter she ever received from her frequently absent mother.

Svetlana, age six, with her eleven-year-old brother, Vasili, in a photo from 1932 taken before their mother committed suicide on November 9.

Svetlana felt she was a quiet, obedient child. Three decades later, she could write: "[Mother] expected a good deal of me," still hurt that there were few memories of tenderness in her mother's treatment of her.[14] But there was one thing in particular that she did recall. It was the memory of her mother drawing a little square over her heart with her finger and telling her, "That is where you must bury your secrets."[15] In the backbiting political world of the Kremlin, Nadya kept her feelings and her secrets hidden, something her daughter, who would become notorious for her emotional outbursts, did not emulate.

As a child, of course Svetlana thought her mother was beautiful. In retrospect, she believed her mother showed her love through her dedication to her children's education, which she took in hand from their earliest childhood and which, for Svetlana, made her the model of the dedicated mother.

Nadya is an elusive figure in the Stalin universe. She was a sixteen-year-old girl when, according to the family and to her daughter, she fell madly, passionately in love with the thirty-nine-year-old Stalin, already Lenin's loyal ally and a star in the Bolshevik firmament. Much to her parents' annoyance, she ran off with him in 1918 to join the Revolution, becoming his secretary. Nadya was headstrong, stubborn, puritanical, and idealistic. To outsiders she appeared cold, but this exterior hid a passionate and volatile temperament.

Nadya's warmth, as well as her frustration, surfaces in a letter to the aunt of her stepson Yakov, Maria Svanidze, of whom she was clearly very fond. Maria and her husband, Alexander, were then living in Berlin, where he was working for the Soviet Bank for Foreign Trade. Nadya wrote the letter just before the birth of Svetlana, who, despite her mother's ambivalence about the pregnancy, obviously treasured the letter, translating it into English herself and saving it:

JANUARY 11, 1926

Dear Maroussya

You write that you feel bored. You know, my dear, it's the same thing everywhere. I have nothing to do with anyone in Moscow. Sometimes that looks even strange: in so many years not to develop close friendships, but that depends on character. It is strange that I feel much closer to non–party members, I mean women. This public is much simpler to get along with.

I regret that I have again took [sic] upon myself strong family bonds [here Svetlana added a footnote: "N. S. Allilueva was expecting her daughter Svetlana at that time"]. This is not so easy in our days, because there appeared to be so many new prejudices, like if you are not working you are a "baba,"* although perhaps one does not work only because one does not have due qualifications. And now when I am going to be with family business, it is impossible to think about one's qualifications. I advise you, dear Maroussya, to obtain some skills for Russia, while you are abroad. I am serious. You simply cannot imagine how unpleasant it is to work simply for earnings, doing any work; one must have a specialty, specialization, which would liberate you from dependence on others. . . .

Well, my dear Maroussya, do not feel lonely, do obtain necessary qualifications and come to us next time. We shall all be very happy to see you. Joseph is asking me to give you his love. He has very good feelings toward you (he says "she is a smart *baba*"). Do not get angry—that is his usual way to treat us, women. . . .

I kiss you and goodbye,

Nadya[16]

Nadya was fed up with being a shadow in the Kremlin and was determined not to be a *baba*. As soon as Svetlana was born, Nadya, then twenty-five, searched for a nanny to care for her infant daughter so that she would be free to pursue her own education. After interviewing prospective candidates, she settled on Alexandra Andreevna Bychkova.

Alexandra Andreevna knew about loyalty. She had been born in 1885 on an estate in Ryazan, southeast of Moscow,

---

* Svetlana defines this in the margin of Nadya's letter as "a peasant woman."

and worked as maid, cook, nurse, and housekeeper until she joined the Saint Petersburg household of Nikolai Yevreinov, a theater director and critic, a member of the prerevolutionary liberal intelligentsia. The Yevreinov family taught the illiterate Alexandra Andreevna to read and write. When the outbreak of the Revolution forced them to flee to Paris, they invited her to accompany them, but she refused to leave the motherland. During the famines of the early 1920s, she fled, with her one remaining son (the other had died of starvation), to Moscow, where Nadya Stalina discovered and hired her. Svetlana's adopted brother, Artyom Sergeev, would say that Alexandra Andreevna was "an absolutely wonderful nanny." She reminded him of Pushkin's faithful nanny, Arina Rodionova.[17]

Alexandra Andreevna was a remarkable storyteller who threaded her conversation with Russian proverbs, filling the children's ears with tales of her village and of her "theater" days in Saint Petersburg. Her greatest gift was her capacity to keep silent as she weathered all the vicissitudes over the years in the Stalin household. Svetlana would say of her, "For me, during my whole life, she was an example of calmness, hard work, warmth, some kind of epic tranquility, and an unending optimism."[18]

Nadya left Svetlana's nanny strict instructions never to let her charge be idle. Svetlana remembered her nanny taking her to preschool for music lessons with twenty other children. Svetlana sang in a children's chorus and was soon taught to read and transcribe music and play the piano. Alexandra Andreevna stayed with Svetlana for thirty years until her death in 1956, serving as nanny for Svetlana's own children. If there was any ethical grounding for Svetlana in the morally ambiguous Stalin universe, it came from her nanny, Alexandra Andreevna. "If it hadn't been for the even, steady warmth given off by this large and kindly person," Svetlana later wrote, "I might long ago have gone out of my mind."[19]

In 1928, when Svetlana was two, Nadya enrolled at the Industrial Academy to study synthetic fibers, a new branch of chemistry. There were also endless Party meetings, and what free time Nadya had she spent with Stalin. She hired tutors to oversee her children's education, while she was mostly absent.

As Svetlana put it with some resentment, "It was not the thing at that time for a woman, especially a woman Party member, to spend much time with her children."[20] All the Kremlin wives had Party jobs. In their spare time, some took up tennis. There were tennis courts and croquet sets on those dacha lawns. It was an uncanny replication of the old tsarist aristocracy's way of life.

Nadya hired a German housekeeper from Latvia, Carolina Til, to run the Kremlin apartment and left everything to her German efficiency. She also hired a governess for Svetlana and a male tutor for Vasili, much as the tsars had done. Svetlana learned to read and write German and Russian by the time she was six.

From left: Carolina Til, the housekeeper, and the nanny Alexandra Andreevna Bychkova.

The life of all the children in the numerous Kremlin apartments followed a similar routine, run by governesses and tutors. But it was not all discipline. Stepan Mikoyan, whose father was an Old Bolshevik and a Soviet statesman, one of the few who survived Stalin's purges, lived in the Horse Guards building and used to play with Vasili and Svetlana. He remembered afternoons when all of the children of government officials, including the staff—there must have been thirty or forty children—raced through the gardens. Svetlana was a tomboy and fearlessly climbed the Tsar's Cannon, the largest cannon in the world, just like everybody else.[21]

There were rollicking children's parties at which twenty or thirty children might read a fable by the nineteenth-century writer Ivan Andreyevich Krylov, imitating the animals and wearing actual bearskins. But they would also chant satirical couplets about "political double-dealers." Their parents would be the audience, and even Stalin might be there, a passive witness, as was his habit, watching indulgently from the sidelines. "Once in a while," his daughter would remark laconically, "he enjoyed the sounds of children playing."[22]

Svetlana remembered her sixth birthday. The Kremlin flat was full of children. They had prepared songs and dances, and she recited some German poetry. It had been a feast, complete with tea and small cakes in cups. Svetlana had to hold this memory in a sealed compartment since she recognized, years later, that much of the rest of Russia had been starving.

Only once did Svetlana recall spending a full day with her mother. She remembered watching in amazement as Nadya furiously cleaned the underside of the claw-foot bathtub and then the rest of the apartment. She was too young to understand that the motive was probably less her mother's obsession with cleanliness, though there was that, than a wife's repressed anger, for there was much unhappiness in the Stalin family.

Stalin and Nadya often fought. Years later Polina Molotov, Nadya's close friend, told Svetlana, "Your father was rough with [your mother] and she had a hard life with him. Everyone knew that. But they'd spent a good many years together. They had a family, children, a home, and everyone loved Nadya." Although it wasn't a happy marriage, Polina asked, "What marriage is?"[23]

Svetlana remembered her mother hitting her only once. A new tablecloth made of disk-shaped pieces of embroidery hung alluringly from the dining room table. When Svetlana took her scissors and cut out one of the disks—they were so beautiful— her enraged mother slapped her across the face.[24] It was a terrible shock. When Stalin heard her cry, he came running to comfort her.

Svetlana reciprocated this role of placater. When her mother and father were arguing, she would run to her father and wrap her small hands around his boot. Only then would he calm down. Nadya's close friend Irina Gogua, witness to such domestic arguments, remarked, "The only creature who softened [Stalin] was Svetlana."[25]

If her mother was cool, Svetlana got the emotional response she craved from her father. She was Stalin's favorite child. He called her his "little sparrow" or "little fly." It was to his knees that she flew, and from him she got the kisses and caresses her mother withheld. She took his constant absences for granted; they made his appearances all the more dramatic and the child all the more needy.

It was Nadya who embraced the Svanidze side of the family. She was particularly protective of Yakov, whom Stalin apparently treated with contempt. The adolescent boy spoke only Georgian when he joined the household. Svetlana thought this was one of the reasons her father seemed to dislike him. Stalin was reportedly self-conscious of his own Georgian-accented

Russian. Svetlana would say that her father "knew Russian well in its simpler, conversational form; . . . in Russian he could not be an eloquent orator or writer, lacking synonyms, nuances, depths."[26] Instead he often used silence to assert his authority, a much more effective tool to control others, who could never figure out quite what Stalin was thinking.

As a child, Svetlana didn't even know that her father's roots were Georgian. Once her brother Vasili, who constantly teased her, told her that the family were Georgians. When Svetlana asked him what being Georgian meant, he said that "they went around in long Circassian cloaks and cut everybody up with daggers."[27] Svetlana claimed that Stalin, seeking to distance himself from his roots, banned visiting Georgian colleagues from bringing the usual gifts of Georgian wines and fruit, raging that such generosity came at public expense, and Nadya concurred.

Looking back, Svetlana said the room she most loved in their Moscow apartment was her mother's room. In her mother's absence, she would retreat there whenever she could to sit on its thick, raspberry-colored Oriental rug or curl up on the old-fashioned Georgian *takhta* (divan) with its embroidered cushions. She loved to touch the books on Nadya's desk and drawing table. Given the dangerous household in which she grew up, Svetlana needed this idealized image of the beloved mother for psychic survival, but the outsider sees only an absent mother and a desperate, emotionally needy child. Of course, the truth was that Nadya herself was barely surviving.

Life at Zubalovo

Buried in the minds of those of us who are lucky is a childhood landscape, a place of magic and imagination, a safe place. It is foundational, and we will return to it in memory and dreams throughout our lives. Despite what her life would become, Svetlana had such a place.

As a member of Lenin's inner circle, Stalin was awarded a dacha called Zubalovo. It was not far from the village of Usovo, about twenty miles outside Moscow. The family lived there weekends and summers from 1919 to 1932, and the extended family continued to visit until 1949, long after Nadya's death.

The dacha took its name from the former owner, Zubalov, an Armenian oil magnate from Baku. The whole area around Usovo had once served as a vacation retreat for the wealthy in prerevolutionary Moscow. After the owners fled during the Revolution, the dachas were divided among the Party elite. Stalin and Anastas Mikoyan got Zubalovo. There was more than a small amount of revenge in this. Both men had directed strikes protesting the long working hours and miserable conditions at Zubalov's oil refineries in Baku, Azerbaijan; and Batumi, Georgia.

On the expansive grounds of Zubalovo, there were three separate houses called the big house, the small house, and the service block, all surrounded by a redbrick wall. The larger one was taken over by Mikoyan and other Old Bolshevik families. Nadya's siblings, the Alliluyevs, and some of the Svanidzes used the service block, while Stalin and Nadya had the smaller dacha. It was always filled with visitors.[28]

Stalin immediately had the dacha remodeled, removing the gables and old furnishings. He had a balcony built on the second floor—"father's balcony"—and a terrace covering the back of the house. Stalin and Nadya occupied the upstairs, while the children and visiting relatives and friends lived downstairs. Purple lilac bushes framed the front of the house, and a grove of white birch stood at a slight distance. There was a duck pond, an apiary, a fenced-in run for chickens and pheasants, an orchard, and a clearing where buckwheat was planted to attract the bees. This Bolshevik estate served much the same role as it had when owned by the industrial elite, "a small estate with a country routine of its own" as Svetlana described it.[29]

As a child, Svetlana knew the landscape like her own skin. She knew where the best mushroom patches could be found; she fished every stream and pond with her grandfather and brother and discovered where the trout rested in the slipstreams. She knew where to pick the berries among the brambles, which left her arms and legs covered in scratches. She brought home buckets of berries for the cook and, happy and exhausted, waited for praise. Svetlana had her own garden plot to tend and her own rabbits to raise. The smell of the larch trees, the white skin of the peeling birches, the flamboyant green of the new leaves, the smell of Russian soil—all this imprinted itself on her mind.

During the summer many children of the ruling elite came to stay. She'd lead them to the poultry yard to collect the eggs of the guinea fowl and pheasants or take them out on expeditions to pick mushrooms. On the estate they had a tree house to climb into and swings and a seesaw to ride. The children went camping in the woods, sleeping in a lean-to overnight and fishing in the local river. They would cook their catches over the fire, and bake pheasant eggs in the hot cinders.

Stalin, who had learned to love Russian baths in Siberia, eventually had a banya built at Zubalovo. It was a roofed hut with birch branches in the eaves sending their fragrance over the bathers. When her father was absent, Svetlana used to read her children's books there, spread out on a rug on the floor.

Relatives floated into and out of Zubalovo: her grandparents Olga and Sergei Alliluyev; her Aunt Anna and Uncle Stanislav; and Uncle Pavel and Aunt Zhenya. Uncle Pavel told stories of the time after the Civil War when Lenin sent him on an expedition to the far north to prospect for iron ore and coal.

They'd lived in tents, ridden reindeer, and made their clothes from reindeer pelts.[30] The Svanidzes also came to the dacha, particularly Uncle Alyosha and his dramatic wife, Maria. Stalin was often there but preoccupied. He could be found sitting at his table working on the terrace.

Svetlana's grandparents, Olga and Sergei, were the dominant presences at the dacha. It was Sergei who brought Stalin into the Alliluyev household. The Russian-born son of a freed serf, he had trained himself as a mechanic and was working at the Tiflis rail yards when he joined the Mesame Dasi (Third Group), the Georgian socialist party formed in the early 1890s. He first met Stalin in 1900, when his future son-in-law was already famous locally for his brilliant organization and political exhortations at the clandestine May Day workers' demonstrations. In those days, Sergei was mostly in charge of printing Marxist propaganda posters and leaflets, for which he was arrested and jailed seven times. Whether he participated in revolutionary violence is unclear, though he seemed to have had no objections when his nine-year-old daughter, Anna, was used by the revolutionaries as a mule to carry explosive cartridges sewn into her undervest on the train from Tiflis to Baku.[31] Sergei offered the family's apartment as a refuge for Stalin when he was hiding out from the tsar's secret police.

Olga was a more complex figure. In 1893, she'd run off with Sergei, who was the family's lodger, to escape her tyrannical father. She was sixteen; he was twenty-seven. She seemed a willing ally in Sergei's revolutionary politics. Her life and the lives of her four children had been a narrative of constant moving from city to city, police searches, fear, keeping secrets, visiting Sergei in prison, and watching friends disappear. She distributed Marxist tracts, as did her young daughters, a dangerous practice that could bring them a jail term as it did their father. It was she who suggested their Saint Petersburg apartment on

Rozhdestvenskaya Street as a hiding place for Lenin in the
summer of 1917, when he stayed for several days before fleeing
to Finland when the Revolution seemed to be dissolving, only
to return to organize the Bolshevik triumph that October. And
she also welcomed Stalin's visits. Stalin was effusive in his gratitude to Olga, writing to her from his Siberian exile:

NOVEMBER 25, 1915

Olga Eugenievna:

I am more than grateful to you, dear Olga Eugenievna,
for your kind and good sentiments toward me. I shall never
forget the concern which you have shown me. I await the
time when my period of banishment is over and I can
come to Petersburg, to thank you and Sergei personally, for
everything. I still have two years to complete it all. . . . My
greetings to the boys and girls. . . .

Respectfully yours,

Joseph[32]

This was the son-in-law who would one day betray her every
trust.

As soon as her youngest daughter, Nadya, turned fourteen,
Olga asserted her independence by undertaking training as a
midwife. When Russia entered World War I, she joined the
Red Cross, tending the wounded who arrived from the German front. She lived mostly at the hospital and, according to
her son Pavel, began to take lovers.

By the time they were in residence at Zubalovo, Sergei and
Olga were completely alienated. He would arrive from one end
of the dacha, she from the other, and they would stare each

other down across the length of the dining room table. Sergei had been sidelined as an Old Bolshevik, though he remained a fervent believer, while Olga seemed skeptical, and was the earliest to suspect the true nature of her son-in-law.

Through those long summers at the dacha, this seemed an explosive, hot-tempered, typically Georgian family—Grandpa Sergei, angry when a child was restless at the table, was known to pour his soup into the child's lap.[33] Olga had reverted to her Eastern Orthodox religion. When the Stalin children and their friends, brought up in the atheistic ideology of Communism, mocked Grandma Olga's beliefs, she would respond, "Where is your soul? You will know when it aches."[34] However, she didn't seem to mind the ascendency and benefits her son-in-law's position gave her.

Svetlana, who inherited Olga's red hair and blue eyes, identified with her grandmother. She claimed that her mother had banned her grandmother from visiting their Kremlin apartment because she resented Olga's constant criticism of her Bolshevik devotion to her career and her failure to stay at home with her children.[35] Svetlana probably picked this up from her aunts, as it is hardly the memory of a six-year-old child. Apparently Olga would shout at Nadya that she'd brought up four children, though Nadya, remembering her fractured childhood, might have found this ironic. Olga was explosive but not particularly self-reflective, traits her granddaughter Svetlana also seemed to inherit.

As a child, Svetlana would not have had much understanding of these complex family undercurrents. What child does? At Zubalovo, her grandparents, and particularly her grandfather, were benevolent parental substitutes. Sergei kept a machine shop in a separate hut at the dacha and invited the children into his workshop to play with his tools and make things. Sometimes he would hang candy from the trees for them to pluck and take them on long mushroom-picking hikes through the forest.

Svetlana's maternal grandfather, Sergei Alliluyev, in the late 1920s.

Many of the Bolshevik Party elite shared those summers at Zubalovo. Svetlana called all of them uncles. "Uncle Voroshilov" and "Uncle Mikoyan" came to the Stalin dacha with their families. One of the visitors she liked best was Stalin's old comrade Nikolai Bukharin, who filled the dacha with laughter and was loved by everyone. He taught Svetlana's nanny to ride a bike and always brought animals to the dacha and the Kremlin gardens: hedgehogs, garter snakes in jars, hawks, even a tame fox. Long after Stalin had Bukharin executed in the final show trial of 1938, his fox still ran through the Kremlin gardens. Other friends came, like Sergo Ordzhonikidze and his wife, Zinaida. As a six-year-old, Svetlana watched the adult parties with a child's curiosity: Semyon Budyonny played the accordion and the adults sang Russian folk songs. Even Nadya might dance the Georgian *lezghinka*, and Stalin, who had an excellent singing voice and fine pitch, might also sing.[36] Only Mikoyan, Budyonny, and Kliment Voroshilov outlasted Stalin. These "uncles" and "aunts" began to disappear in the mid-1930s; many were executed, and some, like Ordzhonikidze, committed suicide. Svetlana remembered only that, as a child, she couldn't understand where everybody had gone. People simply "vanished." No one explained why.[37]

Stalin was forty-eight when Svetlana was born, and he preferred his vacations without noisy children. He and Nadya often took vacations in Sochi on the Black Sea, where the warm baths helped his rheumatism, in all likelihood a product of his numerous Siberian exiles. It seemed that often a whole retinue of Party members would drive south in a flotilla of cars. Svetlana kept her mother's photographs of those trips. There was the image of Abel Enukidze, her mother's beloved godfather, at picnics on the beach. Other Politburo members, like Molotov, Mikoyan, and Voroshilov, would be there. Taking vacations together was part of Party orthodoxy. Stalin had a deformed arm as a result of childhood accidents, as well as webbed toes on one foot, so he never swam. He preferred to stretch out on a deck chair on the beach reviewing documents. Svetlana was five years old before she was allowed to accompany her parents to their dacha in Sochi.

Looking back in her memoir, written when she was thirty-seven, Svetlana could speak only of these leaders' "deaths," not of their murders. "I want to put down only what I know and what I remember and saw myself," is how she keeps the psychological trauma at a distance.[38] But here the split begins: Zubalovo was once a place of light and magic where old friends, revolutionary comrades, gathered to share summers and laughter with their children. And then everything turned murderously black.

In retrospect Svetlana would not deny the paradox of that childhood happiness. Its privileged isolation protected her from the terrible suffering of the time: the brutal internal Party struggles as Stalin asserted his ascendency over his rivals with purges of Old Bolsheviks and the Party elite; the deaths of millions of peasants from man-made famines caused by forced collectivization in the countryside in the name of rapid industrialization. The classless Bolsheviks had replicated the tsarist regime: now the people were the serfs and the leaders walled themselves within safe boundaries. There were not then the bourgeois excesses that the regime would become famous for after the war.

Nor could Svetlana deny the magic of that first world, when she lived with the timeless unconsciousness of a child in a place peopled with beings she loved. Should she merely have rejected this whole world? But she was at the core of a paradox. How could a world that seemed wonderful be also terrible? Her father petted and loved her and showered her with paternal tobacco kisses as, at her nanny's urging, she trotted up to him with presents of violets and strawberries. How could he already be at the same time one of the world's bloodiest dictators, biding his time?

Svetlana called her childhood normal, full of loving relatives, friends, holidays, pleasure. She even claimed that it was modest, and for the child of a head of state, perhaps it was, though the millions of Russians who were starving and displaced would have been outraged.

In her memoir she wrote: "If only out of respect for their memory, from love and profound gratitude for what they were to me in that place of sunshine I call my childhood, I ought to tell you about them."[39]

It was a willful declaration, for the memories were full of paradoxes and frustrations. "I keep trying to bring back what is gone, the sunny, bygone years of my childhood," she would write over thirty years later, as if acknowledging the impossibility of this.[40]

From the child's point of view, the world may have been undiluted sun, though with a child's intuition, she must already have sensed the cracks in her paradise. From an adult perspective, it was a labyrinthine tangle of pain and anxiety.

Chapter 2

A Motherless Child

Nadya with a young Svetlana, c. 1926.

During the afternoon of November 7, 1932, Svetlana stood with her mother at the front of the crowd watching the soldiers march past the Hall of Columns to honor the fifteenth anniversary of the Great Revolution. This was the first time she had been allowed to attend the annual celebrations. It was an extraordinary festival, with stilt walkers, fire-eaters, and circus performers moving into and out of the throng of thousands of people. She looked up at her father on the platform where his giant image hung behind the Party magnates lined up dutifully on either side of the *vozhd*. She was only six and a half, but she understood that her father was the most important man in the world.

Earlier that day, her mother had called her into her room. "I saw my mother so rarely that I remember our last meeting very well." Svetlana sat on her favorite *takhta* and listened as her mother delivered a long lesson on manners and deportment. "Never drink wine!" she said.[1] Nadya and Stalin always quarreled when he dipped his finger into his wine and put it into his children's mouths. She protested that he would turn her children into alcoholics. Her final words to Svetlana were in character. Nadya dismissed as self-indulgence the emotional effusiveness that she associated with her mother, Olga; and her sister, Anna. Crying, confessions, complaining, and even frankness were not in her repertoire. The most important thing was to do one's duty and to hide one's secrets in the small square over one's heart.

As her nanny put her to bed, Svetlana recounted how Uncle Voroshilov led the whole parade riding on a white horse.

On the morning of November 9, Alexandra Andreevna got the children up early and sent them out to play in the dark, rainy dawn. When they were bundled into a car hours later, the staff all seemed to be crying. They were driven to the new dacha at Sokolovka. Stalin had begun to indulge his penchant for building dachas, and that fall the family was using the Sokolovka dacha instead of Zubalovo. The house was gloomy, with a dark interior that seldom got any light. The children knew something was terribly wrong and kept asking where their mother was. Eventually Voroshilov arrived to take them back to Moscow. He was in tears. Their father seemed to have disappeared.

So many apocryphal stories have gathered around what had happened the previous night that it is impossible to sort fact from fiction, gossip from truth, but a rough outline of the night can be reconstructed.

In the late afternoon of November 8, Nadya was in the apartment in the Poteshny Palace preparing for the inevitably boisterous party to celebrate the Revolution. Her brother Pavel, currently stationed in Berlin as the military representative with the Soviet trade mission, was visiting and had brought her gifts, one of which was a lovely black dress. The Kremlin wives always complained that when they met Nadya at the fashionable Commissariat of Internal Affairs dressmaker on Kuznetsky Bridge, reserved for the Party elite, she selected the most drab and uninteresting clothes. They were amused that she was still following the outdated Bolshevik ethic of modesty.[2] That night, in her elegant black dress, she was beautiful; she had even placed a red rose in her black hair.

Accompanied by her sister, Anna, Nadya crossed the snowy lane to the Horse Guards building and entered the apartment of Comrade Voroshilov, the defense commissar, who was hosting the anniversary celebration for the Party magnates and their wives. Stalin sauntered down the lane from his office at the Yellow Palace in the company of Comrade Molotov and his chief of economics, Comrade Valerian Kuibyshev. They had only one or two guards with them, though the Politburo had banned the *vozhd* from "walking around town on foot."[3] The Politburio had concluded that Stalin was no longer safe, so hated were the policies of terror he had already adopted against so-called industrial saboteurs, bourgeois experts, and political terrorists conspiring with foreign powers. Assassination seemed a real possibility.

For everyone this was an occasion to unwind. The food arrived from the Kremlin kitchen—an ample spread of hors d'oeuvres, fish, and meat, with vodka and Georgian wine—served by the housekeeper. The men, many still sporting the tunics and boots that were a throwback to their revolutionary past, and the women in their designer dresses, sat at the banquet table. Stalin sat in his usual spot in the middle of the table, across from Nadya. This was a hard-drinking, exuberant lot, ready to down toast after toast to the old revolutionary triumphs and the new industrial achievements.

In the anecdotal reports in the multiple memoirs left behind by those present at the party that night, stories coalesce around the following details. Stalin was drunk and was flirting boorishly with Galina, a film actress and the wife of the Red Army commander Alexander Yegorov, by lobbing bread balls at her. Nadya was either disgusted or simply tired of all this. There had been gossip about Stalin's current dalliance, with a Kremlin hairdresser. Stalin liked to confine his philandering to those from whom discretion could be ensured, and a hairdresser working at the Kremlin would have belonged to the secret police. Nadya had seen it all before and knew these affairs never lasted, though neither she nor anyone else seemed to know how far they went. Years later Stalin's bodyguard Vlasik made the suggestive comment to Svetlana that her father "was a man after all."[4] That night, Nadya was seen dancing coquettishly with her Georgian godfather, Abel Enukidze, then administrator of the Kremlin complex, a usual stratagem for an angry woman to demonstrate her studied indifference to her husband's flirtations.

Many accounts claim that it was a political toast that inflamed Nadya. Stalin toasted "the destruction of enemies of the state" and noticed that Nadya did not raise her glass. He shouted across the table, "Hey you, why aren't you drinking? Have a drink!"[5]

She replied venomously, "My name is not *hey*," before storming out of the room. The revelers could hear her shouting over her shoulder, "Shut up! Shut up!" as she exited. The room fell silent in shock. Not even a wife would dare turn her back on Stalin. Stalin only muttered contemptuously, "What a fool," and kept on drinking.

Nadya's close friend Polina Molotov rushed out after her. According to Polina, she and Nadya circled the Kremlin a number of times as Polina reminded her of how much pressure Stalin was under. He was drunk, which was rare: he was just unwinding. Polina said Nadya was "perfectly calm" when they said good night in the early hours of the morning.[6]

When Nadya returned to the Kremlin apartment, she entered her room and closed the door. After fourteen years of marriage, she and Stalin slept separately. Her room was down a hall off to the right from the dining room. Stalin's room was to the left of the dining room. The children's rooms were down another hall, and much farther down that hallway came the servants' rooms.

Sometime in the early hours of the morning, Nadya took the small Mauser pistol that her brother Pavel had given her as a gift and shot herself in the heart.[7]

Nobody seems to have heard the shot—certainly not the children and none of the servants. In those days, the guard stood outside at the gate. Stalin, if he was home, seems to have slept through it all.

The housekeeper, Carolina Til, prepared Nadya's breakfast, as she did every morning. She claimed that when she entered the room, she found Nadya lying on the floor beside her bed in a pool of blood, the little Mauser pistol still in her hand. Til ran to the nursery to wake Svetlana's nanny, Alexandra Andreevna, and together they went back to Nadya's room. The two women laid Nadya's body on the bed. Rather than call Stalin, whose anticipated reaction terrified them, they phoned Nadya's god-father, Abel Enukidze, and then Polina Molotov. The group waited. Finally Stalin woke and entered the dining room. They turned to him: "Joseph, Nadya is no longer with us."[8]

Rumors would later surface that, after the party, Stalin had gone to the Zubalovo dacha with another woman and had arrived home in the wee hours of the morning. He and Nadya quarreled, and he'd shot her. Stalin was a kind of magnet for vengeful myths, but this one is unlikely. More convincing is the relatives' certainty that Nadya committed suicide, and they were angry: how could she abandon her children like that?

They also claimed Nadya left a bitter and accusatory suicide note for Stalin, though supposedly he destroyed it immediately upon reading it. Pavel's wife, Zhenya, reported that for the first few days, Stalin was in a state of shock. "He said he didn't want to go on living either. . . . [Stalin] was in such a state that they were afraid to leave him alone. He had sporadic fits of rage."[9]

Nadya and Stalin together at a picnic, from a
photo taken in the early 1920s.

The family needed to believe that he was devastated, and it is possible that he was. He had, in his way, loved Nadya, as his love letters to her attest. Even dictators can be sentimental. But his reaction was cruelly egocentric and focused on himself. Stalin's sister-in-law, Maria Svanidze, recorded in her private diary the moment when she told Stalin that she blamed Nadya: "How could Nadya have left two children?" He responded, "The children have forgotten her after a few days, but I am left incapacitated for the rest of my life."[10] It is hard to imagine a father saying this of his grieving children, but Stalin's self-pity seems convincing. Svetlana always believed, more realistically, that her mother's suicide exacerbated Stalin's paranoia: No one could ever be trusted; even those closest betrayed.

Why did Nadya, just thirty-one, kill herself? We will never know the truth, but speculations abound. The easiest explanation is that she was mentally ill. Initially, even Svetlana believed this. The historian Simon Sebag Montefiore writes: "[Nadya's] medical report, preserved by Stalin in his archive, and the testimonies of those who knew her, confirm that Nadya suffered from a serious mental illness, perhaps hereditary manic depression or borderline personality disorder though her daughter called it 'schizophrenia,' and a disease of the skull that gave her migraines." Nadya suffered multiple other ailments. She had had several abortions, a not uncommon form of contraception in those days, which resulted in a number of gynecological problems.[11] She retreated to spas and German health resorts, an indulgence, indeed almost a fetish, of most of the Party elite.

But eventually Svetlana came to see her mother's despair as motivated by her opposition to Stalin's repressive policies. The question is whether there is any credibility to this idea.

Nikita Khrushchev, her fellow student at the Industrial Academy, claimed Nadya tried to assert her independence from Stalin.[12] When she registered at the Academy in 1928, she retained her own name, Alliluyeva, though in truth this was not unusual among Bolshevik wives. She refused to travel to the Academy in a government car and rode the tram; this was why she had a pistol. Her brother Pavel had brought back two Mauser No. 1 pistols from a trip to England, giving one to Nadya and one to Molotov's wife, Polina. Alexander Alliluyev, Pavel's son, would later remark, "They took the tram to their school, and there was some real danger at that time in Moscow. Because of that, my father brought those two damned pistols from England. And in regards to this, Stalin said to my father, 'You couldn't find another gift?' The gun had tiny bullets, but they were enough for Nadya to shoot herself in the heart."[13]

From her correspondence as a teenager, it is easy to see Nadya as a dogmatic, idealistic young Communist. During the Civil War that raged after the Bolsheviks' triumph, she seemed able to rationalize the violence as necessary to the survival of the Great Revolution. When, in June 1918, Lenin sent Stalin south to Tsaritsyn (renamed Stalingrad in 1925) with 450 Red Guards to secure food supplies for Moscow and Petrograd, the seventeen-year-old Nadya and her brother Fyodor accompanied him as his assistants. A railway carriage was pulled to a siding, and Stalin used it as his headquarters. They hadn't yet registered their marriage, but under Bolshevik convention, Nadya was already considered Stalin's wife.

Immediately Stalin began to purge the city of suspected counterrevolutionaries. When he wrote repeatedly to Lenin demanding sweeping military powers, Nadya typed his letters. When Lenin ordered him to be ever more "ruthless" and "merciless," Stalin replied, "Be assured that our hand will not tremble."[14]

Stalin conducted a campaign of "exemplary terror." He burned villages to show the consequences of failure to comply with the Red Army's orders and to demonstrate what counter-revolutionary sabotage would lead to. His enthusiasm for indiscriminate violence did not seem to faze Nadya, typing away in her railway carriage.

Nadya loved Stalin and seemed comfortable rationalizing, indeed even glamorizing, the Bolshevik cult of violence. The passionate love letters they sent each other when they were apart had an electric, if conventional, intensity. As late as June 1930, when Nadya was in Carlsbad talking a cure for debilitating headaches (another report suggests that she was actually suffering acute abdominal pains, possibly from an abortion), Stalin wrote: "Tatka [his pet Georgian name for her]. Do write to me something. . . . It is very lonely here, Tatochka. Am sitting at home, alone, like a little owl. I have not been to the country—too much work. I have finished my own task. I plan to go the day after tomorrow to the country, to the children. Well, good-bye. Do not stay there for too long, come back soon. I—kiss—you. Yours, Josef."[15] One of her letters to him ended: "I beg you to take good care of yourself. I kiss you warmly, as you had kissed me at my leaving. Yours, Nadya."[16]

But domestic life with Stalin had a different tenor and was extremely volatile. Nadya made a first attempt to leave him in 1926, when Svetlana was only six months old. After a quarrel, she packed up Svetlana, Vasili, and Svetlana's nanny and took the train to Leningrad (as Saint Petersburg was renamed in 1924 after Lenin's death), where she made it clear to her parents that she was leaving Stalin and intended to make her own life. He telephoned and begged her to come back. When he offered to come to get her, she replied, "I'll come back myself. It'll cost the state too much for you to come here."[17]

Perhaps Stalin's worst characteristic as a husband was the tantalizing quality of his affection. With her pride and reticence, Nadya rarely revealed family secrets, but her sister Anna remarked that she was a "long-suffering martyr." Stalin, usually distant and inscrutable, could flare up with an uncontrollable temper and could be callously indifferent to his wife's feelings. Nadya complained that she was always running Stalin's errands—he needed a document in the commissar's office; he needed a book from the library. "We wait for him, but never know when he will come home."[18]

Nadya's second year at the Industrial Academy, 1929, was the Year of the Great Turn and the forced collectivization of the peasantry into kolkhozy, or collective farms. The process was brutal. In order to root out private enterprise, village markets were shut down and livestock was confiscated. Kulaks, or prosperous peasants (owning one cow could constitute prosperity), were deported. Under this policy, known as dekulakization, peasants, "treated like livestock . . . often died in transit because of cold, starvation, beatings in the convoys, and other miseries."[19] By the year of Nadya's death, 1932, the infamous Gulag (forced-labor camps) held "more than a quarter of a million people," and 1.3 million, "mainly deported kulaks," were living as "special settlers."[20]

In 1932 and 1933, famine raged in the Ukraine. Stalin and his ministers were shipping grain supplies abroad to pay for smelters and tractors in order to sustain the rapid pace of industrialization. Though the Ukraine Politburo begged for emergency relief, no assistance came. Millions died. In 1932, a number of Nadya's fellow students at the Industrial Academy were arrested for speaking out about the famine. Nadya, too, was rumored to oppose "collectivisation and its immorality." Critical of Stalin, she secretly sympathized with Nikolai Bukharin and the right-wing opposition.[21] Stalin commanded Nadya to stay away from the Academy for two months.[22]

In the early days, Nadya attempted to exert some influence. When Stalin was vacationing alone in Sochi in September

1929, Nadya wrote him a careful letter, reporting that the Party was exploding over a dispute at *Pravda*; an article had been published without first being cleared by the Party hierarchy. Though many had seen the article, everyone was laying the blame on her friend Leonid Kovalev, and demanding his dismissal. In a long letter with the simple salutation "Dear Josef," she wrote:

> Don't be angry with me, but seriously I felt pain for Kovalev, for I know the colossal work that he has done in the paper. . . . To dismiss Kovalev . . . is simply monstrous. . . . Kovalev looks like a dead man. . . . I know that you detest my interference, but still I believe that you should look into this absolutely unjust outcome. . . . I cannot be indifferent about the fate of such a good worker and comrade of mine. . . . Good-bye, now, I kiss you tenderly. Please, answer me.[23]

Stalin wrote back four days later: "Tatka! Got your letter regarding Kovalev. . . . I believe you are right. . . . Obviously, in Kovalev they have found a scapegoat. I will do all I can, if it is not too late. . . . I kiss my Tatka many, many, many times. Yours, Josef."[24] Stalin did act on Nadya's request and wrote to Sergo Ordzhonikidze, in charge of adjudicating cases of disobedience to Party policies, to say that scapegoating Kovalev was "a very cheap but wrong and unbolshevik method of correcting one's faults. . . . Kovalev . . . IN NO CIRCUMSTANCES WOULD EVER let one line about Leningrad be printed, had it not been silently or directly approved, by somebody at the bureau."[25] Kovalev was eventually dismissed from *Pravda*—not as an "enemy of the people" but rather as "a straying son of the Party."[26]

Nadya wrote back rather pathetically: "I am very glad that in Kovalev's matter you have shown me your trust" and went on to report that the Academy was very friendly. "The academic achievements are judged according to rules: 'kulak,' the 'center,' the 'poor one.' We laugh a lot daily about that. I am already characterized as a right-wing," a strange admission to make to Stalin who would soon destroy the so-called right-wing opposition.[27]

There were clearly mounting tensions between Nadya and Stalin. She wrote in the summer of 1930, "This summer I did not feel that you might be pleased with a postponing of my departure, quite the contrary. The last summer I did feel that, but not now. . . . Answer me, if not too displeased by my letter, or rather, as you wish."[28] He wrote back to say that her reproaches were "unjust."[29] In October she wrote, "No news from you. . . . Maybe hunting quails absorbed you too much, or just too lazy to write."[30] Stalin responded with irony: "Lately you have begun to praise me. What does that mean? Good or bad news?"[31] Nadya's letters to Stalin in Sochi often contained reports of the hunger in Moscow, the long lines for food, the lack of fuel, the disrepair of the city. "Moscow looks better now, but in some places like a woman who covered with powder her defects, especially after rains, when the paint runs in stripes. . . . One wishes so that these shortcomings would one day leave our lives, and people would then feel wonderful and work remarkably well."[32]

By the time of her suicide, it is possible that Nadya was not schizophrenic but rather disillusioned with her husband's revolutionary politics. The night of her death, she refused to raise her glass in Stalin's toast to "the destruction of enemies of the state."

Nadya's friend Irina Gogua, who had known her since their shared childhood in Georgia, when the Alliluyev children, having no bathroom in their own apartment, had come for weekly Saturday baths at her house, remembered how Nadya behaved in Stalin's presence.

[Nadya] understood a lot. When I returned [to Moscow], I understood that her friends were arrested somewhere in Siberia. She . . . demanded to see their case. So she understood a lot. . . . In the presence of Joseph she resembled a fakir, who performs in the circus barefoot walking over broken glass. With a smile for the audience and with a terrifying intensity in her eyes. This is what she was like in the presence of Joseph, because she never knew what was coming next—what kind of explosion—he was a real cad. The only creature who softened him was Svetlana.

Gogua was not surprised when she heard the gossip that Nadya had committed suicide. Though the truth about her suicide was immediately suppressed, Gogua claimed that it was known among the security organizations. She added an interesting detail to her story. "Nadezhda had very perfect features and very beautiful features. But here is the paradox. The fact that she was beautiful was observed only after her death. . . . In the presence of Joseph, she was always like a fakir—always internally tense."[33]

As recently as 2011, Alexander Alliluyev, the son of Nadya's brother Pavel, offered a convincing detail in the puzzle of Nadya's suicide with a piece of the story that came to him from his parents.[34]

Pavel was at work when he heard the news that his sister had committed suicide. He immediately phoned his wife, Zhenya. He told her to stay where she was; he'd be right home. When he arrived, he asked where she had hidden the packet of papers that Nadya had given them. "In the linen," Zhenya replied. "Get them," he told her.

Nadya had been planning to leave Stalin. She intended to go to Leningrad and had even asked Sergei Kirov, head of the Communist Party organization there, about getting a job in the city. In the packet of papers she left with her brother was supposedly a parting letter for him and his wife.

Zhenya kept the existence of the letter secret for two decades and spoke to her son, Alexander, of its contents only in 1954, after Stalin's death. She told her son that Nadya had written that she "could not live with Stalin anymore. You take him for someone else. But he is a two-faced Janus. He will step over everybody in the world, including you." Alexander commented, "We all came to know what kind of a person Comrade Stalin was, but at the time, only Nadya knew about this."

Zhenya asked Pavel what they should do with the letter, and he replied, "Destroy it." The destruction of the letter and documents, of course, makes it impossible to verify the story, as is the case with so many stories about the inscrutable Stalin.

As an adult, Svetlana always believed that Nadya committed suicide because she had concluded there was no way out. How could one hide from Stalin? Svetlana's nanny later told her of overhearing Nadya's conversation with a female friend just days before she committed suicide. Nadya said that "everything bored her, she was sick of everything, and nothing made her happy." "What about the children?" the friend asked incredulously. "Everything, even the children," Nadya replied.[35] Such boredom was a sign of profound depression, but it was a painful account for her daughter to hear. Her mother had been "too bored." Svetlana's responses to her mother would always swing, unresolved, between sentimental idealizations and bitter anger.

Svetlana could not remember how or when she was told of her mother's death or even who told her. She remembered the formal resting in state that began at 2:30 on November 9. The news of Nadya's death had been shocking, and hundreds of thousands of Muscovites wanted to say good-bye to her, even though many were hearing her name for the first time. Stalin kept his family life very private.

Nadya's open coffin rested in the assembly hall at the GUM;
a huge building with atria, it housed government offices as well
as the GUM department store. Irina Gogua remembered that
the lines of people outside were so long that some of the un-
initiated public wondered what the stores were giving away.[36]
Svetlana remembered that Zina, the wife of Uncle Sergo Ordzhonikidze, took her hand and led her up to the coffin, expecting her to kiss her mother's cold face and say good-bye. Instead
she screamed and drew back.[37] That image of her mother in her
coffin seared itself in her mind, never to be dislodged. She was
rushed from the hall.

There are several versions of Stalin's behavior at the ceremony. In one, he sobbed, and Vasili held his hand and said,
"Don't cry, Papa." In another, Molotov, Polina's husband, always recalled the image of Stalin approaching the coffin with
tears running down his cheeks. "And he said so sadly, 'I didn't
save her.' I heard that and remembered it: 'I didn't save her.'"[38]
In Svetlana's retelling, Stalin approached the casket and, suddenly incensed, shoved it, saying, "She went away as an enemy."[39] He abruptly turned his back on the body and left. Had
Svetlana herself heard this? The anecdote sounds like retro-
spective invective and does not seem like the observation of a
six-year-old in hysterics. Perhaps this was someone else's story.

A cortege of marching soldiers accompanied the coffin carried on a draped gun carriage covered in flowers. Vasili walked
with Stalin beside Nadya's coffin in the procession to the Novodevichy Cemetery. Svetlana was not present.

Svetlana believed her father never visited her mother's grave.
"Not even once. He couldn't. He thought my mother had left
him as his personal enemy." Yet there were stories from Stalin's
drivers of secret nocturnal visits to Nadya's grave site, especially
during the coming war.[40]

Mourners walk alongside Nadya's coffin during the procession to Novodevichy Cemetery in November 1932. Vasili is the small boy in the front row. Svetlana was not present.

Pravda reported Nadya's death in a perfunctory manner, without explanation. Her suicide was a state secret, though everyone in the apparat knew about it. The children, along with the public, were told another story: Nadya had died of peritonitis after an attack of appendicitis.

It would be ten years before Svetlana learned the truth about her mother's suicide. Though this might seem astounding, it is entirely credible. The terror that Stalin had begun to spread around him particularly infected those closest to him. Who would dare tell Stalin's daughter that her mother had committed suicide? Many would be shot simply for knowing the truth. It soon became "bad form" even to mention Nadya's name.

Stalin was clearly shocked by Nadya's death, but he got over it. He wrote to his mother:

MARCH 24, 1934

Greetings Mother dear,

I got the jam, the ginger and the *chukhcheli* [Georgian candy]. The children are very pleased and send you their thanks. I am well, so don't worry about me. I can endure my destiny. I don't know whether or not you need money. I'm sending you 500 rubles just in case. . . .

Keep well dear Mother and keep your spirits up. A kiss.

Your son,

Soso

P.S. The children bow to you. After Nadya's death, my private life has been very hard, but a strong man must always be valiant.[41]

But for very young children the scars caused by a parent's death are profound, in part because death is not something their young minds can grasp; they understand only abandonment. Svetlana's adopted brother, Artyom Sergeev, remembered Svetlana's seventh birthday party, four months after her mother's death. Everyone brought birthday presents. Still not sure what death meant, Svetlana asked, "What did Mommy send me from Germany?"[42] But she was afraid to sleep alone in the dark.

A childhood friend, seven-year-old Marfa Peshkova, granddaughter of the famous writer Maxim Gorky, remembered visiting Svetlana after Nadya's death. Svetlana was playing with her dolls. There were scraps of black fabric all over the floor. She was trying to dress her dolls in the black fabric and told Marfa, "It's Mommy's dress. Mommy died and I want my dolls to be wearing Mommy's dress."[43]

Chapter 3

The Hostess and the Peasant

Stalin with Vasili and an eight-year-old Svetlana.

Svetlana always divided her life into two parts: before and after her mother's death, when her world changed utterly. Her father immediately decided to move out of the Poteshny Palace, where the shade of Nadya hovered in every corner. Nikolai Bukharin offered to swap his ground-floor apartment in the Kremlin Senate, also known as the Yellow Palace, where Lenin had once had his private residence. Stalin accepted.

The apartment was long and narrow with vaulted ceilings and darkened rooms and had once served as an office. Svetlana hated it. The only familiar object was a photograph of Nadya at Zubalovo, wearing her beautifully embroidered shawl; Stalin had had the picture enlarged and hung in the dining room over the elaborately carved sideboard. Svetlana filled her bedroom with mementos of her mother. Stalin's office was on the floor above, and the Politburo met in the same building.

Svetlana's home was now full of vigilant strangers. It was run on a military model with a staff of agents of the OGPU (the secret police) who were called "service personnel" rather than servants. Svetlana felt they treated everyone but her father as nonexistent. She was sure her mother would never have allowed such an invasion, but Stalin obviously thought the quasi-military regimen of the household fitting. His children were not to be spoiled. No luxuries, no indulgences. He probably also thought the security was necessary. Enemies were about.

Even Svetlana's beloved Zubalovo had altered. When she and Vasili returned there after their mother's death, she was devastated to find the tree house they called "Robinson Crusoe" dismantled, and the swings gone.[1] For security reasons, the sandy roads had been covered with ugly black asphalt, and the beautiful lilacs and cherry bushes had been dug up. While the extended family still frequented Zubalovo on weekends and Grandpa Sergei lived there most of the time, Stalin seldom visited the dacha again.

Grandmother Olga continued to live in a small apartment in another building in the Kremlin. With its Caucasian rugs, its *takhta* covered with embroidered cushions, and the old chest holding photographs, Olga's apartment was the only welcoming space in this strange new world. When Svetlana visited, she would find her grandmother raging at the new regimen. She called the "state employees" a waste of public money. The staff retorted that she was "a fussy old freak."[2]

Svetlana's maternal grandmother, Olga Alliluyeva,
in an undated photograph.

It was soon clear that Stalin had no intention of living in the Kremlin. Shortly after Nadya's death, he had his favorite architect, Miron Merzhanov,[3] design him a new dacha in the village of Volynskoye in the district of Kuntsevo, about fifteen miles outside Moscow. He called it Blizhniaia, the "near dacha." Stalin was said to have chosen this name for its useful vagueness in telephone conversations that might be overheard by enemies. The sixteen-room dacha, painted camouflage green, sat in the center of a forest. To approach it one had to drive down a narrow asphalt road and pass through a sixteen-foot-high fence with searchlights mounted, within which was a second barrier of barbed wire. Svetlana detested her father's new dacha. She said that the dacha and the Kremlin apartment continued to surface in her nightmares for decades.

By 1934, Stalin had moved to his dacha in Kuntsevo. Most evenings, he came down the stairs of the Yellow Palace to dine at the Kremlin apartment with his children. With him would be members of his inner circle, all men. Svetlana would rush to the dining room. Her father would seat her on his right. As the men talked business, she would stare up at the framed photograph of her mother over the sideboard. Her father would turn to her and ask about her school marks and sign her school daybook. This, at least, was her memory of family dinners. Though she never mentions her brother, presumably Vasili was also there and equally silent. At the end of the meal, Stalin would dismiss his children and continue his discussions with his Politburo members into the small hours of the morning. Then he would head out to Kuntsevo, where he slept. Sometimes he would come upstairs in his overcoat to give his sleeping daughter a good-night kiss.

Stalin's departure was an elaborate ritual. There would be three identical cars with tinted blue windows waiting outside. Stalin would pick one, climb in, and move off in a cordon of guards, taking a different car and a different route each night. The traffic on the Arbat and Minskoye highways was stopped in four directions. He always waited until the last minute to tell his personal secretary, Alexander Poskrebyshev, or his bodyguard, Nikolai Vlasik, that he intended to leave for his dacha.[4]

Life at the Kuntsevo dacha also had a military tone, with commandants and bodyguards. Two cooks, a charwoman, chauffeurs, watchmen, gardeners, and the women who waited on Stalin's table all worked in shifts. They, too, were employees of the OGPU. The commandants and bodyguards, in particular, were high functionaries rewarded for their services with Party privileges: good apartments, dachas, and government cars. Valentina Istomina—everyone, including Svetlana, affectionately called her Valechka—soon joined the household as Stalin's personal housekeeper and stayed with him for eighteen years. According to Molotov, there were many unconfirmed rumors that she was Stalin's bed companion.[5]

Though the nanny Alexandra Andreevna was permitted to stay with Svetlana in the Kremlin apartment, a new governess, Lidia Georgiyevna, arrived in 1933. Svetlana disliked this governess immediately for reprimanding her nanny: "Remember your place, Comrade." The seven-year-old Svetlana shouted back, "Don't you dare insult my nanny."[6]

With her mother gone, Svetlana's devastation was palpable, and she directed her neediness toward her father. She spent August 1933 with her nanny in Sochi. There she wrote to her father, who was in Moscow:

AUGUST 5, 1933

Hello my dear Papochka [Daddy],

How are you living and how is your health? I received your letter and I am happy that you allowed me to stay here and wait for you. I was worried that I would leave for Moscow and you would come to Sochi and I would not see you again. Dear Papochka, when you come you will not recognize me. I got really tanned. Every night I hear the howling of the coyotes. I wait for you in Sochi.

I kiss you.

Svetanka[7]

It had been nine months since her mother's death. A child, afraid of the dark, listens to the coyotes howling in the woods, worried that her father will disappear. She was seven years old. She waited. This unappeasable emotional hunger would return without warning to sabotage Svetlana throughout her life.

Stalin seems to have been somewhat aware of his young daughter's psychological needs. Candide Charkviani, a visiting writer and politician whom Stalin admired and promoted, described in his memoirs how shocked he was to discover that "Stalin, someone who absolutely lacked sentimentalism, expressed such untypical gentleness towards his daughter. 'My little Hostess,' Stalin would say, and seat Svetlana on his lap and give her kisses. 'Since she lost her mother I have kept telling her that she is a homemaker,' Stalin told us."[8]

Stalin had loving diminutives for Svetlana. She was his "little butterfly," "little fly," "little sparrow." He developed a game for her, which they continued to play until she was sixteen. Whenever she asked him for something, he would say, "Why are you only asking? Give an order, and I'll see to it right away."[9] He called her his hostess and told her he was her secretary; she was in charge. He would descend from his office on the upper floor of the Yellow Palace and head down the hall, shouting, "Hostess!"

But this was still Stalin. He also invented an imaginary friend for Svetlana called Lyolka. She was Svetlana's double, a little girl who was perfect. Her father might say he'd just seen Lyolka and she'd done something marvelous, which Svetanka (the affectionate diminutive Stalin used) should imitate. Or he might draw a picture of Lyolka doing this or that. Secretly, Svetlana hated Lyolka.

When he was staying at his dacha in Sochi, Stalin would write his daughter letters in the big block script of a child, signing them Little Papa:

To My Hostess Svetanka:

You don't write to your little papa. I think you've forgotten him. How is your health? You're not sick, are you? What are you up to? Have you seen Lyolka? How are your dolls? I thought I'd be getting an order from you soon, but no. Too bad. You're hurting your little papa's feelings. Never mind. I kiss you. I am waiting to hear from you.

Little Papa[10]

Stalin called himself Secretary No. 1. Svetlana would write short notes to Secretary No. 1 with her orders, and pin these with tacks on the wall near the telephone above his desk. Amusingly, she also sent missives to all the other "little secretaries" in the Kremlin. Government ministers, such as Lazar Kaganovich and Vyacheslav Molotov, had no choice but to play the game.

Svetlana would order her Secretary No. 1 to take her to the theater, to ride the new subway, or to visit the Zubalovo dacha.

OCTOBER 21, 1934

To Comrade J. V. Stalin.
Secretary No. 1
Order No. 4
I order you to take me with you.

Signed: Svetanka, the Hostess

Seal
Signed: Secretary No. 1   *I submit. J. Stalin*[11]

Stalin always spent several months each fall working alone at his southern dacha in Sochi; Svetlana would be left in her nanny's hands. She would write her father loving letters, but one can hear the solicitude and tentativeness in her tone:

SEPTEMBER 15, 1933

Hello my dear Papochka,

How do you live and how is your health? I arrived well except that my Nanny got really sick on the road. But everything is well now. Papochka, don't miss me but get better and rest and I will try to study excellently for your happiness. . . .

I kiss you deeply.

Your Svetanka[12]

Stalin's letters could be affectionate and teasing:

APRIL 18, 1935

Hello Little Hostess!

I'm sending you pomegranates, tangerines and some candied fruit. Eat and enjoy them, my little Hostess! I'm not sending any to Vasya [Vasili's nickname] because he's still doing badly at school and feeds me nothing but promises. Tell him I don't believe promises made in words and that I'll believe Vasya only when he really starts to study, even if his marks are only "good." I report to you, Comrade Hostess, that I was in Tiflis for one day. I was at my mother's and I gave her regards from you and Vasya. She is well, more or less, and she gives both of you a big kiss. Well, that's all right now. I give you a kiss. I'll see you soon.[13]

He signed his letters: "From Svetanka-Hostess's wretched Secretary, the poor peasant J. Stalin."

There were others who remembered the little "hostess." Nikita Khrushchev managed to stay in Stalin's favor after Nadya's death. He recalled Svetlana as a lovely little girl who was "always dressed smartly in a Ukrainian skirt and an embroidered blouse" and, with her red hair and freckles, looked like "a dressed-up doll."

> Stalin would say: "Well, hostess, entertain the guests," and she would run out into the kitchen. Stalin explained: "Whenever she gets angry with me, she always says, 'I'm going out to the kitchen and complain about you to the cook.' I always plead with her, 'Spare me! If you complain to the cook, it will be all over with me!'" Then Svetlanka [sic] would say firmly that she would tell on her papa if he ever did anything wrong again.[14]

The game of the Hostess and the Peasant might have seemed charming, but it had a dark side. Khrushchev claimed that he felt pity for little Svetlana "as I would feel for an orphan. Stalin himself was brutish and inattentive. . . . [Stalin] loved her, but . . . his was the tenderness of a cat for a mouse."

A British journalist, Eileen Bigland, recalled meeting Svetlana in 1936 when she was a "lumpy schoolgirl" of ten. "Her father adored her. He loved listening to her exploits in the Park of Rest and Culture. He patted her delightedly when she played 'The Blue Bells of Scotland' on the piano. He was a rough and tumble father to her, a pincher and a teaser—like a bear with a cub—and you felt at any minute that he might cuff her like a bear. She was a jolly little girl."[15]

The Kremlin contained a small cinema on the site of what had once been the Winter Garden, linked by passageways to the Kremlin Senate. After the usual two-hour dinner, which ended at nine p.m., Svetlana would beg her father to let her stay up. He would feign displeasure and then laugh. "You show us how to get there, Hostess. Without you to guide us we'd never find it."[16]

It was thrilling for the child to race ahead of the procession through the passageways and out across the grounds of the deserted Kremlin. Behind her followed her father, his cronies, the security guards, and at a distance, the slow-moving armored car that now always accompanied the *vozhd*. The movies would end at two a.m. When the last film was over, Svetlana would race back through the empty grounds, leaving the men behind to continue their discussions.

Stalin viewed all new Soviet films in the Kremlin before they were released to the public, so the ones Svetlana watched were often Russian: *Chapayev, Circus, Volga-Volga*. But Stalin loved American Westerns and particularly Charlie Chaplin films, which would send him into fits of laughter—with the exception of Chaplin's *The Great Dictator*, which was banned.[17] She would always think back nostalgically to these times: "Those are the years that left me with the memory that he loved me and tried to be a father to me and bring me up as best he knew how. All this collapsed when the war came."[18]

After her mother's death, as Svetlana put it, her father became the "final, unquestioned authority for me in everything."[19] None was more brilliant at psychological manipulation than Stalin, the "poor peasant" controlling his little "hostess." Svetlana would spend a lifetime trying to rip off the mask of compliance that she had invented for her father. She would often succeed, spectacularly, only to find the mask slipping back over her face. A paradox was forming: a child who could order around the most powerful members of the Politburo as her secretaries, but also a dreadfully lonely little girl who learned to behave.

Though it is often said that the family disintegrated after Nadya's death, the family members refute this. All of them—Grandfather Sergei and Grandmother Olga, Uncle Pavel and Aunt Zhenya, Aunt Anna and Uncle Stanislav, Uncle Alyosha and Aunt Maria Svanidze—continued to visit. For the next two or three years, the Alliluyevs and Svanidzes remained close to Stalin. There were shared trips in the summer to Sochi, and the New Year and birthdays were celebrated at Stalin's Kuntsevo dacha. According to Svetlana's cousin Alexander Alliluyev, the family was fragile but united, still absorbing the shock of Nadya's suicide, all of the relatives asking themselves: "Why did we not see it coming?" Alexander's father, Pavel, felt particularly guilty about giving his sister that small gun.[20]

From left: Vasili, future Supreme Soviet chairman Andrei Zhdanov, Svetlana, Stalin, and Svetlana's half brother Yakov at Stalin's dacha in Sochi, c. 1934.

It is even possible that Stalin was keeping up some semblance of family ties. When Svetlana was nine, he arranged for her, Yakov, and Vasili to visit his mother, Keke, in Tiflis. It was 1935, two years before Keke's death. Though the palace in Tiflis was grand, she continued to live like a peasant in a ground-floor room. The visit was not a success. Keke terrified Svetlana. Sitting up in her black iron cot surrounded by old women dressed in black who looked like crows, she tried to speak to Svetlana in Georgian. Only Yakov spoke Georgian. Svetlana took the candies her grandmother offered her and re-treated outside as soon as she could.

Stalin was not on this trip. Before her death, he did manage to visit his mother in her final illness. It was supposedly on this visit that Keke made her famous rebuke to her son. She asked, "Joseph, who exactly are you now?" Stalin answered, "Remember the tsar. Well, I'm like a tsar." Keke responded, "What a pity you never became a priest." Svetlana reported that her father always recounted this conversation "with relish."[21]

Svetlana was now attending Model School No. 25 on Staropimenovsky Street in the center of Moscow. When she turned seven, Stalin ordered Karl Viktorovich Pauker, in charge of security for Stalin and his children, to check out the best schools.[22] Her brother, Vasili, then twelve and in grade five at the less rigorous School No. 20, was transferred to Model School No. 25 to join her. At 7:45 a.m. each weekday, a Kremlin limousine dropped Svetlana and Vasili off at Pushkin Square. They walked the short distance to the school, through the large oak doors, and up the stairs to the second floor, where their father's and Lenin's portraits hung on the wall of the imposing landing.

Svetlana's school years coincided with the cult of personality. Stalin's image appeared everywhere, and he began to be hailed with grandiose epithets, from the Great Helmsman to Soviet Women's Best Friend. His relative Maria Svanidze insisted this wasn't personal vanity. According to her, Stalin claimed that "people need a tsar, that is someone to whom they could bow and in whose name they could live and work."[23] This disclaimer is not entirely convincing, though it would seem that shrewd political calculation about the impact of propaganda, as much as megalomania, motivated Stalin's cult of personality. In any case, Svetlana climbed the stairs to meet her father's face every morning.

Because she was used to private tutors, the school was a shock. The first day, she walked into the boys' bathroom, as she had always done at home among her brothers and cousins, and was ever after known as the girl who walked into the boys' toilets.[24]

Svetlana in her classroom at Model School No. 25 in Moscow, sitting at the third desk in the second row, in 1935.

Model School No. 25 was no ordinary school. It was considered the best in the country. As one former pupil described it, it was "the school where the big-shot children went."[25] So rarefied was the world of Model School No. 25 in relation to what was happening in the rest of the country that it was like stepping through the looking glass. Palms and lemon trees dotted the hallways, and there were white tablecloths on the tables in the cafeteria. The students included the sons and daughters of the famous and powerful: the children of actors, writers, an Arctic explorer, an aviation engineer, members of the Comintern's Executive Committee and the Politburo, and other high government officials. There were many limousines.

Model School No. 25 was a Soviet lycée with very high scholastic standards. By 1937 the library, with its resplendent banner, WITHOUT KNOWLEDGE, THERE IS NO COMMUNISM, had twelve thousand volumes and subscribed to forty journals and newspapers. Beside the library was a quiet room where children played dominoes, table croquet, and chess.[26]

The school had clubs in theater, ballroom dancing, literature, photography, airplane and automobile modeling, radio and electrotechnology, parachute jumping, and chess. The boxing club and track club trained on the surrounding streets. There were sports competitions, a rifle team, and volleyball tournaments. A doctor and a dentist were in residence. The children went on excursions to Moscow's famous Tretyakov Gallery and to Tolstoy's estate, and they vacationed at sanatoriums on the Black Sea. Even as the train carried them through the famine-stricken Ukraine on their way to their Crimean summer camps in the early 1930s, and though the station platforms were crowded with hungry people devastated by collectivization, students remained under the spell of their school. Their teachers did not discuss the famine.

Model School No. 25 was treated as a "shopwindow on socialism," and thousands, including foreigners, came to visit. Reporters and photographers would follow in their wake. The American singer Paul Robeson placed his son there in 1936, though under an assumed name. When the school needed money, a letter from the director to Stalin or Kaganovich would get a response. One American visitor, Joseph C. Lukes, wrote in the visitors' book: "The standards of lighting, heating, ventilation and cleanliness are up to American standards."[27] Soon the school got more money to renovate and upgrade. Model School No. 25 was meant to be better than American schools.[28]

There were schools outside Moscow that the foreigners did not visit, schools where, by the early 1930s, students went without paper (they wrote notes in the margins of old books) and pens were rationed. Because of a shortage of desks, classes were taught in shifts. Schools closed for lack of firewood or of kerosene for lamps. Outside the capital, the devastation caused by forced collectivization and the attacks on the kulaks, which led to widespread famine, meant that often as many as 40 percent of the students dropped out. Many of them had died.[29]

In 1929, Andrei Bubnov, commissar of enlightenment and head of the Communist Party's Agitation and Propaganda Department (Agitprop), called upon all schools "to immerse themselves in a class war for the transformation of the Soviet economy and society." Students and teachers at Model School No. 25 were meant to internalize the Stalinist credo: "a respect for obedience, hierarchy and institutionalized authority; a belief in reason, optimism and progress; recognition of a possible transformation of nature, society, and human beings; and an acceptance of the necessity of violence."[30] Like all Soviet schools, Model School No. 25 promoted indoctrination with banners hung in the hallways: DOWN WITH FASCIST INTERVENTION IN SPAIN or LIFE HAS BECOME BETTER, COMRADES, LIFE HAS BECOME MORE JOYFUL (Stalin's famous 1935 pronouncement).[31]

All Soviet children were trained in Communism. First they were Octobrists, then Pioneers, then Komsomols. One became an Octobrist in first grade on November 7 (October in the old, Julian calendar) to coincide with Revolution Day. Everyone got a red star with a white circle in which was the head of baby Lenin.

One became a Pioneer in third grade. Children received

triangular red scarves that they were required to wear every day. They also got pioneer pins with the slogan ALWAYS READY! Svetlana proudly wore her Pioneer uniform and marched enthusiastically with the Model School No. 25 contingent in the annual May Day parades across Red Square. "Lenin was our icon, Marx and Engels our apostles—their every word Gospel truth," she would say in retrospect.[32] And it went without saying, her father was right in everything, "without exception."

However, there was a paradox at the core of the Model School. When Svetlana started there in 1933, only 15 percent of the teachers and administrators belonged to the Communist Party. Many of them had questionable backgrounds as part of the prerevolutionary nobility, the White Army, religious organizations, or the merchant class. Model School No. 25 managed to be relatively democratic and fostered an ideologically unacceptable individualism.[33] Some of its graduates became critical opponents of the Communist system, working as reformist editors, historians, attorneys, and human-rights activists.

It is compelling to compare the reputations of Stalin's children at the school; they were polar opposites. Most of Vasili's schoolmates remembered him as an amusing and rambunctious boy who was constantly in trouble. His closest friend was called Farm Boy (Kolkhoznik)—the boy's family had recently migrated from the countryside; his mother scrubbed the school floors.[34]

Vasili was notorious for his pranks. A church had once stood beside Model School No. 25, and the mounds of graves in its abandoned graveyard were still visible. One of Vasili's favorite escapades was to sneak into the graveyard with his buddies to dig up bones.[35] And he was already known for his cursing.

When reprimanded by schoolteachers, he would say he would do better, "remembering whose son I am."

Still, his fellow students considered themselves his equals. When he broke a window and blamed someone else, they beat him up. When he harassed a boy who had poor eyesight, they voted to expel him from the Komsomol.[36] There was an amusing moment when he deliberately interrupted a film being shown to visiting teachers and his instructor shouted, "Stalin, leave the room." They all froze until they saw the diminutive Vasili storm out. Whenever he attempted to intimidate the administration and teachers with his name, reports were sent to Stalin, who had relayed firm instructions that his children were to be treated like everybody else.[37]

Vasili was clearly afraid of his father, but he was already presuming on the authority his name conferred. Aged twelve, he wrote to Stalin. He had taken to calling himself Vaska Krasny (Red Vaska), presumably to please him:

AUGUST 5, 1933

Hello Papa.

I got your letter. Thank you. You write me that we could leave for Moscow on the 12th. Papa, I asked the Commandant if he could personally arrange for the wellbeing of the teacher's wife. But he refused. So the teacher arranged for her to work in the barracks of the workers. . . . Papa, I send you three rocks on which I have painted. We are alive and well and I am studying until we meet again soon.

Vaska Krasny[38]

In this instance Vasili's intervention seems to have been benevolent, but having Stalin's children in their charge made school officials very nervous. Vasili complained to his father:

SEPTEMBER 26 [NO YEAR]

Hello Papa,

I live well and go to school and life is fun. I play in my school's first team of soccer, but each time I go to play there's a lot of talk about the question that without my father's permission I can't play. Write to me whether or not I can play and it will be done as you say.

Vaska Krasny[39]

Only Svetlana seemed to have measured the cost to Vasili of his mother's suicide when he was just eleven. She believed Nadya's disappearance from their lives completely destroyed her brother. He began drinking at the age of thirteen and, when drunk, often turned his venom against his sister. When his foul language and crude sexual stories became too explicit, Yakov, her half brother, would step in to defend her. She later told several interviewers, "My brother provided me with an early sex education of the dirtiest sort."[40] She did not elaborate, but it is clear that she kept Vasili at a safe distance. She said she discovered she loved her brother only after he died.

However, she was grateful for one thing. Svetlana was often ill in childhood, but her father refused to send her to the hospital, presumably for security reasons. She remembered long lonely days exiled to her room in the care of nurses and her nanny.[41] But that changed in her adolescence. Saying she was "fat and sickly," Vasili pushed her into sports. Soon she joined the ski team and the volleyball team and developed the robust health that would characterize her for the rest of her life.

In 1937 Vasili was finally transferred to Moscow's Special School No. 2, where he continued to trade on his name, refusing to do his homework, throwing spitballs in class, whistling, singing, and walking out. But at his new school, the administrators tried to coat over his lapses and even allowed him to skip his final exams. The German teacher who tried to give him a failing grade was threatened with dismissal. Even as an exasperated Stalin ordered the keeping of a "secret daybook" on his conduct, higher officials protected him.[42] There is also a much darker rumor attached to his name. Vasili may have "provoked the arrest of the parents of a boy who bested him in an athletic competition."[43]

In 1938, the seventeen-year-old was sent to the Kachinsk Military Aviation School, where Stalin thought he might find the discipline he needed, but again he demanded and received special privileges. Vasili was learning the power of his father's name, which would eventually prove his undoing.

Meanwhile, Svetlana dutifully brought home her daybook with a record of her academic work and conduct. Over dinner at the Yellow Palace, her father would examine and sign it, as vigilant parents were required to do. He was proud of her. She was a good little girl. Her indoctrination was clear in the words she recorded as a third grader in a testament celebrating the achievements of Nina Groza, the school administrator: " 'Under your leadership our school has advanced into the ranks of the best schools of the Soviet Union.' Svetlana Stalina."[44] Svetlana had become one of the little "warriors for communism."

Until she was sixteen, like many of her fellow students, Svetlana remained an idealistic Communist, unreflectingly accepting Party ideology. In retrospect she would be appalled by how this ideology demanded the censorship of all private thought and led to the mass hypnosis of millions. She called this "the mentality of slaves." Vasili learned cynically to manipulate the system, which, by its very nature, invited corruption. He understood early that the best way to get ahead was to betray somebody else.

Chapter 4

The Terror

Stalin's December 21 birthday celebration at Blizhniaia dacha in 1934. *Top row, from left:* Anna Redens, Dora Khazan (wife of Politburo member Andrey Andreyev), Ekaterina Voroshilova (wife of Soviet military officer Kliment Voroshilov). *Middle row, from left:* Maria Svandize, Maria Kaganovich (wife of Lazar Kaganovich, the "Wolf of the Kremlin"), Sashiko Svanidze, Stalin, Polina Molotov (wife of Vyacheslav Molotov, a protégé of Stalin), Kliment Voroshilov ("Uncle Voroshilov" to Svetlana). *Bottom row, from left:* Anna Eliava (wife of George Eliava, a prominent Georgian scientist), Zhenya Alliluyeva (wife of Stalin's brother-in-law), and Dmitry Manuilsky (a Soviet deputy) and his wife.

On December 6, 1934, two years after the death of her mother, eight-year-old Svetlana found herself at the Hall of Columns attending the lying-in-state of Sergei Kirov. He was one of her favorite "uncles" with whom she'd played the Hostess game. Just days before, the extended Stalin clan had attended a comedy called *The Hangover After the Feast* at the Maly Theater, and then her father had invited them all back for dinner at Kuntsevo. Uncle Sergei had sent them *snetki* (smelts) from Leningrad.[1] Now Uncle Sergei was dead too. "I didn't like this thing called Death. I was terrified. . . . I developed a fear of dark places, dark rooms, dark depths," Svetlana later told a friend.[2]

On December 1, at 4:30 p.m., Sergei Kirov, secretary of the Leningrad Party organization, was assassinated in the corridor of his office at the Smolny Institute, headquarters of the local Communist Party. Kirov's assassin, Leonid Nikolaev, had walked brazenly into the building and shot him. According to the initial reports of the NKVD, Nikolaev's motive was revenge for Kirov's adulterous relationship with his wife, but it was soon announced that Nikolaev was a member of a counterrevolutionary terrorist organization plotting to overthrow the government. At the end of December, Nikolaev, along with fourteen codefendants, was tried and executed.[3]

The Kirovs, the Stalins, the Alliluyevs, and the Svanidzes stood together in the austere Hall of Columns. In her private diary, later confiscated by the secret police, Maria Svanidze described the scene:

> The Hall was brightly lit, decorated with heavy plush banners, reaching the ceiling. . . . The Hall was high, two stories. In the middle . . . was standing . . . a very simple red-cotton coffin with rushes. . . . [Kirov's] face was yellow-green, with nose grown sharp, lips tightly closed, with deep lines on the forehead and on the cheeks, with corners of his lips curled down in suffering sadness. A large blue spot from falling could be seen from the left temple to

the left cheekbone. Around the coffin were many wreaths with ribbons, inscribed by the organizations. . . . Lights for news-chronicles were around . . . security people and on the stage the orchestra of the Bolshoi was playing all the time. . . . Full lights notwithstanding, it was gloomily dark.

At eleven p.m., the leaders appeared, preceded by Stalin.

Joseph steps up the stage to the coffin, his face is twisted with grief, he kisses the forehead of dead Sergey Mironovitch. All this pierces our souls, we know how close they have been, and everyone in the Hall is sobbing. I can hear through my own sobs the sobbing of men around.[4]

Maria recorded that immediately after receiving news of Kirov's death, Nadya's brother Pavel visited Stalin at his dacha. Sitting with his head in his hands, Stalin cried, "I am quite orphaned now." Pavel was so moved that he rushed at once to hug and kiss his brother-in-law.

But Stalin was not at his dacha. The scene of Pavel's tenderness probably occurred several days later. Instead, Stalin was in his Kremlin office. As soon as news of the assassination reached him at five p.m., a much less maudlin Stalin called in his Politburo and Genrikh Yagoda, NKVD chief, to arrange an overnight train to Leningrad. Probably that night he drafted the Law of December 1, "instructing the police and courts to try cases of terrorism without delay, reject appeals, and carry out death sentences immediately upon conviction."[5] The rules of investigation thus simplified, over the next three years, what had begun as the expulsion of counterrevolutionaries from the Party would turn into mass repression.

Some believed Stalin ordered Kirov's assassination. Kirov was too popular and was in favor of slowing down Stalin's policy of rapid industrialization. There is little evidence to support this theory, but certainly Kirov's assassination provided a necessary and important beginning to the subsequent Great Terror, in which hundreds of thousands were swept away in "mass operations."[6]

As a consequence of collectivization and dekulakization,[*] the OGPU (secret police, renamed NKVD in 1934) had already spread its tentacles through every level of society as it hunted for class enemies. Wiretapping, surveillance, pressure on informants, imprisonment in solitary confinement, confessions exacted under torture—all became the norm. Compromising information mutated like a virus, implicating hundreds of thousands.

In 1935 and 1936, as the mass arrests were under way, a collective hysteria took over. At the height of the Great Terror, during "seventeen months in 1937 and 1938 alone, 1.7 million people were arrested, more than 700,000 of them shot, and another 300,000 to 400,000 sent into punishing exile in Siberia, Kazakhstan, and other far-away places."[7]

In 1937, on the twentieth anniversary of the Revolution, Stalin was reported to have told his close associates at a private banquet:

> We will destroy each and every enemy even if he was an old Bolshevik; we will destroy all his kin, his family. We will mercilessly destroy anyone who, by his deeds or his thoughts—yes, his thoughts—threatens the unity of the socialist state.[8]

By 1938, as a result of the repression carried out by the NKVD, the Gulag prison population had swelled to two million.[9]

---

* Dekulakization: Soviet campaign of political repression, including deportations and executions, of so-called wealthy peasants.

As an eleven-year-old, Svetlana could understand nothing of this, but she personally began to feel the impact of this new climate of terror when she returned from her vacation in Sochi at the end of the summer of 1937. Carolina Til, the German housekeeper who'd been with the family for ten years, had been dismissed as unreliable.[10] Lieutenant Alexandra Nakashidze appeared in her place. Nakashidze had totally reorganized Svetlana's room, removing all the furniture that once belonged to her mother and emptying the cupboard of her childhood mementos, her album of drawings, her clay figurines, and her presents from the aunts. The few cherished things that tied her to her mother—an enameled box with dragons, a tiny glass, and some cups—had vanished.[11] When Svetlana asked her nanny to complain about the loss, her nanny replied that there was nothing to do—everything belonged to the state.

Nakashidze worked for the NKVD State Security Forces. A young woman under thirty, she was unskilled as a housekeeper, but housekeeping was not her function. She was meant to get close to Svetlana and her brother Vasili in order to scrutinize their friends and acquaintances.

Starting that fall of 1937, Svetlana was assigned a bodyguard named Ivan Krivenko, a sour, jaundiced-looking man whom she immediately disliked. He followed her everywhere—to school, to the theater, to music lessons. One day she discovered him digging through her schoolbag and reading her diary.[12]

At school she found herself under a new regimen. She was forbidden to use the common cloakroom and had to hang her coat in a small room next to the school's office. She was no longer allowed to eat with the other students. Now she ate a lunch, brought from home, in a small screened-off corner of the lunchroom under the scrutiny of an NKVD officer, which left her blushing with embarrassment.

Then there was trouble with Misha, one of her closest friends. Red-haired and freckled like Svetlana, Misha was a passionate reader whom she'd known since she was eight. They both loved to raid their parents' extensive libraries and discuss the books they found. As eleven-year-olds, they shared a passion for Maupassant and were madly engrossed by Jules Verne and the Indian tales of the American author James Fenimore Cooper. At school they passed each other little love notes on blotting paper, and they phoned back and forth almost every day. Then Misha's parents, who worked for state publishers, were arrested. Svetlana's governess took her little love notes to the school principal and insisted that Misha be transferred to another class. Clearly Misha was a dangerous influence, with his "unreliable" parents, and the friendship was terminated. It would be nineteen years before they met again.[13]

From the early days of the Revolution, Bolshevik ideology had built a tradition of identifying "enemies of the people" and "anti-Soviet elements." Show trials and the fabrication of evidence had been almost commonplace since the Civil War.[14] People were trained to believe in conspiracies against the great Soviet experiment. After the first two great show trials engineered by Stalin in August 1936 and January 1937, in which most of those targeted were from the Old Guard of the Bolshevik Party, Svetlana's Aunt Maria Svanidze wrote in her secret diary:

March 17, 1937:
My soul is burning with anger, and hatred, their death does not satisfy me. They ought to be tortured, burned alive, for all their wicked deeds. Sellers of the motherland, parasites with the party. And so many of them! Ah, they wanted to ruin our society, they wanted to ruin all victories of revolution, to kill our husbands, our sons. . . .
Endless disappearance of persons with big names, who

for years were our heroes, conducted big jobs, were trusted, and many times rewarded—they turned out to be our enemies, traitors of the people, bribed and bought ones. . . . How could we have missed all this?[15]

Maria Svanidze believed in their guilt until she herself was arrested.

On December 21, Maria and Alexander Svanidze were the first members of Svetlana's family to be taken away by the NKVD.

According to Anastas Mikoyan, Alexander Svanidze was like a brother to Stalin. He was deputy chair of the board of the State Bank of the USSR in 1937 and had done sensitive work for Stalin in Germany over a number of years. In April, Stalin ordered Nikolai Yezhov, the new head of the NKVD (the former head, Genrikh Yagoda, was awaiting execution), to begin the purge of the staff at the State Bank.

Pavel and Zhenya Alliluyev were hosting a housewarming party in their apartment. It was a festive, elegant affair. Maria and Alexander had attended and then returned to their own residence. After midnight, the Svandizes' son Johnik, named after John Reed, the famous American author of *Ten Days That Shook the World*, rang Pavel and Zhenya's bell. "Mama and Papa have been arrested," he cried. "She was taken away in her beautiful clothes."[16] Alexander's sister Mariko was also arrested, along with Maria's brother. Johnik, Svetlana's longtime playmate at Zubalovo, soon disappeared too.

To Svetlana it was inconceivable that Uncle Alyosha and Aunt Maria were "enemies of the people." She believed they were "victims of some frightful mix-up, which 'even Father himself' could not disentangle."[17] Everyone in the family was frightened and tried to send messages to Stalin through Svetlana. When she conveyed these, Stalin would say, "Why do you repeat everything like an empty drum?" He ordered her to stop "lawyering."[18]

Alexander Alliluyev, the son of Pavel and Zhenya, tells the story of how Maria Svanidze managed to smuggle a letter to his mother from prison. The letter was written on a shirt: "Zhenya, you cannot imagine what is going on here. I am sure that Stalin does not know about this. I ask for a favor. Please let him know." Without telling her husband, Zhenya typed out Maria's letter and took it to Stalin. Stalin's reply was cold and measured: "Zhenya, I ask you never to come to me with a letter like this again."[19]

That summer of 1938, Uncle Pavel often visited the Kremlin apartment, hoping to plead for the Svanidzes. He would sit dejectedly in either Svetlana's or Vasili's room, sighing deeply as he waited for Stalin.[20] Pavel's own son Alexander explained the futility of this:

Stalin's massive system of informants kept the channels of information flowing. He was systematically eliminating Old Bolsheviks and the higher military echelons as potential rivals. As terrifying as it sounds, people were divided into categories. You could not plead for those about whom Stalin had made personal arrangements.[21]

Soon a purge began in the army. Pavel was deputy head of the Armored Tank Division. On November 1, when Pavel returned from his vacation in Sochi and went to his office, he discovered that most of his colleagues in the Tank Division had been arrested. He had a heart attack on the spot.[22]

The NKVD phoned his wife, Zhenya, to ask what she had given her husband for breakfast. When Zhenya arrived at the hospital, Pavel was already dead. Everyone stood around terrified as Zhenya ripped off her husband's clothes. She was looking for bullet holes. Her husband had told her, "If they come after me, I will shoot myself."[23]

In fact, Pavel had had heart attacks before. This was a *nat-*

ural death, if it was natural for a man to succumb to the terrifying pressures of such brutal times. In his funeral procession,
Pavel's body was mounted on a gun carriage, and the mourners
proceeded to Novodevichy Cemetery. Though Stalin did call
Zhenya to offer his condolences, he did not attend, claiming it
would be easy to organize his assassination at a funeral. In retrospect, Pavel's son Alexander felt that "it was an easy excuse."[24]

The Alliluyev-Redens family in 1937. *Back row, left to right:* Pavel
Alliluyev (Svetlana's maternal uncle); Tatyana Moskaleva (nanny);
Stanislav Redens (Stalin's brother-in-law) holding his son Vladimir;
Stanislav's wife, Anna Alliluyeva Redens. *Foreground, left to right:*
Svetlana's maternal cousins Sergei (son of Pavel Alliluyev) and Leo-
nid (son of Stanislav Redens).

Other family members tried to plead with Stalin to protect
his relatives. Grandfather Sergei would wait for hours on the
sofa in the Kremlin apartment until Stalin arrived in the small
hours of the morning. Stalin dismissed his old protector by
making fun of him. "So you came to see me. Exactly. Exactly,"
repeated Stalin in a way of speaking that Grandfather Sergei
always used.[25]

Grandmother Olga raged against her son-in-law: "Nothing happens that he does not know about."[26] Olga was right: Stalin knew everything. At his Kuntsevo dacha or in his garden in Sochi, he would spend hours on his terrace working over his papers, blue pen in hand. He had 383 "albums," provided to him by the NKVD head, Yezhov, containing the names of 44,000 proposed victims. Stalin would cross out the names of the damned and tick off those to be spared. Despite what must have been an onerous workload for the *vozhd*, Stalin found time to do this task.[27]

The husband of Nadya's sister Anna, Stanislav Redens, was arrested not long after Pavel's death. On November 19, Redens returned from Kazakhstan, where he had been serving as people's commissar for internal affairs. Svetlana knew the Uncle Stanislav who was ebullient, full of life, and kind to children. She did not know the public man. As head of the OGPU in the Ukraine, he had participated in the purges of the early 1930s, but now, as a high official in the NKVD, he himself was a target.[28] Redens was arrested on November 22. Like hundreds of thousand of others, he was a victim of the violence in which he had once participated.[29]

Apparently Stalin himself arranged for Aunt Anna to visit her husband in Lefortovo Prison to offer his personal guarantee of freedom and safety for their children if only Redens would confess his counterrevolutionary crimes. Stanislav sent Anna away, telling her that any promise from Stalin could not be trusted. Stalin approved the execution of his brother-in-law on February 12, 1940.[30]

Nothing happened to Anna or her children. She was even allowed to keep her apartment in the government compound called the House on the Embankment; this was an unusual concession for the wives of disgraced officials. However, Anna and her children were forbidden to visit Svetlana and Vasili in the Kremlin, though they were permitted to see them at Zubalovo.

In 1939, the NKVD tried to get rid of Svetlana's nanny, too.

Agents reported to Stalin that Alexandra Andreevna had been married to a clerk in the tsarist police before the Revolution and was therefore "untrustworthy." When she heard of "the plot" to get rid of her nanny, Svetlana became hysterical and begged her father to intervene. She was almost shocked when he got angry and called off the secret police. "My father couldn't stand tears," she said. She should have qualified this: it might possibly have been true that he couldn't stand his daughter's tears.[31]

One day at school in 1940, Svetlana noted that her girlfriend Galya was crying. When she asked her what was the matter, Galya replied that her father had been arrested the previous night. Her mother had asked Galya to give Svetlana a letter to pass to Stalin. At dinner that night, Svetlana gave him the letter in the presence of his Politburo colleagues and begged him to do something. Stalin was angry and replied, "The NKVD never makes mistakes." Svetlana began to cry and said, "But I love Galya." Stalin replied curtly, "Sometimes you are forced to go even against those you love."[32]

After discussing the case with his dinner companions, including Molotov, Stalin berated Svetlana for a long time, warning her never again to serve as "a post-box" for begging letters from friends at school. But her plea worked. Within a few days, Galya's father was released from prison and returned home. Now, however, Svetlana understood something: "The life of a man depended entirely on a word from my father."[33]

An atmosphere of fear pervaded Model School No. 25, where a propaganda campaign promoting "vigilance" was afoot. There were warnings about anti-Soviet spies and agitators writing in invisible ink, passing secret notes, and burning them.

Though it seems that none of Svetlana's teachers or administrators was imprisoned or shot, the parents of some of her fellow students were not so lucky. However, as long as one parent avoided arrest, the children were allowed to stay at school. It was all terrifyingly confusing and impossible to penetrate. One pupil explained his father's arrest by saying, "I believe in my father's innocence, yet the security organs do not make mistakes. So, he must have been duped into becoming an instrument of our enemies."[34]

But mostly no one spoke about what was happening. Svetlana recalled, "It was all just a kind of misfortune that dragged upon us."[35] The children got on with their schoolwork as best they could, although she always knew when an arrest had happened. The principal would be ordered to remove the child from her classroom as a potentially dangerous influence by "unreliable elements."[36]

A young Svetlana sitting on the lap of Lavrenty Beria, Stalin's notorious chief of the NKVD, while her father works in the background, in a photograph taken in either 1935 or 1936.

Of course, the fourteen-year-old Svetlana could make no more sense of these tragedies than anyone else. As an adult, she would explain thus: "Many years had to go by before everything that had taken place, not only in our family but all over the country, could range itself in my consciousness with my father's name, before I could realize that all of it had been done by him."[37] Her words "range itself in my consciousness" are fraught with the terror of this recognition.

About her lost relatives, however, she could write with undiluted nostalgia. "They formed a circle that sprang up around my mother and vanished soon after she died, not so quickly at first, but finally and irrevocably." She came to believe that if her mother had lived, Nadya would not have accepted what was happening. In her darkest moments, Svetlana believed that her mother, too, would inevitably have become one of her father's victims.[38]

At this stage, Stalin probably was not especially targeting members of his family; he simply refused to save them. They had the misfortune to move in the circles of power that overlapped with those designated for liquidation. They had played the game of power and privilege and lost. And they gave Stalin an effective cover: he could deny that he was leading the purges. He could say, "It's not me. It's happening in my family too."

One of the devices of all dictatorships is the pseudolegality of the judicial system under which the most grotesque crimes are committed. After the arrest of Maria and Alexander Svanidze in December 1937, an extensive "investigation" by the NKVD ensued, lasting three and a half years, before they were both executed:

Investigation [into the case of Alexander Svanidze] continued from December 1937 to December 1940. On December 4th 1940 Military Collegium of the Supreme Court of USSR had sentenced A. S. Svanidze to death, accusing him in alleged "active participation in nationalist group in Georgia," and in alleged participation in an "anti-soviet organization of the right"; he has been accused in active participation in undermining works, and allegedly joined an anti-soviet group of Sokolnikov, promising him his support in all sorts of anti-soviet activities. In Svanidze's case there was a statement about his alleged plotting on life of L. Beria. For more than a month A. S. Svanidze had been kept in a cell with the sentence of death; it was expected that he would ask for pardon, confess his alleged crimes and beg for life. He did none of that.

On January 23, 1941 the plenum of the Supreme Court of USSR replaced his death sentence for imprisonment for 15 years. But on August 20th, 1941, the Supreme Court changed its mind and left in power the previous sentence—execution through shooting. At the same day—on personal orders from Beria—A. S. Svanidze was shot.

His wife Maria Onissimovna Svanidze was sentenced on 29 December 1939 to eight years of imprisonment for "hiding the anti-Soviet activities of her husband, for anti-soviet gossip, for criticizing soviet regime and for speaking openly against one of the leaders of CPSU and Soviet Government/Beria."

On March 3rd, 1942, without any new evidence the Special Commission at NKVD USSR decided to replace imprisonment of Maria Svanidze by execution, which was done the same day. . . .

The sister of A. S. Svanidze, Mariko Svanidze, was sentenced for ten years of imprisonment, but on March 3, 1942, she was shot . . . due to a new decision of the Special Group at NKVD, USSR.[39]

In 1955, after Stalin's death, A. I. Mikoyan ordered this special report on the case of Maria and Alexander Svanidze. On January 6, 1956, the military procurator, V. Zhabin, informed Mikoyan that "after protestations from [the] investigating magistrate the case of A. S. Svanidze and M. O. Svanidze was abandoned due to absence of any crime."[40] The phrasing is convoluted. What it meant was that the case against the Svanidzes as traitors continued long after they were executed. But now they could be posthumously "rehabilitated" because they had committed no crime.

Chapter 5

The Circle of Secrets and Lies

Svetlana, age eleven, in the uniform scarf of the
Soviet youth group Young Pioneers.

For Svetlana, these were "years of the steady annihilation of everything my mother had created, of systematic elimination of her very spirit."[1] The people whom Svetlana had loved and who had made her childhood secure had been taken away, and she didn't know why. A wall of silence surrounded things too dangerous to speak of. When Svetlana asked her grandmother what happened to their relatives, Olga said, "It was just something that happened. It was fate." Her nanny counseled her, "Don't ask."[2]

The family found ways to paper over the horror and carry on—either through denial or by retreating into consoling myths. Though Stalin had personally told Anna Redens that her husband, Stanislav, had been executed, she always insisted that he'd escaped to Siberia. The family continued to spend weekends at Zubalovo. The young people skied or hiked through the forest, a bodyguard always in tow. Anna's son Leonid recalled a walk that took place when he was eleven years old with his mother, Svetlana, and her nanny and bodyguard. It was early spring. Svetlana, who was three years older, "carefully, bit by bit, slipped away" from the group, taking Leonid with her. They walked for miles beside a small river. At a particularly precipitous point, he lost his footing and fell in. She pulled him out, then removed her jacket and gave it to him. He remembered her kindness. He also thought of this as the first time he realized that she "wanted to jump out of this trap." When they got home, she was roundly reprimanded for running away from her bodyguard.[3]

At fourteen, Svetlana was anxious to assert her independence. She wrote to her father suggesting that she was no longer a child: "Hello my dear Father, I will not wait for any more orders from you. I am not little in order to be amused by this."[4] A few weeks later, she wrote again. Oddly, it was as if she'd assumed her mother Nadya's demanding, coquettish voice. Perhaps this was the only way to get Stalin's attention.

AUGUST 22, 1940

My dear, dear Papochka,

How do you live? How is your health? Do you miss me

and Vasya [Vasili]? No. Paposchka, I miss you terribly. I keep waiting for you and you keep on not coming. I feel with "my liver" that you are trying to trick me again—I refer to a lack of joy—and there's no directive and you will not come. Ay, yai, yai . . .

Now with Geography, it's a mess again. Because 5 more republics have been added, there's more territory, more population, and there's an increased number of industrial spaces but our textbook is taken from 1938, and especially because we have the economic geography of the USSR, there's lots of stuff missing from the textbook. . . . There's a lot of crap in it. . . . Scenes of Sochi, Matsesta, different resorts, and, in general, these images are not needed by anyone. . . .

Papochka, please write me right away because you will forget after, or you will be busy. And by that time, I myself will come. OK. I kiss you deeply my dear Papochka. Until we see each other again.

Yours,

Svetlana[5]

How would Stalin have responded to his lippy fourteen-year-old daughter criticizing her textbook as full of crap? Unsurprisingly, Stalin was a misogynist. On one occasion, Svetlana overheard her father and Vasili discussing women. Vasili said he preferred a woman with conversation. "My father roared with laughter: 'Look at him, so he wants a woman with ideas! Hah! We have known that kind: herrings with ideas—skin and bones.'"[6] Was he talking about her mother? The remark cut deeply enough that she never forgot it.

Svetlana was turning into an intelligent young woman. At school she loved literature and valued the exotic. Her favorite memory of Zubalovo in her teenage years was of the two yurts that sat on the front lawn at the dacha. Her Uncle Alyosha Svanidze, now dead, had brought them back from a trip he'd made to Guangxi in China. As young teenagers, she and her four cousins—Leonid, Alexander, Sergei, and Vladimir—would sit in those strange dwellings and imagine their inhabitants.

The yurts were round wooden structures made of slats, with walls insulated by patterned felt and floors covered with thick felt rugs. In each yurt, a bronze Buddha sat in a wooden box positioned on top of a small red chest. The Buddha's demure smile and mysterious third eye captivated Svetlana. It was the first icon of a god she had ever seen. A half century later, she could describe those yurts to a friend with precision.[7]

Svetlana's fascination with other cultures is implicit here, but her father did not share this curiosity. Stalin detested travel; he had no real interest in other cultures and, once in power, left the Soviet Union only twice—for Allied peace conferences. Svetlana was never permitted to travel outside the frame of Sochi and Moscow. She would be twenty-nine (and her father dead) before she visited Leningrad. Though this was the norm for Soviet citizens, it was a deprivation for a curious young mind.

When Svetlana was fifteen, the yurts disappeared, as did her entire world—in one fell swoop.

World War II came suddenly, though not without warning, to the Soviet Union. On June 22, 1941, at 4:00 a.m., Stalin, asleep on his couch at his Kuntsevo dacha, was awakened by a phone call from his chief of staff, Marshal Georgy Zhukov, informing him that German planes were bombing Kiev, Vilnius, Sebastopol, Odessa, and other cities. A total of 147 German divisions had crossed the border and were already proceeding at a fierce pace through the Ukraine.[8]

For months, Stalin had received reports from British and Soviet intelligence agencies that Hitler was planning to stage an invasion, code-named Operation Barbarossa, on June 22. According to Stepan Mikoyan, Stalin had even been warned again that very midnight. In the presence of Mikoyan's father and several other Politburo members, Stalin was informed that a defecting German soldier had just been apprehended and was claiming the attack was coming in the morning. But as Mikoyan's son explained, "Stalin's attitude to intelligence data reflected his extreme mistrust of people. In his opinion everyone was capable of deceit or treason." When his agents in the field sent him "alarming reports," Stalin ordered them recalled and deported to the camps to be "ground into dust."[9]

Stalin insisted that Hitler would keep to the nonaggression pact the two leaders had signed in 1939. The USSR would not *provoke* a war. Privately he knew that the Soviet army was not ready—his purges of the armed forces had cut too deeply. Now the front was in anarchy; Russian troops were in flight, and Stalin was to blame. Hitler had disastrously outmaneuvered him.

On June 29, when the Germans encircled four hundred thousand defending Russian troops and took the city of Minsk in Belarus, giving themselves a direct route to Moscow, Stalin climbed into his car waiting outside the Kremlin and turned to his comrades. "Everything's lost," he said. "Lenin left us a great legacy, but we, his heirs, have shit it out our asses."[10] Cursing all the way to Kuntsevo, he announced his resignation. For two days, Stalin kept silent in his dacha. There were rumors of a breakdown, but this is unlikely. More convincing is the idea that Stalin was testing his comrades to see whether his leadership would survive the crisis.[11]

A contingent of frightened ministers, including Beria, Mikoyan, and Molotov, headed to Kuntsevo to ask him to return to work as head of a new "super–war cabinet." They couldn't imagine running the war without Stalin. Anastas Mikoyan explained, "The very name of Stalin was a great force for rousing the morale of the people."[12]

On July 3, Stalin addressed the nation with his new title, supreme commander, and declared the coming struggle to be the Great Patriotic War. He exhorted the people to "rally round the Party of Lenin and Stalin." Stalin was something *other* now, an Idea, no longer just himself. He warned that, in this "merciless struggle," all "cowards, deserters, panic-mongers" would be ruthlessly crushed.[13]

Looking back from adulthood, Svetlana would say that her father refused to admit that Hitler had tricked him. "He considered himself infallible . . . his political flair unmatchable." After the war was over, she recalled his habit of repeatedly saying, "Ech, together with the Germans we would have been invincible!" And then he would add, "So they thought they could fool Stalin? Just look at them, it's Stalin they tried to fool!" Svetlana was always appalled when her father spoke of himself in the third person, always amazed that it never occurred to him that "he might fool himself."[14]

Even as he attempted to control the war disaster, Stalin took measures to protect his daughter. He asked his sister-in-law, Zhenya, to take the family to his dacha in Sochi. "The war will be long," he told her. "Lots of blood will be shed. . . . Please take Svetlana southwards."[15]

Amazingly, Zhenya refused, saying she had to join her husband (she had hastily remarried after Pavel's death) and to safeguard her own children. Nobody said no to Stalin. He never forgot or forgave a single betrayal, and he could wait years to exact his revenge, as Zhenya would discover.

Stalin next turned to Nadya's sister, Anna, for help. Threading through the crowds of untold thousands of evacuees desperately trying to leave Moscow, Anna hustled the anxious little troop of Stalin's relatives aboard a train heading south to the Black Sea. Anna and her own two sons; her parents, Sergei and Olga; Yakov's wife, Yulia, and their daughter Gulia; and Svetlana and her nanny squeezed together in bewilderment into a private compartment. Even though her school had been practicing war drills for years—she kept a school photo of her class practicing a gas-mask drill in 1935—now Svetlana discovered the real terror of war, and the racking fear for loved ones left behind.

On June 23, one day after the German invasion, Stalin sent his sons, Yakov and Vasili, and his adopted son, Artyom, to the front. Artyom reported rather cryptically in retrospect:

Jacob and me joined the artillery, and Vasili became a pilot. All of us went to the front—from the first day; Stalin telephoned to have us taken there immediately. It was the only privilege we got from him. There remain several letters from Vasili to his father. In one of them from the front, he asked his father to send him money. A snack bar had opened in his detachment and he wanted a new officer's uniform. His father replied, "1. As far as I know the rations in the air force are quite sufficient. 2. A Special uniform for Stalin's son is not on the agenda." Vasili didn't get the money.[16]

The family spent the summer in Sochi. Svetlana's friend Marfa Peshkova had also been evacuated to Sochi and visited Stalin's dacha one morning. Svetlana came into the room, looking distraught and, as Marfa reported, said, "I had a very strange dream last night. It was as if I saw a large nest in a tree. There was an eagle in the nest with little babies next to it. And suddenly the eagle takes one of the babies and throws it out of the nest. The baby falls and dies." And then Svetlana cried. "You know, something terrible has happened to Yasha [the family's pet name for her brother Yakov]." Her last good-bye to him had been over the telephone, just before he left for the front.[17]

Not long after her dream, Svetlana picked up the phone and heard her father's voice on the other end. She asked about Yakov, and Stalin replied, "Yasha has been taken prisoner." Before she had time to respond, he added, "Don't say anything to his wife for the time being." Yulia was sitting anxiously on a nearby couch, scrutinizing Svetlana's face. Svetlana thought her father was being solicitous and so mumbled to Yulia, "He doesn't know anything himself."[18] She could not bear to tell her the truth.

Svetlana was devastated by her father's call. In the last few years, she had become very close to her half brother. Though he was nineteen years older, they would study together in the banya at Zubalovo, spreading their blankets among the fragrant birch branches, curled up with their books.

Stalin's relationship with his older son had always been poor. According to the family, he bullied Yakov relentlessly, calling him soft and worthless. Stalin disapproved of Yakov's first marriage, and in despair twenty-year-old Yakov had attempted to shoot himself, but the bullet only grazed his chest. Stalin wrote to Nadya from Sochi: "Convey to Yakov from me that he has acted like a hooligan, applying blackmail and I do not have anything else in common with him,"[19] and the story circulated that Stalin had laughed and said, "Ha! He couldn't even shoot straight."[20] Yakov left for Leningrad and didn't see his father again for eight years, but Svetlana always defended him. "Yakov's gentleness and composure were irritating to my father, who was quick-tempered and impetuous even in his later years."[21]

After the tragic death of his first child, Yakov's marriage

ended in divorce. Perhaps to reconcile with his father, he left his career as an engineer and entered the Frunze Military Academy in Moscow in 1935. In 1936, he married Yulia Meltzer. Again Stalin did not approve. According to Svetlana, this was because Yulia was Jewish, and her father "never liked Jews, though he wasn't as blatant about expressing his hatred for them in those days as he was after the war."[22] Their daughter, Gulia, was born in 1938. Summers until the war, they would come to Zubalovo, where Yakov, still desperate for approval, tried to ingratiate himself with his father.

Yakov with his daughter, Gulia, 1939.

By early September, Sochi was no longer a safe refuge, and the family returned to Moscow. The ravages of the war were already apparent. From the windows of the Kremlin apartment, Svetlana could see a gaping hole on the corner of the Arsenal Building opposite, where a German bomb had hit. Vasili had been in the apartment and had been thrown from the bed as the windows shattered.[23] She was terrified to discover that a bomb had fallen on Model School No. 25. Of course, it had already been evacuated. Construction crews were hastily building a bomb shelter inside the subway for the War Cabinet.

After their arrival, Stalin explained to Svetlana that there would be new arrangements: "Yasha's daughter can stay with you for a while. But it seems that his wife is dishonest. We'll have to look into it."[24] Svetlana was appalled and had no idea what her father was talking about. How could Yulia be dishonest?

Yulia was arrested and incarcerated in the Lubyanka prison. Was it possible that another family member could disappear like this? When the last wave of family arrests had occurred in 1938, Svetlana had been twelve. Now she was fifteen, but she still did not understand. Who was doing this to her family?

On August 16, Stalin had issued Order 270, condemning all who surrendered or were captured as "traitors to the Motherland." Wives of captured officers were to be arrested and imprisoned.[25] Yakov was a traitor; Yulia must be arrested. There would be no exception made for Stalin's son.

Meanwhile poor Yulia was held in solitary confinement in the dark bowels of the dreaded Lubyanka. The "investigation" would take a year and a half. As the Germans advanced, she was transferred to a prison in Engels, on the Volga.[26] When she was eventually freed, in the spring of 1943, her five-year-old daughter, Gulia, did not recognize her and had to be encouraged to approach her mother. No explanation was ever offered to Yulia for her imprisonment. She was simply told she was free to go. She never spoke to Stalin again.

The news of what had actually happened to Yakov filtered out slowly. One report came from Ivan Sapegin, commanding officer of the 303rd Light Artillery Regiment. When Yakov's armored division was encircled and overrun at Vitebsk in Belarus on July 12, 1941, the divisional commander had fled the battlefield, but Yakov was separated from his unit and had been taken prisoner.[27]

Yakov served as a Red Army artillery officer in World War II, and he was captured by the Germans on July 16, 1941.

The German command immediately informed Stalin by flash cable of his son's capture and then used it for propaganda purposes. Pamphlets with a photograph of Yakov in his uniform without belt or epaulets, surrounded by German officers, were dropped on Soviet troops.

> Stalin's son, Yakov Dzhugashvili, full lieutenant, battery commander, has surrendered. That such an important Soviet officer has surrendered proves beyond doubt that all resistance to the German army is completely pointless. So stop fighting and come over to us.[28]

Yakov languished in various POW camps until the spring of 1943, when, after their disastrous defeat at the Battle of Stalingrad, the Germans attempted to exchange him for Field Marshal Friedrich Paulus. Stalin refused the prisoner exchange. That spring Yakov either was shot or committed suicide; it would never be known which. It would be several years before Svetlana knew her brother's fate. In this she was like millions of her fellow Soviets.

With the Germans on Moscow's doorstep and an invasion of the city imminent, the town of Kuibyshev to the southeast was chosen to be the alternative capital. In early October 1941, government personnel, foreign diplomatic missions, and cultural institutions began a hasty evacuation. Lenin's mummified body had already been removed from its mausoleum and sent by secret train to Tyumen in Siberia.

As Moscow filled with smoke from the bonfires of burning archives, the Stalin family's belongings were packed into a van. Most of the family was already in Kuibyshev, but it wasn't yet clear whether Stalin would evacuate too, though it was assumed he would. The Kuntsevo dacha was booby-trapped, and a secret train to transport Stalin stood waiting at a railway siding.

In Kuibyshev, a small local museum on Pioneer Street was emptied of its exhibits and newly painted to house the Stalin family, along with bodyguards, cooks, and waiters. Svetlana's nanny came with her, as did Mikhail Klimov, her personal "secret police watch-dog," as she called him. Vasili's young wife, Galina (they had married in 1940, when Vasili was nineteen), was there. While Grandmother Olga came, Grandfather Sergei had decided he would return to Tbilisi and spent most of the war in Georgia. At Svetlana's urging, Yakov's baby daughter, Gulia, was soon permitted to join them.

Stalin elected to stay in Moscow to conduct the war. Svetlana wrote to her father from Kuibyshev on September 19, 1941.

My dear Papochka my dear happiness. Hello.

How do you live my dear Secretary? I am fine here. In our

school there are other kids from Moscow. There are many of us so I am not bored.

I only miss you . . . now especially I want to see you. If you allow me, I could fly on a plane there for two or three days. . . .

Recently a daughter of Malenkov and the son of Bulganin . . . left for Moscow, so if they can fly why can't I? They are the same age as me and in general they are in no way better than I am. . . .

I don't like the city very much. . . . There are many, and I don't know why, people who are blind. . . . Every 5th person is a disabled man. Very many poor people and urchins. In Kuibyshev during the war, many people came from Moscow, Leningrad, Kiev, Odessa and other cities and the locals treat the incomers with an anger they don't hide. . . .

And now Hitler will come and will bomb this place. . . . Papa, why do the Germans keep coming and coming? When will they finally get a kick in the neck? After all we cannot give up all our industrial areas.

Papa, I have one more request for you. Yasha's [Yakov's] daughter Galechka [Gulia] is right now in Sochi. . . . I would very much like for Galechka to be brought to me here. Now she has no one. . . .

Dear Papa . . . I wait for your permission to take a flight to Moscow. But only for two days . . . I don't know when you are free and that's why I don't call. . . . I kiss you many many times once again.

Svetanka[29]

The fifteen-year-old Svetlana was by turns petulant, begging, naive, and then, finally, generous. She was a daughter fearful for her father so far away and in danger, a daughter with expectations: she must be flown to see him. On October

28, Stalin gave her permission to travel to Moscow. It was the day the Bolshoi Theater, the university buildings on Mokhovaya Street, and the Central Committee building on Staraya Ploshchad (Old Square) were bombed. She found her father in his bomb shelter, reached by an elevator descending ninety feet into the ground. The commissars had exactly replicated his rooms at Kuntsevo, lining the walls with wood paneling, though now they were covered in maps. The same dining room table had been installed for his dinner guests, who were the same men, but now uniformed officers. The table was also covered with maps, and telephone lines snaked through the rooms. Stalin was constantly in contact with the front. Svetlana was, of course, in the way.

As millions starved in the cities under siege, life in Kuibyshev often had a strange, surreal normalcy. Musicians who had been evacuated from Moscow formed a philharmonic orchestra, and there were concerts. Shostakovich's Seventh Symphony was premiered in Kuibyshev and broadcast around the world. The war was a shadow presence. Health centers and most of the city's hospital facilities were turned into base hospitals as the wounded arrived with devastating injuries.

A makeshift cinema had been constructed in the ex-museum next to the kitchen, and there everyone watched the newsreels from the front. The cameramen were in the trenches and accompanied the advancing tanks. Svetlana watched battles on the outskirts of Moscow. She soon lost her naïveté about the meaning of war.

That spring in Kuibyshev, Svetlana made a devastating discovery that she claimed shattered her life. Her father had instructed her to keep up with her English language skills now that Britain and the United States were Russia's allies, and so she had taken to reading any English or American magazine she could lay her hands on. She read *Life*, *Fortune*, *Time*, and the *Illustrated London News*. One day that spring (she had just turned sixteen), she came across an article about her father. It mentioned, "not as news but as a fact well known to everyone," that his wife, Nadezhda Sergeyevna Alliluyeva, had killed herself on the night of November 8, 1932."[30]

The shock of this revelation was heart-stopping. Svetlana rushed to her grandmother, article in hand, and demanded to know if her mother had committed suicide and why this had been hidden from her. Olga replied that, yes, it was true. Nadya had had a small gun. It had been a gift from Pavel. Olga kept repeating, "Who would have thought it?"

Marfa Peshkova remembered Svetlana showing her the magazine with the article. "I remember this very well. She showed me this photograph. It was a photograph of her mother lying in the coffin. She had never seen this. And somewhere . . . she did not know for sure about the death of her mother. It was rumored then that she died from appendicitis, from a failed operation or something like that. For her it was a shock."[31]

When Svetlana had read the article, she hadn't wanted to believe it, but her grandmother had confirmed it. Her mother had killed herself. Only she, her daughter, seemed not to know. Her anger at her mother's betrayal of her must have been profound. And she turned that anger on her father. She knew how he could be. She had seen him become mean, even brutal. She was certain it was his cruelty that had caused her mother to commit suicide. Now she began to switch her allegiance to the memory of her mother, but like all orphans of suicides, she would need decades to forgive Nadya for abandoning her.

Things that had been mysterious before suddenly became clear. When her father had said to her over the phone, "Don't say anything to Yulia for the time being," it hadn't been solicitude he was expressing. It was suspicion. The idea of Yulia and Yakov betraying their country was inconceivable. Svetlana began the slow process of realizing that her father was capable of condemning innocent people to prison and even to death.

She would look back and say, "The whole thing nearly drove me out of my mind. Something in me was destroyed. I was no longer able to obey the word and will of my father and defer to his opinions without question."[32] This is the voice of an adult, but certainly Svetlana's adolescent confusion must have been overwhelming. Which was more devastating: her belief that her father was responsible for her mother's death or her discovery that her mother had not loved her enough not to kill herself?

Everywhere—at home, at school—her father was called the wise, truthful leader. Stalin's name was linked to winning the war. He was the great Stalin. Only he could save Russia. To doubt him was an act of *blasphemy*. But Svetlana had begun to doubt.

Chapter 6

———

Love Story

Svetlana, age sixteen.

By January 1942, the Red Army had driven the Wehrmacht from Moscow's gates. The skeletal remains of German tanks lay like burned husks outside the city. Hitler had drastically miscalculated both Russian wiliness in tactical defense and the brutality of the Russian winter. It is estimated that one million Russians, both military and civilian, died, but Stalin won the battle for Moscow. In June Svetlana and her retinue were given permission to return to Moscow. The previous autumn, a fire had almost destroyed the Zubalovo dacha; the family moved into the surviving wing. By October an ugly new house, painted camouflage green, was built in the shell.

Svetlana did not see her father until August, when she was summoned to his Kuntsevo dacha to attend a dinner for Churchill. The British prime minister had flown to Moscow for a consultation about Allied strategy. The news Churchill was bringing was not good. There would be no Allied second front to distract Hitler from his assault on the USSR for a good while yet.

Svetlana had no idea why she was summoned to this dinner. Her father forbade any interaction with foreigners, and she was never included in diplomatic circles. When he introduced her to Churchill and said she was a redhead, Churchill remarked that he too had been a redhead but, waving his cigar over his bald pate, said, "Look at me now." She was too shy to respond. Very soon, her father kissed her and told her to run along. Reflecting on this strange moment much later, she concluded that her father had been performing for Churchill, demonstrating what a charming domestic life he had.[1]

Svetlana was still a schoolgirl in the tenth grade. She was reading Schiller, Goethe, Gorky, Chekhov, and the poets Mayakovsky and Yesenin. She loved Dostoyevsky, even though her father had banned his books. Slowly she was growing into an independent-minded young woman. But according to her friend Marfa Peshkova, Stalin was becoming more and more disapproving of his teenage daughter. If she wore a skirt above her knees, wore shorts, or wore socks instead of stockings, he would rage: "What's this! Are you going around naked?" He ordered her to wear *sharovary* (baggy pants tight at the ankles) and had a dress made for her that covered her legs.[2] His reprimands often brought Svetlana to tears, but she was stubborn and staged her rebellion shrewdly. She heightened the hem of her dress slowly until it was back above her knees. She knew her father was too busy to notice.

In the autumn of 1942, a new student, Olga Rifkina, entered Model School No. 25. Olga had an unusual background for this elite school. She was from a poor Jewish family living in a one-bedroom communal apartment shared with two other families. Her mother kept them all going by working as a journalist for *Pravda*. The year 1941 had been terrible. That June the government had issued a directive for the evacuation from Moscow of all children under the age of three. Olga and her mother, grandmother, and baby brother Grisha left for Penz. When they returned to Moscow in May 1942, Olga had missed a year of school.[3] Model School No. 25 had special placement for such children. She was enrolled and sent to live with her grandmother.

Olga's memories of the school were mostly unhappy. While the teachers never singled out students who were poor, the other children made her aware of her inferiority. She would look back and say, "Only one person, who seemingly had the most reason to preen, . . . was a true 'personality' not tied to her position. This was Svetlana Stalina."[4] Olga remarked in an interview:

I really did like Svetlana very much right away. . . . She was a particularly humble person. And even shy. And she had a lot of charm and femininity. She attracted my attention. I always looked admiringly at her. And our friendship survived all our lives. Until the last day.[5]

Soon the two girls became deskmates. After school they would take long walks along the Moskva River, though these walks were often interrupted when Svetlana would suddenly say, "I can't be late. My Papa is coming. I haven't seen him in two weeks." Olga had the impression that, like most people, Svetlana thought of her father as the "great, big Stalin, but not exactly a father."[6]

Because of the food shortages caused by the war, most people, including Olga's family, often went hungry. Olga recalled that, after coming home from school, she would eat a bowl of soup and then, with a glass of *kakavella* (a drink made from boiled cocoa pods), do her homework. When there was no food for the evening, her grandmother would tell her to go to bed while she still wasn't hungry; otherwise she'd never be able to sleep. Olga remarked, "Svetlana, of course, could not imagine any of this. At the time she was artificially isolated from regular life. . . . She never had to buy anything, she could barely tell the denominations of money apart."[7]

At school, Svetlana did not parade as Stalin's daughter. She often complained that the other students looked on her as if she were an "insider" and had access to secret information. But she assured Olga, "I don't know anything, nor do I really care." She hated the teacher who made her write out lists of all the things that carried her father's name: the mountain in Perm, Stalingrad on the Volga, the ZiS car (Zavod imeni Stalina, Factory in the Name of Stalin). Olga recalled: "Poor Svetlana. She wanted so much to be equal with everyone else. I remember once she stepped on a young man's foot and he called her a 'ginger cow'—she even beamed with joy."[8]

One indication of her status, however, was that Svetlana had her bodyguard, Mikhail Klimov, who had accompanied her in the evacuation to Kuibyshev. Most of the elite children had bodyguards—the Molotov children had three. The bodyguards had their own separate room beside the school cloakroom, where they spent their day. Both Olga and Svetlana played piano, and they often went to the conservatory together to hear music by their favorite composers: Bach, Mozart, Tchaikovsky, or Prokofiev. Klimov would buy the tickets. If there was violin music on the program, he would complain: "We are going to saw the wood again" and sit behind them, shuddering.[9] Svetlana claimed to have grown fond of Klimov, but it was disconcerting to have someone always shadowing her.

Both girls were readers. Svetlana had a copy of the 1925 *Anthology of Russian Poetry of the Twentieth Century*. Together they would read the subversive work of Anna Akhmatova, Nikolai Gumilyov, and Sergei Yesenin. While still in grade ten, Olga gave Svetlana a notebook full of her poems. She felt Svetlana was a kindred spirit: she, too, had had her happy childhood shattered by misery; she, too, was deeply attached to her absent mother. In response, Svetlana wrote a poem to Olga:

Through poetry, as if through clear tears, looking
Into her soul, again and again
How can I not understand her, if I too am
Waiting in vain for my dear mother? . . .

To the lovely girl with the eyes of spring
I find I am unable to speak
About myself and about how close and clear
Are her thoughts, her dreams, and her grief.[10]

Though addressed to Olga, the poem was really an elegy for Nadya, now dead ten years. It spoke to Svetlana's terrible isolation. Nothing of the pain of loss had healed. Olga slowly came to realize that Svetlana was "essentially an orphan."[11]

After her return to Moscow, Svetlana spent much of her

time at the Zubalovo dacha while her father, preoccupied with the war, was mostly in his bunker hunkered down with his Politburo. Her brother Vasili also lived at Zubalovo with his wife, Galina. Now twenty-one, Vasili had graduated from the Lipetsk Aviation Institute. In October 1941 he became a captain. By February 1942, he had been promoted to colonel. His friend Stepan Mikoyan, wounded and in the hospital, recalled his surprise when Vasili visited him in Kuibyshev in his colonel's uniform. According to Mikoyan, Vasili later explained that his father had taken him aside and told him he didn't want him to fly. Too many sons of the elite had already been lost: Mikoyan's brother, Khrushchev's son, the war hero Timur Frunze. Vasili was appointed chief of the Air Force Inspection Command to keep him grounded. He flew only one or, at most, two combat missions. Though Stalin was often strict and rude with Vasili, Stepan Mikoyan believed he actually loved his son. Vasili soon had a grand office in Moscow on Pirogov Street.[12]

Stalin's younger son, Vasili, was a colonel of the Red Army Air Force by the time this photo was taken in 1943.

Vasili surrounded himself with fellow pilots and treated them like courtiers. He liked to fete them at Aragvi, his favorite Georgian restaurant, where the food was lavish even when the war was raging and Moscow was still being bombed. An orchestra played the latest dances, and the Russian elite sang into their vodka.[13]

That fall Vasili turned Zubalovo into a party house; he particularly liked pilots, actors, directors, cameramen, ballet dancers, writers, and famous athletes. Stepan Mikoyan thought he gave these late-night drinking parties in subconscious imitation of his father, who used to summon select members of his Politburo to Kuntsevo and keep them up drinking until four or five a.m.[14] Most who came were somehow involved in the war—the pilots were flying bombing missions; the filmmakers were shooting footage at the front, often from inside the trenches or with cameras mounted on tanks; the writers were working as journalists covering the war. The evenings had a Hemingwayesque flamboyance. Everyone came to watch films in the small private cinema at the dacha and to listen to the American jazz tunes that were constantly churning on the record player. There would be long drunken nights with people dancing the fox-trot. For many the hard edge of death framed the moment with an intensity unknown in peacetime.

Vasili insisted that his sister come to the parties. Svetlana mostly watched the bacchanal from the sidelines. Friends who attended, like Marfa Peshkova, noted that she had suddenly turned into an attractive young woman, though she still seemed closed off in her own private torment. Sometimes the parties got out of hand. On one occasion, when Vasili was very drunk, he insisted that his pregnant wife tell a joke. When she refused, he hit her, though luckily she fell back onto a couch. Enraged, Svetlana threw her brother out of the house along with his drunken buddies. Yet the parties continued.[15]

Svetlana with her friend Stepan Mikoyan, the son of the long-standing Soviet official Anastas Mikoyan, in 1942.

Svetlana assumed that no one noticed her, but she had caught the attention of Aleksei Yakovlevich Kapler. The Jewish Kapler, then thirty-eight, was one of the most famous screenwriters in the USSR. He was the author of the epic films *Lenin in October* and *Lenin in 1918*, and in 1941 he had been awarded the prestigious Stalin Prize. Kapler was supposedly working with Vasili on a film about air force pilots, though evenings were spent mostly drinking, and the film was never made. Kapler was within the inner sanctum of the head of state—best friends with the dictator's son, who was wild and outrageous. It was heady stuff. He was obviously a man who loved risk. Though he was married, he and his wife were separated, much to his distress, and he was on his own.

One night the Zubalovo group was invited to a film preview on Gnezdnikovsky Street, and Svetlana found herself talking with Kapler about movies. All those years of watching films in the Kremlin with her father paid off. Kapler was intrigued.

Describing his impression of her to a journalist years later, Kapler said that he had been surprised. Svetlana was not like the other girls in Vasili's retinue. She was not what he expected. He was taken with "her grace and intelligence . . . the way in which she would talk to those around her, and the criticisms she made on various aspects of Soviet life—what I really mean is the freedom within her."[16] Her "judgments" were "bold and her manner unpretentious." She was not decked out like the other women in their gorgeous outfits, preening for attention. She wore "practical, well-made clothes."

An undated photograph of a young Aleksei Kapler, probably one of the two hundred photographs stolen from Svetlana's desk by the KGB agent Victor Louis.

On November 8, a party was organized at Zubalovo to celebrate the anniversary of the Revolution. The guests included the famous, like the writer Konstantin Simonov, whom Svetlana admired, and the documentary filmmaker Roman Karmen. Much to her surprise, Kapler asked her to dance. She felt awkward and clumsy. She was so young. He asked her why she seemed sad and asked about the lovely brooch she was wearing, a decorative touch to her austere outfit. Was it a gift, he wondered? Svetlana explained that it had belonged to her mother and this day was the tenth anniversary of her mother's death, though no one else seemed to remember or care.[17] As he held her, she poured out her life. She spoke of her childhood, of the losses she had endured, though she didn't talk much about her father. Kapler understood that "something seemed to separate them."[18]

Charming, daring, knowledgeable, experienced, Kapler was irresistible to an idealistic girl of sixteen. And he seemed to be equally drawn to her. The first film they saw together was *Queen Christina* (1933), starring Greta Garbo and John Gilbert, a biopic of the seventeenth-century queen of Sweden, which distorted and absurdly romanticized her life. It is not hard to imagine the film's impact on the impressionable young Svetlana as war raged in Moscow.[19]

"Spoils, glory . . . what is behind those big words? Death and destruction. I want people to cultivate the arts of peace," says Garbo's Queen Christina. The film is about "great love, perfect love, the golden dream." The queen falls in love with Antonio, envoy from the king of Spain. "I have grown up in a great man's shadow," Garbo cries. "I long to escape my destiny." "There is a freedom which is mine and which the state cannot take away." Kapler recalled how they both identified with the film. She was the rebellious "royal daughter" demanding her own life; he was poor Don Antonio, the lover aspiring above his station.

Kapler brought Svetlana books that were forbidden, including Hemingway's *For Whom the Bell Tolls*. He'd gotten hold of a Russian translation that was circulating privately among friends.[20] The novel had been officially banned; Hemingway's portrait of the murderous Communist commissar who directed the purges of Trotskyites in the Spanish Civil War was too revealing.

The couple looked for pretexts to be together. Of course the meetings had to be kept secret from her father. Kapler would wait for Svetlana outside her Model School, lurking, embarrassed, down the lane. They would walk in the woods, he holding her hand in his pocket, or amble along the Moscow streets under blackout, or go to the unheated Tretyakov Gallery and wander the halls for hours. They went to private film showings at the Cinema Artists' Club and at the Ministry of Cinematography on Gnezdnikovsky Street. They saw musicals starring Ginger Rogers and Fred Astaire, as well as *Young Mister Lincoln* and Walt Disney's *Snow White and the Seven Dwarfs*. They met at the Bolshoi and were most happy when they got the chance to stroll through the foyer during the performance.[21]

Mikhail Klimov, Svetlana's bodyguard, was always a few paces behind them. Kapler even enjoyed his company, offering him the occasional cigarette. Svetlana felt Klimov was kind and even pitied her "absurd life."[22] Perhaps they thought he wouldn't betray them, but in fact Klimov was terrified by their growing liaison. He knew that Stalin had his daughter's phone tapped and her correspondence opened, and that NKGB agents made daily reports to him on all her activities.

After all, what were they doing? With her guard constantly on their heels, they could never be physical lovers, and this charged their relationship with a romantic desperation. She thought Kapler the "cleverest, kindest, most intelligent person on earth."[23] For him, she was a bright Lolita, a child longing to be taught about the world. She was so appallingly lonely, "surrounded and oppressed by an atmosphere worthy of a god." "Sveta really needed me," Kapler said.[24]

The lovers blithely enjoyed their little deceptions. Kapler's friends called him Lyusia (which sounds like a woman's name).

Svetlana would go over to her grandmother's apartment in the Kremlin to phone Kapler. Grandma Olga always thought she was talking to a girlfriend.[25]

Soon Kapler left on an assignment to cover the guerrilla war in Belarus, one of the most dangerous of the partisan fronts, and then he traveled to Stalingrad to cover the Battle of Stalingrad for *Pravda*. In the December 14 issue of *Pravda*, he published an article called "Letters from Lieutenant L from Stalingrad—Letter One," by Special Correspondent A. Kapler. The letter purported to be a soldier's description of Stalingrad to the woman he loves:

> My love, who knows whether this letter will reach you? A really difficult journey awaits it. I will nevertheless hope this letter will reach you, that it will carry, under the enemy's fire across the Volga, across the prairies, through storms and blizzards towards our lovely Moscow, my tenderness towards you, my dear.
>
> Today it snowed. It is winter in Stalingrad. The sky descended and became low as the ceiling in an *izba*. This gray, cold weather is especially agonizing on a day like this. One thinks of their loved one. How are you doing now? Do you remember Zamoskvorech'e? Our rendezvous in the Tretyakov gallery? How, while it was closing, the guard was kicking us out by ringing his bell, and how we could not recall which painting we sat in front of all day, while looking into each others' eyes. Until now, I know nothing about that painting except that it was wonderful to sit in front of it, and I thank the artist for that.[26]

Kapler went on to describe the war to his lover. The article reads like a film script about the heroic purity of war, in which love, suffering, friendship, and death are focused a million times more intensely than in ordinary life. Caught up as they were in the frenzy of romantic obsession, it was as if the lovers, too, were living in a film. Kapler ended his letter on a note of longing:

It is almost evening. It is also almost evening in Moscow. You can see the ragged Kremlin wall from your window and the sky above it—Moscow's sky. Perhaps, it is also snowing there right now.

Your,

L.

It is impossible to imagine Stalin's outrage as he read this and recognized the reference to Svetlana. Kapler later claimed he hadn't intended to send the article to *Pravda*. "Friends had played a trick on him."[27] But he had dared to write a love letter to the dictator's daughter, an indiscretion that should have been unimaginable. Marfa Peshkova remembered Svetlana bringing the newspaper to school. Though Svetlana understood the danger of Kapler's words, it was also clear she was deeply moved.[28]

When Kapler returned to Moscow for the New Year's celebrations, Svetlana told him they must not meet or even call each other. They managed silence until the end of January and then resumed their phone calls. They developed a code. He or she would call and blow air twice, to say, without words, "I'm here. I remember you," and hang up.[29]

One evening at the beginning of February, Kapler got a phone call. The gruff voice on the other end of the line was that of Colonel V. Rumyantsev, second in command of Stalin's security detail. He told Kapler the security agents knew everything and suggested he leave Moscow immediately. Kapler replied, "Go to Hell."[30]

Through February, Kapler and Svetlana resumed their walks in the woods and their theater outings, with her bodyguard in tow. At the end of February, they arranged a last rendezvous. They found an apartment near the Kursk Station used by Vasili's pilot friends for assignations. But the faithful Mikhail Klimov stayed with them. Svetlana persuaded him to sit in an adjoining room, though he insisted on keeping the door open. In silence the lovers kissed for the last time. They were ecstatic at touching, grief-stricken at parting; their leave-taking was devastating to Svetlana. It was February 28, her birthday. She had just turned seventeen.

Kapler was preparing to leave for Tashkent to shoot a movie based on his screenplay *In Defense of the Fatherland*. As Kapler reported it, on March 2 he drove to a committee meeting for the film industry. As he got out of his car, a man approached, flashed an identity badge, and told him to get back in. The man got into the passenger seat, and when Kapler asked where they were going, he replied, "To Lubyanka."

Kapler responded, "Is there any reason for this? Have I been accused of anything? Is there a warrant against me?"[31]

The man said nothing. Kapler could see there was a black Packard following them. In the passenger seat, he recognized General Nikolai Vlasik, chief of Stalin's personal security, and knew he was doomed. They drove into Lubyanka Square, where the statue of Felix Dzherzhinsky, the founder of Lenin's secret police, the Cheka, stared across at the dreaded prison. The heavy gates of the Lubyanka swung open. The massive neo-baroque building was synonymous with the terror of the NKVD. Under the tsars it had been an insurance firm, and it still retained its imposing marbled entrance and wooden parquet floors. Below, in its labyrinthine basement, were the cells and torture chambers that had seen much service in the late 1930s.

The KGB's infamous headquarters and prison on Moscow's Lub-yanka Square (informally known as "the Lubyanka"), where Beria had his office, still looks much as it did during Stalin's time in power.

Kapler understood that he was a top priority when Deputy Minister Bogdan Kabulov arrived. No mention was made of Svetlana. And Stalin's name did not come up. Kapler was being accused of contact with foreigners—which was irrefutable; he knew all the foreign correspondents in Moscow—and of spying on England's behalf.

Kabulov intoned, "Aleksei Yakovlevich Kapler, on the basis of Article 58 of our law, you are under arrest for having made known in your speeches your anti-Soviet and Counter-revolutionary opinions."[32] No trial was needed. No defense could be mounted. However, instead of the usual ten years for this offense, Kapler was sentenced to only five years in a labor camp.

Kapler's belongings were confiscated and itemized for his signature. He was not allowed to communicate with his wife, Tatiana Zlatogorova, and certainly not with Svetlana. But Kapler was too famous to merely disappear. The war had released some tongues, especially in the military and at the front, and his arrest was a major scandal.[33] Neither his epic films nor the appeals of his more courageous colleagues helped, however. Everyone knew that the cause of his arrest was his indiscreet affair with the daughter of the *vozhd*.

In retrospect, Kapler would say he knew that the relationship with Svetlana would inevitably end, but he was strangely enthralled. Asked why he didn't heed the general's advice, Kapler replied, "Who knows? It was also a question of self-respect."[34] What drew him to Svetlana was what he called "the freedom within her," her "bold judgements." In his mind, it was an "innocent enchantment," not a seduction. He recognized her desperation; he felt he understood her.

Vasili's son, the theater director Alexander Burdonsky, would later comment that Kapler was an intelligent and charming man:

> Yes, he was enamored of Svetlana—when a young girl is looking at you with infatuated eyes—but he did not anticipate the outcome of all this. He had a risk-taking personality. He was ordered not to return to Moscow. He came back. He got kicked in the neck. But, you understand, this was an affair of the century that surpassed the boundaries of accepted norms. Eisenstein dreamed of making a film about it. He even wrote a script—set in a different country. He saw how Kapler suffered and he mixed himself and Kapler because he too was in love with Svetlana. All this can really thrill a man of a particular nature. Even when threats like Stalin come up.[35]

On March 3, Stalin arrived at the Kremlin apartment just as Svetlana was getting ready for school. Her nanny, Alexandra Andreevna, was still in the room. Apoplectic with rage, he demanded that Svetlana hand over her "writer's" letters. He spat out the word *writer*. He said he knew the whole story. He was carrying their taped phone conversations in his breast pocket. "Your Kapler is a British spy," he seethed. "He's under arrest." Petrified, Svetlana gave up everything Kapler had given her: letters, photographs, notebooks, and even a draft movie script about the composer Shostakovich, protesting to her father that she loved Kapler.

He turned to her nanny with withering irony, "Oh, she loves him," and then slapped his daughter across the face. It was the first time he had hit her. "Just look . . . how low she has sunk. . . . Such a war going on and she's busy the whole time fucking." Her nanny managed to stammer, "No. No. No. I know her." Stalin turned to Svetlana. "Take a look at yourself. Who'd want you? You fool! He's got women all around him."[36] The irony that he himself had been thirty-nine and Nadya sixteen when he'd fallen in love with her was lost on Stalin.

Svetlana was in such shock that it took her a moment to realize that her father had called Kapler a British spy. She was appalled. She knew what this meant. When she returned from school that night, Stalin was in the dining room reading and tearing up Kapler's letters. "Writer!" she reported him saying. "He can't write decent Russian! She couldn't even find herself a Russian." Svetlana believed that in her father's mind, "the fact that Kapler was a Jew was what bothered him most of all."[37] She made no attempt to contact Kapler. She knew she couldn't even speak to his friends without its being reported to Stalin, and Kapler's fate would be worse. She now understood that her father "*was* the state."[38]

Kapler was held for a year in solitary confinement at Lubyanka prison before being transferred to Vorkuta in Siberia. For the Italian journalist Enzo Biagi, he recalled the ride in the "black crow," the prison truck in which he was accompanied by other "deviationists . . . terrorists, Trotskyites, ex–Social Democrats." Vorkuta was the locus of a prison complex in the coal-mining center in Komi Autonomous Republic. The complex had a reputation for profound brutality and exploitation.

But Kapler's luck held. The camp director, Mikhail Mal'tsev, who'd been appointed the previous year to turn Vorkuta into a model city, selected him, as the most famous prisoner in the camp, to be the official photographer of the city and prison complex. Kapler was designated one of the *zazonniki* (prisoners without borders) with permission to live and work outside the prison zone.[39] Kapler soon joined the Vorkuta Musical Drama Theater, a prisoners' collective, where he met the actress Valentina Tokaraskaya, who became his lover. In the Soviet Gulag there were always surreal distinctions that dictated survival or death.

When he'd completed his five-year sentence, Kapler was released and warned that under no circumstance was he to return to Moscow. He decided to go to Kiev, where his parents lived, but not before slipping into Moscow in the hope of seeing his wife. He stayed only two days and made no attempt to meet Svetlana. As he boarded the train for Kiev, plainclothes policemen surrounded him. They hustled him off the train at the next station. He was sentenced to another five years, this time to hard labor at a mine in Inta, also in the Pechora coal-mining basin, where conditions were brutal. Only visits by his lover, Tokaraskaya, with her food parcels kept him alive and sane.

Svetlana's cousin Vladimir Alliluyev remembered the turmoil at Zubalovo that immediately followed Kapler's arrest. As he put it, "Everyone was kicked out of there. Everyone got hit on their brains quite harshly." Stalin ordered Svetlana "banished" from the dacha for "moral depravity." Vasili was sentenced to ten days in an army prison for degeneracy. Grandfather Sergei and Grandmother Olga were sent to a ministry sanatorium for failing to intervene. The housekeeper, Lieutenant Sasha Nikashidze, who had spied on the lovers and read Kapler's letters, was fired. Zubalovo was closed.[40]

When Kapler was shipped off to Siberia, Svetlana knew that her father had ordered it. "It was such obvious and senseless despotism, that for a long time I was unable to recover from the shock."[41] But Kapler's imprisonment and the discovery of her mother's suicide had finally "cut the soap-bubbles of illusions. My eyes were opened and I could not any more claim blindness."[42]

Chapter 7

A Jewish Wedding

The House on the Embankment, across the river from the Kremlin in Moscow's Bersenevka neighborhood, was constructed to house the Soviet elite—and was the first home of the newlyweds Svetlana and Grigori Morozov.

A fter five months of brutal urban warfare that left over one million dead, the Battle of Stalingrad ended in a Russian victory on January 31, 1943, when Field Marshal Friedrich Paulus, commander of the German Sixth Army, and his staff surrendered.[1] Stalin's son Yakov Djugashvili, who had been languishing in a POW camp since his capture in 1941, was a valuable hostage. Count Folke Bernadotte of the Red Cross approached the deputy chairman of the Council of Ministers, Vyacheslav Molotov, to offer a prisoner swap: a field marshal for Stalin's son. Molotov conveyed the offer to Stalin. According to Molotov, Stalin adamantly refused. "All of them are my sons," Stalin said.[2]

Since the arrest of Aleksei Kapler in early March, Svetlana had seen little of her father. One morning he called her into his office and told her curtly, "The Germans have proposed that we exchange one of their prisoners for Yasha. They want me to make a deal with them! I won't do it. War is war." Her father said nothing further about her brother, but shoved an English document from his correspondence with Roosevelt at her, barking, "Translate! Here you have been studying all this English. Can you translate anything?"[3] Then the audience was over. It seems out of character for Stalin to involve his daughter in a state secret, but if her account of this moment is accurate, her father's delivery of the news was brutal. In her mind, he was "washing his hands" of his son.[4]

By the middle of April 1943, Yakov was dead. Looking back, Svetlana believed her father had been informed by his intelligence services of his son's death but kept the knowledge secret.[5]

In 1945, after the war ended, reports about Yakov began to filter out of Germany slowly. One came from SS Commander Gustav Wegner, head of the battalion guarding the POW camp near Lübeck where Yakov was held. He claimed to have witnessed Yakov's death. When the prisoners were taking exercise, Yakov crossed the no-man's-land toward the electrified fence. The sentry shouted, "Halt," but Yakov kept walking. Just as he reached the fence, he was shot. He collapsed on the first two rows of electrified barbed wire, where his body hung for twenty-four hours, until it was removed to the crematorium.[6]

Another report came from I. A. Serov, deputy to the minister of internal affairs of the Soviet administration in Germany, who in 1945 was assigned to discover the specifics of Yakov's fate. Serov added another detail. When the sentry shouted, "Halt," Yakov ripped open his shirt and yelled, "Shoot, you scum!"[7]

Stalin failed to save his son, but even Yakov's family believed he had little choice in rejecting a prisoner exchange. He could not be seen to be protecting his own son when millions of Russian sons were dying. In the first year of the war, two thirds of the three million Soviet POWs, taken largely in the June encirclement in 1941, were dead by the end of December. By the end of the war, at least three million of the five million Soviet POWs had died.[8]

Svetlana believed her beloved half brother died a "quiet hero. His heroism was as selfless, honorable and unassuming as his whole life had been."[9] And she did not forgive her father. Like many Russians, she felt Stalin had betrayed all his soldiers by the draconian Order 227, announced on July 28, 1942, and known colloquially as "Not a Step Back." The order included the statement: "Panic-mongers and cowards are to be exterminated on sight." Penal brigades of deserters were established and sent into the fiercest fighting.[10] When Soviet POWs were released from German camps in 1945 and repatriated, many were sent on to Siberian camps with sentences of up to twenty-five years for surrendering to the enemy. "I think that Yakov understood that returning back to our country after the war's end would not bode well for him," Svetlana's friend Stepan Mikoyan remarked pointedly.[11]

That spring Svetlana graduated from Model School No. 25. Her father summoned her to his Kuntsevo dacha and asked what she intended to study in college. When she replied, "Literature," he scoffed, "You want to be one of those Bohemians!" and insisted she reenroll in history at Moscow University.[12]

Sixty-two years later, she wrote to her friend Robert Rayle about this. None of her bitterness toward her father had abated.

> My own Father, a very possessive man, and <u>a Dictator of all + everybody + everything</u> . . . <u>did not let me</u> start, as 17 yr. old, my <u>own life</u> and <u>profession</u> . . . <u>he</u> wanted me to become an educated Marxist—to follow him, to be with him, to be a "valid member" of the CPSU (the <u>party</u>). That was his dictatorial love to me . . . everybody obeyed his wishes (during WWII, 1943!) and <u>I began</u> to study Modern History, although <u>I loathed</u> it with all my heart.[13]*

Svetlana was secretly hoping to be a writer. Olga Rifkina understood her friend's despair and decided to change her own program. Olga's mother, then working as a senior reader of American reports at *Pravda*, suggested that the girls major in the modern history of the United States. Although they had missed the deadline for enrollment, when the head of the department learned that it was Stalin's daughter who was applying late, he ordered that their applications be accepted.

In the program she undertook, Svetlana was required to be knowledgeable about American geography, history, and economics, for the moment all ideologically acceptable because the United States had become an ally. She wrote essays on Roosevelt's New Deal, on US-Soviet diplomatic relations in the 1930s, on American trade unions, and on US foreign policy in South America and Europe. She would end up knowing more about the United States than many European and even some American students.

---

* In her letters Svetlana underlined, capitalized, and added marginal notes and the occasional drawing, which uncannily gave them the emphasis of her speaking voice.

At least initially, social life in college was difficult. Olga Rifkina recalled that people came to lectures to look at Svetlana and her bodyguard, though gradually "they got used to her and treated her with sympathy."[14] Svetlana always claimed that her new university friends separated her from her father. Many of the students' parents or relatives had gone through the repression of the late 1930s, but she maintained that "it was the same in our family and it changed nothing in their feelings for me."[15] Of course, this was wishful thinking on her part. People may not have dared to speak out against Stalin, but as Stalin's daughter, Svetlana must often have been viewed with suspicion, while some may have seen her as a quick route to coveted privileges. Friendships could rarely have been as disinterested as she hoped.

Most of the children of the Kremlin elite, the "Kremlin set" as Svetlana called them, sought life outside the fortress. They had a running joke. When they left the Kremlin for a particular destination, they would say: "The subjects have gone to the objects," imitating the parlance of the secret police.[16] Svetlana found ways to slip the noose of scrutiny. With her Alliluyev cousins, she would drive for hours around the Moscow suburbs at night, though her father had not given her permission to drive. Then in December she asked her father to dismiss her bodyguard; it was humiliating to have a "tail." She was seventeen and a half and wanted to be able to walk down the street by herself. She recalled her father's response: "To hell with you then. Get killed if you like. It's no business of mine."[17]

Svetlana did not invite her new school friends to the Kremlin, embarrassed that they needed a pass to enter the gates. Olga Rifkina remembered only one occasion when Svetlana invited her home. It was 1944. The last exam at the end of their first year involved assembling a rifle. The university armory room was closed, but Svetlana said she had a rifle at home. Olga remembered passing Stalin's well-guarded door in the Kremlin apartment. Svetlana's nanny served them food while they practiced assembling the rifle.[18]

After that last exam, however, Svetlana began to distance herself from her group. She seemed to be spending her time with a fellow student named Grigori (Grisha) Morozov (the family's name was actually Moroz, but the family members had changed it to hide their Jewish origins).[19] Four years older and a close friend of Vasili, Morozov was someone Svetlana had known from her high school days. They began to date, often going to the theater or cinema.

Svetlana may have gotten rid of her personal bodyguard, but the security forces were still watching her. Soon she received a phone call from General Vlasik, Stalin's chief of security. The conversation was clipped: "Listen, this young Jew of yours—what is it between you?" She replied, "The Jew?" She was shocked. Nobody openly made ethnic distinctions—yet. It would be a couple of years before anti-Semitism became state policy. She said she knew Grigori Morozov from school. They were dating, that was all.

General Vlasik told her that he knew everything—for instance, he knew that Morozov wanted to get into the new Institute of International Relations but needed a military deferment. "We can help. Do you really want him released from the army?" When she said yes, the general replied, "OK. We'll do that. We'll release him." General Vlasik, too, could decide the fate of people with a phone call.[20]

Svetlana was not in love with Morozov—she was still pining for Aleksei Kapler—but she was looking for a way out of her Kremlin life. She felt her father now treated her with a kind of contempt, as if she had somehow been "soiled": "I wasn't his little girl anymore. I grew up wrong." Morozov phoned continually. When he eventually proposed, she agreed to marry him.

"He was sweet. I was lonely, and he loved me."[21] She said she would ask her father.

Svetlana claimed that when she went to Kuntsevo to get Stalin's permission, her father said flatly that he did not approve of the marriage because Morozov was Jewish. He fumed. "The Zionists put him over on you." It was "impossible to convince him that this was not so."[22]

Svetlana believed that her father was deeply anti-Semitic, and that this trait increased as he became more and more convinced of the existence of a Jewish conspiracy against the Soviet Union. In the end apparently he told her, "To hell with you. Do as you like."[23]

But Stalin also ranted that Morozov was studying at a university while other young Russians were dying at the front. Svetlana said nothing about her successful efforts to get Morozov a military deferment. When Stalin contacted Vlasik to say, "Our little girl is going to get married," Vlasik assured him, "We know the fellow. He's a good Communist. He's all right."[24] Stalin did not stop the marriage, but he categorically refused ever to meet Morozov, and though he continued to support the couple financially, he kept to his word. Morozov never met his father-in-law. Because it was wartime, there was no wedding celebration.

With Stalin's permission, the young couple moved into the House on the Embankment. This was a huge complex of 505 apartments, designed by the architect Boris Iofan and completed in 1931. Built on the banks of the Moskva River facing the Kremlin, the complex covered three acres and was the largest apartment block in Europe. The House on the Embankment was intended as a residence for Party officials and other members of the elite. It had a theater, exclusive stores, and a collective kitchen where residents could order pre-prepared dinners. A number of Svetlana's relatives had moved there in

1937, including the families of Aunt Anna and Aunt Zhenya. It was, however, a sinister building. In tsarist times, a tunnel had been built under the river, and this tunnel was made to align with Block 12 of the new complex when it was built. Secret police could come up the back stairs.[25] Svetlana and Morozov lived in apartment 370 in the ninth entrance.

Marfa Peshkova recalled that, once out of the Kremlin, Svetlana seemed to become much more independent. She held parties in the apartment for her literary friends, at which they read and discussed their poems. When friends came over, she always made a point of turning her father's portrait to the wall.[26] But soon the eighteen-year-old was pregnant. When Stalin learned of Svetlana's pregnancy, he had Zubalovo reopened, saying a pregnant mother needed country air. As always, the message from Stalin was mixed—just enough demonstration of family ties to keep his daughter dangling.

On May 9, 1945, radios blared the announcement of the end of the European war. Jubilant crowds poured into the streets of Moscow. American Ambassador George Kennan stood on the balcony of the American Embassy watching the thousands of people on the pavement below tossing people into the air and passing them over friendly hands. And cheering America. The United States had helped the USSR defeat the Germans—war aid had included everything from weaponry to Spam. Kennan waved to the throng below, stepped up, and shouted, "Congratulations on the day of victory. All honor to the Soviet allies." But he remained pensive. He feared Stalin's intentions. Fascist Italy and Germany had been defeated, but he felt that "a third totalitarian state was poised to dominate much of the post-war world." Kennan would eventually turn out to be a significant figure in Svetlana's life, but for the moment, he didn't even know that Stalin had a daughter.[27]

Svetlana phoned her father. "Congratulations on your victory, Papa! I just heard that the war is over." Stalin replied, "Yes, thank you very much. Yes, we have won." He asked her what she was doing. She said she was about to have her child. He said, "Well, all right, and take care of yourself."[28] And that was it. He did not invite her and her husband to celebrate the victory with him. Svetlana and Morozov had their celebratory party in their own apartment.

The war was over, but the price to the USSR was astounding. Of the 34.5 million men and women mobilized, an incredible 84 percent were killed, wounded, or captured. The total military deaths are estimated at 8.6 million, though estimates have gone as high as 23 million; at least 17 million civilians died, but the number is imprecise because statistical records do not include the hundreds of thousands who starved to death. "The Soviet population suffered out of all proportion to the sufferings of Soviet allies." No part of the country escaped the carnage. It had been the "disaster of a century."[29]

Svetlana and Morozov's only child, Joseph, was born two weeks after Victory Day. She insisted that the name was not a covert appeal to her father. Both of the child's grandfathers were named Joseph. She finally took the infant Joseph to see his grandfather at his Kuntsevo dacha that August. It happened to be the day the Americans bombed Hiroshima. "[My father] noticed me, of course, but my news—that I'd had a baby— didn't matter very much in this context. I went back home."[30]

Svetlana had few ties with her father now. If she phoned, Stalin might say he was busy and bang down the phone. It would take her weeks to find the courage to phone again. She and Morozov continued their studies. Their child lived mostly at Zubalovo with his two nannies: Svetlana's old nanny, Alexandra Andreevna Bychkova; and the nanny who looked after Gulia, Yakov's daughter. Most Soviet women left their children like this. While the elite left their children with nannies, the majority left them at nurseries on Monday morning and picked them up late on Friday; otherwise they left them with their babushkas (grandmothers). Even if this was common practice, Svetlana seemed not to remember how bitterly she had resented her mother's absences. Svetlana's relatives would comment laconically, "She wasn't a warm mother," but then add that she'd never learned what a mother was.[31]

By most accounts, Morozov was a charming young man, and the marriage began well. Decades later Svetlana could recall how simple life had been and how happy they were as students.[32] Yet, later, she would also characterize her young husband to her daughter Olga as a "shirt-tearer." He would become outraged at something and yell at her while literally tearing his shirt.[33]

On December 1, 1945, a year and a half into her marriage, Svetlana wrote to her father, who was vacationing in Sochi. In early October, she'd sent him a photograph of her son, and he'd sent a gift of mandarins in return:

> Hi my dear Papochka,
>   I've never been happier than today when I received your letter and the mandarins. . . . I'm waiting for you in Moscow and maybe you will send another kind letter like that one. Kissing you, my dear daddy.[34]

Svetlana was trying desperately to repair relations with her father. It would seem that her marriage was already in trouble. She would soon be twenty, and married life was not what she'd expected. When she was distraught, Svetlana would turn to her father to seek emotional support.

There were probably a number of reasons for the alienation between her and Grigori, of course, but one, according to her friend Marfa Peshkova, was the multitude of Morozov relatives coming to visit and asking for a better apartment or for their children to be placed in various elite schools and institutions.[35] Her cousin Vladimir Alliluyev dismissed Morozov as an opportunist. "Svetlana's husband filled the apartment with his friends and continuously asked for various comforts and favors. Svetlana found herself shoved into the back corner."[36] Svetlana was still shy in any public gathering, and this portrait of her becoming a shadow in her own home among her husband's guests is not unlikely.

Rumors in Kremlin inner circles claimed that Stalin engineered the divorce, though Svetlana always denied this. The main problem was elsewhere. She'd just turned nineteen when she had Joseph, and soon she found herself pregnant again. She claimed to have had three painful abortions in her three-year marriage.[37] This might seem shocking, but abortion had always been a common form of birth control in the Soviet Union until, along with homosexuality, it was declared illegal after the census indicated a drastic fall in population—and even then, exceptions were always made.[38] When Svetlana finally became seriously ill after suffering a miscarriage, she decided to flee. She told Grigori she was moving back to the Kremlin and taking Joseph with her.

Years later, she would write to her friend Rosa Shand:

In fullest sincerity I can tell you to-day—looking back from years of search and experience—I should have stayed together with my very First Young husband. There was nothing wrong with him. We were so young—so foolish—just didn't know a damn thing about life. And it was always me who was dissatisfied, and tried to run away to find "something better."[39]

Consoling a friend who was going through a divorce, Svetlana reflected:

I was <u>never</u> used to a family life, and for that reason it was easy to break it. But still I felt lonely afterwards, and made many mistakes, trying immediately to find some substitute for the lost companionship . . . how young and stupid I have been![40]

Grigori and Svetlana's marriage ended in 1947. Divorce in the Soviet Union was not particularly complicated. It involved a two-stage procedure: the couple submitted an application to a district court, and within a month they would be divorced. But for poor Morozov, divorce was even simpler. One day Morozov was not allowed back into the House on the Embankment. Svetlana's brother Vasili had taken the matter in hand. When a couple married in the Soviet Union, the wife's Soviet passport—all Soviet citizens were required to hold passports—was stamped and included the husband's name. A new stamp indicated a divorce. Vasili took Morozov's and Svetlana's passports and had them returned to their virgin state by simply removing the original stamps. It was as if the marriage had never occurred.

Stalin was pleased with the divorce. He had built a new dacha at Kholodnaya Rechka, north of Gagra on the Abkhazian coast, and now ordered a small dacha constructed for Svetlana nearby. She visited. It was the first time father and daughter had been together for any extended period in a long time.

Stalin kept his usual schedule—waking at 11:00 a.m. and dining at 10:00 p.m. Svetlana remembered Andrei Zhdanov, Lavrenty Beria, and Georgy Malenkov coming over from their nearby government dachas. As usual, the meal would last until 4 a.m. For Svetlana, dinner with her father had always been an ordeal. As a teenager, she had often been the butt of Stalin's jokes. If he noticed she'd slipped away after some coarse joke, he would shout, "Comrade Hostess! Why have you left us poor unenlightened creatures without giving us some orientation?

Now we don't know where to go! Lead us! Show us the way!"
That joke, a parody of the slogan "Comrade Stalin Leads the
Way," went on for years.[41] But now the collective dinners at his
dacha merely appalled her. Stalin, as usual, forced his comrades
through endless toasts—it was said he liked to get them drunk
to see what they might reveal in unguarded moments—and the
dinners would end with the bodyguards carrying home their
charges "dead drunk," many, as Svetlana remembered, "having
lain for some time in a bathroom, vomiting."[42]

When she and her father were alone, it was difficult to find
subjects to talk about, other than the food they were eating or
the botanical details of nearby plants. She was careful not to
talk about people, in case she might mistakenly say something
about someone that might arouse her father's suspicions. She
never knew what to say or, more important, what not to say. It
was easiest when she read to him.

Dejected by the whole ordeal, Svetlana returned to Moscow
after three weeks, but as soon as she was back in the Kremlin
apartment with her son Joseph, she felt she was again trapped
inside a sarcophagus. She grew desperate. Given her psychological history, Svetlana did not know how to be alone. Alone,
she felt totally exposed. She thought she would be safe if only
she could entwine her life in another, but then, once she had
achieved this, she would feel suffocated, a pattern that would
take her decades to break, if she ever succeeded.

Now she thought of Sergo Beria, the son of Lavrenty Beria,
as a potential partner.

She and Sergo had been children together, watching cartoons
in the Kremlin and going to Model School No. 25. Sergo Beria
and her close friend Marfa Peshkova had just gotten engaged
that year. She confronted Marfa, saying that Marfa should
have known that she, Svetlana, had always been in love with

Beria. And ended their friendship. This was childish, petulant, and high-handed, the action of a princess in the Kremlin. She would look back with regret and say that she had thus lost two friends, Sergo and Marfa.[43] Focused only on her own need, Svetlana seemed incapable of thinking rationally or pragmatically about what it would mean to have Lavrenty Beria as her father-in-law. Sergo's mother, Nina, had already warned her son against such a union, certain that Stalin would think Beria was worming his way into power and would turn against them all.[44] The twenty-one-year-old Svetlana seemed willfully naive about the perfidy of the closed political circle she lived inside.

After Marfa and Sergo Beria were married, Stalin called the young man to his dacha. Sergo described the encounter in his memoir. Though Beria is not always a reliable witness, the conversation has a certain plausibility. Allegedly Stalin said:

> "Do you know your wife's family? . . ." He then told me what he thought of that family: "Gorky himself was not bad in his way. But what a lot of anti-Soviet people he had around him. . . . I regard this marriage as a disloyal act on your part. Not disloyal to me but to the Soviet State. . . . I see your marriage as a move to establish links with the oppositionist Russian intelligentsia." This idea had never even crossed my mind. My wife was pretty, plump like a quail, but not very intelligent and with a rather weak character, as I was to discover later. Stalin went on, . . . "It must be your father who urged you into this marriage, so as to infiltrate the Russian intelligentsia."[45]

Two things are obvious from this conversation: the degree to which Stalin meddled in the private lives of his political allies and their minions and the fact that Svetlana had had a lucky escape. Had she succeeded in marrying Sergo Beria, her life would have been impossible. Sergo's contempt for his wife is unpleasant, but the rivalry between Stalin and Sergo's father, Lavrenty Beria, would have made her life a living hell. However, when driven by need, Svetlana seemed to lose the instinct for self-preservation.

Chapter 8

The Anti-Cosmopolitan Campaign

By the end of the 1940s, Stalin had turned on many of the relatives who had celebrated his birthday with him in 1934. *Top row, left:* Anna Redens was arrested in 1948 (her husband, Stanislav, had been executed in 1940). *Middle row:* Maria Svanidze (*left*) was executed in 1942; although Sashiko Svanidze (*third from left*) survived, her sister Mariko was executed in 1942; Polina Molotov (*at Stalin's left*) was arrested in 1948. *Bottom row, second from left:* Zhenya Alliluyeva was arrested in 1947.

A fter the war, everyone in the Soviet Union expected an easing of restrictions. The Great Patriotic War had been won at immense cost and through heroic sacrifice. So much reconstruction had to be undertaken. Surely now the long-promised era of socialist plenty was at hand. Instead, a new wave of repression was about to begin. With the cult of personality he'd fostered, Stalin had consolidated his power and assumed the template of the dictator. His adopted son, Artyom Sergeev, remembered an incident during which he heard Stalin upbraiding his son Vasili for exploiting the Stalin name.

"But I am a Stalin too," Vasili had said.

"No, you're not," replied Stalin. "You're not Stalin and I'm not Stalin. Stalin is Soviet power. Stalin is what he is in the newspapers and the portraits, not you, no not even me!"[1]

Power, its preservation and execution, had filled the vacuum of a human being. Stalin was an idea now, infallible. And he was still fighting a war. Propaganda made it clear that the Soviet Union had enemies out to destroy it.

It was Winston Churchill who inserted the term Iron Curtain into the public imagination. On March 5, 1946, in a gymnasium at Westminster College in Fulton, Missouri, Churchill declaimed: "From Stettin in the Baltic to Trieste in the Adriatic an iron curtain has descended across the Continent."[2] Americans, who still thought of Stalin as Uncle Joe, believed Churchill was meddling. But their attitude would soon change.

Within a year after the end of World War II, the Cold War was under way, dividing the world into capitalist and communist spheres. In the background loomed the terrifying threat of the atomic bomb detonated over Hiroshima. Stalin was now sure the United States intended to attack the Soviet Union sooner or later. In 1946, he placed the meticulous bureaucrat Lavrenty Beria in charge of atomic research. Highly restricted fenced-off settlements for Soviet scientists were constructed in remote regions. Well-trained Soviet spymasters soon brought Stalin the atomic secrets he wanted.[3] The first Soviet atom bomb was detonated in 1949.

Even as the playing field of atomic war was being leveled, suspicions between the two countries had grown exponentially since 1946. In 1947, President Truman signed the National Security Act establishing the Central Intelligence Agency. By early 1948, the CIA had already helped to swing an election in Italy away from the Communists.[4] Now the deadly game of international intelligence gathering was afoot.

The CIA spied on its own citizens in a domestic campaign of fear. Beginning as early as 1945, the House Committee on Un-American Activities (HUAC) began hunting for Soviet spies and Communist sympathizers. Senator Joseph McCarthy created paranoia with his reckless Red Scare propaganda, and his sensationalized public hearings targeted thousands of Americans. But Stalin went much further. He turned his secret police, the MGB (Ministry of State Security), even more murderously against his own people. To instill and then control through fear had always been his strategy, and as he had learned from the earliest days, he had to keep the fear going. His solution was to engineer a campaign of ideological purification that became known as the Anti-Cosmopolitan Campaign. All contacts with the West and Western culture were declared subversive. To be seen engaging in any conversation or transaction with any foreigners was forbidden; to seek to marry a foreigner was a crime. Foreign travel was restricted to high Party officials or those accompanied by "handlers." A shroud of silence blanketed the country. No one dared to express criticism of the Great Stalin, who had won the war. As Sergei Pavlovich Alliluyev put it, "It was not done by anyone. It just wasn't accepted, nor was it possible."[5]

By late 1947, the new wave of repression hit the Stalin family. At five p.m. on December 10, Zhenya, Pavel Alliluyev's widow, now forty-nine and remarried, was at home in her apartment in the House on the Embankment. She was busy with her dressmaker, sewing a new dress to celebrate the New Year. Zhenya's married daughter Kyra, twenty-seven, was visiting and was in the dining room rehearsing Chekhov's *The Proposal* with her theater friends. Zhenya's sons—Sergei, nineteen; and Alexander, sixteen—were also there, as was her frail mother, who lived with them. The doorbell rang. Kyra answered it. Two military men, Colonel Maslennikov and Major Gordeyev, stood at the door. "Is Eugenia Aleksandrovna at home?" they asked. "Yes, come in," Kyra replied and went back to rehearsing the play. Then Kyra heard her mother say, "Prison and bad luck are two things that you can't avoid."[6]

They took Zhenya away in what she was wearing. Hastily kissing her children good-bye, she told them not to worry since she "had no guilt of any sort." Other agents arrived; their search of the flat lasted well into the night. As they tapped the potted plants, Kyra asked, "What are you looking for? An underground passage into the Kremlin?" But irony was never a good idea with the NKGB. Anyone who came to the flat that evening was ordered to sit and wait. The agents took away all family photos with Stalin and Svetlana and Vasili in them, as well as all autographed books.[7]

Transported to Vladimir Prison, Zhenya was accused of spying; of poisoning her husband, Pavel, who had died of a heart attack nine years earlier; and of interactions with foreigners. She was kept in solitary confinement. Her children were not permitted to contact her.

Zhenya confessed to all the accusations. She later told her daughter, "You sign anything there, just to be left alone and not tortured!" In prison, bombarded by the screams of victims begging for death, she swallowed glass. She lived, but suffered the consequences in stomach problems for the rest of her life.[8]

The nighttime arrest had been so surreal that the fear kicked in only later. Alexander Alliluyev remembered that his brother

Sergei would lie in bed, waiting breathlessly to hear whether the elevator stopped on their floor. Rustlings or other sounds on the staircase would cause him to tremble. A few weeks later, at about six in the evening, the elevator did stop. Kyra was visiting, as, of course, the secret police knew. She was sitting reading *War and Peace*. When she answered the knock on the door, it was the commandants again. Her brothers stood behind her to protect her. As the agents read Kyra the arrest warrant, her grandmother cried. "Grandmother, don't humiliate yourself, don't cry, you mustn't," Kyra remembered saying.[9]

Kyra was taken to a waiting car. As they drove across Moscow and she watched the streets disappear behind her, she wondered if she would ever see her city again. The journey across the nocturnal city took place in oppressive silence until the heavy gates of the Lubyanka prison swung open and the car drove into the courtyard. She remained stoic until they took everything from her and put her in a cell. Then she wept.

Her interrogator accused her of spreading rumors about Nadya's suicide. She was dumbfounded. She didn't know that Nadya had committed suicide. She had always believed the story about appendicitis. "I belonged to the kind of family where it wasn't accepted to talk more than necessary. There was no gossip. . . . They needed something to accuse us of, so that was what they pinned on me: I was supposed to have talked to everybody."[10]

She was kept in solitary confinement for six months. Her salvation was her memory. It was vital to hold on to the belief that a real world still existed outside the walls of that madhouse. She visualized all the movies and musicals she knew. She was permitted to read. She paced her cell, asking herself what she had done. She had always been a good Pioneer, a good Komsomolka. She could not understand. It had to be Lavrenty Beria, who had always had it in for her family.

My only clue was that I was a relative of Stalin and I knew that Beria was bound to say something to Stalin that he would believe. My mother was very outspoken, she was freedom-loving, she was forthright with Stalin and equally truthful with Beria. He had evidently taken a dislike to her from the moment they set eyes on each other. I realized that all this had to be instigated by Beria. Stalin by this time was deeply under his influence.[11]

People advised Kyra to write to Stalin from prison, but she refused. It was better not to remind Stalin of her existence. But so twisted was her (and indeed most people's) logic in this climate of fear that she could still rationalize, indeed justify, Stalin's motives. Her brother Alexander explained:

We could only surmise there must be some minor guilt, something to do with purely personal relationships and loyalty to Stalin. We definitely thought that without Stalin's knowledge this arrest simply could not have taken place. And so far as he decided on such an extreme thing as to arrest his own close relatives, so, thought we, there must be a reason. It was a cruel step from our point of view. But from his point of view it had to be a legitimate one.[12]

Zhenya's second husband, N. V. Molochnikov, a Jewish engineer, was soon arrested. When Zhenya's sons asked what they were to tell friends about the absence of their mother and stepfather, the NKGB instructed them to say, "Our parents are on a prolonged trip." "But until what time?" they asked. "Until a special announcement."[13] A number of Kyra's friends were also arrested.

On January 28, 1948, they came for Svetlana's aunt Anna, who was Nadya's older sister and the widow of Stanislav Redens.

Her sons—Vladimir, twelve; and Leonid, nineteen—were in the apartment. Everyone was asleep. A colonel, followed by a number of agents, knocked on the door at 3:00 a.m. They showed Anna the arrest warrant. As she was being taken away, Anna said, "What a strange array of misfortunes come upon our family Alliluyev." The children sat up with their nanny as the search was under way. In their memory it lasted a day and a night.[14]

Accused of slandering Stalin, Anna Redens was arrested in 1948 and was not released until 1954.

Anna was accused of slandering Stalin. Her interrogators had collected denunciations from family, friends, and acquaintances. However, when they demanded that she sign a confession, her son Vladimir claimed she refused. He said proudly, "When they arrested my mother, they couldn't get her to sign anything, not even by force. She was stubborn, they couldn't break her, even by putting her into solitary."[15]

In 1993, forty-five years later, when the files of former prisoners were opened to families, Vladimir Alliluyev was permitted to examine his mother's rehabilitation file, P-212.[16] The final dimension of the tragedy was that Zhenya and Kyra had been forced to sign condemnations of Anna.

The House on the Embankment earned a new nickname: The House of Preliminary Detention. (The Russian acronym DOPR is the same for both.) It was now a ghost house as Zhenya's and Anna's children drew together for comfort. Uncle Fyodor, Nadya's brother, lived in the same complex and visited often. "Everyone was shocked—shocked, depressed, surprised. But we all kept holding together, as we always had done, and even more so now," recalled Leonid, Anna Alliluyeva's son.[17]

Svetlana tried to intercede with her father. When she asked him what her aunts and cousin had done wrong, he replied, "They talked a lot. They knew too much and they talked too much. And it helped our enemies." Everyone was required to shun the families of people who were purged, and they hadn't done this. When she protested, he threatened: "You yourself make anti-Soviet statements."[18]

Zhenya's son Alexander remembered meeting Svetlana on the Stone Bridge that winter. They both understood that it was too dangerous to speak openly. Alexander's maternal grandmother had warned him: "Do not write to the freckled one." They met occasionally, surreptitiously, at the skating rink amid the spruce trees.[19]

Grandmother Olga was still living alone in the Kremlin, where she would sit brooding over the fate of her four children. Her older son, Pavel, and her younger daughter, Nadya, were dead. Her second son, Fyodor, was mentally disabled, living a half life as a consequence of trauma suffered in 1918 during the Civil War. And her older daughter, Anna, was in prison. Olga couldn't comprehend why Stalin put Anna in prison. She would give Svetlana letters for Stalin, appealing for her daughter's release, and then would take the letters back. What was the point?

After the arrests, the grandchildren were soon banned from visiting the Kremlin, so Olga would go every weekend to visit them in their apartments in the House on the Embankment. To Olga it was very clear that Stalin was responsible for their mothers' imprisonment. Zhenya's son Sergei remembered her visits in those days. "Grandma would refer to the place where our mothers were confined as nothing other than the Gestapo, although she didn't say it to Stalin's face. She knew what that word was about! Her dark humour! She knew things; she had no illusions. She was not far from the truth, either, as we all realized later."[20]

Grandfather Sergei had died in 1945. Luckily, he did not live to witness the arrest of his elder daughter, in his memory the child who had once carried live ammunition for the revolutionary cause and refused to wash her hand for a whole day after Lenin had shaken it. But Sergei's ideals had died long before he did.

Despite Grandmother Olga's comments, the family chose to focus their anger on Lavrenty Beria. Someone had to be targeting them. It must be Beria carrying tales of their disloyalty and perfidy to Stalin.

Beria was a Mingrelian from Western Georgia. The family believed he had sought the death of Anna's husband, Stanislav Redens, in 1938 because Redens knew secrets about his past.[21] Ten years later, they still believed he was out to destroy them. But however much Beria might have inflamed Stalin's paranoia, Stalin was always in control. Rather than looking into the utter blackness and the erasure of all trust that locating the blame squarely on Stalin would have involved, the family held to their illusions. Zhenya's son Sergei Alliluyev admitted that it made things easier. It was "simpler to explain everything this way." Alexander Alliluyev said, "It is a natural protection." To repress a terrible idea "keeps one from going completely mad, from losing one's mind."[22]

Looking back, Sergei would add, "What was so terrible for the country in the thirties and the forties is that when they started arresting people here and people there, people began to get used to this, as if this were normal. *That* is what was so horrible! Everybody believed that this was what had to be."[23]

In the meantime, Stalin was bent on a larger campaign, which took all his attention. The Anti-Cosmopolitan Campaign was evolving into the gradual and methodical elimination of Jewish influence on the country's social, political, and cultural life.

Stalin was particularly incensed by the Jewish Antifascist Committee (JAC), created in 1942 and headed by Solomon Mikhoels, the director of Moscow's State Jewish Theater. Then it had served as a good propaganda tool to gain the support of American Jews and tens of millions of dollars in financial aid, but now it was evidencing "bourgeois nationalism" in seeking to promote Jewish national and cultural identity.[24]

On the night of January 12, 1948, Solomon Mikhoels was killed. Svetlana claimed to have been a witness to the murder. She overheard her father on the phone:

> One day, in father's dacha, during one of my rare meetings with him, I entered his room when he was speaking to someone on the telephone. Something was being reported to him and he was listening. Then, as a summary of the conversation, he said: "Well, it's an automobile accident." I remember so well the way he said it: not a question but an answer, an assertion. He wasn't asking; he was suggesting: "an automobile accident." When he got through,

he greeted me; and a little later he said: "Mikhoels was killed in an automobile accident."

When Svetlana went to her classes at the university the next day, a friend, whose father worked with the Jewish Theater, was weeping. The newspapers were reporting that Solomon Mikhoels died in an "automobile accident." But Svetlana knew otherwise.

[Mikhoels] had been murdered and there had been no accident. "Automobile accident" was the official version, the cover-up suggested by my father when the black deed had been reported to him. My head began to throb. I knew all too well my father's obsession with "Zionist" plots around every corner. It was not difficult to guess why this particular crime had been reported directly to him.[25]

Mikhoels had been sent to the town of Minsk in Belarus to review a play that was being considered for the Stalin Prize. He checked in at his hotel. The next morning, street workers discovered his battered body dumped in a snowdrift. There was no investigation, no effort to explain why Mikhoels might have been outside his hotel in the middle of the night or how such a deadly car crash could have occurred on a quiet back street in the city of Minsk.[26] In an elaborately staged public funeral, Mikhoels's body lay in state at Moscow's State Jewish Theater for a full day as mourners filed past. But many remained unimpressed by the sham ceremonial send-off of one of the Soviet Union's most famous directors and actors.

Ironically, for strategic reasons, Stalin's was one of the first governments to recognize the state of Israel, in May 1948, and that fall he welcomed Golda Meir, the Israeli ambassador to the USSR. Stalin was hoping that the new Jewish state would take a pro-Soviet stance, but when Israel leaned toward America, he was furious. Thousands had greeted Golda Meir that May when she attended a synagogue in Moscow on Rosh Hashanah.[27] It was clear to Stalin that Russian Jews who enthusiastically supported Israel were dangerous Zionists. They had friends and family ties in the United States. If war with America broke out, they would betray the USSR.

Articles began to appear in *Pravda* and *Kultura i zhizn* in 1948 accusing literary, music, and theater critics, most of whom were Jewish, of "ideological sabotage." They were branded as "rootless cosmopolitans." They were "persons without identity," and "passportless wanderers."[28] Jews were disloyal by definition. Jews resisted the Soviet project of complete assimilation of national ethnicities. They identified themselves as Jews. In 1952, twelve members of the JAC would be executed.

Unwittingly, Svetlana played a minor role in this intrigue. Knowing he was a target, Solomon Mikhoels had, months before his murder, sought information about Svetlana and Grigori Morozov, hoping that the Jewish Morozov might intercede with his father-in-law to cool the virulent anti-Semitic campaign that was emerging in Moscow. This unforgivable approach to his own family confirmed Stalin's resolve to eliminate Mikhoels. The crime was specific: "Mikhoels conspired with American and Zionist intelligence circles to gather information about the leader of the Soviet government."[29]

In late 1948, Joseph Morozov, the father of Svetlana's ex-husband, was arrested. When Svetlana discovered this and went to her father to appeal for the old man's release, Stalin was furious. "That first husband of yours was thrown your way by the Zionists," he again told her. " 'Papa,' I tried to object, 'the younger ones couldn't care less about Zionism.' 'No! You don't understand,' was the sharp answer. 'The entire older generation is contaminated with Zionism and now they're teaching the young people too.' "[30]

But when it came to her family, her father's motives were personal.

Trying to defend her aunt Zhenya, Svetlana wrote her father a strange letter on December 1, 1945:

Papochka

In regards to Zhenya and now that the conversation about her has started. It seems to me that these types of doubts came to you because she remarried very quickly and the reason for this she shared with me a little bit. I didn't ask her myself. I will definitely tell you when you come. If you have doubts like this in another person it is undignified, terrifying, and awkward. In addition it [the problem] is probably not in Zhenya and in her family struggles, but the principal question is—remember that a considerable amount was said about me. And who were they? They can go to hell.

Svetanka[31]

We will never be privy to that conversation, but Svetlana seemed to believe that her father was still angry with Zhenya for her hasty remarriage after her husband Pavel's death in 1938. Rumors circulated, of course, that Zhenya had quickly married to avoid Stalin's unwanted attentions. She and Stalin had been close. More convincing, however, is the idea that Zhenya's unseemly haste made her unreliable in Stalin's eyes. Svetlana assured her father that all was gossip and she could explain.

But it may have been more than this. Stalin was now carefully guarding his reputation, and the aunts "talked too much." Looking back, Svetlana would conclude, "There is no doubt that [my father] remembered how close they [the aunts] had been to all that happened in our family, that they knew everything about Mamma's suicide and the letter she had written before her death."

Svetlana also remembered Zhenya's description of her father at the outbreak of war in 1941. "'I had never seen Joseph so crushed and in such confusion,' was the way she described it. . . . 'I was even more frightened when I found he was almost in a panic himself.'" Svetlana was certain that her father recalled this. She added with rancor, "He didn't want others to know about it. And so Yevgenia [Zhenya] Alliluyeva got ten years of solitary confinement."[32] Could the reason for Zhenya's imprisonment be as simple as the fact that she had seen Stalin in a moment of weakness?

It seems unlikely that Stalin's imprisonment of Anna was an act of personal revenge, however. He called Anna "an unprincipled fool . . . this sort of goodness is worse than any wickedness."[33] During the final years of the war, Anna had helped her father, Sergei, to write his memoirs. His carefully self-censored book was published under the title *Proydenny put'* (A Traveled Path) in 1946, the year after his death. Meanwhile, Anna had decided to write her own memoirs. When she submitted the manuscript of *Reminiscences* for official vetting, it was heavily edited by a journalist named Nina Bam and ended safely with the triumph of the Bolsheviks in 1917. It seemed a harmless, moving, personal memoir, but family members were terrified. They begged her not to publish the book. Anna only laughed and said she was working on volume two.

When *Reminiscences* came out in 1946, it was praised,[34] but the family had been right to warn her. In May 1947, a savage review appeared in *Pravda*, written by Pyotr Fedoseyev and titled "Irresponsible Thinking." The attack was shocking. Fedoseyev dismissed "memoirs by small people about grand figures with whom they were somehow connected." Gorky was quoted as lamenting Tolstoy's experience: "How large, how clingy was the cloud of flies that surrounded the famous writer, and how annoying were some of these parasites who were feeding off his spirit." Anna was a parasite feeding off Stalin and claiming family intimacy. Official hagiography and encomiums were mandatory, but it was forbidden to write intimately of Stalin. He did not want personal stories obscuring the icon.

But the reviewer, Fedoseyev, had a larger point to make:

It is especially intolerable when authors of such kind attempt to write a memoir about the development of the Bolshevik Party, about the life and the struggle of its outstanding participants. V. Lenin said that the Bolshevik Party was the intelligence, honor, and conscience of our epoch. The history of the Bolshevik Party and the biographies of its leaders embody the historical experience of the struggle for freedom of the proletariat against the capitalist enslavement, for the creation of the fairest, freest way of life on earth. The great achievement of the Bolsheviks and their leaders serves as a source of inspiration for millions of people in their struggle for the complete victory of communist society. During the lessons about the history of the party and its leaders, millions of working people learn how to live and struggle for the interests of society, for the free, joyful, truly human life.

In order to protect the "free, joyful, truly human life" that Soviet society supposedly was, Anna was sentenced to ten years. It is hard to credit, but a large portion of the Soviet population, bombarded by propaganda and cut off from the rest of the world, believed this version of their lives.

The real error of Anna's memoir, however, was that she didn't place Stalin at the center of the story. Her portrait of the Revolution was wrong:

The decisive speech made by Comrade Stalin against Lenin's appearance at the court tribunal against the counterrevolutionaries convinced Lenin to go underground and hide from the provisional government. The short biography of I. V. Stalin expressly states the significance of Stalin's stance at this time. "Stalin saved Lenin's precious life for the party, for the people, and for all humanity by decisively taking a stance against Lenin's appearance at the tribunal and by resisting the suggestions made by the traitors Kamenev, Rukov, and Trotsky" (*Joseph Vissarionovich Stalin: Short Biography* p. 63). This is the real truth in regard to the question that A. Alliluyeva distorted and twisted in her pseudo-memoirs.[35]

The reviewer concludes that Anna was "a narcissist," "an opportunist," "a self-advertiser" hoping to receive large royalties. Readers were advised to consult the "scientifically constructed" *Short Biography* of Stalin (written, of course, under Stalin's supervision) for the truth. Svetlana could see her father's stock phrases threading the review.[36]

In retrospect, Svetlana would explain thus: "My father needed . . . to throw out of history, once and for all, those who had been in his way, those who had actually founded and created the Party and had brought about the Revolution."[37] What Anna did wrong was to speak of Stalin as a human being. In his mind, he was already a historical personage.

No such review could have appeared without Stalin's prior vetting. Anna's arrest occurred almost a year after the review was published, but this was characteristic of Stalin's methods. In order to obscure his involvement, he waited patiently for revenge against enemies. The book was banned and Anna disappeared.

Svetlana had seen little of her father during this torturous time, but in early November 1948, while he was on vacation in the south, he summoned her to visit him at his dacha. When she arrived, he seemed angry with her. He called her to the dinner table and "bawled me out," as she put it, "and called me a 'parasite' in front of everyone. He told me 'no good had come' of me yet. Everyone was silent and embarrassed."[38] She, too, remained silent. Her father was terrifyingly changeable. The very next day "he suddenly started talking to me for the first time about my mother and the way she died." It was in fact November 8, the anniversary of Nadya's death. "I was at a loss," she recalled. "I had no idea what to say—I was afraid of the subject."

Stalin was still looking for culprits. "What a miserable little pistol it was," he remarked. "It was nothing but a toy. Pavlusha brought it to her. A fine thing to give anybody!" Then he remembered how close Nadya had been with Polina Molotov. Polina had been a "bad influence." He started cursing the novel *The Green Hat*, which Nadya had been reading shortly before she died. He claimed on several occasions that this "vile book" had distorted her thinking.[39]

The Green Hat, published in 1924, was a potboiler romance, probably acceptable in Bolshevik circles because it satirized the British upper class. Nadya had been in charge of Stalin's library and of ordering his books. It is doubtful that Stalin read *The Green Hat*, but she must have discussed it with him. In the novel, the aristocratic high-minded heroine, betrayed by her lover, commits suicide as a gesture of her contempt for approval from her elite circle. A book did not kill Nadya, but Stalin believed it had an influence on her decision to commit suicide. This similarity paints a portrait of Nadya as a young woman with an icily unbendable pride and a strange sense of idealism.[40] In cultural circles in the 1920s, multiple suicides, especially those of the poets Mayakovsky and Yesenin, had made a kind of romanticized cult of suicide. Of course this was only among the intelligentsia. Ordinarily, suicide was looked on as treason against the collective.

Svetlana found the whole conversation with her father utterly painful. She felt he was looking for anything *but* the real reason for her mother's suicide—he refused to look at the things that made Nadya's life with him so unbearable. And she was suddenly frightened. Her father seemed to be speaking to her as an adult for the first time, asking for her trust. "But I'd rather have fallen through the ground than have had that kind of trust."

That November Svetlana returned with her father to Moscow by train. When the train stopped at the various stations, they'd descend for a stroll. There were no other passengers on the train, and the platforms had been cleared. Stalin strolled to the front engine, chatted with the engineer and the few railway workers who had security clearance, and then got back on the train, seeming not to notice that the whole thing was a "sinister, sad, depressing sight," as Svetlana saw it. Her father was a prisoner of his own isolation, an isolation he had constructed. Before the train pulled into the Moscow station, it was diverted to a siding, and the two passengers descended. General Vlasik and the bodyguards were there to greet them, puffing and fussing as Stalin cursed them.[41]

Father and daughter parted, each dissatisfied with the other. It was impossible to be with her father. He had sacrificed everything human in him to the pursuit of power. After seeing him, she always needed days to recover her equilibrium. "I had no feeling left for my father, and after every meeting I was in a hurry to get away."[42] This, however, was not entirely true. Svetlana could never wholly repudiate her father. His black shadow always remained over her, impossible to exorcise. There was the father to be pitied and there was the dictator. She would always believe that in some part of him, the father loved her.

Chapter 9

Everything Silent, as Before a Storm

**Svetlana with her first two children,
Joseph and Katya, in 1953.**

By 1949, Svetlana was living in the otherwise empty Kremlin apartment again. As he had done for years, her father lived at his Kuntsevo dacha. Ivan Borodachev, a commandant of State Security, ran the Kremlin household with rigor. He kept a list of any books Svetlana took from her father's library to the dining room table to read and crossed them off when she returned them to the shelves. After the war, Stalin had initiated a regimen of having all of his food tested. Special doctors chemically analyzed every scrap of food that came from the kitchen. All foodstuffs came with official seals: NO POISONOUS ELEMENTS FOUND. From time to time, "Dr. Dyakov would appear in our Kremlin apartment with his test tubes and take samples of the air in our rooms." Svetlana commented drily, "Inasmuch as . . . the servants who cleaned the rooms remained alive, everything must have been in order."[1]

Svetlana was now a divorced woman with a four-year-old son. Her nanny, Alexandra Andreevna, was taking care of Joseph at the Zubalovo dacha. That spring Stalin visited the dacha to meet his grandson for the first time. Svetlana was terrified at the prospect of her father's visit. Because he had refused to meet Grigori Morozov, she was worried he would reject their child as well. "I'll never forget how scared I was," she said in retrospect. Joseph "was very appealing, a little Greek- or Georgian-looking, with huge, shiny Jewish eyes and long lashes. I was sure my father wouldn't approve. I didn't see how he possibly could."[2]

Yet Stalin responded warmly to the child, playing with him for half an hour in the woods. Her father even praised young Joseph: "He's a good-looking boy—he's got nice eyes"— affectionate words from a truculent man who offered little praise. Stalin would see his grandson only twice more. Ironically, Joseph would remember his grandfather with love; he always kept a photograph of Stalin on his desk.

Svetlana graduated from Moscow University in June 1949 with a major in modern history. She immediately entered the masters program in Russian literature. This time her father was indifferent to her passion for "those Bohemians!"

If Svetlana's version of herself was that she was passive and vulnerable, this was not always how others saw her. Her cousin Vladimir called her character "harsh and unbalanced," though she was "courageous and independent, with her own principles, in line with the traditions of Alliluyevs," as he put it.[3] Her friend Stepan Mikoyan felt her shyness was half camouflage. "Svetlana was very shy and quiet when everything was quiet; and when she was against something, she was very strong."[4]

Candide Charkviani, by now first secretary of the Communist Party of Georgia, who had first encountered Svetlana as a child, remembered meeting her again on Lake Ritsa, where Stalin was vacationing. Svetlana had come to visit. They had been cooped up in the dacha for days until the rain finally lifted, and they set out for a walk, led by Major General Alexander Poskrebyshev, Stalin's trusted private secretary.

Suddenly Svetlana veered off the paved road and headed toward the raging river. A large log formed a bridge to the other side and Svetlana was determined to cross. She told the others, "Don't worry . . . nothing is going to happen to me." "We found ourselves in an awkward position, a woman perched on stilt-like heels was clearly challenging us to cross the wildly gushing river." Poskrebyshev stood his ground, but Charkviani followed, then was disgusted to discover that all Svetlana wanted was to pick a cluster of frozen flowers on the other bank. She skipped back across the log in her spike heels, while he crawled along the log, terrified of the river raging below. It clearly amused Svetlana to challenge her father's comrades.[5]

Charkviani's version of Svetlana was that she was stubborn and could stand up to her father. A few evenings later at the dacha, in the presence of guests who included Molotov and Mikoyan, Svetlana told her father she wanted to leave for Moscow. Stalin didn't want to let her go. Charkviani recalled the conversation. Apparently Stalin replied,

"Why rush? Stay for some ten more days. You are not in a stranger's house, are you? Could it be so very boring here?"

"Father, I have urgent business to look to, please let me go."

"Let's stop discussing this, you will stay here, with me."

We all thought that was the final decision. Yet for Svetlana, Stalin's words were not final. . . . Throughout the whole evening, as the ongoing conversation permitted, she would start repeating her request.

Finally Stalin lost patience:

"All right, if that's what you want—go. I cannot make you stay by force," he said to his capricious daughter and she happily went to her room, probably to pack her bags.

When we left the dining room, Mikoyan noted: "She has taken after her father; whatever she puts into her heart, she definitely has to do it."[6]

But her rebellions were minor. In the fall of 1949, according to Svetlana, her father arranged for her to marry Yuri Zhdanov, son of the late Supreme Soviet chairman and his former second in command, Andrei Zhdanov, who had died the previous summer. She recalled: "My father . . . always hoped the two families might one day be linked in marriage," as though it were a marriage of dynasties.[7] Stepan Mikoyan concurred that the marriage was Stalin's idea. He knew—he had been one of the candidates under consideration until he himself married.[8]

According to Molotov, among his ministers "Stalin loved [Andrei] Zhdanov best. He valued him above everyone else."[9] Zhdanov was humorous, lighthearted, and not a threat. Stalin had made him head of Ideology in charge of carrying out the Anti-Cosmopolitan Campaign of repression against artists and intellectuals, which he did so ruthlessly that it acquired his name—Zhdanovshchina, the period of Zhdanov.

Stalin was equally attached to Zhdanov's son Yuri, who,

from early adolescence, often stayed at Stalin's dacha in Sochi. Yuri was only twenty-eight and had barely completed his degree in chemistry when Stalin appointed him head of the Science Department of the Central Committee. Yuri would later tell Svetlana he hadn't wanted the job. "Oh, you know those places. The entrance is free but you pay at the exit," he'd said.[10] But one did not refuse Stalin.

Even so, it was remarkable that Yuri stepped so blithely into this marriage; he had already tasted Stalin's wrath. The previous year, he'd become embroiled in what came to be called the Lysenko Affair.

T. D. Lysenko was a quack agronomist who ruled the world of Soviet botany. Rejecting modern discoveries about genetics, he claimed to have produced new vegetables through a process of hybridization: his most famous was a tomato-potato. He also claimed to be working on a new disease-resistant strain of wheat to solve the wheat shortages that had ravaged the country since the war. It was absurd science, but Stalin loved it, so no one dared challenge Lysenko.[11]

On April 10, 1948, Yuri gave a lecture that was "mildly critical" of Lysenko's theories, though he did not mention Lysenko by name. Yuri; his father, Andrei; and two others, who had approved the lecture, were summoned to a meeting of the Politburo in Stalin's Kremlin office the next day. Stalin was furious. "This is unheard of. They presented a report by the young Zhdanov without the knowledge of the Central Committee." Stalin is reported to have said, "We must punish the guilty in exemplary fashion. It is necessary to question the father and not the children."[12] Two months later, Andrei Zhdanov, a heavy drinker, suffered a heart attack and was sent to a sanatorium in Valdai to recover. He died at the end of August of a massive coronary thrombosis.

Yuri Zhdanov soon published a letter of apology in *Pravda*, addressed to Comrade I. V. Stalin, admitting his "mistakes," which were caused by "inexperience and immaturity."[13] His apology was disingenuous, of course, but the terrified young man put his life ahead of his science. To Svetlana, he said privately, "Now genetics are finished!"[14]

Clearly Stalin had forgiven him. According to Sergo Beria, who loved to gossip, Stalin played matchmaker. "I like [Yuri]," Stalin told Svetlana. "He has a future and he loves you. Marry him."[15] Svetlana claimed she was tired of resisting her father—he was old now—and she simply gave in. Stalin even added a second floor to his Kuntsevo dacha, apparently expecting the young couple to live with him. When both resisted the idea, he converted the extension into a cinema room. Stalin did not attend their elaborate wedding, but the government arranged their honeymoon on the Black Sea. It went badly. She loved the sea; he got seasick. He loved the mountains; she suffered from altitude sickness.

Relatives and friends felt Yuri made a pleasant impression. Stepan Mikoyan remembered him as "calm and intelligent, but fun at the same time." He was a good amateur pianist.[16] Yuri immediately adopted Svetlana's son, Joseph, and mother and son took up residence in the Zhdanov family's spacious apartment in the Kremlin.

A witness to Svetlana's life at the time was the actress Kyra Nikolaevna Golovko.[17] Kyra had first seen Svetlana as a teenager sitting with her father in his official box at the Moscow Art Theater (MKhAT) around 1943. Kyra had just returned to Moscow from evacuation in Saratov and was starring in Alexander Ostrovsky's *Hot Heart*. The actors had been warned that "He" was in the audience. When Kyra caught a glimpse of Stalin's black mustache out of the corner of her eye, her knees almost gave way. To her relief, Stalin loved the play, and "watched it, as he did *The Days of the Turbins*—ten or fifteen times and maybe even more."[18]

Kyra met Svetlana and Zhdanov in the summer of 1949 when she and her husband Arsenii, who was chief of staff of the navy of the USSR, were vacationing at the same health spa. The couple soon moved into the House on the Embankment. They hadn't wanted to move to "the Detention Center" from their comfortable three-bedroom apartment, but the suggestion had come from Stalin. As Kyra put it, "[Stalin] asked himself in passing whether or not we wanted to move. He rarely simply asked straight out about these types of things."[19] But it could be fatal not to pick up on his innuendo. The couple were given the five-room apartment of a navy admiral who had been arrested for passing military secrets to the British and Americans.

Kyra was worried about being so visible. Artistic friends were being repressed. Her husband's former lover, a ballerina at the Bolshoi, had been arrested for having links with foreign intelligence, and Arsenii was fearful that the woman might denounce him. Pervaded by jealousy and betrayal, the theater world was full of "whisperers" as they were called—the informants. If Kyra was selective about whom at the MKhAT she introduced to her spouse, Arsenii was equally selective about his military associates.

At the House on the Embankment, the couple held small parties for family and close friends. The first night that Yuri and Svetlana showed up, Yuri immediately went to the piano and played, inviting Kyra to join him in a duet. The house parties were lively, with singing, dancing, listening to records, and arguing. But Kyra noticed that Svetlana sat in the corner, "somehow pulling away from the whole company," talking quietly and never dancing. She dressed somewhat strictly in well-tailored dresses of expensive materials, often adorned with a small diamond or garnet brooch. Kyra noted that she was slender, with a beautiful athletic figure. She wore low heels and stooped slightly, probably because her husband was shorter. As they became friends, Kyra and Svetlana laughed quietly about those evenings at the MKhAT with Stalin in attendance.

One day Svetlana asked Kyra how she had trained her voice. Kyra replied that she had a wonderful teacher, a former aristocrat named Sofia Raczynskaya. Svetlana was excited. She complained that she had, by nature, a very quiet speaking voice, and now, as a graduate student, she had to give lectures at the university. Besides, Yuri had a wonderful voice. "He's very sociable and loves to sing, while I, as you can see . . . Yuri's at the piano, and I sit alone." Kyra promised to ask her teacher to give Svetlana voice lessons.

When Kyra approached her the next day, Raczynskaya almost had a heart attack. She slumped and her hands shook as she said, "Kyra! What are you doing to me?" Kyra helped her to sit. She explained how nice Svetlana was. After much coaxing, Raczynskaya agreed. "Well, Kyra, for your sake."

A few days later, Raczynskaya sat waiting for her new pupil to arrive. She lived in a communal apartment on Vorovskogo Street in one very large room filled with antique cabinets, a piano, stacks of books, and boxes of memorabilia. Two hours before the lesson, there was a knock on the door. Three men in civilian dress entered. They searched her room, turning everything upside down. Nothing was said. Before the men left, everything was put back exactly in its right place.

Svetlana, unaware of what had just happened, arrived twenty minutes later carrying flowers, a box of candy, and two bags of food. Raczynskaya had refused to accept payment for the lessons, but even so, she felt a little embarrassed at this largesse. Raczynskaya soon learned not to speak to friends about Svetlana. When she told one acquaintance about her new pupil, he disappeared from her life for years.

Svetlana didn't have much of a voice, but Raczynskaya believed all people had the potential to be vocalists; one just had to open them up. The lessons continued. Each time, three plain-clothes policemen arrived two hours before Svetlana to "shake up" the room. Each time it was a different three men, but each time they acted identically. Unnerved by this mechanical mimicry, Raczynskaya took to phoning Kyra to report on the trinity of suits. Feeling guilty, Kyra said she would ask Svetlana to stop her lessons. Raczynskaya replied, "No, no! If Svetlana needs this, we will continue." As Kyra put it, "Sofia Andreyevna, in spite of her age, was a gambling woman."

This was the way much of the Soviet intelligentsia, especially in Moscow, lived. Spies, informants, secret police were legion. It was never possible to understand what was going on behind the scenes; one only felt the impact. It was like living on a bed of quicksand and pretending that the ground was solid.

It was willful blindness that Svetlana, who placed the highest value on art and literature, should have followed her father's directive and ended up in the Zhdanov household. As the enforcer of Zhdanovshchina, Yuri's father had been the official most hated by artists and intellectuals. He'd suppressed the music of Prokofiev, Khachaturian, and Shostakovich as "alien to the Soviet people and its artistic taste" and had banned the work of many writers, including the poet Anna Akhmatova. Of Akhmatova he infamously said, "She is a half-nun, half-harlot or rather harlot-nun whose sin is mixed with prayer."[20]

The Tretyakov Gallery, where Svetlana had once gone with her beloved Aleksei Kapler, mounted a show that winter of 1949 in honor of Stalin's seventieth birthday (actually his seventy-first). Every canvas was a grotesque portrait of Stalin: the kindly grandfather, the war hero, the legendary knight.

When she saw the exhibition, Svetlana was devastated. Art was being prostituted to gratify her father. But here she was in the Zhdanov family where Zhdanovshchina had originated. What did she expect?[21]

The whole marital exercise proved a disaster, another mistake. Even after Zhdanov's death the previous year, the Zhdanov family kept up the rhetoric of *partiinost* (party-mindedness). The apartment was filled with war booty—vases, rugs, works of art—carted back from Germany after the war. "The most orthodox Party spirit reigned in the house I lived in, but . . . it was all hypocritical, a caricature purely for show."[22] Svetlana found that she detested her mother-in-law, who, she felt, had her son tied to her apron strings. Yuri called her "the wise old owl."

Svetlana was soon pregnant again. Through the entire first winter of her marriage, she was very ill. She entered the hospital that spring of 1950 and remained there one and a half months. It turned out that Svetlana and her husband had incompatible blood types, which caused her to develop toxicosis affecting her kidneys. She almost died. Her baby daughter was delivered in May, two months premature, and after the delivery Svetlana spent another month in the hospital.[23]

Feeling alone and unloved, she turned to her father to pour out her woes, telling him about his new granddaughter, Yekaterina (Katya). He replied:

Dear SVETOCHKA!

I got your letter. I'm very glad you got off so lightly. Kidney trouble is a serious business. To say nothing of having a child. Where did you ever get the idea that I had abandoned you?! It's the sort of thing people dream up. I advise you not to believe your dreams. Take care of yourself. Take care of your daughter, too. The state needs people, even those who are born prematurely. Be patient a little longer—we'll see each other soon. I kiss my Svetochka.

YOUR LITTLE PAPA[24]

Though her father did not visit her in the hospital, she was pleased to get his letter. But there was always the barb—the state needed her premature baby, who was just then fighting for her life.

The marriage lasted another year, but it was obvious to both Svetlana and Yuri that it was doomed. Yuri's mother and Svetlana could not stand each other. At the Science Section of the Central Committee, Yuri continued to feel the noose tightening. Instead of drawing together, both withdrew into their own woes. Svetlana complained:

> He wasn't home much. He came home late at night, it being the custom in those years to work till eleven at night. He had worries of his own and with his inborn lack of emotion wasn't in the habit of paying much attention to my woes or state of mind. When he was at home, moreover, he was completely under his mother's thumb. . . . [He] let himself be guided by her ways, her tastes and her opinions. I with my more easy-going upbringing soon found it impossible to breathe.[25]

It's hard to think of Svetlana's upbringing as easygoing. What she probably meant was that the home was full of emotional noise: Grandma Olga, Anna, and Zhenya all spoke their minds. And she, behind the docile public façade, was "vehement about everything."[26]

But it was more complicated than facades. It was not possible for either her or her husband to go into the interior dark spaces where the fear and anger raged. It was not possible to engage real emotions in these families where nothing was said.

Did she and Yuri discuss his father, her father, what was happening in the world beyond their walls? That seems impossible. Was what she called an "inborn lack of emotion" simply an inability to speak truthfully? And yet it was also true that in orthodox Bolshevik circles, certain kinds of emotion were seen as weakness or self-indulgence.[27]

Her old acquaintance, the actress Kyra Golovko, was passing the Kremlin one day. To avoid the crowded trolleys, she often walked to the Moscow Art Theater over the Stone Bridge, past the Kremlin. Once, as she passed the Borovitskie Gates, she heard a voice calling her name. She shuddered in fear, but then looked up to see Svetlana approaching her. They had lost touch, each consumed by her own worries.

Svetlana begged Kyra to walk with her. She needed to talk. Kyra remembered how upset she seemed, and recalled the conversation, particularly because this was the only heart-to-heart they managed to have. Svetlana had always been so private and restrained, and few dared to speak openly with her.

Svetlana told Kyra that she wanted to divorce Yuri. Kyra was shocked. To her, Yuri and Svetlana had seemed so much in love: those voice lessons, wearing low heels, "all was done for Yuri's sake." And there was her new daughter, Katya.

Kyra recalled Svetlana's words:

"It's Yuri's mother. From the outset she was against my marrying him. And now we are all on the brink of disaster. It came to the point that I even rushed to my father."

"And what did he say?" I asked.

"He said that marriage is an endless chain of mutual compromises and that if you give birth to a child, you must somehow save the family."

"You told Yuri about this conversation?"

"Yes, but it had almost no effect. His mother thinks I ruined his talent as a scientist and as a pianist."

By this time, the two women had reached the Moscow Theater, where they parted. Kyra remarked, "Thus ended my relatively close relationship with Svetlana."[28]

Svetlana and Yuri separated. Knowing that they would not be allowed to divorce without Stalin's permission, she wrote warily to her father, signing her letter "your anxious daughter":

FEBRUARY 10 [NO YEAR]

Dear Papochka,

I would like to see you very much to let you know about how I live. I would like to tell you all of this in person—tête-à-tête. I tried several times and I didn't want to bother you when you weren't very well and you were very busy. . . .

In connection with Yuri Andreevich Zhdanov, we decided to finally separate even before the New Year's . . . for two years, [we] have not been husband or wife to each other but have been something indescribable.

Especially after the fact that he proved to me—not with words but with actions—that I'm not dear to him, not one bit, and I'm not needed. And after that he repeated, for the second time, that I should leave my daughter with him. Absolutely not . . .

I'm done with this dry professor, heartless erudite, he can bury himself under all his books but family and wife are not needed by him at all. They are well replaced by his numerous relatives. . . .

So, Papochka, I hope that I will see you, and, you, please

do not be angry with me that I informed you about these events post-factum. You were aware of this even before.

I kiss you deeply.[29]

In the summer of 1952, Svetlana got her father's permission to divorce Yuri.

Again it is Candide Charkviani who reports the story of how Svetlana approached Stalin to tell him of her final intentions:

My third meeting with Svetlana was so peculiar that I remember it rather well. Before it was 1 PM, I had already arrived at Stalin's Kuntsevo residence. After a brief discussion, J. Stalin excused himself. "Don't get bored," he said and left the room. Some while later he returned freshly shaved in a well-ironed service jacket and trousers. Before we started discussing the issues I came with, there was a knock on the door. The guest turned out to be Svetlana. Stalin greeted her with enthusiasm, kissed her and, while pointing to his jacket, said: "Look how I got dressed up for you, I even had a shave." Svetlana shook my hand and we all sat round the table.

As some banalities were exchanged, a silence fell. Stalin expected Svetlana to start; however she kept silent.

"I know what you are going to say," said Stalin finally, "so you still insist on your decision to divorce?"

"Father!" pleaded Svetlana.

As I felt the conversation was to touch on family matters, I got up and asked J. Stalin for permission to go for a walk in the garden.

"No!" cut in Stalin categorically, "you need to be here. It is necessary." Then he turned to Svetlana and promised to be the first one to spread her news to the world.

I had no other way but to be an unwilling witness to an unpleasant discussion of private matters. I took my seat rather far away; however the host was conversing in such a loud voice that it was impossible to escape hearing it all.

"What's besetting you? What's your reason for wanting a divorce?"

"I cannot stand my mother-in-law. I have not managed to adjust to her ways," mumbled Svetlana.

"And your husband? What is your husband saying?"

"He is supporting his mother in everything." . . .

"All right, if that's what you have decided, get a divorce. Such matters cannot be settled by force. Yet I want you to know that I don't like your attitude to family life."

That was J. Stalin's final verdict in this awkward affair. Svetlana, probably satisfied but blushing because of embarrassment, said goodbye and left us.[30]

In retrospect, Svetlana would say that Zhdanov was very intelligent, cultured, talented in his field, and a wonderful father but that they lived in different universes. He, too, wanted a divorce. He remained friendly toward her and devoted to his daughter, Katya, and would take both of her children on his hiking and archaeology expeditions.[31]

Stalin gave his twice-divorced daughter permission to leave the Kremlin, assigning her an apartment in the House on the Embankment. Her old nanny, Alexandra Andreevna, came with her, perhaps more of a responsibility now than a help. The apartment, number 179 on the third floor, entrance seven,[32] was modest—four rooms with a kitchen—but certainly extreme luxury in comparison with the communal apartments into which most Muscovites were crammed, where several families might share a single room separated by sheets of plywood and where there were always fights over the communal kitchen and toilet and constant reports to the Housing Committee about noisy children being brought up like hooligans.

Svetlana was now twenty-six and in the last year of her MA studies. Her father asked her how she would survive. Having left Zhdanov, she was not entitled to a government dacha or an officially chauffeured car. A new law in 1947 had decreed that relatives of members of the government would no longer be fed and clothed at public expense. She recalled he almost spat at her: "What are you, anyway—a parasite, living off what you're given? . . . Apartments, dachas, cars—don't think they're yours. It doesn't any of it belong to you."[33]

She explained that she didn't need a dacha or a chauffeur. Her stipend as a graduate student was enough to pay for her and the children's meals and the apartment. He calmed down. Thinking it a magnificent sum, he passed her several thousand rubles. He didn't know that the currency had been so devalued that the amount would barely cover living expenses for a few days. Svetlana said nothing.[34]

However, Stalin offered to buy her a car, but only if she got her driver's license first. This would become one of her fondest memories. She would always recall the one and only time she took her father out for a drive. His bodyguard sat in the backseat, rifle across his knees. Stalin seemed so pleased to discover that his daughter could drive.[35]

But, in truth, Stalin and his daughter were growing more distant. On October 28, she wrote to him:

OCTOBER 28, 1952

My Dear Papa,

I very much want to see you. I don't have any "business," or "questions" to discuss. I just want to see you. If you would allow me and if this wouldn't bother you, I should like to ask if I could spend some time at the Blizhniaia [Kuntsevo] dacha—two days of the holidays—the 8th and 9th of November. If it's possible I will bring my little children, my son and daughter. For us this will be a real holiday.[36]

Svetlana took the children to Stalin's dacha on November 8. It was the first time he saw the two-and-a-half-year-old Katya and the only time he, Svetlana, and his two grandchildren were together. It was also the twentieth anniversary of Nadya's death, though this was not mentioned. Svetlana wondered if her father remembered that this was the date on which her mother had committed suicide.

Svetlana looked at her father's dacha with loathing. His rooms were ugly. In cheap frames on his walls he had huge photographs cut out from the magazine *Ogonyok*: a little girl with a calf, some children sitting on a bridge. Strangers' children. Not a single photograph of his own grandchildren. The unchanging rooms—a couch, a table, chairs; a couch, a table, chairs—frightened her. The little party went off well, but Svetlana felt her father's response to her daughter was indifference. He took one look at Katya and burst out laughing. Svetlana wondered if her father would have liked to be a family again. When she had fantasies of herself and her children living under the same roof with him, she realized that he was accustomed to the freedom of his solitude, which he claimed to have come to appreciate during his long Siberian exiles. "We could never have created a single household, the semblance of a family, a shared existence, even if we both wanted to. He really didn't want to, I guess."[37]

She went alone and without a present to celebrate his seventy-third (seventy-fourth) birthday on December 21. Beria, Malenkov, Bulganin, and Mikoyan were at the birthday party. Khrushchev came in and out. Molotov was unwelcome; Stalin had singled him out for savage humiliation at the Nineteenth Congress that

October, and his wife, Polina, had been exiled to Kazakhstan for speaking in Yiddish at an official cocktail reception and declaring recklessly that she was a "daughter of the Jewish people."[38]

Stalin was ebullient. The kitchen staff had laid out a Georgian feast. Even with the "poison tests" conducted in the kitchen, Stalin still made sure someone tasted any dish before he ate it. Khrushchev remembered the drill: "Stalin would say, 'Look, here are the giblets, Nikita. Have you tried them yet?'" Khrushchev would reply, "'Oh, I forgot.' I could see he would like to take some himself, but was afraid. I would try them and only then would he start to eat them himself."[39]

When Stalin put Russian and Georgian folk songs on the gramophone, everyone had to dance. As Khrushchev described him, "He shuffled around with his arms outstretched. It was evident he had never danced before." Then Svetlana appeared. Khrushchev recalled:

> I don't know if she'd been summoned or if she came on her own. She found herself in the middle of a flock of people older than she, to put it mildly. As soon as this sober young woman arrived, Stalin made her dance. I could see she was tired. She hardly moved while dancing. She danced for a short time and tried to stop, but her father still insisted. She went over and stood next to the record player, leaning her shoulder against the wall. Stalin came over to her, and I joined them. We stood together. Stalin was lurching about. He said, "Well, go on, Svetlanka [*sic*], dance! You're the hostess, so dance!
>
> She said, "I've already danced Papa, I'm tired." With that, Stalin grabbed her by the forelock of her hair with his fist and pulled. I could see her face turning red and tears welling up in her eyes. . . . He pulled harder and dragged her back onto the dance floor.[40]

Svetlana denied that her father had ever pulled her onto the dance floor by the hair, but this birthday party would turn out to be her last encounter with him. Stalin was certainly drunk. Perhaps he was gloating. He was in the midst of engineering his last and most terrifying ideological campaign, the "Doctors' Plot."

On January 13, 1953, the TASS news agency published a government statement officially announcing the plot.

> From the latest news.
>
>   Arrest of a group of subversive doctors.
>
>   Some time ago, the bodies of State Security uncovered a group of terrorist doctors who set themselves the task of cutting short the lives of prominent public figures in the Soviet Union by administering harmful treatments.[41]

The editorial in *Pravda* that day was titled "Evil Spies and Murderers Masked as Medical Professors." The "killer doctors" were called "murderers in white coats." Nine doctors, six of them Jewish, were identified by name.

Dr. Yakov Rapoport, a distinguished Soviet pathologist, was arrested on February 3. In a memoir, he described the atmosphere of the time:

> We were aware of a marked thickening of the political and social atmosphere, a thickening oppression that was near the point of suffocation. The feeling of alarm, the premonition of dire and inevitable disaster, achieved a nightmare intensity at times, supported, moreover, by actual facts.[42]

The public, whipped into a frenzy by news reports, cursed the bloody killers and thirsted for revenge. People refused to be treated by Jewish doctors.

Dr. Rapoport was arrested as a murderer and a member of an anti-Soviet terrorist organization. Like all the doctors, he was submitted to a "secret lifting," the MGB* term for a sudden disappearance. The MGB men came for the targets in the middle of the night, searched all their belongings, and confiscated savings passbooks, bonds, and any money. This was a strategy to impoverish the families in order to see which fellow conspirators would come to their aid. Encountering the wife or children of an arrested person on the street, people averted their eyes. The prisoners were carted off to Lubyanka or Lefortovo prisons. Having no clue as to what was going on, the remaining family members waited in terror for the secret police to return.

Dr. Rapoport remembered that "initially the Doctors' Plot had no nationalistic coloring; both Russian and Jewish doctors were implicated. But before long it was given an anti-Semitic slant."[43] Jews could be found in all strata of Soviet society, and Russia's long history of anti-Semitism could be counted on to induce people to believe any slanders against them. All Stalin needed was the doctors' confessions. The well-tried strategy was simple: "If they confess, it must be true."

It is also virtually certain that a "Writers' Plot" would have come next. A report from a source at the Writers Union, sent to the Central Committee's Department of Propaganda, claimed that the *Literary Gazette* "pandered to Jews and was dominated by Jews." Its editor, the well-known writer and war hero Konstantin Simonov, was purportedly Simonovich, born to a Jewish family and the son of a publican on the estate of Countess Obolenskaya. In fact, Simonov was not Jewish. He was the son of Princess, not Countess, Obolenskaya and his father was Mikhail Simonov, a colonel in the tsar's army. Si-

---

* The NKGB (People's Commissariat for State Security) was renamed the MGB (Ministry for State Security) in 1946.

monov laughed when he heard this slander, but he would soon grow very concerned to discover that he was identified as head of a group of people in Moscow's literary world connected to the cosmopolitan conspiracy. His editor warned him: "There are some bastards out to get you who want to dig your grave, come what may. And just remember, absurd though it is, it was all said with such seriousness that I couldn't believe my ears."[44] This was how one became a target.

Svetlana recalled the atmosphere of that last year. "During the winter of 1952–1953 the darkness thickened beyond all endurance."[45] It was "terribly trying for me, as for everyone. The whole country was gasping for air. Things were unbearable for everyone."[46] So many relatives, friends, and acquaintances were in jail or camps: her aunts and cousin for "babbling" too much, Polina Molotov for Zionist plotting, and Lena Stern as a member of the Jewish anti-Fascist Committee. She had consulted Stern for advice on the treatment of tubercular meningitis for the child of a close friend.[47]

Svetlana listened as Valechka, her father's faithful housekeeper, told her that Stalin was "exceedingly distressed at the turn events took." Valechka had heard him say that "he didn't believe the doctors were 'dishonest' and that the only evidence against them was the 'reports.'"[48] But even Svetlana must have known by now that this was pro forma for her father. Stalin, the consummate actor, pretended to sit back as others brought reports to him of enemies, whom he could not refuse to punish, while of course he was the puppet master manipulating the strings behind the scenery.

At the time, Svetlana heard rumors that a third world war with the West was imminent. A friend of her brother, an artillery colonel, told her, "Now it's the time to begin, to fight and to conquer, while your father is still alive. At present we can win."[49] Was this war plot truly afoot? Vasili's friends were hotheads and unreliable, but George Kennan, the American ambassador to the USSR, was expelled after only four months. Still, it is unlikely that Stalin was planning outright war. Some historians believe he was in the process of organizing a major deportation of Jews, though this is based only on hearsay. Whatever was going on, the doctors' fates hung in the balance. And the pressure was unbearable. Everyone was afraid to speak. Everyone was silent, "very still as before a storm."[50]

And then Stalin died.

Chapter 10

The Death of the *Vozhd*

Svetlana at her father's funeral in March 1953.

On March 2, Svetlana was summoned from her French class at the Academy of Social Sciences and told that a car was waiting outside to take her to Kuntsevo. She felt a sudden vertigo. No one but her father ever phoned her from Kuntsevo. Something was wrong—she hadn't been able to reach him in days. When she'd phoned, the guards told her not to come, it was not a suitable time, and to stop phoning.[1]

On the evening of the first, she'd felt so uneasy that she'd driven to the dacha of her friend Lucia Shvernik. They'd watched a silent movie called *The Station Master*, based on a story by Pushkin in which an old man dies at the roadside searching for his long-lost daughter. When the daughter finally returns to her village, she finds only her father's grave. "I wept over that movie," Svetlana recalled. "It absolutely hit me. [My father] was calling me. It was a silent call. I was probably the only person in the world he would have called for."[2] The comment is poignant but hardly true. As he lay dying on the evening of March 1, it is unlikely that Stalin was sending a silent call for help to Svetlana, however much she may have longed for him to do so. It is heartwrenching that she imagined he was.

Everything to do with Stalin involves some mystery or intrigue. His slow death is no exception. What actually happened in his last days? The broad outline is as follows.

On the night of February 27, Stalin went to the Bolshoi Theater to attend a performance of Tchaikovsky's *Swan Lake*. The next day was Svetlana's twenty-seventh birthday, but her father did not invite her to accompany him.

The next evening, he summoned four members of his Politburo—Beria, Malenkov, Bulganin, and Khrushchev—to the Kremlin for their usual evening film, again completely ignoring his daughter's birthday. Of the dinner on the evening of February 28, Khrushchev reported that Stalin appeared "sprightly and cheerful." The men returned to his Kuntsevo dacha for the usual Georgian buffet. Supposedly, one of the subjects Stalin brought up was the interrogation of the doctors.

"Have the doctors confessed?" Stalin is reported to have asked. "Tell Ignatiev [head of the MGB] if he doesn't get full confessions out of them, we'll shorten him by a head." Beria replied, "They'll confess. . . . We'll complete the investigation and come to you for permission to arrange a public trial."[3]

The credibility of this conversation is questionable—after the fact, each participant shaped his own version for self-serving ends—but the suggestion that a public show trial of the doctors was in the making is not far-fetched.

Khrushchev described the end of the evening thus:

> As usual dinner lasted until five or six o'clock in the morning. Stalin was pretty drunk after dinner and in very high spirits. He didn't show the slightest sign that anything was wrong with him physically. When it was finally time for us to leave, he came into the vestibule to show us out. He was joking boisterously, jabbing me playfully in the stomach and calling me "Nikita" with a Ukrainian accent, as he always did when he was in a good mood. So after this particular session we all went home happy because nothing had gone wrong at dinner. Dinners at Stalin's didn't always end on such a pleasant note.[4]

According to the report of his guards, Stalin then lay down on the divan in his "little dining room," and told them, "You can take a nap too. I won't be calling you."

The following morning, March 1, Stalin's staff waited for his summons. He usually rose around eleven a.m. The guards' anxiety mounted as no sound emanated from his room all day. Still, none of them had the nerve to disturb him. Finally at six p.m., a light went on in his room. Stalin was obviously awake, but he didn't call, and unless he called, no one dared enter the room.

Around ten p.m., the Kremlin courier arrived with a packet of mail from the Central Committee. Stalin's bodyguard, Pyotr Lozgachev, in charge of mail delivery, walked with a firm step along the corridor toward his suite—one never crept up on Stalin. He described the scene:

> There was the Boss lying on the floor holding up his right hand. I was petrified. My hands and legs wouldn't obey

me. . . . He couldn't speak. . . . I hurried up to him and said: "Comrade Stalin, what's wrong?" He'd wet himself while he was lying there. . . . I said, "Shall I call the doctor, maybe?" He made some incoherent noise—like Dz—dz . . . all he could do was keep on "dz"-ing. His pocket watch and a copy of *Pravda* were lying on the floor. . . . [The watch] showed 6:30, so 6:30 was when it must have happened. . . . I raised the receiver of the house phone.[5]

By the time the other guards arrived, the boss was unconscious. They moved him onto the sofa in the large dining room. They phoned Beria; Ignatiev, who was now in charge of Stalin's personal security; and Malenkov, who phoned Khrushchev and Bulganin, and then they waited. Lozgachev claimed that his hair turned white that night.[6] No one phoned a doctor.

Stories conflict. Supposedly the five men came at different times, saw Stalin sleeping peacefully, and left, annoyed that the guards had called. "Don't cause a panic," Beria is reported to have reprimanded them. Khrushchev said that they didn't need to be there when Stalin woke up to discover himself in such an "unseemly" condition: he had lain in his own urine all evening.[7]

The doctors were not called until seven a.m. (other reports say nine a.m.) on the morning of March 2, twelve and a half hours after Stalin's fall and nine hours after he'd lost consciousness. Theories percolate that the delay was a deliberate effort to deprive Stalin of necessary medical attention. It is just as likely that all those present, including Stalin's colleagues, were too frightened to make any decisions. If Stalin regained consciousness, he might see the summoning of a doctor as a treasonous plot to seize power. Certainly it was not the most opportune time for Stalin to require the services of a doctor.

When Stalin's personal physician, Dr. Vladimir Vinogradov, had last examined him, he had diagnosed arteriosclerosis and recommended a rigid course of medical treatment. He also suggested that Stalin retire. Vinogradov was a principled doctor but an imprudent man. Outraged, Stalin ordered the destruction of his medical records. Vinogradov was arrested on November 4 in connection with the Doctors' Plot.[8] Any treatment was further hindered by the fact that a number of the country's top specialists were now incarcerated.

When a team of doctors, led by Professor P. E. Lukomsky, arrived, "they were all trembling like us," observed the bodyguard Lozgachev. The hands of the dentist who removed Stalin's false teeth were shaking so hard that he dropped the teeth on the floor. A neuropathologist, therapist, and nurse stood vigil. Oxygen cylinders were wheeled in.[9]

When Svetlana's car arrived, Khrushchev and Bulganin greeted her in tears. She thought her father was dead. But then they told her to enter; Beria and Malenkov would inform her of the situation.

The usually silent dacha was in chaos. A crowd of doctors surrounded her father "applying leeches to his neck and the back of his head, making cardiograms and taking X-rays of his lungs. A nurse kept giving him injections and a doctor jotted it all down in a notebook."[10] In her initial recounting of the incident after the fact, Svetlana claimed to be satisfied with the treatment—"everything was being done as it should be." The one oddity was that she was told her father had been found on the floor at three a.m. In fact he had been discovered at least five hours earlier. Given Stalin's condition, were the leaders hiding the delay?

Svetlana knew that a special session of the Academy of Medical Sciences was even then meeting to discuss her father's case. She thought this was ridiculous. "Everyone was rushing around trying to save a life that could no longer be saved." Fear flooded the room and the hunt for experts to save him began.

On the evening of March 2, Dr. Yakov Rapoport was in his cell in Lefortovo Prison awaiting another torture session. He had been told that the hours for a "voluntary admission" of his guilt were running out. Stalin himself was following the course of his investigation, and was "displeased." When his interrogator entered his cell, Rapoport was taken aback. He expected this was his end, but his torturer told him he needed his expert opinion. Would the doctor tell him what "Cheyne-Stokes respiration" was? Presumably Stalin's doctors had ventured this as their diagnosis.

Rapoport replied that it was "spasmodic, interrupted breathing," found in infants and adults suffering "lesions of the respiratory centers in the brain . . . as in brain tumours, cerebral haemorrhages, uremia, or severe arteriosclerosis." Could someone with such a condition recover? his interrogator asked. "In the majority of cases, death is inevitable," Rapoport replied.[11] He was asked to recommend a Moscow specialist to attend such a patient. He named eight specialists but said that, unfortunately, they were all in prison. Rapoport assumed that the MGB was cooking up a case against one of the doctors. He had no idea until after his release from prison that the patient his interrogator had been inquiring about was Stalin himself.

To Svetlana the scene of Stalin's dying was a black comedy. She watched in disgust as an artificial respirator was brought in. None of the attending doctors knew how to work it. They stood around speaking in whispers or tiptoeing past the body on the divan. When Professor Lukomsky approached the unconscious Stalin, he must have been thinking of the fate of his colleagues in their various prison cells, for he was shaking with such trepidation that Beria shouted, "You're a doctor, aren't you? Go ahead and take hold of his hand properly."[12]

Vasili soon arrived, completely drunk, screaming that the doctors had killed his father. They had poisoned him. He then raced out of the dacha. Each time he returned, he shouted the same accusations. Svetlana felt her brother was acting "like the crown prince who's just inherited the throne."[13]

Svetlana was the only member of Stalin's immediate family to attend the long vigil of his dying. Her cousins who could have been there had been banned from the dacha. Her aunts were in jail. For comfort she occasionally sat with the servants in the kitchen.

She was shocked by the complexity of her own emotions, alternately love and relief:

It's a strange thing, but during those days of illness when he was nothing but a body out of which the soul had flown and later, during the days of leave-taking in the Hall of Columns, I loved my father more tenderly than I ever had before. . . . During those days, when he found peace at last on his deathbed and his face became beautiful and se-rene, I felt my heart breaking from grief and love. Neither before nor since have I felt such a powerful welling up of strong, contradictory emotions.[14]

Perhaps she saw the face of the man he might have been had he not, as she felt, subsumed all his humanity to an idea—the idea of *Stalin*, the symbol of Soviet power. And strangely, she felt guilt—she had not been a good daughter. "I'd been more like a stranger than a daughter, and had never been a help to this lonely spirit, this sick old man, when he was left all alone on his Olympus."[15]

Grief distorts reality. Svetlana had little real influence over her father. Her fantasy that she might have saved him required an en-emy who had corrupted him. She watched Beria scuttling around Stalin's bed, leaning in obsequiously to assure the leader of his loyalty when Stalin opened his eyes and they thought he might

regain consciousness, then assuming the dominant role of para-
mount leader and ordering the others around when he was sure
Stalin would die. She decided Lavrenty Beria was that enemy.
He was the "artful courtier" who had succeeded in deceiving her
father, his Iago, who had "used his cunning to trick" her father
into many of his crimes.[16] This was absurd, a willful blindness
that many in the family colluded in rather than face the evil that
Stalin, a man whom they had loved and who had professed love
for them, had perpetrated against them. They wanted to believe
that Beria had fed Stalin's vindictiveness until it became paranoia.

This might have been partially true. All the Politburo members and their apparatus could be accused of stoking Stalin's
plots. All were perpetrators, but everyone knew that Stalin was
in charge, and each had much to fear, none more so than Beria.
Beria had begun to suspect that Stalin was setting him up for
a fall. Beria was a Mingrelian from Western Georgia. In 1951,
a Paris-based Mingrelian nationalist group was denounced as
running an espionage network in Georgia, a conspiracy that
became known as the Mingrelian affair, and a number of
prominent Mingrelians were soon arrested. The leader of the
group was identified as the uncle of Beria's wife.[17] This was
coming very close. Beria knew Stalin's methods. He must have
prayed for Stalin's death.

Stalin's death throes were agonizing. For several days he lay
unconscious, choking on his own fluids as the cerebral hem-
orrhage spread throughout his brain. His face gradually darkened, his lips turned black. He was being slowly strangled. In
his death agony, he opened his eyes and lifted his hand in what
seemed a final gesture. It was probably a last gasp for oxygen,
but Svetlana's confusion over the gesture was telling:

At what seemed like the very last moment he suddenly
opened his eyes and cast a glance over everyone in the

room. It was a terrible glance, insane or perhaps angry and full of the fear of death and the unfamiliar faces of the doctors bent over him. The glance swept over everyone in a second. Then something incomprehensible and awesome happened that to this day I can't forget and don't understand. He suddenly lifted his left hand as though he were pointing to something above and bringing down a curse on us all. The gesture was incomprehensible and full of menace, and no one could say to whom or at what it might be directed. The next moment, after a final effort, the spirit wrenched itself free of the flesh.[18]

Khrushchev, too, noted the gesture. He thought it simply the final reflex of a dying organism.

Stalin's Kuntsevo dacha, with its forbidding rooms, would return in Svetlana's nightmares throughout her life, always cold, dark, and suffocating. Running down its endlessly gloomy, labyrinthine halls, she would awake in terror. Her father had loved the dacha. She believed his soul was trapped there. After his body was removed, she visited the dacha again only once.

Stalin died at 9:50 p.m. on March 5, 1953. Svetlana remembered how they all stood in frozen silence around Stalin's bed. Many of them, she believed, shed genuine tears. Khrushchev recalled, "Each of us took Stalin's death in his own way. I took his death very hard. To be honest, I took it hard not so much because I was attached to Stalin—although I *was* attached to him. . . . More than by his death itself, I was disturbed by the composition of the Presidium which Stalin left behind and particularly by the place Beria was fixing for himself."[19] The corpse was still warm when Beria shouted for his car and driver. The plotting had begun.

As the leaders rushed for the door, Svetlana found herself alone, fighting contradictory emotions of sorrow and relief. She had lost a father and experienced pain and terror, but she also felt that a "deliverance of some kind" was coming. A burden was being lifted from the hearts and minds of everyone, and this "liberation" would be for her, too.

She watched as the servants filed in for a final leave-taking. Stalin's housekeeper, Valechka, laid her head on his body and wailed at the top of her voice in the tradition of village mourning. Svetlana was amazed and almost jealous. She found that she herself remained frozen. She could not cry.

At dawn the next morning, the body was placed on a stretcher and taken for an autopsy. Svetlana waited with the servants in their dining room for the official notice on the 6:00 a.m. news. The announcer intoned, "The heart of Lenin's comrade in arms, of the enlightened inheritor of Lenin's struggles, of the wise master, of the Head of the People's Party, has ceased to beat."[20] Stalin was reported to have died in the Kremlin—a lie, of course, but suddenly, to Svetlana, her father's death was real. She finally wept, surrounded by Stalin's servants. She felt she was not alone. "All of them knew me, too. They knew that I had been a bad daughter and that my father had been a bad father, but that he had loved me all the same, as I loved him."[21]

This was the one fact she had to hold on to, as if, were she to let go of this belief, she would disappear. Once she said, "It was as though my father were at the center of a black circle and anyone who ventured inside vanished or was destroyed in one way or another."[22] She needed to believe, as an act of survival, that he had loved her.

Immediately after her father's body was taken away, the MGB arrived with trucks to remove every piece of furniture, including the telephones, from his rooms.[23] Molotov claimed that Stalin was so frugal that he had no clothes in which to be buried and an old military suit had to be cleaned and repaired.[24] The body lay in state in the Hall of Columns for four days of mourning from March 6 to 9. Svetlana and Vasili, with their children, were among the official mourners, but the rest of the family—Uncle Fyodor, Anna's and Zhenya's children—were pariahs and were allowed to view the coffin only from the restricted area opposite the mausoleum reserved for people whose function at the funeral was to represent ordinary citizens.[25]

The country came to a standstill: theaters and cinemas were closed, and school classes were suspended. The crowds converging on Red Square and moving down to the Hall of Columns to view Stalin's coffin were so large that the militia could not control them. On nearby streets, over a hundred people, including children, were trampled to death in the crush. To those who had suffered, like Dr. Rapoport, it was as if "even his corpse thirsts for new victims."[26]

The author Konstantin Simonov, who had thought he might be next on the list for repression, was informed by the funeral commission that he was to report to the Hall of Columns on March 7 to join the writers' delegation. It took him two hours to force his way through the silent turmoil. He had to crawl under and through the trucks that blocked off Neglinnaya Street, where the crush was so great that he couldn't even reach into his pocket for his Central Committee identity card until he found a way to slip around the back of the Maly Theater. While stationed in the Hall as part of the writers' guard of honor, Simonov noted Stalin's daughter emerge from the family group. Svetlana quietly climbed the few steps up to the platform on which her father's coffin was resting and stood there for a long time gazing at his face. And then she turned her back and walked down the steps. No tears, no farewell kiss.[27]

On March 9, the coffin was placed on a gun carriage and moved to the Mausoleum to take its place beside the sarcophagus containing Lenin's embalmed corpse. The dignitaries lined up and climbed the steps. The upper part of Stalin's body had been covered with a semicircular or concave glass window. As his turn came to view the body, Simonov, used to the "long waxy face of Lenin," was shocked at how "horrendously," "terrifyingly alive" Stalin still looked. It was as if a living person lay there covered under glass. He was reminded of the "sensation of fear and of danger" he had recently had about the future, a fear that still gripped him, as he had no idea what turn events would take.[28]

Millions of Russians lined up to pass the corpse and pour out their grief. For many, this was not hypocritical. A young Oleg Kalugin, who would become a general in the KGB, remembered his adolescent hero worship of Stalin:

> It is difficult for most people to imagine how a nation worshipped such a monster, but the truth is that most of us—those who had not felt the lash of his repression—did. We saw him as a man who led the country through the war, turned a backward nation into a superpower, built up our economy so that there was employment and housing and enough food for all. His propaganda machine was all-powerful. . . . I revered Stalin.[29]

Stalin, the Man of Steel who had ruled for a quarter of a century, was dead. Even those who hated him had to mask their relief at his death. It was not safe to express anything but enduring devotion to the leader. Who knew what regime would succeed him?

PART TWO

The

Soviet
Reality

Chapter 11

The Ghosts Return

This 1932 photograph shows prisoners at work in a forced-labor camp, one of many run by the "Gulag"—the government agency that operated throughout the Soviet Union from 1930 to 1960.

After Stalin's death, people began to emerge from the Gulag. Like everyone, Svetlana was shocked at the numbers. "Many people have come back, thousands and thousands who managed somehow to survive. . . . The scale on which the dead have come back to life is difficult to imagine."[1]

On March 27, 1953, the new collective leadership, which

had been appointed by the Central Committee the night Stalin lay dying, declared an amnesty for nonpolitical prisoners. According to the historian Stephen Cohen, "Nearly one million camp inmates, mainly criminals serving short terms," were immediately released.[2] It was Lavrenty Beria who took the initiative to release prisoners. Ironically, the Gulag had become an enormous strain on the public purse, not to mention its increasing instability. The Gulag population of the 1930s had been relatively docile, but now the camps housed a huge number of formerly armed men, including Soviet and German POWs.

The initial amnesty was for actual criminals serving terms of five years or less, as well as for those about to be convicted and expected to serve terms of five years or less. Of course it was difficult to determine who was a criminal, to be released, and who was a political prisoner. The freeing of prisoners classified as "'politicals' unfolded slowly over the next three years, agonizingly for those still there."[3]

The amnesty was a highly risky move for the new government. Would innocent people wrongly imprisoned be thirsting for revenge? Nikita Khrushchev recalled, "We were scared. We were afraid that the thaw might unleash a flood, which we wouldn't be able to control and which would drown us all." Mikoyan warned that they must proceed slowly: if all the "enemies of the people" were declared innocent, it would be clear "that the country was not being run by a legal government, but by a group of gangsters."[4]

On April 4, one month less a day after Stalin's death, the 6:00 a.m. news was interrupted by an official announcement from the USSR Ministry of the Interior. The doctors accused of being involved in the Doctors' Plot were declared innocent.

The USSR Ministry of the Interior has carefully examined all materials of the investigation and related data concerning a group of doctors accused of sabotage, espionage, and other subversive activities aimed at doing harm to certain Soviet leaders. It has been established that the arrests of the doctors allegedly involved in the plot [fifteen doctors were named] by the former Ministry of State Security, were illegal and completely unjustified.

It has been established that the accusations against the above persons are false and the documentary materials non-authentic. All evidence given by the accused, who allegedly pleaded guilty, was forced from them by the investigators of the former Ministry of State with methods strictly forbidden by Soviet law.[5]

This was unprecedented. Not only were the doctors being exonerated, but it was also being officially acknowledged that the charges against them were trumped up and their confessions coerced.

On April 3, the day before the announcement, Dr. Rapoport had been taken from his cell and was invited to sign his own release papers. He waited in a cubicle as his confiscated belongings were itemized with bureaucratic slowness and returned to him. The same officers who had arrested him then chauffeured him home. It was three in the morning when he arrived at his apartment complex on Novopeshchanaya Street. Of that journey, Rapoport wrote:

It is difficult to describe what I felt during that ride across nocturnal Moscow, which for decades had been wreathed in blood-curdling legends, as I made my way back from the netherworld, a world full of horrible mysteries. . . . I was blissfully conscious of the fact that I was going—not being transported—home, that I could stop the car and get out.[6]

In the apartment three floors up, Rapoport's dog, Topsy, recognizing her master as soon as he entered the vestibule, started to bark. As he put it wryly, "My dog was the first to announce to the world the end of the Doctors' Plot."[7] When he entered his apartment and embraced his astonished wife, she asked him if he knew Stalin was dead. He had not been told. Only then did he understand why he had been released.

It took a long time for the Soviet Procuracy to process the release of Gulag prisoners. The millions of prisoners, including those who had died, had to be issued "certificates of rehabilitation," and there were endless and often deliberate procedural delays. No officials wanted to admit that a prisoner had been arrested on fabricated evidence or that they themselves were involved in the fabrication.

According to Svetlana, Khrushchev helped search the jails for her aunts, each sentenced in 1948 to ten years in solitary confinement. It seemed nobody knew where they were being held. After the March amnesty, both Anna and Zhenya spent more than a year in prison before they were freed. Like other families, the Alliluyevs waited in anguish, with no guarantee that their relatives were still alive. Many people had been arrested "without right of correspondence"—a euphemism for execution.

Anna returned home in the spring of 1954. Her son Vladimir recalled that the family received a phone call telling them that their mother would be coming home. Her niece Kyra, who had already been released, went to pick her up. Dressed like a vagrant in the ragged clothing all prisoners wore, Anna looked decades older and seemed totally disoriented. When Kyra brought her to the flat where Svetlana and the family were waiting, Anna did not recognize her youngest son. The young man who stood to embrace her bore no resemblance to the boy of twelve she had left behind. When Anna asked about her mother, she was told Olga had died in 1951, still stoical about the catastrophes that had devastated her family.

Svetlana's memory of Anna's homecoming remained raw. "Aunt Anna was very sick when she emerged, she didn't even recognize her children, or anyone else. She was just sitting there, and her eyes were not her eyes. They were fogged, misted."[8] Kyra recalled, "She had hallucinations, heard voices talking to her, and talked to herself a lot."[9]

Like many Gulag prisoners, Anna rarely spoke about her years in solitary confinement. Though she knew the people who had denounced her, including Zhenya and Kyra, she said she understood. "Stalin did arrest me according to your reports—but it was not your fault; it was mine."[10] What she meant by these words is unclear. "My aunt, Anna Sergeyevna, was forgiving of Stalin," Zhenya's son Sergei remarked, but only up to a point. She let the past go "for the sake of [Stalin's] children, Svetlana and Vasili, whom she loved so very much."[11] But actually Anna was not unusual. Tragically, many, even in the Gulag, continued to insist that Stalin knew nothing. It was evil advisers who were responsible.

Anna's death ten years later was a tragedy. In 1964 she was hospitalized in a psychiatric facility. As Svetlana recounted bitterly:

After six years in prison she was afraid of locked doors. She had ended up in hospital, very disturbed, talking all the time. She would walk the corridors at night talking to herself. One night a stupid nurse decided that she should not walk in the corridor, so she locked her into her room, even though it was known that she couldn't stand locked doors. In the morning they found her dead.[12]

Zhenya Alliluyeva returned home in the summer of 1954. One day she showed up at the apartment in the House on the

Embankment, where, according to her astonished son Alexander, her first words were "I knew it! I knew Stalin would release me!" In Alexander's memory, his brother Sergei responded dryly, "He did not release you, he died."[13] Svetlana rushed over to comfort her aunt, who couldn't stop crying.

Her son Alexander recalled the first days of his mother's freedom:

> My mother could not talk when she returned; all the muscles of her mouth had been idle for such a long time while she was in solitary with no one to talk with. But gradually the capacity returned to her.[14]

Not long after her release, Zhenya asked Svetlana to take her to Stalin's Kuntsevo dacha. "I want to see what remains," Zhenya told her. Svetlana remembered that visit:

> The room was empty; they had wiped out all [my father's] belongings and furniture, taken everything away and put back other things which were not his. There was a white death mask standing there. [Zhenya] was in her mid-fifties, and after prison she was quite weak. She stood there holding my hand, and she cried and cried and cried. She said: "Everything is hurting. Everything. The best days of our life have gone. We have such good memories. We will keep those, and everything else has to be forgiven."[15]

While her Aunt Anna and her mother had been sentenced to ten years in solitary confinement, Kyra Alliluyeva had been exiled for a five-year term to the town of Shuya, 180 miles northeast of Moscow. She always claimed that her exile had not been terrible:

In exile, I worked for a local theater for the first three years, then I worked with retarded children—I love children! . . . On stage I always had a part with singing and dancing, in musical comedies and vaudeville. It was all very helpful—not heavy stuff. I was in my own creative atmosphere, although I was lonely without my family. But there were always good people who came my way . . . people who never rejected me as an "exile"—they had been warned about that, yet still they were good friends to me.[16]

Kyra's term expired in January 1953, shortly before Stalin's death. When she returned to Moscow with a "tainted passport" (indicating she had a prison record), she found her brothers living in two rooms of their six-room apartment in the House on the Embankment. The other rooms had been handed over to MGB female clerks. Kyra thought it better to live elsewhere. Zhenya would spend years fighting to get their apartment back under her control.[17]

In this family, it was better not to analyze the whys of fate but simply to accept stoically the hand life dealt. And the family shared one survival strategy. Zhenya's son Alexander explained: "Even after our mothers returned from prison, nobody in the family could believe Stalin himself to be an initiator of those arrests. They always thought the evil initiative came from somewhere else and they could not therefore blame Stalin directly, or alone, for their misfortunes." His brother Sergei added, "We see Beria's influence on Stalin as being very evil, because this way it makes things better for us. It would be much simpler to explain things this way." Beria was their "sworn enemy," who had polluted the mind of Stalin against them.[18]

Svetlana shared this response. She blamed her father for the family's tragedy, but she blamed Beria more, and yet she always marveled: "It's very strange that the family didn't show any anger."[19] Perhaps she understood that in some ways they were protecting her.

By the time of her aunts' release, Beria was already dead. Khrushchev had taken only a few months after Stalin's death to stage a leadership coup. In July 1953, Beria was arrested and accused of heading a group of conspirators who intended "to seize power and liquidate the Soviet worker-peasant system for the purpose of restoring capitalism and the domination of the bourgeoisie."[20] He was court-martialed, and shot in December, though the date of his execution is disputed.[21] For the Alliluyev family, this was a huge relief. "It was a great holiday for us!" said Zhenya's son Sergei.[22] With Beria's death, an epoch had ended.

Svetlana's brother Vasili never recovered from his father's death. After Stalin's funeral, he was summoned by the Ministry of Defense and offered a provincial command. When he insisted that he would command only in Moscow, the ministry refused. Vasili took off his insignia and resigned. He spent the following month, April, carousing in restaurants and bars, often falling into drunken rages during which he denounced government officials, who, he claimed, had murdered his father. The Ministry of Defense was not pleased. After a drinking bout with foreigners, he was arrested on April 28, 1953.

Vasili was accused of dereliction of duty, of beating junior officers, and of being involved in illegal deals and high-level intrigues that had ended in some people's being sent to prison and even to their deaths. His former flatterers denounced him, and a military collegium sentenced him to eight years in Vladimirskaya Prison, 110 miles northeast of Moscow. He could not understand how this could happen to Stalin's son. From prison he sent begging letters and letters of outrage, which went unanswered. Unlike his sister, Vasili didn't understand that, his father dead, he was now nobody.

In the winter of 1954, Khrushchev took pity on him and had him transferred to the Barvikha Sanatorium. Soon his old cronies showed up with vodka, and again he went on drunken binges. He was sent back to prison. His third and current wife, Kapitolina, and Svetlana visited; he'd beg them to intercede, but there was nothing they could do.[23]

As she had sat keeping vigil over her dying father in early March 1953, Svetlana had believed that a "deliverance of some kind" was coming. In fact, there was no liberation. She continued to live with her two children in apartment 179 in the House on the Embankment. Looking out from her balcony, she could see below in the courtyard a small sixteenth-century church with beautiful onion domes and across the river, the Kremlin, where she had spent her childhood. As before, she continued to feel hemmed in by "the attention of some, the dislike of others and the curiosity of absolutely everyone." Her father's ghost haunted not just her but the country. She lamented, "He is gone, but his shadow still stands over us all. It still dictates to us and we, very often, obey."[24]

As her children grew up, although both her ex-husbands visited, Svetlana was essentially on her own. She learned to be domestic, cooking a bit, sewing, using the gas stove—all things servants had done before. Her nanny was now living with her own son in a Moscow apartment. Svetlana was awarded a government pension of two hundred rubles a month (about fifty dollars in 1950s currency), and the children each received one hundred rubles.[25]

Looking back, Svetlana's son, Joseph, would say their life was very quiet. His mother didn't like going out much, seldom invited guests, and received only friends who sat with her in the kitchen, as was the Soviet custom. There they ate their lunches and had their evening tea. For dinner, they mostly picked up precooked meals from the House on the Embankment kitchen. Svetlana took the children to symphony concerts at the conservatory, and they went to exhibitions at the Tretyakov Gallery. As with all Communist children, much of their life was organized by the state. Katya and Joseph became Octobrists, then Pioneers, and finally joined the Komsomol.

Svetlana had a small car called a Pobeda (Victory). When the Management Department of the Central Committee of the Communist Party demanded that she exchange it for a Volga, a more appropriate car for the daughter of Stalin, according to a friend, she "refused on principle."[26] She'd also been assigned a sumptuous dacha, but her adopted brother Artyom Sergeev said she asked to be given a smaller dacha instead. She told him, "I don't want to be in a large Sovnarkom [Council of People's Commissars] dacha."[27] As a Soviet, she had no problem with the state controlling all property; she simply wanted to be treated as *ordinary*. Of course, compared with the vast majority of Soviets, she still had a very privileged lifestyle.

The modest dacha she found was in Zhukovka, just outside Moscow, where she and her children spent summers and weekends. When she was short of money, knowing she would be recognized at the shops, she would ask her cousin Leonid's wife, Galina, to sell some of her coats or jewelry for her.[28] It would have provoked a scandal if Stalin's daughter were caught selling her clothes. In Zhukovka she tried to re-create the pleasures of her own childhood. The children played in the woods, rode their bikes at breakneck speed through the village lanes, swam in the streams, and camped in tents under the stars.

Relatives visited. Her nephew Alexander Burdonsky, her brother Vasili's son, remembered the dacha fondly:

Zhukovka was not even a village. It was just scattered dachas in a forest that belonged to the Soviet Ministry. . . .
On this giant territory that stands on the Rublevsky highway, Svetlana had a small property surrounded by a small
fence. There was a house and a garden of flowers, not a
vegetable garden. It was a small two-story house. Downstairs there was a hallway, next to it the dining room and
then two rooms and a glassed terrace. To the right, there
was a kitchen. And upstairs there were three bedrooms—
Joseph's room, Katya's room, and Svetlana's. It was not a
large dacha. . . . There was already some furniture there—
real dacha furniture made of wicker. It was quite sweet.
All the knickknacks—different vases, etc.—were hers. I
really loved that dacha.[29]

Anna's son Leonid and his new wife, Galina, also visited.
Galina remembered Svetlana as adventurous at that time. She
loved pranks. The route to Zhukovka was guarded at intervals by
sentry boxes in which stood vigilant policemen whose job it was
to keep outsiders off the highway. Nearby were the dachas of the
rich Party officials and also the special compound for scientists.

One day Galina saw the gates of Svetlana's dacha suddenly open and her car come flying through. Two police cars
roared after her and pulled her over, and the officers jumped
out. There was a moment of shock when they recognized the
woman they were following; then they beat a hasty retreat. As
Svetlana had come to the sentry post where she was meant to
stop, she stepped on the gas. "She was terribly delighted with
herself," Galina recalled. She loved to thumb her nose at the
bureaucrats.[30]

In 1954 Svetlana completed and defended her disserta-
tion, "Development of Russian Realist Traditions in the Soviet

Novel," and was awarded her graduate degree.[31] The books on the bookshelves in her apartment ranged from Chekhov and Dostoyevsky to Jack London and Maupassant. She also had the Russian moderns—Akhmatova, Ilya Ehrenburg, and Konstantin Simonov—and read many foreign authors as soon as their writings were translated, occasionally working as a translator herself. On the living room wall was a small silver-framed photograph of her father in his marshal's uniform, one of her mother with her as an infant in her arms, and photographs of Joseph and Katya.

Svetlana's solution to keeping herself and her children safe was to disavow politics. She called this abstention "my weird and preposterous double life."[32] Outwardly she lived on the fringes of the government elite, enjoying its material comforts. Inwardly she felt total alienation from the elite. She longed to be anonymous, but most people continued to see her as the princess in the Kremlin. The GUM department store still sold the perfume called Breath of Svetlana. The government had made it clear that she must not speak out publicly about her father. Anything connected to Stalin was state property, and this, she understood, made *her* state property too. In any case, she didn't believe that anything Stalin's daughter could say would be helpful. It would inevitably be filtered through people's responses to her father and distorted. Few were neutral about Stalin: people either worshipped or reviled him.

On one occasion, however, she did speak out publicly. She had joined the Communist Party in 1951 when her father had insisted that it was "unseemly" for the daughter of Stalin not to be a member. Mostly she sat silently through hours of mandatory, boring Party meetings, knowing her absence would have been noted. When the journalist Ilya Ehrenburg published his novel *The Thaw* in 1954, the Party was outraged and wanted him censured. Courageously Svetlana came to his defense. She deeply admired him.

The winter after Stalin died, Ehrenburg rushed to complete his new novel. It was an immediate sensation, and its title entered the Russian lexicon—the post-Stalin era was called the Thaw, at first with optimism and later with cynicism. The novel's main character was a brutally indifferent factory manager who forced his workers to live in wretched conditions in order to fill industrial quotas. Through one of its minor characters, a Jewish doctor, it was also the first novel ever to convey the dread created by the Doctors' Plot. The treatment of its central love story advanced the idea that the state surveillance apparatus had no right to enter private lives.

The regime came down hard on Ehrenburg. Konstantin Simonov, then editor of *Novy Mir*, attacked the novel as "too dark." He said it falsely portrayed Soviet life "as a great deal of misery and too little happiness" and that "it imitated Western patterns."[33]

Svetlana stood up at a Party meeting and defended Ehrenburg, saying that she "could not understand in what way Ehrenburg was to blame, when our own Party's press admitted the mistakes of the past, and innocent people, wrongly condemned, were returning from prisons." She was bluntly told that her statement was "irresponsible and politically immature."[34] She later wrote Ehrenburg a fan letter. "I am truly grateful for your rare ability to find words of truth, to say them out loud, without the duplicity which, for many of us members of the modern Soviet intelligentsia, became second nature."[35]

She may have had in mind Ehrenburg's project *The Black Book*. In 1944, before the war was over, he organized a team of two dozen writers, including Vasily Grossman, to compile and edit testimonies of survivors of German atrocities against Soviet Jews. One and a half million Jews had been killed by execution units that followed the Wehrmacht into Soviet territory. Ehrenburg left the project in disgust when the role of

Soviet collaborationists in the betrayal of Jews was edited out. *The Black Book* went unpublished for decades.[36]

In her private life, however, Svetlana continued to feel isolated. A friend at the time, Olga Kulikowsky, described her as "one of the loneliest women I have ever known."[37] Another friend, Tatiana Tess, said, "Her search for happiness was boundless."[38] A die-hard romantic, she longed to meet someone who wouldn't think of her as Stalin's daughter. In 1954, at a Congress of Soviet Writers in the Kremlin, she thought maybe she had found that person.

As she walked through the dazzling gold glitter of Saint George's Hall, unexpectedly and to her shock, she ran into Aleksei Kapler. For a second she was frightened that he might ignore her, but he was his usual ebullient self. He simply stepped out of the entourage of film people surrounding him and said, "Hello." Then he took her hand and laughed. Everyone watching the encounter knew the resonance of his gesture.

Kapler had been released from the Inta Labor Camp in 1953, shortly after Stalin's death, and had returned to Moscow with his new wife, the actress Valentina Tokaraskaya, whom he'd married three months after his liberation. Her visits and food parcels had kept him from dying, and furthermore, marriage gave them the legal right to a large flat in Moscow.

Svetlana and Kapler left the Congress together, walked across Sokolniki Park to a tiny café, and picked up the relationship that her father had terminated so viciously eleven years before. She was terrified that Kapler would hold her responsible for the horrors he had endured and begged him to understand why she had never attempted to contact or help him. Had she done so, his sufferings would have worsened. He didn't reply.

However, he did tell her about his release from the Gulag. After his case was reviewed, he was told he had been "rehabilitated": "You can go home now." He was given a telephone, but he could think of no one to call. He finally phoned his sister in Moscow and said, "Hello, I will be seeing you soon. Sit at home. I'm coming." He walked slowly from the Lubyanka prison. It was summer, July. Suddenly he felt his feet could no longer carry him. He sat down on a bench. The children were playing in the park, the leaves were rustling in the sunlight, and he burst into tears. He told Svetlana, "I sat there and cried rivers of tears. Then I went to my sister's. Thank God I cried it out before I got there." A disheveled man crying alone on a bench in a park didn't arouse any curiosity in those days.

The old attraction flared up again. They were soon secret lovers. She was astonished that he was "still the same." She would look back fifty years later and marvel: "He just laughed at everything. He laughed away everything. He could do that. Not many people could."[39]

By 1954, Svetlana had reunited with Alexei Kapler, who took this photograph of her on the shore of the Black Sea.

With her son, Joseph, she drove in her little Pobeda to Crimea, where Kapler had an assignment. They spent magical seaside days of lovemaking as he took endless photographs of her, but he assured her that their assignation could never be more than a fling. He would not hurt his wife. His marriage to Valentina was not happy, but he felt loyalty to her because she had gotten him through the brutal five years at Inta. He told Svetlana categorically that he would never marry her.

Friends warned her that she mustn't take Kapler seriously. He was chronically unfaithful, but Svetlana was not to be dissuaded. She described their reunion to Ilya Ehrenburg: "The miracle stayed alive. . . . We looked in each others' eyes and it turned out that not one word we said to each other back then had been forgotten, that we can talk, continuing the phrases that we started . . . understanding one another with the same ease and effortlessness."[40]

Kapler told her it was impossible for their affair to last. It would be "like taking a burning match to the river and expecting the water to go up in flames. It can't happen." She remembered his lovely words, but not their meaning. She asked, "Why can't it happen?"[41]

One evening Svetlana showed up at the stage door of the theater where Kapler's wife was performing and asked to be admitted to her dressing room. She confronted her with the news that she and Aleksei were lovers. Valentina only laughed, saying that she knew all about it. She informed Svetlana that Aleksei was "perpetually unfaithful, and had really only loved his first wife." Svetlana should "not let her imagination get the better of her, because even this would not last." "Slowly there came into Svetlana's alert face a look of helplessness."[42] Perhaps Svetlana was hearing her father's words: "Take a look at yourself. Who'd want you? You fool! He's got women all around him." Svetlana immediately withdrew, humiliated.

Kapler recounted the ending of the affair to the Italian reporter Enzo Biagi:

> My wife was a very reserved, polite kind of person. She never made a fuss, or caused a row. She told me of their meeting, of that strange, unexpected visit. I was shocked at the way Svetlana had behaved; to me it seemed wrong, silly, and also unnecessary. Svetlana had said nothing to me, and had acted with no consideration for anyone else, except herself. That was the end of my second marriage, the end of that second part of my life with Sveta.[43]

Of course, it was easy for Kapler to overlook his own culpability. Certainly Svetlana's behavior was outrageous, though not untypical of a woman caught up in a romantic obsession, but he was not exactly uxorious. He was clearly entertaining lovers behind his wife's back. It took a year after his relationship with Svetlana ended before Kapler left Valentina and moved in with a young poet named Yulia Drunina, the woman who would become his third wife. And there would be a third phase in his relationship with Svetlana when Yulia suggested they help her in a particularly dark time.

Svetlana picked up the pieces of her shattered expectations and moved on. In 1955, she obtained permission to visit Leningrad. Russians still needed permission to travel from one city to another, just as they needed permission to change houses or jobs. The fact that this was her first visit to her mother's beloved city was a measure of how narrow her life was. Though Nadya was born in Baku, Azerbaijan, she had moved to Saint Petersburg,[44] as the city was then called, at the age of six.

In Leningrad, Svetlana visited her grandparents' apartment at 17 Tenth Rozhdestvenskaya Street. The Party had claimed it as a museum. When Lenin hid out there in July 1917, he stayed in her mother's room—such a tiny room with its narrow iron bedstead, a dresser, and a table. On the wall were pictures of her family, of her grandparents, of her mother, of her aunts and uncles as children. In Pavel's room, there still hung a portrait of the English poet Byron, reminding her how romantic and idealistic they had all been in the initial stages of the Revolution.[45]

Everything seemed so intimate and yet so hopelessly lost. She walked through the apartment thinking of her mother as a schoolgirl. This was the place where her sixteen-year-old mother had fallen in love with her father. "I felt a breath of family warmth and love. There was still something vital and alive in the air. I could feel my mother's spirit and sense that it never left this cozy place at all, that it never really lived in the Kremlin and couldn't stand being there. The Kremlin never was the place for her."[46]

Now they were all gone. Nadya dead in 1932; Pavel dead in 1938; Grandpa Sergei dead in 1945; Grandma Olga dead in 1951; Yakov dead in a German POW camp; Anna and Fyodor inaccessible in their private, eccentric worlds; Vasili in prison. She was the only survivor among the ghosts.

In 1956, just after her seventieth birthday, Alexandra Andreevna died. She'd been Svetlana's nanny for the first thirty years of her life. Svetlana could say, "After the many losses I have suffered, the death of my nanny . . . was my first real loss," by which she meant the loss of someone she had known intimately and continuously, someone whom she had loved and who had loved her unconditionally in return.[47]

Chapter 12

The Generalissimo's Daughter

Nikita Khrushchev on February 25, 1956, giving his famous
"Secret Speech" in which he denounced Stalin.

L ate one afternoon in mid-February 1956, Svetlana received a telephone call. Anastas Mikoyan, deputy chair of
the Council of Ministers, was on the line. He said he needed
to speak to her urgently and would send a car to bring her to
his home in the Lenin Hills. When she arrived, he told her
that Khrushchev was soon to give a speech about her father;

the document would be made public at the Twentieth Party Congress on February 25 in the following week. He needed to prepare her. He led her to the library and gave her the document. "Read this. Afterward we'll discuss it, if necessary. Don't hurry. Think it over."[1] Once she had finished reading it, she could join the family downstairs for dinner.

Svetlana spent several hours alone in the library reading what would become known as Khrushchev's "Secret Speech." When he delivered it at the Party Congress, it lasted four hours. The Secret Speech was a devastating attack on Stalin, whom Khrushchev described as a "very distrustful man, sickly suspicious." He accused Stalin of "originating the concept *enemy of the people*," and engineering a "cult of personality." Beginning in 1935, Stalin had directed the "mass arrests and deportation of many thousands of people, executions without trial" and the murder of so-called spies and wreckers, who "were always honest Communists." Khrushchev said, "Confessions of guilt . . . were gained with the help of cruel and inhuman tortures. . . . Stalin personally advised judges on which investigative methods to use: These methods were simple—beat, beat, and, once again, beat." Khrushchev made no mention of his own support for Stalin's atrocities nor of his masterminding the purges in the Ukraine.[2]

The speech was agonizing for Svetlana to read, because she "believed every word of it." She later wrote, "If only I could have refuted it all, not believed it; if only I could have exclaimed, 'It's a lie! He didn't do it!' But I could not. . . . All this was so terrible that I felt like howling and running away from everyone, myself included."[3] She came downstairs to join the Mikoyans and said simply, "It's all true." Mikoyan replied, "I hoped you would understand."[4]

Terrified that she would be identified with her father and hated, Svetlana withdrew into isolation. She did not even seek the consolation of her family. They learned of the denunciation of Stalin by reading reports of Khrushchev's speech in the newspapers.[5] How she prepared her children is unclear, but most likely she said little. Eleven-year-old Joseph continued to revere his grandfather, whose portrait always stood on his bedside table. Six-year-old Katya probably was unaware of the truth at the time, and in later life, she chose a career that took her to the isolation of far-off Kamchatka, where she was reputed to be a staunch Stalinist. Certainly it must have been a complex fate to be Stalin's grandchildren.

The Secret Speech was not really secret. Khrushchev ordered it read at Communist Party meetings throughout the country. A copy of the speech even reached the *New York Times*, which ran extracts on its front page on June 4.

The revelation of Stalin's crimes was cataclysmic. The propaganda icon—"the creator of happiness," "the savior of the Russian people," and "a genius among mortals"—had been a fraud all along, just another ruthless and cruel politician who had committed horrific crimes with impunity.

Examining his own generation in retrospect, the writer Konstantin Simonov wrote:

> If we are honest, it is not only Stalin we cannot forgive, we cannot forgive anyone, including ourselves. . . . We may have done nothing bad, at least at first glance, but what is bad is that we [became] accustomed to . . . what now seems incredible and monstrous, somehow gradually became some kind of norm, seemed almost customary. We lived amidst all this like deaf people, as if we did not hear the firing going on all round us all the time, people being shot, murdered, people vanishing.[6]

Simonov confessed that he had lived for a long time in a duality, knowing and refusing to know, "partly through cowardice, partly through stubborn efforts to reassure myself, partly through coercion of myself, and partly through a reluctance to touch on some things even in thought."[7]

After March 1956, the outward manifestations of the cult of Stalin began to disappear. Portraits of Stalin were taken down at the Museum of the Revolution. All those names glorifying her father, which, as a young girl, Svetlana had had to write out in lists for her teachers, were changed. The ZiS car was renamed the ZiL, in honor of the scholar and Gulag survivor Dmitri Likhachov. Mount Stalin in Pamir became Mount October. Even Stalingrad would eventually be renamed Volgograd.

A number of Svetlana's friends turned their backs on her, but some felt only sympathy. Aleksei Kapler's new wife, Yulia, suggested that Svetlana must be devastated since everyone seemed to be deserting her. Kapler called to invite her to visit, and she gratefully accepted.[8]

That year, 1956, was very difficult for Svetlana. The actress Kyra Golovko remembered encountering her at the apartment of friends. She was "even more closed and clamped up than twelve years ago. She looked awful and was dressed very strangely." Kyra was performing in a play at the MKhAT, and someone suggested they all go. Svetlana said, "in a quiet voice, but which was definitely scary: 'I do not go anywhere except the Conservatory.'" The play, Kyra suddenly realized, contained several attacks on Stalin's cult of personality. The room remained silent. Svetlana said that it was time to go and left.[9]

Svetlana had begun to work as a junior research fellow at the Gorky Institute of World Literature in early 1956. The researchers at the Institute were warned in advance that Stalin's daughter would be joining them. "Don't make a fuss," they were told. "Treat her normally, like a regular person." Portraits of Stalin still hung on the walls. As she inadvertently sat under a portrait of her father, a student remarked cruelly, "Do you think she resembles her father? Yes, of course she does!"[10]

One of her colleagues at the Gorky Institute, Alexander Ushakov, had already met Svetlana briefly when she was enrolled at the Academy of Social Sciences. It was during the tumultuous early days of the Thaw, when students were excitedly debating the possibility of freedom of thought. Ushakov had come late to the Academy's general assembly. The hall was full, with nearly all the seats occupied, but then he saw a woman sitting alone with an empty chair beside her. He casually sat down, and they exchanged a few brief words. During the intermission, a friend came up to him and asked, "How do you know Stalin's daughter?" "What Stalin's daughter?" he replied. "You are sitting with Stalin's daughter!"

When they met again at the Gorky Institute, Ushakov asked Svetlana if she remembered him. She had been wearing a bright green dress on the previous occasion, and she replied, "I remember the green dress but not you." They both laughed. Gradually Svetlana "came to life a bit," as Ushakov put it. "But she was a very uptight person." Ushakov recalled:

Our group met often. We drank alcohol, drank tea, told each other stories. In these moments each person wants to share something. But she usually sat silently; sometimes she smiled and laughed. . . . She smoked a lot then—she would sit in a chair—she always slouched a bit—and while others talked, she always remained silent. Some difficult processes go on inside a person. She had difficult processes, but they never came out.

Many saw her as a strange person. People like me had to explain to our colleagues: "You understand, she is the daughter of Stalin. She lived in particularly harsh conditions. Always next to her, there was a person from the authorities. . . . Don't think of her as being similar to us. . . ."

She was closed-in. She did not like to open up her soul and to throw out everything that was inside of it. And of course, she was the victim of this whole system to a large degree. . . . She was not like those who were, let's say, imprisoned and terribly abused by the Soviet authorities. . . . But the epoch drove right through her because she was Stalin's daughter; all the pluses and minuses of this system went straight through her.[11]

By the end of March 1956, every institute in the country had received a copy of Khrushchev's Secret Speech. When it was read from the podium at the Gorky Institute, many were devastated by its revelations. Svetlana sat quietly in the audience without saying a word, but the extent and cost of her ostracism are clear from a brief encounter. When the soon-to-be-famous writer Andrei Sinyavsky, who also worked as a researcher at the Gorky Institute, approached her after the speech and kindly made the gesture of helping her on with her coat, she burst into tears.[12]

Soon she joined Sinyavsky's research team, compiling documents related to Russian literature of the 1920s and 1930s. The team had access to books banned to the public. She discovered Yevgeny Zamyatin's dystopian novel *We*, the exuberant literature of the 1920s, and the works of artists arrested and destroyed in the 1930s. This was a narrative of Russian literature more subversive and more candid than the "canonized lies" she'd been forced to study under the spirit of Zhdanovshchina. Dostoyevsky's novel *Demons* overwhelmed her. She saw it as a prophetic template of her father's world, in which the revolutionaries, impelled by internal, paranoid conspiracies, climbed the ladder of power over the corpses of their fellows.[13]

After his Secret Speech, Khrushchev began to institute a number of political and cultural reforms. In the arts, censorship was relaxed, and some foreign publications were allowed into the country. It was a utopian moment that, borrowing Ehrenburg's title, came to be characterized as the Thaw. It suddenly seemed "as if the horrors and rigours of Stalinism were going to have a happy ending. . . . People were excited and started talking and arguing in a way they hadn't done in decades. . . . If you were young and reform minded, . . . it was something you never forgot."[14] At the Gorky Institute, Sinyavsky and his friends were obviously a route to a new freedom of thought that Svetlana had not believed was possible.

In this euphoric atmosphere, Svetlana, too, was becoming something of a rebel. A friend at the time, Galina Belaya, recalled that Svetlana used to invite friends to her apartment in the House on the Embankment. In particular, she remembered when they all gathered—Svetlana's children were there, and she'd had to run off to borrow forks and spoons from the Molotovs—and Andrei Sinyavsky and Anton Menshutin sang their subversive "criminal" songs satirizing the old Soviet "songs of the masses."[15] Both Galina and Svetlana knew that Sinyavsky was publishing his work abroad under the name Abram Tertz. The KGB now tolerated samizdat (literally, self-publication), more or less, but to smuggle a manuscript to the anti-Soviet West for publication was still strictly forbidden.

In September 1957, Svetlana decided to change her name from Stalina to her mother's name, Alliluyeva. She said the metallic sound of the name Stalin lacerated her heart. Voroshilov, chairman of the Presidium of the Supreme Soviet, who had been her mother's friend, showed no surprise and merely said, "You have done right." Yet the first official who saw her new documents could not believe she had rejected her father's glorious name: "So they forced you to change your name?" He refused to believe she had initiated the change herself.[16]

Even though she had long ago abandoned that edifice, Svetlana was still the princess in the Kremlin and an object of intense scrutiny. In the early days of the Revolution, women, like men, were often freewheeling in their sexual behavior, but now Svetlana's hungry, searching, self-directed sexuality made her vulnerable to gossip. Ironically, it was her father who had ushered in this bourgeois puritanism. People gossiped about her two marriages and her "numerous" sexual affairs.

She actually did have a brief love affair with Yuri Tomsky, the son of Mikhail Tomsky, a trade union leader who, when faced with arrest by the NKVD in 1936, had committed suicide. Yuri was raised as an orphan in the Gulag. The gossip regarding them was cruel but showed the degree of contempt she'd inherited as Stalin's daughter. The writer Boris Runin described the affair in his memoir:

> Suddenly, yesterday evening, Svetlana Alliluyeva rolled into Koktebel on her "Pobeda" with Yuri Tomsky. Long ago, young Tomsky was in the same Young Pioneers groups with Svetlana. Obviously—in the Kremlin. And now, after years of serving his time in the camps, he is, apparently, in a marital union with her. Shortly after they married, Svetlana put him in her car and brought him here, to the sea. However, The House of the Arts did not allow them to stay there without a vacation package. They spent the first day on a shore, still empty at that time. They spent it in their car—and what could they do—they had to carry out basic tasks. Svetlana tried to cook something, wash something. And the rumor started going around the House of the Arts which quickly gathered lots of curious onlookers on the shore: a Princess doing chores.[17]

Runin was wrong. Svetlana was not married to Tomsky, and the delight taken in her humiliation was mean-spirited: the princess reduced to washing her linen in public while the audience leered.[18]

Many believed that Svetlana changed after her father's death. Her cousin Vladimir remarked, "It took [Svetlana] a while to understand that the majority of people who sought her out did so [not sincerely] but as a means to their own opportunistic ends. . . . All this fuss and commotion that revolved around her left a negative imprint on her character. Gradually, she understood that she would never experience sincere human feelings and began to search for entertainment and to treat people as if they were toys."[19] Her cousin Kyra concurred. "Svetlana was regarded as a means of achieving a certain goal . . . and she knew this. She was barred from the real feelings of people."[20]

However, there were other versions of Svetlana. Thinking about Svetlana's marriages and love affairs, Stepan Mikoyan would write:

> I am sure she was genuinely in love, or believed herself to be in love, with each of them. Every time she got carried away with someone she would say that "this time it is real," and then be disappointed a few months later. When it happened, she would come to our place nearly every day . . . and cry it all out on Ella's shoulder.[21]

In the late 1950s, Svetlana met the Jewish poet David Samoilov and fell deeply in love. Only six years older, he was handsome, with an open, remarkably candid face that often bore an ironic smile. He had already garnered a reputation as something of a sage and playboy and would become one of the best poets of the postwar generation, writing some poems about the war but also some expressing an almost mystical sense of nature that must have appealed to Svetlana.

Their first encounter occurred when Stepan Mikoyan's wife, Ella, gave a birthday party to which she invited Boris Gribanov, her coworker at Children's Literature Press. Ella and

Stepan lived in a five-room apartment in the House on the Embankment. Gribanov decided to invite his close friend David Samoilov, who was keen to see how the elite of the country lived.

At dinner, Samoilov was surprised to find that his seating companion was Svetlana Alliluyeva. He found her exceedingly attractive, but couldn't rid himself of the idea that he was actually speaking with Stalin's daughter.

With Anastas Mikoyan at the head of the table, according to Gribanov, Svetlana and Samoilov were soon engaged in a passionate flirtation:

> After only 15 minutes, without paying any attention to Mikoyan himself—for Svetlana it was more than natural; she was used to seeing her father's comrades as her servants, and for Samoilov the poet, ranks didn't mean anything at all—in short, after 15 minutes they were kissing passionately. My wife and I left, leaving my friend to his own devices.[22]

The image of the couple kissing passionately in public is not in keeping with the rather demure image of Svetlana that most others paint, and Stepan Mikoyan did not recall such an erotic encounter,[23] but whatever happened, Samoilov and Svetlana went home together. The next morning, Boris Gribanov received a phone call at his office. Samoilov was on the other end of the line, "giggling."

> "Borya, we fucked him!"
> [Gribanov asked,] "And what do I have to do with it?"
> I was appalled.
> "No, no, don't argue. I did it in both our names!"[24]

But soon, what started as a "prank," to use Gribanov's word, turned into a love affair. Samoilov had not counted on being drawn in by Svetlana's intelligence and obvious sincerity. And she must have found his mind thrilling: a lyric poet, a member of the left-wing avant-garde, and like her, more devoted to the muse than to politics.[25]

Svetlana still aroused fear in others, however. Gribanov remembered the occasion when he, Samoilov, and Svetlana visited his friend Tak Melamid. It happened to be March 5, the anniversary of Stalin's death. During the denunciations of Stalin that were inevitably part of the conversation, Svetlana remained quiet. As they were leaving for the elevator, Melamid's wife asked Gribanov who was the "lovely woman" they had brought and almost had a heart attack on hearing the name Svetlana Alliluyeva.

The next morning, she phoned Gribanov, saying hysterically that they should have been warned. She and her husband had spent a sleepless night trying to remember everything they had said. Gribanov tried to calm her, assuring her that Svetlana was a very cultured woman and was not moved by anything being said about her father, but the habit of fear was so ingrained that the Melamids would not be appeased.[26]

The lovers would meet at Svetlana's Moscow apartment or at her small dacha in Zhukovka. Boris Gribanov was an occasional witness. He usually joined them at a restaurant at the Moscow Race Course on days without races, or they lunched at the restaurant Severny (Northern) in the Maryina Roshcha district. On May 9, the two men liked to gather with their war-veteran buddies at a restaurant called Berlin to celebrate Victory Day. The celebrations would end with Samoilov saying, "Borya, I think it would be appropriate to conclude a day that began so beautifully at the Generalissimo's daughter's."[27]

Samoilov and Gribanov took to stopping by Svetlana's apartment with a bottle of cognac for long quiet conversations. Gribanov noted that there wasn't a single portrait of Stalin on the walls (by now she must have put the small silver-framed photo of her father away). There was only a huge photograph of her mother. Though both men were curious, neither of them wanted to exploit Svetlana as a source of information about her father, and he was not often discussed.

There was one problem in Svetlana's relationship with Samoilov, however—she wanted him to marry her. She would go to the publishing house where Boris Gribanov worked, pull him out of his office, and drive him into the country, always for the same conversation:

> "Borya," she said. "He must marry me."
>
> "Svetik [as he affectionately called her], . . . it will never happen."
>
> "But why?" she asked indignantly.
>
> "Because he's a poet, and you—a princess," I answered unequivocally.[28]

Gribanov would write in retrospect: "Svetlana was a very emotional, amorous person, ready to give in fully to each new love affair, ready to sacrifice everything for the sake of the man she loved. But at the same time she had an obsession: an obsession that that man, whom she loved, should marry her. This greatly complicated the relationship."[29]

Svetlana's compulsive need to rush into marriage arose in each of her love affairs. It was as if, regardless of what experience had taught her, she believed marriage would provide a bulwark against otherwise inevitable loss. At core she was an emotional orphan with a tragic fragility that always threatened to sink her. How could it be otherwise? Things would crack when she pulled others into her emotional maelstrom.

In his book *Daily Notes*, published years later, Samoilov wrote about Svetlana. He describes the ending of the relationship in an entry dated November 17, 1960:

Today, Svetl. unexpectedly came over and . . . threw a glove at me. In the morning on the phone, yet again, I tried to avoid a conversation with her. It is as difficult to talk as it is to get over a sickness or to write an epic poem. She, as always, committed an act of a princess—she appeared in front of me and threw a glove, a volume of [the poet Konstantin] Sluchevsky, and an old cross of Saint George on the table—pitiful souvenirs of my infatuation.

Only in retrospect can one appreciate the touching absurdity of her actions that were dictated by the intensity of her feelings, tempestuous temperament of her father, and loneliness. At that moment you experience a difficult feeling of pity, admiration, and indignation. She is a slave to her passions; inside a slave, a tyrant always dwells. . . .

Never in my life have I been so directly shaken and captured by the tragedy of another person. And never had I had such an intense need to run from a person, from the circle of her unresolved and suffocating tragedy.[30]

In 1967, when Samoilov learned the news of Svetlana's defection, he wrote, somewhat chastened, in his diary, "She is more magnificent than I thought." In chagrin, he added, "I understood and valued little in women who were close to me."[31]

The tragedy, according to Samoilov, was that "Svetlana was doomed to carry the cross of her origin for the rest of her life." She could never completely renounce her father, even though she defiantly renounced his "spiritual legacy"—a paradox or duality that was impossible to live.

Svetlana's situation may have been even more complex than this. Surely it is one thing to be the dictator's son but quite another to be the dictator's daughter. The son is required to be *like* his father and often becomes a parody of his father, disastrously so as in Vasili's case. But Stalin had a special attachment to

Svetlana. He had given her his paternal love, such as it was—perfunctory, intermittent, crude, often cruel. It required abject submission. It was laced with contempt: "Take a look at yourself. Who'd want you? You fool!" Nevertheless, to her it often *seemed* tantalizingly real. The truth was that Svetlana did not know what love was. Some deep part of her probably believed she couldn't be loved. She was still looking for a romanticized, idealized substitute for love. In this she was not unlike many women, though perhaps her case was extreme. She felt she needed a man to invent her or complete her. Her desperation came from the terror of being alone, but who among the men she was drawn to would bind themselves to Stalin's daughter and take on that darkness?

Chapter 13

Post-Thaw

In 1962, Svetlana converted to the Russian Orthodox faith and was baptized in Moscow's Church of the Deposition of the Shroud. This was firmly against Communist doctrine.

In the late 1950s and early 1960s, Moscow was an exciting place. It was an international city—with music, film, and dance festivals, world congresses of literature, international delegations of artists, foreign student exchanges, and an exciting nightlife. Yet behind this facade of cosmopolitanism, everything was still under the control of the cultural commissars; the secret police remained active.

Almost from the outset, Khrushchev's Thaw invited political chaos. In March 1956, immediately after the Secret Speech, as Georgians gathered in Tbilisi to celebrate the third anniversary of Stalin's death, student demonstrators rioted. Dozens (some say hundreds) were killed by Soviet troops. Ironically, the students were protesting Khrushchev's policies of de-Stalinization. Khrushchev had defamed Georgia's favorite son. In October, Soviet tanks were rushed to Budapest to crush the uprising in Hungary, where students were demanding liberalization and an end to Soviet domination. The stability of the whole Soviet bloc was threatened. Soviet citizens waited anxiously to see what would happen.

In Russia, a *thaw* means both an easing and a muddy mess. Khrushchev's Thaw went back and forth. In its early days, no one knew just what to expect, but it was soon clear that repression was still Party policy, though now it was intermittent. Khrushchev followed zigzag policies, retreating when necessary to save his own authority.

The fate of writers was a kind of barometer. In October 1958, when Boris Pasternak was awarded the Nobel Prize, he sent a telegram to the Nobel committee: INFINITELY GRATEFUL, TOUCHED, PROUD, SURPRISED, OVERWHELMED. Four days later, the Politburo, which had banned his novel *Doctor Zhivago* as antisocialist and forbade its publication in the USSR, forced Pasternak to send a second telegram renouncing the prize.[1] In February 1961, the KGB seized and destroyed the manuscript of Vasily Grossman's *Life and Fate*. Yet in November 1962, despite objections from top Party members, Khrushchev allowed the publication in *Novy Mir* of *One Day in the Life of Ivan Denisovich*, Alexander Solzhenitsyn's harrowing account of life in the Gulag. No one could predict which was coming: a thaw or a freeze.

The spring and summer of 1961 were particularly hard for Svetlana. She was thirty-five. It is not a comfortable age. If one is still alone, one believes one will stay alone. Her children, now sixteen and eleven, were at school. Katya had her compulsory Pioneer meetings, and Joseph had joined the Komsomol. Svetlana recalled, "I was melancholy, irritable, inclined towards hopeless pessimism; more than once I had contemplated suicide; I was afraid of dark rooms, of the dead, of thunderstorms; of uncouth men, of hooligans in the streets and drunks. My own life appeared to me very dark, dull, and without a future."[2] Beneath Svetlana's carefully controlled exterior, there existed sorrows and suspicions, rages and frustrations, psychic wounds that she did not know how to face, let alone heal.

Gradually she had drawn close to Andrei Sinyavsky, her friend at the Gorky Institute, where she worked, and turned to him for consolation. Clearly he found her compelling. They were sitting on a small bench near the Kropotkin Gate when Svetlana mentioned the subject of suicide. Sinyavsky replied, "A suicide only thinks that he is killing himself. He is killing only his body, and the soul after that languishes, for God alone can take the soul."[3] Svetlana may have remembered Grandmother Olga's words: "You will know your soul when it aches."

This is an intimate conversation that suggests there were other conversations. It was a serious mistake to awaken Svetlana's expectations. A love affair began. According to her fellow researcher, Alexander Ushakov, gossip soon circulated in the Gorky Institute that one day Svetlana showed up at a dinner party at the apartment of the writer Andrei Menshutin, carrying her suitcase and demanding that Sinyavsky leave with her.[4] Sinyavsky's wife, Maria Rozanova, later confirmed the incident in an interview:

Once Sinyavsky and I were having dinner at his colleague's place . . . Andrei Menshutin, who, like us, also lived in a communal apartment not far from us. Suddenly the doorbell rings three times—Svetlana Alliluyeva.

The Menshutins had a very small room. I, together with Lida, started to scurry to get her another chair, but Svetlana declared, "I will not sit down. Andrei, I came for you. Now you will leave with me?" I asked, "Svetlana, what about me?" Alliluyeva told me, "Masha, you took Andrei away from his wife, and now I'm taking him away from you."[5]

It was as if Svetlana were still the little "hostess" in the Kremlin, commanding love and expecting her command to be obeyed. Rozanova described how her husband's "jaw almost fell off"; she said to him coyly, "Andrei, don't you think that while studying the history of the USSR, you've gone too far?" "Of course, I asked him about it, very matter-of-factly. Yes, he fucked her once. So what?"

Rozanova found it easy to blame Svetlana. She was "a hysterical woman—to have such a father." Sinyavsky was just being a man. She recalled his famous joke. He used to say, "If I'm sitting in a train car with a woman, I have to make her an offer, as a polite human being." Rozanova added that in a relationship, sexual fidelity "is not important. [This] is not what connects people. Without me he would not be able to work, nor live. To live—it is not the same as making soup." But she would never forgive Svetlana.

Svetlana didn't seem to understand the sexual double standard that flourished everywhere in the 1950s and 1960s. She was the "sexually deranged" one, while the artist Sinyavsky was forgiven his sexual dalliance, necessary for his work, which had so raised her hopes. The women became rivals and enemies, while the husband stood blithely by. And Svetlana was far from unusual in believing that her only route to a creative life was adjacent to a man. She retreated once again, but it must have been embarrassing to face down the gossip at the Gorky Institute. Later she would write admiringly of both Sinyavsky and his wife in her second memoir *Only One Year*, never alluding to this humiliation, and would assume she could pick up her friendship with them both.

However, Sinyavsky did have a lasting impact. As a committed Christian, he probably influenced her decision to convert to the Russian Orthodox faith. In the spring of 1962, she was baptized in a small Byzantine church named Deposition of the Shroud, beside the Donskoy Cathedral, the same church in which Sinyavsky had been baptized a few months earlier.

A second influence was, ironically, her father. Stalin had introduced her to Christianity when she was an adolescent. She'd been rooting around in his library and had come across a book called *The Life of Christ*. She was appalled and, indoctrinated as a good atheist, expressed her shock to her father: "You know it's a lie, it's mythology." And Stalin responded, "No, he was a real man. He actually lived." That afternoon, calling on his training in the Tbilisi seminary, he recounted for her the life of Christ—her father, of all people! The memory of sitting on Stalin's lap as he recounted the life of Christ hugely amused her.[6]

Though it was illegal, many Russians were secretly converting to Christianity in the early 1960s as a protest against Communism. For some, this was a nostalgic return to a vanished Russia. Others felt a genuine longing for spiritual values. But for Stalin's daughter to break the Party rules was dangerous. In order to protect them both, Father Nikolai Alexandrovich Golubtsov baptized her privately and did not record her name in the church register. She would always recall Father Nikolai's words of reassurance. "He said God loved me, even if I was

Stalin's daughter."[7] The remark suggests a depth of loneliness that is devastating.

Accustomed as she was to ideological conformity, Svetlana must have been deeply moved to find herself in the Church of the Deposition of the Shroud, with its beautiful onion domes, hidden in a Moscow suburb. The tiny vaulted stone chapels drawing the gaze upward, the burning incense and many candles lighting the gloom, and the hypnotic chanting of the choir, would have been intoxicating after the gray uniformity of Moscow. Since the days when she had wondered at the smiling Buddhas in the yurts at Zubalovo, Svetlana had tasted metaphysical longing. Her compulsive search through world religions began with her baptism. She read voraciously—about Hinduism, Buddhism, Christianity—and would eventually try many in her search for inward peace.

She must have had many motives for converting, but one, she maintained, was her brother's death. In January 1961, Khrushchev had arranged his release from Vladimirskaya Prison, but Vasili lasted only three months, racing around Moscow and drinking with his Georgian cronies at his favorite restaurant, Aragvi, before he disappeared. The family finally located him in Lefortovo Prison, but he was so ill that he didn't have to serve out his term. With his retired general's pension, he moved to Kazan. Broke and broken, he died on March 19, 1962, at the age of forty-one, after a bout of drinking, leaving behind four wives and several children. Svetlana remembered the boy who had shown such promise before his mother abandoned him. She no longer hated him.[8]

That same year, 1962, Svetlana reconnected with her past in a way that was both moving and devastating. She met her cousin, Ivan (Johnreed) Svanidze, whom she had not seen since the arrest of his father and mother in 1937. Stalin had had his father executed in 1941. His mother was executed in 1942. As a child, Svetlana had adored her aunt and uncle. It was Uncle Alyosha who brought the yurts to Zubalovo, told the children stories of the ancient Persians and Hittites, and recited Georgian poetry. When Svetlana met their son, Ivan (as he now called himself, having dropped the Johnreed), after twenty-five years of silence, probably at the Institute for African Studies, where he was a researcher, they both plunged back into that past with fervor. But the encounter had its dark side.

Svetlana was devastated when Svanidze showed her letters his parents had written him from prison before their executions. They had assumed he was being taken care of by his relatives, but this was not the case. Knowing the price exacted for associating with children of "enemies of the people," the family had been afraid to shelter him. When Svetlana's brother Yakov tried to help him, his wife pleaded that they would be putting themselves at risk.[9]

Under Stalin's iron rule, children of "enemies of the people" became enemies themselves. Supposedly, after the Svanidzes' arrest, his nanny took in the eleven-year-old Ivan, until she herself was denounced. He was then sent to an orphanage for children of the condemned and lived for several years in a compound behind barbed wire. Orphans in wartime were like flotsam, dispensable, the last to be fed. To this boy who had spent his childhood in affluent Germany and later in London and Geneva when his father was head of the Soviet Bank for Foreign Trade, the shock must have been incalculable.

At seventeen Ivan was exiled to Kazakhstan to work in the mines. He was finally given permission to live in Moscow in 1956. Like most survivors, he came back broken and haunted. On his return, he made no effort to contact his relatives. He enrolled in Moscow University, obtaining a doctoral degree in African studies, but never fully recovered his health.

Svetlana would later say, "We suddenly found each other. . . .

I simply couldn't let go."[10] In late 1962, she married Ivan Svanidze in the Russian Orthodox Church. It was as if two neuroses met—though his experience was much darker than hers, they were both Stalin's victims. The marriage was doomed from the outset and lasted less than a year. Yakov's daughter, Gulia, remembered Svetlana and Svanidze visiting, but as Gulia put it, "Ivan had suffered a great deal; he was nervous, susceptible, and also had an extremely difficult character."[11]

Svetlana and Ivan separated, and though she always spoke of him warmly, she didn't publicly admit to the marriage. Perhaps she was ashamed. Salving her own loneliness, she had only exacerbated his pain. A divorce notice was published in the evening newspaper *Vechernyaya Moskva*.[12] It must be said that while she was accumulating divorces—she now had three—she was not the only Soviet citizen to do so. Under the emotional trauma of decades of dictatorship, divorce was common.

Svetlana sought solace in her circle of close friends, many of whom were members of the intelligentsia. Dmitri Tolstoy and his wife, Tatyana, lived in Leningrad. She would slip away for a few days to visit them whenever she could. Dmitri was the son of Count Aleksei Tolstoy, cousin to the more famous Leo Tolstoy. The count, revered in the Soviet Union for his historical novels, had divorced Dmitri's mother, Julia Rozhansky, and had lived in a mansion in Moscow while the countess lived in penury in a communal apartment stuffed with the tattered remnants of her former life. Svetlana loved the feel of history in the Tolstoy apartment—the eighteenth-century Dutch cupboard, the precious cheval glass, the antique chairs.

Dmitri Tolstoy was a composer, but, because he'd refused to become a member of the Communist Party, his operas went unproduced, while he earned his living giving music lessons. Yet however reduced the Tolstoys' circumstances, they still gave parties where they read the works of prerevolutionary poets and passed around illegal samizdat manuscripts, like the banned poems of the new rising star in Leningrad, the poet Joseph Brodsky. Brodsky would be put on trial for parasitism in 1964 and sentenced to five years of internal exile.[13]

It was at one such party that Svetlana met Lily Golden. Golden remembered her first impression of Svetlana thus: "A red-haired, green-eyed, rather short woman who was dressed very simply and whose eyes reflected the immense pain of knowledge denied to others."[14] Lily Golden was a researcher at the Institute of African Studies and the author of numerous books and articles on African music and culture. She was also the first to research the impoverished and isolated black communities in the Caucasus, descendants of former slaves who had escaped to the mountains of Abkhazia and whose existence the Soviets would have preferred to keep secret. She had an extraordinary history. Her father, Oliver Golden, was a black American who had fled Mississippi after World War I and ended up in Chicago, where he became a dedicated Marxist. He always said, "The first white American to shake [my] hand and shake it as an equal was a Communist."[15] Her mother, Bertha Bialek, was Jewish. Because it was impossible to live in America as an interracial couple, they had sailed to the Soviet Union in 1931, dreaming of helping to build a just, more equitable society. They personally escaped the repression of the 1930s, but watched helplessly as friends disappeared. Their only child, Lily, one of the few black Russians in Moscow, had grown up in Tashkent.

The evening Lily met Svetlana at the Tolstoys' party, the group paid a visit to Professor Victor Manuylov, a literary critic and historian of Russian poetry who lived in a communal apartment nearby. His single room was stuffed with books that overflowed into the communal bathroom. He greeted them kindly, lighting the samovar and speaking of Saint Petersburg in the old days, and then suddenly said to Lily and Svetlana, "Show me your hands! Sometimes I have success in palm reading."

When he examined Svetlana's hand, he exclaimed that he "had never seen a hand like it. This belongs to an extraordinary person!" Lily remembered his prediction for Svetlana: "Your life divides into three periods. The first, finished long ago, was one of cloudless bliss. Your present period is difficult. You are fighting to get together with a foreign prince . . . he will sicken and die. Then you will begin the third period, when you will cross oceans and travel far away."[16] Uncannily, he had described the exact trajectory of Svetlana's life. She would meet a prince, an Indian rajah named Brajesh Singh, and would eventually cross oceans.

Lily became curious. "Who is this Svetlana?" she asked Tatyana Tolstoy and was told, "Svetlana Alliluyeva, Stalin's daughter." Lily was shocked. "It was difficult to place this simply dressed, modest young woman . . . amid the horror that must surround her life."[17]

As she came to know Svetlana, Lily would say, "She was a very kind, tender-hearted person. . . . It was impossible for her to escape her terrible heritage. She simply couldn't trust people; how could you if you were Stalin's daughter?" People treated her "as some kind of freak."[18] Svetlana came to love Lily, who brought gaiety and freshness into her household. They would comb through Lily's large collection of recordings of African folk songs and spirituals. She taught Svetlana's son, Joseph, to dance the twist.

Soon Lily began to see what it meant to be Stalin's daughter. In the Moscow streets, people looked at Lily with curiosity because she was black. But when Svetlana walked out, people often looked with contempt. When Svetlana got a job at the Institute of World Economics and International Affairs—she wanted to leave the Gorky Institute—she lasted only a few days. "Every few minutes the door would open and someone would stare in with undisguised hate. The fact that the raw emotion was directed against her father was unimportant."[19]

Lily also knew Ivan Svanidze as a talented scholar at her institute. She believed that in marrying him, Svetlana was seeking absolution for Stalin's crimes. She told her own daughter, Yelena Khanga: "[Svetlana] did everything she could to help people who returned from the camps in the late fifties."[20] Lily also understood why the relationship ended abruptly. Svanidze had been "deranged" by his multiple imprisonments and was impossible to live with. According to Lily, he had become paranoid about his own Jewish origins and removed all his Jewish mother's portraits from the walls. And he hated Svetlana's son because Joseph was half Jewish.[21]

Lily had a special reason to be grateful to Svetlana. She was aware that Svetlana rarely exploited her privileges and contacts to gain special favors, but she made an exception in Lily's case. When Lily's husband, a political revolutionary from Zanzibar, was assassinated and Lily was left in poverty to bring up her daughter alone, Svetlana used her influence to get Lily a monthly allowance. Lily would remain at Svetlana's side through many of the coming traumas, even helping her children after she defected.

Another of Svetlana's crucial friends was Fyodor Volkenstein, a professor of chemistry in Moscow and Dmitri Tolstoy's half brother. During their long conversations together, Volkenstein began to urge her to write a memoir of her family. "But how can I do this?" she demurred. "Write! Write! You can do it," he told her. "Start as if you were writing me a letter, the rest will come of itself."[22]

In 1962, Svetlana received an unexpected visit from a French writer and editor, Marquis Emmanuel d'Astier de la Vigerie. His friend Ilya Ehrenburg had discouraged him from seeking her out because it was dangerous, but he had found her address on his own. He simply arrived at her doorstep and explained that he was writing an article about her father and wanted to check some biographical facts. By law, she should have refused to admit him because he was a foreigner, but she was tired of Soviet rules, and they talked for hours. Among Moscow intellectuals, d'Astier was considered pro-Communist but a liberal pacifist.

Shortly after d'Astier's first visit, Deputy Chairman Mikoyan invited Svetlana to his dacha and, while he assured her it wasn't forbidden to meet foreigners, he said it was "better not to." Then Mikoyan asked her if she'd ever considered writing her own memoirs. If she had, it would be unwise to give them to foreigners; she would never have peace again. Sensing a risk, Svetlana assured him she had no intention of writing a book. D'Astier took to visiting each time he came to Moscow, and after each visit she was summoned to the Central Committee and asked—but politely—"What did that Frenchman want?"[23]

In fact, Svetlana *was* writing her memoir. She had taken Fyodor Volkenstein's suggestion and was writing her story in the form of letters to him. She would call this book *Twenty Letters to a Friend*. Her old friend Olga Rifkina remembered how, at one point in the summer of 1963 working in her Zhukovka dacha, Svetlana became very secretive about what she was writing. "She started to get worried that the authorities would get interested in it. That they would take it away . . . That they would destroy it."[24] In thirty-five days, she wrote her book as a conversation with an "unidentified interlocutor." For his safety, she never named Volkenstein as the friend. She was writing, as they said in the USSR, "for the drawer."

She managed to get her manuscript to Professor Manuylov, who had read her and Lily Golden's palms that evening in Leningrad. He called her in the middle of the night. "Oh, this is so wonderful, I cannot put it down," he said. Knowing her telephone was bugged, she asked, "What are you talking about?" Recovering himself, he replied, "Oh, yes, I'm talking about one book I'm reading here." He was so excited, he'd forgotten the Soviet rule of *discretion*.

Svetlana took the next train to Leningrad. "My dear, it's a finished book. How have you done it?" the professor asked.[25] "We can publish this abroad." She wasn't surprised to discover that he might be able to do this—he may have been responsible for getting Joseph Brodsky's manuscript out of the country—but she replied, "No. I don't want anything like that right now." She knew it would cause a great scandal, and she had to protect her children. "I perfectly understand," he said, but he did take the manuscript to a typist, who typed three copies to be circulated among trusted friends.

Twenty Letters to a Friend is not a confession. It's an exorcism. By writing her book as if to a friend, Svetlana was able to speak intimately and to dismiss all the censors sitting on her shoulder, including her father. She wanted this book to be about people, not about a political era, about all those whom she had loved and lost. The conceit of letters (there are no Dear Friend salutations) soon vanished under the weight of the story she had to tell.

Twenty Letters to a Friend begins with the terrible days of Stalin's death, as if Svetlana needed to exorcise her father's ghost in order to speak freely. She does not convey the monumentality of the event—the *vozhd* is dying—but rather she recounts the death as a daughter would. "Who loves this lonely man?" she asks, watching his ministers ricocheting between fear and ambition, Beria scrambling for ascendency. Only his servants. When a comatose Stalin raises his arm in his last moments, she sees this as a gesture of rage against life itself. He had wished to dominate life, but life had finally defeated him. His Kuntsevo dacha, with its emptiness and coffinlike gloom, is the monument he built. But there had been a sunnier, happier house, the Zubalovo of her childhood.

In a second letter, she conjures that house, before her mother died. It is a fantasy, of course. She introduces the Alliluyevs, in her mind benevolent figures, early idealistic revolutionaries with "no axes to grind." They are "sincere, honest, kindly" and on an equal footing with her father. The "uncles," like Mikoyan, Molotov, and Kliment Voroshilov, visit. She knows that, given a longer lens from which to view it, this world is cruel and murderous. Beneath the bucolic surface, a Dostoyevskian nightmare of competing ambitions will lead to the deaths of most of these people, but she wants the friend to whom she is writing to know Zubalovo as she knew it in her childhood.

Her intervening chapters recount the lives of her family—the Svanidzes, the Alliluyevs, the Redenses, all broken in different ways, all turned into enemies and sucked into the black hole that was her father. It is a double life, and perhaps this is her most important insight. On the surface, it is normal; beneath, it is a world of cruel bereavements. She watches this terrible theater from backstage, seeing the illusion. It is scripted with a brutal fatality, and there is nothing she can do but watch, including viewing the audience out front, which, as she imagines it, sits incredulous, openmouthed, silent.

Finally, though she has put it off from grief, in the middle of the book she tells her friend about her mother's suicide. She paints a portrait of the adolescent Nadya by including her mother's letters to a friend, written when Nadya was living through the turbulent years of 1916 to 1918 and being pulled slowly into the "full fervor of revolutionary idealism." By 1918 Nadya's letters hint that she has fallen in love with Stalin. Svetlana explains that Nadya "had only begun to grow when the Revolution broke out, whereas he [Stalin] was already a man nearly forty, an age of hardened scepticism and cold calculation and all the other qualities important in a politician."[26] It is from her nanny's account that she writes about the night of her mother's suicide.

Then come "letters" recounting the fate of her family after 1932. People appear and disappear as they did in life, until there is almost no one left. She reserves a special letter for Aleksei Kapler, whose fate made clear the cruelty of which her father was capable. Unburdening herself, she talks of her marriages and children. Looking back, she sees her life as one of "cruel bereavements" and "disappointments and losses."

And yet her last letter is devoted to her nanny Alexandra Andreevna, who, with her gaiety and kindness, is offered as an embodiment of all that is good and unchanging in Russia, a person without whom she would have "lost her mind." She paints Alexandra Andreevna as a kind of Tolstoyan epic figure who watches the revolutionaries with stoicism, knowing they too will pass. Svetlana seems to suggest that it was her nanny who gave her a sense of morality and a conscience.

Svetlana ends her book thus:

> We are all responsible for everything that happened. Let the judging be done by those who come later, by men and women who didn't know the times and the people we knew. Let it be left to new people to whom these years in Russia will be as remote and inexplicable, as terrible and strange as the reign of Ivan the Terrible. But I do not think they'll call our era a "progressive" one, or that they'll say it was all for the "good of Russia." . . . They'll read through this page in their country's history with a feeling of pain, contrition and bewilderment, and they'll be led by this feeling to live their lives differently.[27]

The book is personal, saturated with a kind of wistful lyricism, and ambiguous in its judgments of those involved. Svetlana is at once nostalgic, romantic in her idealizations of certain people, especially her mother, and sometimes biased in her testimony, yet remarkable in her clarity of memory. This is not the book one might expect from a daughter of Stalin. It revealed no state secrets. It had no political points to make, beyond the condemnation of Stalin's regime and the repudiation of a system in which the goals of the so-called collective good, exacted through ideological conformity, made the individual meaningless. In some ways, the book is a love letter to enduring Russia, with its ancient heritage and astonishingly varied geography. Svetlana assured her friend that no one who loved Russia ever left, but it would be only four years before she did exactly that.[28]

Chapter 14

The Gentle Brahman

An undated photo of Svetlana and Brajesh Singh, a rajah's son and a former Communist official whom she met in 1963 in Kuntsevo Hospital.

In October 1963, Svetlana entered Kuntsevo Hospital for a tonsillectomy. Hospitals had changed slightly under the Khrushchev Thaw. There were still government sanatoriums for members of the Party elite and their relatives and for famous actors and athletes in high-society Moscow, but now more foreigners were admitted. Each year Communist Party organizations abroad received invitations from Moscow to send patients for care. Their presence was not surprising, perhaps, but now they were often placed in the same wards as Soviet patients and even allowed to mingle without interpreters or watchers. But Soviet patients were still discouraged from too close intimacy with the foreigners.

Svetlana noticed a small, stooped, gray-haired man roaming the halls. He was Indian and that interested her. She was reading a biography of Gandhi and wanted to ask this stranger about the Mahatma, but she was too shy to initiate a conversation with a foreigner. However, when they bumped into each other in the hospital corridor, they sat on a couch and talked avidly for an hour. They spoke in English. He asked what organization she belonged to, and when she said, "None," he seemed pleased. Brajesh Singh was no longer the fervent Communist idealist he had been in his youth.

He was the son of the rajah of Kalakankar in Uttar Pradesh. He had studied English under tutors at a college in Lucknow and then spent much of his life abroad. In London in 1932, he had become a Communist. This seemed to him the best way to fight for Indian independence. According to friends, he was a kind of Puck, with a mischievous sense of humor that he brought to "the game of politics."[1]

Svetlana was relieved that Singh had no idea who she was. When he began asking about life in the USSR after Stalin, she replied that, though there had been superficial reforms, fundamental aspects of Soviet society remained unchanged.

When she finally decided to tell Singh she was Stalin's daughter, his only response was a British-inflected "Oh!" She claimed he never once questioned her about her father.[2]

Over the days of their hospital stay, they wandered the halls in their bathrobes or ate together in the hospital dining room, much to the consternation of their Soviet fellow patients, who didn't approve of Singh and resented Khrushchev's incursions on their privileges with his "liberal" reforms. English-speaking patients were encouraged to eavesdrop on Svetlana and Singh's conversations, but the two went silent when anyone approached.[3] For the Soviets, Singh was too ebullient. As they passed the dour officials in the hallway, laughing, Svetlana feared for him.

Svetlana discovered that Singh was chronically ill. He suffered from bronchitis and emphysema, and his lungs were collapsing. Soon both were sent to recuperate at a sanatorium called the House of Rest in Sochi on the Black Sea. They spent their time walking on the boardwalk under the disapproving eyes of their fellow patients. More than one resident pulled her aside to say, "Your father was a great man. You wait, the time will come when he will be remembered!"[4] Then they would tell her to stick to her own kind. Some even expressed shock that she had dropped her father's name, though afterward they might ask to be photographed with her. Svetlana was certain the patients and staff were sending reports to Moscow about her bad behavior.

At the age of fifty-three (Svetlana was thirty-seven), Singh was lonely. In Vienna during the war, he had met a Jewish girl and, to help her escape the Nazis, they had married and fled to India, where they lived for sixteen years. She then moved to England with their young son. Singh joined her, but after his failure to find work in England, they divorced, and he returned to India alone.

He and Svetlana became deeply attached. Although (or perhaps because) he was sixteen years older, she sensed that she had found a lover, a guide, and a friend. His world was far richer spiritually than hers; he seemed to have an inner peace and equilibrium. It was her capacity to think for herself that moved him. He called her Sveta, or Light; it was one of the few Russian words he knew. By the terms of his visa, after his discharge from the hospital, Singh was scheduled to return to India, but now he and Svetlana made new plans. He would return to Moscow and find work as a translator of Russian texts into Hindi. Impulsive as always, Svetlana invited Singh to live with her.

The Indian ambassador to Moscow, Triloki Nath Kaul, had been a friend of Singh's since his youth. It wouldn't be hard to get a Soviet work visa. It appalled Singh that Svetlana had spent her whole life within the confines of the USSR. He would come back, and they would travel to India; he would show her Europe. It was a lovely fantasy, and this was the time of new hope, the time of the Thaw.

Singh left for India in December. Svetlana waited, but something was wrong. A visa for Singh should have come easily. He had recommendations from Kaul and from the secretary general of the Indian Communist Party, Shripad Amrit Dange. Though Svetlana and Singh wrote to each other constantly, they soon found that their letters did not arrive.

Svetlana suspected that reports had reached Moscow that she had consorted with a foreigner at the House of Rest in Sochi, but in fact she was mistaken. Through Ambassador Kaul, Singh discovered that a young Indian named Chandra Shekhar, secretary of a group of Indian Communists in Moscow, was reporting that Singh was unreliable. Shekhar worked in radio and supplied the Central Committee of the Soviet Communist Party and its Foreign Division with information about India. When he visited Svetlana and Singh before Singh's departure for India, he had laughingly said that Singh was not a Communist but a rajah.[5] It was still normal for issues of ideological purity to derail a person's career, and the best way to advance in the system was to betray another.

Svetlana went to see Deputy Chairman Mikoyan. Mikoyan told her he had spoken with Khrushchev, who had been sympathetic. Mikoyan said that everything would be fine and she should bring Singh for a visit. He would be happy to meet him.

The delays were excruciating for Svetlana, but in March 1965, sixteen months after his departure, Singh finally got his visa to return to Moscow. Svetlana and her son, Joseph, went to meet him at Sheremetyevo Airport on April 7. The man who stepped off the plane was ill and had aged visibly. Svetlana did not hesitate. Though Singh had been assigned a state apartment, she insisted he come home with them. Joseph and Katya welcomed him. Joseph would later say:

> Singh was a nice sort of person, cultured, kind. . . . It was very enjoyable to be with him. . . . He was calm and patient and also knew how to look upon things with a certain sense of humour. . . . He came to live with us, and to Katya and I he was our mother's husband, and we treated him with respect. I think she was happy.[6]

Svetlana was, indeed and at last, very happy. An Indian friend of Singh's, Dr. Ram Manohar Lohia, a member of the Indian parliament and head of the Socialist Party, recalled his visit with Singh. Although Singh was suffering from a painfully swollen leg and his asthma was very bad, the two men went to Lohia's hotel. They had been friends for thirty-seven years. Lohia asked Singh about Svetlana.

> He spoke of her with great affection and respect, and I, for one, could understand that she could care deeply for him. Brajesh had a quiet charm and poise, a willingness to listen to one, which grew out of his innate sympathy. He had humor, too, and a certain something I can't quite define in his eyes, which women would undoubtedly find attractive. . . .
>
> Suddenly, it seemed, it was midnight. I wanted to go to Red Square and look around, but Brajesh said that Svetlana

would be very worried by now. We took a taxi to his home. As we turned into his street, we saw Svetlana standing in the road, obviously looking for Brajesh and deeply worried. She was standing nearest my side of the taxi, and I leaped out. Although we hadn't been introduced, I began at once to josh her out of being so upset.

"Are you so much in love with this man?" I asked.

Svetlana said gravely: "Things happen, you know— auto accidents and things like that!"

I could guess at what she really meant but was not saying.

When Lohia spent several hours the next day with the couple, he was deeply impressed by her sincerity. He told a journalist in an interview:

I compare her to a flower, not to a rose, for roses are not so tender, but to jasmine or orchids, which have a subtle scent that doesn't intrude or pounce on you.

I thought her also a woman of many sorrows and that a life of sorrows had transmuted her into a quietly charming woman. In all those hours we spent together, I did not hear her speak loudly or boisterously even once. The only time I heard an edge to her voice was later, in India, when she said in a harsh, rasping tone: "I hate politics! I hate politics![7]

Even Svetlana's cousin Vladimir concurred:

Only a true feeling toward this very sick man can explain why a young, interesting, intelligent, passionate woman calmed her fervent spirit and movingly cared about him, a completely helpless man, until his death in 1966. There was something otherworldly about this relationship. It was love based on grace.[8]

Now Svetlana had a new plan. She was determined that she and Singh must marry. Of course, there is a question as to why Svetlana was so eager to marry him, she who had so precipitately married three times before, but in this case, in addition to her usual longing for permanence, she had a very pragmatic reason. Singh needed the status of a Soviet citizen, which marriage would give him, to be safe from expulsion. At first, she had wanted to be married to him so that they could fulfill their fantasy of traveling in Europe. But now the idea of marriage became urgent. Singh was very ill. Svetlana thought that if they went to India, to a climate he was used to, she could save his life. He refused to return without her, and she needed to be his wife to travel with him.

But the political winds that had always shaped Svetlana's life had again shifted for the worse. In October 1964, Khrushchev was deposed. He had made too many mistakes: his drinking, his mishandling of the Cuban missile crisis, his wildly unpredictable Thaw that disturbed the political status quo in the Soviet Union and Eastern Europe. Slowly a palace revolution engineered him out. Leonid Brezhnev was elected first secretary of the Presidium, in effect the country's leader, sharing power with Aleksei Kosygin as chairman of the Council of Ministers and Nikolai Podgorny as chairman of the Supreme Soviet. Soon these conservatives stopped the minor reforms.

Svetlana had felt somewhat invisible since her father's death, unnoticed and anonymous as a public citizen. It had been wonderful to be almost forgotten. Now she was once again Stalin's daughter, the bearer of the famous name and, to the conservative Communists back in power, this involved responsibilities. Even Mikoyan had forgotten what had been said about Stalin at the Twentieth Congress. One day he invited Svetlana and her children to his dacha for dinner. As they were leaving, he passed Katya a present. "Here's a present for you—a rug. You can hang it up on your wall," he said. When they got home and unrolled the rug, they discovered it was woven with a portrait of Stalin. Svetlana rolled it up and put it away.[9]

On May 3, she and Singh visited the Moscow office where marriages with foreigners had to be registered. The very next day, Svetlana was summoned to the Kremlin. It was an eerie experience. She passed through the Spassky Gate and entered the Senate building designed by Matvey Kazakov. She had lived for over twenty years in that first-floor apartment, and it was the same dreary building, with the same red rugs, the cold wood-paneled walls, the vaulted ceilings. She entered Kosygin's office on the second floor, the office that had once been her father's. She faced the stranger who sat at her father's desk. She had never met him before.

His first question was why had she had stopped attending Party meetings. He insisted she must "rejoin the collective, occupy [her] rightful place." She explained that she had to take care of her family and now she had a sick husband.

At the word *husband*, Kosygin responded angrily. There is only Svetlana's record of the conversation, in which Kosygin sounds like the mad dictator Alice found when she went through the looking glass—the Red King, so to speak.

What have you cooked up? You, a young healthy woman, a sportswoman, couldn't you have found someone here, I mean someone young and strong? What do you want with this old sick Hindu? No, we are all positively against it, positively against it![10]

Whatever the shading of the conversation, it was now official. Kosygin, in the name of the government, refused her the right to register her marriage to Singh. It would never be allowed. As she left, she felt the Kremlin sarcophagus closing in on her again.

Svetlana again approached Anastas Mikoyan for help regarding her marriage. He had already assisted in getting Singh a contract with the Soviet publisher Progress, but this new request became the occasion for a terrible rift between Svetlana and her close friend Ella Mikoyan.

As Stepan Mikoyan explained it, Svetlana asked his wife, Ella, to arrange an interview with her father-in-law. Mikoyan agreed and suggested he and Svetlana meet at his dacha. However, this turned out to be the day an internationally acclaimed pianist was performing at the Moscow Conservatory, and when Mikoyan heard that Ella was attending, he wanted to go. He asked Ella to phone Svetlana to postpone the meeting until the next day. Apparently Svetlana was furious and turned her anger on Ella. Stepan Mikoyan recounted the rupture:

> Uncharacteristically raising her voice, Svetlana attacked Ella with an avalanche of accusations and insults. The gist was that Ella had plotted against her and deliberately enticed her father-in-law with the idea of attending that concert to prevent Svetlana's meeting with him. Svetlana slammed down the receiver.

That night, after the concert, Ella returned home to find a hand-delivered letter from Svetlana. She read it in tears and showed it to Stepan. "I could not believe what I read. It was flagrantly unjust and cruelly insulting." Much later she showed the letter to her father-in-law. Mikoyan responded, "Her own father all over—can't do without enemies."[11]

Was this a fair appraisal? Svetlana certainly had an imperious side. From childhood—after her mother's death, in a world where everything was secret, too dangerous to speak about, even in such an atmosphere—Svetlana had learned her power. She knew how to get things from people. And when she was frustrated, she had no emotional blocks. Anger would well up in her and she would spew it out regardless of the consequences. People on the receiving end of her rage would not always know the cause.

And yet, in this instance, she must have been thinking, *A concert! And Singh's life was on the line!* But her response was also intemperate. She accused Ella of sabotaging her when all poor Ella was trying to do was help, and Svetlana had probably not explained the gravity of Singh's need. Her father's teaching: "Don't ask. Command."

Apparently, despite Svetlana's tirade against Ella, the meeting with Mikoyan took place the next day. He was unhelpful. "Why is it necessary to marry?" he wanted to know. He and his wife had lived as common-law partners for forty years. "Formal marriage has no significance in love." He then warned against her friendships with foreign ambassadors. "This Kaul is very pushy," he said. "Not at all like other Indians. Keep away, keep away from him."[12]

That fall, in 1965, the Gorky Institute, where Svetlana continued to work, was in turmoil. In September her friend Andrei Sinyavsky and his fellow writer Yuli Daniel were arrested for spreading anti-Soviet propaganda. They were accused of allowing their novellas, depicting Soviet society as surreal and menacing, to be reproduced as samizdat—typed copies passed clandestinely among friends. They had even allowed their work to be published in the West under the respective pseudonyms Abram Tertz and Nikolai Arzhak. Khrushchev's Thaw was officially over. The repressive Brezhnev era had begun. Now anyone caught with samizdat could expect to be brutally punished, and everyone was frightened.

On December 5, Constitution Day, a few brave souls organized a public rally to demand an open trial for the writers. This was the first independent political rally in Moscow since 1929. Only two or three leaflets announcing the rally were posted at Moscow University, but soon the whole of Moscow knew. A young dissident, Alexander Yesenin-Volpin, was carrying a poster: WE DEMAND AN OPEN TRIAL FOR SINYAVSKY AND DANIEL. A KGB officer ripped out the word *open* from the poster. "It seemed he especially disliked that word." About fifty people gathered at the Pushkin Monument in central Moscow, though thousands stood on the opposite side of the street. They had come to see what would happen to the demonstrators. "Would they be shot then or later?"[13]

The trial of Sinyavsky and Daniel opened on February 10, 1966. Despite the attempted intervention of organizations like PEN International, Daniel was sentenced to five years and Sinyavsky to seven years of hard labor in prison camps.[14]

Svetlana was appalled. This was grotesque, ugly, unconscionable. She came home each night to Singh with tales of the kind of meetings that were going on at the Gorky Institute, and he would ask, "But why? Why? . . . Seven years of prison for writing books? Just because a writer writes books?"[15]

By this time, her friend Alexander Ushakov had become secretary of the Party organization at the Gorky Institute. The atmosphere was tense. Even before the so-called trial, organizations like the Union of Writers were required to condemn Sinyavsky and Daniel in mass proclamations, as in the old days when Stalin had established the system of collective condemnation and shunning. After the trial, Party committees at the various institutes circulated an official letter to the *Literary Gazette* approving the sentences. Campaigns were launched against those who abstained from signing.

Ushakov remembered chairing the meeting of the Party

bureau at the Gorky Institute. "Suddenly Sinyavsky was arrested. No one knew. . . . We had to take some kind of stance about this." Ushakov said to the Party members, "We should not think this is our doing. Everything is so turbulent in our country and this is the context in which Andrei existed," the implication being that Sinyavsky knew what he was getting into by publishing his books outside the country. Ushakov then described Svetlana's sudden entrance.

> Svetlana came in. She was not a member of the Party bureau. She came to the Party bureau and after I made my speech, it was understood that I supported the idea of keeping everything inside the Institute. Suddenly she gets up and delivers a political speech in defense of Sinyavsky. And I say, "Who invited you?" I say, "There's the door. We did not invite you here." Later she told some of my acquaintances, "Sasha [Ushakov] has become rude. He kicked me out of the Party bureau." I was not rude, but she should have known. She could go to Red Square or write a letter to the TsK [Central Committee]. As if anything depended on us![16]

Svetlana was no dissident. She avoided what she called politics, but for the second time, she made a public protest, saying in her speech defending Sinyavsky that the Gorky Institute should have publicly supported him and the staff should never have been forced to sign an open letter denouncing him. It was shameful that those who had refused to sign were subjected to a witch hunt.[17] Fed up with the brutal hypocrisy of it all, that summer she quit the Institute.

Singh was very worried. The Politburo was spearheading the return to Communist Party orthodoxy. Tensions in Moscow between the old guard and the reformers were building and were splitting families and friendships; ideological battles raged. Singh, who always encouraged Svetlana's writing, said that she must send her manuscript of *Twenty Letters to a Friend* abroad. Any apartment could be searched by warrant, any manuscript confiscated. Everyone knew by now that the KGB (the Russian initials of the Committee for State Security, the omnipresent secret police and spy agency, so renamed in 1954) had raided Vasily Grossman's apartment and taken away not only his manuscript of *Life and Fate*, but also his carbon copies, his notebooks, and even the typewriter ribbons. (A surviving typescript of the novel was microfilmed, smuggled out of the country, and published in the West in 1980, sixteen years after Grossman's death.) Singh arranged to get a copy of Svetlana's manuscript to Ambassador Kaul, who took it with him to India in January 1966, safely carried in his diplomatic pouch.

After the trial of Sinyavsky and Daniel, at least ten well-known Moscow intellectuals were arrested, and one disappeared. The wife of V. V. Kuznetsov reported that on November 1, 1966, at 6:00 a.m., her husband was seized and driven in a police car to the Moscow Regional Psychiatric Hospital.[18] She hadn't heard from him since. Singh had every reason to be concerned.

Now the isolation of Singh began. He had fallen under the shadow of the government's displeasure, and old Indian friends stopped visiting. His nephew, Dinesh Singh, who had risen to become deputy minister of the Department of Foreign Affairs under the pro-Soviet government of Indira Gandhi, stopped corresponding. Only his brother Suresh Singh continued to write from the village of Kalakankar. Only Singh's old friends, Ambassador Kaul, and Ambassador Murad Ghaleb from the United Arab Republic, continued to visit.[19]

Soon Singh's work as a translator at his publishing house, Progress, was called into question. The chief editor of the

English Division, Vladimir N. Pavlov, who had been Stalin's translator at Yalta and elsewhere and had been in charge of Stalin's correspondence with Churchill, questioned Singh's capabilities. The chief editor of the Hindi Division corrected his Hindi translations. It was clear that forces were at work to discredit Singh as incompetent so as to rescind his legal right to stay in the USSR. Clearly Svetlana had been correct. Only if he were married to her would Singh be safe from expulsion.[20]

But all these political machinations soon became irrelevant. It was clear that Singh was terminally ill. He was admitted to the Intourist Polyclinic, where he was wrongly diagnosed with tuberculosis. Finally Svetlana got him back into Kuntsevo Hospital. He made multiple visits, each time more ill. Rules had changed even at Kuntsevo. Foreigners were now isolated on a special floor, and friends had to secure official passes to visit. Still, his friends the ambassadors came.

Svetlana began to spend the whole day with him. When he was strong enough, they would go to the garden. She would sit at his feet, and he, eyes closed, with his hand on her head, would speak of India and sometimes read the Vedic hymns. At night at home, she would discuss his case with Joseph, who was now studying medicine at the university. Joseph would consult his books. The outlook was not hopeful. Singh wanted to return to India. Desperate, Svetlana wrote to Brezhnev, begging to be allowed to take him there. Her stay would be short. He would not live long.

It was not Brezhnev, but Mikhail Suslov, the Party's chief ideologue, who responded. He summoned her to the Communist Party Headquarters on Old Square. When she again asked for permission to register her marriage, he replied that her father had established a law against marriages with foreigners. It had been a good idea. He told her that she would not be

allowed to go abroad. Why would she want to? It was unpatri-
otic. If Singh wanted to go back, that was his business. No one
was preventing him.

Suslov predicted that there would be political provocations
if she traveled to India. Journalists would hound her at the airport. She was Stalin's daughter. He demanded that she return
to work at her collective; she should take up "a place suitable
for [her] famous name."[21] She tried to suggest that if Singh
died now, it would be a public blot on the Soviet Union. Suslov
replied coolly that Singh was getting good care. If he died, he
died.

Singh only laughed when Svetlana reported her interview
with Suslov. For Indians, Suslov was an internationalist, a
model modern Marxist, though his wife and children had
never ventured outside the Soviet Union.

Finally Singh asked Svetlana to get him out of the hospital and take him home. On Sunday, October 30, friends and
colleagues from Progress dropped by. When they were finally
alone, Brajesh told Svetlana, with a calm resignation that was
both disconcerting and moving, "Sveta, I know that I will die
today." He said he had had a dream of a white bullock pulling
a cart. In India when you have that dream, it means death is
coming.[22] She did not believe him.

At seven a.m. that Monday, he pointed to his heart and then
to his head and said that he could feel something throbbing.
And then he died.

Into her mind came the memory of her father's death, the
only other death she had witnessed. She recalled her father's
outrageous struggle, his fear in the face of death, his terrifying
last gesture of accusation. Singh's death was quick and peaceful, his last gesture toward his heart. She thought, *Each man got
the death he deserved.*

With Singh's death, Svetlana felt that something had

changed in her. "Some inner line of demarcation" had been drawn. Something was totally lost. She did not yet know what this meant. Oddly, she also felt a kind of peace. She did not cry. She felt Singh's comforting, benevolent presence, hovering.

She hastily called Singh's Indian friends. She didn't want Singh's body to fall into the hands of the Soviet bureaucracy. The friends came. They read some of the verses of the Bhagavad Gita in Sanskrit. They burned sandalwood. They took Singh's body to the crematorium.

There, on November 1, 1966, some of her friends from the Institute of World Literature showed up as she took her leave of Singh, whom they had never met. Svetlana was moved when her son, Joseph, kissed the body on the forehead to say goodbye. Singh had expressed a wish to have his ashes scattered over the Ganges, though he didn't expect this to happen. As she placed his urn in her bedroom, she made a resolution. She would personally scatter his ashes over the sacred river.

Expecting to be repulsed, she wrote to both Kosygin and Brezhnev. The morning after her letters were delivered, she was summoned to the Kremlin. Astonishingly, Kosygin told her she could go. Singh's nephew Dinesh Singh, a shrewd politician, had intervened with Indira Gandhi to secure a traditional funeral for his uncle. Svetlana would be allowed to attend as long as the Indians ensured that she would avoid any contact with the foreign press. That night she collected her relevant documents, signed by the head of the General Department of the Central Committee, Konstantin Chernenko.[23]

On November 7, she wrote an elegiac letter (in English) to Singh's brother and sister-in-law:

My dear Suresh and Prakashwati:
    It's very difficult for me now to try to express my feelings

and my grief. But I know about you so much from my dear Brajesh, who loved you and was attached to you so strongly. . . .

I need . . . to spend a few quiet days at the bank of the Ganga, to see its quiet waters, to watch its great waves. I'll have my visa for two weeks only, but even a week spent at Kalakankar will give me the greatest satisfaction and consolation. . . .

My son who is 21 and my daughter who is 17 now have become deeply attached to Brajesh. Everyone who knew him here was charmed with his quiet nature, with his humor, his patience, his good nature—although he was so badly sick for the last six months. . . .

I was so happy with him—notwithstanding the illness, doctors, hospitals, and all that. He'd taught me so many good things. . . . I'm so grateful to Fate that I could meet Brajesh and for three long years my life was full of him and of his love.

Svetlana[24]

Her passport was issued on November 11. She received a polite letter from Singh's nephew Dinesh Singh with an invitation to stay at his home, but he was also asking her to delay her visit until December 12, when the Indian parliament would be in recess and he would be free. Clearly Dinesh would be responsible for Svetlana.

For the month and a half she waited, Svetlana rarely left her apartment. She was guarding Singh's urn, as if she feared it might be abducted if the government changed its mind. Joseph announced that he and his girlfriend were going to get married. At the end of November, they held a short civil ceremony. Though Svetlana and Grigori Morozov, Joseph's father, had been divorced twenty years and he had remarried, he and Svetlana stood together at the ceremony, holding hands. The event was joyous. Svetlana believed Singh was present, his "cheerful soul . . . warming us."[25]

On December 19, 1966, Svetlana waited in her apartment with her son, Joseph; his wife, Elena; and her daughter, Katya, to find out if her 1:00 a.m. flight out of Sheremetyevo Airport would actually be leaving for India. The weather was terrible. Snow fell, covering the city. A blizzard was building. The phone was busy all night. She kept calling the dispatcher for updates on the flight, and friends kept calling to ask if it was really true that she had gotten permission to travel outside the USSR. It was an extraordinary privilege—to be traveling to India.

Finally her handler, a Mrs. Kassirova, from the Ministry of Foreign Affairs, showed up. There was a kerfuffle before Svetlana's departure. Joseph's wife, Elena, had grabbed Svet-lana's overnight bag to hand it to her. She'd shouted, "Don't touch that!"[26] Elena didn't know that it contained the porcelain urn carrying Brajesh's ashes. Joseph was angry at his mother's sharpness, Elena looked offended, and Svetlana was distraught. She hadn't had time to give more than a peck on the cheek to Katya. She had mismanaged her farewell.

She left for the airport around ten p.m. with her son, her friend Lily Golden, and Mrs. Kassirova. In the car, all was silence. At the airport, Svetlana was rushed to the segregated section for "passengers leaving for foreign parts." She barely had time to hug Joseph, who was brooding. She glanced be-yond the glass partition to see the sad face of her son. It was the last glimpse she would have of him for eighteen years. For his part, Joseph remarked, "I did not dream what epilogue that journey would have."[27]

And then she was on the plane with Mrs. Kassirova. Singh had always promised that she would see his village, Kalakan-kar. This was the version that fate assigned her, his urn occupying the seat beside her on the flight to India. The irony was not lost on her that, because she was Stalin's daughter—"state property," as she bitterly called herself—she had been refused permission to accompany Singh to India while he was alive but had been granted a visa to carry his ashes back to his country after he was dead.

Chapter 15

On the Banks of the Ganges

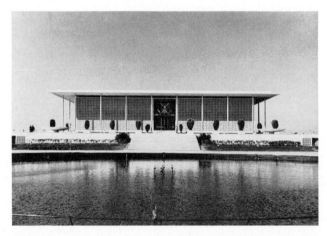

On March 6, 1967, Svetlana walked into this building—the United
States Embassy in Delhi—and announced her intention to defect.

W hen Svetlana descended from the plane in Delhi on
December 20 in the company of her minder, Mrs.
Kassirova, she found Second Secretary Surov and two other
officials from the Soviet Embassy waiting to greet her. They
whisked her underground so hurriedly that the Indian press
never got wind of her visit. Her passport, visa, and plane ticket
were confiscated. Though she had expected to stay at the home

of Brajesh's nephew Dinesh Singh, she was driven to a guest-house on the grounds of the Soviet Embassy in downtown Delhi and told this was where she was meant to stay. The room she was assigned was bare except for a bed and table. It had been sanitized—the telephone had been removed. She would have to make all phone calls at the embassy building next door, where there would be a staff to monitor her conversations.[1]

Ambassador I. A. Benediktov was currently out of town, but she was taken to meet the chargé d'affaires, Nikolai Smirnov. Breakfast was set in the embassy dining room; on the table sat a large bottle of cognac. A round of toasts was drunk to the much-loved Mr. Brajesh Singh. Svetlana was then told that plans had been altered. The situation in Delhi was unstable. The elections were looming in February, and the opposition, particularly the pro-American Swatantra Party, was mounting attacks on Mrs. Gandhi's Socialist government. It would be unwise for Svetlana to go to Kalakankar. A solemn and digni-fied ceremony would be held at the embassy, and Mr. Singh's ashes would be taken back to his village by his nephew.

Smirnov said that Mrs. Kassirova would take Svetlana shop-ping and sightseeing; she knew all the stores in Delhi. Cer-tainly Svetlana could visit the Taj Mahal. She would stay in the Soviet compound. Smirnov mentioned that Dinesh and T. M. Kaul were friendly to the Soviet government, of course, but it would be quieter and more peaceful at the guesthouse. They didn't trust Kaul. He had outraged Moscow by violating the rules for foreign diplomats that restricted their travel to a twenty-five-mile perimeter outside Moscow, and had even taken foreign visitors to Pasternak's grave in Peredelkino.[2] There was a return flight to Moscow on January 4. This would give her a comfortable two weeks.

After the overnight flight, Svetlana was exhausted, but she gathered her wits for the bargaining. She agreed to stay at the guesthouse while she was in Delhi, but only *she* could take her husband's ashes to Kalakankar. She was a guest of Dinesh Singh and Suresh Singh, longtime friends of the Nehru and Gandhi families. After a long session with Chargé d'Affaires Smirnov the next day, it was agreed that she could go to Kalakankar as long as she kept her visit a secret, avoided all contact with the press, and traveled in the company of Mrs. Kassirova. She would return to Moscow January 4.

Soon Svetlana extended her liberties. She walked in the streets around the Soviet Embassy alone, encountering locals with an insouciance she had never thought herself capable of. On one walk she noted the US Embassy, with its wide, imposing steps and Christmas trees, only a few hundred yards from the Soviet Embassy. She imagined the festivities inside and kept walking.

Expressly avoiding Mrs. Kassirova, Svetlana spent three days touring Delhi with Ambassador Kaul's daughter Preeti. The chaos of rickshaws and cyclists careening through the boulevards, street vendors selling garlands of flowers, brilliantly colored saris in cluttered shopwindows, and endless beggars importuning as they passed was like nothing she had seen before. She discovered that she was a good traveler with a keen eye and soon had a sense of the social strata in Delhi. The layering of eras and cultures, of classes—the colony of beggars outside the first-class Hotel Oberoy, the luxury vehicles, the billboards blaring the names of English films, like *Doctor Zhivago*, left her marveling. For someone who had been locked inside a single culture for forty years, this sample of another culture was intoxicating.

She visited the Kaul household and the ambassador mentioned to her that he had her manuscript. His daughter had read him the first few pages. She thanked him but did not retrieve it. Perhaps she had no plans for it, but more likely she knew her room at the Soviet compound would be searched.

On December 25, she took the flight to Lucknow, but not without some frustrations. When Dinesh, who was to accompany her, didn't show up, she insisted that Surov drive her to Dinesh's house. They were intercepted by Smirnov's limousine on the highway. He wanted her to return to the guesthouse, but she resisted. The Soviet officials were in a difficult position. They had to follow Moscow's orders but also not offend the Indians. When she reached the Singh household, Dinesh said he couldn't travel to Lucknow, but she could go with his daughter Reva. Dinesh seemed very friendly, so Svetlana took a risk. Only a few days into her visit, she asked him to tell Mrs. Gandhi that she wanted to extend her stay in India. It was an impulse. He offered to take her to Mrs. Gandhi that day, but she said she was not prepared for an interview and asked if he could put in a good word. He assured her he would and then added that Mrs. Gandhi would be traveling to Kalakankar soon to give a speech as part of her campaign for reelection.

At Lucknow airport, Svetlana and Reva, shadowed by Mrs. Kassirova, were met by the family car and driven the three hours to remote Kalakankar, an ancient village on the edge of the Ganges. They arrived at the Raj Bhavan, the Palace of the Rajah, a huge white building at the end of a long driveway. It looked like a large steamer, docked and ready to sail. A guard stood in the yard with a raised spear beside the locked gates. The palace belonged to Dinesh Singh, who had inherited the role of rajah from his father, which meant that Brajesh and his brother Suresh had in effect become the poor relations. Dinesh held public office as the local parliamentarian and headed a family foundation, while his uncles lived in comparative poverty. Even so, they were still part of the local ruling family.

As soon as Svetlana, Reva, and Mrs. Kassirova arrived, the funeral ceremony for Brajesh began. Suresh took the urn from Svetlana's arms.

A procession of men, led by Suresh, headed to the sandy shore. Only men were allowed to carry the ashes. Svetlana and the women watched from the terrace as the boats set out for the deep water. In the middle of the river, Brajesh's ashes were slowly immersed in the Ganges. Svetlana found herself weeping the tears she had held back for months.[3]

Svetlana was invited to stay at the palace but chose instead to follow Brajesh's brother Suresh to his more modest house nearby and was given the room where Brajesh had lived when he was in India. The house was crumbling, the impoverishment of its residents apparent, but the part they occupied was warm and cozy. Beside Svetlana's room was a small terrace surrounded by ashoka trees and ten-foot cacti overlooking the sandy shores of the Ganges. It was like a sanctuary. She took to sitting there for hours. Here she felt "peaceful, so utterly well."[4]

She felt as if she had returned to family. Everything was as Brajesh had described it. The beauty of the Ganges, the gardens, the dust, and all the family squabbles. She decided she would not return to Moscow on January 4 but stay in India. Her Indian visa had been stamped for one month, and the consular division in Moscow had approved this. She would insist on staying until that visa ran out on January 20. She wrote to Smirnov and Ambassador Benediktov the next morning, making her intentions clear, and told Mrs. Kassirova to take the letter to Delhi, a clever way of getting rid of her minder. Thinking her career was being jeopardized, Kassirova became hysterical but eventually complied. When Svetlana stood her ground, she was impossible to dissuade.

Svetlana had reached one of those transformative moments that seemed to recur in her life. After the exhaustion and sorrows of the last three years, the intrusions and constraints on her private life, she had reached a limit. This would be a turning point, though where she would turn was not yet clear. Her hope was that she would be allowed to live in Kalakankar. But how? She thought of her manuscript. Perhaps she could sell it. It was not, she believed, political; it was a family memoir, and yet she knew there would be intense public interest. The family she was talking about was Stalin's. She wrote to Kaul, saying she intended to stay longer in Kalakankar and asking him to send the manuscript to her.

Suresh and his wife were deeply moved at how easily Svetlana adapted to their way of life. When asked by a journalist to characterize Svetlana, Suresh said:

> She was, after all, the daughter of the one-time ruler of Russia, and we thought that perhaps we lived too simply here. But Svetlana is the simplest of women. She has not the slightest pretensions or airs about her. She would take household chores upon herself that my own wife is not accustomed to do. We have servants, but Svetlana washed and pressed her own clothing, helped clean and cut up vegetables and was not the least trouble to us. We hope she will come back. We learned to love her, and we believe she loves us.[5]

Svetlana entered wholeheartedly into Indian life, wearing a sari and eating the family's vegetarian food. She walked about the village and visited with Brajesh's old friends, but she had no illusions about the complexities and compromises of life in India. She found the caste system, with its seemingly ineradicable rules, disturbing. However run-down Suresh's house was, his wife, Prakash, still had a retinue of servants, each with duties assigned by caste. Only the cook, who was a Brahman, could cook; another servant brought him the food, but was not permitted to cook; he also washed the dishes. Two indoor servants served at meals, but could not eat the same food; they also ironed the clothes; an untouchable washed the floor and cleaned the bathrooms. It was absurd, but everyone respected the tradition. When Svetlana tried to wash her own clothes, the servants concluded she was of "common origin" and therefore, to her amusement, treated her in a friendly manner. Still, it was impossible to walk through the village and not see the poverty. She resolved to found a small local hospital in Brajesh's name, if she was permitted to stay and if she sold her manuscript. She was frustrated that Kaul had not sent it.

She wrote to Paris to Louba Krassin, the wife of the publisher Emmanuel d'Astier, who had visited her on at least four occasions in Moscow. She told Krassin she was in India and didn't want to return to the USSR. Did she think there was a possibility of publishing her book abroad? Sending such a letter was a risk, but it seemed safer than asking anyone in India. A few days later, she received a cryptic telegram from Paris: YES, POSSIBLE.[6]

Within the week, Second Secretary Surov traveled to Kalakankar to bring Svetlana back. She was not to be persuaded. He reluctantly returned to Delhi without her.

Meanwhile, Mrs. Gandhi's visit to the village was scheduled for January 16. Svetlana was determined to meet her, but suddenly she was receiving letters from Kaul to return to Delhi. Dinesh was avoiding her. She felt the reason was that the Soviet Embassy did not want her to meet the Indian prime minister. She wrote an angry letter to Kaul, asking why he had not sent the manuscript. Had he given it to the Soviet Embassy? This was typical of Svetlana. Whenever she thought the machinations of Moscow were operating, she lashed out in anger at anyone she supposed might be involved. Kaul was offended and wrote back testily. If she thought he could betray her trust, their friendship was over. He was probably being sincere, because if the Russian embassy officials had known of the manuscript's existence, they would have escorted her immediately out of India.

Svetlana told Dinesh she planned to stay to the end of her visa, January 20, and then take the next plane back to Moscow. Because there was only one flight a week, this meant that her departure date would be January 26. In the company of Suresh Singh's wife, Prakash, she did manage to meet Indira Gandhi when Mrs. Gandhi was campaigning in the area. When Svetlana expressed her desire to stay in the country, the prime minister was surprised but wished her luck. It was clear to Svetlana that Dinesh had never spoken to her. It was also clear that if the Soviets refused her request to stay on, the Indian government would not jeopardize relations with them by helping her. The whole thing was a show. Now Svetlana decided to advance the argument that by law Soviet citizens visiting relatives may extend their visas by two or three months. She would write to Kosygin.

While in Kalakankar, Svetlana read on her balcony overlooking the Ganges. One of the books she picked up from Suresh's library was *Ambassador's Report* by the American Chester Bowles. She was totally captivated. Bowles's knowledge of India was inspiring, as was his reverence for Mahatma Gandhi.[7] She was so enthusiastic about the book that Suresh's family began to talk of a new plan. The Singhs' son worked in Seattle as an engineer. Why didn't she go to the United States? Then she could become an American citizen and return to India.

Svetlana became alarmed. If word leaked back to the Soviet Embassy of such an idea, she would be in grave trouble. And anyway, it wasn't yet *her* idea. She dismissed this talk, saying it was absolutely not a step she would ever take. But the thought embedded itself in her mind. If only she could talk with Ambassador Chester Bowles. She began to visualize the embassy building back in Delhi, which she had passed so casually a month before. The idea "hovered, reappearing again and again, recalling itself to me with unexpected tenacity."[8]

Second Secretary Surov returned to Kalakankar a third time and, repulsed again, sent her letter asking to stay directly to Moscow. It was a pointless gesture, she knew, but it delayed her departure. Finally Dinesh delivered her manuscript from Kaul. He was intensely curious about it. His wife had told him Svetlana had sent a letter to Paris. He asked if her intention was to send the manuscript to a French publisher. She was evasive. She warned him, however, that if the embassy officials knew of her manuscript, they would immediately confiscate it. He replied, "Are you sure they don't already know about it?" She assured him that Kaul had said nothing.[9]

Out of the blue, Dinesh Singh told her he didn't think the Americans would help her, though of course they'd publish the book and turn it into a movie. He said he knew Ambassador Bowles personally and found him charming, but that was not the right route to take. Clearly his wife had been relaying the household gossip. Svetlana assured him that all she wanted was to stay longer in India before returning to the USSR. She had sent a formal request to that effect. "It may work," he said. She felt that Dinesh looked relieved.[10]

Again Second Secretary Surov visited. He said that she had already overstayed her travel permit. She had done what she had come to do. The Indian Ministry of Foreign Affairs had prolonged her visa to March 15. She must fly out of India on March 8.

Svetlana was still equivocating. Part of her wanted to begin a new life. Part of her was terrified at the prospect. How could she live? Was she counting too much on her manuscript as her ticket out? She was thinking of her children. Could she part from them? If she left the USSR, she would never be allowed to return, and things would have to change immeasurably there before her children would be permitted to visit her.

She thought of the loving letter she had just received from

her son: "Mama, my dear, hello! . . . Here everything is in good shape. With the documents you sent us, we obtained coupons for ready-cooked dinners. Everything is well, except that Katya misses you terribly. I too miss you very much and want to see you."[11]

Finally she agreed to go back to Delhi with Surov. As she was getting into the jeep to leave Kalakankar, she glanced back at the village and told Suresh Singh that one day she would return. He smiled warmly. He didn't understand that this would be possible only if she decided never to return to her family and her country.

Arriving in Delhi on March 5, she was met by Dinesh Singh, who had become extremely friendly—he seemed delighted that she was finally leaving. He assured her that next year he would invite her and her children back to Delhi. She was skeptical. After she had so long delayed her return, the Soviets would not allow her out again. Although he offered her the run of his house until her departure on March 8, she said she preferred to stay at the embassy guesthouse.

She spent the evening of March 5 at the home of Ambassador Kaul and his family. It was an anxious evening for Svetlana. He, too, seemed glad to be getting rid of her. Oddly enough, he asked whether she had her manuscript with her. It was a curious question. Instinctively she replied that she had sent it to Paris. She was terrified lest the Soviet Embassy should learn of its existence and take it from her or that Kaul would somehow intuit the plan that was slowly forming in her mind—could she possibly go to the US Embassy?

The morning of March 6, she was picked up by Surov, who drove her to the guesthouse, where everything was in chaos. The embassy was preparing for the celebration of International Women's Day. There would be a lecture and an artistic program. The thought of a vodka-filled evening appalled her. The embassy women in the yard were talking of shopping, of all the things they would buy and then sell on the black market in Moscow. It was always the same.

Surov took her to lunch at Ambassador Benediktov's home. The meal was elaborate, but she barely touched the food, having become accustomed to her Indian diet. Benediktov was contemptuous of her vegetarianism, which he considered an affectation, and railed about India's backwardness. He, too, would be glad to be rid of her. He invited her to their soiree for International Women's Day. She replied that she had promised to dine with the Kauls. "That English agent!" he had said. But it was an automatic response. The Indian press considered Kaul to be in the pocket of the Soviet Embassy.

Benediktov congratulated her on the success of her stay and himself on the "concessions" they had made: "It seems to me you have nothing to complain about." Svetlana held back the retort that was on the tip of her tongue. She needed to ask this man for her passport. "Well here I am," she said, "all packed with gifts for my family. Now may I have my passport and papers returned to me?"[12] To her shock, Benediktov commanded Surov to fetch them. This was against regulations. Passports were to be given back to Soviet citizens only at the airport. This mistake can be explained only by Benediktov's relief that Svetlana was apparently leaving. She had played her part well.

She returned to her guesthouse at three p.m. Her first idea was to dine with the Kauls and go to the American Embassy the next morning. She packed her large suitcase with the manuscript and the bag of presents. She went out to the Indian watchman and asked how to call a taxi. He showed her where the telephone box was: outside, under the staircase. She would phone a taxi the next morning after breakfast. She was certain no one suspected her plan.

She paced the room. She ironed the scarf she had received

from Preeti Kaul. She gazed at the presents she had bought for her children. She worked on logistics. Her coat over her left arm, dragging her big suitcase, the taxi call.

Suddenly it occurred to her. Why wait? It must be now. Otherwise, she might change her mind. In the morning, there would be people about. She would lose her nerve. It would be better to leave under cover of darkness. The Soviet Embassy was holding a reception to honor Marshal Matvei Zakharov, chief of staff of the Russian armed forces.[13] The International Women's Day party was already in full swing at the embassy club. Everyone would be getting drunker. Benediktov and his staff assumed she was dining with the Kauls. No one would look for her. She would leave tonight.

She decided to take only her small suitcase, in which she packed a guesthouse towel, the soap dish, a pair of shoes, a summer coat, and the bag in which she had carried the urn of Brajesh Singh's ashes. Into this she put her manuscript.[14] She unpacked her large suitcase, scattering its contents about, so that to anyone looking into her room, it would appear as if she were still in the process of packing. On the bed lay her presents for her children: a hookah from Benares and gold embroidered slippers for Joseph and his wife, bracelets from Lucknow for Katya. She doubted they would ever get those presents, and for a moment, her resolution faltered.[15]

It was shortly after six p.m. She went to call the taxi. It was dark under the stairs. She fumbled at the numbers. The dispatcher asked where she was. The Russian Embassy? No, the Russian Guesthouse.

She waited at the gate. No taxi came. Embassy guests passed in cars. Her terror built; she was afraid that Preeti would arrive to pick her up for dinner, that she would be noticed loitering. Everything would fall apart. After twenty minutes, she phoned again. A cab appeared. She returned to the guesthouse for her small suitcase and then climbed into the backseat. "Do you know the American Embassy?" she asked. "Why, yes," the driver said, surprised, "it's just nearby." But as if he understood what she was up to, he first turned into a dark alley, passed the Soviet compound, and only then entered the long driveway of the US Embassy. She glanced at the beautiful pool. Suddenly she was standing at the bottom of the wide staircase. She climbed it on shaky legs. The young marine guard got up from his desk and unlocked the door. As he tried to explain that the embassy was closed at this hour, she showed him her Soviet passport. Without speaking he led her to a small room, sat her down, and told her to wait. Then he disappeared into the far reaches of the building.

PART THREE

Flight *to* America

Chapter 16

Italian Comic Opera

The CIA officer Robert Rayle, posted to the embassy in Delhi, was charged with spiriting Svetlana out of India before the Soviets discovered that she had defected.

T he ten-hour time difference between Washington and New Delhi worked in Svetlana's favor. She was already in the air on her way to Rome when the diplomatic machinery in Washington went into overdrive. Undersecretary of State Foy Kohler was obviously angry at Ambassador Bowles's precipitate decision to help the defector. He began damage control immediately.

On March 6, Secretary of State Dean Rusk sent a secret flash telegram to Llewellyn Thompson, the US ambassador to the Soviet Union, to inform him that Svetlana Iosifovna Stalin, daughter of Joseph Stalin, had requested asylum in the United States. She was traveling on an open ticket to Rome in the company of an embassy officer. She had no reservation beyond Rome. Rusk explained:

> Ambassador Reinhardt [US ambassador to Italy] has been advised that we feel it would be undesirable for Svetlana to proceed to the US, both politically and from point of view of her own security. We consider it urgent that every effort be made arrange other safer asylum in Switzerland, Spain, or Italy and have asked Ambassador Reinhardt to make every effort to have her persuaded that such a course [is] in her best interest.[1]

Dean Rusk phoned President Lyndon Johnson at 4:30 p.m. that day to brief him on the situation.[2]

On March 7, Ambassador Llewellyn Thompson sent a return telegram from Moscow to advise Dean Rusk: "The more we can disengage from this operation the better from point of view of our relations with Soviets. They will in any event blame U.S. for facilitating subject's departure from India and possibly charge us with kidnapping."[3]

Svetlana's timing was terrible. Though she may have been the most famous defector ever to denounce Communism and, under different circumstances, would have been an invaluable propaganda tool in the Cold War standoff between the United States and the USSR, she had chosen the wrong moment. The

Johnson administration was in the midst of ratifying a consular convention with the Soviets.[4]

The convention was intended to establish consular functions in both countries. It would give full immunity from criminal prosecution to consular officers and staff, and ensure the protection of nationals. Each government would be notified of the arrest of one of its citizens within two or three days. At that time, a US citizen visiting the USSR could be held incommunicado for nine months or more awaiting charges. Approximately eighteen thousand Americans traveled on business or tourist visas to the USSR annually. But the ratification of the convention, first signed in 1964, had been rough. A bloc of senators had stalled it, citing the Red peril and suggesting it would open vast opportunities for Russian secret agents to operate in the United States. At that very moment, the treaty was being debated in the Senate, and the last thing Rusk and his staff wanted was a famous defector derailing the process.

How seriously both governments took the treaty is clear from the gestures of goodwill each offered. A few months earlier, a young Arkansan, Buel R. Wortham, had been sentenced to three years in a Russian labor camp on charges of "changing dollars into black market rubles, and stealing a cast-iron bear from a Leningrad hotel." On March 11, five days after Svetlana's defection, the Soviet Court of Appeal reversed the sentence, releasing Wortham with a fine of 5,000 rubles. On the American side, Igor Ivanov, a Soviet agent convicted of spying in 1964 and sentenced to twenty years' imprisonment, was currently on bail pending an appeal for executive clemency. The Soviet ambassador to the United States, Anatoly Dobrynin, had made it clear that because of the reversal on Wortham's case, the Soviet Union expected a "certain amount of credit" toward clemency for Ivanov.[5]

Aleksei Kosygin, chairman of the Council of Ministers, was set to arrive in the United States in late June for discussions on everything from the Mideast to the Vietnam War to arms control. Détente was in the air. Svetlana was not just an inconvenience; she was a threat. Harboring this high-profile defector might set things back irrevocably. The Johnson administration didn't need her on its hands. She had to be contained.

Even as Bob Rayle and Svetlana were in midflight, the CIA station chief in Rome called the head of the Italian intelligence service, Admiral Eugenio Henke, to say that the CIA had a defector coming in and needed the Italians' help. "You wake me up in the middle of the night to tell me that?" Henke had replied. "Yah, well, let me tell you who it is," the CIA head replied. Henke was furious. "OK," he said, "she can come in, but she's got to leave tomorrow."[6] He said he'd wait until the morning to tell the minister of foreign affairs, Amintore Fanfani, who would not be pleased. The Communists at that time had a strong delegation in the Italian parliament and, if urged on by the Soviets, could make a lot of trouble for the Christian coalition government in power.

As Bob Rayle and Svetlana stepped off the Qantas flight in Rome at six a.m. on March 7, Rayle was convinced that this was just a stopover and that they would proceed immediately to the United States. He was shocked, then, when the deputy chief of his office in Rome met them at the arrivals gate with the bad news.

Rayle was informed that the State Department was categorically refusing to allow Svetlana to proceed to the United States. Foy Kohler was claiming that relations with the USSR were warming up. There was even the possibility of a *thaw*. Rayle and many of his colleagues believed that this thaw was "wishful thinking and existed mostly in Kohler's imagination."[7] But Kohler's decision meant that Svetlana was grounded. From the airport, Rayle and Svetlana were conducted to a safe house, a small apartment in Rome, where they settled in to wait.

When Admiral Henke informed Fanfani that morning that Stalin's daughter had landed in Italy, Fanfani exploded. "Get those people out of this country immediately and I don't want there to be any evidence that they were actually in the country." Admiral Henke replied, "OK, technically we'll say that the International Transit at the airport in Rome is extended to include the international apartment where they are temporarily housed."[8] By this ruse, Svetlana and Rayle would never *legally* be in Italy.

During the next few days, the State Department contacted the governments of Australia and New Zealand, but both refused Svetlana asylum. South Africa was willing to take her in, but given its history of apartheid, she refused to consider it.

As Svetlana and Rayle waited in their safe house guarded by Italian security officers, word came from the Swiss that they would consider accepting Svetlana for a short term. In keeping with their tradition of neutrality, they insisted that her visit remain private and that she make no political statements. This condition of silence was exactly what the State Department wanted. Walt Rostow, special assistant to the president, wrote to President Johnson: "About the lady, we can relax. Switzerland has agreed to take her."[9]

But the Swiss decision could not be confirmed until the Swiss Council (or cabinet) met, which took several days. The Italians were furious at the delay, but as Rayle put it, "Admiral Henke was unwilling to arrest us and deport us."[10] The State Department promised the Italians that if the Swiss didn't come through by Friday morning, the two fugitives would leave immediately for the United States.

Over the next few days, Rayle and Svetlana became friends. Their Italian flat had a small sitting room and one bedroom, assigned to Svetlana, and the phone rang constantly. With each phone call, Rayle looked paler and more distraught, but he was pleasantly surprised by Svetlana's tranquillity. She later said, "I had been trained not to make decisions for myself, to wait and to be patient, above all to remain well-mannered."

Rayle was amused that every morning Stalin's daughter made him breakfast, prepared meals from the groceries delivered by the security guard, and washed the dishes. When they had Chianti for dinner, she recalled that her father had loved good wines and knew all the best brands and years. He found her very intelligent. She was "not spoiled or demanding," as one might expect of the princess in the Kremlin. Though the boredom in the apartment was excruciating, they had good laughs together.

She told Rayle that her defection had been an impulsive act taken in rage and frustration. Had she returned home, she was certain she would have been punished for her deliberate disobedience in extending her stay in India. Her passport would have been confiscated. With her defection, she had slapped the Soviet government in the face. She had fooled them all. But she now began to think of the revenge the Soviets might exact.

Rayle watched her fall into moments of deep sadness as she spoke of her son, Joseph, and her daughter, Katya, whom she had left behind. She had convinced herself they would be all right.

In a dark moment, she sat down and wrote them a six-page letter:

MARCH 9, 1967

My Dearest Children, Kate, Helen [Joe's wife Elena], and Joe!

I am afraid that all sorts of lies will be told to you—and

to everybody—about me. Perhaps you will be told that I'd become mad, or that I've been kidnapped, or that I am no more. Do not believe anything. I want to explain myself how the decision not to return to Russia has come to me. I did never expect to do so when I was leaving Moscow in December. Then I have not even taken your photographs with me. . . .

I could live in Russia—as many others are doing—being a hypocrite, hiding my true opinions. More than a half of our people live like that. We have no opportunity to criticize, we have no press, no freedoms, and also nobody wants to risk. Everyone has a family, children, a job, which is too dangerous to lose. I've lived like that for many years and could live still longer—but the fate has made me to do my resolute choice. . . .

My husband's death changed my nature. I feel it impossible to be silent and tolerant anymore. It is impossible to be always a slave. . . . My sweet darlings . . . please keep peace in your hearts. I am only doing what my conscience orders me to do.

Your mother[11]

When Svetlana asked the Americans to send her letter to her children, she was told it was too political. The letter was never delivered.

Meanwhile, the *New York Times'* reporter in New Delhi, Tony Lucas, had been piecing together the story. Through anonymous sources, he discovered that, in the early hours of March 7, Svetlana had flown out of India in the company of someone said to be the US Embassy second secretary, Robert Rayle. By checking the passenger manifest for all flights out of New Delhi, he concluded that Svetlana and her escort were in Rome. Obviously he wasn't the only journalist to do so.

At three a.m. on Friday, Rayle and Svetlana were awoken with the news that the international press had tracked them down to Rome. The Italians wanted them gone. They waited for the next five hours to be moved out. Finally they left for the airport under guard and were just about to board the 3:00 p.m. flight to London and on to America, when Rayle phoned a friend at the embassy to say good-bye. "Don't get on the plane," his colleague said. The Swiss had come through.[12]

They were to meet the Swiss consul at the airport at 8:00 p.m. to get Svetlana's visa. A young woman from the US Embassy brought her a dark green raincoat; dark sunglasses, which she refused to wear; and a small red suitcase for her few clothes and her manuscript. Because she was not legally in Italy, she could not step on Italian soil and so could only glance at the passing sights of Rome from the car window as they drove to the airport, she and Rayle laughing and singing "Arrivederci, Roma."[13]

Svetlana must have thought she was in a film. Obtaining her visa turned into a car chase. Two cars, she in one and the Swiss consul in the other, circled the flowerbed in front of the airport for what seemed ages until finally she was transferred to the other car. A secretary with a bottle of ink and a rubber stamp stamped her visa, joking about the undercover operation. She returned to her car. But Swissair Flight 615 to Geneva was four hours late. Svetlana and Rayle retreated to the safe house to wait.

Then the movie became a farce. When she and Rayle returned to the airport, international journalists and photographers were swarming the terminal. A TV film truck had managed to turn its floodlights on the departure gate. Afraid that Rayle and Svetlana might be photographed together, the Italians insisted they board the plane separately.

Rayle slipped through immigration and onto the plane easily, but when the car carrying Svetlana arrived at the gate, it was swarmed by paparazzi, and the car turned back. A new plan was hatched. Svetlana would be smuggled to the plane in one of the small tractors that pull the baggage carts. She squeezed in behind the nervous driver.

But as the tractor approached the plane, an Italian official rushed toward it. There were too many reporters. *Back, back,* he gestured wildly, and the distraught driver swerved, the engine stalled, and, once it was going again, they headed across the empty tarmac to the other side of the airfield. Meanwhile Rayle was standing at the open door of the plane, refusing to budge until his "wife" boarded. "My wife went to the ladies room in the terminal and hasn't come back. We have to wait for her," he said. The portable stairs were wheeled away, but Rayle planted himself at the open hatch and refused to move. He managed to delay the flight for fifteen minutes. Finally an Italian security officer gestured to him. Svetlana would not be boarding. The stairs were returned and Rayle disembarked, fearing that the Italians had arrested Svetlana.[14]

He was taken to a room in the basement of the terminal where about forty security officers were swarming. The colonel in charge was madly shouting into a phone. Eventually Rayle learned that the baggage handler had driven Svetlana to a warehouse on the edge of the airport and abandoned her in an empty hangar.[15]

Alone in the dark hangar, Svetlana found a door and walked into what looked like an airport storehouse, where she sat crouched in a stairwell and waited in the eerie silence for almost an hour. Awake since three a.m., she was exhausted and truly frightened. When Rayle found her, though they embraced and laughed, her composure had finally dissolved. The two found refuge in the apartment of a local police officer and waited. The worst news was that her small red suitcase with her manuscript had been checked onto the plane and was already on its way to Geneva.[16]

The frustrated Italians were so anxious to get rid of their unwanted charges that they demanded the Americans charter a plane. A Vickers Viscount airliner was stationed in a far, dark corner of the airfield, ready for the flight to Geneva. Apart from the full crew, Rayle and Svetlana were the only passengers on that 1:00 a.m. flight. This would be her first trip into Europe. Rome didn't count. She was never *officially* in Rome.

On the plane to Geneva, Rayle kept repeating that he wanted to show Svetlana "Washington, the Lincoln Memorial, everything." In fact, he said this to reassure her; he had little hope of her getting to Washington soon.[17] He gave her some pertinent advice. She must not admit that she had ever left the international transit lounge in Rome; if the press pestered her with difficult questions, she must simply say, "No comment." She must not accept the first publisher who wanted her book but instead get the best possible deal. As Rayle wrote to his superiors, "She plans to support herself in the West as a writer so this manuscript right now is all that stands between her and the poorhouse."[18]

On Friday, March 10, the *New York Times* published the first of many stories. Citing unidentified sources, the article was tentative:

> Svetlana Stalina, the daughter of Stalin, was reported to have left the Soviet Union for good. . . . Some reports indicated that she may be in danger. She was said to be seeking visas and may have approached United States officials in New Delhi. It could not be determined why she left the Soviet Union.[19]

Svetlana was still a mysterious figure, and there were many errors in the piece. It was claimed that she had married Mikhail

Kaganovich, son of the Politburo member Lazar Kaganovich, in 1951 in a wedding that cost $280,000 and that after Stalin's death, she had been banished from Moscow. The American Embassy in Delhi and the State Department refused to comment.

But there was soon another dimension to the story. Tony Lucas of the *New York Times* discovered through anonymous sources that Robert Rayle was an undercover CIA officer. Lucas phoned the US Embassy in Delhi and said that if he didn't receive a disclaimer, he would file the story.[20] The embassy refused to comment. Bob Rayle's cover as second secretary was blown. Svetlana's defection in the company of a CIA officer soon became headline news around the world.

When Rayle later submitted a mandatory report to the State Department on the defector's "personality" and her "adaptability to different environments," he described Svetlana as "the most completely cooperative defector I have ever met." He said she'd remained cheerful and optimistic throughout the week as they waited in the safe house, even as she took in the shock that the Americans were refusing her asylum. As Rayle put it, "She recognizes that she cannot be considered a normal, ordinary human being and that her actions have political implications. . . . You'll find her a warm, friendly person who responds to warmth and friendliness. I think you'll find her genuinely likeable." He added, "She is a very stable person."[21] But he warned that she seemed quite naive, as if she'd never lived "in any real world," and would need help in finding her way in the West.

In the early morning hours of March 11, Svetlana "stepped over the invisible boundary between the world of tyranny and the world of freedom."[22] Of course, it could never be that simple. The strange journey of the second half of her life was about to begin, but if she hoped to escape the shadow of her father's name, she was tragically mistaken.

Chapter 17

Diplomatic Fury

Because he had been the US ambassador to the Soviet Union at the time of Stalin's death, the diplomat George Kennan, photographed here in 1966, was given responsibility for Svetlana as she began her new life in the United States.

Early in the morning on Friday, March 10, the first and second secretaries of the Soviet Embassy in New Delhi arrived at the Singh estate in Kalakankar. They said Svetlana had disappeared from the Soviet compound and demanded to know where she was. Brajesh Singh's brother Suresh said that he hadn't the least idea. Just then the caretaker of the estate rushed in to say the BBC was reporting Svetlana had reached Rome. The face of the first secretary blanched in terror.

"Now we're through! We're done for! Oh, my God!"

"So you do believe in God after all, don't you?" Suresh teased.

"Please, Lal Suresh," the first secretary said. "This is terrible. I cannot discuss God just now!"[1]

This is the story Suresh Singh liked to tell, and it may have been true, but Moscow already knew that Svetlana had left India. Perhaps the secretaries had rushed to Kalakankar hoping against hope that it was all a mistake and she might have returned there. Her defection was on *their* heads. They had shown insufficient vigilance. Had Stalin been alive, they would have been shot.

Behind the scenes, international shuttlecock diplomacy moved at a frenzied pace. In New Delhi, Ambassador Chester Bowles received a letter dated March 9 from Mr. Chandra Shekhar Jha, Indian foreign secretary in the Ministry of Foreign Affairs. Its contents and the ambassador's response were precisely recorded:

MARCH 9, 1967

The Ministry of External Affairs presents its compliments to the Embassy of the United States of America and has the honour to inform the Embassy that it has come to the knowledge of the Government of India that Madame Svetlana Aluleva [*sic*], a Soviet citizen, who had been on a visit to India and was about to return to the Soviet Union, was given a United States visa and a plane ticket and was escorted to the United States by an officer of the US Embassy . . . in full knowledge that she was an important personality.

The Ministry of External Affairs wishes to point out that the above action taken by the US Embassy in such haste without giving any inkling to the Ministry of such impending action, is a source of serious embarrassment to the government of India. . . . The Government of the Soviet Union have strongly protested to us about what they have characterized as kidnapping of Madame Svetlana Aluleva, a Soviet citizen, by the US Authorities here. . . .

Having regard to all the circumstances of this case . . . the Government of India strongly urge that Madame Svetlana Aluleva be immediately sent back to Delhi. On her return to India, the Government of India will deal with her in an appropriate manner consistent with international law and practice.[2]

Luckily for Svetlana, Ambassador Bowles was mostly on her side. The next day, March 10, he wrote to Jha in a "frank and informal way" responding to what he characterized as Jha's "secret protest note," the contents of which were "in no way justified by the facts."[3] Bowles replied that "Mme. Aluleva [*sic*] had entered the embassy on her own initiative." No one at the embassy even knew of her existence. She had a valid passport, and her departure had been entirely legal. Numerous employees at the airport could attest to the fact that there had been no coercion. Any attempt by the USSR to suggest otherwise would be "demonstrably false and malicious."

Bowles assured Jha that, in making his decision, he'd had India's best interests in mind. If Svetlana had gone to the press as she threatened, India would have been in the middle of a diplomatic nightmare. He'd helped her on her way in accordance "with American tradition stretching back to our earliest years as a nation."

This was all in the style of diplomatic damage control. However, at the end of the National Archives and Records Administration (NARA) file containing Bowles's letter to Jha is attached a disconcerting note, written several days later, containing gossip that the American ambassador in Moscow had collected from a UPI reporter's poker game.

FROM MOSCOW, 13 MARCH 1967

Ambassador reports following possibly useful background. Pls pass to appropriate persons in Department. Shapiro comment made in course casual conversation at weekly poker game evening 12 March. Shapiro said he had interviewed children and sent story.

From Ambassador: Shapiro of UPI says Svetlana Stalin reputed to be a nymphomaniac. He says her children convinced mother will return and think possible she mentally upset by death of husband. Shapiro says she was comfortably well off by Soviet standards and that children attractive and appear fond of her.

END OF MESSAGE[4]

The gossip that Svetlana was a nymphomaniac was the kind of helpful information that could be filed away for future use if the game got dirty. The initial reaction of the USSR to Svetlana's flight was controlled silence, but soon it had to respond publicly. News of her defection was reaching the Soviet people through Radio Free Europe and on the grapevine, and the regime was worried.[5] Svetlana was reportedly carrying a book she'd written. What did she know? It was not likely that her father would have let his daughter in on state secrets, but what gossip might she offer about the current leaders? She knew all their stories. Soviet state television reported coolly:

In reply to the enquiries of journalists, it is confirmed that Svetlana Alliluyeva, the daughter of Joseph Vissa- rionovich Stalin, is out of the country. In 1966 she was given an exit visa for New Delhi in order to accompany the remains of her deceased husband, an Indian citizen who died in the Soviet Union. How long Svetlana Alllilu- yeva will remain outside our country is her concern only.[6]

The same brief notice appeared in *Pravda*. Any Soviet cit- izens reading this would have seen through the lie. None of them were free to travel as they wished. Had she read it, Svet- lana would have responded bitterly. *Now* the government called Brajesh her husband.

At first the Soviet authorities had been unable to believe that Svetlana had fled and actually searched to see if somehow she had slipped back into Moscow. According to her cousin Leonid Alliluyev, the KGB came to his and his wife's apartment in the House on the Embankment and, in their absence, questioned his mother-in-law. But for most of the family, there were no immediate repercussions. As Leonid Alliluyev put it, "When Svetlana left, the only person in our government who made a comment was Kosygin . . . a few words and that was all. This is why they were the authorities. They did not speak of anything that was not supposed to be spoken about."[7]

Of course, that was publicly. Behind the scenes, the Polit- buro and the KGB were already planning their revenge against Svetlana and the Americans. They were certain that this de- fection was a US conspiracy initiated to embarrass the Soviet government on the soon-to-be-celebrated fiftieth anniversary of the Russian Revolution. The regime was determined to get back at Svetlana in whatever way it could. Secret telegrams to Dean Rusk, the secretary of state, flew from American embas- sies as far-flung as Tehran and Hong Kong, reporting rumors that Soviet plans were being set in motion for defamation of her personally, and of her book.[8]

When Svetlana and Robert Rayle descended onto the tarmac at Geneva airport—the only two passengers to exit the plane—they were spirited away from reporters shouting questions. Reunited with her little red suitcase containing her manuscript, Svetlana was reminded of the conditions of her stay: no political statements. But her arrival was world news, and every journalist wanted the story. The CBS reporter Marvin Kalb stayed in Switzerland for three weeks, longer than any of the others, but he never got close to Svetlana. "There was lots of intentional lying in Switzerland," he reflected in retrospect.[9]

Svetlana was driven to an inn at Beatenberg near the Jungfrau, in the Bernese Alps, and given papers under the name Fräulein Carlen, with the story that she was an Irishwoman recently arrived from India.[10] It was an absurd ruse. Even if she could talk about India and supposedly had been away from her native Ireland too long to remember it, it is hard to imagine her Russian-accented English being taken for an Irish accent. Alone in the dining room of the inn, she listened to the radio announcing, in crisp German, the defection of Stalin's daughter. She missed Robert Rayle. At the Geneva airport, he'd immediately jumped into a waiting car, which was chased to the French border by eager reporters. By now he was already on his way back to India. When he arrived home, he would find a dinner invitation from Ambassador Chester Bowles waiting for him and his wife. The ambassador was making it clear, particularly to the Indian authorities, that he stood behind Rayle 100 percent.[11]

The US State Department handed responsibility for Svetlana over to the Swiss, who insisted that the Americans stay in the background, at arm's length. Antonino Janner, the fifty-year-old chief of the East European section of the Swiss

Foreign Ministry, took charge. As it became clear that international journalists were zeroing in on Beatenberg, Svetlana was whisked off to a hospice run by Catholic nuns as a rest home for priests at Saint Antoni, then to the Visitacion de Saint Marie, a convent near Fribourg, where her identity remained mysterious. The nuns were instructed not to ask. She had just seen *The Sound of Music* in Delhi and must have felt that she was in a trailer for the movie.[12] Fribourg Canton plainclothes policemen assigned to her as bodyguards took her on sightseeing ventures and allowed her to drive their Volkswagen Beetle. Her first response was euphoria. "I had a feeling of wonder that I had escaped the Soviets! This I will recall even when I am dead," she later told a friend.[13]

Hundreds of letters from strangers, some addressed simply *Switzerland*, began to arrive, many with propositions of marriage. A former Soviet circus performer, now an Australian citizen, offered to marry her, as did an English naval officer. The owner of a motorboat in Florida, indignant she had not been granted immediate entry into the United States, invited her to stay with his family.[14]

On Friday, March 10, ex-ambassador George Kennan received a phone call. Donald (Jamie) Jameson, an expert on Russia at the CIA and Kennan's friend, was on the line. Jamie said, "We have a tremendous defection here."[15] He wanted Kennan to read a manuscript and tell him what he thought of it. It was, of course, Svetlana's *Twenty Letters to a Friend*. The CIA had made multiple copies of it in Rome. Jameson asked if, having read it, Kennan would be willing to fly to Geneva to meet Svetlana. The CIA needed a civilian because the Swiss wouldn't permit any American officials to visit her.

It was Chester Bowles's suggestion that Kennan be selected to take charge of Svetlana. Bowles had written to Dean Rusk that they should see "[Svetlana] as an opportunity to enable us to promote our policy objectives." But someone like Kennan was needed to keep her in line and encourage her to "see herself in a special position to help improve relationships between the USSR and USA." Kennan should also give her advice about a publisher. "Since she needs money badly, she is likely to settle with the wrong people on the wrong basis," Bowles said.[16]

George Kennan was indeed the right man. He had a long, romantic attachment to Russia and served briefly as ambassador to the Soviet Union before Stalin expelled him in 1952. He was the author of the American postwar policy of containment of the Soviet empire. The Soviets should be left free to operate within their own sphere of influence, essentially the Eastern bloc, as long as they didn't challenge American supremacy. He was certain that Communism would eventually self-destruct from its own paranoia and inefficiency. Shortly after the formation of the CIA in 1947, he'd advised the agency to work specifically with Soviet defectors and expatriates to counter the USSR's dirty tricks in international espionage.[17] Having retired from the diplomatic service, he was currently a faculty member at the Institute for Advanced Study in Princeton, and therefore technically a civilian, but he still had close ties to the US government.

Now Kennan was about to read a book by the most unexpected defector of all. When Svetlana's manuscript finally arrived in the United States and was delivered to him on March 16, though he was ill in bed, he read it through the night. He was deeply moved. He thought it was a brilliant book that would be of interest to hundreds of thousands. He went down to Washington the next day to meet Attorney General Nicholas Katzenbach.

Though Kennan had lived in the Soviet Union for nine years, Svetlana had been so well hidden within the Kremlin that he'd never encountered her. Clearly the idea of meeting her excited him, but he also saw her as a problem. He told Katzenbach that if the government brought her to the United States poverty stricken, it would have to put her up in a safe house. However, if her book was sold in advance, she would arrive with money in her pocket and not as a ward of the government.[18]

Chester Bowles was now suggesting to the president's assistant, Walt Rostow, that Svetlana should be viewed not as a potential time bomb, but rather as an asset. She just needed to be persuaded to rewrite her book. "If, after dealing with the Stalin years, her emphasis were on the new more liberal Soviet generation and hopes that it can develop a more cooperative relationship with America, the favorable impact could be very great."[19] He thought Kennan was exactly the man to persuade her. But Svetlana had just witnessed this "new liberal regime" condemn Andrei Sinyavsky and Yuli Daniel to hard labor in prison camps for publishing books. She would have asked the Americans what universe they were living in.

Kennan believed that if the book was sold, Svetlana would need a good lawyer who understood the delicacy of the situation she and her book posed. He immediately thought of his old friend and Princeton neighbor Edward Greenbaum, whom everyone affectionately called the General. (He'd served as a brigadier general in World War II.) Greenbaum, now seventy-seven, was a partner in the prestigious New York firm Greenbaum, Wolff & Ernst, which counted among its clients Tennessee Williams, Carl Sandburg, and the firm of Harper & Row.[20] Kennan felt he would be putting Svetlana in good hands.[21]

The day before Kennan left for Geneva, his wife, Annelise, phoned Greenbaum at six p.m. to say Kennan needed to see him urgently. Greenbaum crossed the Princeton lawns. He didn't need to read Svetlana's book to understand the value of the enterprise. Kennan asked him to stand by for a flight to

Geneva. If Svetlana agreed to have Greenbaum represent her, he would send a curt telegram: ARRANGEMENTS COMPLETED.[22]

Kennan flew to Switzerland on March 22. His arrival was top secret. To avoid press inquiries, he had a cover. He was supposedly visiting his daughter at her Swiss school and was giving lectures at the University of Geneva. Janner told Svetlana, "It's a big honor and very lucky for you, this meeting. He's one of the greatest experts on Russia. I'll bring you his books."[23]

Svetlana had been taken aback when she was told in Italy that the US government didn't want her in the United States. Now she had no idea what to expect from Kennan. She was so confused that she didn't even know what she wanted herself. Perhaps she should try to stay in Switzerland, but then the Swiss had forbidden her to make any political statements. What about her book? "What sense was there in leaving my country in order to remain silent here?" she asked herself.[24] In truth, the only place she really wanted to be was India, but that was impossible.

Preparing to meet the man who would possibly determine her fate, Svetlana read Kennan's book *Russia and the West Under Lenin and Stalin*. His attack on Stalin and Communism was relentless. To her mind, it was accurate. She wondered if he would be able to separate her from her father.[25] Two policemen drove her to Janner's house, near Bern, where Janner greeted her enthusiastically: "I have already spoken to Kennan. He has read your manuscript and thinks it should be published."[26]

When the courtly diplomat arrived, they sat on the sofa, and he congratulated her on her memoir. It was soon clear that he had read it thoroughly. Kennan had made a decision. He would protect Svetlana but also guard against her being used in the United States for anti-Soviet propaganda. In his ongoing relationship with her, he had always to balance two things: "his genuine admiration for her and his *other responsibilities*."[27] He would later tell the *New York Times* that help for Svetlana in adjusting to her new life would best be given "by private parties, not by governments or by anyone who had a commercial interest in her future."[28] In effect, however, the State Department would be pulling the strings.

Kennan assured Svetlana that if she wanted to go to the United States, she would certainly find a publisher. There was international interest in her book, and she would be offered substantial sums of money. She'd need lawyers to negotiate with publishers and arrange her visa. He suggested Greenbaum. He had been careful to ensure that Janner, as a Swiss representative, was present at their discussion, and he emphasized that he was only offering suggestions. It was up to her to decide, because "this was the essence of the free society in which she now found herself." She smiled wryly and agreed, but then added realistically, "What choice, after all, do I have?"[29]

Over a candlelit dinner, Kennan talked of his family and American friends eager to meet her. He said he was impressed by her mastery of English. For Svetlana, the pace of things falling into place felt surreal. Soon she was telling Janner and others that Kennan was "like a God to me" and that a "whole new world had opened" when he put his counsel at her disposal.[30]

Kennan reported to the State Department that he was very impressed by Svetlana's "intelligence, stability, sincerity." He was sure her decision to present herself at the US Embassy in Delhi had not been an "irrational caprice." Her book had literary merit. She was implacably opposed to the Soviet regime. Moreover, he wrote, "She has iron in her soul."[31]

She would later say this was the kind of gamble she always took. When she'd left the Soviet Compound in Delhi, she had only the address of the American Embassy.

What I would need to do after, on the next day, I did not know about it and I did not think about it. Not planning ahead—as always—I only vaguely imagined what my new life would be. . . . Sometimes at night I dreamed of the streets of Moscow, the rooms of my apartment; I woke up in a cold sweat. This was the nightmare to me.[32]

The nightmare was both what had happened in that city and the thought that she might be forcibly returned to it.

Chapter 18

Attorneys at Work

When Svetlana defected, she left Joseph and Katya behind, and in October 1967, they appeared on West German television with an open plea to her to return.

O n March 25, Edward Greenbaum traveled to Switzerland with his legal assistant Alan Schwartz. Schwartz knew only that they were going to help a "lady in distress." It wasn't until they were in midair that he was advised their client was Stalin's daughter. The two men stopped in Milan, where Kennan was waiting to brief them, and were then driven to Bern. Their mission was to ensure a book deal for Svetlana, so that she could enter the United States as a private person, reducing the political liability she represented for the State Department. When they met the Swiss official Antonino Janner, he warned them that not only the press but also the Russians were looking for Svetlana like crazy.[1]

That evening Janner drove them to a remote hotel and, as Alan Schwartz remembered it, "*There she was.* She was a very warm person. She charmed the two of us." It wasn't yet certain what the American government was going to do with her. They offered their services as her attorneys.

On March 29, Svetlana signed two powers of attorney to the firm of Greenbaum, Wolff & Ernst. The first granted her attorneys the right to act on her behalf in all immigration matters; the second assigned them all rights over any current or future books she would write.

When she signed the documents, Svetlana had only one thought in her head: to be cooperative. She knew how things happened. The leaders at the top spoke to each other and suddenly you vanished. When Greenbaum assured her that her book could make money, she said she hoped she might earn enough to have a car and a dog. She joked: It "should be a 'gypsy' dog since she was leading a gypsy life."[2]

On March 30, Greenbaum and Schwartz returned to New York. Now they needed to get Svetlana a visa to America. Greenbaum arranged a meeting with Attorney General Nick Katzenbach, along with Charles Bohlen from the State Department, who was an expert on the Soviet Union; and a number of CIA officers, including Donald Jameson, CIA branch chief in charge of handling Soviet defectors and other covert operations. By now Jameson, a victim of polio, was confined to a wheelchair; most likely he'd contracted the poliovirus from an East German defector whom he interrogated in 1955. Jamie, as he was called, was charming, deeply read in Russian literature, and personally committed to helping Svetlana.

Alan Schwartz was present at the meeting.

They were all at this table, talking about what happened, and it became clear the American government still didn't want any part of this, at least on the surface. But we had to get some kind of security, knowing that if she came here, she wouldn't be thrown out, she would have some documentation allowing her to stay. Without the intervention of Donald Jameson, I don't know what would have happened to her. The best we could obtain for Svetlana was a six-month tourist visa.[3]

Next Greenbaum telephoned Cass Canfield, the president of Harper & Row, with whom he'd recently worked on a lawsuit brought by Jacqueline Kennedy involving a biography Harper & Row was publishing. He asked if he could drop by Canfield's home on East Thirty-Eighth Street that evening to talk about an urgent matter. When he got to the house, Canfield and Evan Thomas, the executive vice president, were waiting for him. He informed them that he represented Svetlana Alliluyeva, who in 1963 had written a book, which she was eager to publish. He assured them nobody knew she'd written a book. He added a proviso. The Swiss government had asked him to keep the existence of the book secret, and "there were other considerations that made it essential to keep this news confidential."[4]

Greenbaum did not explain the "other considerations," but certainly he was alluding to the State Department's wish to play this one low-key. In view of the need for secrecy, he said he and Alan Schwartz decided not to open Svetlana's manuscript to general bidding, which would "disturb her security," but to offer it only to Harper & Row. Canfield was indeed interested. After negotiations, on April 14, Harper & Row signed the contract, paying $250,000 for US English-language rights.

Greenbaum next called Arthur Sulzberger, then the publisher of the *New York Times*, about serialization rights (he was close to the Sulzberger family). Sulzberger offered $225,000 for six installments. In a cooperative agreement with the *Times*, *Life* bought the rights to serialize the book two days after the *Times* for the sum of $400,000. Still to come would be Book of the Month Club rights ($325,000), and foreign book and serial rights. Greenbaum had accomplished all this by mid-April.[5] No one had actually read the manuscript, but everyone was certain a book by Stalin's daughter was eminently marketable.

Now Greenbaum needed a translator. Kennan proposed several names, and soon Priscilla Johnson McMillan, a thirty-nine-year-old journalist and translator, was approached.[6] McMillan had worked as a translator at the US Embassy in Moscow in the mid-1950s and had even met Svetlana briefly in 1956 when she tried to audit a course, The Soviet Novel, that Svetlana was teaching at Moscow University. The course was canceled; Khrushchev had just delivered his Secret Speech. Now McMillan was working on a book about Lee Harvey Oswald, whom she'd interviewed in Moscow in 1959 when she'd worked as a reporter for the North American News Alliance. The CIA had already vetted her.

McMillan flew immediately to New York to meet Greenbaum. Svetlana's manuscript had been delivered to Harper & Row at 10 East Fifty-Third Street, where it was kept under lock and key. She read the manuscript, written in longhand, over the course of a week, but wasn't allowed to take it out of the building. When she was asked to write a précis needed to sell foreign rights, she had to do so from memory one night in her hotel room. The book moved her deeply. "I just couldn't believe my eyes: to think that Stalin's daughter was capable of writing this. And I never got over the great respect and awe that reading that manuscript imbued in me."[7]

Greenbaum thought it imperative for McMillan to meet Svetlana and persuaded Harper & Row to send her to Switzerland. As Greenbaum prepared her for the trip, she found herself in the middle of a comedy.

> The General [as friends called Greenbaum] delivered his instructions to me at the Williams Club in New York City, a very crowded restaurant where I ran into a couple of people I knew, and at the Algonquin, where everyone in New York would gather. General Greenbaum was very deaf and he would deliver me my instructions at the top of his voice and, so that he could hear me, I had to answer him at the top of my voice. It was a miracle that the whole thing wasn't in the newspapers long before it was. . . . He drilled me on what I was supposed to say if I ran into any of my newspaper friends in the lobby of the hotel in Zurich. "If you run into Marvin Kalb in the lobby, what are you going to say? Well, Marvin, isn't it wonderful, don't you love skiing here?" I went secretly to Frankfurt and took a train to Zurich.[8]

McMillan's encounter with Svetlana went well. The two women met once at Janner's home and again at a sort of B & B in Neuchâtel, where neither Svetlana nor McMillan was staying. McMillan had brought a sample chapter of her translation, which she showed Svetlana upstairs in the lobby with a parrot screeching in the background. This amused McMillan—she was pretty sure the parrot didn't have a direct line to the *New York Times*. "Svetlana's comment was that I stuck too close to her original but otherwise she liked it. Her English was excellent, as I already knew from that 1956 meeting." Within days, McMillan was back in the United States.

While the flurry continued in New York, for Svetlana the euphoria of escape had passed, and she fell into a brutal depression. She was missing her children. On April 4, she finally received a letter from her son, Joseph, lamenting that they had had no word from her.

Greetings, dear Mama!

We were very surprised when, on March 8, we went to the airport and did not find you. . . . When *Tass* came out with an announcement that you had been granted permission to remain abroad as long as you wished, we more or less stopped worrying, and life returned to its normal routine; that is if one discounts that to this day Katya cannot get back on track; and we, to tell you the truth, just don't understand anything.

I even called up the Swiss Embassy, asking them to help us in contacting you. . . . At last we got your card, in which you said you didn't know how to get in touch with us. Can you explain why we have to write you through a government department? . . . Mama, all your friends are asking after you. It would be good if you wrote and told us what to say to them. Until we see you. We kiss you. Joseph and Katya.[9]

Svetlana turned to Antonino Janner in desperation. There must be a way to telephone Joseph. Janner drove her to a small hotel in nearby Murten (Morat), where they rented a room with a phone and called Moscow using a fictitious name. To Svetlana's shock, her son answered, though Katya was not at home. They spoke for half an hour, and yet it seemed nothing was said. He asked no questions, and she only stammered repeatedly that she was not coming back. She thought it would be dangerous for him to know too much. He replied, "Yes, yes I hear you."[10] Then the phone line was cut. From that point on, whenever she tried to reach her son in Moscow, the operator replied that the line was dead.

After this painful phone call, Svetlana phoned her friend Lily Golden. When Lily picked up the phone, she heard Svetlana's voice asking, "Is anybody in your home?" Lily said no, but she was dumbstruck by the absurd question. "Every espionage agency in the world had to be listening to her phone calls, at least the KGB and the CIA." Svetlana seemed almost hysterical, and as Lily remembered it, "she began to list all the names of the government and the Communist Party, and gave all their crimes and terrible deeds that she had learned about them abroad and about her father. I stood, holding the phone, numb with terror." Lily shifted the conversation to express her dismay at the toll Svetlana's departure was taking on her children and asked how she could leave her friends.[11] Lily was soon called into the offices of the KGB and interrogated, as each of Svetlana's friends would be, but she refused the interrogators' demand to pronounce Svetlana "crazy."[12]

When the truth of Svetlana's defection hit home, the KGB approached her children, demanding that they denounce their mother. Leonid and Galina Alliluyev believed that Joseph might initially have resisted. "As a result of some pressure on him," Joseph and his young wife left their apartment in the House on the Embankment and moved to the suburbs, but soon they were back in the center of Moscow, and Joseph was offered the opportunity to work in the faculty of the First Medical Institute, from which he'd graduated.[13] The Soviet press now reported that Joseph said his mother was "unstable." Perhaps he felt: why should he be loyal, when it was she who had deserted them?

Looking back more than thirty years later, Joseph would tell an interviewer that he had kept Katya in the dark about the whole situation, and he himself was not pressured by the KGB: "Nobody tortured me with hot irons or fire," though he added that an officer from the KGB did drop by the university once and leave his phone number.[14] Stating that he loved both his grandfathers, he said his mother "had ruined herself."[15]

Olga Redlova, the daughter of the chemist Fyodor Volkenstein, who was the secret interlocutor for Svetlana's *Twenty Letters to a Friend*, recalled: "My father had the manuscript of this book. I remember that when Svetlana left, Osia [Joseph] called my father and asked if he had anything left of Svetlana's things. And my father said, 'Yes, I have. I have a small bag in the hallway, wrapped in newspapers, but I've never opened it. I don't know what's in it.' Well, of course it was Svetlana's manuscript. Joseph came and picked up the manuscript."[16] When the KGB came to visit Joseph and Katya at the House on the Embankment, the agents confiscated not just the manuscript, but also family photographs from Svetlana's locked desk.

Svetlana spent her time in Fribourg brooding in the convent garden. Robert Rayle had bought her Boris Pasternak's *Doctor Zhivago* in Rome—it had finally been published in Russian in Milan. This was the first time she was reading it, for she'd never managed to get a samizdat copy in Moscow. She walked among the thuja trees in the garden and wept: over the book, over her children, over her lost country. And wrote a public letter "To Boris Leonidovich Pasternak," who had died in 1960.

In it she lamented her "beloved, long-suffering baffled Russia," where she had left her children and friends to the "unbearable Soviet life, a life so unlike anything else that it can never be imagined by Russians abroad, whether friendly or hostile."

She thought of her friend Andrusha (Andrei Sinyavsky), exiled for seven years in a concentration camp, carrying buckets of water, his clothes in tatters, like Pasternak's character Yuri Zhivago. Nothing had changed. "As before, it is given to gendarmes and policemen to be the first critics of a writer's work. . . . Now you can be tried for a metaphor, sent to a camp for figures of speech!" The "Party hypocrites and Pharisees! . . . these miserable compilers of dossiers and denunciations" were still in control.[17] What had she done to her children, who would be subjected to slanders and possibly worse? She begged them: "Let them all condemn me—and you condemn me as well, if that will be easier for you (say whatever you like: it will only be empty words, and they will not hurt me), only do not reject me in your hearts."[18]

Svetlana felt lacerated to the bone. She wondered if she'd really understood that she was losing her children when she'd made her impulsive decision not to return to Russia. "Probably not."[19] But when she read *Doctor Zhivago*, the reality hit like an electric shock. The tragedy of separation from a child imposed by a regime that knew no constraints was also Zhivago's and Lara's story.

In mid-April Alan Schwartz flew back to Switzerland. The contract with the law firm of Greenbaum, Wolff & Ernst was now ready for Svetlana's signature. He landed in Frankfurt and took the train to Basel, feeling "fairly spooked out, looking around all the time to see who was there." The Russians, the Indians, the international press, and, by now, other international publishers were looking for Svetlana. Antonino Janner was waiting for Schwartz when he stepped off the train. Janner drove him to meet her. That night over dinner, Svetlana warmed to her young lawyer. She kept telling the thirty-four-year-old Schwartz that he "reminded her of her brother, Yakov, who had died in a German internment camp."[20]

Two Swiss lawyers, William Staehelin and Peter Hafter, joined her legal team, and in a two-day meeting, they reviewed the contracts regarding her manuscript.

Greenbaum had invented for Svetlana a company called

Patientia, in Liechtenstein, where taxes, of course, were low. On April 20, Svetlana signed the rights in her unpublished manuscript to Copex Establishment, Vaduz, Liechtenstein. The contract read in part:

> NOW, THEREFORE, in consideration of an amount of US $1,500,000.00 (US Dollars One Million Five Hundred Thousand) MRS. ALLILUEVA hereby assigns to COPEX ESTABLISHMENT all of her right, title and interest throughout the world in and to the above manuscript. . . .
>
> The price of US $1,500,000.00 shall be paid as follows:
> * a down payment of US $73,875.00 has been made today;
> * the balance of US $1,426,125.00 is paid in notes which have been delivered to MRS. ALLILUEVA today.[21]

A million and a half was an astonishing sum back then, but the deals with Harper & Row, the serial rights with the *New York Times* and *Life*, and the foreign sales had been exceedingly lucrative. Svetlana was to be paid in installments. Alan Schwartz recalled: "I think the reason for the notes must have been taxes. Because a note comes due, you're taxed on the money you get. It might've been a way to spread out the payments—instead of paying $750,000 in taxes on $1.5 million."[22] Even Greenbaum must have been surprised at the amount of money Svetlana's book was bringing in. Only Churchill's memoirs had sold for more. Friends sent letters to Edward Greenbaum congratulating him on his coup in representing Stalin's daughter.

Svetlana would look back and say she had understood nothing. What did she know about money, about contracts, about American law? When she asked the lawyers what Copex was, she was told it was a "legal body." Fresh out of the USSR, she couldn't conceive what a *legal body* might be.[23] She didn't even know what a bank account was. She sat passively through the two-day meeting trying to follow the discussions, her English barely adequate with regard to her lawyers' legalese. All she could think was that she must not create problems. She must not be sent back to the Soviet Union. She had to sign everything the lawyers gave her.

When she'd walked through the impoverished streets of Kalakankar just a few weeks back, she'd imagined setting up a hospital in Brajesh Singh's name. She now told Greenbaum she wanted to use her money to do this. As Alan Schwartz remembered, "We were very skeptical about setting up a foundation in some hospital in India in remembrance of her former lover, but we acceded to her wishes."[24]

Two trusts were established: The Alliluyeva Charitable Trust and the Alliluyeva Trust. Her charitable trust would eventually pay $200,000 to build the Brajesh Singh hospital, with $250,000 set aside in investments to pay for the hospital's maintenance. The rest of Svetlana's money went into the Alliluyeva Trust, from which she received $1,500 every month to live on. She felt this was more than enough.[25]

Robert Rayle had warned her that her manuscript was all that stood "between her and the poorhouse." It had turned her into a millionaire.

This was possibly the worst fate that could have befallen her. She was no longer a principled defector who had rejected Communism; she was a very wealthy woman. "What did she intend to do now that she was rich?" was one of the first questions journalists asked when she eventually reached the United States.

The propaganda blowback was intense. The commissars were delighted to point out that Svetlana had always been *only after the money*. Alliluyeva "is a first-class slanderer of the Soviet system and even of her own father. We will only emphasize that dollars will hardly bring success to the woman without a country, who abandoned home, country, and family and pleased herself in the services of anti-Communism."[26]

It was suddenly remembered that in 1941 the Germans had dropped propaganda leaflets on Moscow claiming Stalin was secreting huge sums of money in Swiss banks, ready to flee. No one had believed this at the time, but now his daughter had stopped in *Switzerland*.[27] Even ordinary Soviet citizens were disconcerted.

The rumors made it to Washington. On June 15, in an article entitled "$300 Million in Gold for Svetlana," the *Washington Observer Newsletter* wrote that Svetlana herself had insisted on stopping in Switzerland. "The real reason is that she wanted to pick up the $300 million in gold deposited in a Berne bank!" The article claimed that "old 'bloody Joe' Stalin" had stashed it in a secret numbered account during the siege of Moscow, and had named Svetlana as "sole beneficiary." It was reported as a fact, confirmed by "an American intelligence source," that "Svetlana submitted documentary evidence proving her true identity. . . . The Swiss bank officials have ruled that she has established a valid claim to the Stalin fortune."[28] For now, Svetlana was unaware of the gossip her newfound wealth was provoking.

The Swiss were pressuring the Americans to take Svetlana off their hands. Although they found her to be undemanding and were fond of her, her security was a burden to their small Foreign Office. Secretary of State Dean Rusk advised President Lyndon Johnson that he now believed Svetlana should be permitted to enter, but strictly as a private visitor.[29] The State Department informed the media that she was traveling to the United States on a six-month tourist visa at the invitation of her American legal firm, Greenbaum, Wolff & Ernst, in order to consult her publishers about her book. Even the Soviet journalists at the Foreign Correspondence Center in Moscow said this was a "diplomatic master stroke."[30] The State Department had kept its hands clean.

Very early on the morning of April 21, Alan Schwartz was picked up at his hotel. Svetlana was already in the car. They were scheduled to take a Swissair flight to New York under assumed names. Schwartz recalled: "The airport was surrounded by security guards in uniforms with guns. Svetlana was determined to make sure she got out of there in one piece, and I was too." On the flight, Schwartz warned her, "They're going to ask you to say something when you get there. Do you want me to say something for you?" She replied, "'No, no, I want to speak for myself."[31]

But Greenbaum had already hired a public relations firm to handle Svetlana, and Kennan had drafted the statement she was to make on disembarking:

> I have come to this country because I am faced with the problem of making a new life outside Russia and would like to make some acquaintance with the United States, but also because it is here that I intend to publish material I have written, and I would like to be in close contact with my publishers. I do not know how long I shall remain here. . . . I am tired, now, from the journey, and I would like to have a few days of privacy before I meet with the press again.[32]

Kennan's job was to keep Svetlana from saying anything that might compromise American relations with the Soviet Union. But Kennan did not yet know Svetlana. She didn't intend to use his carefully crafted diplomatic speech. She wanted to be very clear about why she left the Soviet Union. It was not simply to publish a book, but rather to protest her treatment and the treatment of Russian artists and intellectuals at the hands of the current Soviet government.

In placating the Soviets, had the American government distorted her poignant rejection of life under Communism?

The British Foreign Office thought so. Because the BBC was planning to broadcast the Russian text of Svetlana's "To Boris Leonidovich Pasternak," the Foreign Office scrambled to determine its "policy about the Svetlana story." Many were puzzled about why the Americans were "taking so restrained a line." On May 1, nine days after her arrival, Sir Paul Gore-Booth, permanent undersecretary for foreign affairs, sent a secret memo to twenty-three heads of mission at the Foreign Office:

Miss Stalin's Defection:

The defection of Miss Stalin seems to me to be something of quite a different order from the normal world of defection in which one scores plusses and minuses, and tries to exploit the plusses and, by a deep professional yawn, to submerge the minuses.

If any person said to you in 1950 that in seventeen years Miss Stalin would defect to the West, you would rightly have considered that person certifiable. She has now done it, with impressive smoothness and conviction. She has made it clear . . . that the reason for her defection . . . is because she can no longer accept a society in which you are told that there is only one point of view from which politics, and indeed life itself, must be judged. . . . This may not be a new doctrine, but its relaunching by the daughter of Stalin, in the fiftieth anniversary of the Communist Revolution in Russia, is immensely important, indeed so important that quite a lot of people haven't noticed it.[33]

Svetlana could have told the State Department that its efforts to placate the Kremlin were pointless. Nothing the Americans could say would ever convince the Soviets that the CIA had not "prepared, arranged, and financed" Svetlana's defection.[34] At the deepest level, Soviet officials needed to believe she'd been kidnapped. They could not accept the idea that she had acted freely, and so their first response would be to try to kidnap her back. In an interview held later that August at the home of Harper & Row's executive vice president, she explained this belief to journalists puzzled by the Kremlin's fury:

> They cannot believe that an individual, a person, a human being, can make decisions on his own. They still cannot believe that I left Russia just by my own decision, that it wasn't a plot, it wasn't organized, there wasn't help. They cannot believe it. They only believe in actions which are ruled by some organization—the collective, yes—and they are always very angry to see that although they have tried to make people in Russia for fifty years think the same way, have the same opinion . . . the same political point of view, . . . when they see that the whole work done for fifty years was in vain and people still have something of their own, they are very angry.[35]

Chapter 19

The Arrival

On April 21, 1967, Svetlana stepped onto American soil for the first time at New York's John F. Kennedy Airport.

The FBI was watching a Soviet operative named Vasily Fyodorovich Sanko. On April 13, 1967, the State Department's Bureau of Intelligence and Research sent the FBI a memo advising that a G-2 visa had been issued to Vasily Sanko to attend the Fifth Special Session of the UN General Assembly. J. Edgar Hoover personally acknowledged the memo, indicating that the subject, Vasily Sanko, had participated in the attempted abduction in Australia of a Soviet citizen in 1954. Svetlana Alliloueva (*sic*) was mentioned in the FBI document.[1]

Enzo Biagi, an Italian freelance journalist, and Martin Ebon, a German American author, both of whom were working on stories about Svetlana and had sources inside the Soviet Union, reported that a KGB operative named Vasily F. Sanko arrived in New York on April 20 (one day before Svetlana) on a diplomatic passport.[2] He was identified as a chauffeur with the Soviet Mission to the United Nations. In 1954 Sanko, along with three other agents, had kidnapped Yevdokia Petrova, wife of Vladimir Petrov, a KGB officer who had defected in Australia seventeen days earlier. The Soviet agents forced Mrs. Petrova aboard an Australian airliner in Sydney bound for Moscow, but the pilot received instructions to land at Darwin airport. Mrs. Petrova was freed and, along with her husband, granted political asylum.

Obviously alerted to a possible abduction plot, on April 19, Greenbaum called into his office Albert and George Paloesik, two brothers who ran the Fidelity Detective Bureau. They claimed to have expertise in guarding celebrities; they had once guarded Errol Flynn.

On Friday, April 21, Svetlana and Schwartz, using their assumed names, managed to slip unnoticed onto the Swissair DC-8 jet bound for New York. Svetlana's presence on board was not announced to the media until one hour after takeoff. Even the flight crew didn't know she had boarded. When the plane arrived at Kennedy Airport, six representatives of the Fidelity Detective Bureau were on the tarmac to greet her.

Svetlana was the last of the forty passengers to disembark after the flight touched down at 2:45 p.m. Dozens of plain-clothes policemen were stationed around the arrivals gate, and a tight security web surrounded the airfield. Members of the

New York City Police Department's Bureau of Special Services peered from the observation deck of the International Arrivals Building, which had been closed to the public at 2:30. Svetlana's arrival was a sensation. There were more people to greet her at the airport than had been there for the Beatles in 1964. Reporters remarked how she "bounded down the stairs" onto American soil and seemed unable to stop smiling. She climbed onto a small box to elevate herself into camera range and, facing scores of journalists cordoned off behind police barricades, said, "Hello there, everybody. I'm very happy to be here."

The firm of Hill & Knowlton, which Greenbaum had hired to handle Svetlana's public relations, had decided that she would make only a brief statement at the airport and give a press conference later. The Hill & Knowlton executive in charge, John Mapes, later remarked, "I talked with Foy Kohler of the State Department on the way to handle the thing."[3]

Apologizing for her clumsy English, Svetlana assured the public that leaving the USSR had been her own decision, based on the anguish she had felt over the death of her husband, Brajesh Singh, and her subsequent treatment by her government. She had come to the United States to seek the self-expression so long denied her in her own country. She was part of a new generation, as were her children, who didn't want to be fooled by the old ideas. "I do believe in the power of intellect in the world, no matter in which country you live. Instead of struggling and causing unnecessary bloodshed, people should work more together for the progress of humanity. I believe that one's home can be anywhere that one can feel free." She added, perhaps as a conciliatory gesture to George Kennan, that publishing her book would "symbolize for me the main purpose of my journey here."[4]

Coincidentally, the Soviet poet Andrei Voznesensky had arrived at Kennedy Airport just two hours before Svetlana for his

American tour. When asked to comment on Svetlana's defection, he said that he would speak only about "literary topics, not politics."[5] Svetlana was not offended. She knew that Voznesensky was under tight KGB control. Back home he was adored as one of the generation of liberating poets of the 1960s, and his recitals could fill whole stadiums. Moscow sent him on international tours as a "cultural envoy," but he knew the terms—never to speak out about the truth of repression he and other writers suffered. His fate embodied the reason Svetlana left the Soviet Union. When Voznesensky got back to Moscow after the tour, his travel permit to return to the United States that summer was revoked because he had not publicly condemned her.[6]

The KGB agent Vasily Sanko seemed to have kept to his chauffeur duties, although the CIA and the FBI continued to take the possibility of an "extraction plot" seriously. Was the threat credible? In his obituary of Vladimir Semichastny titled "Top KGB Plotter Dead at 77," the Reuters correspondent Ron Popeski wrote, "Semichastny, head of the KGB in 1967, told reporters he was removed by Brezhnev and replaced by future Communist Party chief Yuri Andropov after a failed attempt to smuggle Joseph Stalin's daughter, Svetlana Alliluyeva, out of the United States."[7] Whether this is reliable or hearsay is unclear, but Andropov *was* appointed the new head of the KGB on May 18, 1967, three weeks after Svetlana's arrival in the United States.

In any case, Svetlana's personal security detail stayed on. It is unlikely she was aware that it was she who was paying for their services.[8]

In his statement to the *New York Times* the day after her arrival, George Kennan asked Americans to rise above their "Cold War reflexes." He said, "Mrs. Alliluyeva loves her country and hopes, with her writing and activity outside Russia, to bring benefit to it and not harm" in the "new era" that was "dawning."[9] He didn't seem concerned that Svetlana didn't believe in this "new era."

Harper & Row's executive vice president, Evan Thomas, also spoke to the *Times*, characterizing Svetlana's book as a high literary achievement, although he admitted he'd not read it. "What politics there are are by implication. It is largely personal."[10] This insistence that Svetlana was not politically important seemed to mask an anxiety that, in fact, she was.

After her brief encounter with the press, Svetlana climbed into the backseat of a car with Alan Schwartz. Svetlana's translator, Priscilla Johnson McMillan, had offered her father's estate in Locust Valley as a refuge. Svetlana and Schwartz were traveling in a convoy of three cars. Albert Paloesik drove the first car, his brother George drove the second, and one of their men from the Fidelity Detective Bureau followed in a third. As they drove out the Van Wyck Expressway to Sunrise Highway, Albert was sure they were being followed. He went into evasive techniques.

> [Our] third car detained the one that was following us . . . known as the crash car technique. We went north on Meadowbrook Parkway, and by the time we reached East Gate Boulevard, we had determined, talking to each other on the car radios, that we were being followed by another car. This one was a limousine, with a chauffeur and with two men in the back—I thought immediately of the Russian Embassy. When I turned off at Roosevelt Field, I made a left, a right, another left, and stopped. We were in a narrow lane. My brother stopped and the limousine drew up behind him. My brother got out and started toward them. . . . I shot forward.[11]

It turned out the men in the limousine were reporters. Paloesik was sure Svetlana didn't notice any of this—she thought he was just talking on the radio with his other cars. He probably underestimated her. When they arrived at the estate of Priscilla McMillan's father, Stewart Johnson, the Paloesik brothers, armed with shotguns, set up guard posts.

Priscilla and her father had been waiting for Svetlana. Now a widower, Johnson was excited by the distraction of sheltering Svetlana, with all the cloak-and-dagger brouhaha this involved. That night in the stately, wood-paneled reception room, they watched news clips of Svetlana's arrival. It embarrassed McMillan that the news clips were continuously interrupted by commercials. Svetlana didn't seem to mind.

Greenbaum had scheduled Svetlana's first press conference for April 26, four days after her arrival. It was to take place in the Terrace Room of the Plaza Hotel and be broadcast via satellite feed through Telstar. The day before her performance, Greenbaum rehearsed her on likely questions and reported to George Kennan that he was "optimistic about Svetlana's conduct in a press conference." He said he had "grilled her 'brutally' about some of the more sensitive aspects of her life" to see how she'd stand up, and was astonished by her "composure and skill," as if she'd been giving press conferences all her life.[12]

Greenbaum did not indicate what these "sensitive aspects" were, but US intelligence sources were already confirming that the line the Soviets were taking about Svetlana was that she was promiscuous, abnormal, non compos mentis, and certainly incapable of writing a book. In fact, they were going to try to pin her book on the CIA.[13]

The next day, Svetlana was driven to the Plaza Hotel. Reporters had been directed to submit questions in writing an hour and a half before the 2:00 p.m. press conference. From the more than three hundred questions, her public relations firm—Hill & Knowlton—selected about forty. At the hour-long session, Alan Schwartz read the questions to Svetlana, assuring the audience that she had not seen them in advance. The full transcript of her interview was published the next morning in the *New York Times*.

One of the first questions came from Bob Schakne of CBS News, who asked if she disapproved of her father's regime. She responded, "Of course I disapprove of many things but I think many other people who still are in our Central Committee and Politburo should be responsible for the same things for which he alone was accused. . . . Those horrible things, killing people unjustly, I feel that responsibility for this was and is the Party's, the regime and the ideology as a whole." When Gabe Pressman of NBC asked what caused her to "re-evaluate conditions in Russia" and to defect, she responded that the government's opposition to her marriage to Brajesh Singh was "disgustful," but also added that another factor was the trial of Sinyavsky and Daniel. "The way two writers were treated and sentenced made me absolutely disbelieve in justice. I lost the hopes that I had before that we are going to become liberal." If the State Department people expected that Svetlana would refrain from expressing her political opinions, they were disappointed.

She spoke of her children. "They are not guilty at all and I believe they cannot be punished for anything." Of her newfound wealth: "I'm not going to become a very rich woman. It is absolutely impossible for me to become a rich woman here." She planned to give most of the money away. To the question of whether she minded the media fuss, she replied, "I cannot understand why, if they write something about new person, why it should be mentioned . . . what he is eating for his lunch." But she added, "More information is better than no information at all." Asked if she would become an American citizen, she said that "love must come before marriage" and burst out laughing. "If I will love this country and this country will love me, then the marriage will be settled."[14]

Her performance was described as "stunning, surefooted, breathtaking." John Mapes, the head of her PR handlers, remarked to reporters, "She is an intellectual exhibitionist. She needs an audience. She's a female Nabokov, quite strong-willed."[15] At the end of the press conference, the press corps gave her a standing ovation. She was swiftly taken back into seclusion.

The next day, however, Svetlana received a devastating letter from her son, Joseph, which she showed to Priscilla with shaking hands. Greenbaum had held the letter back until after the press conference, knowing how much it would devastate her. It was a cold, angry letter in response to their phone conversation in Switzerland:

> When we spoke on the telephone and I heard all you had to say, I was so lost I was unable to answer you coherently. It took me several days to think it over, for things are not at all as simple as you seem to think. . . .
>
> You must admit that after what you have done, your advice from afar to take courage, to stick together, not to lose heart and not let go of Katya, was, to say the least, strange. . . . I consider that by your action you have cut yourself off from us and therefore, please allow us to live as we see fit. . . .
>
> Since we have endured fairly stoically what you have done, I hope from now on we shall be allowed to arrange our own lives ourselves. . . . Joseph[16]

Svetlana could not stop weeping. She wanted to run away, to hide from all the hospitality and curiosity of people who didn't understand and seemed to believe that everything was fine now that she was *free*.

Basketsful of mail for Svetlana began to arrive, friendly notes of welcome to America, marriage proposals, invitations to join religious organizations, as well as the occasional variation of "Go back home, Red dog! Our cat is better than you. She takes care of her children." That one cut particularly deeply.[17]

The defection of Stalin's daughter was an event of such consequence that the international press was swarming the Johnson estate. Newsmen parked outside the fence and spied from the shrubbery. Helicopters circled overhead taking pictures. Local police kept the house under surveillance twenty-four hours a day. Svetlana liked to take long restless hikes through the nearby woods, but the Paloesik brothers insisted on accompanying her. They grew very fond of Svetlana, particularly when she took a rose off her own suit jacket and gave it to Albert. "She's so nice. I'm almost beginning to like Russians," Albert said.[18]

Meanwhile, Priscilla and Svetlana worked on the translation of *Twenty Letters to a Friend*. On one occasion, to give Priscilla a break from the pressure of having the author sitting across from her knitting or reading as she translated, Priscilla's sister Eunice took Svetlana shopping. The next day, a photograph of Svetlana bending down to try on shoes appeared in the *New York Times*. It was reported that she bought three pairs of stockings, slacks, a sweater, and the shoes. "The cost of the slacks and sweater was $46.82."[19] The existence of paparazzi and the invasive curiosity of "the public" were astonishing discoveries for a Soviet citizen. There was no public in the USSR.

But domestic life at the Johnson estate provided a welcome shelter. Soon Svetlana assumed Priscilla's mother's seat at the head of the table—Mr. Johnson would be at the other end, with Priscilla relegated to the middle. To Priscilla, Svetlana was like the "chairman of the board, a very able and capacious person." The name of Aleksei Kosygin would come up and Mr. Johnson would say, "Oh, I suppose he's a very nice man," but Svetlana would respond, "Oh, no indeed." Priscilla remembered: "One by one, whoever's name came up, she would give a very good sketch of all of them, accurate brief sketches. It was very impressive."[20] She would read the Soviet attacks on her reported in the newspapers and explain what they were really saying.

Priscilla thought of herself as something of a Kremlinologist but Svetlana's "touch, her feel as to what they were really getting at was incredibly accurate, much, much better than mine and I think much better than anybody's would have been."[21]

But soon the Johnson house began to feel like Grand Central Station. Everyone wanted to meet Svetlana. People Priscilla hadn't seen in years began to drop by. The phone rang ninety-eight times a day. Anyone who walked downstairs at night would stumble over a private detective. It was all too much. When Priscilla's siblings visited and saw the chaos, they insisted Svetlana would have to leave. There were so many unwanted people in the house that they were afraid their father's old servants would abandon him. But Priscilla's father loved having Svetlana as his guest. He had a good sense of humor and would say, "Svetlana likes me because I remind her so much of her father."

Priscilla went to see Greenbaum, suggesting that a time for Svetlana to leave needed to be set. "Would you save me from having to take the blame?" she asked. "I guess I realized that whoever, so to speak, kicked her out of our house, she was going to be furious, because I must have understood early that partings and leavings and not being welcomed were going to induce that reaction."[22] She hated to make Svetlana feel unwelcome yet again.[23]

Priscilla took a trip to Atlanta, Georgia, to see her husband, who was threatening to divorce her because of her long absences; they had married just the previous December. One night Svetlana phoned, raging. "You urged them to restore the cuts in my book. You're not supposed to. That's not your place!"

She got angrier and angrier. "You're getting into editorial matters that aren't any of your business." Priscilla was thrown for a loop. "It was like having a very heavy tank or truck run over you."

George Kennan had recommended minor cuts to the manuscript. One was a letter to Aleksei Kapler that Svetlana had included. Because Kapler was still alive, it might be dangerous to him to reveal so much.[24] Another cut was the comment that Stalin didn't engage in blood sports because he couldn't stand the sight of blood. Kennan must have thought this statement was too offensive.

Priscilla had a secret motive in wanting to restore the cuts. When the manuscript was in longhand, she'd been asked to estimate its length and had given a wildly erroneous word count. The publisher had oversold serial rights, and she was afraid there'd be little left over for the book. But she was hurt and also puzzled by Svetlana's uncontained rage in her phone call. Svetlana seemed to find it so easy to disregard all the hospitality she'd received in the Johnson household during her six-week stay. Where did her rage come from? Was it simply that her vanity as a writer was piqued? Her Russian friend Professor Manuylov had told her never to allow anyone to change a word in her book. Whatever the case, after the blowup, apart from business calls, she and Priscilla remained permanently estranged.

Chapter 20

A Mysterious Figure

With the advance from her book *Twenty Letters to a Friend*, Svetlana bought a Dodge sedan in 1968. She imagined driving across America.

George Kennan had asked his daughter Joan to host a luncheon for Svetlana in her Princeton home. It was a daunting prospect because it all had to be carried out in secrecy even though other famous guests were invited, like Arthur Schlesinger and Nicholas Nabokov, the son of the novelist. Joan cooked lobster stew without washing off the brine, and the meal was inedible. Only Svetlana emptied her plate, declaring the dish delicious—it reminded her of the Black Sea. Joan found her endearing.

It was now decided that Svetlana would spend the summer with Joan and her family. George Kennan and his wife, Annelise, would be in Africa, where he was engaged on a lecture tour. On June 6, the Paloesik brothers drove Svetlana to Kennan's remote two-hundred-acre farm in East Berlin, Pennsylvania.

Called the Cherry Orchard after Chekhov's play, the farm felt like a Russian landowner's country estate. The farmhouse was filled with mementos the Kennans had brought back from Russia: old engravings, porcelain, Fedoskino lacquered tables. They'd even hung up a framed photograph of the Kremlin Embankment. Built in the nineteenth century, the house had two large columns in the front that created a kind of porch. Joan remembered many evenings when she and Svetlana sat there looking out over the fields, Svetlana talking nostalgically of the Russian steppes. Joan's two children would already be in bed and her husband was working in the city and came only on weekends.

After two weeks Svetlana told the Paloesik brothers that she didn't like being guarded, that in America she had more guards than she'd ever had in the Kremlin. The brothers gave her a ballpoint pen as a parting gift, inscribed: To Svetlana. Use with happiness. Al and George.

When Svetlana had received her son's devastating letter a few weeks back, she'd written to George Kennan in despair. Now his consoling reply from Johannesburg finally came in the mail.

> You should not permit it [the letter] to shake your confidence in yourself. . . . You, in doing what you did in Delhi, followed the deepest needs of your own nature. Had you gone back to the USSR at that time, you would have gone back not only as an enemy of the system but in a sense as an enemy of yourself. All this would have done your son no good either. . . .

Dear Svetlana, even in the face of this greatest sorrow, be confident that in some way of which probably neither you nor I are now able to conceive, all this courage and faith will be vindicated—and for him as well.[1]

On June 23, the long-awaited summit between President Johnson and Premier Kosygin took place in the small town of Glassboro, New Jersey; this was the meeting that demonstrated the thaw between the two countries, in the name of which Foy Kohler and the State Department had initially rejected Svetlana's request for asylum. The *New York Times* reported that the talks about the Mideast, Vietnam, and nuclear arms control lasted five hours, to little effect. "Not only were the difficult questions between them not resolved, but there appeared to have been no subsidiary agreements in relation to them."[2]

Two days later, as Svetlana and the Kennan family sat in the farm kitchen eating dinner and listening to the radio broadcast, they heard Kosygin's press conference at the United Nations. The Third Arab-Israeli War (the Six-Day War) had ended just two weeks earlier, and, denouncing Israel, Kosygin was declaring Soviet support for the defeated Arabs. Almost as an afterthought, Kosygin was asked about Svetlana. She heard Kosygin's familiar voice:

Alliluyeva is a morally unstable person and she's a sick person and we can only pity those who wish to use her for any political aims or . . . [to] discredit the Soviet country.[3]

Joan and her husband, Larry Griggs, laughed, but Svetlana could hear Kosygin's anger. She could also hear that the translator was modifying his tone. She knew what this meant. The Central Committee, the Party, and the secret police had all conferred. The anti-Svetlana campaign had begun. In fact, though she probably didn't know it, the KGB already had a code name for her—*kukushka*, a word that has the double meaning of "cuckoo bird" and "escaped convict."[4] From Kosygin's seemingly offhand remark, she understood that the new head of the KGB, Yuri Andropov, was out for revenge.

Damning articles began to appear in *Pravda* and *Izvestia*. The worst was a commentary by Sergei Izvekov, Patriarch Pimen I, the Russian Orthodox metropolitan (bishop) of Krutitsy and Kolomna, published in *Izvestia* on July 1. Pimen was following the Kremlin line:

> Lately our press and the press abroad report that the conscience of many honest people has been revolted by statements made by Svetlana Alliluyeva. This woman, who has had several husbands, who has abandoned her children, who has become a traitor to her people and exposes her father's nakedness, attempts to speak about religion, about her belief in God.
>
> The moral image of this woman, who has sold everything for dollars, can only arouse revulsion and anger.[5]

Soon the anti-Svetlana campaign went international. A shorter version of Pimen's commentary appeared in London's *Daily Express* and *Evening News*, and an Italian Communist paper, *Paese sera*, ran an article that claimed Svetlana suffered frequent nervous crises and attacks of hysteria and had done so all her life.[6]

It was an unfortunate coincidence for Svetlana that she happened to defect in 1967, the fiftieth anniversary of the Great Russian Revolution of 1917, celebrated on November 7. Worse still, her publisher, Harper & Row, had decided to bring *Twenty Letters to a Friend* out in October. The KGB was certain the Americans were out to humiliate the Soviet Union on the eve of the USSR's most important celebration ever.

A KGB operative named Victor Louis was chosen to handle Svetlana. He'd already tried to contact her at the Johnson residence in April. When Priscilla McMillan had answered his call, she'd been disgusted. She'd known Louis in her days in Moscow. "I never hated knowing anybody as much as I hated knowing Victor Louis."[7]

Vitaly Yevgenyevich Lui (Victor Louis) was a mysterious figure. In his exposé of Soviet spies, the American journalist John Barron identified Louis as the most celebrated KGB disinformation agent.[8] As a nineteen-year-old student, Louis had been arrested in Moscow. He claimed it was because of his association with foreigners, but it was more likely that he was a common black marketer. He spent nine years in the Gulag, where fellow prisoners, like the dissident writer Arkady Belinkov, who would soon become Svetlana's friend, claimed to have clear evidence that Louis worked as an informer for the camp directors.[9]

When Louis was freed from the labor camp, his lavish lifestyle—a Volkswagen, foreign suits, meetings at the American Embassy cocktail bar—should have been enough to get him arrested as a spy, but nothing happened. He was soon working abroad for the *London Evening News* and eventually the *Evening Standard*, where, presumably, much of his work was to leak KGB-doctored documents to the English press. But he seemed able to play both sides. He was also involved in the publication of dissident manuscripts forbidden in the Soviet Union. By 1965 he had already accumulated enough wealth to buy a lavish country house in the writers' colony of Peredelkino outside Moscow.

Victor Louis came up with an ingenious strategy to sabotage Svetlana's book. Nikita Khrushchev's son Sergei, whom Louis later approached with an offer to sell his father's memoirs in the West, had the story from Louis himself. "Every step Svetlana took resonated loudly in the corridors of power in the Kremlin." With the prospect of an October publication looming, "Vitaly Yevgenyevich proposed, on his own responsibility, as a private person, to make some cuts in the book to remove those passages that most alarmed the Kremlin and to bring the book out a few months earlier than the official launch date."[10] When the real book came out, it would be old news. Louis informed the KGB that the proceeds from the sale were to belong exclusively to him because he would bear the inconvenience of the project. The KGB agreed.

The KGB, after getting a copy of the manuscript from Svetlana's son, Joseph, handed it over to Louis, who promptly sold it for £5,000 to the London publisher Flegon Press. Alec Flegon, a Russian Romanian, had a reputation among London publishers as a pirate who published banned Soviet literature smuggled out of the USSR by tourists, students, and possibly more nefarious sources but never paid royalties to the writers back in the Soviet Union.[11]

Svetlana's British publisher, Hutchinson, which had paid £50,000 for the book, sight unseen, and *The Observer*, which had bought serial rights, were furious, but it was tricky to go after Flegon. He claimed to be an innocent third party who had obtained the manuscript legally from his "invariably honest" agent, who had brought the manuscript out of Russia on July 27. Flegon declined to name his "agent" so as not to jeopardize future delivery of dissident literature. Victor Louis had come up with a clever ruse—in the name of protecting writers, he could do the KGB's bidding and sabotage them.[12]

Because the Soviet Union was not a member of the International Copyright Agreement, Hutchinson could not claim breach of copyright. Instead, on July 31, the company filed an injunction in the High Court in London for breach of confidence, on the grounds that Svetlana had entrusted the manuscript to people who had no right to share it with others. The injunction was granted. Harper & Row and Hutchinson immediately rushed a Russian version of the book into print.

Ironically, the KGB's plot backfired. If Victor Louis hadn't tried to preempt the publication of *Twenty Letters to a Friend*, the book's release might have been delayed until the fiftieth anniversary of the Revolution was over. Influential Americans like Arthur Schlesinger were pressing for a November date. Schlesinger told his friend Patricia Bohlen that, during his recent visit to Moscow, the Soviets had appealed to him to ask the US government to delay publication.

Bohlen had been outraged. "What business had Arthur, who makes a fuss about Soviet censorship, to try to get our government to interfere with plans of publishers?"[13] In fact, though, Evan Thomas had been waffling, suggesting Harper & Row would consider November 13 as a possible date, but when it became clear that Victor Louis was selling a pirated copy, it was imperative to get the book out as soon as possible.[14]

Victor Louis managed to sell his pirated version of Svetlana's book, as well as a collection of two hundred photographs, to the German magazine *Stern*. In mid-August, *Stern* published the first of four articles on the "Secret Album of Stalin's Daughter," summarizing anecdotes from Svetlana's book, which it called "a tame bunny," and printing the private photographs confiscated from her desk in the House on the Embankment. The images were mislabeled and not flattering, including a photo of a slightly overweight Svetlana in what looked like her underwear at a private beach. A caption lied: "On her flight, Svetlana could not take along her photo album. Her children are now publishing it." No mention was made of Victor Louis.[15]

In *Stern*'s "conversations" with Joseph in an article titled "Mother Is a Little Bit Screwed Up," Joseph is quoted as referring to his mother's "unstable character," her "fickleness," her "wild character," and her "vacillating mental states." Joseph then allegedly described a private visit he and Katya made to the Mausoleum on Red Square to view the embalmed Stalin. "I took Katya by the hand and we went up to the coffin on tiptoe. . . . It was dark and quiet. I can't remember if I felt anything. It was something like fear and awe as we saw our grandfather lying there lifeless and waxed. . . . It's no secret that I'm proud of my grandfather to this day." Joseph seemed to be following KGB directives. The KGB wanted Svetlana slandered and had already begun the rehabilitation of Stalin's image. *Stern* commented drily, "The shadow of their grandfather offers a lot of conveniences: 200 rubles of government pension and two government apartments. . . . Katya has her own horse. Joseph went for a vacation in the Caucasus after four months in the army."[16]

Meanwhile, the Italian journalist Enzo Biagi had been working on the Svetlana story. Perhaps because he was known for his Communist sympathies, he was given access to Svetlana's relatives. (Without official permission, he could never have met them).

In an interview with Joseph Alliluyev, Biagi asked, "If your mother appeared on the doorstep, what would you do?" Joseph responded coldly. "Obviously I wouldn't shout for joy. . . . It is she who left us." Joseph told Biagi, "We will meet again only in one situation: if she comes back. . . . This is our country."

Biagi also interviewed a number of Svetlana's Moscow friends. The journalist Tatiana Tess condemned her.

Everything has been left for her just as it was in her father's lifetime: apartment, dacha, the large one as well, and she chose Zhukovka, because it was easier to keep up; she did not have to pay for anything, and could use the State's car at any time; she could go into any kind of rest home. . . . We were very close friends; I loved her very much. . . . Her children were very dear, they loved her and she could be proud of them. . . . She had an erratic personality; she has the childish complexes of a princess. Nothing is impossible or forbidden for her, because she has been used to having her own way since she was a little girl. . . . One shouldn't abandon one's children.[17]

Biagi spoke to Svetlana's old lover, Aleksei Kapler, who said he was shocked at her defection. "When I heard of her departure I couldn't believe it. I have my own ideas about Russian women; I have known many. . . . I believe something terrible, something abnormal must have happened to Svetlana, perhaps an illness of some kind." Her act was unforgivable. Kapler paraphrased Turgenev: "Russia can do without us, but no one can live without Russia."[18]

When Biagi asked the writer Ilya Ehrenburg about Joseph's comments on his mother, Ehrenburg replied cryptically: "He would do better to venerate his father [Morozov] who is Jewish, and has his own troubles."[19] He was implicitly supporting Svetlana's repudiation of the current government by himself critiquing its policies of anti-Semitism, though only those used to reading Soviet citizens' coded language would understand this. For Ehrenburg to say more would have been dangerous.

By July, Biagi had turned his research into a short book, *Svetlana: The Inside Story*. It was immediately released in Italian and hurriedly translated into English. For Svetlana, the effect of reading it, as well as the slanderous clippings from European newspapers sent to her anonymously, was shattering. While she knew that her friends and her son were under the scrutiny of the KGB and had to denounce her defection, it was excruciating to have her private life smeared. "Why did they have to go after my children?" she asked. But of course she knew why.[20]

One day at the end of the summer when there was no one else at the Kennan farm but the children and their babysitter, Svetlana called them all out to the veranda. She asked Joan's son Christopher, who was seventeen, to bring her the lighter fluid for the barbecue. She told the children they were witnesses to a solemn ceremony: "I am burning my Soviet passport in answer to lies and calumny." They all watched wide-eyed as the passport flared brightly. When it was over, Svetlana "carried out the handful of ashes and blew on them. The wind carried them off."[21]

There was one consolation, however, that restored a modicum of her dignity. That June the *Atlantic* had published her article "To Boris Leonidovich Pasternak." She'd worked with Pasternak's British translator, Max Hayward, to whom Priscilla McMillan had introduced her before their falling-out. In his brief preface to the article, Hayward had offered lavish praise: "Svetlana Alliluyeva's reflections illuminate the sense of Pasternak's work as no other comment has ever done."[22] She had drawn parallels between Zhivago's terrible fate and the devastation in her own lost family and country. As Hayward was the translator of *Doctor Zhivago* into English, his words carried weight. He was invited to visit the Kennan family at Cherry Orchard farm at the beginning of the summer.

Joan Kennan had been surprised when Svetlana chose to settle herself on the third floor of the farmhouse, which got unbearably hot in the summer months. There were other, more comfortable rooms below, but Svetlana had picked this space because it was where Kennan had his study. One wall was covered with bookshelves painted white, as her bookshelves had been in Moscow, and the shelves were full of Russian books, newspapers, and journals. The huge plain wooden table flooded by sunshine, which served Kennan as a desk, now served as hers. But the third floor also had the convenience of a door that closed off the upper reaches of the house. Joan Kennan remarked that Svetlana and Max would go up to the third floor and close the door. "There was a romantic interest, certainly on Svetlana's part, and I think she was pretty starry eyed for a while because I think she thought they would be going off into the sunset together."[23]

Max Hayward was an interesting figure. Two years older than Svetlana, he'd begun his career in the world of diplomacy, working in the late 1940s at the British Embassy in Moscow, once serving as the British ambassador's translator on a visit to Stalin in the Kremlin. He was currently a professor of Soviet literary politics at Saint Antony's College, Oxford.

Saint Antony's was the "spy college,"[24] rumored to have connections with the London branch of the Congress of Cultural Freedom, one of the CIA's most effective Cold War covert operations, which supported journals and set up international congresses to reach intellectuals behind the Iron Curtain. That very May 1967, it was finally confirmed that the CIA, through the CCF, had been secretly funding the prestigious British magazine *Encounter* for more than ten years.

When Svetlana's article on Pasternak came out that June and the KGB realized that Max Hayward was working with her, he was called a CIA spy in the Soviet press. There was no evidence for this, but Max Hayward was certainly one of the foreign academics who were personae non gratae in the Soviet Union. In the frenzied 1960s world of intelligence intrigue, it made sense that Hayward was thought to be safe to manage Svetlana. He was well known to George Kennan and Arthur Sulzberger from summers spent together on the Greek island of Spetses. But Hayward was more of a gadfly than anything else. Looking back, he liked to boast of the wealthy Americans whom he'd "managed to con" into generously supporting his lifestyle.[25]

Svetlana was delighted by Max. They spent their time in her third-floor room speaking in Russian about Russia, about "everything under the sun." No one understood her problems and worries better than Max Hayward. He was at the farm so often that Joan Kennan ended up doing his laundry.[26]

Before long, Svetlana was in love with Max. He was flattering and he clearly admired her, but he soon discovered he was in over his head. As Priscilla McMillan, who knew him well, explained:

> Max was a person whose idea of heaven was to come to New York and stay at the Chelsea, where [Bob] Dylan, [Judy] Collins, Leonard Cohen had stayed, and drink a lot. There was one time he left to go to supervise the Maltese translation of *Doctor Zhivago*. We were all laughing. Or when it came to translating [Solzhenitsyn's] *One Day in the Life of Ivan Denisovich*, I and my friends locked him up in a room in the Russian Center here and took him his meals so he couldn't get out and drink all night and could translate it in time for the deadline.

In Priscilla's opinion, whoever had an affair with Max had to be smart enough "to know he wasn't marriageable material. But Svetlana had a tropism towards men and wouldn't have applied that kind of sophistication."[27]

Joan Kennan remembered picking up Max at the train station in Harrisburg on one of his visits. He was clearly distraught at having entangled himself with Svetlana. He said that she seemed to expect to marry him. Joan wasn't sure whether they had an actual physical affair or who seduced whom, but in any case, Svetlana was expecting to be with Max. By the middle of August, he beat a hasty retreat to England. However, Svetlana was not so easily discouraged.

When George Kennan returned from Africa at the end of

the summer, though Max had asked her not to, Svetlana discussed her plans with him. Max, she assured Kennan, had said he was coming back to the United States for a month at Christmas, and had invited her to join him in Oxford. He was going to help her write a second book. Kennan knew Hayward. He advised Svetlana, gently, that it would be hard for her to get to England now that she had burned her Soviet passport.

That October, she finally received a letter from Max saying it was impossible for him to leave Oxford. She wrote to Joan Kennan that she didn't know what happened. It had to be the slander from Moscow. She ranted, "Why have I escaped from USSR, indeed, to meet here, in this free country, something which again makes me feel the 'Government property' but not the free human being?"[28]

She lamented to Joan that she was terrified of being alone. "I cannot imagine my own life just alone—it is not my nature to live just by my own. My life can only wind itself around somebody—and you know how much I have lost. . . . To remain alone just in the beginning of some kind of the new life seems for me absolutely unbearable."[29] Svetlana may have been gullible, but she was also extremely willful. She was looking to Max to save her.

Poignantly, she refused to see through Max's evasions. She believed in Max's feeling, his compassion. There was a future with him, but the world condemned her to solitude. Love was a melodrama, a longing for the person who never came; and fidelity to that person. Who but her father had taught her the dynamics of love? But this was not something that Svetlana could examine, for it would have meant confronting the psychological scars, traumas, and losses of her terrible childhood. The affair with Max fizzled out.

Svetlana decided there had to be an enemy, and the enemy became George Kennan, who was worried about "what people would say." In Moscow they said she was a "very bad woman."

She complained to Joan: "And so for the sake of my own good name, and also the honor of this country . . . I must keep away from Max Hayward and he should stay away from me." She said, "I still have great faith in Max, in his feeling, in his compassion, in everything he has given me—and can give more. But I can see that his own life becomes only full of pain because of me—and nothing else."[30] Max was probably feeling more embarrassment than pain.

The relentless KGB-staged attacks—from her son, her friends, her countrymen—appearing in Soviet and international newspapers were lacerating, and she must have felt totally exposed. Who could possibly understand what she was going through? She had turned to Max Hayward, the erudite and impeccable Russian translator, for protection. Given her outward strength, Hayward probably had no idea of her vulnerability. Uncharacteristically, Svetlana rarely spoke publicly of Max Hayward again or wrote about him in her books.

Svetlana had now tasted the intoxicating freedom of escape, but to what? From the total silence of the USSR, she had stepped into the world of the free press and was an object of everyone's scrutiny. She knew "the lies spread about me would be believed sooner than anything I might say or write. My father's name is too odious, and I am living under its shadow."[31] She was now an exile: her country, her roots, her children, and all those she loved had been amputated. When her new acquaintances closed their doors and retreated to their families, she was entirely on her own. It is hard to imagine a human being more alone than Stalin's daughter.

Chapter 21

Letters to a Friend

By 1969, Svetlana was hard at work on her second book, *Only One Year.*

Svetlana left the Kennan farm in the middle of August and headed to New York to prepare for the publication of *Twenty Letters to a Friend.* The autumn would be frenetic as she moved from household to household, often the guest of people she'd met casually who offered to take her in. It might have been fun if not for the campaign of vilification against her book and the constant intrusive attention of journalists looking for Stalin's daughter.

On August 15, while staying at the home of Evan Thomas, she met with fifteen editors of the various magazines that were serializing her book, including ones from England, Finland, Japan, Israel, Greece, and Brazil. Publicity about *Twenty Letters*, particularly the slanders from Victor Louis, had raised some concerns. Svetlana was almost amused by their initial response to her.

How they eyed me at first! I don't know what they had expected to find—a proverbial Russian baba in bast shoes, or a dark-haired Georgian with a moustache and a pipe in her mouth, like my father? Whatever it was, after two hours they warmed up to me. The conversation was un-constrained and interesting. They could not guess, of course, how much I would have liked to continue talking to them for a few more hours, ask them questions, go to a restaurant with them, have a long heart-to-heart talk with every single one. If only they could have understood what a yearning for the outside world is experienced by all of us, the cloistered and incarcerated Soviets![1]

Her demeanor impressed the editors; she was not the un-stable woman Victor Louis and others portrayed. But she was frustrated that they didn't seem to understand her main point. Russia was a paradox; her whole life consisted of paradoxes, and until Westerners fully recognized this, nothing would ever be clear. She wanted them to understand that while so-called revolutionary Russia had become a reactionary, repressive state, many Russians still miraculously maintained a climate of psychological freedom and a longing for internationalism that made it an exciting country. Russia was not only the Gulag prison system and the police state that the West focused on in its portrayal of dissidents. Among the tiny community of intellectuals, it was a vibrant, creative milieu, at least in private kitchens, and she missed it deeply. There was so much paranoid propaganda that she despaired of the West's ever understanding the conundrum that was Russia.

Svetlana spent the next two weeks in Nantucket with Alan Schwartz and his family. The place plunged her into a meditative and restorative nostalgia. She felt she was back in Koktebel in the Crimea, a seaside village where artists and friends gathered.

> Nantucket was all subdued colors: gray, overcast skies, yellow dunes, purple heather in the marshes, and, of course, the ocean, changing every day, every hour. Inconstant, capricious, at times gray, at others blue, and then again black with the white foam of rage. One never grew tired of contemplating that difficult, changeable temperament. Perhaps that was why all Russians loved the sea so. . . . To reach the blue sea, to feel in one's heart its expanse, its freedom, see its glitter in the sun, enjoy it to the full and dissolve in it. . . . Pushkin talked to the sea. Pasternak listened to it. Gorky said: "The sea laughed."[2]

In Nantucket she'd met Eleanor Friede, the widow of an Estonian immigrant from Russia, who invited her to stay at her summer home in Bridgehampton on Long Island for a couple of weeks. Friede had a small one-story cottage on the ocean. She kept a portrait of Emperor Nicholas II on her living room wall. Svetlana was amused when Eleanor offered to remove it, thinking it might offend her Communist sensibilities. The portrait stayed on the wall. They walked on the beaches collecting stones and driftwood, and Svetlana talked of her rambles along the Black Sea Coast. Though Truman Capote had a house nearby, she declined an introduction. She longed for privacy.

She was with Eleanor Friede on September 10 when the first of twelve installments of *Twenty Letters* appeared in the *New York Times*. When she eagerly opened the newspaper, she was shocked to find herself staring at a photograph from her own collection. The photograph had been taken in Sochi. She was seven years old, squirming in her father's arms as he kissed her and tickled her with his mustache. The extract was called "The Death of My Father." There were other photographs: of her father's funeral cortege; of Lavrenty Beria, with the caption "monster"; of herself sitting among the birches at Zubalovo. How had the newspaper obtained her photographs?

Over the subsequent days, for twelve issues, she read the distressing subtitles: "How My Mother Killed Herself," "My Love Affair with Kapler," "Two Marriages End in Failure," "My Brother Dies in Disgrace," "Beria Takes Over Our Household." A number of the photographs were mislabeled. In one her governess was misidentified as her mother; in another the child was not her but a stranger. She thought the newspaper must have bought the photographs from Victor Louis, because the captions contained the same inaccuracies as his article in the *London Daily Express*. There were also errors in the text.

Why hadn't the newspaper checked with her? The Greenbaum firm had neglected to ensure that preapproval rights were in her contract.[3] She complained to Evan Thomas that extracts taken from here and there in her book and illustrated by stolen photographs made her feel confused and unhappy, but there was nothing to do.[4]

In late September she moved to the home of her publisher Cass Canfield in Bedford Village. It was here that she got her first copy of *Twenty Letters*. The book was a consolation after the serialization. It was pristine; there were no photographs or lurid titles. It seemed suddenly miraculous that she was here, in America, holding in her hands a book that she had written for the drawer four years earlier in Moscow. She had never imagined then that people would be able to read it.

Soon she moved to New York, living as a guest at the Brooklyn home of her lawyer Maurice Greenbaum (though he was an executive partner of the firm of Greenbaum, Wolff & Ernst, he was not related to Edward Greenbaum). She was grateful not to be in hotels, where she would have been at the mercy of reporters, and spent much of her time with Greenbaum's twenty-two-year-old niece, who introduced her, incognito, to Manhattan. She found it easy and absorbing to be with the young woman and her friends, and as they talked of their summers in Greece and Canada, she thought how constrained the lives of her own children were. Her son had never been given permission to travel as a tourist, even to Yugoslavia.

Nevertheless, she still had reason to feel anxious. The KGB had her in its sights. She received an unexpected letter from a woman named Madame Boyko, an employee at the Soviet Embassy whom she had known slightly in Moscow. Madame Boyko wanted to meet and talk with her, even offering her services in delivering a letter or parcel to her children. "I often think of you in the evening. Is there a single person here with whom you could talk? I know Americans, they are indifferent to the lives of others, uninterested."[5] All of a sudden this stranger was concerned about her *loneliness*. She was certain that KGB officers at the Soviet Embassy had dictated the letter.

In October, CIA officer Donald Jameson wrote to George Kennan:

As perhaps you have learned from Svetlana or Alan Schwartz, there have been a series of interesting new approaches to her from the Soviets. The affair of the letter from Madame Boyko [is] . . . only part of the story. Two KGB officers in New York have mentioned her recently to contacts of theirs. In both cases the content of their comments seemed to foreshadow an attempt to urge Svetlana to return to the Soviet Union for family reasons.[6]

Reviews of *Twenty Letters* began to appear in late September, and predictably, they were more about the reviewers' politics than about the book. Bertram Wolfe, who had written biographies of Lenin, Trotsky, and Stalin, wrote in the *Chicago Daily News*: "[Alliluyeva's] memoirs take us into a world whose people and way of life are utterly strange to us, a world of gloomy Kremlin splendors, intrigues and suspicion, espionage, preposterous accusations and blood purges."[7] Arthur Schlesinger ended his review in the *Atlantic* by commenting that the Russians were upset by the book and asked: "How would Americans have felt at the celebration of the fiftieth anniversary of the Declaration of Independence if the British, a month before July 4, 1826, had published a book by a daughter of George Washington exposing the glorious experiment as a racket and a fraud?" But he said the Russians were wrong. "This book is not the work of a sensationalist or a traitor. It is wrung from an agonized conscience and a sickened heart."[8] In the *New York Times Book Review*, Olga Carlisle, a writer of Russian extraction whose family had been forced into exile after the triumph of the Bolsheviks in 1917 and who later helped to smuggle Alexander Solzhenitsyn's *Gulag Archipelago* to the West, expressed astonishment. "To be Stalin's daughter and to remain human is itself admirable—and we have every evidence that Svetlana Alliluyeva remained so."[9]

But there were also negative reviews. In the *Times* of London, Arthur Koestler dismissed the book. "One was certainly not prepared for the voice of this nice, homely woman, treating us to nice homely reflections."[10] The journalist Alexander Werth's review in the *Nation* was titled "Svetlana: Who Needs

Her?" Werth insisted, absurdly, that Alliluyeva misdated her affair with Kapler. He had been in Moscow when the affair was the subject of gossip.[11] Elizabeth Hardwick complained that Svetlana had been so overexposed by the press that her book had the staleness of old news.[12]

On October 18—Svetlana remembered the date because the encounter mattered so much to her—she met Alexandra Lvovna Tolstoya, the eighty-three-year old daughter of the famous author of *War and Peace*. Imprisoned by the Bolsheviks in 1920 but released, Tolstoya had chosen exile in the United States. Svetlana traveled to visit her at Valley Cottage in Rockland County, a colony she'd established dedicated to her father's principles of nonviolence—surely an epic meeting of daughters. Svetlana worshipped Tolstoy and had visited his home in Yasnaya Polyana in Russia several times. Over a Russian dinner of borscht, buckwheat kasha, rye bread, herring, and vodka, she told Tolstoya she would like to help her Tolstoy Foundation.

By the end of October, as she had said she would, Svetlana began to distribute money from her charitable trust. The *New York Times* reported in a blazing headline, MRS. ALLILUYEVA DONATES $340,000.[13] The donations included $90,000 to organizations helping needy Russians abroad, $50,000 to the Tolstoy Foundation, $10,000 to the New York–based Russian Children's Welfare Society, $5,000 to the Fund for Relief for Russian Writers and Scientists in Exile, $5,000 to *Novy zhurnal*, a dissident Russian literary journal in New York noted for its opposition to the Daniel/Sinyavsky trial, $10,000 to the Russian Children's Home in Paris, and $10,000 to the Pestalozzi Children's Village in Switzerland. It was her lawyer, Edward Greenbaum, who phoned the *New York Times* to report the donations.

Alexandra Tolstoya had assumed Svetlana's offer was casual.

Interviewed by the *Times*, she said she found Mrs. Alliluyeva "a fine woman, very sincere. I think she suffers. The Russians ought to be kinder to her." The editor of *Novoye Russkoye slovo*, the oldest Russian-language newspaper in the United States, remarked cryptically, "If children were to be punished because fathers were guilty, we would do the same thing the Communists did in Russia."[14]

When the jubilee celebration of the fiftieth anniversary of the Great Russian Revolution took place on November 7 and the Soviet Union was greeted with endless praise for its socialist progress on American radio stations of the radical left, Svetlana turned off the radio. To her, this was a day of mourning; she spent the day brooding over her mother's death.

Like many exiles from the Soviet bloc, Svetlana did not approve of the radical left. She watched the hippie movement and anti–Vietnam War protests of 1967 with dismay. "There is no ideal society," she said curtly, but at least "here a person can leave."[15]

By the end of October, she'd found a home of sorts. Colonel Ruth Biggs, whom she'd met through George Kennan, invited her to stay at her home in Bristol, in Newport County, Rhode Island. Biggs was actually a lieutenant colonel, now retired, who had served with the Women's Army Corps in World War II. She had good connections in Washington and tried, unsuccessfully, to help Svetlana search for information about her half brother, Yakov, whose death in the Nazi prisoner-of-war camp in 1943 remained unclear: had he committed suicide or been executed? Svetlana spent the next month and a half with Biggs. They passed their days weeding the garden overlooking Narragansett Bay and taking long walks by the ocean, while the colonel kept the newsmen at bay. Svetlana desperately needed this respite. She wrote to Joan Kennan:

I had such a difficult time—and finally, now, when [I am staying with] Colonel Biggs (with black cats) and when I can relax and try to forget all the worries—now I feel completely exhausted. It seems to me that all my strength has gone—the last summer, autumn, the book, the reviews, TV interview and all that propaganda of slander which continues to go from Moscow—all that finally has ruined me. I feel no more strength to resist all that.[16]

In the December 9 issue of the *New Yorker*, the literary critic and expert on Russia Edmund Wilson, who had not yet met Svetlana, wrote a long article that completely vindicated her complaints about being misunderstood. Few critics carried Wilson's authority. He castigated the press—in its eagerness to exploit the sensational aspects of her story, it had vulgarized her. The magazine *Stern* had cast doubts on her veracity. The TV journalists who had interviewed her were hostile, as if they wished to degrade their subject. *Esquire* magazine reached the lowest point with a cover photograph of Svetlana painted with Stalin's mustache, implying that she was trading on her father's infamy.

Wilson lashed out:

Thus America has exploited Svetlana and at the same time accused her of exploiting herself. The Soviets denounce her as a traitor and a tool of the United States, and intimate that she is off her head, while the more fantastic White Russian émigrés, who do not want to believe that the daughter of Stalin can have anything good about her, declare variously that her sojourn in Switzerland was for the purpose of collecting money that her father had stashed away there, and that her interest in religion is an impudent pretence, since she is really a Soviet spy. The last idea that any of these critics seem to be able to entertain is that . . . she may have left the Soviet Union with something like a sense of mission—to repudiate her father's "system" and to try to make amends for his crimes. No one seems to ask himself what it would be like to be Stalin's daughter, brought up on the gospel of the class struggle and later a witness to the horrors that this gospel was made to produce, and at the same time to find oneself a serious, affectionate, and spiritually minded woman. . . . Why are the only motives imagined for her so often only sordid ones?[17]

This review mattered deeply to Svetlana. She had become accustomed to the merciless attacks against her father in the USSR during the Thaw, attacks that had also fallen on her, but in the West she had naively expected a different reception. It's astonishing that she absorbed the blows and continued. She had an undaunted optimism, honed by years of surviving so many cruel bereavements, so many disappointments and losses. Somehow she continued to believe in the future. Was this merely the product of growing up at the top of the pyramid and learning to wield the power there? Detractors said so, but she said her optimism was founded in a spiritual sense of the profundity of nature and the Good.

In 1963, still trapped in the USSR, she had ended *Twenty Letters to a Friend* with an epilogue addressed to future generations who would look back "at their country's history with a feeling of pain, contrition and bewilderment":

I hope they won't forget that what is Good never dies— that it lived on in the hearts of men even in the darkest times and was hidden where no one thought to look for it, that it never died out or disappeared completely.

Everything on our tormented earth that is alive and breathes, that blossoms and bears fruit, lives only by virtue of and in the name of Truth and Good.[18]

It's a remarkable statement from Stalin's daughter. Many wanted to dismiss this as rhetoric, sentimentality, self-delusion, or hypocritical evasion. And yet she would never let go of this belief in the Good. How to explain it? Perhaps when human beings are tested to the depth that Russians were tested, they find other dimensions of the inner self. Andrei Sinyavsky had taught Svetlana much about belief in the Good. It sustained him through his years in the Gulag. It had less to do with Western notions of goodness, the absence of evil, than with the will to affirm good in the face of evil. Svetlana kept going when others would certainly have quit. Something drove her to pick herself up each time. And the tests would continue almost indefinitely.

Chapter 22

A Cruel Rebuff

In a photo taken in 1969, Svetlana stands proudly outside 50 Wilson Road.

In December 1967, George and Annelise Kennan had good news for Svetlana. They'd found her a house to rent in Princeton. She had been a nomad for nine months now, living as a guest in other people's houses, and it would be a relief to be settled. The house at 85 Elm Road belonged to Dorothy

Commins, a professional musician whose husband, a New York publisher, had recently died. Commins was setting out on a world tour to collect children's songs and musical games, leaving her substantial home to Svetlana to rent for a year.

The house had a living room large enough for musical recitals, a library filled with musical scores and records, and a grand piano. There were fine engravings and watercolors on the walls, and old silver and bronze decorative objects scattered throughout the rooms. Everywhere, there were also plastic flowers, which Svetlana stuffed away discreetly in drawers. She brought only her boxes of books, sent to her by strangers from around the world, and the clothes she'd collected since her arrival.

Svetlana claimed that when she went down to the cellar of the house, she found men installing wires. They said these were for a fire alarm, but she was certain the men were from the CIA or FBI. She complained to Kennan, who responded that, well, yes, it was possible, but he couldn't prevent it. Anyway, he was concerned for her safety. She laughed. Here she was in the free world, still bugged. No matter.[1] Was she actually being bugged? Svetlana sometimes gave in to paranoia, but the FBI had certainly been informed as soon as she moved into 85 Elm Road and kept tabs on her, believing, accurately, that the Soviets had not given up on Stalin's daughter.[2] They knew she was working on a second book. If she left Princeton for more than two days, she felt uncomfortable unless she put her papers in a safe-deposit box in the bank.

On December 19 she sat at a small table at the Princeton Inn with Annelise Kennan and Louis Fischer. It had been exactly a year since she had left her son at the Moscow airport in a raging blizzard and flown to New Delhi. Who could have predicted that the flight would land her at this table? "Let us drink then to this *year of freedom!*" Louis Fischer said.[3] Svetlana had met Fischer a little over a month before at a dinner at the Kennans' home on November 12, and he had taken it upon himself to show her how to live in America. There was so much she didn't know. One of the first things he did was to accompany her to a Princeton bank to open a bank account and show her how to balance a checkbook.[4]

On December 21, Svetlana was alone and in an antic mood and decided to play a joke. She put out snacks and wine on the table and dialed the emergency number for the police. When the police arrived, she said, "Merry Christmas" and invited them in. It was the same spirit of mischief that had led her to step on the gas when she passed the sentry post in Zhukovka. It amused her to test authority, though only someone used to wielding it would find this amusing. The police replied, "We're on duty. We don't drink,"[5] though apparently one of them laughed. Gossip soon traveled around Princeton and even reached the newspapers that she had dialed the emergency number to summon the police because she was so desperately lonely.[6]

Svetlana was actually excited by her new life of freedom, though she was, not unexpectedly, looking for someone to share it. She was deeply attracted to Louis Fischer. Fischer was seventy-one when he met Svetlana, but he was still as charismatic and vital as he had been in the days when he had out-Hemingwayed Hemingway. It is hard to imagine a more volatile career and a more seductive man.

Fischer grew up in the Jewish ghetto in Philadelphia, the son of Russian immigrants. After serving with the British army in Palestine in World War I, he married a Russian and began working as special European correspondent for the *Nation*. "We correspondents were one big, almost permanent poker party," he recalled.[7]

Fischer knew Russia well. Enthusiastic about the Russian Revolution, he'd lived for nine years in Moscow until the Great Terror of 1937, when he quit the country, leaving behind his wife and two sons. Through the intercession of Eleanor Roosevelt, he eventually got his family to the United States, but he abandoned them again, saying he preferred to live in hotels.[8]

Fischer was most famous for his coverage of the Spanish Civil War. He'd worked with Hemingway, with the novelist André Malraux, with John Dos Passos; he'd met Gandhi and Churchill. There were few among the famous whom Fischer hadn't encountered. By the time Svetlana met him, he had published ten books, including a somewhat hurriedly written biography of Stalin completed in 1952, and a biography of Gandhi. Fischer was now a professor at Princeton, affiliated with the Woodrow Wilson School of Public and International Affairs. He radiated confidence. The sheer scale of his life, its encyclopedic breeziness, was thrilling.

And now Fischer sat across from Stalin's daughter in a restaurant in Princeton. To him, of course, she was an opportunity. Svetlana would have the inside story. From the beginning, it was clear that Fischer was less interested in Svetlana than in the idea of Svetlana—as Stalin's daughter, she was at the center of the maelstrom of twentieth-century history.

Fischer was obsessed with Stalin. In 1927, with a delegation of American labor leaders and intellectuals, he had spent six hours interviewing him. He described Stalin as having "crafty eyes," a "low forehead," and "ugly short black and gold teeth when he smiles," but he was impressed. Stalin was "unsentimental, steel-willed, unscrupulous and irresistible."[9] *Irresistible* was not quite the word one would expect, but according to accounts of those close to Stalin, the *vozhd* could be charismatic and even seductive.

The Yugoslav author Milovan Djilas corroborated Fischer's assessment. He knew Stalin well and described him shrewdly as a "cold calculator," a man of "fanatical dogmatism," but said that "his was a passionate and many-sided nature—though all sides were equal and so convincing that it seemed he never dissembled but was always truly experiencing each of his roles." Whatever he wanted "he could approach by manipulating and kneading the reality and the living men who comprised it."[10] Stalin had a capacity to focus so intently on whomever he was talking to that the person felt intimately connected, almost, for the moment, as if living in the reality he, Stalin, invented. One could almost say the same of Fischer. This gift of attention made him a brilliant journalist and a consummate seducer.

Svetlana would claim that Fischer was the first man to capture her imagination with the intensity of her long-ago lover Aleksei Kapler. At forty-one, she must have felt sixteen again. Indeed, she behaved as if she were.

Perhaps it wasn't surprising that Svetlana found Louis Fischer attractive. He was an outsize figure, larger than life. But in her way, so was she. Her old lover, David Samoilov, had said that there was something of the tyrant in Svetlana's emotional exuberance. When she was drawn to someone, she dived into the relationship until it consumed everything else. She demanded a drama.

The affair with Fischer had been building for some time, but for Svetlana the climax came when Fischer invited her to accompany him to the memorial service for Dr. Martin Luther King at the University Chapel in Princeton. She'd phoned Fischer when she heard the news of Dr. King's assassination on April 4. The shock and distress in his voice had been palpable.

After they'd spent the night together, she wrote to Fischer that at the memorial service, as they had sat under the filtered light from the blue and yellow stained glass windows and the organ played, she'd had a "strange feeling" that she and he were "joined together." "It was our wedding, the union of two souls to be always together, to do only good to each other. That was something that Martin Luther King left for you and me—

because he, certainly, left his heart with us, with everybody, <u>who was present</u> that afternoon at University Chapel."[11]

But Fischer seemed unmoved by Svetlana's romanticism. He was not looking for a soul mate. The central motive of his life was his own work, and at seventy-one, he cherished his independence. On their next encounter a few days later, he was decidedly cool. "I felt the strongest pain of uselessness," she complained.

> Well, dear, you have taken my life in your hands, now, DO SOMETHING with it: throw it away, press it to your heart, put it aside gently, put it in the freezer for a while, to keep it there—DO SOMETHING, if you really are concerned about me and my feelings. BUT, please, PLEASE, do not just play the game with it. . . . My only peace is near you, when I embrace you and your hands ARE AROUND ME. Svetlana[12]

Having clearly raised her expectations, Fischer seemed to have been in retreat from her all-consuming passion. He warned her that he needed his independence for his work. She countered: "You do not need a mistress—forgive my vulgar words. Neither I ever looked to find a lover. We both need something else—warmth, friendship, understanding. . . . It is love. Everyone needs it."[13] By June she was assuring him she would follow his "way." "I will not come and will not make telephone calls."[14] She even promised to write shorter letters.

Unfortunately, she could not control her anger. In a burst of fury, she stormed over to his house and returned all his things, including a ring he had given her. Three days later, in a five-page letter, she tried to explain why she had been so upset. It is a very sad letter.

She had come home from an unsatisfactory meeting with

him—she realized he had made sure to have his housekeeper present to avoid her passionate expectations. Then she found out inadvertently that his excuse for cutting their encounter short—that he had to meet an ambassador for lunch—was a lie. He had really been having a casual lunch with Dmitri Nabokov and his wife.

She got home in a horrible mood, which as usual she acknowledged was her own fault—she should not have barged in on him. Then she found that a rat had come to die in her garage. It was an ordinary domestic drama—a neighbor had probably set out rat poison—but for Svetlana it was traumatizing.

The animal looked dying, breathing heavily, could not run away and looked at me with that terrible expression of a dying creature, not much different from a human being. I am not afraid of rats and mice, as some people are, but that was different, that was frightening because it was death. May be simply my nerves were already strained. The rat could not go away from my garage, she came not from my home, from outside, and she just came here to die. I locked the door from the garage to the kitchen, and could not eat any supper. From time to time I opened the door to see. The rat was slowly crawling over from one place to another. The big flies were already sitting on her back.

Louis, that night was really a nightmare. I did not sleep, thinking about that animal in my garage. We were two alone in the whole house. . . . I was thinking about myself in the most gloomy and tragic ways—just something like that rat, whom nobody really can love or need. . . . This rat was like something very BAD in my own soul.

And—in half an hour—Burgi called to tell me the terrible news about Robert Kennedy. . . . [Kennedy had been assassinated at midnight on June 5.]

And, of course, I was already in a tragic mood and horrible news only PROVED that there is NO justice in this world, so the answer came back to my mind very quickly. Everything is so bad, because Louis does not love me anymore.[15]

It is hard to know how a man like Louis Fischer would have reacted to such a letter. Her candor and the intensity of her feeling may have moved him. He knew her history—few were more intimately acquainted with death than she. But he was far too cynical and far too worldly to want to take on her raw need.

The affair continued but remained secret. When the Kennans invited her to dinner, Svetlana would suggest it might be nice if Mr. Fischer joined them. Fischer took to phoning her every day at 10:00 a.m., and he would drop by 85 Elm Road to sit for an hour or two while she read him pages from the new book she was working on. When he was away, as he often was, she sent him chatty letters and settled for the assurance of his continued attachment. There was another explosion when she suspected he was seeing a young woman named Deirdre Randall. Her suspicion was right, of course, but he must have reassured her. He remained *tentatively* in her life.

The hook for Svetlana was that, as Fyodor Volkenstein had once done with her first book, Fischer was encouraging her to write. She was working hard on her new manuscript, but she wrote to him, "I need a help. It does not mean that I need an editor or advisor or co-author, no, but I badly need the help of sircumstance [sic], the help of an atmosphere which surrounds me. . . . I need your presence . . . even a silent one."[16]

However, to understand this love affair, it is important to know who Fischer really was. He was a romantic predator. He drew women in but had no desire to fulfill their expectations once he'd raised these. Svetlana was simply one in a long line of women who'd fallen for him.

Meanwhile, fifteen months after her defection, political intrigue continued to swirl above Svetlana's head. When Robert Rayle and his wife, Ramona, returned from India that April, Rayle's boss at the CIA asked him to serve as Svetlana's case officer. He would be responsible not only for her welfare but also for her "exploitation" for the maximum benefit to the US government. The idea now was to make Svetlana the center of a "propaganda campaign" against the Soviet Union.[17]

Rayle told him this was a bad idea. If the CIA tried to make Svetlana a "featured, public spokesperson against the USSR," she would feel manipulated and might turn against the United States. He refused the assignment. Instead, he worked on covert actions to help émigré groups and facilitate the transmission and publication of dissident literature. It was exciting work: one of his student contacts came back from the Soviet Union with "a footlocker of manuscripts by Nadezhda Mandelstam."[18]

Rayle's boss next turned to Donald (Jamie) Jameson. This was a wise choice. Svetlana soon trusted Jamie and became very fond of him. When he visited her in Princeton, she would tell Louis Fischer that her "'invisible friend' from Washington" was in town.[19]

It was probably Jameson who facilitated her application for "residence status." In June 1968, she took the bus to New York to get her resident card and her reentrance permit. Alan Schwartz accompanied her to the INS.[20] "We were both so worried, like schoolchildren before an exam," she wrote to Fischer. "Actually I feel a little different after this, somehow calmer. Driving home on the bus yesterday feeling totally, totally at home."[21]

She told Fischer that while she was in the city, the General (her lawyer, Edward Greenbaum) gave her yet another "astronomy lesson," as they called his talks about her finances. "I find it so difficult and I understand very little, but I'm trying."[22] Her money was invested in the name of the firm of Greenbaum, Wolff

& Ernst in a New York bank, which sent regular monthly transfers to her bank account in Princeton. When she wanted to buy a large item, she had to ask her lawyers to send her an advance.[23]

One of the items she bought that summer was a bottle green, four-door Dodge sedan, which she kept for ten years. She had fantasies of driving across the country, but she didn't have a driver's license. Evenings, she sat behind the wheel of her car, remembering her days as a teenager when she drove surreptitiously through the streets of Moscow with her Alliluyev cousins. Finally the gardener's son offered to teach her to use an automatic transmission. She passed her driving test. Now she felt free; she could go anywhere.

That July, after she'd submitted an outline and a first chapter of her new book, she signed a contract with Harper & Row for an advance of $50,000 (Copex Establishment was not involved). The amount reflected the middling sales of *Twenty Letters to a Friend*. As Pamela McMillan had feared, Greenbaum had oversold the serialization rights; people read the extensive extracts and didn't buy the book. But for Svetlana, money had no real meaning; she was simply happy to be back at work.

She spent her days writing. Placing a low stool on her back terrace and her typewriter on a chair, she sat barefoot in shorts and T-shirt, smelling the freshly cut grass, and worked. She still wrote in Russian, and the ideas flowed quickly. She would take breaks and head to the local grocery store on Nassau Street to buy her food or to Urken Hardware to buy supplies from friendly Mrs. Urken. Sometimes she would take the bus to New York to see her editor, Dick Passmore, at Harper & Row, and it became their habit to go out for a quick supper at the Jolly Shilling on Lexington Avenue, where the steaks were good and a blind pianist played with his Alsatian dog resting beside him.[24]

Svetlana was still getting so much mail that she longed for a secretary rather than all her lawyers and agents. One letter in particular must have moved her deeply. It was from the Russian writer Arkady Belinkov:

AUGUST 18, 1968

Dear Svetlana Iosifovna,

I read your book four months ago in Moscow, but, of course, couldn't write to you from there about its enormous meaning, high literary achievements, and role in our fate. Books like these people read at night and all in one go, from them are written out quotes that are passed around the city and return to you as almost unrecognizable tales. You Muscovites, you all remember this so well.

The first book that was given me on my day of freedom was yours. Now I gift it myself so that each of my new friends will be tempted to bring me great spiritual happiness.

I write to you as an authoress, author of an astounding book, showing your incredible knowledge of the agonizing history of Russian cultural thought; you are a comrade in this difficult craft of writing.[25]

In 1944, at the age of twenty-three, Belinkov had been arrested for writing an anti-Soviet novel and circulating it among friends. Betrayed by a *stukach* (informer), he was sentenced to death until Count Aleksei Tolstoy interceded with Stalin. He spent twelve years in the Gulag, one of those years in a cell once occupied by Aleksei Kapler. "The chamber was still full of stories of him," he wrote to Svetlana.[26] Belinkov was freed in 1956, but the repressions of the Brezhnev government led him and his wife, Natalia, to flee to West Germany in 1968 and then to the United States. That Svetlana's was the first book he read as he prepared to leave for the West and that he gave it to friends was the deepest affirmation she could wish for.

Svetlana immediately phoned to say she would love to meet the Belinkovs. She would drop by on her way back from a trip to Boston. The idea that someone could so casually drop over still shocked them. In a book Natalia and Arkady Belinkov wrote together, Natalia described that first meeting in Greenwich:

> She was of an average height, a fragile, red-haired woman who was warmhearted and gentle. At the same time, Svetlana's resemblance to her father made anyone speaking with her a bit uncomfortable. . . . Imagine a house that I already described as "rural" in the suburbs of New York. (Tranquillity in the park beyond the windows.) The face of comrade Stalin is leaning over his escaped victim, and the hands of his daughter gently touch Arkadii's stooped shoulders. And a quiet voice: "Everything will be all right. Everything will be all right." Who was Svetlana persuading that time: him or herself?
>
> Our "foreign" fates were so similar! We agreed that as soon as we would get the chance, we would come to Princeton. "And we will drink tea in the kitchen! Yes?" (Svetlana felt joy from the renewal of Moscow customs.) "Some evening in the kitchen, over a cup of weak Moscow tea, could be a revelation" . . . she wrote in one of her books.[27]

The previous January she had written to the critic Edmund Wilson to say she was grateful for his review of *Twenty Letters to a Friend* in the *New Yorker*, and now she wrote to him again to ask him if he might be interested in the work of her friend Arkady Belinkov. Wilson asked her for more information about him, and she replied that Belinkov was an intelligent and charming man who had suffered terribly, and she wanted to help him. The circles he had landed in at Yale were inviting him to lecture, but their liberal delusion that "capitalism and socialism [could] meet halfway" drove Belinkov crazy. He had been imprisoned in the "socialist" Gulag. She told Wilson she rather enjoyed the fact that Americans seemed healthy, naive, and openhearted. It was a relief after "Russian psychological complexities," but Belinkov was finding it hard going.[28]

On September 10 the Belinkovs took the bus to Princeton. They were impressed by Svetlana's spacious house on Elm Road, with its grand piano, and amused to find bouquets of plastic flowers jumping out from the linen closets where Svetlana had stuffed them. The three spent most of their time in the large kitchen drinking tea and talking of their escapes, their common friends in Russia, and the current repression under Leonid Brezhnev. The Belinkovs were already aware of the tactless behavior of the Russian émigré community toward Svetlana. As Natalia Belinkov put it, "Some treated Svetlana with utter spite because she was the daughter of a tyrant; others fawned over her as if she were a crown princess; yet others were not against marrying her or, at the very least, borrowing money from her."[29] The Belinkovs were eager to assure her that their friendship was genuine.

For much of that summer, Louis Fischer was not in Princeton. He traveled often to New York and had flown to Paris in mid-August to work on the manuscript for his new book, *Russia's Road from Peace to War: Soviet Foreign Relations 1917–1941*, published by Harper & Row in 1969. The night of August 20, 1968, Soviet tanks rolled into Czechoslovakia. Everyone was reeling in shock from the terrible news, though Svetlana explained that it was a logical move for the Brezhnev regime. She told George Kennan that the invasion must be an indication of turmoil and dissention at the top in the Politburo, which might lead to further unexpected events.

Soon she was hearing of arrests in Moscow. She wrote to Fischer:

> Did you know that Pavel Litvinov is arrested? Larissa Daniels, and many others? Arkady says that he knows them all well, and that he recently received a letter from Moscow which said they just started grabbing them and choking them—so far events in Czechoslovakia are steal-ing the attention of the public from such "minutia" like some poets and intellectuals—horrible. It's necessary to pay attention to the news every minute.[30]

As the repression continued, she worried for friends—the au-thorities were arresting so many—and was desperate for news of her children. She knew that the Komsomols and the Communist Party would be exerting brutal pressure on all youth—the slight-est statement or action would lead to expulsion from a university. "All of this seriously complicates my contact with my children," she wrote to Fischer. "That's unavoidable. I'm really trying to avoid danger. I'm always trying to guess whether Katya has ap-plied/been accepted to MGU [Moscow State University]."[31]

At a distance, the relationship with Fischer continued smoothly. She sent him chatty letters, tried to reply to his ques-tions about Politburo members like Zhukov and Mikoyan, and reassured him: "Be good and calm, dear Louis, I embrace you tenderly, like always. Kiss your dear eyes, your hands, your face."[32] By the end of August, Louis was on a beach in Tunis editing the manuscript of his book, and sent Svetlana brief notes on hotel stationery. She responded with her chatty loving letters.

One piece of good news was that she'd found a house to buy at 50 Wilson Road. The Kennans had noticed it was for sale and urged her not to miss the chance. She'd decided to look at it because it wasn't far from Fischer's house near Bayard Lane, and once she saw it, she knew she must have it. She was rather appalled at the price—$60,000—but this was not extravagant for Princeton. She had $50,000 from the advance for her new book, but she still had to request the remaining $10,000 from her New York lawyers. She had begun to be annoyed that she had to ask for her own money.

It was a typical New England frame house, cozy and compact, with a big study, a screened-in porch, a lovely terrace, and a small backyard filled with dogwoods, forsythia, crab apples, and lilac bushes. It reminded her of her dacha in Zhukovka, where she'd spent each summer with her children. The rooms upstairs were even laid out the same way Katya's and Joseph's had been. "I'm having strange premonitions about this house," she told Fischer. "Strange analogies: nice and sad. This house is calling me in to itself. These rooms upstairs, it's as if they're waiting for my children. I can't describe to you what the feeling is like."[33] She was tired of living in other people's houses, and at least Fischer would finally discover what her personal "lifestyle" was like. She would be able to move in on December 20.

Fischer was due home from Tunis on September 17. Svetlana went to his house to bring some welcome-home flowers to greet him on his arrival. When his housekeeper, Mrs. Duffs, let her in, she found on a shelf intimate possessions of Deirdre Randall, who was working as his "research assistant." Svetlana wrote in fury to Fischer about this "evidence of [his] lies" and demanded that he choose between them. She concluded: "I could never <u>expect you</u> to be so dishonest to me."[34]

But in this soap opera Fischer was staging (it must have been addictive to have women fighting over him), this was exactly what she could expect. As usual, the women turned each other into enemies. Randall reported coyly to Fischer that Svetlana had phoned—her voice had had "the elaborate sinisterness of people in Eisenstein movies"—and had asked, "Are you wearing your beautiful nightgown?" Deirdre told Fischer that she had replied, "Of course not. Most of the time I was in bed naked." Her attack on Svetlana was cheap:

> I think she's absolutely crackers and that one of us is going to end up with an icon buried in her heart. My mommy told me not to fool around with married men. If you get home at a reasonable hour, better call her. I really feel awful. I hate being bullied and I hate most of all being afraid and she's so crude I feel I know what it was like to talk to Stalin.[35]

Svetlana resolved to end the relationship and wrote to Fischer that it was best if they parted. But she could not so easily exorcise her feelings for him. By the end of October, she confessed:

> I'm so frightened without you . . . my whole life is falling apart, I can't do anything, I'll either die or go crazy. . . . Don't leave me without any live contact with you—that's inhuman. I cannot think, I cannot work, everything is falling out of my hands.[36]

She asked to meet him on October 31. She said it was a sad and meaningful day for her, two years since Brajesh Singh died. They could have breakfast. She wouldn't offer this to anybody but him on *that* day; he must at least acknowledge this. She wouldn't call, since he had told her not to, but she begged him not to leave her completely alone on that day. Fischer did not come.

There was one piece of good news during this dark time. She received in the mail a photograph of the walls of her hospital in Kalakankar. She named it the Brajesh Singh Hospital. She wrote to Joan Kennan: "You know, what does the medical help mean for a large rural area, where thousands of people—women and children—have no doctor. This hospital will provide for them a *free* treatment. It makes me feel perfectly satisfied that after all—I have done something for the real people."[37] Joan, who had worked for the Peace Corps in Tonga, would understand, unlike other people who "often do not care about others at all." The barb was clearly directed at Fischer. She told Joan she had finished her new book. All she needed was one more month to reshape and edit it.

Yet Svetlana could not stop brooding. On November 22, she asked Fischer to return her love letters. She said it disturbed her to think his archive was under the administration of Miss Randall. She wanted to destroy her letters herself; she couldn't trust him to do it: "I no longer BELIEVE A SINGLE word you say, so I won't calm down until these documents have been returned to me."[38] Fischer replied officiously:

NOVEMBER 24, 1968

Dear Svetlana,

Letters belong to the recipient.

Your letters to me are therefore mine and you have no right to them and no right to ask for their return either politely, much less "categorically." However, since you are eager to have them, I shall send them back to you when I find time to search my files.

Fischer obviously kept a carbon copy of this letter since it remained in his archive and he certainly never found the time to return Svetlana's letters.[39]

The note was a cruel rebuff. By this gesture he had washed his hands of all responsibility. This is probably when Svetlana marched over once again to his house, this time to demand the return of her letters and other things. What happened next is sad.

Like all stories attached to Svetlana, it would eventually become available for public consumption. Years later the journalist Patricia Blake, who had worked as Fischer's co-translator, would write in a *Time* magazine article:

> One autumn evening in 1968 [Svetlana] arrived in fury at Fischer's house. He was inside with his editorial assistant, Deirdre Randall, but ignored Svetlana's knocks and shouts. As Randall remembers the scene, Svetlana raged outside the house for over an hour, weeping and demanding the return of her presents to Fischer: a travel clock and two decorative candles. When Svetlana shattered the glass panels on the sides of the door in an attempt to break in, Fischer called the police. Two officers arrived and found Svetlana hysterical, blood dripping from her cut hands.[40]

The gossip buzzed around Princeton, a town unused to such emotional extravagance: Svetlana was unstable, but what could you expect? After all, she was Stalin's daughter. Blake did not identify Randall as Fischer's lover.

One might have hoped at least for some discretion, if not sympathy, from Deirdre Randall, because she knew who Louis Fischer was. In one of her letters she chastised him: "What manner of a man sees three women in as many hours? Who would allow such a thing? Well, I just want to be the last."[41]

She told his son George that "Lou" had a "horrible hard, tough, thick-skulled frightening ego," but she adored the man, and she did manage to be the last of his girlfriends.[42] Fischer died a little over a year later, on January 15, 1970. Randall worked for the next two years on the final preparation of his book.

The gossip soon swelled. In a rage, Svetlana drove her car into Fischer's house. Princeton hostesses invited Svetlana to important dinner parties where she disappointed the guests who had wanted to meet her. She sat in stony silence and once broke into tears and abruptly left. No one thought to ask why.

Seven years later, Svetlana was still a good subject for conversation at dinner parties. Priscilla McMillan remembered one party where the episode of her breaking the glass on Louis Fischer's front door came up. In her memory, George Kennan described how he'd been summoned from a party to the police station. He appeared in his dignified suit, white handkerchief in his pocket, every inch the diplomat, and the police had said, "Oh, you again."[43] Joan Kennan asserted that, in her memory, Svetlana had been taken to the police station only once.[44]

One thinks of Svetlana at that door, banging for an hour until she broke the glass and her hands bled, and imagines that she was beating in fury against all the ghosts of her past who had failed her: her mother, her father, her brother, her lovers. And now, this new life.

Chapter 23

Only One Year

As much as she was committed to her new life, Svetlana could not forget her past—here she's photographed in 1969 while looking at family photographs.

Svetlana took possession of her new house at 50 Wilson Road on December 20, 1968. The move was hardly the joyful event she'd anticipated. She phoned her old friends Albert and George Paloesik of the Fidelity Detective Bureau and

asked them to help her move. She had bought useful, cheerful furniture for the living and dining room and a writing desk for the study; on the desk she placed the pen set Al and George had given her the previous summer. Dried flowers from the vacuum cleaner salesman sat on her kitchen table. She hated dried flowers, but these had been the salesman's gift—he said he usually charged for them—and so she kept them.

On December 24, she received a card from her children. The date, so close to the New Year's celebration, was suspiciously precise. She doubted they sent it. She was sure it came through the Soviet Embassy and was a sadistic taunt. Why was she alone? If she returned home, she could be with her children.

At some point, Louis Fischer phoned to thank her for her Christmas card and gift. She wrote to him the day after Christmas to say that she'd sent neither a gift nor a card but was simply returning his things. He sounded as if he expected to joke and chat again. If he thought their friendship could resume, she told him, "Forget it."[1]

At the end of January, Edmund Wilson and his wife, Elena, invited her to visit them at their home in Wellfleet on Cape Cod. Wilson was passionate about all things Russian and spoke the language well. He'd visited the Soviet Union in 1935 and come back an advocate of a Soviet-style socialism, but after the show trials of 1937–38 and Stalin's 1939 pact with the Nazis, he'd completely repudiated Soviet Communism. Svetlana and her courageous act of defection fascinated him. His wife, Elena, whose roots were partly Russian, was very nervous about meeting her; she told her husband she had a prejudice against Stalin's daughter. But Svetlana turned out not to be what they'd expected. Wilson wrote in his journal:

Svetlana made a hit with everybody. She is over 40 but does not look her age. She is very pretty and with her character and brains must have had men after her all her life. Her appearances on TV and in photographs give a misleading impression of her because they make her look much bigger and more substantial than she is. She is small, with nice soft brown hair, rather large round eyes of a peculiar pale color of green, a somewhat elongated and pointed bird-like nose and a small mouth. She has small hands and feet. Elena says that the way she uses her hands shows that she has been frightened all her life: she flicks her thin little fingers as if she were accustomed to warding something off. She is simple and well bred—rather shy but with very firm opinions.[2]

Soon Wilson discovered how fierce Svetlana could be. When they discussed the Soviet Union, he found her very pessimistic. He asked her if there wasn't some political opposition in Russia now, and she replied with disdain that five or six people protesting over a literary trial (the trial of Daniel and Sinyavsky) in a country of two hundred million, a handful of ignored poets in Red Square while tanks invaded Prague—what did that amount to? She thought Brezhnev and Kosygin were complete mediocrities, quite incapable of governing Russia, and would soon be pushed out, and things would get worse. When Wilson mentioned that the writers Leonid Leonov and Valentin Kataev seemed "good fellows," she replied, "We have a different opinion of them," and told him that both had voted against Pasternak at the Union of Writers.[3]

Wilson's purpose in inviting Svetlana to Wellfleet was for her to meet his friend Paul Chavchavadze, who he thought would be an excellent translator for her new book. Chavchavadze, a Georgian prince in the Caucasus, had fled to Romania and then America, where he'd worked in a shipping office. Recently he'd turned to writing novels and doing translation work.

The maiden name of his wife, Nina, was Romanov. Her father, the tsar's uncle, had been shot by the Bolsheviks as he was attempting to leave Russia. Her mother had been queen of Greece, and Nina herself was a grand duchess. Apparently both Nina and Paul were charming and could be great fun and never complained of the catastrophic change in their fortunes.

At dinner that first night, Svetlana remained restrained and silent. When Nina Chavchavadze mentioned that she'd visited the Kremlin, Svetlana replied, "Your Kremlin and my Kremlin are different."[4] She was not amused by Paul's joke that reports would soon be surfacing that the two great families of Georgia and Russia—the Chavchavadzes and the Stalins—had met. And yet when Svetlana and Nina had a chance to talk privately, Svetlana's warmth surfaced. They talked of their children, and it was clear to Svetlana that Nina did not judge her.

Svetlana was soon regularly taking the bus to Wellfleet to visit the Chavchavadzes. Nina always delighted in telling friends about Svetlana's first visit to her house with George Kennan. There'd been an accident in the kitchen. The sink had blocked and two inches of water covered the kitchen floor. Svetlana said, "I can do this. Leave it to me," and rolled up her sleeves and mopped the floor. Nina remarked, "If somebody had told me that one day Stalin's daughter would be scrubbing my kitchen floor, I'd have thought them mad."[5] For Svetlana, the Chavchavadzes seemed a relief after the conventionality of Princeton, where she complained that the ladies "put on stockings" to walk a block or two on the streets.

Not unexpectedly, Svetlana's relationship with Louis Fischer could not be so easily abandoned. In early February, they accidentally ran into each other on High Street in Princeton. She wrote to him on February 3:

Dear Louis,

    I can't seem to forget your face, which I only saw for a

moment when you accidentally looked into the car. It looked thin, to me, tanned, but not very healthy.

This state of malice and pain that we're both now in, is counter-intuitive and unfair. . . . But the worst part is knowing that I did it all myself. . . . To forget you and everything else, all that was, isn't in my hands—there's no use trying. The foolishness is forgotten and all the good things remain. . . . But a dead end is a dead end; and I know I know how to get out of it.

Svetlana[6]

Fischer agreed to meet her in March at their old haunt, the Princeton Inn. On March 5, she wrote to him that she'd been frightened she would open old wounds, but as she put it, "It turned out you were so emotional and I was so happy." He wasn't to worry; she wasn't going to call him. She would wait for him to call. This woman who had had the strength to defy the Kremlin was again twisting herself into emotional knots. She resumed translating his biography of Mahatma Gandhi into Russian, a task she'd begun, unpaid, as a gesture of love. She told Louis she could feel him between the lines, though she complained—"You USED to be better, I'll have you notice."[7]

By the end of March, she could say, "I miss your voice—if only I could hear it for a little everyday." She knew that for Fischer she had been "Too Much, too hot, and too exhausting. What to do? . . . I hope you remember that I'm not asking for anything. Don't worry and panic when I call. . . . Please try to understand me."[8] By mid-April she could say that all she needed was his smile over the phone. She assured him she was "re-making myself in the spirit of Gandhi. It's very hard, but possible. Kisses."[9]

At the end of April, she wrote to Annelise Kennan, who had been on the sidelines of the drama, to reassure her that she and Louis had succeeded in making peace. "Do not worry, Annelise my dear—there will be no more broken glasses [*sic*]."[10] She told Annelise she was holding birthday parties for her children. Katya turned nineteen on May 4; Joseph, twenty-four on May 22.

When she visited Harper & Row in June, she casually asked her publishers how much they were paying Paul Chavchavadze for his translation, because she knew he needed money badly. The amount was satisfactory, but then she was told Louis Fischer was paid $4,000 for editing. Shocked, she wrote to Fischer:

> I do not understand it at all. Should friendship be paid for by the publishers? Do you really believe that you have done such amount of work with my manuscript, which could be estimated in such high figures? What about warmth and encouragement—which was the most important part of your participation in my work? Did you refuse to receive this payment from Harper & Row, or did you feel that it's OK? . . . I still have hope that it is a mistake. But I would like to hear from you about that.[11]

She could not believe that Fischer had taken money. He had only encouraged her. The book was hers.

Fischer did not respond, but in early August he sent her the manuscript of her translation of his Gandhi biography, obviously hoping she might resume her work on it. She sent it back, addressing him as "Mr. Fischer," saying he could easily find a better translator. She wished him "good health and a peaceful life."[12] She rarely mentioned Fischer again.

Svetlana now undertook the ordeal of seeing her new book through publication. Like her first book, *Only One Year* was autobiographical. It was an account of the extraordinary journey she'd made from the Soviet Union to India to Switzerland to the United States, all in a single year. She'd wrestled with the first section because it mattered to her a great deal, offering as it did a loving portrait of Brajesh Singh and recounting their long battle to marry, ending in his death and her journey to India. In a second section, called "Interlude," she told her version of her dramatic escape from India and her brief sojourn in Switzerland. In a section called "We Shall Meet Again," she offered portraits of the many friends she'd left behind in Russia. The last section of her book was about her new life on another continent—"another planet," as she put it. But *Only One Year* had a political dimension her first book lacked. In subsections she made uncompromising criticisms of Stalin and his regime.

Her US publisher, Cass Canfield, had warned her British publisher: "We are dealing with a rather complicated lady and what I advise has little effect. She makes up her own mind."[13] He assured her translator, Paul Chavchavadze, that she was very amenable to suggestions about style, "but she's not receptive to suggestions as to the shape and content of the book. She feels that the book must be wholly her own and must stand as it is."[14]

Many reviewers had concluded that her purpose in *Twenty Letters to a Friend* was to exonerate Stalin by placing the blame for his crimes on Beria. She felt they did not understand that her first book had been a private family memoir, written almost as a catharsis four years before she defected. She published it without revisions because it was authentic as to how she had felt then. Beria *had* targeted her relatives because of their Georgian connections—they knew too much about him.[15]

But since 1963, she had read much and been exposed to other cultures. She *knew* who her father was. Her description in *Only One Year* of her gradual recognition of his crimes is devastating.

In the family in which I was born and bred nothing was normal, everything was oppressive and my mother's suicide was most eloquent testimony to the hopelessness of the situation. Kremlin walls all around me, secret police in the house, in the kitchen, at school. And over it all a wasted, obdurate man, fenced in from his former colleagues, his old friends, from all those who had been close to him, in fact from the entire world, who with his accomplices had turned the country into a prison, in which everyone with a breath of spirit and mind was being extinguished; a man who aroused fear and hatred in millions of men—this was my father. . . .

My generation was trained to think this monument [Stalin] was the embodiment of all that was most beautiful in the ideals of Communism, its living personification. . . .

But later I began to doubt. . . . Little by little it became more than obvious not only that my father had been a despot and had brought about a bloody terror, destroying millions of innocent people, but that the whole system which had made it possible was profoundly corrupt; that all its participants could not escape responsibility, no matter how hard they tried. And it was then that the whole edifice, whose foundation rested on a lie, crumbled from top to bottom.[16]

She wanted to offer a real portrait of Stalin. After all, she knew him intimately.

[My father] knew what he was doing. He was neither insane nor misled. With cold calculation he had cemented his own power, afraid of losing it more than of anything else in the world. . . . To explain things in this way—as madness—is the easiest and simplest thing, but it isn't true, and it isn't an explanation.[17]

He believed not in ideals but only in men's realistic political struggles. Nor did he romanticize people: there were
the strong, who were needed; equals, who were in the
way; and the weak, who were of no use to anyone.[18]

I don't believe he ever suffered any pangs of conscience.[19]

But Svetlana had a larger point to make. Her father was not
alone responsible. A dictator needs accomplices. In 1966, before she defected, she read Milovan Djilas's *Conversations with
Stalin* and Isaac Deutscher's *Stalin: A Political Biography* and
was able to understand the history of the political struggle for
supreme power that Stalin had waged in the Communist Party
against all his former colleagues. Stalin had reedited, altered,
and added to *A Brief History of the CPSU* (Communist Party
of the Soviet Union) in order to exclude all rivals, in particular Trotsky. This text served as *official* history and was distributed in millions of copies. "My father needed this 'textbook' to
throw out of history, once and for all, those who had been in
his way," she wrote.[20] But it was not the *true* history. The true
history was that there were many participants in the political
roulette game that Stalin had won, and after his death, the
Party continued to play it.

Svetlana agreed that Khrushchev had raised "the banner
of liberation" and would be remembered for his effort "to call
things by their real names. The timid half-efforts of this vital,
jolly, pig-headed man, broke the silence of many years."[21] But
Khrushchev was also responsible for the bloody events in Hungary and the killing of university students in Georgia, students
whose bodies had lain in the streets because their relatives were
forbidden to collect them. His eleven years in power were a
pseudoliberation. Nothing had changed. "Sputniks, festivals,

jubilees, and consciousness drowned in Vodka on every occasion: 'We are the greatest!' 'We are the best, the fastest, the foremost!'"[22] Anti-Semitism was still rife—no Jews on the Central Committee. In the 1960s in the Soviet Union, you could be refused a job because you were Jewish.

Then, in her book, Svetlana did the unthinkable. She not only criticized the current Soviet government as neo-Stalinist, warning that reinstating Stalin's "merits" would be disastrous not just for the USSR but for the world. She also traced the Soviet system back through Stalin to its roots in Leninism. This was sacred territory.

> Lenin laid the foundation for a one-party system, for terror and the inhuman suppression of all dissenters. He was the true father of everything that Stalin later developed to its furthest limits. All efforts to whiten Lenin and make a saint of him are useless. . . . Stalin became the embodiment of [Lenin's ideal], the most complete personification of power without democracy, built on the suppression of millions of human lives.[23]

Edmund Wilson received an advance copy of *Only One Year* for review and wrote to his friend Helen Muchnic that he thought Svetlana's new book was "terrific—quite different from the first—and I am afraid it may get her into trouble."[24] When he saw Svetlana in early September, he suggested that her book was such a bombshell that the Soviets might just ignore it. She said they weren't bright enough for that. "They would say, as they had done with her first book, that it had been written by the CIA and circulate scandals about her personal life."[25] A reporter for *Look* magazine interviewed her and asked how the Russians would receive her book. She replied, "It is an anti-Communist book. They will receive it as they receive anti-Communist books."[26]

She was exactly right. *Only One Year* infuriated the KGB. She had maligned Lenin! The surviving minutes of a Government Safety Committee meeting directed by Yuri Andropov outlined the plot of deliberate obfuscation the Soviet government was hatching in order to sabotage her book. The Soviets would spread the word that Svetlana had not written the book at all. The enemy had written it as part of an anti-Soviet campaign. The enemy was bent on defaming the name of Lenin on the hundredth anniversary of his birth.

Top Secret:
USSR
Committee
Government Safety, on the advice of the Ministers of the USSR

NOVEMBER 5, 1969

No. 2792-A
Reference: Moscow

On the information of the Safety Committee, the analyst is examining the publication of a new book by S. Alliluyeva, "Only One Year" as one measure of an expanding anti-soviet campaign underway in time for the 100-year anniversary of the birthday of Vladimir Lenin.

Recently in the newspaper "The New York Times" and other American publications, a number of pieces have appeared highlighting the publication of "Only One Year" which propose the idea that STALIN was unjustly blamed for "dictatorship and the police state." In truth, he inherited everything from LENIN and "it is precisely LENIN who is responsible for everything that is happening in the USSR." "STALIN was not a perversion of LENIN. He was the sole possible outcome after LENIN."

Keeping in mind the aforementioned, in the goal of distracting the global public from the slanderous campaign carried out by the enemy using S. Alliluyeva's book "Only One Year," the following action is recommended:

Through letters between Joseph Alliluyev and Ektarine Alliluyeva and the Politburo "TsK KPSS" in which indignation at the quisling behavior of their mother is discussed, to prepare and publish abroad letters of S. ALLILUYEVA's children addressed to a famous political correspondent H. Salisbury [Harrison Salisbury], an editor at the New York Times who interviewed S. ALLILUYEVA and who had a personal acquaintanceship with her.

This action will be ensured by the publication of the aforementioned letters and interview with the children of S. ALLILUYEVA in one of the leading European journals/ magazines.

To publish in Western print, the thesis that the new book by S. ALLILUYEVA is the result of the collective efforts of individuals who may include: D. [*sic*] KENNAN, L. SCHIFER, M. DJILAS, G. FLOROVSKY, A. BELINKOV, and others who recommend themselves as enemies of the USSR, specializing in falsifying the history of the Soviet Government. At the same time to include in those materials currently at the disposal of the KGB, information to personally compromise these individuals.

To direct a letter to the address of S. ALLILUYEVA from the known Soviet intelligentsia, who are personally acquainted with S. ALLILUYEVA (the writer Soloukhin; the cinema director Kapler, editor in chief of the journal "The

Soviet Screen," Pisarevsky; professor Myasnikov who was academic advisor to S. ALLILUYEVA when she defended her thesis, and others), which would contain a motivational protest against the falsification of the facts surrounding the Soviet government, slandering V. I. LENIN. Such a letter may be sent to S. ALLILUYEVA via the KGB, with the calculation of it being worthy of publication abroad.

In preparing for the publication, in the soviet press, of these letters/articles in order to expose the construction of these lies, it is imperative to include the thesis that these pieces dirty the "facts" of the material available to the people, in that they are inadequate in a personal and public sense. With that comes the need to show the attempts of the enemy to undermine the greatness and authority of V. I. LENIN, while instilling distrust in our system with the help of such figures as S. ALLILUYEVA, discrediting the memory/eulogy of (Aleksander) KERENSKY and relying in her book on the demagoguery of TROTSKY.

Allow the Propaganda division of the TsK KPSS to analyse the book "Only One Year" in order to determine the new position and direction/strategy of the enemy, which may be present in the text, and on the basis of which the ideological campaign will be set in play to undermine the 100th anniversary of the birthday of V. I. LENIN.

Please consider.

Representative for the Committee on Government Safety,

Andropov[27]

This top-secret document was among Svetlana's personal papers. How or when she obtained it remains a mystery, though it is probable, if not verifiable, that it came to her through the CIA. How she reacted can be guessed. She would probably have thought, *Yes, this is how the secret police work in my country,* and found their scheme to distort reality and steal her book both repulsive and predictable. The clear evidence of their blatant manipulation of her children would have been exceedingly painful, if also predictable. Of course, she would not have blamed Joseph and Katya; she knew that, like all those who came under KGB scrutiny, her children had little choice.

However, the terrible thing was that the suspicion of treachery and espionage was so ingrained that the accusation stuck; many Russians believed the KGB propaganda. Even members of Svetlana's own extended family suspected that she didn't write *Only One Year*.[28] It was too different from her first book.

In the acknowledgments, Svetlana had made the generous mistake of thanking all those who had read her manuscript in Russian. Among others, she thanked George Kennan, Louis Fischer, Robert Tucker, Georges Florovsky, Milovan Djilas, and Arkady Belinkov and his wife. This was where the KGB got its list for the "collective" authorship.

Arkady and Natalia Belinkov had indeed read the manuscript. In their memoir published in 1982, Natalia Belinkov explained:

Like many writers, who have been cut off from their familiar milieux and have not yet adapted to the new one, she needed readers. While we visited [Svetlana] we took on that role. Arkadii thought highly of this manuscript. He only had doubts about the chapter that was most important to Svetlana—"The Shore of the Ganges." Perhaps it slowed down the development of the main plot. . . .

We did not know, and neither did Svetlana, that at the same time as we were reading the book, it was being read in all the right places. It was read more than carefully. As a result, the head of State Security, Andropov, in December of 1969, ordered the Department of Propaganda "to spread ideas into the Western press that the new book is the result of a collective work of people like Kennan, Fischer, Djilas, Florovsky, and A. Belinkov" and ordered "to include materials in the possession of the KGB that individually compromise every person on the list." No, he [Andropov] was not concerned about "The Shore of the Ganges" slowing down the main plot of the book. He was saving Lenin's reputation.[29]

Kennan had read part one of *Only One Year* and told Svetlana it was very good. She didn't offer him the rest to read. He made a few editorial comments, but nothing substantial.[30] Georges Florovsky was a professor at Princeton; mentioning him was a courtesy, as was mentioning Djilas, whom Svetlana had met only once.

Svetlana gave the Russian typescript to the Princeton historian Robert Tucker. He and his wife were neighbors whom she'd met shortly after she arrived in the United States when he'd tried to persuade her to lecture at Princeton University. Tucker posed questions, offered suggestions, and advised her to change the title. Svetlana told Louis Fischer in March that Tucker had "made 'comments' on almost every page, but I didn't bother listening to him."[31]

In a portrait of Svetlana written for the *Washington Post* in 1984, titled "Svetlana Inherited Her Tragic Flaw," Robert Tucker complained that she had taken almost none of his advice and that her unnecessary thank-you to him in her afterword caused him an "unpleasant moment" when he visited Moscow State University in 1970. His Soviet escort had pounced on him in an unguarded moment and told him in an intimidating way that he had read *Only One Year*, remarking nastily that it was American anti-Soviet propaganda.

We knew her as a student here and she couldn't even write a course paper on her own. . . . Then he leaned very close to me and said in an intense voice: "You wrote that book." If he believed that, I answered, he didn't understand Svetlana. She was not one to accept easily a person's critical suggestions, much less to allow somebody else to write her book. It would offend her pride of authorship. At that, the exchange ended with a frosty smile on our escort's face.[32]

Louis Fischer's role was initially important. He was her lover. She had read the first part of her manuscript to him during those days in Princeton when their affair flourished, but he had already left for Paris and Tunis in mid-August while she was still in the midst of writing the book. And by the time he got back, their relationship was so acrimonious that he could hardly have offered his services as a reader. However, his presence in the initial stages of the writing probably influenced her tone. *Only One Year* was a more political book than *Twenty Letters to a Friend*, but, as she told her friend Lily Golden in her telephone conversation from Switzerland, she now knew so much more about the crimes of the Soviet government, and she was outraged.

Twenty-five years later, Meryle Secrest, who'd written a biography of the American architect Frank Lloyd Wright and approached Svetlana with the idea of writing her biography (an idea Secrest eventually abandoned), asked her directly about the "collective authorship" of *Only One Year*. Svetlana stated, "No one has written anything for me. I wrote it all,"[33] but said she did feel that, by posing questions to which she felt obliged to respond, her editors at Harper & Row swayed her to write a more polemical book than she'd initially intended. Fischer encouraged her to remove references to her belief in God in the first part, but she rebuffed his suggestion, retaining the chapter "Destiny," about her baptism in the Russian Orthodox faith in 1962. She decided to keep it in the book after the Yugoslav dissident Milovan Djilas visited her in Princeton, and said that, if she believed in faith (he didn't), she should write about it, because he would like to understand the impulse toward the spiritual. This was why she'd included him in her acknowledgments.[34]

In fact, rather than influencing her, Louis Fischer had stolen from her. It was she who reported in *Only One Year* that she had heard her father on the telephone responding to the murder of the actor-director of the Yiddish State Theater, Solomon Mikhoels, in 1948 with the comment, "Well, then, a car accident." In his 1969 book, *Russia's Road from Peace to War*, Fischer reported the story: "Stalin received the news by telephone and apparently . . . said . . ."[35] Fischer offered no source for the anecdote. He edited Svetlana out of the story.

It mattered. The international Jewish community was desperate to know what had happened to Mikhoels. Svetlana's book came out after Fischer's, and thus it was as if she were copying *his* anecdote and claiming it as her own. When she confronted Fischer and asked why he hadn't acknowledged her as his source, he said he'd forgotten, but when she asked his editors at Harper & Row (she and Fischer shared the same publisher), they told her they'd advised him to include her name, but he'd refused. It was a deep betrayal. When Fischer died in 1970, this scandal of "literary theft" fizzled out.[36]

Ironically, the one area where Svetlana would later admit she'd not been candid in *Only One Year* was in her description of her experiences in Italy and Switzerland. The US State Department had made it clear that she was never to reveal the role the Italians played in her "stopover" in Rome, because it had been illegal, and the Swiss had asked her not to discuss their political role in her defection.

That fall Svetlana read chapters of her book over the Voice of

America. The Soviet Foreign Office immediately protested to the US Embassy in Moscow, which replied that what a writer read over the air was the writer's private concern. The Soviet government was so infuriated that on December 19, two days before the ninetieth anniversary of Stalin's birth, the Presidium of the Supreme Soviet (executive council of the parliament) passed a decree stripping Svetlana Alliluyeva of her Soviet citizenship. She was charged with "misconduct, defaming the title citizen of the USSR," a crime her father had invented in 1938 during the Great Terror.[37] When American media asked her for her reaction to this news, she said she was overjoyed. She commemorated the event by climbing with a friend to the top of the Empire State Building.[38]

The reviews of *Only One Year* were mixed. Edmund Wilson in the *New Yorker* was effusive in his praise, claiming that *Only One Year* was "a unique historical document, which will take its place, I believe, among the great Russian autobiographical works: [Alexander] Herzen, [Peter] Kropotkin, Tolstoy's *Confession*."[39]

Margaret Parton wrote in the *Saturday Review*: "Her character remains the same: gentle, nature-loving, profoundly religious. What seems new is the clear-eyed, almost hard objectivity with which she describes Russian society and her father who had terrorized her. She is even capable of occasional irony; explaining why her father left no will, she remarks that 'He lived above material interests at the expense of the State.'"[40]

However, some reviews were nasty. *Life* published a review titled "Svetlana Faces Life." "Who needs it, after all? We have had better harder-eyed witnesses to these truths."[41] The political Left hated the book for its "fairytale version" of the United States. In his review titled "The Princess" in *Commentary*, Philip Rahv wrote that he didn't believe Svetlana went to India with the sole purpose of scattering her husband's ashes. "Her eyes were already riveted on distant America, so big and so glamorous." She knew that her book would be "the ticket to another life." She built up "a fancy-picture of America staggering in its naiveté. . . . Now that she knows the horrid truth about [her father], she has found another cult-object she can worship, and this time it is nothing less than a whole country. . . . The term 'democratic socialism' is not mentioned in her book; nor is the term 'capitalism.' . . . Clearly, Svetlana is not a woman capable of communing with history. She is merely its victim."[42]

From her letters to friends, it is clear that Svetlana was growing tired of these attacks. She was feeling buffeted, bruised, pushed around, and often not a little paranoid. And soon she was dealing with problems with the French translation of her book.[43] Apparently pages, paragraphs, and phrases of her text had been omitted. Odd jokes and humorous phrases had been inserted. Some criticisms of the Soviet regime had been softened, and friendly attitudes toward the Americans had been omitted. The translator had imposed his own political agenda. Harper & Row and the firm of Greenbaum, Wolff, & Ernst demanded that the translation be withdrawn.

But there was a much more serious concern—*Only One Year* was causing dangerous repercussions for her friends in the Soviet Union. In writing the section of her book titled "We Shall Meet Again," Svetlana wanted to honor the Russian intelligentsia and to protest their treatment.[44] These Soviets were not the gray conformists the West thought them to be, but rather were highly original, uniquely talented individuals. But she should have known that her portraits of friends would put them at risk.

One of the unwritten laws in the Soviet Union was that you never spoke. She had changed names, but it was not hard for the KGB to identify the people she meant. Certainly her disguise of the black specialist in African song and culture under the name "Bertha" was no protection for Lily Golden. Lily found herself increasingly followed and watched. Party hacks who had long been trying to kick her out of the Institute for African Studies were encouraged to harass her. She discovered that one "friend" was checking the titles of books she borrowed from the library while another was reporting all her meetings with foreigners. She had already been blacklisted from travel to scholarly conferences abroad, and any hope that this ban might be lifted was now gone. Lily fought back and endured the isolation but was shocked that Svetlana had exposed her.

Lily's daughter, Yelena Khanga, thought perhaps Svetlana had been caught up in the enthusiasm a writer feels when she creates a book, not measuring the consequences. Perhaps the dizziness of freedom to speak out in the West had dulled her censors, leading her to break the code of *loyalty and discretion* among friends in the USSR.[45] Her cousins Alexander and Leonid Alliluyev later claimed that none of her relatives, indeed not even her children, had suffered.[46] However, Lily Golden maintained that all of the friends Svetlana mentioned were put on a list and banned from traveling.[47]

It is unclear whether Svetlana knew about the impact her book was having on her friends in the Soviet Union, but she told people she was sick and tired of writing books. Though she had an idea for a new book based on the letters she was receiving from around the world, she now said she didn't plan on writing anymore. It would be fifteen years before she published her next book. But it was not exhaustion or disgust over the reception of her books that caused this interruption. She was heading into a completely new and heartbreaking disaster.

Chapter 24

The Taliesin Fiasco

Svetlana married Wesley Peters, the head architect of Frank Lloyd Wright's Taliesin Foundation, on April 4, 1970, at the Taliesin West compound in the Sonoran desert.

Svetlana had been in the United States three years now and was still receiving letters from strangers around the world. In November 1969, persistent letters began arriving from

Olgivanna Wright, the widow of the architect Frank Lloyd Wright, exhorting her to come to Arizona to visit the Taliesin Fellowship. Svetlana didn't know much about the famous architect, and friends tried to warn her gently that the "Fellowship," as Wright's School of Architecture was called, was *strange*, but in the books and pamphlets Olgivanna was sending, Taliesin looked exceedingly beautiful.

Svetlana had planned a monthlong trip to California to meet a number of her new pen pals, and then intended to go on to Hawaii to visit a Russian-born American painter she had met on Long Island. She decided she would stop in Phoenix for a week. It would be an American experience to add to her list. Truthfully, she was desperate to put Louis Fischer and Princeton gossip behind her.

There was an unexpected hook in Olgivanna Wright's letters. Olgivanna wrote that her eldest daughter, Svetlana, had died in a car accident twenty-five years earlier. What a strange coincidence that Svetlana should carry the same magical name, which means "enlightened." The name itself was a talisman. According to Olgivanna, they were destined to meet.

Svetlana had an equally compelling fantasy. She knew that Olgivanna was Montenegrin and was only four years older than her own mother, Nadya, would have been if had she lived. She imagined a woman with the dark Georgian looks of her mother. As she remembered it, "We both expected something very important to come out of this meeting, both caring for beloved images and fantasies. . . . Apart from this strange connection, I really did not expect anything exciting from the Arizona desert."[1]

Svetlana had no idea that she was about to encounter a titan who'd already plotted the role she was to play in the world of Taliesin. Few could stand up to Olgivanna Wright.

Olga Ivanovna Lazovich was born in the kingdom of Montenegro in the Balkans in 1897, and her genetic inheritance was fierceness. Her father was a chief justice and her mother was a general in the Montenegrin army who'd once ridden on the back of her father's saddle into battle against the Turks. Olga viewed her mother, the general, with awe and fear. At the age of fourteen, she was sent to Batum (Batumi) on the Black Sea to live with her sister. While visiting friends in Tiflis, Olga found her escape route. Now nineteen, she married a Latvian architect named Valdemar Hinzenberg. She weathered the Bolshevik Revolution of 1917 in Tiflis and learned what near-starvation was. Soon she gave birth to her daughter Svetlana. In Tiflis she met the Armenian "spiritual teacher" Georgi Ivanovich Gurdjieff. Coincidentally, the Gurdjieff family knew Joseph Djugashvili before he was Stalin. He'd rented a room from them when he was a student at the Tiflis Seminary. He made himself memorable by stiffing them for the rent.[2]

By the time Olga met Gurdjieff, he'd transformed himself into a mystic, teaching his spiritual discipline of cosmic dance based on his theory of astral bodies, through which one could achieve the higher consciousness of the true "I" and work out the laws of the universe. To avoid the Bolsheviks, Gurdjieff fled to Constantinople, where he established the first version of his Institute for the Harmonious Development of Man. With her three-year-old daughter, Svetlana, Olga joined him. The route to becoming Frank Lloyd Wright's wife was arduous and led through France to Chicago, where Olga met Wright at a theater performance in November 1924. He claimed he immediately fell in love with Olgivanna, as he renamed her. By the end of January, she had moved permanently to Taliesin. She was twenty-five.

Wright built the first Taliesin on his estate in Spring Green, Wisconsin, in 1911. Three years later, while he was on business in Chicago, a servant, in what was presumed to be a fit of insanity, set fire to the house after nailing all the doors shut, leaving only a small hatch open. As the people inside crawled through the hatch, he killed each one with an ax. Devastated, Wright vowed to rebuild, and by 1932 he had established the Taliesin Fellowship. Seven years later, he expanded Taliesin to include a second estate, Taliesin West, in Arizona, which served as the Fellowship's winter home.

Frank Lloyd Wright originally designed the Taliesin West property as his winter home.

Taliesin was not a school; it was an experiment in revolutionary communal living. Wright's eccentric genius—his spectacular buildings, his colorful antiauthoritarian harangues, and his clarion call for an "organic architecture"—drew aspiring architects to Taliesin. Students paid a large yearly tuition to participate; it was they who hewed the rock with backbreaking labor and built the structures, tended the gardens, collected the garbage, did the domestic labor, served meals, and, in what little time was left, worked at their drafting tables. The students who chose to stay thought of themselves as social radicals, remaking the United States in terms of Wright's grandiose vision of a vast landscape of Broadacre Cities, a network of *natural* villages linked by modern communication and transportation systems. Since Wright's death in 1959, Olgivanna had run the whole enterprise and, though she knew nothing about architecture, had the last word in everything.

By most accounts, Wright had not been interested in Gurdjieff's teachings, though Gurdjieff did visit at Taliesin, but after Wright's death, Olgivanna assumed the role of reigning queen and spiritual guru of the Fellowship. The dance rituals she organized at Taliesin, called "cosmic" dances, were Gurdjieff rituals. Every Sunday morning, she gave compulsory lectures on the pursuit of higher consciousness, often reading from Gurdjieff's books. She claimed to have absorbed Gurdjieff's methods for deconstructing a person and *remaking* him or her in pursuit of the true "I."

At Taliesin, even under Frank Lloyd Wright's direction, there had always been a split between a coterie of insiders and those on the outside. To the disenchanted, the insiders who worked on architectural projects were "the studio crowd," and the outsiders were the leftovers, many of whom were wives. When Meryle Secrest interviewed residents for her biography of Wright, one of the wives, Mary Matthews, spoke to her of Olgivanna's special project for the outsiders:

> Mrs. Wright wanted to set up her own coterie with all those who were not exactly architects. They were supposed to come and sit at her feet. You gave her your spirit and she molded you. . . . She would see an opportunity when someone was uncertain or slightly at fault, and she would tear them to shreds to see how they would react. . . . I was not about to let her get the upper hand, and she finally

said, "The trouble with you is you stand before me like a rod when you should bend like the grass before the wind."[3]

Olgivanna's acolytes defended her. They said she "sometimes had to crack heads open to put something new in them."[4] One of the apprentices, Rupert Pole, although he admired Olgivanna, admitted that she was "a very designing woman, powerful and egotistical." She insisted on supervising everything—down to the style of the apprentices' hair and the color of their socks. She had an inner circle that came to be known as "the kitchen crowd" because people would wait in the kitchen for hours to consult her. Bill Calvert, another apprentice, claimed that he often accepted her criticisms as valid, but drew the line at the "kitchen talks," where you were expected "to kiss and tell." "I knew that a lot of fairly freewheeling liaisons were being arranged in the 'little kitchen.' . . . I knew what Olgivanna was capable of."[5] The marriages of apprentices were often arranged during those kitchen talks.

While claiming that, like a second mother, Olgivanna was warm and accepting, even her staunch supporter Bill Calvert remarked, "Keep in mind that Mrs. Wright was running a branch of the czarist court, and absolutely anything was possible. I am not exaggerating a bit. She was a master of intrigue. . . . She wasn't an ogre. It's hard to convey. She was operating on a different principle. Her goals were to keep . . . Taliesin intact, and she did it brilliantly."[6] Olgivanna had a dictator's gift for smart politicking.

Kamal Amin, an Egyptian American architect who trained under Frank Lloyd Wright and stayed with the Fellowship, explained that Olgivanna collected famous people, especially if they were wealthy. "She needed to sustain the extravagant lifestyle." Olgivanna had read *Only One Year*, and as Amin put it, Svetlana was "a hot news item."[7] She had clearly heard and, perhaps because she had grown up in the Balkans, believed the gossip that Svetlana had stopped in Switzerland to collect the gold and millions of rubles that Stalin had stashed for her in a Swiss bank. Her plot was simple. She would marry Svetlana to her chief architect, William Wesley Peters, and the foundation would claim her money.

Wesley Peters's story was complex. He had arrived at Taliesin Fellowship as a twenty-year-old apprentice in 1932 and had immediately fallen in love with Olgivanna's daughter, Svetlana. Just eight months after the Fellowship opened, he and the sixteen-year-old Svetlana fled Taliesin. Three years later, the rebels, now married, returned, perhaps understanding that only the cocooned environment of Taliesin could nurture the aesthetically beautiful lives they aspired to. During his absence, Peters had gotten his architect's license and, with his engineering skills, he now proved a valuable asset to Wright. By 1946, the couple had two children and Svetlana was again pregnant. The gossip at Taliesin had it that this was actually the child of Gene Masselink, Wright's private secretary and Peters's best friend. Whether Peters knew this rumor or not, it was clear both men were in love with Svetlana.

And then the fatal car accident occurred on September 30, 1946. Svetlana was returning from town with her two children when her jeep flipped over on a narrow bridge crossing a slough on the Wisconsin River. She and one of her sons drowned. She had continually complained to Peters that the soft-topped jeep she was forced to drive was dangerous and had begged him to buy a conventional closed-in car, but he had always refused. Peters believed the accident was his fault. Now he owed Mr. and Mrs. Wright not only loyalty, but also a crippling blood debt. Henceforth, people said, he was totally under Olgivanna's power. His apprentice Aris Georges explained that Olgivanna had "a grip on Wes that was actually very disturbing. She would call him in and diminish him to pieces. And yet turn around and build him back up since he was the pillar she could not have done without after Wright died."[8]

It took money to run this enterprise of two large estates and to sustain the architects, their wives, and the apprentices, who, along with Olgivanna, her daughter Iovanna, and her daughter's two children, numbered sixty-five people. Benefactors were needed. Olgivanna had targeted Svetlana as a benefactor.

Svetlana flew to Phoenix in March and was met at the airport by Iovanna. On the twenty-six-mile drive from Phoenix to Scottsdale, Iovanna told Svetlana about the death of her half sister, Svetlana, repeating the name as though it held some magical significance. "I hope you will be my sister!" she said. They drove through the vast desert of Paradise Valley with its dusty sweeping plains and sunburned rocks under a bowl of brilliant blue sky up into the high mesa, which felt like the top of the world. The journey was completely mesmerizing.

Olgivanna, with her large black Great Dane at her feet, waited amid the arcades of bougainvillea. Small, thin, dark-haired, elegantly dressed with a turquoise hat protecting her pale skin, she looked every bit the regal widow. Olgivanna embraced Svetlana, repeating her name several times, as if she were addressing her daughter. She was not what Svetlana was expecting. "There was nothing of that dreamy beauty of my mother, of her shyness, of her humility," Svetlana recalled. This was an image from photographs; she had no visual memories of her mother, nor could she imagine what her mother might have looked like in old age.[9] Still, Olgivanna was extremely warm and welcoming.

This photograph of Olgivanna Lloyd Wright, the architect's third and final wife, was taken in 1971, by which time she'd been widowed for over a decade.

Svetlana was shown to her own private guest residence and told to prepare for a welcoming dinner in Mrs. Wright's quarters. Because she didn't have a floor-length gown, the requisite attire for Taliesin West festivities, Iovanna offered several of her own dresses. They were exquisite creations of chiffon and silk, but Svetlana was still too self-conscious to put on such a costume and stuck to her own conservative short green dress.

She was out of place. The men and women gathered around the Taliesin fireplace wore tuxedoes and elegant gowns. She was introduced to a tall, distinguished man in his late fifties wearing a sand-colored tuxedo and a lavender ruffled shirt, with a gold pendant at his neck and numerous rings on his fingers. He looked like a peacock, but his face was stern. "Svetlana, this is Wes. Wes, meet Svetlana," said Olgivanna, seemingly moved to be linking those names again. Svetlana had not expected to meet the long-ago husband of Olgivanna's dead daughter.

In the dining room, elaborate Chinese tapestries hung on the heavy stone walls. The table was set with gold cutlery and crystal goblets around an elegant bouquet of desert flowers. Svetlana was seated next to Peters, who remained reserved and mostly silent through dinner. From his face, she immediately concluded that he was "sad, lonely, and utterly unhappy." Even in his "crazy suit," he seemed somehow "noble" and different from the rest.[10]

Though arranged for her, the whole evening made Svetlana feel inadequate. She had no idea who the eager young men in bright ruffled shirts attending the guests were or, indeed, who even the other guests might be. But it was all so tasteful and luxurious. She decided to let herself enjoy this exoticism. She had her ticket for San Francisco in her suitcase.

The next morning, Wesley Peters knocked on her door. He said he had been instructed by Olgivanna to show her around Taliesin. On the tour, still excited by Wright's concept of organic architecture, he explained how the buildings, with their horizontal lines and their texture of rough-hewn stone, blended perfectly into the desert landscape. He said Wright and his students had built it all by hand, whittling the gigantic rocks from the hillsides. Svetlana hid her dismay. To her it all looked gloomy, "like ancient graves."

But her guide was "agreeable and gallant" and seemed to have "an old fashioned decency." When Peters drove her to Scottsdale in his Cadillac, she found it "difficult not to be charmed." His silent, relaxed companionship spoke to her of shyness. "I suddenly felt complete security and peace near this man; something I had not experienced for a long time—a sign more significant to me than many words."[11]

In Scottsdale Peters took her to shops selling West Coast Native American jewelry. She decided she wanted to buy a ring as a memento of her visit, and he insisted on picking out the best one for her. When she put the ring he'd selected on her finger, she felt a sudden shock and a thought went through her. "Am I going to marry this man? I was frightened by the thought because I cherished nothing more at the time than my newfound freedom and independence. The question did not go away, and I did not hear myself with a definite 'no.' This was danger."[12]

On the drive back to Taliesin, Peters was mostly silent. She watched him. "Doesn't matter what he says; we do not chat; I just sit next to him." He reminded her of Brajesh Singh, who also spoke little. "It was this same sense of quiet, of peace, of inner serenity." She told herself in panic, "Don't get into this. . . . I have to be careful! I have to be careful!"[13] She began to be impatient for the day of her departure.

When Saturday evening came, this time Svetlana wore Iovanna's blue chiffon tunic dress and joined the glittering masquerade of music and dancing, for a moment shedding her conservative, shy persona. She found she liked being one of these exotic birds of Paradise Valley. When she informed Olgivanna that she would soon be leaving, Olgivanna insisted she stay at least for the Easter celebrations, and Svetlana found it impolite to refuse. As was the tradition, she sat with the architects and their wives and painted Easter eggs. She wondered when these people worked. When did Wesley Peters work? He was always showing her around. She even asked herself: "What did all this mean, really?" Yet she delayed her departure.[14]

At such crucial moments, Svetlana always fought her own skepticism and gave in to her feelings. She called it submitting to fate, the river that carried her forward. It didn't seem to occur to her that Olgivanna had orchestrated this particular fate. Perhaps she was naive or simply needy, or perhaps Olgivanna was a brilliant manipulator and set the trap well. Kamal Amin explained that from the start, Olgivanna "wrapped Svetlana in an invisible, impenetrable layer of protection." And Olgivanna was thorough. When Amin told her that his friend would be visiting at the same time as Svetlana, she changed the friend's ticket to ensure that the two traveled on different flights. "He will start a relationship with her," Olgivanna complained. Amin greeted Svetlana with a welcoming bouquet of roses at the dinner table that first night, but the next day, his seat was moved to a distant table, and his future contacts with Svetlana were severely limited. Clearly, Olgivanna had a design.[15]

Olgivanna had selected Wesley Peters for Svetlana. He was tall, handsome, charismatic, with a tragic past, and was completely under her control—the perfect candidate. Everyone at Taliesin enjoyed watching the progress of the increasingly "whirlwind" courtship. The fact that Svetlana and Peters were sexually attracted to each other was palpable to everyone.

It didn't occur to Amin to warn Svetlana. He saw in her a person of raw need. "She coexisted with pervasive uncertainty, inconsistency, and insecurity about what her future held." He found her "soft-spoken, attractive, and a pleasure to be with," but she would occasionally withdraw into some private recess where she became inaccessible.[16] Having read her books, he knew her history—the shattering loss of her mother to suicide; the arrests, imprisonments, and murders of her relatives and friends. Amin thought that perhaps Wes could make her happy, though he doubted it.

By the second week, Wesley Peters invited Svetlana to dinner at Trader Vic's in Scottsdale. Now he opened up, talking about the first Svetlana, his beloved wife, and the tragic car accident for which he felt responsibility. Although he had been a widower for twenty-four years, he spoke as if the accident had just occurred. He listened as Svetlana talked about her childhood, her broken marriages, the death of Brajesh Singh. As the restaurant closed, they were still talking.

Svetlana said, "I like you very much," and suddenly it seemed they were talking of staying together. As Svetlana remembered it, Wes said: "Oh, I'm very glad. I'm going to tell Mrs. Wright."[17]

On April 4, just three weeks after her arrival at Taliesin West, to the shock of many of her friends back in Princeton, Svetlana and Wesley Peters were married. In fact, what friends did not understand was that this man was irresistible to her precisely because he proposed marriage and not a casual affair. She may have failed three times at marriage already, but Wesley Peters seemed "so clean, so decent, and so sad."[18] She expected to entwine her life in his.

A joke went around Taliesin. It was said that Svetlana should call her next book *Only Three Weeks*.[19]

A handful of guests were invited to the afternoon wedding, which took place in the small living room at Taliesin. None of the guests were informed why they had been invited until they arrived. Mrs. Wrigley of the vast Wrigley gum fortune was there,[20] as was Ed Murray, the editor of the local newspaper, *Arizona Republic*. By keeping the wedding secret and assuring Murray of the scoop, Olgivanna was calculating that his sense of indebtedness would serve her in the future.

Olgivanna introduced Svetlana to each of the guests triumphantly: "My daughter, Svetlana!" Svetlana was suddenly frightened, but her worry was that she might merely be a substitute for another woman and would be expected to remain in her shadow. How could she "ever fulfill everyone's desire" to take the first Svetlana's place?[21] Her father's voice was still in her head: "Take a look at yourself. Who'd want you? You fool!" But it was too late for doubt. She did not want to believe that anything about this precipitate marriage could possibly be amiss.

Only one guest, Alan Schwartz, represented the bride at the wedding. Svetlana had called Schwartz at his office and said:

"Alan, remember when I was telling you about my brother, and you said, 'If you ever need me, I'll be there'?" I said, "Yeah, I do." She said, "I need you to come here to Taliesin. I need you to come tomorrow." I asked, "Why?" And she said, "I just need you to come. Do you have a pink tie?" So I said, "I think I have a pink tie." She said, "Bring the pink tie."[22]

Schwartz traveled to Taliesin without a clue as to why he was so desperately needed. He was met at the airport by a car and driven to Taliesin. Svetlana was standing at the entrance of the compound beside a tall stranger. "Alan, this is Wes," she said. She then led Schwartz to the guest quarters and asked if he wanted a gin and tonic. "I better have something," he replied, "because I don't know why I'm here." He was already somewhat suspicious, having noted that, though there were phone jacks, the phones in his room had been removed. Svetlana said, "I'm getting married in an hour."

That night there was a huge party with all the architects, students, and guests in attendance. The only thing Alan Schwartz really remembered was Svetlana's almost girlish happiness. "One got caught up in her impulsiveness. She'd pull you in and you felt helpless."[23] He also noted that Olgivanna Wright made sure she knew where he was every minute.

He had been scheduled to fly out after the wedding, but Olgivanna persuaded him to change his ticket for the following afternoon so that he could stay for the party. She knew

Schwartz was Svetlana's lawyer. The next morning, she arrived in her golf cart to take him on a tour of the grounds. "She showed me where this had happened, where that had happened. She wanted to make a good impression on me, but she wanted to make sure I saw and heard only what she wanted me to see and hear."

Kamal Amin recalled: "The glow of the event lingered on for some time as the international media picked up the story, placing Taliesin at the center of intrigue—a favorite place for Olgivanna."[24]

There was a dimension of Olgivanna's intrigue that would be discovered only afterward. Even as the wedding was under way, at 2:30 p.m. on April 4, a quitclaim deed was filed in Dodgeville, Wisconsin. Wesley Peters had used his entire family inheritance to buy the foundation a large acreage called Hillside, adjacent to Wright's original estate in Spring Green. Peters's name was removed from the deed to the Hillside property. The title was reregistered in the name of the Frank Lloyd Wright Foundation, blocking any future claim Svetlana might have to the property as the new wife.[25]

It didn't take Svetlana long to discover that her rights as a wife were a little ambiguous. According to O. P. Reed, one of the fellows at the time, it was immediately made clear to Svetlana that Olgivanna was in charge—her "sway extended into their nuptial bedroom. Somehow Olgivanna convinced Wesley and Svetlana to spend their wedding night in separate bedrooms."[26] Somewhat later Olgivanna would try to engage Svetlana in one of her "kitchen talks," asking about her sex life with Wes, at which Svetlana bridled. "Mrs. Wright, I am not seventeen!"[27]

The morning after the wedding, Svetlana moved into Wes's quarters. Though he was the chief architect, he had only a small room with a sofa bed, a shower cabin, and a terrace. The bride took her breakfast in the communal dining room. And discovered that, now that she was no longer a guest but a member of the Fellowship, she was expected to attend morning and afternoon tea, as well as the shared noon and evening meals. Though she protested to her new husband that she would prefer some privacy, Wes had been living as a bachelor since his first wife's death and had no intention of changing his ways. He tried to make her understand that they were now a *public* couple. Tour groups tramped through the halls of Taliesin, bringing in money, and some had come to see Stalin's daughter. Wes told her she should have expected to be on view.

There was very soon a second demonstration of Olgivanna's supremacy. She called one night at 1:00 a.m., urgently commanding Wes to appear in her quarters to solve a crisis. The fellows were used to these calculated disruptions. For some, to be selected was flattering; but Svetlana responded, "But, Mrs. Wright, it's one o'clock in the morning and we were asleep." She had missed the point. Svetlana might be the wife but Olgivanna was in control. When Olgivanna shouted at her, Svetlana replied, "Don't shout at me. I do not like it when people shout at me."[28] And hung up. Wes's response was to ask his wife not to interfere with his work.

The day after her marriage, she noted that Wes was not as "charmingly silent as on the first day" nor as "sad" as she had imagined. She now felt she was constantly displeasing him. He seemed to love the endless parties and wanted her there, though she thought they were a terrible waste of time. She didn't understand that the foundation was always engaged in a desperate hunt for needed revenue. As fishing expeditions for patrons, the parties *were* the work. However, Svetlana had a will equal to Wes's. She was determined to be happy and to *stay* happy. As she put it, "I was launched upon the path of domesticity, and nothing could stop me."[29]

The first problem was that Wes was a compulsive spendthrift;

this impulse, as Olgivanna had warned her two days before her marriage, reached the level of pathology. Though he was unsalaried, Wes used his numerous credit cards to buy himself new cars, dogs, extravagant gifts for the apprentices, jewels and gowns for the Taliesin women, and even presents for people he barely knew. He was on the verge of personal bankruptcy, and his family farm was about to be repossessed. Olgivanna called it a strange weakness and was expecting Svetlana to keep him under control.

Soon after she was married, Svetlana informed her New York lawyers that she would be assuming control of her personal trust and demanded that her money be transferred to her husband's law firm Lewis, Roca, Scoville, Beauchamp & Linton, in Phoenix. She told George Kennan, "My own financial independence has now become very important for me. . . . Please do not worry about me, I rely on Wes, on his love and his protection."[30] She planned to pay off Wes's creditors. It would be her wedding present, and anyway, this was what an American wife would do. In retrospect, she explained, "I was trying to heal all old hurts of my husband."[31] She seemed to think that once her love "healed" him, Wes would be cured of his addiction to money.

Despite her lawyers' valiant efforts to dissuade her, Svetlana remained firm; she seems not to have balked when she and Wes went to the bank and she discovered that his debts amounted to half a million dollars. Her own living for the past three years had been so frugal that she had barely touched her $1.5 million advance from Harper & Row.

People at Taliesin never took vacations, apart from their biannual weeklong treks across the country as they moved from their winter residence in Arizona to their summer residence in Wisconsin. Nevertheless, Svetlana and Wes managed a four-day vacation in San Francisco to stay with Wes's sister, Marge, and her husband, Sam Hayakawa. From family conversations, Svetlana understood that Wes's extravagance had been a problem since his youth. While they were in San Francisco, Wes spent every spare moment in the city shopping: buying art, tapestries, jewelry. Svetlana saw this simply as his love for beautiful objects. He bought Svetlana dresses of silver-and-gold brocade. She was amused to model them for him. She recalled with nostalgia, "I enjoyed immensely seeing him choosing clothes for me—no one had ever done that for me in my whole lifetime!"[32]

For now, she was delighting in indulging Wes. When Joan Kennan visited Taliesin with her new husband, Walter Pozen, Pozen remembered Svetlana's glee as she said, "I want to show you something." She led them to her and Wes's apartment. "We went into the bathroom and there were about sixteen different aftershave lotions, and she said, 'That's my garden of fragrance.'"[33]

At Taliesin, Svetlana seemed content to enjoy her new status. Standing beside this handsome man, she was thrilled to be addressed as Mrs. Peters. It would appear, however, that she wasn't quite the docile wife she pretended to be. At one of the fancy dinners where she was required to play hostess, she turned in fury on Wes. It wasn't clear what occasioned the argument; paying his debts, perhaps she'd discovered he was still buying extravagant presents for the wives of apprentices. To the shock of the gathered guests, Svetlana slapped Wes's face.[34] They had been married only a month.

It was just a tiff. In June she was writing to her friend Jamie (Donald Jameson), who was still managing her case file at the CIA, that Wes was going to take her citizenship into his own hands:

He does know many influential politicians in Arizona and California (Wisconsin, too) both republicans and democrats, and he, too, feels that being my husband he has to worry about me and to take care of all my problems. He is a darling, indeed. What a blessing for me to have met that man![35]

Jamie was organizing her papers so she could travel to Iran, where Wes was working on construction of a $6 million project, the Pearl Palace (Morvarid Palace) for Princess Shams Pahlavi, the daughter of the shah of Iran. Wes had a romantic side, at least in architecture, and so loved excess that he'd based his design for the palace on *A Thousand and One Nights*. Although it seems he'd initially invited Svetlana to accompany him to Iran, in fact she never got to go on this business trip. In her chatty letter, she told Jamie that she'd seen another new state of this "blessed country." She and Wes had driven to the town of Alma in Michigan to attend the dedication of a church he'd recently designed.

Jamie was obviously a conduit for information about her children. She asked him:

> If you happen to hear a word about my kids from the source <u>more</u> reliable than the Soviet reporters, please, let me know. I've sent them "Happy Birthday" cards in May as usual, but I have not heard anything <u>from them</u> since December 1968. I understand why, but still I'd love to learn at least some news. Do you think I should just write a long letter to Katya and send it by ordinary mail. Why not? Or— better not? How do you feel about that?[36]

She sent Katya an "absolutely unpolitical" book, *Horses of the West*. Naturally she had no answer. She had wanted to send her son a small gift too but had stopped herself. It might bring him trouble. Determined to convince Jamie, and perhaps herself, that she had the perfect marriage, she ended her letter:

> May I tell you how happy I am to have a 28-year-old son, Brandoch Peters, who is a charming young man. He is running his father's farm at Spring Green, Wisconsin, although he is a musician by profession. I am too lucky indeed . . . best wishes from Wes.[37]

Beneath her enthusiasm about her new stepson lay her ongoing anxiety for her own children. She was always looking for secure routes to information about them. When she heard that the young architect Kamal Amin would be visiting his native Egypt, she asked him to write to her friend the Egyptian ambassador to Moscow, Dr. Murad Ghaleb. Dr. Ghaleb did not reply, but by chance Amin ran into him in the elevator of the Sheraton Hotel in Cairo and immediately launched into the subject of Svetlana's children, asking for his help in getting some information about them. The ambassador turned his back and left the elevator without a word. There was fear in his eyes.[38] The KGB had not forgotten Svetlana. Svetlana had many reasons to be looking for security.

Chapter 25

The Montenegrin's Courtier

John Amarantides, an architect and a student of Frank Lloyd Wright's, took this candid photo of Wesley and Svetlana at Taliesin in 1970.

Every summer the architects and their apprentices made the long trek by car back to Taliesin East in Spring Green, Wisconsin. Svetlana and Wes set out in his Cadillac. Finally she had him to herself, and soon she felt the loving Wes had returned. As they traveled through the Grand Canyon, Monument Valley, Mesa Verde, Colorado Springs, and the flats of Kansas and into the beautiful green fields of Wisconsin, he sang her funny songs, recited limericks, and told her fascinating stories of the history of the places they were driving through. He seemed to want her to know his America. Despite the constant business calls to and from hotels and in telephone booths en route, this drive would become a precious memory. She believed Wes would be hers as long as she could get him away from the Fellowship.

When they arrived in Spring Green, Svetlana discovered that Wes's accommodations in Taliesin East consisted of two rooms, with a kitchen and bathroom next to his office, an improvement certainly, but the same hordes of tourists roamed through the halls. She was settling in when she got word from her lawyers at Greenbaum, Wolff & Ernst in New York that the trustees of the Alliluyeva Charitable Trust had received a letter from the Frank Lloyd Wright Foundation requesting a donation of $30,000, to be given annually.

The trustees had replied that this was absolutely impossible because the Trust was small, with an annual yearly income of much less than $30,000, and the money was already committed to funding the Brajesh Singh Foundation Hospital in India. It took Svetlana a while to process this. She remembered that Olgivanna had hinted that, once married, she could turn over her personal assets to the Frank Lloyd Wright Foundation, where she would live and be well taken care of.[1] Svetlana turned her rage on Wes. She was paying *his* bills, not the F. L. Wright Foundation's. He remarked with a sigh, "My dear, try your best to remain good friends with Mrs. Wright. Because if you don't, we shall meet tragedy." She was still basking in the happiness of their trip together and so decided that this money business was a misunderstanding. She also dismissed his warning.[2]

The best times were her visits with Wes to his farm, which he called Aldebaran. It consisted of a small old-fashioned farmhouse, outbuildings, and considerable acreage of bucolic woods and fields. His surviving son, Brandoch, was tending it. Though he had reached the level of cellist with the Munich Symphony, Brandoch had given up music. The rumor was that he realized he didn't have the talent to be a soloist; supposedly Olgivanna had told him he was just a "stand player. You don't stack up."[3] It is also likely that a broken love affair had sent him back to Taliesin, where he'd seemingly fallen into an emotional paralysis.

Brandoch now confided to his stepmother that he dreamed of owning a cattle-breeding farm. Svetlana came up with a new plan. She would pay off the liens on Wes's farm and finance a joint agricultural venture. She, Wes, and Brandoch would be co-owners, though the money would remain hers. In other words, she would be in control. Both of "her men," as she liked to call them, seemed excited by the idea. Privately, she thought she could be done with Taliesin. At least in the summer, Wes could work at Taliesin and live at the farm.

Soon it was time to return to Taliesin West in Arizona, but in September, Svetlana had astonishing news to tell Wes. As she walked the fields of her new property, she had begun to feel young and vital, with a sensation of centered well-being that she'd felt twenty years back. When she visited the doctor, he confirmed that she was pregnant.

Svetlana was thrilled. At her age, forty-four, this was a great gift. The child would be fate's compensation for her abandoned Russian children, and it would finally cement her relationship with Wes. When she told him, he was certainly shocked but he seemed happy. However, when he reported the news to Olgivanna, she was furious—there was no place for children at Taliesin—they diverted "energy from the work." In Wright's last years, women with babies had been exiled to a tent at the farthest edge of the compound in Arizona, and applicants with children were rejected. Svetlana must get rid of the child. "Women of Svetlana's age don't give birth in America," Olgivanna told Wes. How had he been so careless?[4]

George and Annelise Kennan had visited Svetlana at Taliesin East that August. They had so impressed Olgivanna that she'd claimed them as her own guests. Now she turned to them. In a rampaging phone call to Princeton, she demanded that they talk Svetlana out of this folly.[5]

It took Wes some time to summon the courage to confront Svetlana, but he finally asked, "You are not going to do anything about it?" She sensed Olgivanna behind Wes's question and answered angrily. "Why does that dictator always interfere with human lives? Well, of course, because that is the nature of all dictators."[6] Her words eventually got back to Olgivanna.

When they finally undertook the fall trek back to Arizona, Svetlana was reminded why she loved Wes. Away from the Fellowship, he was still warm and chatty. He drove less recklessly. She thought he was thinking of their child. She now believed the problem was that Wes was in thrall to Olgivanna, and many agreed. Edgar Tafel, who had worked at Taliesin, remarked, "Wes Peters approaches the age of 60, and he cannot have any feelings of his own without consulting his superiors."[7] It shocked her to think that her large, imposing husband was "afraid of that little old lady with the wrinkled parchment face."[8]

She and Wes decided they must renovate his small apartment to make space for the baby. She was hoping for a kitchenette and bath, but he concluded that these were not necessary; they would ruin the design. As they fought continuously over the renovations and he dismissed her suggestions, she was taken aback by how stubborn he could be. At the end of the three

months of work by the unpaid assistants, she was presented
with a bill for $30,000, the exact amount the foundation had
requested from her charitable trust.[9]

Svetlana endured the winter as things deteriorated. Having
turned down the Frank Lloyd Wright Foundation's request for
an annual bequest, she now found that architects in the halls
shunned her. She sought solace among a few people she met
outside Taliesin who detested the Fellowship as much as she
did. Olgivanna concluded that Svetlana was spreading gossip
about her and doing harm to her reputation. One of their quar-
rels turned into a great battle, which ended with Olgivanna
screaming at Svetlana that she "behaved just like Stalin."[10]

Svetlana could not imagine having her baby at Taliesin and
gratefully accepted an invitation from Wes's sister, Marge Hayakawa, and her husband, Sam, to come to California for the
delivery. Wes took her to Mill Valley and then left for Iran. To
remind her that he was with her in thought, he arranged for
the local florist to send flowers every day, with cards that he'd
left behind: "I am missing you."[11] Those fifty little handcrafted
cards were among the things she always saved. To an outsider,
they are uncannily reminiscent of the notes her father sent her
when she was a child, declaring his love in absentia. She'd been
trained to feed her longings on so little, and even when contrary evidence was staring her in the face, she always tried to
will her version of reality into being. But her domestic fantasy
held little meaning for Wes.

Svetlana gave birth to a beautiful healthy child, Olga
Margedant Peters, on May 21, 1971. She'd chosen to name
her child after her grandmother Olga, though Wes was probably delighted to be able to ingratiate himself with Olgivanna.
When her contractions started, her new brother-in-law, Sam
Hayakawa, drove her to the hospital. Wes showed up a few days
later, bringing with him a local TV crew to film mother and

child. He loved publicity. Svetlana thought the public interest in the birth of Stalin's granddaughter was brutally invasive. He was not the one receiving the letters that said, "How awful at your age!" and "America does not need Stalin's heirs," though in truth most of the letters were warm and congratulatory.[12]

Svetlana and Olga, photographed in 1971 in Arizona.

From her long conversations with Marge Hayakawa, Svetlana had come to understand that Wes's devotion to Taliesin was absolute. "He has invested too much of himself there," Marge told her. Svetlana concluded sadly, "It was for me to comply, to adjust to his ways, to alter my whole nature if necessary, in order to follow after him."[13] She flew back to Wisconsin with her new baby.

Wes seemed happy with his new family. He said he had always wanted a daughter. She would cherish his lovely words spoken when they were visiting friends in Wisconsin with the infant Olga: "You have returned me to life. I was dead all these years." She was astonished. "It was more than I had expected to hear from anyone."[14]

Svetlana still had hopes for the cattle farm at Aldebaran. Brandoch was delighting in his new role as cattle breeder. Though the herd of Holstein cattle she'd bought him had died over the winter, she'd sent money for another herd—the second one cost $92,000.[15] He'd built a new silo, improved the old barn, and purchased a stud bull from Colorado. As she sat with her baby on the porch while her men inspected the farm, she had a moment of bliss. She would write about that moment over fifteen years later:

> I couldn't forget the one happy hour years ago in the summer of 1971 when Wesley and I had a small farm near here. Olga had just been born three months ago and I was tending the baby-buggy while sitting on the wooden porch of a small farm we had. A big Irish wolfhound was peacefully lying at my feet as I rocked in an old, comfortable rocker. It was the evening hour, the golden rays from the low sun were filling everything in sight. A herd of cows was returning home down the road, with cow-bells tinkling. I could see, down the road near the gate, Wesley and his grown son, hands in their pockets slowly walking home while discussing farm affairs. The rocker was rocking, Olga was sleeping, and I thought then, here it is, the greatest, the happiest moment of my life. Stop! Hold this moment forever. I have a family, a home in my new country and from here on, my life will be like this: harmonious, secure, and filled with evening light. I thought then that nothing, no force in the world, could undermine this seemingly well-established life in which everything was harmonious and secure. Never before had I such a complete moment of sat-

isfaction and peace. . . . I had everything: a good husband, a healthy child, good friends, beauty, and plenty.[16]

What's astonishing is that this is all she got of domestic life on her farm: one hour.

As Wes and his father returned to the porch, Brandoch made it very clear that if she had any ideas of moving in, she wasn't welcome. He said that he needed privacy for himself and his girlfriend, who often visited. Wes concurred, telling her that he didn't want her "meddling" in the business and that he needed her at the apartment at Taliesin. Svetlana was shocked and hurt. She suddenly understood that Brandoch had never considered himself her son; she was only his banker. There was no warmth; they had never been a family. But she was not ready yet to give up on Wes. Launched on her "path of domesticity," she had to keep fighting.

She confessed to Annelise Kennan.

I feel I am egotistic, self-centered and absolutely have <u>no</u> experience of married life. I spent almost all my life alone, divorced, and with my children. I do not know <u>how</u> to be a good wife in the most usual normal way. And this <u>is</u> what Wes badly needs. . . . I know (and you know too) that life in Taliesin as such has its enormous difficulties for an individualist like me. But apart from that, there is something within <u>myself</u> that deprives me of a possibility to be a real good wife. . . . I <u>have</u> to find ways to overcome that and to <u>learn</u> to be a good wife. Pretty late—isn't it? Please, do not laugh at me. Please, do help me. You know, you <u>are</u> so perfect in this difficult field of knowledge. . . . Annelise, I just <u>cannot</u> break this family. I <u>have</u> to save it, and even more, to make it a pleasant thing to live. Some trick within myself has to be found and has to work—up to now I never knew <u>how</u> to do this. A divorce always seemed to me <u>the</u> best way; but I do <u>not</u> feel that way anymore. . . . It still seems to me that not for nothing the Fate has joined us together and blessed us with that sweetest child. . . . But I do not know <u>how</u> to build my home, how to create, please tell me—how?[17]

To see into the heart of a relationship, to understand the impinging of one personality on another, is virtually impossible. Certainly Wesley Peters must have sometimes felt he had invited a tornado into his safe bachelor's existence, but he had willingly turned Svetlana into one of Taliesin's collectibles. As his apprentice Aris Georges, who deeply admired both Wesley Peters and Svetlana, admitted ruefully, Wes and Olgivanna together played Svetlana, though he claimed Wes was not without feelings of guilt.[18]

It's hard to exonerate Wesley Peters, however. His freewheeling use of Svetlana's money was immoral. In retrospect, at her bitterest and most insightful, Svetlana could see that she had been used. "He married me because of my name; if I were Nina or Mary he would never have looked at me. But the main attraction was money."[19] Stalin's mythical Swiss gold, his long shadow, had enveloped her. It was all very sad. Even sadder was that Svetlana was perfectly tailored to their needs. She carried an idealized template in her head of the man who would offer permanent security and serenity and who would need her. For now, she was still not ready to give up, but Wesley Peters was never the man for the domestic life she imagined.

Back at the Fellowship, Kamal Amin watched the animosity build between Olgivanna and Svetlana, but he assigned much of the blame to Svetlana. "The residue of resentment [between them was] exaggerated by Svetlana's brooding nature. . . . Her soft, sweet demeanor camouflaged forty years of bottled-up anger accumulated during her life in the Soviet Union."[20] But one might also ask how she had contained her anger for so long.

The last straw, just before the trek back to Arizona, was a summons from Olgivanna to her private quarters for a talk. Olgivanna was making it clear that the warfare between them was entirely Svetlana's fault.

When Olgivanna asked what she so disliked at Taliesin, Svetlana couldn't say, "Everything," so she said she simply wanted peace. She assured Olgivanna that everything would be all right. Suddenly Olgivanna pulled Svetlana to her and looked deeply into her eyes. Svetlana was appalled.

> She began to breathe deeply and slowly, still staring. I lost all volition and stood there riveted; fear entered me like a cold wave, but I could not move. After a few moments of strain I broke down in tears, still holding her hands. And then I did something I would never have done of my own accord: I kissed those hands of hers several times. Only then did she release me. She was pleased. "One never forgets such moments," she said slowly.

Svetlana ran to Wes, still trembling and weeping, and said that Mrs. Wright had attempted to hypnotize her. She would never again go to see that woman. As she recalled the scene, Wes, with a cold indifference, called her hysterical and lectured her.

> Mrs. Wright loves you, but you are unable to respond to her in the same way. She is very much upset by that. She loves everybody here like a mother. . . . You have no understanding of this place whatsoever. It is a privilege to

live at Taliesin, the best way of life imaginable. I thought I gave you this chance by our marriage. If you do not appreciate this, I do not know what our future will be. You cannot stay at our farm because I want my wife to be where I am. You must find some way to adjust.[21]

The smugness of his response, as Svetlana reported it, probably accurately, is shocking, given that he and Olgivanna had set her up.

Svetlana now saw Taliesin as an uncanny and sinister echo of something she knew all too well. Olgivanna was just like her father. Her brown eyes had "the yellow wildcat sparkle" Stalin's eyes used to have that said, "Here is the boss."[22] She looked deeply into your eyes, digging for what you were trying to hide; her father "had a way of looking like that, too."[23] At dinner Olgivanna controlled the table, and everyone was careful to anticipate her response, just as at Stalin's table. Like Stalin, Olgivanna rewrote history to correct anything that diminished her role, claiming that only after Frank Lloyd Wright met her did his genius flower, though he was then sixty and already world famous. How had Svetlana landed herself at a place in America that echoed her father's oppressive world with its "cult of personality"?

Svetlana wrote to George Kennan that Taliesin was "ruled, suppressed, dominated, and indoctrinated in the most dictatorial Slavic (Montenegrin) way by the old woman (69) who is a good politician, who has very sharp common sense, and a tremendous desire to RULE." She had left dictatorship and false ideology in her country and now, in this "most democratic and free country in the world," she had landed "in a small Montenegrin Kingdom," with "a court and devoted courtiers, just like in my father's residence in Kuntsevo."[24]

Svetlana made a decision. She would neither bend to that psychological yoke nor allow her daughter, Olga, to be tethered in this way. She was appalled at the thought that she would have to leave. For solace, she took to driving along the back roads of Spring Green. This was her baby's motherland, and she wanted Olga to receive its beauty in her blood. She would gather wildflowers and sit on the banks of the Wisconsin River wondering at her life.

On one of her drives, she stopped to visit the cemetery beside the local Unitarian church and searched for the grave of the first Svetlana. There it was, Svetlana Peters, her own name on the gravestone, and with it the name of the dead child, Daniel. She had seen photos of the child, and he looked like her Olga, who resembled her father. Perhaps truly paranoid now, she began to be afraid of driving with Olga, afraid of a car accident. She knew she was falling under the spell of an idée fixe, but she couldn't stop herself. Perhaps she was meant to repeat the life of the first Svetlana down to the last detail.

This time, when the Taliesin caravan headed to Arizona, instead of taking their lovely drive across the country, she, Wes, and Olga flew. When Wes returned to work in Iran, she was on her own. There was now open warfare between her and Olgivanna. Kamal Amin remembered one particularly brutal dinner. He, Olgivanna, her daughter Iovanna, and Svetlana sat at the exclusive table. Svetlana began to complain, slightly hysterically, about Wes's work schedule. "He works too hard all the time; he's going to die." Olgivanna replied through clenched teeth in a tone of steel: "So are you."[25]

Svetlana had had enough. When Wes's friends Don and Virginia Lovness visited, Virginia claimed that Svetlana asked them to take her and Olga away with them. Apparently she told Virginia, "Someone tried to burn Taliesin before and they didn't do a good job. But I'm going to burn it down and I'll do a good job."[26] Believing Svetlana might really set fire to Taliesin, Virginia warned Olgivanna, who hired a private guard to protect the estate. Svetlana withdrew into her room with Olga. When Wes returned, he was delegated to bring their food.

According to Kamal Amin, "Olgivanna had the unusual ability to design and implement conflict, then cleverly retire into a solitary posture, assuming the role of victim. . . . In the process she gathered around her the small circle of yes people who in turn tried to widen the circle by disseminating the party line."[27] The party line was that Svetlana was the recipient of the Frank Lloyd Wright Foundation's beneficent largesse. Olgivanna had facilitated her marriage to a wonderful man. Taliesin was a place where she could nourish her creative abilities, which she had failed to do. Svetlana was "stubborn and ungrateful."

That Christmas, Olgivanna staged a final gesture of reconciliation, clearly to secure her own exoneration. She went to Svetlana in bare feet and presented her with diamond earrings. Svetlana threw them out into the desert, saying, "You cannot buy my friendship!" When Olgivanna's daughter Iovanna heard this, she screamed, "I'll kill her! I'll kill her."[28] They had come to the end, and Wes finally agreed that they could move out of Taliesin.

But now Svetlana began to worry about money. The Aldebaran farm was proving a sinkhole. Since the initial outlay, she had spent an additional $500,000 in repairs and land purchases, a total of about two thirds of her initial $1.5 million advance. The tax accountant complained that he could find no proper bookkeeping. Tax returns had not been filed for the last two years.[29]

When Svetlana wrote to George Kennan to ask for his advice, he immediately turned to his daughter Joan. Her husband, Walter Pozen, worked in the Washington office of the prestigious law firm Stroock & Stroock & Lavan. For months, Joan had been receiving strange, unexpected presents in the mail from Svetlana and Wes: Native American turquoise jewelry, expensive perfumes, and, once, four exquisite evening dresses in a single mailing.[30] The presents disturbed her, and she worried about Svetlana.

Pozen began to look into Svetlana's finances. The lawyer who represented the Valley National Bank indicated that the bank was extremely anxious about Svetlana's account and the endless loans that were being made against it. Pozen began to feel that "something awful" was going on. He sent one of his partners, an estate lawyer, to Spring Green, first to Taliesin and then to the bank. Both were shocked. "How could she have done this? She just assumed debts, assumed all the debts, assumed all of Wes Peters' personal debts, and there was much, much more."

To Pozen the whole farm fiasco felt like a fraud. When he confronted Svetlana, she said, "Oh, Walter, we're going to do this with this cow and that with that cow Charlie." And he thought, *My God, she's completely unaware she has nothing.*[31] Pozen concluded that her husband and stepson had almost wiped her out.

Svetlana's stay at Taliesin had lasted just short of two years. A few days after Christmas 1972, she moved out with infant Olga. She had found a two-bedroom house with a small terrace and fireplace, fully furnished, about fifteen minutes away. She signed the deed in the names of Mr. and Mrs. Peters, hoping Wesley would follow her. A young local resident, Pamela Stefansson, who'd served as Svetlana's babysitter at Taliesin and was devoted to Olga, moved in, and Svetlana was grateful for this.

Svetlana had managed to establish one very close friendship in Spring Green with a woman named Elizabeth Coyne. Coyne had a child at the late age of forty-five and knew what Svetlana was coping with as an older mother. Svetlana made one last gesture of rebellion before she left Taliesin. There was a piano at Taliesin that no one seemed to use. Because supposedly nothing belonged to any individual fellow, Svetlana played the innocent. The piano was public property. She asked Coyne if she wanted a piano. The movers showed up at Taliesin, loaded the piano, and took it away. When Herb Fritz, the actual owner of the piano, showed up, his piano was gone.[32]

Wes decided not to accompany Svetlana to their new house. He now said she had deserted him and taken his child, though she was only fifteen minutes away. He was soon demanding that she either come back to the Fellowship or divorce him. "I am not fit for any compromise," he said.[33] On her doctor's advice, Svetlana sought out a psychiatrist, who, having talked with the two of them, told her that she and Wes were completely incompatible and that Wes wanted out.

Svetlana's psychiatrist counseled that she never return to Taliesin, however much she might be tempted. Of course, she was unable to hold out. She drove there one night. Parking a short distance away, she walked via the back route and noiselessly entered Wes's apartment through the terrace. She stood watching him.

> Then I came close and touched his shoulder, weeping. He stood up, his face just as it was when I had seen him for the very first time; very sad, with deep vertical lines down his cheeks. He looked pale, exhausted, and could not talk. "You must go," he said, fearing that someone might see me. "You shouldn't. You shouldn't." He was unable to say anything more. He started towards the door in his dressing gown, and I followed. He knew which way I had come, and he walked with me towards the car, parked amidst rocks and cactuses. No one was around, only the stars were shining. We did not talk; what was there to say?
>
> I drove slowly away, still crying; I could see him in the

driving-mirror there by the roadside. The same beautiful desert road cut amidst savoaras and choias through which I came the first time. A bumpy, rocky road, leading to Taliesin from the asphalt highway. That was the last time I saw it.[34]

At the end of February, the Frank Lloyd Wright Foundation issued a statement that Wesley Peters was seeking a divorce. Reporters descended on Svetlana. To their questions, she replied that she didn't want a divorce; she simply could not live at Taliesin. "I believe in private property. They live a communal life at the foundation. They share their incomes, their food, their living. Everyone works, including the children [presumably she was referring to Iovanna's two adolescent children]. That's why I left Russia."[35] The *Danville Register* and the *New York Times* both had the headline STALIN'S DAUGHTER LEAVES HER HUSBAND.

In the *Danville Register*, Wes retorted, "I'm afraid her mind has been conditioned by years of Communist training to the point she rejects the highly individualized life. She views [Taliesin] with the eyes of one conditioned to reject the real principles of democracy in operation."[36] He added that Svetlana "came here and was anxious to marry me too fast."[37]

In a second article in the *New York Times*, STALIN'S DAUGHTER DISPUTES HUSBAND ON SEPARATION, he showed a little more grace, saying, "The last thing I want to do is say anything against Svetlana. I'm very fond of her," and "It was a mistake on my part to allow her to marry a person such as I am." Their separation was "one of the great tragedies of my life."[38] Wesley maintained that Taliesin was "the quintessence of democracy. Frank Lloyd Wright taught a higher degree of individuality than anyone I know. . . . Of course there is leadership."[39]

Positioned right beside this second article, the *Times* ran a piece called "Custodian of a Tradition: Olgivanna Lloyd

Wright," in which Olgivanna is quoted as saying, "Our Taliesin life is based on the democratic principle—young people are treated according to their merit. With those few of wealthy or aristocratic background we have more difficulties." Foreigners with titles, Olgivanna explained, found it hard "to submit to the orders of people whose backgrounds are much more modest than theirs." The *Times* then identified Svetlana as having grown up "in effect a Soviet princess, daughter of Stalin." Svetlana was trumped.

When Olgivanna's daughter Iovanna was interviewed much later, she claimed, "Nobody rejected her at all. It was she who rejected and was so suspicious." And then she added gratuitously that Svetlana's book "had been shadow written by somebody in the government. She was a murderer's daughter."[40]

As news of their separation spread, friends came to comfort Svetlana in her new home. When the Hayakawas visited, Wes came too and stayed for an hour. Perhaps for reinforcement, he also brought an old friend from Munich and a couple from Switzerland. He sent flowers at Easter. She wrote to Joan Kennan:

> Dearest Joanie,
>   I feel so sad. I feel pity for [Wes]—he is a weak man, he cannot lead his own way. This is his nature. He depends on "mother" complex. I can only hope & pray that old witch will die one day. Then he'll have a sort of rebirth of his own. Love to you dear.
>   Yours, as ever,
>
> *Svetlana*[41]

According to Walter Pozen, at this stage it was Svetlana who actually wanted a divorce and Wes who was delaying. In

Pozen's opinion, "He wasn't about to give up this woman." He was refusing a settlement agreement because it would have prevented him from having access to Svetlana's future earnings, and he was continuing to write checks on their joint account, already overdrawn by $1,000.[42] Pozen soon had their bank accounts separated.

Walter Pozen tried to make Svetlana understand her financial position, but he despaired, saying she had no concept of money. As part of the Soviet elite, she hadn't needed to understand it. When she finally had money, she gave it away—to found the Brajesh Singh Hospital, as donations to charities for children, and to support literary endeavors. According to Edmund Wilson, she was also sending $300 a month to Nina, the widow of her translator Paul Chavchavadze, who had recently died and of whom she had been so fond.[43] She gave her money unconditionally to Peters and his son. Joan Kennan would say, "It seemed to me the wealth from *Twenty Letters* had never been real to her—just one more turn of Fortune's wheel. The village in India, Wesley's troubled son on the farm, all those animals, the expensive gifts to friends."[44]

Pozen managed to get Svetlana a small loan from the Valley National Bank on the strength of future earnings from her books. In consultation with Cass Canfield at Harper & Row, he found out that Greenbaum had terminated the Copex Establishment, and all accrued earnings from her books had already been disbursed. In Canfield's judgment, her potential earnings over the next five years would total approximately $15,000. Clearly, she was in a mess.

Pozen was certain there had to be some way of working things out. If Wes and his son had taken all her money, she was owed that money back; the farm really belonged to her, or at least she had a legal interest in it, though of course Brandoch was fighting this. Pozen finally found a solution, a friend of

Brandoch who was willing to lend him the money to buy Svetlana's interest in the farm. He concluded that Wes would probably sign a settlement agreement for a divorce and future child support in exchange for settling the debt. This at least would leave Svetlana with some money, which, if properly invested, would provide an income.

It had taken Pozen about ten months to negotiate the agreement. Numerous lawyers were involved. Svetlana continually phoned Pozen in Washington, to the point that he dreaded to hear that Mrs. Peters was on the line. She would say, "Walter, I don't know . . ." Finally an agreement between Wes and Svetlana was ready to be signed the next day. Pozen was having dinner with Joan when the phone rang. It was Svetlana. Pozen recalled her words: "Oh, Walter dear, do you think we are doing the right thing? And this and that, and I don't need the money, and so on and so forth, and I'll give him this and I'll give . . ." Pozen would always regret his exasperated response. He said, "Svetlana, you can't buy this man back." She hung up the phone.[45] No agreement was signed.

Though his remark about buying Wes had been unkind, he was astonished that Svetlana could give up ten months of effort in a fit of pique when she might have had the money that would have liberated her. But this is not how Svetlana saw things. She complained to Joan Kennan that all Americans talked about was money. Ending this marriage, she "wanted no conflicts, no hatreds, no claims."[46]

When Joan replied with a reassuring letter, Svetlana wrote again to explain why she had changed her mind at the last minute. She knew that Walter had acted wisely and that they might indeed have "won the game." "We were just 5 minutes from it." But she insisted, "I have to <u>save</u> as much as possible friendship and peace with Wes because of Olga. . . . I cannot fight him." On the morning of Olga's birthday, she told Joan she had attended the service at the Greek Orthodox church in Phoenix. "I cried for him, for myself, for our small child, and gradually I felt that all my hatred—or whatever it was—was leaving me. . . . I've lost the game, in a way. But from the other point of view I've won something, too. Qne day Wes will recognize that, if he is not able to do that now."[47]

When she finally signed a settlement agreement with Wes in July, Svetlana renounced any interest in the farm and did not demand income or child-support payments. What was the point? No one at Taliesin, not even the lead architect, Wesley Peters, received a personal salary. All monies from projects went directly to the Frank Lloyd Wright Foundation, which paid the architects' expenses. Olgivanna claimed they were well compensated with accommodations, a car, and health benefits, and anyway the survival of Taliesin came first. No one complained. To demand support payments from Wes would only have meant ongoing acrimony.

When Wes finally filed for divorce a year later, Svetlana did not appear in court. She said she still had money in investments that would provide her a comfortable income. In fact, according to Walter Pozen, she may have salvaged between $200,000 and $300,000 in sheltered investments, though Pozen believed it was probably less and would not generate enough money to live on.

Svetlana decided her only option was to return to the familiar ground of Princeton. As her possessions were loaded into the moving van and she looked at the For Sale sign on her house, occupied for three months, she felt only a cold devastation. Wes had agreed to fly with her and Olga to Philadelphia. On the flight, they barely spoke. What was there to say? When her Princeton taxi arrived, Wes kissed her and then was gone. It felt like a defeat, but ironically, out of the whole debacle had come her greatest gift—her daughter. Without Olga, it is questionable whether Svetlana would have survived.

Chapter 26

Stalin's Daughter
Cutting the Grass

Joseph, the son Svetlana left behind, poses with his passport in 1975 in this photograph that George Kennan received from an anonymous American journalist.

W hen Svetlana and Olga arrived in Princeton in early August 1972, the Kennans, who were in Europe, lent Svetlana their home until her furniture arrived from Wisconsin and she could move back into 50 Wilson Road. Her first glimpse of her old house was disappointing. The interim owners had painted the white house red and added a screened-in porch and a two-car garage, which cut into the lovely terrace and backyard, ruining them. But this was the house where she had known comfort and safety, and she wanted it back. She still had doubts—had she left Wes too soon? She wrote to Annelise Kennan that she was still in love with him. "Only now I can see the full size of my unhappiness."[1] Wes kept promising to visit. He was always friendly on the phone.

Svetlana was now a forty-six-year-old single mother bringing up an infant. These were the cards she had turned up in her last gamble, and she was determined to make the best of them. Mostly, she feigned contentment. She told Annelise, "We are quite happy on our Wilson Road."[2]

For Olga's second birthday, Wes sent magnificent flowers and toys but, to Svetlana's shock, did not appear. She wrote to George Kennan:

> After he [Wes] "won" the divorce, I phoned him to ask if he is happy now; he talked to me as a bitten dog, complaining that he is terribly unhappy, etc. But about visiting Olga he said "perhaps in the summer." So she will never, I guess, have much attention from a daddy like this. I feel terribly unhappy about the whole thing, too. All my life I was used to idealize and romanticize a man I loved, and it always took me a long and painful time to be able to see a man as he really is; only then I would have relief. Although Wes showed us that he does not care about us too much, and in many ways he was not kind to me even when we lived together, I still cannot get rid of the good memories I do have.[3]

Now she told Kennan, "The only goal of my life is to bring up this precious child the right way—the right American way—about which I truly do not know much."[4]

Svetlana could no longer afford a housekeeper and a gardener. She went back to Urken Hardware, where Mrs. Urken greeted her warmly, to purchase the cleaning supplies she needed. As the newspapers announced that Wesley Peters was seeking a divorce, she was buying a lawn mower and joining the noisy chorus of husbands cutting the lawn on weekends. All her neighbors pretended it was not Stalin's daughter cutting the grass.

Everything about American domestic life had to be learned from scratch. Hella McVay, a teacher at a local private school, the Stuart Country Day School, remembered running into Svetlana at the Acme grocery store. Svetlana was standing in the aisle with Olga in the shopping cart, looking completely lost. McVay must have seemed approachable. "Svetlana came up to me and said, very shy, very quiet, 'Excuse me. I would love to make ice cream cone for my daughter. Tell me how to do this?'" McVay hid that she knew who Svetlana was and took the task very seriously.

So I said, I like cones for my—I have two daughters— and I like sugar cones. Maybe she likes sugar cones too. I knew the little one's name was Olga but I didn't use it. She wanted to give her little daughter something that was American. And I showed her the cones and then I took her to the ice cream. Look, oh my God, how much ice cream we have here! All the flavors. Just pick your favorite flavor. Maybe you want to put vanilla at the bottom and maybe raspberry on top, or maybe chocolate and then vanilla, and make little scoops and then just let her lick and have fun and get messy all over. And she just thought it was so wonderful! And thanked me up and down and then picked up several packages, and then we kissed good-bye.

Hella McVay and Svetlana became friends.

I felt very strongly not to violate her privacy because one always read about the fear Svetlana had that she was only Stalin's daughter. I mean I think women in general know that we are always in the shadow of a man up to a point, but being in the shadow of a monster who killed more people, I mean ten times more people than Hitler did . . . Svetlana wanted to disappear. And she always said she had two children but they were not free children. She wanted a child late in life here, a child born in a free country. . . . That was the phrase she used. I remember that.[5]

When Olga turned two, Svetlana took her to the Presbyterian Cooperative nursery school and served happily as a "helping mother." The younger mothers frowned upon her age—it was somehow unseemly to have a child in one's midforties. Svetlana had begun to go under the name Mrs. Lana Peters and believed that no one knew it was she, Stalin's daughter, who was changing the children's diapers. But in small-town Princeton everyone, down to the local taxi drivers, knew who she was.

Of course she was lonely. Old friends like Paul Chavchavadze and Edmund Wilson had died, but there were still the Kennans and a few new friends as well. And she continued her voluminous correspondence. She had met the writer Jerzy Kosinski in Princeton in 1970; they had talked for hours, and she had felt that, because he was Polish, he understood her and she him. She wrote to him:

When it comes to talk—the way we, useless Russian intellectuals are used to talk—then I have to knock my head against the wall. I am trying my best to become "Americanized" in that—that is <u>not</u> to talk (or think) in those old, outdated Russian intellectuals way. I made some success. I can have a good American cocktail—chat by now pretty well. But sometimes I <u>miss</u> that luxury of talking-for-an-hour-with-someone-who-understands. I <u>had</u> plenty of this <u>luxury</u> in Russia—nothing else, but a lot of <u>this</u>. . . . It was very refreshing, you know. I have had a bit of the same luxury with George Kennan, with Alan.[6]

She joked that if their conversation in Princeton had continued, she might have fallen in love with him, but "God saved us both from that. I'm afraid that would be quite a mess." She had heard he was unwell. Her closing was charming. She wished him "luck (the writers <u>need</u> luck). What else? Much laughter, which gives good health. Some inner peace, if you like that (some people don't)" and reminded him he had *freedom*, even more than she.

In his novel *Blind Date*, Kosinski introduced Svetlana as a character, and caught perfectly the shock that any expatriate Russian would have felt meeting her. By chance, his fictional character, Levanter, becomes a next-door neighbor to Stalin's daughter in Princeton:

> Her name alone, even over the telephone, was enough to call up visions of his Moscow past, and for him she became a direct link to the awesome power that Joseph Stalin had wielded. Levanter had to remind himself again and again that he was a lecturer in Princeton now, not a student in Moscow, and that he was talking with a woman who was just another neighbor and only happened to be the daughter of Stalin.
>
> Levanter showed [his friend Romarkin] a few photographs of Svetlana Alliluyeva. Picking up the snapshots reverently, as if he were handling fragile and irreplaceable heirlooms, Romarkin carefully spread them out on the café

table and studied each one. "It can't be," he whispered. "The daughter of Stalin an American. It can't be." He shook his head. "If within a quarter of a century you and I can go through life under Stalin and then go halfway around the world and meet his daughter as an ordinary next-door neighbor, well, I guess that means anything can happen."[7]

Knowing the complex responses she evoked, Svetlana mostly avoided the Russian community. Evgeniya Tucker, the wife of the eminent historian Robert Tucker, recalled one friend saying about Svetlana, "Not in my house!" And when Evgeniya replied, "Well, *she* didn't do it. It was her father," the friend simply said, "Why should I shake her hand?"[8]

Svetlana had only her faith in God left and sought out a church for solace. Her idea of God was, as she called it, "informal." She detested all claims of the superiority of one faith over another. Because all religions were the same, the church didn't matter, though she avoided the Russian Orthodox community.

A new assistant minister had arrived in Princeton at the Episcopalian Church of All Saints. He and his wife, Rosa, had just returned from nine years of missionary work in Uganda. Rosa Shand remembered her first impression of Svetlana, kneeling one row ahead of her across the aisle in church on Sunday. "She was curled so low I saw her as a ball of untamed orange hair."[9] Her eyes lowered, her pose was penitential. What was she repenting? Her abandonment of her children? All her failures? She was so private that no one dared disturb her.

Rosa Shand had read her book *Twenty Letters to a Friend*. Svetlana, seated there in a suburban Princeton church, was the closest she had come "to the dark wellsprings of history." After the service, Svetlana invited the Shands to visit her at her home. She'd found something in the young couple she responded to intuitively; perhaps they, too, seemed shell-shocked by their reentry into affluent Princeton. And soon Svetlana visited them, though she requested that no one else be present when she came, saying it was hard to encounter unexpected strangers. In a very short time, Rosa underwent back surgery.

It happened quickly, as all things happened quickly when Svetlana made up her mind, and she made up her mind that she would be our friend. It was scarcely three weeks later, after I'd gone through a back operation, that Svetlana took me into her home. It was the first—though far from the grandest—of those Russian gestures that struck me with awe, made me feel our own inhibiting caution. . . . I don't mean this spontaneous act of hospitality was particularly odd. Not then, but one already could feel the germ in her: that refusal to calculate. . . . At this point Svetlana's gesture was a reaching out . . . a simple impulse toward companionship and kindness. In any case, it was a gesture I scarcely imagined a member of my own family offering.[10]

Svetlana argued that Rosa needed time to recuperate. Her husband, Philip, could take care of the children. "You must have peace and breakfast in bed," she said. Rosa was apprehensive. Svetlana's "thunderous history pressed the air from my lungs." What might they talk about? But she was in such pain that she gratefully accepted Svetlana's offer.

It turned out that they talked mostly about children and played with Olushka (Svetlana's endearing nickname for Olga). Svetlana said that she was not too worried about her daughter Katya. Katya had discovered her passion for science at the age of eleven and was very close to her father, Yuri Zhdanov. It was Joseph who worried her. By now he was a doctor, but what scars did he carry? Not only from her abandonment of him, but did he feel guilty about the way he had been forced by the KGB to vilify her? It was nothing! What choice did he have? She spoke so longingly of sitting with her son at the kitchen table, laughing, crying, discussing everything in their old apartment in the House on the Embankment, that Rosa imagined she almost knew him.

Rosa was shocked by the total absence of any signs of Russianness in Svetlana's home and by the collection of modern gadgetry in her kitchen. How had she found such an item as an electric garlic press? "Television," Svetlana told her. She seemed to be eternally mopping the already spotless kitchen floor. "She didn't mean to be different, she meant to get things right, master the American ways."

One morning, when Svetlana was unaware she was already awake, Rosa glimpsed her in the kitchen through her open bedroom door.

It seemed to me I looked on all she had thoughtfully hidden. I looked on desperation. She wasn't moving, but you could not call her resting. She was perched on a stool in the middle of the kitchen, her mop tossed down, her back erect, stilted, gripping her automated eggplant peeler as if she had to fit like a robot in the tin-bright sheen of this kitchen. She stared out the window hopelessly, anxiously, so weary with faking she belonged with gadgets it was clear she wouldn't survive them. Abruptly I felt my helplessness in the face of the losses gnawing her. . . . What in the name of the twisting corridors of history was Svetlana doing here, clinging to an eggplant peeler in the rarefied elegance of Princeton?[11]

But Rosa could talk books, and to Svetlana this was a salvation of sorts. Over vodka, they discussed the ideas of the Danish philosopher-theologian Søren Kierkegaard, whose existential theories of faith as passion so moved Svetlana. They talked of Simone Weil, the French theologian and mystic, and of her tragic history. And there was always Pasternak. But Svetlana's writer was Dostoyevsky. Ah! That story *The Gambler.* Rosa said she preferred Chekhov. When Rosa mentioned that she delighted in the sassy poetry of Marina Tsvetayeva, Svetlana erupted as only she could: "Tsvetayeva's nothing. Leave her—she was weak—she committed suicide."[12] Rosa must read Anna Akhmatova's *Requiem.* That poetry had moral grandeur.

Requiem was Akhmatova's cycle of poems about the horrifying years in Russia under Stalin's Great Terror in the late 1930s, when she had lined up each day for seventeen months at the prison in Leningrad to deliver a package to her son Lev, arrested for counterrevolutionary activities. It began with the famous moment when an old woman in the line had whispered, "Can you describe this?" and Akhmatova said, "Yes, I can." The poetic sequence was her requiem to Moscow, its streets bloodied by the wheels of Black Marias, the Kremlin towers like the "wailing wall," and "hieroglyphics cut by suffering on people's cheeks."[13]

As Svetlana talked, Rosa was examining the photographs in the book *Pasternak par lui-même.* When she looked up, she saw that Svetlana was crying. "She had her elbows on the table, her hands in front of her mouth, her knuckles white. Tears rained down her freckles. She said, 'Akhmatova lost her son. Did you know she lost her son?'"[14] Akhmatova eventually recovered her son. Lev was released from the Gulag in 1957, four years after Stalin's death, but he was bitter when he returned from the camps, believing that his mother, who had fought so hard for his release, had not done enough to save him.

Svetlana had a vague notion that maybe she could buy a bigger house and Rosa, Philip, and their daughters could share it, but the family soon moved to Texas, where Philip had been offered a teaching post, though the friendship continued in letters for years.

As soon as Olga was old enough for preschool, Svetlana set about searching for a private institution. She had a Russian émigré's suspicion of state-controlled public schools—she thought parents who recommended them were deluded by some notion of "benevolent" socialism. She wanted "no State schools; no State *anything*."[15]

Millie Harford was the founding director of the Stuart Country Day School of the Sacred Heart. Harford recalled how she first met Svetlana. She'd recently accompanied her academician husband on a visit to the USSR, during which she'd visited Russian schools. Interviewed in the *Princeton Packet*, the local daily, on her return, she'd said it was a fascinating experience; schools in the USSR had interesting curricula, hardly different from those in the United States.

Out of the blue, Svetlana called Millie Harford and chewed her out for her newspaper diplomacy—"diplomatic" was a word Svetlana detested. Millie had never met Svetlana, but she agreed that she had not been truthful. She'd actually found the Soviet schools restrictive; the children seemed to be discouraged from self-expression and taught to conform. Svetlana said, "I want to meet you."

"We met. She was disarming. I liked her immediately."[16]

Three-year-old Olga was soon enrolled in a class for preschoolers at the Stuart School. Fees were high—$1,500 a year. Though Princeton was divided between new and old money, many of the students at Stuart were culled from the international set. The husband of one of the teachers had grown up in Communist Poland and remembered all the books with propaganda photographs of Svetlana, the "Little Sparrow," seated on her father's knee, as an example for Polish children, of the beloved youngster. He found it ironic that his child should be playing with Stalin's granddaughter.[17]

Svetlana and Millie Harford became close friends. Harford often invited her to dinner with discreet guests, but one dinner in particular was seared in her mind. The gathering that night was intimate.

> Svetlana told that story, which is so well known, of how in the evening when her father and his companions were drinking and she was already asleep or reading, he would drag her down by her pigtails and say: sing and dance for us. And that was very painful, very painful. I think what made her speak was that my husband asked our son, who was a Beatles fan and had just learned to play guitar, to play for us. And Chris refused. And Jim said, "Come on, Chris." And he said, "No, I don't want to do it." And that's when Svetlana got up and said, "Let him be. Let him go. Because when I was his age, my father would pull me out when I was very quiet and by myself and have me come out to his parties. Male parties, men parties. And put me on the table, and said, 'Dance.'" And she showed us how she danced. She went into the coat closet and got a hat and a cane and she did the dance. She actually went to the floor and kicked.[18]

As she danced, the guests looked on, appalled at the heart-break of it.

Svetlana was aiming for a normal "American" life. She invited guests to her home: the Hayakawas came, and her old friend Ruth Biggs. She had the neighbors to dinner. People she met through Olga's school dropped by. That summer of 1974, she put a small in-ground swimming pool in her backyard, paid for on a monthly installment plan. She wrote to Rosa Shand that they'd had a lovely relaxed summer at their own "little private beach."

"We've had guests all the time—couples, singles, families—with children, and whatnot. All this quite unexpected and unusual for us—but *very* pleasant anyway."[19] But the next July, terrible rains hit Princeton and the pool collapsed under the weight of the floods, leaving a trench of mud in the yard as if after a bombing. It was "sad" but "OK," Svetlana reported. "Some people had much worse damages and losses on the same very day."[20] She had a Russian's stoicism. One never counted on anything's lasting.

Moreover, she was never entirely free from fear. The letters from strangers had decreased. Now there were perhaps only ten a day. Some saddened her. One man had wanted to know why her father treated his people the way he did, but even she, his daughter, didn't know. However, other letters caused deep anxiety. She wrote to tell Jamie (her CIA minder) that right after their regular telephone call, on November 6, she'd received a "terrible hate letter" from a woman who presented herself as a professor at the University of Rome. "I do not mind to be cursed, but she cursed Olga too. This is—I think—something beyond politics; an animal feeling."[21] The thought that Olga might be harmed was unnerving. She told Jamie she'd felt safer in Arizona; it was so isolated. Why had she ever moved back to Princeton?

Wesley Peters holds his daughter, Olga, in 1974, by which time he and Svetlana were divorced.

She had other worries about little Olushka. Everyone at the school found Olga a darling child, lively, independent, with large black eyes that drew one in, but Olga did not speak. Svetlana was referred to a speech therapist, who asked her to fill out a questionnaire. When the doctor read it, his face blanched. Svetlana summarized: "Olga's parents were old. My mother had a nervous breakdown and committed suicide. My brother died an alcoholic." She seems not to have mentioned who Olga's grandfather was. Perhaps she didn't need to. She was told by the nervous doctor to bring the child back. They would check her ears; maybe she couldn't hear. Svetlana felt sick. "I returned home in tears, fearing that no doubt now they would try to find all sorts of inherited defects in my daughter."[22] But by the time Olga turned four, Svetlana was thrilled to be able to tell Annelise Kennan that Olga "keeps *talking* all the time! I never saw such a talkative child! The last thing she's brought from her summer school was: 'Mummy I think I have a baby in my tummy. When one eats a lot you know, one gets a baby in one's tummy.' She was so sure about it, I did not know what to say!"[23]

Svetlana didn't believe that the KGB had given up on her. In June 1974, she received a letter from her son, Joseph. She never spoke of its contents but clearly did not trust that it came from him. She told Annelise Kennan she'd sent the letter to a graphologist, along with a sample of Joseph's authentic handwriting. The graphologist reported that the letter and the sample were not written by the same person.[24] In Svetlana's mind, who else but the KGB would forge a letter from her son? But why?

She wanted *real* news from Moscow. In the closed universe of the Soviet Union, where mail was censored and official eyes kept watch, the safest route to her children was brutally labyrinthine. Her neighbor on Wilson Road, Roman Smoluchowski, attended a conference of astrophysicists in Moscow that July. He came back with news that Katya, twenty-four, had graduated in geophysics from Moscow University and was now teaching. She was still unmarried and was living with her grandmother, Yuri Zhdanov's mother, whom Svetlana had so hated that she'd told her father all those years back that she was leaving her marriage because of her domineering mother-in-law. But Svetlana consoled herself that at least her totally impractical Katya was not living alone. Joseph had a very good job at one of the best clinics in Moscow. She was not surprised to learn he was divorced. She had tried to warn him that he'd been too young to marry.[25] She discovered for the first time that she was a grandmother. Joseph had a four-year-old son.

That month, November 1974, was particularly hard for Svetlana. She wrote to Rosa Shand that she'd fallen into a desperate gloom, believing God had abandoned her. "Everything abandoned me—even the words of prayer." For her, November was the black month of death, the month of her mother's suicide. Reading the theologian Dietrich Bonhoeffer, she'd found the words for what she'd been through. She told Rosa it was a "crisis of faith," "a temptation of the Spirit. If you've never been through that, I wish you never have it."[26] When the desolation of her terrible aloneness confronted her, Svetlana could only try to hold on.

Believing it would endanger them, Svetlana had always been very careful not to try to contact her children in Moscow directly. But then on August 5, 1975, George Kennan received an astonishing letter from an unidentified American journalist in Moscow, delivered by diplomatic pouch through the State Department. It read: "Dear Mr. Kennan: I am writing on behalf of Joseph G. Alliluyev who has asked that I get in touch with his mother regarding his desire to visit the US." The journalist said that Joseph was asking his mother to obtain a three-month tourist visa for him. This was a very strange request. In the mid-

1970s, virtually no citizens of the Soviet Union were permitted to travel, unsupervised, outside the Eastern bloc, and any and all contacts with foreigners inside the USSR were still considered treasonous.

Signing his letter only "A Friend," the writer explained that, through an acquaintance, he'd met Joseph, who was now a teaching physician at the First Moscow Institute, divorced, with a five-year-old son. Apparently Joseph told the writer that he'd denounced his mother in 1967 because he was bitter and felt betrayed, but also because "considerable pressure was brought to bear on him to denounce her." Now, however, Joseph recanted, saying, "I absolutely understand her. It took nine years." Joseph wanted his intentions kept secret. No one, not even his father or his half sister, Katya Zhdanov, knew of his desire to visit his mother. Joseph never spoke openly of defection, though there were hints that he might not want to return to his country.[27] Inside the envelope were several photographs, including one of Joseph holding his passport. The anonymous journalist said he was jeopardizing his own job by acting as an intermediary, but wanted the exclusive scoop if Joseph did indeed follow through with his plans.[28]

Kennan immediately took the letter and photographs over to Svetlana's house. It looked suspicious. Who was this journalist? Why the diplomatic pouch? Why was the letter addressed to Kennan and not to her? Kennan advised Svetlana that it might be a trap meant to damage relations between the United States and the USSR.

It is not hard to imagine Svetlana's state of mind at this news. If the journalist was credible, her beloved son Joseph was asking to join her in America; he'd forgiven her for abandoning him. She also understood that his contacting her in such a clandestine manner through the American Embassy was exceedingly dangerous for him. What would happen if his plans were discovered? And if he really wanted to join her in the United States and didn't receive an invitation from her, would he ever forgive her?

But there was a second possibility. The whole thing might be a new KGB plot, as Kennan certainly suspected, which meant that her son was being used against her once again—the photographs were clearly authentic. But what was the point? So that the KGB could say that the vile daughter of Stalin, a tool of the American imperialists, was luring her son to become a traitor to his country, but he'd valiantly exposed her?

It was impossible to penetrate. Anguished, she agreed with Kennan. She could not respond. Kennan went to his colleague Mark Garrison, director of the Office of Soviet Union Affairs in the State Department, who had passed him the letter, and asked him to send a message to the journalist that "Joseph's mother still loved him deeply," but that "if he wanted to come to America, he should send a letter by ordinary mail."[29]

The anonymous journalist soon sent a second letter to Kennan. This time he identified himself as George Krimsky. He worked for the Associated Press and often dealt with the dissident community. He explained what had happened. A young man named Alexander Kurpel had approached him in Moscow that spring asking for a lift. As they chatted in the car, Kurpel told Krimsky that he was a close friend of Joseph Alliluyev, to whom he would like to introduce him. Krimsky went to Joseph's apartment, where Joseph invited him for a walk in the local park so that they could talk more freely. Joseph asked Krimsky to pass a message to his mother "about a possible visit."[30] It had obviously been Krimsky's idea to send the letter to George Kennan.

This second letter clarified little, and Svetlana was distraught. Perhaps this Alexander Kurpel, who had first approached Krimsky, was working as an agent provocateur for the

KGB when he'd offered to get Krimsky in touch with Joseph in the first place. Yuri Andropov, then head of the KGB, was certainly ingenious at the tactics of Cold War intrigue. Was Kennan right? Kennan was sure the KGB was out to embarrass the Carter administration by demonstrating that the CIA was still plotting against the USSR through Svetlana. It was an easy conclusion for him, but, tragically, she was still the pawn in the middle, her motherly heart wrung by the politics of the Cold War.

Next George Krimsky made a brief trip back to the United States and phoned the Kennan household. He spoke with Annelise, who told him her husband refused to be involved. Krimsky then phoned Svetlana, and despite her longing to see her son, she mostly followed Kennan's advice and spoke with him only briefly.

Still, Svetlana thought of another possible plan. George and Annelise Kennan were set to visit the USSR in November. Kennan might try to contact her son to know his real intentions. Unfortunately, things had suddenly deteriorated in the USSR. The Nobel Peace Prize had just been awarded to the nuclear scientist and dissident Andrei Sakharov, and the Soviets were furious. It was still not clear whether Sakharov would be allowed out of Russia to receive his prize. (He wasn't.)

Svetlana wrote to Kennan on October 15. As if thinking out loud about the implications of trying to contact her son, she parsed the possibilities. With the Soviets so angry about Sakharov's Peace Prize, the timing was very bad. Any mention of her son's name would be traced back to her. "After your departure from Moscow, God knows what they might incriminate him in, and we will not be able even to learn about it." That would be "the WORST possibility, to gain nothing, but to ruin my son's rather peaceful existence." But there might be a second possibility. George could meet with Joseph openly and ask him if he wanted to visit his mother. If he said yes, George could convey his request to officials. Surely the Soviets would not dare to refuse George.

The worst mistake would be to go halfway. She added that if things went wrong, "This would be the REAL tragedy. . . . I would certainly prefer to stay in the same position of 'no communication' with them both, THAN to see them in trouble due to my own blunders. . . . Complete separation from me . . . is the most secure way in the crazy society of the USSR."

She concluded her letter thus:

> I love my children dearly, George; they deserve it. You would love them, too. But . . . one cannot do anything to fight FATE; we HAVE to wait for better times, when GOOD THINGS will be possible. Even the Decembrists [Russian military officers who revolted in 1825] were returned from their exile, and were allowed to die peacefully in Europe! Such is Russia's history—was and still is.[31]

In the end, Kennan decided it was better not to attempt to contact Joseph, and Svetlana concurred, though the silence from Russia was unnerving.

George Krimsky later reported that after he returned to the USSR, he went to see Joseph again. Indicating that his apartment was bugged, Joseph led him outside and said, "This all has to stop." The KGB had hauled him in. "They knew everything about his contacts with the West. If he continued, he would soon be exiled from Moscow. If he was lucky, he would find himself practicing medicine somewhere deep in Siberia."[32] This conversation would seem to confirm that, in fact, Joseph himself had initiated the request for a visa, but of course that doesn't mean the KGB wasn't playing him at the same time. Penetrating such cloak-and-dagger intrigues required the mind of an espionage specialist. It would be another year and a half before Svetlana would discover the truth about the Krimsky/Kurpel affair.

That Christmas of 1975, while she and Olga were in California visiting the Hayakawas, she gave in to an irresistible impulse and phoned her son. "Bunny, is that you?" she asked, as she had always called him affectionately as a child. He replied curtly: "Do you think you sound like yourself after nine years?" and then the line went dead.[33]

Chapter 27

A KGB Stool Pigeon

Svetlana and Olga, age six, pose together in 1977 for this Christmas photo sent to Rosa Shand from "the Peterses."

Suddenly, seemingly out of the blue, Svetlana pulled up stakes in March 1976, sold her Wilson Road house in Princeton, and moved with Olga to California. While staying with the Hayakawas that Christmas, she'd accepted an invitation from the journalist Isaac Don Levine to visit him in Carlsbad, near San Diego. As she sat in Levine's living room, she stared at the blue Pacific and suddenly felt at home. The smells of eucalyptus, of orange and lemon trees, of the pine forests, stirred

old memories. Emotionally she was leaning back to the Black
Sea of her childhood. Life in Princeton was expensive and her
income from stocks and bonds inadequate. Levine suggested
California was cheaper.

It was not surprising that Don Levine had sought her out.
A journalist of Belarusian background, he was a staunch, even
virulent anti-Communist. He was known to help Soviet dissidents but also occasionally to use them for his own propaganda
purposes. He must have thought that Stalin's daughter could
prove a powerful propaganda weapon in his arsenal. When
they met, Levine had given her an earful about East Coast
liberals like George Kennan who served the State Department
and catered to the Soviets. Almost immediately she became
suspicious that Levine was manipulating her—he was invei-
gling her to sign protest telegrams—and she cut off any potential friendship. Unfortunately this meant that she and Olga
were very much on their own in California. She had hoped
that the Hayakawas would be her family, but Sam Hayakawa,
though still very fond of her, was running for the US Senate
and had little time for his relatives.

It was not Levine or his politics that drew Svetlana to California. The truth was, she'd left Princeton in part because of
a personal entanglement. It had been over four years since her
separation from Wesley Peters, and perhaps she was ready to try
again. She met Douglas Bushnell, a wealthy businessman, at a
Princeton party, and his tragic history had drawn her in. A few
years earlier, his wife had committed suicide, leaving behind
her teenage daughter and two sons. Bushnell still seemed broken by the tragedy. "Things like these were well known in our
family. MAY BE IT IS TRUE that a difficult life produces a
better human being," she later told George Kennan.[1] Svetlana,
it seems, was always drawn to the *broken*. For a brief moment,
they'd almost seemed a family. Little Olga was crazy about

this amusing white-haired joker and loved his visits, when he'd swing her through the air and give her shoulder rides. Svetlana thought Bushnell might become a kind of father to Olga since Wesley Peters had virtually disappeared from their lives. After four brief visits to Princeton, Wesley had stopped visiting and rarely called. He didn't show up again for five years, at which point his daughter didn't recognize him.[2]

However, Bushnell soon made it very clear to Svetlana that he wanted only casual relationships with women. "It ended," Svetlana explained, "with a bad outburst from both sides—as it should be <u>expected</u>."[3] Any man drawing close to Svetlana might have been frightened. Who could cope with her life? She lived on such a large stage, with the drama of Cold War politics and with the KGB as a subtext, and there was her own emotional insecurity to contend with. Her past held private drawers filled with too much pain. She and Bushnell parted but remained friends. He sent warm letters to her in California with news of his children and queries about Olga, and she replied in kind. Svetlana's solution to disappointment was to move on, but it must have been in her mind that she should now *expect* to remain alone.

When she arrived on the West Coast, Svetlana rented an apartment in Oceanside, but soon found a small, inexpensive pseudo-Japanese house to buy in Carlsbad; it had a lovely inner courtyard and a small rock garden. She registered five-year-old Olga in a Montessori school, and then set about resuming her creative life. She wanted to write another book, but she found herself unable to work. Her days grew empty. She would drive Olga to school, to her music lessons, to her dancing and swimming classes. Waiting to pick her up, she would sit in the parked car at the edge of the beach and watch the breakers for hours. Under the multiple pressures she'd endured, Svetlana was slowly falling apart.

In July, she wrote to Joan Kennan that since her separation

from Wes, she'd been breaking down, both physically and mentally, and she was truly frightened. "I've had something really like a nervous 'fit' (or 'break-down'). . . . My increasing <u>habit of drinking alone</u> (at the cocktail hours—so to say), brought me to the verge of absolutely uncontrolled—and totally unbalanced—emotions, which started to rule <u>me</u> instead. Joanie, I know only too well, how <u>this sort of thing could</u> develop. It killed my own brother at age 41."[4] She explained that her sudden escape from Princeton had been an effort to change her environment completely.

It seemed that the only thing she could manage to do was to keep moving. In the next sixteen months in California, she moved from Oceanside to Carlsbad to La Jolla, buying and selling two houses. Her explanation to herself and others was that she was searching for a good school for Olga, but truly, she was lost.

In November, she wrote a long, devastating note to Jamie (Donald Jameson). She began with her usual optimism, telling him she was trying to write a book. It would be about the United States and the USSR, a dialogue that could illuminate both countries for ordinary people. But she could find no one she could trust to work with, and she'd lost her courage.

And then her letter took a deeply unnerving tone.

Since I came to Taliesin—and left it, to my own great unhappiness—I have had a strange feeling of being hypnotized, influenced, directed, or whatever you wish to call that. Very often—since then—I have NOT BEEN MYSELF. . . . I have had moments of utmost despair, such that I did not know what to do with myself. . . . When such a depression comes upon me, I cannot think about anything, Jamie, [but] that some Soviet secret experimentators [*sic*] are, probably, testing on ME their secret, newest, psychological weapons. Para-psychological weapons, if that makes any sense . . .

Somebody has been trying—desperately—to reach MY CONSCIOUSNESS. . . . The result—on this end—was my extreme nervousness / without any visible reason/ and above all, the constant desire TO MOVE, TO CHANGE PLACE, to go somewhere else, where those WAVES could not reach me. . . .

Sometimes—at night—I have terrible fear about Olga, that she might be kidnapped, and I would NOT be able to pay the ransom. This IS my worst nightmare of all. Myself, I do not care about what might happen to ME. . . . But—most of all—I DREAD THE SITUATION when I could be OK, but SHE could get into the hands of some political speculators. . . .

It is easy to notice, if my behaviour becomes disordered. . . . IT IS disordered, Jamie—you could see it even from this very letter. I have lost some controls, and I am not able to pull it all back into my hands. Jamie, I need help sometimes— because I am afraid to be alone, with this dear child.

In the envelope, she enclosed a clipping from the *Christian Science Monitor*, dated November 22, 1976, and titled "DIA Cites Soviet Microwave Research."

A newly declassified Defense Intelligence Agency report says extensive Soviet research into microwaves might lead to methods of causing disoriented human behavior, nerve disorders, or heart attacks.

"Soviet scientists are fully aware of the biological effects of low-level microwave radiation, which might have offensive weapons applications," says the report, based on an analysis of experiments on animals conducted in the Soviet Union and Eastern Europe.[5]

The clipping was meant as proof that such experiments were under way in the Soviet Union. She continued:

> I have deadackes [*sic*], heartaches, sudden high blood pressure, sudden depressions, bad eyesight, and what not—and all I can do is JUST try to pull myself together again—like Humpty-Dumpty. Sometimes it works; the presence of any NICE person is a help. . . .
>
> I feel at the present time desperately opened, unprotected and half-destroyed. . . . We have just moved into that apartment. But I already am going to move back to the house I bought—WHY? I DO NOT KNOW. That URGE CAME—and I will go. Everyone will be once again surprised. I have to say something to explain. But I do not know. *I am already in some sort of dead end.* . . .
>
> Please let me know what do you think about all this.
>
> Yours,
>
> *Svetlana*[6]

Deeply disturbed by her letter, Jamie rushed to California to see how he could help. His visit was welcome, but other than urging her to return to the East Coast, there was little he could do.

It was as if all the self-control that it took to be Svetlana was failing. As the fears and terrors broke through, she felt invaded and occupied. She had always censored her feelings of betrayal. Now she would have to confront them. She faced a dark winter trying to hang on. In the spring, still desolate, she wrote to George Kennan:

> Dear George,
>
> I am definitely not a stone wall, neither a block of concrete. Nor do I possess those nerves of steel, famous

enough, which have made a name for my father. Rather from my mother's side comes oversensitivity and capacity to react to minor things. . . .[7]

I respond TOO EASILY, George, to the ideas, wishes, suggestions, and desires of other people: instead of PRESSING MY OWN instinctive wish, which IS very often the most right one. My father noticed this in me, when I was a teenager, and used to say angrily: "Don't you repeat to me what others want you to say, like an empty drum! Say what you really want: Yes or No!" I am afraid he noticed that weak point in me. The GOOD things to see was not HIS talent. But he was pretty smart about human weaknesses, and despised those.[8]

Her self-contempt is obvious, still filtered through her father's voice.

Finally, in March Svetlana consulted her family doctor and, through him, found a psychiatrist. What precipitated this desperate gesture was her sudden realization that her undigested bitterness at Wes was affecting her relationship with Olga. She told Joan Kennan that if Olga was stubborn or bossy, she saw her child as "a copy of Wes." That was "unhealthy (I knew that!) and wrong." She was panicked. "Olga is my dearest child (no matter who is the father)."[9]

She began to visit the psychiatrist once a week. She never identified him, calling him simply Peter, but it was important to her that Peter had once been a Jesuit. He did not judge her or rush to conclusions. One can imagine the shock to the West Coast psychiatrist of finding Stalin's daughter on his couch, but she told Joan Kennan she was able to speak to this kind, gentle man about her "whole life." He gave her the simple acceptance she craved.

It may have been her psychiatrist who helped her to see that the bedrock of her current despair was located in her broken marriage. It was not Soviet experiments in mind control that were paralyzing her. It was grief. After her defection, the disaster of Taliesin had been the second total break in her life, and it had been a brutal betrayal. She had to find a way to exorcise the rage that resulted from the death of what she'd thought had been love from Wes, from the litany of betrayals during her father's murderous attacks on her family, and from that terrifying moment in 1932 when her mother had abandoned her and she was psychologically orphaned.

Because of Wes, she had lost money, of course, and money is freedom, especially in the West, and is the only route to physical security. But more important than this, she had lost herself. Wes had totally shattered her self-confidence. It had taken her a long time to see and admit this. Now she had to reconstruct herself from scratch. It was a brutal fate, but she assured Joan Kennan that she was recovering the courage and pride she had felt in her act of defection in 1967 and was beginning to imagine again that maturity and tranquillity would be hers.[10] She started attending meetings of Christian Scientists. Though she wasn't convinced by their ideology, their methods of self-discipline allowed her to control her drinking.

In February 1977, a scandal erupted in the international press. The Soviets expelled the journalist George Krimsky (the man who had attempted to help Joseph to defect in the spring of 1975) on charges of spying for the CIA. *Time* magazine's Moscow bureau chief Mark Clark claimed, "The real reason for Krimsky's expulsion was his coverage of dissidents."[11] The Carter administration retaliated by expelling a Soviet reporter. However, mysteriously and to Svetlana's relief, her son's effort to defect was not mentioned.

Then, in March, just around the time she began to see her psychiatrist, she received a letter from Alexander Kurpel, the

Russian who had taken George Krimsky to meet Joseph in Moscow. Kurpel had somehow discovered her California address.

In his fourteen-page handwritten letter, Kurpel ranted in incoherent English in a scrambled, frightening way. He began, "I'm belling the cat not to consider you to be an indifferent person in my destiny. Since the end of January, 1977 everything has gone upside-down and that very comforting so-called 'steel curtain' has flown away in nowhere." He stated that after George Krimsky was expelled as a CIA agent, he, Kurpel, had been hauled in for a seven-hour grilling by a KGB officer named Sevastianov,

> whose sincere intimidations and sincere feelings to collaborate with his organization—"choose yourself right now: either a labor camp or deep heart confession and guaranteed liberty" . . . How much blood have they spilt me and finally had a nerve to say: "We have a failure that we could succeed in coming true and convincing your US instigators that you're a harem-scarem stool pigeon of KGB." . . .
>
> I was dishonorable to play these merely doggish tricks in order to blacken and discredit intentionally such bona fide people as Mr. Krimsky and let alone a most high-skilled journalist, but not a CIA agent and so on.[12]

Kurpel spoke intimately of her life and of her children. He described meeting Katya, who'd "grown thin and has a well-built figure." He suggested that Svetlana write to the White House on Joseph's behalf. He said he was trying to emigrate. Could she help? He had seventeenth-century icons to exchange for hard currency.

Who was this terrifying man? His ranting letter was absurd and sinister. Panicked, she wrote to George Krimsky. In early May, she received a reply on the letterhead of the Associated Press in Nicosia, Cyprus. George Krimsky wrote back:

MAY 2, 1977

Dear Mrs. Peters,

It was a great pleasure to hear from you again. I must confess I have felt a bit guilty for not writing. . . . Frankly, I didn't have much news for you. I felt that, under the circumstances, it was best to "let the dust settle" regarding your son.

Yes, Alexander Kurpel was the one who introduced me to Joseph, and I will tell you what I know about him. First, let me caution you to be very wary of establishing any contact with him. Although I have no proof about his motives, he is a very questionable character, and I regret ever having met him. I do not believe Joseph is served well by him, as you correctly surmised in your letter.

In my opinion Kurpel is quite mixed up and/or is working for the KGB. As to the former I have no doubt; as to the latter, much circumstantial evidence points in this direction but, of course, one seldom can be sure.

Kurpel . . . introduced me to Joseph in the spring of 1975. . . . Your son was rightly suspicious of him because of the young man's loose tongue and his rather unbelievable and conflicting tales. He is also, I might add, an admitted homosexual and extremely effeminate in appearance and actions. I mention this because we both know what that means in the USSR, and it raises questions as to how and why such a person can operate as openly and widely as this fellow did (does) without problems from authorities.

Joseph and I decided to meet privately, without Kurpel's knowledge, to discuss his situation but somehow Kurpel seemed to know this. He was very upset. . . .

After I returned from the US in October 1975, . . . I was unable to see Joseph. As a matter of fact I never saw him again, except briefly in front of his apartment when he refused to talk with me. It was obvious that he was under tight surveillance; Joseph signaled to me silently that he was being watched and did not want to see me. . . .

There were two themes always put forth by Kurpel in his reports to me about your son: (1) How dejected and embittered Joseph was . . . ; and (2) how if only his mother could be informed of this, Joseph could somehow be helped.

I strongly suspected (paranoia?) a trap was being prepared for you, possibly to reap some propaganda windfall. ("Traitor Svetlana tries to get son to defect"), and perhaps I would also be a victim ("Journalist-CIA man in league with Traitor Svetlana to get son to defect"). . . .

Kurpel always had an almost morbid fascination with your history. He knows your birthday and follows any news of you that he can find, over VOA, snippets he comes across in the western press etc. His access to information most Soviet citizens are not privy to always amazed me.

Krimsky believed that Kurpel was behind his expulsion from Moscow. The Soviets didn't mention Joseph's effort to defect and the role that Kurpel had played as a reason for Krimsky's expulsion. "Why?" Krimsky asked Svetlana. "I can only think that the reason was to allow this fellow to continue operating freely and not be exposed in a formal manner by being named as a conspirator in the official press."

Krimsky added in caps:

HOWEVER, IF THEY COULD GET YOU TO INITIATE SOME MOVE TO HELP JOSEPH, THEY WOULD BE ABLE TO CLAIM THAT YOU LAUNCHED A CAMPAIGN TO HELP THIS LOYAL SOVIET CITIZEN WHO HAS DENOUNCED HIS

MOTHER'S TRAITOROUS ACTIVITIES TO LEAVE
THE COUNTRY HE LOVES.

Do you get my point? I doubt they will raise this issue
unless they can show you are trying to get Joseph to leave.

Now this puts you in a very difficult position. Naturally,
you have Joseph's best interests at heart. They are undoubtedly
hoping that your renewed concern over Joseph's situation
(sparked by Kurpel's letter) will prompt you to act. This is
a decision only you can make, but, again, I would be very
cautious.

Although I have no way of knowing, I guess that Joseph
is probably nervous but physically alright. I think he believes
his tentative campaign to see you had backfired before it
could really get started.[13]

What would Svetlana have noted from Krimsky's letter? The
most important thing was that Joseph had initiated the effort
to contact her. He missed her and longed to see her as much
as she longed to see him. The next thing was that Krimsky
believed Kurpel *was* a tool of the KGB. His March letter had
been a provocation. She had been right to remain silent. Any
response from her would have harmed Joseph irreparably. The
final thing was that Kurpel was exceedingly dangerous. His
obsession with her was worse than creepy. One can imagine
Svetlana's disgust and fear.

The KGB was still up to the same old dirty tricks, but who
in the West would believe it would go to such lengths to get
at the Traitor Svetlana after almost a decade? Non-Soviets did
not understand! She was Stalin's daughter. Like Kurpel, the
KGB was obsessed with her. She was a living symbol of the
failure of the Soviet system and the KGB was determined to
make her pay.

After Svetlana received George Krimsky's letter, her first impulse was to protect Joseph from Kurpel by writing to his father, Grigori Morozov, who was now an eminent professor of international law. He was also high up in the Party, close to Georgy Arbatov, a Russian political scientist known in the United States as a spokesman for Soviet policies in the Cold War standoff. Grigori could shield their son. Knowing that her letter would, of course, be read, she wrote to him via the Soviet Embassy, to assure him that she wasn't trying to lure Joseph to the West.

Her ex-husband had grounds for being angry with Svetlana. When she defected in 1967, his pending three-year assignment at the United Nations had been canceled. But he was kind and genuinely fond of her. He was also very anxious for their son. He wrote back immediately, mailing his letter in New York, where he'd stopped en route to Moscow after attending a conference in Mexico.

NYC: 6-29-77

Dear Svetlana,

I have received your letter. I want to tell you frankly I was overjoyed; it has clarified a very serious situation, created by people, who, without any authority from you, have been using your name in their own purposes.

Characters, whom you call "bastards," have already done a lot to confuse Joseph and to mess up his life here—and I have been very worried about that; he is just as dear to me as he is to you.

I am in total agreement with you that a trip to the USA at the present time is impossible for Joe for many reasons—including those which you have mentioned. I must say that I am glad, that in a very complicated situation, which real provocateurs have created for him, he showed himself being mature enough a person. Your letter to me has helped him a lot and he is in agreement with [our] opinion, which I could call yours and mine.

Right before my leaving Moscow for Mexico, after I have received your letter, one of those "bastards" already mentioned, tried to approach Joe again—as if on your behalf. And not only Joe, but he tried also to approach Katherine the same way. He tried to arrange that she would go with him to meet one of the most important dissidents, one of the most outspoken anti-soviets. Katherine has just thrown that fellow out, without much talking with him.

I am convinced that all these activities are being performed by people who would do anything possible to create a "noisy" affair, especially when it is sensational enough to attract the foreign press. Now I am convinced that you were really worried about Joe, who could easily have become the object of these provocations; those characters would love to use Joe and Kate—and your name—for their own purposes. It is just unbelievable how far human meanness can go. . . .

Finally, let me tell you . . . I was glad to hear from you. There have been many difficult things during all these years, but I do not want to dwell on that. There have been good things in the past too, and your letter, your worry about Joe, has reminded me about that very strongly.

Thank you so much for Olga's photograph. I have passed it to Joe. . . .

Take care,

Gregory[14]

Svetlana felt extraordinary relief that Joseph was safe. Her ex-husband had given her his own address, which meant that he was inviting her to contact him for news about Joseph and

Katya. Svetlana thought that one day Grigori might possibly be permitted to visit the United States on some scientific mission, and she might be able to see him again. In fact, however, their correspondence ended here. Though she wrote to him several times, she never received another letter.

She immediately wrote to George Kennan, sending him both Alexander Kurpel's screed and Grigori Morozov's response, and Kennan replied with an affectionate letter. He concluded that Kurpel's delusional letter was too clumsy to be a direct KGB provocation.

> The impression I derive from the document is that the author is a seriously unstable person whose head has been turned, and whose imagination has been over-fired by exposure to the weird atmosphere of deception and counter-deception prevailing today between—or rather, among—the dissidents, the KGB, the foreign journalists, and probably a few unwise lower-ranking diplomats, and who, in addition to that, wants to make himself important by inserting himself into the affairs of important people. . . . I am delighted that you spotted all this and decided to have nothing to do with him. . . .
>
> I continue to think of you with deep affection and concern. . . . When you give careful thought to your problems, and do not act impulsively, your insight and your judgments are first-rate—none better. . . .
>
> Affectionate greetings from us both,
>
> *George K.*[15]

But Svetlana was not sure Kurpel could be so easily dismissed. She knew the KGB better than George Kennan did.

In a book called *Last Interview*, published in 2013, the Russian journalists Ana Petrovna and Mikhail Leshynsky included an earlier interview with Joseph Alliluyev in which they asked him about his attempt to join his mother in America in the mid-1970s. Joseph explained: "I went through a difficult time; there was a failing in my personal life, things weren't coming together at work. All of a sudden it occurred to me that the only way out was to go to my mother, to connect with my only dear relative. No such thing, as I now understand, to my luck, ended up being possible."[16]

It wasn't his bad luck but rather Yuri Andropov, head of the KGB, who frustrated his longing to join his mother. In an undated memo to the Central Committee of the Communist Party, found by Petrovna and Leshynsky in the Party archive, Andropov wrote:

> In a letter that we intercepted, Joseph Alliluev [*sic*] complains about his loneliness after the divorce from his wife, about how he misses his mother, wants to see her. It is established that he has intentions to go abroad. In the past years, Joseph Alliluev developed irritation, lost interest in social life, abuses alcoholic beverages. It seems rational for the Ministry of Health of the USSR to offer him more attention as a young doctor and for the Soviet Ministry of the USSR to exchange his apartment for a better one.[17]

The tone of benevolent concern is hardly convincing. Joseph had been very frightened when he realized the KGB had intercepted his letter to his mother and recorded his contacts with foreigners. He had warned Krimsky, "This all has to stop," or he'd end up practicing medicine in Siberia. For Andropov to have instigated such an upgrade in his circumstances, he must have made it very clear that he had no intention of defecting. But the tragedy of the secret police's interference in family life is caught in his reference to his mother as "my only dear relative," whose consolation he had needed and been denied for years, especially when his life was dissolving.

Svetlana could take comfort in the fact that she'd not been responsible for destroying her son's peace. Now she began to reassess her life in America. It had been ten years since she'd arrived, but sometimes it felt like forever. She'd come through a terrible psychological crisis and felt she was back to herself. She'd begun work on a book that would take the form of a notebook—moments from a human life that would be like talking to oneself. The strange blending of her Russian past and her American present would provide its texture.

That spring of 1977, Donald Jameson from the CIA phoned to say that it was now time for her to think about applying for American citizenship. In 1978 she would have completed the ten-year "quarantine" required for applicants who had once been members of the Communist Party. She began the slow process of filing the necessary documents and getting finger-printed at the local police station in Carlsbad. That fall she wrote to Jamie to say she was ready, but she wanted the confer-ral of her citizenship to be more than a symbolic gesture. She'd decided she would become an American citizen in Princeton among people who cared for her. One of the kindest letters of support came from George Kennan. In September 1977, he wrote reassuringly:

> I think I understand some of your difficulties as well as anyone could; but my own basic faith in you—in your decency and sincerity—and concern for you in your strange

and, to most people, incomprehensible Odyssey has never been shaken. Your friendship and understanding have also meant a great deal to me, and have been a source of strength to me in the more difficult moments. It will always be so.[18]

In January, she headed back across the continent with Olga, their belongings in tow. She would take the Oath of Allegiance in a New Jersey courtroom, among her friends.

Chapter 28

Lana Peters, American Citizen

An iconic shot of "Generalissimo" Stalin, taken c. 1920.

Whuhen Svetlana arrived in Princeton in January 1978, she found a perfect house to rent. She'd become adept at finding houses. At 154 Mercer Street, she was close to downtown and across from a large park, Marquand Park, which made the area feel almost like country. The house was a modest semidetached affair with two bedrooms. On the living room wall, she hung the decorative straw plate that Joan Kennan had sent from Tonga, and on the other walls she tacked up seven-year-old Olga's colorful drawings. She moved in her battered furniture, her books and archive of letters, and Olga's toys. She mowed the lawn and planted flowers and vegetables. Life could begin again.

On June 18, Svetlana filed her application for American citizenship. It amused her that it happened to be Father's Day. She could imagine her father's reaction. He would have killed her. She thought her mother would have approved.

Around this time, she found a letter in her Palmer Square post office box addressed care of Princeton University with a return address in Sweden. The letter was from Alexander Kurpel. She felt a sudden cold shudder at seeing the name. The man was now in Sweden! How had he managed to get out of the USSR? She thought the KGB must have sent him on some mission. She put the letter, unopened, back in the mail marked Return to Sender and worried. Was it a coincidence that he had just happened to write when she was applying for her citizenship?

She wrote to George Kennan. "I would not be surprised that Soviets already know about it [her citizenship application] and will use Alex Kurpel and his possible writings abroad to present me in some unpleasant way—the mission that was ten years ago given to Victor Louis. . . . Anyway, they love to put pressure on me." She asked Kennan, who was then lecturing in Sweden, to keep a lookout for anything about Kurpel in the Swedish newspapers, and worried that the man would try to come to Princeton to meet her. She protested: "What a game I have to play, my God, and why!?"[1]

Understandably, she was concerned about her examination under oath, which was the next stage in her naturalization. It was to take place on September 29. Kennan wrote a reference on her behalf to the Immigration and Naturalization Service.

> I have no hesitation in saying that I find Mrs. Peters in every way fitted, and indeed outstandingly fitted, for American citizenship. . . . She has never wavered, since her arrival here, in her desire and resolve to become a citizen as soon as the normal procedures permitted. During all this time, she has lived quietly and with dignity here, has avoided publicity and controversy, and has done all in her power to assure that her presence here should not prove a burden or an embarrassment to the United States government.[2]

Was this really what she had been doing—trying to avoid being a burden or an embarrassment to the US government? Why should she be an embarrassment? But in any case, she was grateful for Kennan's support.

When she asked Millie Harford, her old friend from Stuart School, to drive her to Newark and serve as one of her references, Millie replied that she was afraid to drive, that she was a terrible driver. But Svetlana could be very persuasive. They headed up the highway to Newark and were soon lost on the complex turnpikes leading into the city. Svetlana suddenly said, "Millie, we're going over the bridge. That's New York!" Millie made a turn on the on-ramp and headed back, the cars honking, as Svetlana rolled down the window and leaned out, shouting, "Excuse us! We're peasants from the country." Millie thought this was wonderful. "There must have been angels driving the car."[3] Somehow they made it to Newark without a police escort.

Svetlana needed witnesses to stand up for her during the examination under oath required of all immigrants. Probably with Donald Jameson's help, she managed to locate Corporal Danny Wall, the marine guard who, on that long-ago evening in New Delhi, had admitted her into the American Embassy. She was indeed closing the circle. With a smiling Wall on one side and Millie on the other, she passed her examination without a hitch.

On November 20, Svetlana returned to Newark to take the Oath of Allegiance. When Mrs. Lana Peters was called to the front of the room to sign her documents, she noted the intense gaze on the faces of the ninety fellow applicants watching her. She was thrilled. They scrutinized her with the same intensity they trained on every other new citizen, and saw only someone named Mrs. Peters. Not Stalin's daughter.

When the ceremony was over, Svetlana gave Millie her citizenship manual—it was marked up and underlined on every page, so carefully had she studied it. Millie remembered Svetlana beaming after the ceremony, though she did complain that when she had taken the Oath of Allegiance, she was bothered by her solemn promise to "bear arms to protect the Republic." She said, "I could never shoot anyone, in any circumstance."[4] Millie gave a little party for Svetlana in Princeton that afternoon, with George and Annelise Kennan among the guests. There were no announcements in the US press, and the Soviets made no public statements.

If Svetlana thought that in returning, she might find the Princeton she'd known even a few years back, she was wrong. She was no longer the draw she had once been at Princeton dinner parties. She was now a single mother in straitened circumstances and in need of a babysitter.

She was unwelcome in the Russian exile community. When she and Millie Harford drove to Rockland County to visit Tolstoy's daughter Alexandra, Millie remembered Alexandra's tart rebuke: "She said Svetlana hadn't done enough with her life."[5] The American director of Radio Liberty, George Bailey, who knew Svetlana, remembered those words as harsher. When Svetlana declined to join her "in her struggle against communism," Tolstoya had called her a *svoloch*, a scoundrel. It didn't matter to Tolstoya that Svetlana felt activism on her part might harm her children in Moscow.[6]

Svetlana began to feel there was a growing anti-Soviet sentiment pervading Princeton, the legacy of Cold War propaganda. At school she noticed that Olga was seldom invited to her friends' homes. She told Joan Kennan she was worried for Olga. Would Olga, too, be forced to live in "the constant shadow of her grandfather's name"? Svetlana was indignant that people never identified Olga with her American grandfather. "I just don't know how she'll live her life," she said.[7]

For now, Olga lived in a world of adults—of the "uncles," like Jamie, who came to visit, or the remaining good friends who sat at the dinner table. "My best buddies in those days were people in their forties and fifties and sixties," Olga recalled. "The only Russian words I knew were the swear words Mom still used when she was angry at something. When she had her Russian friends over, and all the conversation was in Russian, I would be sitting there going insane, trying to intervene with these awful swear words."[8]

Svetlana began to brood over public perceptions of her. Looking back, she now thought that her arrival in the United States had been "vulgar." She felt she had been presented not as a principled defector who rejected the repressive Soviet government, but rather as a woman selling a book. She believed everyone thought she was still a millionaire. She had promised to give three quarters of her money to charity, and she hadn't done that.

During her first summer back in Princeton, Bob Rayle and his wife, Ramona, invited her to join them on their vacation in the Outer Banks of North Carolina. As soon as they met, she and Bob reminisced, as they always did, about that long-ago March day in 1967 when Rayle had been called to the embassy in New Delhi with news of a defector. They replayed the whole thing: his first meeting with the "Russian lady," her explanation that she was Stalin's daughter, and George Huey's response: "You mean *the* Stalin?" They especially loved to redo the Keystone Kops episode when she was never "legally" in Italy. She told Bob she hadn't really understood why she couldn't go to the United States. There were simply "various reasons." Expecting the Soviets to be furious and knowing they would be maligning her, she had focused all her effort on being as pleasant as possible.[9]

She would always be grateful to the people at the embassy in India, particularly to Ambassador Chester Bowles, who had courageously taken a risk in saving her, and to Bob Rayle, whose career she felt she'd ruined when he was outed as a CIA officer. He always assured her that he'd simply been reposted. But now she began to see that her entry into the United States had been orchestrated by the State Department so as not to offend the Soviets. Why? If they had asked her, she could easily have told the officials that the Soviets would not be appeased. They would be humiliated. They would have to hold to their propaganda lie that her defection was a CIA plot. There was no point in the Americans' trying to placate them. Why hadn't they just asked her? There had been many publishers looking to publish her book. Why hadn't she been allowed to meet them? George Kennan would have said the officials had protected her from the thousands of reporters and publishers desperate to get at her. He would also have admitted she was a diplomatic liability, and naturally he had to protect the State Department's interests too.

Reading the past with a now cynical eye, she concluded that she had always been under the CIA's control. In comparison with those of the KGB, its strings had been silk, but never-theless, there had been strings. She began to feel she had been controlled and supervised since her arrival. The Americans had tried to make "this strange defector," as she described herself, the least dangerous of them all.[10]

She was bitter, and in the book she was writing, she got it off her chest.

> The public, through the world Press, were misinformed by the State Department. They were making the whole picture increasingly confused and controversial. Decisions were attributed to me that I had never made. The public imagined for years that "She went to Switzerland to collect money her father left for her in Swiss banks." This fantasy of my father behaving like some Western million-aire caught hold in some quarters and took root. . . . This idea was so easily believed.[11]

If she hadn't stopped in Switzerland, would this calumny have persisted? The State Department said *she* had chosen to "retreat to Switzerland for rest and recuperation." But it had never been her decision. She now felt she had been set up for a fall.

The rumor of all that gold and the wealth from her book had made her vulnerable to Olgivanna Wright, whose plan, as Svetlana explained to Joan Kennan, had been "to sell out her best man for big money."[12] Svetlana had been catastrophically naive. It hadn't occurred to her then that a man would marry for money. That was a plot she'd seen in films. Her father had been so mistrustful that he had the air in his rooms chemically tested, never ate food that wasn't first tasted in front of him, and elim-inated anyone who roused his slightest suspicion. But she, his daughter, had trusted too much. She thought she'd been loved.

Her encounter with Taliesin had been the "turning point"

in her "whole American experience." She later wrote to Joan, "As to Wes, he continues today to behave the same way—he pretends to live 'as a wealthy man,' but doesn't pay his bills and <u>never</u> remembers how much I've done for him—paid 0.5 million for his <u>old</u> debts as a gift for our wedding."[13]

She was angry with Wes and with herself. Perhaps she was thinking of Alexandra Tolstoya's remark that Svetlana "hadn't done enough with her life." She wrote to George Kennan with remorseful regret. She assured him that she never identified him with her "New York lawyers," but why hadn't they done things differently?

> BUT WHEN 10 years ago, George, I suddenly, just out of a blue moon made millions with my very mediocre memoir, IT WAS EXTREMELY IMPORTANT—THEN—that my very next step would be the RIGHT ONE. And the only right step to do then was: to give away as much of that money as possible. To give it to US charity, to the world charity through the United Nations, to Russian Emigrees scattered all over the world, to OTHERS whoever they might be . . . But to GIVE IT AWAY, as I have promised in my own words, in my press-conferences, in my TV appearances in spring 1967.
>
> That this has not been done is MY fault, of course. I did not have enough guts to insist on what I considered then to BE RIGHT. I kind of softened under all that murmur of pleasant publicity and fame and nice talk and innumerable friendly letters. I was overwhelmed with all that—and gave up.
>
> I gave up THEN, dear George, and there is no one to blame ten years later. I should have stood firm like a rock, defending my OWN plans, my own ideas. . . . I did not. And all my dear trustees, of course, were NOT able to think my thoughts at this point, all but you.

Ten years ago I could have destroyed a bad reputation of "Stalin's daughter" by giving away 80% of my royalties from my first book, I sensed this; I knew this was the ONLY and the RIGHT step to do; and I missed it. I just missed it as in tennis one falls down instead of doing the right backhand.

I was a loser in my game of high stakes. . . .

Today I am not able to forgive myself; and I cannot find an excuse for all others involved.[14]

Was Svetlana revising the past? Had she really intended to give most of her money away? Quite possibly. To the end of her life and to the astonishment of friends, she was always giving things away. But she did not fully admit that it had been her own impulsiveness that had sent her in Wesley Peters's direction, and this certainly must have been in Kennan's mind as he read her letter.

Now, ironically, money was a constant concern for Svetlana. A Princeton friend suggested she should reprint her first two books in a single volume. It probably wouldn't mean much money, but why not? She'd been a best-selling author twelve years ago. Surely there must be a new readership for those books. But she soon found that she could not yet reprint *Only One Year*. It was still in print and supposedly selling, though she could find no copies in bookstores. Also, to her shock, she now discovered that she was not the owner of the copyright to her first book, *Twenty Letters to a Friend*.

In Switzerland in 1967, the firm of Greenbaum, Wolff & Ernst had created Copex Establishment in Lichtenstein to handle her visa and her book rights. This had been a convenience and also a tax dodge, but certainly legal because she was not an American citizen. But unwittingly, she had signed away all her rights to Copex.

In 1967, the Greenbaum firm had set up two trusts for Svetlana. When she had demanded that her money be sent to her and Wes's bank account in Wisconsin in 1970, the personal trust, the Alliluyeva Trust, had been dissolved. But the second trust, the Alliluyeva Charitable Trust, continued. For tax reasons, it had been converted in 1968 to an irrevocable trust, run by a board of trustees, of which she was a member. According to the Princeton copyright lawyer she hired, E. Parker Hayden Jr., when Copex was dissolved, in 1972, the copyright and royalties to her book had been assigned, not back to her, but to her irrevocable Alliluyeva Charitable Trust. Even though she was a board member, she was never informed of any of this. Why hadn't the lawyers simply given her back her copyright? Edward Greenbaum had died in 1970, and there may have been some confusion, but no effort was made to correct the error, if it was one. Svetlana believed the lawyers had stolen her book. She was furious. As any author might have, she felt it was a profound personal violation.

Determined to regain control of her professional life, she wrote to George Kennan's secretary to request that all mail be sent directly to her, not to the Institute for Advanced Study at Princeton. And she expected a lot of mail. The upcoming hundredth anniversary of her father's birth, December 21, 1979, would bring endless requests for interviews and she wanted to receive and decline these requests through her own lawyer.

E. Parker Hayden Jr. wrote to the firm of Greenbaum, Wolff & Ernst to suggest that Svetlana had not understood what had been done through Copex Establishment in 1967–68. According to Svetlana, the firm replied, "We did inform you about everything, you were aware of all we were doing," and "we have done our best to help you."[15]

Svetlana now did something she had avoided doing for years. She invited a journalist, Sharon Schlegel of the *Trenton Times*, into her home to interview her. She wanted the world to know that she wasn't a millionaire. Schlegel's long article was reprinted in the *Washington Post*, titled "I Don't Want to Be Svetlana Any More." Schlegel began with a portrait of Svetlana's modest living conditions and repeated the story of Svetlana's defection, her divorce from Wesley Peters, and her lost money.[16] She quoted Svetlana as declaring, "I am not a greedy person who came here to make money. . . . I came here to live in the free world, as an enemy of communism. I made certain sacrifices [she was referring to her children]." Svetlana also said she had learned that "the legal fees charged by her original American lawyers . . . were exorbitant."

Schlegel interviewed representatives of the firm of Greenbaum, Wolff & Ernst and reported their response: "Lawyers [unnamed] connected to both the sale of her book and its serialization deny that she was never fully informed and stress that she was actually anxious for world-wide serialization. They call her account 'pathetic and confused—she's been through a lot of unhappiness.'"[17]

Toward the end of her article, Schlegel reported Svetlana's angry response to a newspaper clipping that stated, "At 53 Mrs. Peters is hiding from the public."

"Well, I'm not hiding from the public. I'm bringing up this child. And it takes so much of my strength and I'm tired much of the time. . . . This is the No. 1 interest of my life now and I don't see such tasks as second-rate." Svetlana did not understand American misogyny. In Soviet culture, especially after purges and war had so drastically reduced the ratio of men to women, a single mother bringing up a child alone was almost the norm.

Finally Schlegel asked, "Has it been worth it, after all the misunderstanding and disappointment that have followed in these 12 years?" Svetlana replied: "Oh yes! Oh yes! . . . I turned my life from one road to another with my own effort. . . . It was a unique chance—I had never been out of the country before, you know. Once in your life you can take it or not take it. I took it. I will never be sorry."

Svetlana was bitter about the published piece. It was condescending and clarified nothing. She sent it to George Kennan, with the comment "Our dear Greenbaum, Wolff & Ernst now dares to say that I 'was actually anxious for worldwide serialization' and even 'knew every detail of their money-making.' And so on, without end. Their name is not mentioned [Schlegel had not identified the law firm]—neither is yours, but MINE is always opened for any slander."

Kennan did not respond. She wrote again, scathingly.

Hypocrisy, even much honorable and presented as a "good image," will never take one to a desired destination. All efforts will be fruitless. Better to be "vulgar" and outspoken—not quite so dignified, not so in the best taste. . . . Goodbye George. I feel sorry that you have associated yourself with my name for such a long time—in the public eye that is—I hope I did not smear your IMAGE too badly by my very existence. You will be OK, honored and respected. . . . Please do not bother about me any more.[18]

Svetlana remained a Russian. An angry letter from her could feel as if she were ripping your flesh. She knew this. She thought part of her problem was her "clumsy English." Even when Americans spoke directly, they always offered "polite decorations." Unfortunately, she'd never been very good at this, even in her native tongue, but "in a foreign language every thought inevitably looks simplified to a certain degree of unpleasant vulgarity. And directness sounds almost rude."[19] She was like Grandmother Olga, who always said, "My tongue is my enemy." Moving past anger, Svetlana was soon writing

Kennan a letter of apology. Though she didn't expect their close friendship to resume, she wanted Kennan to know she wasn't, as she put it, "an ungrateful *swine*."

But she wrote more candidly to his daughter Joan:

> At 53, I feel tired, disgusted, and very <u>bitter</u> about many things I went through in USA since 1967. I am <u>not</u> the same person you and Larry used to know <u>then</u>, Joanie! . . . So, we'll stay where we are, <u>not</u> liking it, but tolerating. What else <u>can</u> I do? Nothing. It is important not to make things even worse.[20]

Kennan eventually did make an unsuccessful effort to help Svetlana regain her copyright, but he always rejected the idea that she had been in any way manipulated. Kennan explained to Donald Jameson of the CIA, that, yes, he had suggested the Greenbaum firm. Greenbaum was his neighbor, and this meant that "I could handle the matter through him without danger of its leaking prematurely to ten thousand hungry publishers and editors, dying to get at her." Certainly the attorneys had charged her "a handsome sum for their services; but since they left her a wealthy woman . . . this was no more than was to be expected." That they deliberately took advantage of her was "wholly out of the question." She probably didn't understand all the details of the arrangements, but what client hadn't been in that position? He advised that, after so much time, the copyright should be returned to her if "legally possible. But this should be without reflection on her attorneys."[21]

By now, Svetlana was exaggerating the conspiracies against her, but she was right about some things. The Greenbaum firm had not been enthusiastic about her creating a charitable foundation. As Alan Schwartz put it, "We were very skeptical about setting up a foundation in India in some hospital in remembrance of her former lover."[22] But most important, the firm had not protected her copyright. It had probably been bureaucratically convenient to transfer her copyright to her irrevocable trust, though Svetlana could be forgiven for believing it was revenge. She had gone against the lawyers' advice when she dissolved her personal trust in 1970 and transferred her money to Wesley Peters's account.

Svetlana was now on her own and discovering that she didn't have the skills to survive in a capitalist system. In her first forty years, she had never managed money; when she had been desperate, she could ask her nanny Alexandra Andreevna, who actually received a salary, for a loan. In her circle of intellectual friends, those with a little shared what they had. Everything in America seemed to be about money and success, and she had neither. She had worked at the prestigious Gorky Institute and could have attached herself to an American university, as many former dissidents did, but she knew that as Stalin's daughter she would always be a freak, a curiosity. She must earn money by writing, but she couldn't reissue her first two books and couldn't get a contract for a third.

Svetlana didn't need much money for herself—she lived very simply—but she was driven by a fixed idea that came from her mother. Her daughter must have the best education, and that meant private school. She watched her income decline—she now had about $18,000 a year from investment, not a meager sum in the late 1970s, but she needed several thousand just for the Stuart School. Her solution was to keep moving. She moved four times in the next several years. When it came to a choice between paying Olga's private school fees or paying the mortgage, she downsized her house. That first year, she took in a teacher from the Stuart School as a boarder.

When her lease on Mercer Street was up in January 1979, she bought a house at 40 Morgan Place and then, in the spring of 1980, sold it. She told friends it was a lousy property, too expensive to maintain, and she was glad to be rid of the worries of ownership. She found a rental at 53 Aiken Avenue. She wrote to her old friend Rosa Shand, who had stayed with her in those early days in Princeton when Rosa was recovering from back surgery, to say that the new house was within walking distance of downtown Princeton. Though it was not large, she assured Rosa that if she wanted to send her daughters to school in Princeton, they could be squeezed in. She was planning to stay put, unless the rent went up beyond her limits.

The truth is, there was a part of Svetlana that loved to move. Olga remembered Mother's Day on Aiken Avenue when she was nine. She'd prepared and brought her mother breakfast in bed. She watched her mother lying there, gazing pensively out the window as if looking in the far distance. Svetlana said, "It's Mother's Day, I feel like doing something special for myself." Olga responded, "OK," assuming her mother wanted to go for one of their long drives in the country. But Svetlana asked, "How do you feel about moving again?"

In the spring of 1981, when the rent on her Aiken Avenue house was raised from $550 to $600 a month, Svetlana started searching for another place to buy in Princeton, but she could find nothing she could afford. Olga was now tall, long-legged like her father, very pretty, and more remarkably stubborn than her stubborn mother. Svetlana drove her to her private lessons in piano and guitar, French, and horseback riding. But it seemed Olga was unhappy at Stuart School.

The principal had changed, and in her memory decades later, Olga recalled that she had come to hate the school. The children didn't know that Olga was Stalin's granddaughter—Stalin meant nothing to them—but they knew she was part Russian, and they had absorbed their parents' suspicion of Russkies. Olga was sure she was not a Russky; she was American. She insisted on changing her name to Chrese. Hereafter her mother must call her by the American nickname she'd chosen for herself.

Ironically, there was an added prejudice. Not only was her mother divorced and Russian, but she was also a non-Catholic. When Olga reached the fourth grade in 1980, she encountered the teacher from hell. "It was horrible what they put non-Catholic girls through."[23] She and two other girls—Rebecca and Jasmine, one Jewish, the other Polish—were the only three unbaptized girls in the school, and found themselves ostracized. "There was prayer assembly, but not for everyone. You weren't allowed to take communion. You went home early on Ash Wednesday, because you couldn't participate in the ceremony." Olga remembered going home to her mother and asking, "So, can I be a Catholic?" But that wasn't going to happen. When Svetlana had asked earlier to be baptized as a Catholic, she was told she had already been baptized in the Russian Orthodox Church and couldn't be baptized twice.

Olga recalled: "I didn't know that there was a Russian hype going on. I didn't know who my grandfather was. I didn't know there was a problem with a woman being divorced, with no father around. I didn't know any of these things. I just felt the wrath. . . . I would be pointed out in class, taken aside, embarrassed, humiliated, caned on the hand. . . . I was actually a really sharp child who liked to learn, but I was very, very shy and terrified of my environment. Those were the days I hated to go to school. I hated it."

One morning, Olga, who had just turned ten, ran away from home. Having prepared her breakfast and gone to her room to wake her, Svetlana found her daughter's bed empty. Olga had left a note: "Mommy I have left home. Meet me at the bus station on Wednesday. I am sorry but I must go."

° Svetlana was petrified. Still in her housecoat, she ran into the lane and across the street, banging on neighbors' doors. No, her daughter wasn't there. The bus stop for New York was around the corner on the main street. Where was Olga heading? One kindly neighbor simply walked to his Oldsmobile and, waving reassuringly, set out to find her. Svetlana reported her disappearance to an indifferent police officer. She was panicked. Should she search for her daughter? Should she sit and wait? Had she been "too severe on this independent spirit, too demanding"? Recounting the incident later, she said, "I was truly scared out of my wits."[24]

Soon there was a knock at the door. Her neighbor, grinning broadly, was standing with Olga at his side. She was holding out a bouquet of daffodils and offering them tentatively to her mother. She had been in a shop buying a pencil and a notebook when he'd found her. Olga leaped into her mother's arms and said she would never run away again.

Svetlana began to think how costly her solitary life was to Olga, an exuberant and extroverted child who was suddenly receiving terrible report cards at Stuart School. She told friends her bright daughter needed "more freedom and less 'uniformed' surroundings."[25] They would move; they would find another house.

Svetlana understood that friends often believed that some kind of psychological instability was the root cause of her constant migrations, and she had once thought so herself. But now, in her mind, Olga's education was always the motive for her moving. However, in Olga's own childhood memories, she and her mother moved every November, the month when Svetlana's mother, Nadya, had committed suicide—that greatest of all losses that still consumed her; the month that, according to her daughter, Svetlana associated with "death, dying, the dying of everything."[26] In fact, they often moved in the spring, but to the child, it was her mother's sorrow that sat in her memory as the reason they moved. Olga was intuitively shrewd, of course, as children often are. Svetlana was funneling all her multiple anxieties into the fate of her child. It was the one fate she could somewhat control.

Chapter 29

The Modern Jungle of Freedom

Sir Isaiah Berlin, whom Svetlana first met in 1970.

L uckily for Svetlana, her friend Rosa Shand had moved back to New York with her family in the winter of 1981. Svetlana soon visited, eager to reintroduce Olga to Rosa. She told Rosa she wanted to take her daughter to the museums and galleries in a cosmopolitan city, as she had once done in Moscow with her older children.

The General Theological Seminary of the Episcopal Church had assigned Rosa, her husband Philip, and their two daughters an apartment in an eighteenth century neo-Gothic gray-stone on Ninth Street. The twelve-foot ceilings gave an old-world appearance to the cavernous space, the center of which was the kitchen, where Rosa had pasted postcards on all the cabinets. As soon as she visited, Svetlana gravitated to the kitchen, where they drank tea, or vodka "sparingly,"[1] and resumed their conversations about faith, literature, and children. Svetlana's eyes played across the glass-doored cabinets. "Glass cabinets, she said—it was the kitchen she grew up in. It was the kitchen she'd not supposed America possessed."[2]

It had been almost ten years since Rosa had sat across a table from Svetlana. Though she'd put on weight, Svetlana was still pretty when she smiled, with her striking pale blue eyes, her hands slicing the air for emphasis. Rosa was amused by the way Olga ordered her mother around. She thought that, with her daughter, Svetlana was both "ultra-solicitous and steely." She would say, "Do not interrupt me," but the next moment, the two would be giggling in each other's arms.[3]

Svetlana took to visiting Rosa as often as she could. They would have dinner in the dining room by candlelight. One memorable night, opening a bottle of champagne, Philip fumbled with the cork, and Svetlana took over. Much to the family's delight, she quickly had the cork flying and the champagne deftly poured into an adjacent glass, explaining, "[My] father took his time to teach the important things quite well."[4]

Suddenly Svetlana was evoking her beloved Moscow—"its onion domes in snow, the dripping evergreen beauty of its quiet little hidden graveyards, the glittering icicle world," and the tiny ornate church that consoled her as she looked out from the window of her apartment in the House on the Embankment. Rosa's daughter Kristin slipped over to the piano to play the theme from *Doctor Zhivago* as a backdrop to Svetlana's stories. Svetlana was not the only one weeping under cover of darkness in the candlelit room.

Svetlana and Rosa tramped through the winter streets of New York with Olga, visiting bookstores and museums, and lumbering up the stairs inside the Statue of Liberty. When Svetlana was in town on a Sunday, they attended services at an Episcopalian church in Greenwich Village. They also went to concerts throughout the city, and these made Svetlana nostalgic for the days when she had taken her son, Joseph, to concerts at the Moscow Conservatory—she could almost see him sitting beside her. How strange the twists of fate, how strange that she now had Olushka at her side in America. On one occasion, Vladimir Ashkenazi sent Svetlana box seats for his concert at Carnegie Hall, and Rosa learned that he was a friend whom Svetlana had not seen in six years. He'd been living in Iceland and then Switzerland since his defection in 1963, when the continual pressure from the KGB to turn *stukach* (informer) had proved too much. She also met her friend the cellist Mstislav Rostropovich, who had defected in 1974 and like her had had his Soviet citizenship revoked in 1978 for speaking out against the lack of freedom in his homeland.

That May, Rosa saw a wonderful new film called *Oblomov*, released in Russia in 1979, that seemed made for Svetlana. She phoned to tell her she must come to New York to see it. Svetlana said that in her student days, she'd known the star, Oleg Tabakov, as well as the director, Nikita Mikhalkov. Mikhalkov had survived the Soviet censors by making lyrical films about the seasons in Moscow, films without people.[5]

Leaving Olga to walk in the Village with Philip, Rosa and Svetlana went to the cinema for the matinee. As the film opened with the image of a child waking, running through a warm kitchen, and dashing gleefully out over a green steppe filled with summer flowers filtering dazzling sunlight, Svetlana was immediately transported back to the kitchen at Zubalovo, where her nanny, Alexandra Andreevna, had bathed her in the iron tub with the hot water pouring in from the tank, the logs burning, the fire cracking, and the room filling with steam. She still remembered her nanny's fat warm hands. Her mother was always off doing something more important. When the film ended and the credits played as the curtains closed, Svetlana sat in stunned silence. They remained in the dark abandoned cinema for an hour as Svetlana cried. To Rosa, the moment was somehow transformative. "I knew: this was another order of experience. This was beyond my grasp of being moved by art. This was Russian, or Svetlana, or a disparate color of soul."[6]

Oblomov totally overwhelmed Svetlana. She wrote to Rosa that she'd slipped back to New York on her own to see the film again and that night she had spent many hours "in the same position as Oblomov, who sat overnight under the rain, thinking—I was stunned and could not move." She was shocked that the Soviet censors had approved a film about nineteenth-century tsarist Russia. Could this mean that the USSR was changing?

She told Rosa the film had taken her back to Moscow in 1962 and to her spiritual mentor, Father Nikolai, whom she revered and whose words she always remembered. "He did not say that Christ cannot love me, Stalin's daughter."[7] He had baptized her.

She had had a reassuring dream about Father Nikolai just before moving to Princeton in 1967. In September 1970, she saw him again in a joyful dream, predicting wonderful news, and then discovered she and Wes were going to have a child. Many years of silence had followed. These were her worst years, but she had dreamed about him again this very March and was certain something important was coming. She had never imagined it might be this film. She begged Rosa to understand.

Please do not think I am exaggerating the importance of some movie production. You know: in Soviet Russia, in that silent society, e v e r y sign is important, every little symbolic move, word or even ballet dance is a communication. One has to learn to read those silent signs. I have learned to do so. . . .

I cannot tell you what a magnificent, and also mysterious effect the last photographs convey. One must be, of course, familiar with that gentle green land . . . the meadows and the skies, those pale clouds, those gently rustling groves, those wild flowers. MOTHER, childhood, love, gentleness . . .

Here it is not a sentimental image at all. It is not "Mom & Apple-pie" of Protestant virtue, righteousness, and all good things. . . . Here it is Life itself, in its every little sweet moments of existence, fragrant, immensely peaceful, filled with that blessing and grace. . . . Life as Oblomov was able to perceive it. Although he was indeed a lazy, sleepy man, he had a gift of communicating with grasses, flowers and clouds, that gift of contemplation which is in fact, the essence of Russian Orthodoxy.[8]

But the film had a more heartwrenching element that Svetlana did not mention to Rosa. The film begins and ends with images of Oblomov as a child running rapturously through green meadows. It is a dream sequence, a memory of waiting for, longing for, his mother, who has returned from a long journey and whom the child is instructed not to waken. The mother never appears in the film; she is only an absence. It is impossible not to imagine Svetlana shaken by the child's voice crying with such rapturous anticipation for the mother who will never appear.

Oblomov brought Svetlana back to her Russian roots. She had vehemently insisted that her daughter would be American, giving Olga the best American education and deliberately eliminating all things Russian from the child's life. She refused to teach Olga the Russian language. Clearly she was insulating her daughter from her history. She knew the cost to Olga of being identified as Stalin's granddaughter, but she had never examined the toll this sacrifice had taken on her own psyche. She lamented to Rosa that she had cut herself off from the "music and fragrance of my native tongue. I have suppressed all this and made it silent. Stay there, inside, but shut up!" It was a terrible surgery. "My soul was crying, like in prison and I did not know why. Now it is released."[9] This was *Oblomov*'s message.

And then, that summer of 1981, there was silence. Rosa did not hear from Svetlana until September, when she wrote to say that her life had again plunged into chaos during the summer and she had lost her peace, remarking with rueful irony that after the film "some kind of fresh breeze came strongly through my whole being—but for a while only."[10]

Needing to find a cheaper residence than 53 Aiken Avenue, in June Svetlana spent a frenzied month hunting for a new home. Finally she signed a contract to buy a small house in nearby suburban Lawrenceville, about twenty minutes from Princeton. She had decided to give the public school system a try and enrolled Olga in the Lawrenceville Intermediate School.

And then, at the beginning of July, she left on a trip to England. That February the British journalist and media personality Malcolm Muggeridge, notorious for his conservative Christian propagandizing, had written to invite her to do an interview with him on the BBC. He was proposing a discussion about the resurgence of Christianity in the Soviet Union. He said that she, who had been at the very center of the "materialist-atheist apparat," must have some insights.[11] At first she refused, complaining that after every public appearance, her words were always twisted, and she was tired of the hate letters that followed "from the left and from the right and from the very middle." As a strange non sequitur, she added, "Men are able to easily disregard all this; I cannot." She just wanted to live in peace and avoid "unnecessary hatred."[12]

But gradually the thought of traveling to England became too seductive. She felt it was cynical on her part to agree to be interviewed, because she had turned down so many American invitations. Nevertheless, she accepted, but on one condition: "Could you please, somehow, try to separate me from my father's name, life and philosophies? It is very necessary to do so, otherwise you will keep trying to communicate with my father through me."[13] Of course the request was pointless. The reason Muggeridge wanted to interview her was that she was Stalin's daughter: this made her thoughts on the new Christianity in Russia all the more sensational.

Svetlana set out for London in early July 1981. With the BBC paying for her stay at the Portobello Hotel near Stanley Gardens, she spent three days in the city walking through the streets and found it thrilling. She felt nostalgic for "old stones." She spent five days with Malcolm and Kitty Muggeridge at Park Cottage, their country house near Robertsbridge in East Sussex. The resultant interview, "A Week with Svetlana," culled from twenty hours of talk, was eventually broadcast on BBC 2 the following March. The visit proved to be a quiet interlude; the bucolic walks down English country lanes were therapeutic. She may have reflected that her life might have been this comfortable if she hadn't lost all her money.

She'd sent Olga to Wisconsin to spend the month of July with her old friends, Herbert and Eloise Fritz, who ran a summer camp near Spring Green, and was hoping her daughter might reconnect with Wesley Peters. Secretly, Svetlana often thought of herself as still married to Wes, perhaps because he and Olga were so much alike in character. In Olga's memory, the meeting was a bust. Yes, she met her father, but he was "just some reserved stranger."[14] Whenever Svetlana said Wes liked something, Olga would snap back, "So what?" to which her mother would reply timidly, "It ought to matter."[15]

During her trip to England, Svetlana began to conceive of a new plan. Olga needed stability, continuity. England was so pleasant; the people were so kind. She wrote to the Muggeridges that she wanted to find a good boarding school for Olga in England and live nearby. Did Kitty know any good schools? She would need to have an income, of course, but she could work as a companion to an elderly lady or old couple "who would be educated and sophisticated enough . . . to enjoy having a misfit like me as a companion. . . . I can cook, sew, clean, drive, shop, take photographs, type (slowly), handle mail."[16] She loved old people and would do this with pleasure. She was currently helping a ninety-three-year-old woman in Princeton.

On her return, Svetlana plunged back into the chaos of her life, resuming the ritual of unpacking and scouting out her new neighborhood. She immediately disliked it. There was no place to walk. The streets were filled with cars in the evenings; she missed the lovely trees of Princeton. But she had signed a contract to buy the house and was trapped. She berated herself. She should have known better than to listen to real estate agents. She waited anxiously for Olga to return from Wisconsin. Without her daughter, she roamed the empty house, hoping for things to fall into place.

Then she discovered, to her horror, that the principal and most of the children at Olga's new school were Ukrainians. How would the Ukrainians respond when they found out who Olga was? So many of the hate letters she received were from Ukrainians telling her "to drop dead, or go back to red Moscow where you belong."[17]

A key to Svetlana's psychology was that she would sometimes convince herself of paranoid explanations in order to do what she really wanted to do—in this case, move. If the school administrators had found out that Olga was Stalin's granddaughter, would they have said anything? Stuart School protected Svetlana's and Olga's privacy.

Of course, paranoia was a reflex response for most Soviet political exiles, let alone for Stalin's daughter. It was an automatic self-defense. The purges and famine in the Ukraine had been particularly brutal during Stalin's regime. It would take only one person to begin a hate campaign. Svetlana decided she couldn't take the risk. They couldn't live in Lawrenceville. They must move again.

Whenever she felt cornered, Svetlana acted precipitately, making frenzied decisions. She found another house, this time in nearby Pennington, and bought it, further depleting the principal of her investments. Now she owned this house and the Lawrenceville house and was almost out of money. She wrote to Kitty Muggeridge ruefully, "I feel I am a bad mother."[18]

At least Pennington was an old town with sidewalks. The house at 440 Sked Street was a traditional Cape Cod on the outskirts of town with two bedrooms upstairs, a living room with a wood-burning stove, a dining room that Svetlana turned into her study, and a big kitchen overlooking a sheltered backyard. The large trees in the distance screened her from her neighbors' view. She set about digging up the back lawn and planting her garden. She enrolled Olga in the Toll Gate School in Pennington.

But she was already restless. She wrote to Kitty Muggeridge:

Oh I wish there were no fence, and fields and hills would go endlessly—or the sea, the lake, the river—something that is not limited, not bordered. Frankly I do not need that vegetable garden because the peasant roots in me are not stronger than those gypsy roots from my Grandpa Alliluyev. I wish I could go on those innumerable trips all over the world, preferably by slow freighter ship, with a small cabin, so that we would stand for a long time in every port, where tourists do not go.[19]

Poignantly, Svetlana always claimed her maternal grand-parents' bloodline. Grandma Olga was from German/Geor-gian peasant stock and Grandpa Sergei was part Russian, part Gypsy. It was an ancestry she could celebrate. If she hadn't lost her money, she would have traveled—back to India, to Japan, China, South America, Spain, Greece. But as she told Kitty, 99 percent of people live very far from their dreams. At least she had her sweet daughter. "So I go back to my laundry . . . and my house repairs."[20]

Svetlana had renewed contact with an old Georgian friend, Utya Djaparidze, now a professor at Hartford College, in Con-necticut. Utya was horrified to learn she was living in suburban Pennington. Pennington would ruin Olga! They would both end up as "Archie Bunkers." Olga needed New York City to know the world. Utya suggested a number of private schools. Svetlana wrote to Rosa: "I was SO HAPPY that someone was telling me all this. And she was already taking in her hand our lives."[21]

One of the worst legacies of Svetlana's childhood was her terror of acting independently and getting things wrong. And almost invariably, it was a man she turned to. She told Rosa, "I know I failed to make my own way in this modern jungle of freedom to which I have run fourteen years ago," and reported Utya's words. "'Ludka [Utya's son] is a man and he CAN take your life in his hands and help you and Olenka'—she was shouting at me—and I was melting like ice-cream under sun, and swelling with tears, hot tears of love and gratitude, happy to accept all this and obey and to agree—because I know she understands—I know she knows." Even as she thought of her own submissiveness as a failing, Svetlana seemed unable to resist. She told Rosa, "I have lost my own will completely. Unless something or somebody takes my hand and pulls it strongly in the right direction, I would not be able to do things myself."[22]

Some would diagnose Svetlana as manic-depressive, or bipolar, but such a diagnosis would not take into account the pressures she still lived under as Stalin's daughter. It was as if Svetlana had two modes: abject submission and total rebellion. She had married a Jewish man against her father's wishes long before she had defected from his country, for which act she believed, accurately, that he would have killed her. Her father's censure lurked in her mind long after his death. She was always fighting to find her own authority, her own way. She would abjectly accept others' advice and then rebel. Each new step was inevitably fraught with misgivings. Was she doing the right thing? Yet it could also be said that part of this dynamic was a trait of Soviet psychology. To survive in the Soviet Union, it was customary, indeed necessary, to identify a patron or protector under whose wing one could shelter.[23]

Svetlana was thinking not of New York, but rather of Europe. Like many European émigrés, she believed American children were undisciplined. Olga was already a little rebel. Svetlana told Rosa: "We act exactly as it is described in all those dreadful Mother-Daughter books I have seen. . . . My American daughter gives me all that constant disagreement about everything."[24] Olga was a very bright child doing badly at school. If she could adapt, an English or Swiss boarding school with high educational standards would put her back on track.

Svetlana sent out requests to British and English-speaking Swiss boarding schools for brochures, warning friends, if they made inquiries on her behalf, never to mention who she was. The last thing she needed was reports in American newspapers that she was abandoning the United States. She preferred to remain invisible. When she'd recently been invited to attend a presidential luncheon at the White House to commemorate Franklin Delano Roosevelt's hundredth birthday, she'd written to Nancy Reagan to say she was sick.[25] The prospect of serving as her father's stand-in appalled her.

In February 1982, when Svetlana was visiting Rosa and she and the Shands were all sitting down to a candlelit dinner with the music of Handel playing in the background, the phone rang. It was the British philosopher Sir Isaiah Berlin asking for Svetlana. Rosa was intimidated by the voice of the great man, the very man who had traveled to Russia to meet Anna Akhmatova. Svetlana explained that Berlin was a friend whom she'd first met in 1970. He was in New York and she was going to talk with him about moving to England. He was one of those who could tell her what was best for her. Being told what to do was what she needed now.[26]

Svetlana told Berlin she wanted to return to an intellectual life. How strange it was that even under the severe pressures of cultural life in the USSR, it was easier to have an intense intellectual life there than in the United States, where she had been sleepwalking for fifteen years.[27] Berlin said she had to resume her writing. Forget writing about America. She should go back to the beginning and attempt to see her life whole. She should write about family life with her father. But Svetlana replied that the problem was, she'd "missed a family life." Her father had never been "interested in what she was doing, though she had wanted him to be. But then, to be fair, she was not interested in what he was doing either." She and her father had spent their time together in silence, he mostly fuming in anger.[28]

When she suggested to Berlin that she might serve as a companion to a British retiree, he said this was a little far-fetched, as was her notion of living in a London attic. "I cannot see you in the décor of the first and last acts of *La Bohème*." On the other hand, he was sure she was right in assuming that she would be less visible in England.[29] The British valued privacy. Berlin offered to send a letter of recommendation to Hugo Brunner, his editor at Chatto & Windus, warning her that regarding publishers, it was, of course, always better to be skeptical and then to be agreeably surprised.

On April 6, Svetlana set out for London to meet Hugo Brunner, who found her charming and compelling. She told him she had two projects in mind: a collection of stories about America, which would be a warm-up exercise for the big book she intended to write; and a long autobiographical work that she was not ready to define explicitly. Brunner provided her with the letter she needed for her visa application:

APRIL 8, 1982

Mrs. Lana Peters, who wishes to live and work in the United Kingdom, is a distinguished and successful writer. She will pursue her career in this country. She is at present at work on two books and it is our intention to publish them both.[30]

Rosa arranged for Svetlana to stay in London with friends whom she and Philip had known since their days as missionaries in Uganda. Through them, Svetlana met Terry Waite, then serving as assistant to the archbishop of Canterbury, though in a few years he would become well known when, attempting to negotiate a hostage crisis in Lebanon, he was himself kidnapped and held hostage for almost five years.

By coincidence Rosa was in England visiting friends in Cambridge when Svetlana arrived. The children of Rosa's hosts were attending a Quaker school called Friends' School in the nearby town of Saffron Walden, and Rosa thought perhaps Svetlana might be interested in seeing it. Having arranged a meeting with the headmaster, Waite, Rosa, and Svetlana set out on Easter Sunday for Saffron Walden. Svetlana found the two-hundred-year-old property beautiful and the headmaster sympathetic. She wrote to Aline Berlin that, being more liberal, the Quakers seemed not only tolerant of but indifferent to Olga's background; this was unlike the attitude in America, where suspicion of Russians seemed "a national hysteria of sorts."[31] At Waite's intercession, Olga was enrolled. In Svetlana's mind, the future was set. She was working with a publisher. From his generous letters, she assumed Berlin had taken her on as his protégé.[32] Olga passed the entrance exams for Friends' School. All Svetlana needed to do was survive until the fall.

But then Svetlana's visa application was proving difficult. Sir Isaiah wrote to his friend Francis Graham-Harrison, describing Svetlana as "a dignified, serious, intellectually inclined, somewhat melancholy (not surprisingly, in her circumstances) lady, of considerable presence and charm." He did feel she behaved somewhat like a "Princess from a minor German court," or like "a distinguished exile in an alien land," but he had read her books and she clearly had literary talent. His letter concluded: "My interest in this is that of someone who found Mrs. Peters's predicament a difficult one, and herself a rather noble, certainly touching, human being. . . . I can see no objection myself to letting her come and live here for some time, but I shall be guided by what you think."[33] Graham-Harrison sent a note to the Home Office. Svetlana's visa came through.

By August 1, Svetlana had managed to sell her house in Lawrenceville and the one in Pennington and recouped much of her capital. Rosa's friends found her an apartment in Cambridge that she could afford. At the end of August, she and Olga flew to Britain to begin their new life.

PART FOUR

Learning
to Live
in the West

Chapter 30

Chaucer Road

**In this photograph from 1984, a thirteen-year-old
Olga poses with a bulldog at a British fair.**

Svetlana moved into her flat at 12-B Chaucer Road. The house belonged to Dr. Robert Denman, a professor of land economy at Cambridge. It was damp and gloomy with that peculiar claustrophobic atmosphere typical of an English Victorian house, though there was a substantial and beautiful back garden that ran down to a brook. Chaucer Road was on the edge of Cambridge, and the walk into town went past the botanical gardens along a meandering stream. Svetlana's attic aerie was a hangover from the nineteenth century—small, with no central heating—almost worthy of *La Bohème*. The hot water trickled into the tub and the cold wind blew through ventilation holes behind the gas range. She joked in letters to Rosa Shand that the construction reminded her of "my old Russia." "Very Nostalgic and <u>cold</u>."[1] There were two other tenant apartments in the house, occupied by an elderly Irish librarian on a pension who was always inviting Svetlana in for a cup of tea beside her gas fire, and a South African couple with two children.

Olga boarded at Friends' School while Svetlana took the trip by bus or train from Cambridge to collect her on weekends. The school, founded in 1702 as a Quaker institution committed to internationalism, dominated the medieval market town of Saffron Walden, with its narrow streets and alleyways into which the houses leaned like friendly neighbors. Initially somewhat intimidated, hiding her insecurities, Olga asserted her Americanness—ultrapatriotic, she complained that everybody hated Americans; it was appalling that the Brits didn't celebrate Thanksgiving. But within a few weeks, she began to delight in her school. To Svetlana's amusement, she aped a Cockney accent in order to talk like a Brit.[2]

Olga recalled: "We had always been moving. It was back and forth between California, Carlsbad, Princeton, round and round New Jersey—it was a new house all the time." With her newfound stability, she established intimate friendships with the girls in her dorm. Her closest friends came from Brunei, Kuwait, Uganda, Zimbabwe, South Africa, and, of course, England. She soon felt a wonderful sense of belonging.

The press were buzzing about when we moved to England, but somehow Mom managed to keep me really sheltered. I still didn't know anything about my grandfather.

[Friends'] was an incredible school where I was accepted and flourished. I was actually able to have a personality, for the first time. Ever."[3]

Without Olga around to structure her days, Svetlana tried to pick up the threads of her writing life. After her long silence as a writer, in her attic where the damp English cold penetrated to the bone, she went through a painful autumn of self-doubt. She was reading Vladimir Nabokov's *Speak, Memory*. His work was so good. Why would she have the temerity to think of writing in English? She would open herself to ridicule. And yet she found she could not write in Russian.

She'd written to Berlin soon after her arrival. "Hugo Brunner wants me to write in my native language. . . . Of course, having been raised on Russian literature and poetry, it is only natural for me to write in Russian." But she told Berlin that writing in Russian brought "a feeling of pain, since it's bordering on guilt." It evoked the past: her father, her mother's suicide, all those disappeared lives, the suffering of friends, her abandonment of her children—all the losses that she had been retreating from "behind the American curtain." After fifteen years, was it not time to get rid of her "funny and hypocritical camouflages"?[4] But she could not get to work. She confessed that she needed constant encouragement. She imagined that Berlin's circle must be something like that of the Tolstoys in Leningrad or even of her colleagues at the Gorky Institute— Berlin was Russian-born, after all—and she could indulge again that wonderful "useless" habit of Russian intellectuals: arguing for hours for the sheer pleasure of it as if it were a sport.

But meanwhile she had pressing concerns. Her savings were now reduced—she had an annual income of between £8,000 and £9,000, but that had to last and was quickly being depleted as she paid Olga's boarding-school fees and the costs of her own frugal maintenance.[5] Her visitor's visa to the United Kingdom dictated that she was in the country as an independent writer at the behest of her publisher. She was expressly prohibited from taking on work, whether as a translator, a tutor, or a lecturer. Her only solution was to publish a new book, which she was determined to do. She was sure that all she required was a clear directive from her publisher, a contract, and Berlin's moral support.

When she arrived in England in August, however, Berlin had been in Italy; he was unable to meet her until mid-November, when they finally had lunch in Piccadilly. Their initial encounter was stimulating as she described her plans for work, and she found herself doing something unexpected. After their luncheon, she took a taxicab to Covent Garden to break her long silence with an old friend, Mita, the ballerina Sulamith Mikhailovna Messerer. Mita had defected to Great Britain in 1980 at the age of seventy-two, ending a distinguished career as a dancer and ballet coach with the Bolshoi. Svetlana left a note with her phone number at the stage door. Mita called her in Cambridge the next day.

Svetlana's memories of Mita dated back to 1943 and the days of her romance with Aleksei Kapler. In 1945 Mita had been one of the close friends at her apartment celebrating Victory Day. She had suffered deeply in the Stalinist purges of the late 1930s, when her sister Rachel had been arrested. Despite the risks of consorting with "enemies of the people," Mita had adopted her sister's daughter, Maya Plisetskaya, coaching her to become one of Russia's greatest ballerinas.

Mita had fond memories of Svetlana and never blamed her for her father. Over tea, they talked of the current Soviet Union. Mita assured Svetlana that while the bosses in the Kremlin might have changed, the system had not. She said it was better to work as a ballet coach in London than under the regime, whatever the cost in comfort. They laughed somewhat sardonically at the naïveté of the Western press, which was always talking of détente. Impressed by Mita's stamina at seventy-two, Svetlana returned to her own manuscript, now called "The Faraway Music." She wrote to Sir Isaiah Berlin to say that perhaps she should be geographically closer to him so that she would be prompted more often to work.[6]

November, the month Svetlana always identified with "the dying of everything,"[7] had brought its usual painful spiral down. But then, on December 17, after fifteen years of silence, Svetlana received a phone call from her son. He spoke casually, as if a phone call were a normal occurrence and not a seismic shock. It seemed that the Soviet government had given him permission to contact his mother. Svetlana was elated. Soon affectionate phone calls and letters passed between them. She discovered that Joseph had remarried—he was hoping that one day she might meet his new wife, Lyuda. Ilya, his son, was now thirteen and living with his mother, Elena. When she asked about her daughter Katya, Joseph told her that Katya was now married, had a little girl, and was living in remote Kamchatka in Siberia, where she worked as a geophysicist, but he couldn't tell her much else. He and his sister were no longer in touch. He had no photographs of Katya to send her. His letters often included requests for a particular medical text. Olga and Svetlana would rush off on expeditions to scour the bookshops of Cambridge and London, searching for volumes that might cost as much as £200.[8]

When Joseph finally sent Svetlana a current photograph of himself, she was shocked. The stranger in the photo was balding, middle-aged, with a sad expression in his eyes. He somehow resembled her brother Vasili. She rushed to the telephone, woke Joseph in the middle of the night, and, without preamble, shouted, "You're drinking. I know those swollen eyes." He was furious, of course, but he must have let the eruption pass, for she was soon writing to Rosa Shand, "Time and distance have not changed anything. . . . Somehow I do feel all 3 of [my children] now together with me."[9] She was sure that one day Joseph would be permitted to travel to see her.

She resumed her voluminous correspondence. On one of her daily walks to the postbox, she met Jane Renfrew, a Cambridge professor and highly regarded archaeologist. Knowing who she was, Renfrew invited her in for coffee. They took to sitting in Renfrew's warm kitchen for regular chats. Soon Svetlana was telling Renfrew of her past in the USSR. She talked about her father—how difficult it was to grow up and realize exactly who he was. Renfrew recalled thinking, *You can't choose your father.* "It was hard for her, very hard. After all, he was her father, and her father did show a certain amount of affection for her." She said, "I just wanted her to talk, because she needed to talk."[10]

Philippa Hill, widow of a well-known physicist with some remote family connections to Russia, also lived on Chaucer Road and she, too, grew fond of Svetlana, whom she recalled as very warm. She only "needed steering out of her grumbles and then she could be a fascinating teller of stories from her past."[11] But Hill understood that Svetlana could be difficult. "Svetlana didn't know how to manage life, really, I suppose. That was the truth of the matter." Hill thought of her as "almost a gypsy": "She lived a wandering life."[12]

One of Olga's closest school chums was a girl named Emily Richardson, and Emily's mother and Svetlana soon became friends. Rosamond Richardson lived in a lovely thatched cottage in Saffron Walden and had converted her garage into a small studio with a sofa bed, which Svetlana used when she stayed overnight. Svetlana christened the studio the dacha. Richardson laughed at the memory of the morning Svetlana came to breakfast and said, "I hope you don't mind. I've changed around the furniture." She had moved the bed to the other end of the room because she wanted to look in the other direction. "She was absolutely adorable."[13]

> I really loved Svetlana's soul. . . . It's hard to define, but there are some people who just have a dimension and a kind of depth in their core somewhere. . . . She could respond deeply to other people with enormous warmth. . . . There was a kind of deep spirituality about Svetlana. God in the widest possible sense, but always of course, being dissatisfied with its presentation so even Indian mysticism couldn't quite fill the bill. . . . [This hunger] was powerful enough to keep her on that path, as it were, so that she didn't get deflected because she didn't find it.

But Richardson also understood that Svetlana could "change like the weather. She was very tricky." Richardson felt this "had to do with an emotional woundedness that had never been healed." Like Philippa Hill, she thought of Svetlana as a nomad.

> Always expecting that the thing you're lacking is about to be found around the corner . . . I read her as a deeply wounded person who was extremely bright. Her intellect was phenomenal and she was also a great soul. She had such optimism and incredible energy, which of course could get channelled down the wrong alleyway for her and into a lot of anger. To me that's part of the whole story of her personality. She is both this and that.

Richardson thought Svetlana was exhausted by the misrepresentations that people casually attached to her.

> She wanted control over all that, didn't she? To some extent it's understandable, because she had so many in-

terpretations laid upon her, she wanted control over the material. But the way she did it was very extreme. . . . It didn't knock her off course. It knocked everybody else off course. Flattened everybody else like skittles, but she carried on.

Richardson saw this as Svetlana's tragedy. Everyone reflected back to her the fact that she was Stalin's daughter—people couldn't help themselves—so that an uncontaminated self-knowledge was almost impossible. "I'm not sure she could see herself as she really was." But Richardson felt that the one thing holding Svetlana in the world was her love for Olga. "Their mutual love was never destroyed or squandered."[14]

That December Svetlana decided to officially convert to Catholicism. She joined the Catholic Church of Saint Mary and All English Martyrs and even attended several days of a retreat at the convent of Saint Mary in Suffolk. She now determined that Olga should move to the Chelmsford Catholic School in Essex, where she would receive a more disciplined education. But Olga wanted none of this. She loved Friends' School. When she took the entrance exams for the new school, she marked X's in all the wrong places in the multiple-choice questionnaire and managed to fail. She was delighted with herself, but her mother was furious. She knew Olga had done this deliberately. When they got home, Svetlana lit into her. But Olga's will was stronger than her mother's. She stayed at Friends' School until she was eighteen. When Svetlana complained to Terry Waite that the school wouldn't get her daughter into Oxford or Cambridge, he replied, "You don't understand. She's got to be accepted. She's going to be a teenager. Quakers are the only people who are going to give her what she needs. She's going to get a good education here, but the most important thing is she's going to be safe."[15]

Waite was right. At Friends' School, bullying was unacceptable. As Olga remembered it, if you were caught smoking or drinking, or kissing a boy, you'd get a detention. "But any form of racism, sexism—God forbid!—fighting: instant expulsion. Even name-calling was unacceptable." The school protected her and this would prove invaluable. The first test came at the beginning of April during her first year at the school.

The *Daily Mail* had discovered that Stalin's eleven-year-old granddaughter (she would be twelve in May) was living in Saffron Walden and that her mother resided in Cambridge on Chaucer Road. The reporters descended on Friends' School just before Easter break in the first week of April. Olga looked back on that incident with a kind of annoyed amusement.

> All the kids were leaving; some of us were staying an extra night. I was due to stay an extra night. And suddenly one of the teachers told me that she was going to drive me home. To Cambridge, which was about an hour and a half away. I thought that was really weird. But we didn't have a car, so I just figured Mom didn't want to come up on the bus to get me. I had to duck down as we drove out of the gates. The teacher told me to lie down in the backseat and cover myself with a blanket. And there were paparazzi all around the gates. And I could not understand what was going on. And I assumed—I remember thinking, I assumed that it was happening to all the kids—they were having to smuggle the kids out of the school for some reason, I didn't know why! So I got home and there were reporters outside on the sidewalk and outside the front of the house.[16]

Svetlana was very angry. She had wanted to tell Olga about her grandfather in her own way and only when she thought her daughter was ready. She sat Olga down and showed her a picture of Churchill, Truman, and Stalin at the Potsdam Conference in Germany in July 1945 and said, "That's your grandfather." Decades later she recalled: "Mom told me about it all, and showed me the photos and tried to explain. I mean, I barely had a grasp on American presidents at this point." Svetlana consoled her. "Never mind about that, you're American as apple pie, your father's American."

Svetlana knew that more had to be said, but she couldn't bring herself to say it. How do you tell your child that her grandfather was Joseph Stalin? She asked Jane Renfrew if she would speak to Olga about Stalin, but Renfrew demurred, suggesting that Svetlana instead ask the headmaster of Friends' School.[17]

When Olga returned to school at the end of the week, again driven by a teacher, reporters were still lurking. Her picture had been in all the newspapers. Reporters played riffs on the nickname she'd acquired at school, "Jolly Hockey Sticks," referring to her long legs and American origin. None of the adolescents had much of a grasp of who Stalin was, but Olga did remember that one of her roommates in her dorm exclaimed, "My God, I've been sleeping next to a Russian this whole time. I could've been killed in my sleep."

The newspaper articles that followed made public the details that Svetlana had guarded so carefully: the school Olga attended, its fees ($3,000), a description of Svetlana's flat, and the name of her landlord. When the reporters contacted her, she replied briskly, "I do not grant interviews to anyone. . . . There is absolutely nothing to add to the full truth that we are here in England for the education of my daughter." By late May, even the *New York Times* had picked up the news: "Stalin's Daughter Living in British University Town." The source of much of the information seemed to be Malcolm Muggeridge, who was quoted as saying that Svetlana was a woman broken by her fear of her father, whose death had come as a relief. It was crude; it was painful. The truth was so much more complex than this.[18] Concluding that Muggeridge was the leak, Svetlana was livid. He had violated her daughter's privacy. He had exposed her. In her unbridled rage, she wrote to him: "I curse the day I wrote you. . . . You are one of those obsessed demonic natures who ought to be <u>avoided</u> at all costs."[19]

At the same time as the press was harassing her, Svetlana was expressing her frustrations to Isaiah Berlin and his wife. Since her arrival, they had met her only twice for luncheons in a café. Was that friendship? Berlin had led her to expect so much more. He was the one who'd sought her out in America. It had been his advice that brought her to England. She'd pulled up all her roots on his recommendation, and yet he had not introduced her to a single friend.[20]

That summer, she managed to resume work on her manuscript and soon sent a draft of two hundred pages to Hugo Brunner at Chatto & Windus. Expecting a Kremlin family memoir, Brunner was not pleased. He wrote back that he was impressed by how much she'd written, but he thought the manuscript would be better placed with an American publisher. He wished her good luck and told her he would love to hear how things went.[21] The brisk casualness of Brunner's dismissal cut deeply.

Svetlana was caught in a bind. People were interested only in the Kremlin Svetlana, in what she might say about Stalin. She knew she could make a fortune writing about Stalin, but she refused to be her father's biographer.[22] She wanted to tell her own story. Her manuscript, "The Faraway Music," was a narrative of her arrival in the United States, her marriage to Wesley Peters, and Olgivanna Wright's unscrupulous treatment of her. She also outlined her manipulation at the hands of lawyers and included her contracts with Copex in an appendix. Renouncing her paternity, she dedicated her book to the spirit of her mother, Nadya. "I am a daughter of Nadya Alliluyeva, not of Stalin," she wrote defiantly.[23]

She sent the book to Peter Jovanovich, the managing director of a London subsidiary of the US firm Harcourt Brace Jovanovich. Jovanovich found the book a moving "odyssey and a search" but said that it had structural problems.[24] He was right. Though it had lovely lyrical moments, the book was driven by undigested invective. Had Svetlana been willing to be edited, it might have become a compelling book, but Jovanovich suggested so many changes that Svetlana decided he was altering her work. Eventually he withdrew his offer.

She now turned her attention back to Isaiah Berlin, asking him to read her manuscript. When he did not reply, she was shocked. She thought his secretary, Pat Utechin, must have turned him against her.

Utechin had been exceedingly friendly, even before Svetlana arrived, and helped her to settle in Cambridge. When Svetlana mentioned that her son, Joseph, had phoned her after sixteen years of silence, Utechin said she knew many Oxford dons who traveled to Moscow. They might manage to meet her son and bring her news of him. But after her initial excitement, Svetlana had second thoughts. Perhaps she was remembering the Krimsky/Kurpel affair of seven years back. Suddenly she was sending Utechin long epistles—would the person Utechin had in mind know what he was doing? Otherwise it might be dangerous for her son. Would the Oxford dons be discreet? If not, she herself might become a subject of gossip in Oxford. Though British, Utechin had been married to a Russian and had deep connections in the Russian exile community. Svetlana was certain she had become the subject of rumors.

Utechin became the enemy. Had Berlin palmed her off on his secretary? Perhaps the woman had not delivered her letters to Berlin or had not offered him a clear portrait of her circumstances. She wrote in a rage to Berlin: "I fail to understand what went wrong." She had expected more from a humanitarian of his stature. "May God give you full justice, in accordance with your false promises and your hypocritical assurances. Your Secretary is simply a phony bitch, an intelligence agent (be careful!) and a liar. I hate the day when I talked with you in New York in January 1982: you had [*sic*] messed up my life."[25]

Svetlana was clearly out of control, but one could not raise her expectations and dash them without consequence. Berlin had offered friendship; she had a typical Russian understanding of friendship. It was all-consuming and without borders. She expected the world from Berlin. It didn't seem to occur to her that his support had been based on a casual kindness; he had his own very busy professional life with its own priorities. When feeling hurt, Svetlana would lose all restraint. She had even admitted earlier to Berlin that, once she had begun "to make my own speculations, trying to 'visualize' things, . . . I get carried away and everything becomes messed up completely."[26]

Berlin was shocked at what he called "her bitter, violent, and very wounding letter."[27] He had done what he had offered to do: he had recommended her to his publisher and written a letter to intervene with the Home Office. She replied more temperately that she never expected to make him a "scapegoat" for all her misfortunes, but she did expect more understanding from someone like him. He ought to have shown more magnanimity and generosity. She was bitterly disappointed.[28]

By the summer, she seemed to have regained her equanimity. She'd been reading Jung's *Memories, Dreams, Reflections* and was fascinated by his theory of the necessary integration of the persona and the self in the evolution of the psyche. She wrote to Berlin to apologize for her "very bad manners and lots of ill temper." It was too late in life for her to change her *Georgian* temper, as she called it, but she felt ashamed. She had become "mad in a more hot way. I became mad with too many people, here in GB, there in US. . . . This state of mind being unhealthy, I could not cool it off quickly." But now she could see herself in her "ridiculous pose."[29] Had Svetlana known, however, what was going on behind the scenes, she would have been apoplectic, even frightened. Vera Suvchinskaya Traill, a well-known Russian émigré and writer whose grandfather had been minister of war in Russia's provisional government before the October Revolution, lived in Cambridge and had taken a proprietary interest in Svetlana and her daughter.

Traill wrote to Sir Isaiah Berlin that March to ask how long he'd known Svetlana. She had met Svetlana only the previous September, "but even in these few months my feeling is that she is getting worse—acute paranoia, obviously inherited from . . . (three guesses)." Traill was worried for Svetlana's daughter, "being at the mercy of a mother in such a state."[30] In Traill's view, Olga had to be saved. She explained to Berlin:

> We all feel helpless, particularly as S. has by now lost every friend she had here. She lives under the delusion (sincere of course—delusions always are) that the world is conspiring against her. . . . If you need any evidence in support of the paranoia diagnosis, I can send you some samples of the sort of letters she writes—"international intrigues," "KGB agents," "triple agents," etc., etc. In her Dad's days, people were shot for less.[31]

Traill had convinced herself of her own high-minded motives but in fact would not have been interested in Olga's welfare if Svetlana were not Stalin's daughter. Sublimated within her concern was an unacknowledged vindictiveness. Berlin wrote back to say that Olga's security was indeed worrying, but he couldn't help. He had broken with Svetlana. He suggested that Traill write to Olga's father, Mr. Peters, who lived in some kind of commune of architects in Tucson, Arizona.

Oblivious of this gossip, Svetlana seemed to have emerged from what she called her "unhealthy state of mind." She bought a new residence, saying it would be cheaper than paying rent. By June, she was sending friends her new address—55 Bateman Street, Flat 3. The apartment overlooked the Cambridge botanical gardens and was a bit closer to the center of town. It had one large room, which served as living room, dining room, and study, and adjacent bedrooms. She set up her pine desk with her typewriter and her bookshelves with her photographs of a young Joseph and Katya. She had a few of her possessions, including her two lovely Navaho rugs, shipped from America, where they had been stored with friends. She and Olga went to the Scilly Isles for a two-week vacation, spending time on the beach and visiting Tresco Abbey. By now she had almost exhausted her small savings. Everything seemed in a strange kind of suspension.

That summer Lancer International Press in India finally published *The Faraway Music*. Lancer paid very little, but Svetlana was still pleased. She wrote to Rosa Shand, "I HAVE Author's copies in my hands: you know the feeling when one sees one's ms finally PRINTED."[32]

And she had a second reason for joy. She had recently received a letter from Joseph telling her that the Soviet government was willing to give him permission to travel to Finland—he was certain the government would let him out. She merely had to get herself to Finland and they would hold each other. Svetlana told Olga that she would soon be meeting her brother.

Svetlana rushed to speak with her friend Jane Renfrew. She asked, "If my son comes from Moscow, would you see him?" and was delighted when Renfrew replied, "Of course." But soon she slipped from giddy euphoria to the depths of a darkness she knew all too well. She told Renfrew that Joseph had telephoned and said, "Mother, I haven't seen you in seventeen years. I'm seriously ill. I really want to see you."[33]

The thought occurred to her that she should go to Moscow to see him. She chose to mull over the idea with only one friend, Philippa Hill. She told Philippa that Joseph was in the hospital. He needed her. Philippa had children and grandchildren. She must know how Svetlana felt. All Philippa said was, "Well, I think you have to go, don't you?" though she worried for Olga, who didn't speak a word of Russian.[34]

There had already been hints of Svetlana's loneliness and disillusionment. She'd written to her friend Jerzy Kosinski in September, "If I ever defect back to Moscow, no one should be surprised. . . . What I confronted in this so-called Free World, was enough to kill . . . the enthusiasm of even a strong man. I am NO strong man, and I have no 'Nerves of Steel' [alluding to Stalin]. . . . My son is my only friend. . . . To be with Joseph is my only wish, which I still cannot achieve. He will fail in the Free World as I did, so the only way is to go back."[35]

Earlier, in March 1984, she had told a journalist, "Sometimes it's almost a superhuman effort not to drop everything and run and get a ticket to go and see them. Sometimes I don't care what the regime is. I just want to see my grandchildren."[36] Yet there was Olga to consider. Svetlana felt it was ironic that she had blood ties in both countries, but couldn't find a home. Still, she concluded bravely, if unconvincingly, "Home I have inside me. I take it with me like a snail wherever I go."[37]

But the truth was, she had reached the end of her endurance. She had very little money, certainly not enough to last more than a few months. She was stranded in a foreign country, but a retreat to the United States offered no change in her prospects. She had not found a paying publisher and seemed to be washed up as a writer. She could no longer afford Olga's education, and her sense of herself as a mother, based on her own mother's model, was that she must provide her daughter an excellent education. Most devastating of all was that her son was ill in the hospital and he'd asked her to come. She knew that her defection back to the Soviet Union would be shocking, but she no longer cared whether she provoked another international incident. Her personal reasons trumped those of the state. Perhaps a part of her even wanted to give the finger to those she felt had let her down.

On September 11, 1984, Svetlana took the train from Cambridge to London to track down the Soviet Embassy—the address was unlisted for security reasons. In her handbag, she carried a letter to the Soviet ambassador requesting permission to return to the USSR. When she identified herself and finally made it through the security checks, a man in the familiar brown suit of a Soviet official greeted her noncommittally and accepted her letter, telling her it would be sent to Moscow. "We do not decide anything here, you understand." She should come back in a week.[38]

A week later, the chargé d'affaires greeted her enthusiastically and invited her for tea. He said she could return immediately. Plans were already set. They must avoid Heathrow Airport, where she might be recognized; Gatwick would be better. The embassy would fly her and her daughter to Greece, where they could stay for a few days at the Soviet Embassy, and then the plane would take them to Moscow. Nothing ever happened this quickly in the Soviet Union. Svetlana demurred. She said she couldn't leave so soon. Her daughter was still in school and she hadn't yet told her. They must wait for Olga's midterm break. The chargé d'affaires reluctantly agreed that she could depart at the end of October.

On the train back to Cambridge, Svetlana sat in a daze, watching the trees and houses of the Essex countryside float past the window, and wondered how Olga would react. She knew, once again, that she had started a process that seemed impossible to stop. Did it occur to her that there were eerie echoes of her precipitate flight seventeen years back?

At first she told Olga they were taking a trip to Greece, but as Olga watched her mother sorting through their belongings and destroying her papers and correspondence, she knew something was afoot. The night before they were due to leave, Svetlana finally told her daughter they were flying to the USSR to visit her brother and sister.

Olga was furious. Why hadn't her mother told her? How long would they be staying? She hadn't even been allowed to say good-bye to her friends. They had a bitter fight, and for the first time Svetlana relented. "OK," she said. "We're not going."[39] And then she woke Olga at three a.m., just before the airport taxi was due to arrive.

As she locked the door to her new flat behind her, the fridge still half-full of food, and she and Olga climbed into the airport taxi with only the luggage they could carry, Svetlana tried to avoid facing the fact that she had handled this badly. She should have better prepared her daughter, but what choice did she have? It was impossible for Olga to tell her friends. If the news leaked out that Stalin's daughter was returning to the USSR, it would be blasted in headlines all over the international press. The British or the Americans might have tried to stop her.

All Olga could think was, *This is it. Mom's going to love Joseph now.*[40]

Svetlana had invited Rosamond Richardson for lunch the

next day. Richardson trudged over to Bateman Street with her two young sons and knocked on the door. There was no reply. She checked her agenda to confirm that she had the right date, the right time. It was very bizarre. Svetlana was simply gone.

Svetlana had left instructions with a real estate agent to sell her new Bateman Street flat. It fell to Philippa Hill to empty it. As she sorted things into boxes, Philippa decided to mail Svetlana's beloved Navaho rugs to the Soviet Union, but they, along with almost everything else, simply disappeared.

Chapter 31

―――

Back in the USSR

Upon her return to Moscow in 1984, Svetlana held a press conference at the offices of the Soviet Women's National Committee.

It was late October 1984 when Svetlana and Olga left behind autumn in England and slipped utterly unnoticed into the hot, dusty Athens airport and took a taxi to the Soviet Embassy. There a young diplomat, Yuri Andropov, son of the recently deceased Soviet leader, and his fashionable wife welcomed them. At first Svetlana was comforted by the presence of what seemed to her a youthful generation of new Soviet officials, until she was invited to tea with the usual grim, gray bureaucrats, who elicited flashbacks of her meeting in India seventeen years ago with Ambassador Benediktov. Only the high-spirited Olga relieved the artificiality of the situation. Olga was busy in Athens.

> Mom did whatever it was she was doing. I was chaperoned around, being shown the Acropolis. And I was gift shopping. I had been told I had all of these relatives—a brother, a sister, nieces, and nephews. So I had a whole bunch of people to buy presents for. And I had read that Russians really liked Adidas and couldn't get them, so I was buying everyone Adidas.[1]

It didn't matter to a thirteen-year-old that she didn't know the shoe sizes of all these strangers. When Svetlana joined the shopping expedition, she bought an embroidered dress for Katya's daughter, Anya, and some amusing trinkets for Joseph and his wife. In the three days they had before the Aeroflot flight to Moscow, Olga fell in love with Athens. She laughed when she later read a report in a newspaper that she had tried to commit suicide by jumping off the hotel balcony.[2]

On October 25, Svetlana and Olga left the heat of Athens behind and headed into a Moscow winter. As the descending plane circled over the vast empty landscape of Russia further effaced by a blanket of snow, Svetlana was shocked to discover she felt nothing. She was the *exile returned*; she should have been crying.[3]

She'd asked Joseph not to come to the airport—it would have been too emotional to meet in public. The Soviet officials waiting at the VIP entrance seemed tense. A young woman approached with a bouquet of flowers: "Welcome home!" As they drove into Moscow, Svetlana barely recognized the city: the route was lined with block after block of monotonous highrise tenement apartments.

They were escorted to the Hotel Sovietsky, one of the most expensive hotels in Moscow, overlooking the Leningrad Prospect. They climbed its elegant steps and entered its white marble lobby through the revolving doors, and there stood Joseph.

Some part of Svetlana's psyche still carried the image of the young man of twenty-one whom she had left at Sheremetyevo Airport in 1966: slim, good-looking, with humor in his eyes. The thirty-nine-year-old man staring at her seemed tired and more embarrassed than happy to see her. Joseph was looking at a fifty-eight-year-old woman who was his mother but whom he hadn't seen in eighteen years.

Svetlana always constructed a fantasy of how things would be. She and Olga were returning to a family who loved and would embrace them. Uncles, aunts, and cousins would surround Olga and lavish her with affection. There would be no recriminations, no regrets. The frozen moment dissolved, and Joseph's father, Grigori Morozov, who'd always remained close to his son, stepped forward, followed by Joseph's wife and fourteen-year-old son, Ilya. Joseph moved to embrace his mother and then, taking his wife by the hand, said, "Mama, this is Lyuda."

The whole encounter was awkward. Joseph ignored Olga. Perhaps he was preoccupied, concerned that his mother like his new wife. Svetlana didn't. She took an immediate dislike to Lyuda, who seemed so much older than her son, but she told herself not to meddle. The young boy, Ilya, stood by awkwardly. Only Grigori's presence made the reunion less clumsy. He chatted affectionately with Olga in broken English and guided them to the elevator. Otherwise they might have remained frozen to the white marble floor.

The government had assigned Svetlana a luxurious two-bedroom suite. Even here the reunion did not go well, as they stumbled over each other in Russian and English. Lyuda filled a vase with water to hold the flowers the Committee of Soviet Women had given Svetlana. Svetlana thought, *At least she's practical.* Olga stared at these strangers. Grigori said they would meet downstairs in the restaurant, where he'd reserved a table. He reminded Svetlana that the restaurant was once famous for its chorus of Gypsy singers. It always came up in novels. Didn't she remember? She did not. In the bathroom, Olga turned on her mother in anger. *This* was her brother, who supposedly loved her? He had looked her up and down and said nothing. He hadn't even hugged her.[4]

In the restaurant, Joseph and Svetlana held hands, but it was impossible to speak. The music was too loud. Grigori stuck kindly to Olga, trying to keep her entertained. Ilya remained tongue-tied and tense. Lyuda watched coolly. The familiar feast of vodka, caviar, herring, and pickles lay on the table.

Olga remembered the evening as totally unnerving.

This whole, long, huge table full of people drinking and eating and talking Russian, and there's only this one guy [Grigori] who's sitting here and talking to me. And he's talking to me like I'm six. And I'm thirteen. But he was one of the few that spoke English. Really terrible English. That first night was awful, and I thought, Oh my gosh, Mom's going to be reunited with Joseph. This is it. I'm done.[5]

Svetlana had expected an outpouring of love from her son and seemed incapable of anticipating that his reaction might be complex. She believed she had been faithful all these years in her love for her children. But how was he to know this? All Joseph knew was what Kremlin propaganda had reported. She was anti-Soviet, unstable, a wealthy American who brought them Greek trinkets as homecoming gifts. It would take time to dispel this version. Wrapped in her own longing and now distress, Svetlana lost sight of Olga sitting among these strangers and would look back ruefully: "It is amazing how, when the heart has already made a decision, reason only supplies every possible reassurance in detail."[6]

The next day a friend of Joseph's from the Institute of Foreign Relations brought champagne and flowers and prepared Svetlana for the arrival that afternoon of two officials from the Foreign Office who were going to help her "to begin readjustment to the Soviet life." When she tried to ask about Russian schools for Olga, he made it clear that all such questions should be directed to the two officials. Svetlana was being reminded that decisions were made "up there on the top," as they said in Moscow.[7] The first order of business would be to reinstate Svetlana's Soviet citizenship and confiscate her and Olga's American passports.

The international paparazzi were already lurking outside the hotel. When Svetlana and Olga emerged, one reporter asked Olga, "Are you Olga Peters?" Svetlana grabbed her daughter's arm and pulled her back into the hotel. It was the first time Olga began to understand who her mother really was.[8]

On November 1, the Supreme Soviet reclaimed Citizen Alliluyeva by special decree. On November 2, a brief announcement appeared in *Izvestia* and on the evening news:

> The Soviet authorities considered and complied with a request made by S. I. Alliluyeva, who has returned to Moscow, for restoring her to the citizenship of the USSR as well as for granting Soviet citizenship to Alliluyeva's daughter Olga.[9]

The Communist Party was keen to make a propaganda fuss over returnees. Ironically, the same week that Svetlana arrived, another Soviet exile returned, posthumously. The remains of the legendary singer Feodor Chaliapin, who had died in Paris in

1938, were flown to Moscow and reburied with ceremony in the legendary Novodevichy Cemetery, where Stalin's memorial statue to Svetlana's mother, Nadya, still stood in splendid isolation.[10]

"Entrance is free. But you pay dearly at the exit," as Svetlana's second husband, Yuri Zhdanov, used to say.[11] She knew there would be a price to pay for permission to return, and she paid it at a seventy-minute press conference on November 16, held at the offices of the Soviet Women's National Committee before a restricted audience of foreign and Soviet journalists. Accompanied by Foreign Ministry officials and a translator, Svetlana read a prepared statement in Russian, and occasionally corrected the translator, who read it in English. She seemed composed and spoke without emotion, beginning with a brief saga of her life in the West. After her defection to the United States in 1967, she claimed she had found herself in the hands of "lawyers, businessmen, politicos and publishers who turned the name of my father, my own name and life into a sensational commodity. . . . I became a favorite pet of the CIA and those who even went to the length of telling me what I should write and what I should not."[12] Later Svetlana would claim that her Soviet interpreter had mistranslated her. She had said, "They treated me well, for I was everybody's pet" and had never mentioned the CIA. This was probably disingenuous; the statement reflected what she had often said to friends. However, it is probably true that, because she had little choice, she simply acceded to the ministry's demands. "I wanted to talk and answer questions. They wanted certain things to be there. They made me write texts in Russian, which they all approved. I felt very awkward. I wanted to say simply, 'I came to join my children.'"[13]

At the press conference, she described her second book, *Only One Year*, as a "collective production" by those she "ironically thanked" in her author's note. When this comment was reported in the West, the historian Robert Tucker insisted that

Only One Year was entirely her own work and explained, "It appeared that she was trying to dissociate herself from the book," which was "even more anti-Soviet" than her *Twenty Letters to a Friend*.[14]

She told the reporters that she and her daughter had been greeted like the prodigal son in biblical times, and she was grateful. The bulk of her address was about her personal reasons for her return: her longing to see her children, her deeply held religious beliefs, and her concern for Olga's education. In fact, she had run out of money to keep Olga at her boarding school, and she imagined that in the USSR, where education was free, she could find the equivalent of her old Model School No. 25, which had provided her with a brilliant education and had been more of a home than her own home in those brutal times. She concluded by saying that this would be her last press conference. That night, clips from the press conference were featured prominently on Russian TV news broadcasts, but these clips were only from the officially prepared parts of her statement. Her comments about her personal motives for her return and her religious beliefs were edited out.

For the Soviets, Svetlana's return was a propaganda coup. Preparations were under way for a huge celebration the next year of the fortieth anniversary of the Soviet victory over Nazi Germany. The Politburo was busy rehabilitating Stalin as a military genius and brilliant diplomat. Television documentaries showed Stalin addressing the army in Red Square in 1941, with Hitler's troops only twenty miles from Moscow; in his marshal's uniform posing with Roosevelt and Churchill at Tehran and Yalta; and charming Truman and Clement Attlee at the Potsdam Conference, as he outnegotiated his allies. A feature film based on John Reed's *Ten Days That Shook the World* was rejuvenating the Bolshevik revolution as directed by men of passion and principle. But all this propaganda masked a fragile government. Svetlana had returned to the USSR at a very shaky moment. Konstantin Chernenko, general secretary of the Central Committee of the Communist Party, who had succeeded Andropov as the country's leader, was old, ailing,[15] and rarely seen in public; he would be dead within the year. Behind the scenes, as the economy disintegrated, reformists in the Communist Party were battling the old guard.

The Soviet population was still divided about Stalin. Photos of Stalin could be seen dangling from strings on the windshields of cabs in Moscow and trucks on the Trans-Siberian highway, but some people remembered the purges and the price paid in human lives. The younger generation seemed ignorant of that past and ready to accept Stalin as the great commander in chief who guided the Red Army to victory and saved the Allies; the prewar purges of the Soviet command and the postwar treatment of returning soldiers had been edited out. In this context, Stalin's errant daughter's return and public contrition were invaluable to the Party. Of course, there were those who seemed to have no idea who this Alliluyeva woman was.[16] The Moscow correspondent for the *Washington Post*, Dusko Doder, reported being asked by a young taxi driver, "Who is Alliluyeva?" When he responded that she was Stalin's daughter, the taxi driver replied, "I didn't know Stalin's real name was Alliluyev."

The reaction in the US press to Svetlana's return was predictable outrage. Who did she think she was? *Defecting* from the free world back to the Communists! The headlines blared: STALIN'S DAUGHTER BACK IN THE SOVIET UNION AFTER 17 YEARS[17] and SVETLANA'S FLIGHT: BACK WHERE HER TROUBLES BEGAN.[18] Two articles in particular were utterly damning, both by Sovietologists who had known her personally.

Professor Robert Tucker titled his article "Svetlana Inherited Her Tragic Flaw." Acknowledging that he knew her, Tucker described Svetlana as driven by her inner demons, voicing "angry recriminations" against everyone, including her American ex-husband, Wesley Peters. She refused to speak of Stalin because she couldn't admit to herself that "she was—in some sense—like her father": her "low speaking voice," her eyes with their "yellow glint," her "inner imperiousness," her refusal to accept criticism. She had rejected Tucker's editorial suggestions for her book, the principal one of which was his suggestion to change the title to *Leavetaking*. Unlike her father, "who would destroy those with whom he broke," all she could do was flee. "She is her father's daughter in a way that has finally brought her back to unfreedom . . . the last misfortune bequeathed to her by the terrible man who was her father."[19]

The other article was a lengthy piece in *Time* magazine by the journalist and translator Patricia Blake, a member of the Princeton inner circle and a close friend of Max Hayward, with whom Svetlana had fallen in love all those years ago in Princeton. In her article, "The Saga of Stalin's 'Little Sparrow,'" she didn't disclose that she knew Svetlana.

Blake had a complicated reputation and was considered by many as at least a fellow traveler in American intelligence circles. Vsevolod Kochetov, editor of the Soviet journal *Oktyabr*, wrote a vicious lampoon of Blake in which she was "portrayed as a beautiful spy from the CIA's *Encounter* team who slept around in the Soviet literary world."[20] This was slanderous, but she was clearly a presence as a glamorous journalist interested in Soviet intrigues.

For her *Time* article, Blake interviewed Wesley Peters and the Hayakawas, as well as Svetlana's neighbors on Chaucer Road—Jane Renfrew remembered Blake as being particularly hostile.[21] "The story of Svetlana's life is the chronicle of her losing battle with the specter of her father . . . whom she fatefully resembled," Blake wrote. She offered a full chronology of Svetlana's life from her twenty-six years in the Kremlin, where she learned her "lordly" ways, to the dark decade after Khrushchev's denunciation of Stalin's crimes, when she had lived bereft of status and privileges, to her disastrous relations in the United States.

Blake erroneously claimed, "No open arms awaited Svetlana in the USSR," and, "Dissatisfied by the cool official reception she received, she displayed her temper to the Soviet authorities." To insulate her from diplomats and other foreigners, they moved her out of Moscow and refused her a "car, dacha, or any other of the perquisites that families of the Soviet elite enjoy."[22] This was a fabrication made up out of whole cloth.

Blake focused in particular on Svetlana's failings as a mother. She suggested that Svetlana "thwarted" Wesley Peters's efforts to visit his daughter and implied that Olga had lived in Washington with Senator Hayakawa's family from 1977 to 1981. Some English acquaintances seemed eager to rush to condemn Svetlana. Her fellow tenants, the Mansfields, reported that she constantly "hectored" her daughter. "We could hear her even when we turned up the television and closed the windows." At Olga's school a part-time teacher, Fay Black, remarked that Svetlana forbade her daughter "to wear tight jeans and bright tops like the other girls" and to "wander around town after classes." She said, "Her mother clung to her like a warden to a prisoner. The child's only hope was to go back to school."[23]

When Wesley Peters was contacted, he didn't help. "My reaction is surprise and concern, of course, about our daughter going back to Russia, . . . but there isn't anything I know I can do about it."[24] The pronoun "our" must have been awkward for him. After he and Svetlana separated, he'd seen his daughter only four or five times.

When Svetlana eventually read Blake's article, it was a deep blow. The one thing she felt she had succeeded in was bringing up her daughter. And now she was denied even that success. Olga was quick to defend her mother. "Yes," she admitted, she and her mother fought, but that didn't change the love between them:

> For my mother, the primary importance was education. Friends' School obviously wasn't going to put me into Oxford or Cambridge. My mother's way of parenting was not accommodating. If I was being a brat or if I was sulking about something, I would get it. She wasn't going to tolerate any kind of whining or crying. Yes, she might hit me—it was a Russian thing—but she taught me to be a rebel, so she took it on herself. It was just her way of instilling strength in me, really. I never felt abused, or anything like that. I'm saying this with absolute love. She kept me from the edge of the cliff pretty much.[25]

Olga's former babysitter in Wisconsin, Pamela Stefansson, phoned George Kennan on November 2, saying she was very upset about Olga. She wanted to know if Svetlana had the legal right to take her daughter with her. Kennan had no idea. His secretary suggested she contact the State Department's legal office or the Soviet Desk.[26]

Kennan had a long conversation with Fritz Ermarth, national intelligence officer for the USSR and East Europe. The State Department and the CIA were concerned about Svetlana's return, convinced she would be exploited for propaganda purposes and unsure of what she might say. What came out of this conversation remains classified, but certainly reports from CIA operatives would have come back from Moscow.[27] So far Svetlana didn't seem a threat. After her press conference, she made no more public statements.

Meanwhile in Moscow, Svetlana was getting the VIP treatment. Within days, a government-approved teacher was coming to the hotel each morning to teach Olga Russian while

Svetlana hunted for a good school. It soon became clear that Olga's "free" education was not going to proceed as she had imagined. At the first school, the principal suggested that it would be difficult to have Olga in the classroom, and Svetlana understood that it was Stalin's ghost who was unwelcome. In another, from the attitude and style of the deputy head, Svetlana saw that Olga would be treated as a celebrity trophy. Of course, Svetlana should have anticipated this, but she expressed shock that "thirty years after my father's death, the political passions around his name were still so strong and hot."[28] The Russian teacher continued to come to their hotel suite.

After the first two weeks, Svetlana was shown a large luxury apartment in a sixteen-story complex on Spiridonyevka Street (now Aleksei Tolstoy Street) with a panoramic view of Moscow and the Kremlin towers in the distance. An armed guard stood at the entrance. The apartment had belonged to a Politburo member who had recently died. Svetlana and Olga would be able to shop in the luxury government stores reserved for the elite; they would have a car with a driver; Olga would go to the showcase school next door; and Svetlana would receive the state pension that had been assigned to her when her father died. The well-known House of Receptions, where Moscow correspondents met, was down the street. Svetlana had been forgiven her traitorous defection, but she would be expected to perform. She suggested that she and Olga would prefer a more modest flat.

Olga recalled: "They tried to bring us the best of everything— the white stallions—but my mother would point at the donkey and say, we're taking that; it started to get weird pretty quickly." After the relative austerity of their life in England, Olga didn't understand why they were getting such exaggerated treatment. Her mother's refusal of such largesse "made the landing softer, but it was all a shock."[29]

One of the first people Svetlana went to visit was her friend Fyodor Volkenstein, to whom she had addressed her *Twenty Letters*. The intervening eighteen years had not been kind to him. He was old and ill and his wife had died. He was angry with Svetlana. "Why have you returned? Why? We are all used to the fact that you are living abroad. Your children were all right, you knew that. What will you do here now? You can see already that your return is being used for propaganda. You do not need that!"[30] Volkenstein would be dead within a few months.

Olga and Svetlana visited Joseph and his wife in their Moscow apartment and also at their dacha in Zhukovka near Svetlana's old country house. It seemed to Olga that Joseph had a very comfortable life, with everything he needed, including a driver at his disposal, yet they all looked at her as if she were the one wearing the designer labels. Even as a thirteen-year-old, Olga was shocked by how much they drank. Looking back, she would reflect, "Joseph had a drinking problem, a bad liver. When we visited, we understood why: the rich greasy food, the endless vodka, just pouring shots of vodka. He had yellow eyeballs and looked a lot older than he should have for a man his age."

Svetlana was hardly placating. She confronted Joseph about his drinking, and he responded angrily. Her suggestion to Lyuda that she call her "Mama" was met frostily. When Svetlana asked Joseph to drop by the hotel—she needed to talk with him on his own—he found excuses. When he asked her for money, she gave him what she had but asked him why he needed it and he yelled at her. "Well, I have not come to hear this," she said. She was not yet willing to imagine that her son might still carry deep resentments as a consequence of her abandonment of him and his sister. She concluded only that he had been Sovietized in the intervening years.

Svetlana phoned Joseph's first wife, Elena, now remarried, and asked if her grandson Ilya could visit them. Elena replied that her son was applying to the School of Architecture and had to study. She may have felt it was still too risky for him to visit Svetlana, and after all, what did she owe her ex-mother-in-law, who had left behind her own children?

Svetlana had been hoping Katya might visit from Kamchatka. Although it was a long distance to travel, they hadn't seen each other in seventeen years. Svetlana understood that Katya was now widowed. Her husband had shot himself with a rifle, reportedly by accident. When Katya finally wrote back, her letter was cold and abusive. She called Svetlana a traitor to the motherland and refused to see her or to allow her to see her granddaughter.

All the family relations were dissolving. It was November, and Svetlana felt she was doomed and drowning.

Svetlana visited Stepan Mikoyan and his wife, Ella, who had always been kind to her, and Olga spent time with her four uncles. Svetlana still called them the Alliluyev boys—Anna's and Pavel's sons, with whom she had once played in the yurts in Zubalovo and driven through the darkened streets of Moscow behind her father's back. These were enjoyable reunions, but Olga was finding that "Moscow was the craziest, darkest place and the coldest place I'd ever been. It was really terrifying." Shopping was a shock for a young American teenager. "In some stores, the people were killing each other just to get an egg. And then in the government stores they fought over some kind of designer perfume. I saw racism and sexism."

Olga's uncles tried to entertain her with movies, as there was a cinema in her complex. "I saw lots of Russian films that were dubbed in English, and lots of English films with subtitles. My favorites were *Gandhi* and *Faraway Pavilions*, which was a series about Englishmen living in India. I just remember thinking how wonderful India was, but then having to deal with the Russian dubbed commentary about Indian 'savages.'"[31]

One day at seven a.m., Svetlana and Olga showed up unannounced at Lily Golden's door. Lily's daughter Yelena awoke her mother to say a strange woman named Svetlana was asking to see her. In her half sleep, Lily said, "What Svetlana? There are many Svetlanas." When Yelena returned to say it was Svetlana Alliluyeva, Lily immediately told Yelena to get dressed and leave for work and never to mention to anybody that Svetlana had visited. Clearly she felt it was still dangerous to be connected to Svetlana in any way. On Yelena's return late that night, Lily refused to speak to her daughter about the encounter.[32]

It seemed that Lily didn't give vent to her anger at Svetlana's portrayal of her in *Only One Year*, but instead chose to be kind for Olga's sake. Probably she warned Svetlana that Olga would never be accepted in Russia. She would always be either a trophy or a pariah and would never be allowed to be herself. Olga recalled: "When I met Lily, I just remember wanting to cling onto her every word. I just wanted her to stay. I just wanted her to be around all the time."[33]

Svetlana was beginning to understand that she had made a terrible mistake in returning to Moscow, and she found a confidant for her anxious reflections in Alexander Burdonsky, the son of her brother Vasili. When she had last seen him, he was an adolescent. Now he was a well-known theater director in Moscow. Olga, too, recalled him warmly and always delighted in the "great story" of their first meeting:

Uncle Sacha was surrounded by Gypsies. He was directing a musical in a Gypsy theater and we had gone to see the performance. There were lots of other children—we went back to his apartment and there was a big party and there was lots of drinking. I mean, poor mother. Everybody was passed out, and there was no place for lots of us to sleep, so I went home with the Gypsies. Two hours' drive clear across Moscow. And Mom woke up the next morning to be told that I'd been taken by the Gypsies! I spent the night in a very, very small apartment in one bed with an entire family of Gypsies.[34]

Burdonsky's childhood had fractured when Vasili divorced his mother and took custody of the children. He and his sister were often simply locked in a room, left hungry and living in filth and squalor, and frequently beaten by their new stepmother, Katya Timoshenko, while she and Vasili pursued the high life of parties with their retinue of Olympic athletes, racing car drivers, and ace fliers. When he was eventually sent to the tough Suvorov military school, it felt to him like liberation. After putting up with whispers behind his back—"Look. Stalin's grandson!"—he had assumed his mother's last name.[35]

Burdonsky admired Svetlana. "I always liked her household—at the dacha or in Moscow. I learned to have good taste from her. No excess. I remember her excellent library with photographs of Ulanova,[36] Chaliapin, and Akhmatova. It's strange what stays with you as a child." He used to watch, with longing, her tender relationship with her nanny.

I admired her as a woman and as a human being. I cannot say that of all my relatives. I loved her very much. Of course she was difficult. She was a personality, with charisma. . . . I have compassion for her, and it seems, at times, that I understand her very well. Each one of her actions, seemingly unexpected and spontaneous—to me they are understandable. I hold her in my heart. I am always on her side.[37]

Burdonsky and Svetlana had long conversations sitting and smoking through the nights in his apartment or walking his dog Lialka through the dark Moscow streets. Perhaps only he, as a Russian, could understand what no American could—that in abandoning Russia in 1967 she had pulled up her "*whole root system.*" She had had to leave behind not only her children, not just the landscapes and streets, but all the people with whom she was spiritually connected.

Svetlana was able to talk with Burdonsky about her children. She confessed to feeling enormous guilt at abandoning them, but she could not understand why Joseph, in particular, had so categorically rejected her. To Burdonsky, it was not puzzling. "They had not seen each other for almost twenty years. The boy she had left behind was now a different man and she really did not like what he had become." Joseph had a comfortable life as a surgeon with all the amenities this entailed. He was inside the system of security that the elite enjoyed. Burdonsky felt that Joseph "was very dependent on his wife—a woman of little charm. He was very much under her pragmatic, mercantile influence." He understood that Joseph's wife was offended; Svetlana, a rich woman, hadn't even brought them decent presents.

Burdonsky thought that Svetlana had never been "the type of tender, fussy mother—a hen with her chicks." In fact, she was like her own mother. "In our family they always said that Nadya, my grandmother, was not a tender, soft person. She was also a dry person: you could talk with Stalin in a casual manner, but not with her." Svetlana, too, was strict, but she loved her children. "I was on her side and not on the side of her children. I would never behave this way, no matter what my mother did, whom I loved madly."

He remembered her children's reaction when she had abandoned them.

They were still quite young. And they were people who were not used to public revelation and public attention. And they were literally attacked on a mass scale. They felt confusion. Extreme bewilderment. Svetlana understood well—she was a very intelligent woman—that while all of this was at the center of the world's attention, nothing would happen to the children. I mean Joseph and Katerina. Their fathers, after all, stood behind them. Behind Joseph stood Grisha [Grigori] Morozov; and behind Katya, Yuri Zhdanov: fathers who had different attitudes to Svetlana, who had different attitudes toward her departure, and who had different attitudes toward their children. Even though she was a young girl, Katya always was and remained a person with her own views on human relationship, on the world and its events. She was also a little personality. And she did not forgive Svetlana. She perceived it as a betrayal—not of motherland or the flag—but as a betrayal, that her mother betrayed her. She had a closer relationship with her mother than Osia. And Osia, because of his character, he could have forgiven Svetlana everything if she had taken him with her. And Katya, if she were there with her mother, she would not have let her stay. They were absolutely different kids.

Burdonsky and Svetlana talked of Stalin, particularly about his death. Svetlana recalled Stalin's last gesture, which still haunted her—that fist rising in defiance. "It was rage, a raging rejection of death. His soul had finally fractured." She recalled how, toward the end, her father had asked her to visit. "You know, I came there and by the second day I was going mad. It was very difficult to communicate with him because he always had an internal dialogue. It was not possible to get inside that conversation." And she said, "For me it was torture. And he saw this and said, 'Leave. I can see that you are suffering. Leave!'"

Sixty years later, when Burdonsky visited Stalin's dacha with a filmmaker, he was frightened by the loneliness Stalin's rooms exuded. "Power robs a person emotionally, sucks absolutely all the juices out of you. It's never ending. The man of power alone on a cold mountain peak. Svetlana knew this."

Burdonsky understood that Svetlana's attitude toward her father continually changed. "At times one attitude would prevail —a sort of love, yes, but at another, on the contrary, she completely rejected him." Anyone trying to fathom her attitude had to understand its complexity.

Stalin became a kind of sinkhole, a myth, a sort of gutter where everything is drained. His whole identity— contradictory and difficult—became almost invisible in all this. Just a silhouette. Svetlana knew so much truth about him, even in comparison to all of us, not to mention in comparison to those writing about him. Legends attached to his name. This evoked rage in her. I think that some form of explosion—explosions of rage—were characteristic of her. I think this was because of a sense of internal helplessness. Of helplessness to have any effect or influence.

Burdonsky had thought long and hard about his aunt Svetlana.

She was a mixture of traits that do not mix. She had some sort of ceaseless femininity. Simultaneously she had an unbendable will, even maybe a touch of dryness. Svetlana's sharpened feeling of loneliness, her reclusiveness (and she was a very closed-in person) originates from her childhood, of course. The harshness and dryness were natural to her also; they were a form of defensive veil.

Burdonsky believed that his father, Vasili, had been weak. He was "a product of the people, the freeloaders and leeches, who surrounded him." But Svetlana was her father's daughter. She had his "organized intelligence," his "unbelievable will." But she did not have his evil.

It is easy to accuse everyone. The most difficult thing is to place yourself in Svetlana's place. Not one of us has been in that place. And no one knows what it is like. I can only say one thing. . . . Princesses or daughters of some leaders . . . all of their attempts to be more human, to simply be a woman, to simply be a mother, to simply be a citizen—they are all doomed. They are all doomed. There are no desert islands. They will be reached and found everywhere. Her fate is so interesting . . . just on its own it is so interesting—her whole path, her whole search for some spiritual shelter, which she could never find. . . . I understood that she would never find it, even though she thought she would. She is one of the most tragic figures that I know—tragic figures. And fate treated her very cruelly. And unjustly.[38]

But perhaps Svetlana herself is most succinct in describing the tragedy of her life. "You are Stalin's daughter. Actually you are already dead. Your life is already finished. You can't live your own life. You can't live any life. You exist only in reference to a name."[39]

Faced with the disaster of her return to Moscow, Svetlana knew she had to run again. But where could she take Olga now? She thought of Tbilisi, which she had visited only once long ago when she had gone there with Vasili and her half brother, Yakov, to meet Stalin's mother. In her memory Georgia was something like Greece—warm, fertile, foreign.

She wrote to the government asking permission to move to

a remoter part of the Soviet Union, away from attacks by the Western press. She promised to cooperate with the local authorities in Tbilisi and to refrain from speaking to the foreign press or being too visible. She knew how to write this kind of letter and was ready to promise almost anything to get out of Moscow. She was sure life in Georgia would be independent (at least to a degree) from the center, because Georgia existed on the borderland between the Asian and Russian worlds.

Chapter 32

Tbilisi Interlude

In this photograph from 1986, Soviet Politburo members vote during a session. *Front row, left to right:* Premier Nikolai Ryzhkov, Andrei Gromyko, and Soviet leader Mikhail Gorbachev. *Middle row, left to right:* Vitaly Vorotnikov, Lev Zaikov, and Mikhail Solomentsev. *Top row:* Moscow Party boss Boris Yeltsin (*left*) and Foreign Minister Eduard Shevardnadze.

On December 1, 1984, Svetlana and Olga left for Georgia. They had been in Moscow only slightly more than a month. The peaks and valleys of the Caucasian Ridge gleamed white with snow as they flew over what Svetlana remembered as a tropical landscape. It was winter in Tbilisi and cold, though not as cold as Moscow. At the airport, officials again met them, but the Georgians seemed more casual. Mother and daughter were driven to a modern state residence and assigned a two-bedroom apartment at the far end of Chavchavadze Prospect on the edge of the city.

In Olga's young eyes, it was a "palace" where the important people stayed. She remembered it as feeling like a kind of compound; the grounds included a farm with reindeer, which she took to visiting every day. She and her mother were housed in the main building with glass doors and marble floors; the complex had its own cinema. They ate in the grandiose dining room and had a cleaning staff and a driver whom they could call on. All Party members and visiting dignitaries had chauffeurs. Their driver, Jora, turned out to be a wonderful guide to Georgia.[1]

At Svetlana's insistence, they were moved to a smaller, unfurnished apartment in the complex. She and Olga hunted through the local shops and markets, filling the apartment with Georgian crafts and artifacts, which made the place feel better, but they soon found themselves listening to speeches in the dining hall. Svetlana would later complain that the then–Party boss Eduard Shevardnadze had orchestrated all this, placing them on the edge of the city precisely so that they would need a driver who could report on their activities. It was the same VIP treatment as in Moscow, but at least here things were less ostentatious.

For Olga it was dumbfounding.

I was showered with pretty much anything and everything—but it was just so unreal. I was brought friends to play with whose parents were accepted Party members. Everybody was trying to do anything to keep me happy. If I got sick, we'd go to the doctors. There would be a line of people. I'd get shoveled to the front. And always stared at. Everywhere I went, I had a chauffeur who was consequently also a chaperone. I wanted to ride a horse—I loved horseback riding. The next thing I knew, I had a personal trainer and was training for racing. I wanted to swim. No, I couldn't just go swimming. I was trained by an Olympic champion. I wanted to play piano—they'd send a concert pianist. I liked to draw. I was suddenly going to the best art institute. I was thirteen years old! It seemed people didn't have hobbies there. You trained to do something for life.[2]

Olga had private teachers of Russian and Georgian, and lessons in math and geography; she attended the Riding School with her instructor, Zurab, and went for her art classes. Life found a kind of rhythm. She formed a tight bond with the family of her Georgian teacher, Londa Gedevanishvili. She and her mother often visited this family, feeling accepted for themselves and not for their genealogy. Olga called the Gedevanishvilis' affection a particular kind of Georgian love: Londa kept sending them roses and fruit, which they would find at their apartment door.

Svetlana decided one morning to phone a distant relative of the Alliluyev family, Leila Sikmashvili, to ask if she would give Olga music and voice lessons. Leila was a talented musician and actress who had traveled internationally with theater groups playing from London to Australia.[3] When Leila's phone rang and the voice on the other end introduced herself as Svetlana Alliluyeva, Leila thought it was a prank and hung up.[4] Svetlana called again and insisted she really was Svetlana Alliluyeva. Soon Leila was coming twice a week to teach Olga popular Georgian songs. Her Georgian friends took to calling her Oliko and claimed her as one of theirs. Hating the propaganda coming out of Moscow, the teenagers listened raptly to Olga's stories of life in America.

Meanwhile, Svetlana felt like a ghost walking in the streets of Tbilisi. People stared in shocked surprise, both those who worshipped Stalin as the favorite son of Georgia and those who had been victims of his crimes. In fact, Svetlana was often quite lonely. Many people, ingrained with the habit of fear and certain she was under the scrutiny of the KGB, avoided her. Offered the job of teaching Olga piano, the young pianist Tamara Dovgan turned it down. The job came with strings: "I am sure everyone had to report on Svetlana." She felt pity for Svetlana, but friends advised her to keep her distance.[5]

Svetlana and Olga spent their free time scouring the alleyways and streets of Tbilisi, an exquisite city that dates back to the fifth century and was built at a crossroad between Europe and Asia. Some of its streets were still lined with the palaces of nobility exiled under the tsars, and there were market bazaars and souks overflowing with exotic fruits and Georgian crafts. They often passed the seminary where Stalin had studied until he dropped out at the age of twenty to begin his revolutionary career. The seminary was now closed.

Most Sundays Svetlana and Olga attended services at the Sioni Cathedral overlooking the Mtkvari River. Both were enchanted by the exquisite quality of the Georgian choir intoning the liturgy. Only here, it seemed to Svetlana, could people escape the grinding poverty and fearful repression that still pervaded Georgia. Only here did she feel anonymous and at peace. Of course, this was an illusion. Even at the Sioni, people knew who she was. When she sought a private audience with the patriarch, he was comforting. He told her, "You should write to your own children only words of love. Nothing else. They have forgotten what is love and forgiveness. Never blame them; never argue with them. Just tell them how much you love them."[6]

Svetlana kept writing to her daughter Katya, who had said, "No contact whatsoever." All her letters came back. Katya's father, Yuri Zhdanov, by now a professor of biochemistry at the university in Rostov, wrote a kind letter and sent pictures of Katya and her daughter, telling Svetlana to be patient. "Katya is incredibly self-sufficient and independent. Listens to no one's advice."[7] Neither her son nor her grandson wrote or visited. Svetlana decided the authorities had brainwashed her children.

Chauffeured by Jora, Svetlana and Olga would drive into the countryside as Svetlana tried to recover her Georgian roots. They visited the town of Gori, her father's birthplace, where a monstrous shrine with Corinthian columns covered the humble two-room house with the one bed on which the Djugashvili family slept. There was no fireplace; cooking was done in a small pot on a *karasinka* (kerosene burner). Olga was appalled by the misery of it all.

Nearby stood an equally monstrous two-story museum with marble entrance and rising staircase that now traced the history of Stalin's glory. Svetlana detested the display and instead looked for mementos of her paternal grandmother. The only reminder of Stalin's mother was a pair of her glasses. Though Svetlana had met her grandmother only once, she loved her for those last words to her son which had so amused him: "But what a pity you never became a priest." They also visited the local school where Stalin began to study Russian. Svetlana told Olga her father's Russian was quite good, though he never fully lost his Georgian accent. Svetlana had refused the invitation from the museum's chief curator, Nina Ameridzhibe, to attend the ceremony marking the 105th anniversary of Stalin's birth that December 21, just after they'd arrived. Ameridzhibe claimed that one million people visited the museum in 1984, breaking all previous records.[8]

Still, whenever they went to a museum or even the church, people stared. Olga was young and resilient, but for Svetlana it was gut-wrenching.

My greatest burden lay in the need of everyone to tell me "what a great man" my father was: some accompanied the words with tears, others with hugs and kisses, a few were satisfied with only stating that fact. I could not avoid the subject or the confrontations on beaches, in dining rooms, on the street. . . . They were obsessed with his name, his image, and, being obsessed, they could not leave me alone. It was a torture for me. I could not tell them how complex were my thoughts about my father and my relationship with him. Nor could I tell them what they wanted to hear—so they departed from me in anger. I was continually on edge and nervous.[9]

Olga was angry at her mother's mourning over Joseph. "You had me," she would say. "Was that not enough for you? No! You wanted them all too. See what you've got! We should be living in England like we were. You asked for this!"[10]

There were many things Olga loved about Georgia and the friends she made, but there were "a lot of hardships." For one, her mother was drinking too much, and so was she. They would be invited to Georgian feasts that still followed the tradition of the *tamada* (toastmaster) proposing continuous toasts. "I was fourteen! In Georgia, there were endless dinners with four bottles of wine and you had to give toasts in a ram's horn! Including the children. You couldn't not toast."

Even more disturbing was the problem Olga was having with male attention. She had discovered that foreign girls were considered loose by Georgian standards, and already so tall and lovely, she was fair game. "I was always getting groped by older men. It was horrible, and if I was ever left alone . . . I just couldn't stand being left alone. . . . I don't think I'd even thought about boys yet." And there was another problem. At fourteen, Olga was of marriageable age.

In Tbilisi, they had a tradition: it was not unknown for a girl to be kidnapped. If you'd been out of your house, in another building with a man overnight, you had to marry him. Otherwise you were shunned from society. It happened to a fourteen-year-old girl I knew. It was terrifying. And I was a pretty good bachelorette. Kidnapping Stalin's granddaughter would have been quite a prize! It was a risk.

And then there was just the whole dark side to it, the whole behind the Curtain Communist side. I was living this weird sheltered, secluded life with about four different governesses coming every day. My mother stopped me from going out, trying to protect me from getting kidnapped. And what was she going to do? She couldn't write. We were fighting a lot. I was really fiery. I just had a feeling of despair and was not able to plan a future. This is what we're going to be doing for the rest of our lives! Of course it was wonderful going to the ballet, and seeing friends. And there were many good days. But I was playing it, as if I were this shallow social butterfly who could find herself happy in any situation.[11]

Friends from Moscow visited. Stepan Mikoyan, who was with a Soviet Air Force group that was touring all the capitals of southern Russia to publicize aviation, stopped two days in Tbilisi and had dinner with Svetlana and Olga. To him, Svetlana seemed completely alone. "Maybe she was just conscious of a certain estrangement and isolation; quite a lot of people were feeling hostility towards her. The Stalinists hated her for having 'betrayed' her father, and the anti-Stalinists disliked her for being his daughter."[12]

Svetlana invited her cousin Kyra, the daughter of Pavel and Zhenya Alliluyev, to come to Tbilisi for an extended visit. Like the rest of the family, Kyra was able to separate Svetlana from her memories of her incarceration and five years of exile under Stalin.

She and Svetlana had been very close as children. They shared memories of parties in the Kremlin. "The time passed joyously. . . . Grandpa [Sergei] was not very jolly, but grandma [Olga] would pick up a guitar and sing."[13] Kyra remembered how she and Svetlana watched movies, especially the American ones with Deanna Durbin. When Kyra stayed overnight, she would sleep in Svetlana's room. After nanny Alexandra Andreevna left, Svetlana "would ask me to dance. She would sit on the bed and I would dance to Strauss on the gramophone. Svetlana was a very nice girl."[14]

Svetlana thought the ebullient Kyra's adventures as an actress would entertain Olga. The visit went well at first, but soon degenerated into hostility. Kyra complained that Svetlana seemed displeased with everything and Olga was "spoiled and whimsical" and said, "It was hard to be with them both."[15] Kyra's brother Alexander noted that Svetlana and Kyra were both strong characters, both volatile, and they fought a lot. He wasn't surprised when Kyra returned to Moscow.

Back in England and in America, Svetlana and Olga had not been forgotten. In Cambridge, Vera Traill had taken it upon herself to rescue Olga from her mother. She wrote to Sir Isaiah Berlin. "I'm hyper-active about Olga." She had found Svetlana's address in Tbilisi through an old friend and was looking for anybody going to Georgia who might search Svetlana and Olga down. "It must be somebody with perfect Russian (i.e., an émigré), intelligent and discreet," she said. She had found a couple going to Tbilisi, but they were hopelessly naive. "They will return with nothing or be expelled as spies."

Apparently Traill was in contact with Wesley Peters. She told Berlin:

William Wesley Peters (he always signs with both names in full) asked for Olga's address, applied for a visa, was refused both & now is sitting back in despair. He *could* do more, of course—at the very least insist on regular contact by post or telephone—and I keep prodding him, but what holds him back, I think, is that he is uncertain of his welcome. He feels he did not do enough for Olga & feels guilty; also, apparently he saw a letter written by O. from Cambridge, which contained a "hostile reference" to him.

Traill reported that she then wrote to Friends' School. "Explaining that I want to encourage Wes Peters to more effort, I said I wd be grateful if they could ask O.'s friends if she had ever said nice things about her dad." She found the school's reply "monstrous" and sent it on to Berlin. "You'll have to pinch yourself at every par. . . . False, pompous, utterly irrelevant. I feel both bewildered and sick. I thought quakers were do-gooders, they've been known to help in famines & plagues. Why suddenly this frantic fear of 'getting involved'?" Berlin disappointed Traill. She was irate when he too refused to get involved.[16]

But people who genuinely cared about Svetlana were worried. Joan Kennan had somehow found Svetlana's address in Tbilisi, probably through her father. Certainly the CIA would have known it. Svetlana was overjoyed to get her letter and sent back photographs of Olga, lamenting, "My Katya did not want to see me (us) even once! And I thought all these years that they were missing me badly. What blindness."[17]

Rosa Shand had also managed to get Svetlana's address, probably through Utya Djaparidze, her Georgian friend in New York, and wrote to her. Svetlana wrote back to say she and Olga were fine. Olga had learned to speak Georgian and Russian in a remarkably short time. "She makes everyone here so happy when she speaks their tongue."[18] Rosa wrote back:

> Your pilgrimage has been a courageous one, and you go
> on probing, & I trust you will somehow make sense of it

all as your beloved Dostoyevsky did. . . . I love you. I wear that coral necklace that reminds me of your extraordinary generosity. And I send my love to Olga.[19]

The truth was, Svetlana was not finding it easy to make sense of her pilgrimage, and Rosa, underneath her reassurances, was genuinely anxious. Utya Djaparidze wrote to Rosa giving her a clear idea of Svetlana's isolation. Utya had heard from friends of her brother in Tbilisi that he often saw Svetlana and Olga. Utya feared Svetlana was "a dangerous acquaintance for him."[20] He'd spent fifteen years in the camps and his family was still blacklisted.

Underneath her bravado, Svetlana was, in fact, desperately seeking a way out of the USSR. She now realized that Olga wouldn't be able to live in Georgia or anywhere in Russia. She had brought her daughter here, and this fiasco was all her fault. Luckily for Svetlana, things were changing in Moscow. The ailing Chernenko had finally died, and in March 1985, Mikhail Gorbachev had come to power. He was rumored to be a liberal, but Svetlana saw him acting cautiously, still hemmed in by the hard-line Communists he'd inherited from his predecessors. His first reform was a severe clampdown on the consumption of vodka. In December 1985, Svetlana took her courage in hand and wrote to Gorbachev asking permission to leave. They'd been in the USSR one year. She received no reply.

In February she slipped away, leaving Olga on her own in Tbilisi, and took the train to Moscow. She'd made this trip from north to south by train every summer of her childhood— the railway cars with their sleeping berths hadn't changed a bit. But this time the trip was a kind of torture as she contemplated her renewed entrapment. Would she and Olga ever be allowed out of their golden cage? She used her two days on the train to organize the rhetoric she would need to argue with Party officials. She could not afford any missteps, any impulsive words this time.

She stayed with her cousin Vladimir at his home on Gorky Street, much to the rage of Joseph's wife, who phoned demanding to know how he could let that woman stay with his family.[21] On February 25, the day of the Twenty-Seventh Congress of the Soviet Party (the first congress presided over by Mikhail Gorbachev as general secretary), Svetlana headed to the American Embassy. She was now a Soviet citizen, and no Soviet citizen could enter a foreign embassy. She was stopped and taken away by Soviet militiamen. Later that afternoon, two Foreign Ministry officials met with her to discuss her situation. Clearly Svetlana's letters to Gorbachev had reached the top of the echelon. She was informed, "Your daughter can return to her school in England . . . as a Soviet citizen of course, and she will return here to you for her vacations."[22] Svetlana was advised to move back to Moscow to live.

Two days later, back in Tbilisi, Svetlana managed to phone the headmaster of Friends' School to say that Olga would be returning to school. He replied that the school would be delighted to welcome her back. It would be best if she returned by April 16, in time for the beginning of the spring term. Shocked to have gotten through to England on her own phone—the line must have been opened, though she assumed it was monitored—Svetlana called Sam Hayakawa in San Francisco to say that Olga had been given permission to leave. She urged him to get the information into the news so that the Soviets would not be able to back down. She begged him to let the US Embassy in Moscow know that she, too, wanted to return, but her American passport had been confiscated. "You can't imagine what I've gotten myself into!" she lamented. Hayakawa had recently been elected to the US Senate. He reassured her. "It's OK. All will be well."[23]

Olga now had permission to leave, but Svetlana must have been terrified that she herself would be trapped in Moscow and separated from her daughter. Could she lose a third child? She wrote to Gorbachev again, this time including a formal petition to the Supreme Soviet asking to renounce her Soviet citizenship.

Svetlana made it back to Tbilisi in time to celebrate her sixtieth birthday. A few friends prepared a Georgian feast for her and sang to the accompaniment of their guitars. She told them nothing of her plans. Why make them "accomplices"? She recalled the night with fondness: "duets, trios, an endless sequence of traditional melodic songs about love, death, separation and longing, beautiful eyes, and love for the motherland . . . endless, captivating beauty, melancholy old melodies and tunes streaming one after the other like a murmuring brook."[24] She watched Olga sing, accompanying herself on the piano. It was beautiful and sad. She cried and felt grateful for the generosity of these Georgians, who had extended her and her daughter such warm friendship. And for that single moment the weight of her anxieties lifted.

While Svetlana was in Moscow, Olga managed to acquire a little Pekinese puppy, which she named Maka. Svetlana also discovered that her daughter, who would turn fifteen in May, had developed a girlhood crush on an older man. She was worried. Would this be a complicating entanglement? They had to leave immediately. She knew she had to handle Olga carefully. She told her they would soon be going on a trip to Moscow, but not to worry, they'd be back for visits.

On March 20, the night before they were to fly out of Tbilisi, under the unbearable stress of wondering if she would be abandoned alone in Moscow, Svetlana suffered what appeared to be a heart attack. That Thursday evening, she went to bed feeling pains in her chest and left arm and could hardly breathe. She woke Olga and asked her to fetch a doctor. How could this be happening just as she was preparing their escape! Olga was terrified as she watched her mother turning blue. She thought Svetlana was dying.

At the Tbilisi hospital, doctors determined that Svetlana had had not a heart attack but rather a cardiovascular spasm caused by stress. She was ordered to remain in the hospital for two weeks for a thorough checkup. Svetlana was immediately suspicious. Why two weeks and why now? When the acquaintance of a friend connected to the hospital assured her that her condition did not require a lengthy hospital stay, she concluded that these orders came from Moscow. The authorities were trying to prevent her from leaving Georgia.[25]

She was right, of course, in believing that Moscow knew her every move. Indeed, the very night of her hospitalization, the Politburo was discussing her fate. A top secret document, dated March 20, 1986, recorded the minutes of the meeting chaired by Mikhail Gorbachev with at least fifteen other Party officials in attendance, including comrades Andrei Gromyko and Yegor Ligachev.

Among the topics on the agenda were the war in Afghanistan (they discussed the psychological state of the leaders) and a telegram from Aden—the USSR was then Yemen's main backer—requesting permission "to execute 50 people." This was disapproved on the grounds that "these sorts of actions may exacerbate internal conflict." There followed a discussion about naming an icebreaker after Brezhnev. This was agreed to, but the icebreaker would be put in the water without any public fuss. Brezhnev's was not a popular name in these shaky times.

Then Comrade Gorbachev said, "There's one other thing," and read Svetlana Alliluyeva's letter to the men at the table. Comrade Viktor Chebrikov, chairman of the Committee for State Security (the KGB), remarked, "The first letters were good, there was gratitude. It seems there were about 50% of the problems that she didn't even mention. Tonight they drove her to the hospital [in Tbilisi] with a heart attack."

Gorbachev responded, "We need to figure out the opinion of her daughter and meet on a personal level." He didn't want to meet Svetlana himself. "If I go, I'll have to comment on Stalin, Stalingrad, and all that." His family still bore the scars of Stalingrad. After some discussion, it was decided that Comrade Ligachev would meet with her.[26]

Svetlana was right in assuming that the secret police were keeping tabs on her, but her anxiety that the government was trying to control her was paranoid. In fact it didn't know what to do with her. Sadly, this was when her son, Joseph, chose to phone her. He didn't get a chance to offer his commiseration. She was irate. Why was he calling now? He hadn't bothered to call in *fifteen months*. He might at least have called Olga. Had he such close ties to the authorities that he knew immediately that she was in the hospital? She asked him brutally, "What is it? Do you intend to bury me soon? It's not time yet."[27] They both hung up.

She was sure the authorities were going to try to use her son to stop her from leaving. Possibly she had spent too much time in the Soviet Union. The habits of suspicion were so deeply ingrained in her, as they were in her fellow citizens, that nothing could be taken at face value. There was always a subtext.

In fact, the authorities were now thinking it would be a good idea to get her out of the country. As her cousin Leonid Alliluyev remarked, "Svetlana was a bomb: Stalin, her defection. There were already so many governmental problems that they wanted to get rid of her."[28] Svetlana's only thought was how to get out of the hospital before someone "poisoned" her. She simply walked out of the hospital that Sunday when no doctors were around and took the trolley home.

Her and Olga's departure would be one more silent leave-taking. Not a soul in Tbilisi realized it would be permanent. The only one who knew was the ghost of Svetlana's grandmother. Before they left, Svetlana visited the grave of Stalin's mother, Keke, in the small cemetery on Saint David's hill above Tbilisi, asking herself, "My illiterate, hard-working Grandmother managed to live a decent, honest life to her very end. Why is it that I cannot find my own right way?" She thought of the words of her old lover, David Samoilov: "Remember your brother, Alenushka! And never, never come back."[29] But she feared the future.

When Olga's piano teacher, Leila Sikmashvili, later found out they were not returning, she never forgave Svetlana. Looking back, she would say that one of the great regrets of her life was that she should have abducted Olga. Olga could have married that boyfriend—the man never stopped loving her—and she might have had a happy life in Georgia as the mother of six children.[30] The disconnect between a Georgian and an American version of happiness could not have been clearer. When Olga learned she would be returning to Friends' School, she was over the moon.

Svetlana and Olga, carrying Maka, flew to Moscow on March 27. They left behind most of their personal belongings: books, papers, heirlooms. Leaving things behind never bothered Svetlana. As Olga put it, "She was always leaving things all over the globe."[31] It was as if Svetlana refused to carry her history with her. But Olga put her foot down. They were not leaving Maka behind.

They checked into the Hotel Sovietsky. They had a much smaller room this time because Svetlana was paying for it. Olga received a Soviet passport with an exit and entry visa (the special document necessary for travel abroad), which they had requisitioned in Georgia. She would be allowed to travel to England as a Soviet schoolgirl. Svetlana still had no such document. Nothing about her leaving the USSR had been cleared up. They ended up staying in Moscow for twenty nerve-racking days, waiting to hear.

Svetlana spent many late nights walking in the Moscow streets with her nephew Alexander Burdonsky. One night she turned to him and said, "You want to ask me why I intend to leave?" "Yes," he replied. "Can you understand this feeling? I walk around Moscow. . . . There is no one here. Just crosses. Crosses everywhere . . . crosses, crosses, crosses."

He understood she was saying that the "milieu of people who were close and interesting to her were no longer around. None of the people about whom she was nostalgic existed anymore." He would reflect only later that she had

> needed to come here in order to say good-bye to all of this forever. It was necessary to come back to understand that little has changed—in the psychology of the authorities primarily—nothing has changed. And when once again she was offered to live here, to be given an apartment, to be given this, to be given that, to be given a dacha—to once again be settled like a wolf amongst the red flags. All of this for the second time—her whole being categorically and with rage rejected this.[32]

Burdonsky also realized that Svetlana had to leave the USSR in order to protect Olga. He found Olga "delightful, a completely wild creature, with a character that she'd inherited from Svetlana." Under her quiet surface, Svetlana had always been a rebel in a world where rebellion was unthinkable. "No matter how much pressure she received, she was still a disobedient creature. And Olya [Olga] was also a disobedient creature. Like her mother." Burdonsky knew Olga could never survive in the repressive Soviet system. "Of course there was conflict; they were so much alike, but it was clear they loved each other very much."

Ironically, it was Svetlana's old enemy Victor Louis, who had tried to sell her *Twenty Letters to a Friend* in a pirated edition in 1967, who advised the international press that Svetlana was in Moscow seeking permission to leave. He reported it was unlikely that the Soviet authorities would grant her exit papers, although they would probably give them to Olga. "You just can't change your citizenship every few months," he said. "She cannot simply go to the airport and leave. She has to go through the bureaucracy." He added, "It might be embarrassing to them to let her go."[33]

One day a well-dressed, efficient, cheerful young woman from the American Embassy slipped into the Hotel Sovietsky under the pretext that she was visiting another delegation (a visit to a Soviet citizen by an American Embassy official was absolutely forbidden), and knocked on Svetlana's door. Olga hadn't seen an American in a very long time and began to cry on the spot.[34] Svetlana always encouraged her daughter to stand up for herself. When someone asked a question about what Olga thought, Svetlana would say, "Ask her!" Now the American Embassy official asked Olga if she wanted to return to England. Thoughts of a boyfriend waiting in Tbilisi vanished like smoke. "Yes," Olga said, speaking as eloquently and diplomatically as she could. When the woman returned in a week, she opened her briefcase and pulled out two American passports, one for Olga and one for Svetlana. Svetlana believed Senator Hayakawa had used his influence with George Shultz, then US secretary of state under Ronald Reagan, and pulled strings.[35]

On April 3, Svetlana got a phone call from a Foreign Ministry official, who said, "You may leave with your American passport if you do not want to wait until the cancelation of your Soviet citizenship. This will take some time."[36] On April 5, Comrade Ligachev invited her for a talk. A driver took her to Staraya

Ploshchad (Old Square) and the offices of the Central Committee. The corridor with its Kremlin-style carpet runner looked and smelled exactly the same as it had on the day she had met Comrade Suslov to ask permission to register her marriage to Brajesh Singh. She felt she was in a bad movie, a rerun in which the opening and closing scenes were implausibly repeated.

As a secretary sat nearby recording their conversation in shorthand, Ligachev dismissed her. "The Motherland will survive without you. The question is: Will you survive without the Motherland?"[37] And he added: "Behave," by which he meant, of course, no more interviews, no books. And of course Svetlana would disobey. Soviet officialdom believed books were bombs. So did she. Alas, few in the West, where she was heading back, believed books had such power.

A ticket was arranged for Svetlana through the US Embassy. She was booked to fly out the day after Olga on Swissair with a stopover in Zurich before proceeding to the United States. Svetlana and Olga spent their last days in Moscow entertained by "the Alliluyev boys." The international media were already phoning the Hotel Sovietsky. Even Olga's father, Wes, phoned. Svetlana thought, *Better late than never,* though she did wonder whether his motive for phoning was to look after Olga's welfare or to arrange his own public image before the press onslaught that was on its way. In the *Washington Post,* he was reported to have spent a year working for Olga's return. He advised Svetlana that Olga must be "circumspect" in what she said. The situation was delicate. Svetlana responded that Olga was still outspoken. Her father told the newspapers he was glad "that [Olga] wasn't crushed."[38]

Olga's uncles and her mother saw her off at Sheremetyevo Airport. It was a strange moment when she kissed her mother good-bye. She still couldn't quite believe she was leaving. She had dreamed of this moment almost every night and worried she might wake up and it wouldn't be real. "I imagine people dream—not that I want to call this experience prison—but I imagine that people do dream of getting out of prison every night." There was even a moment when she got back to England and thought, *This is a really long dream.* At the airport, Olga could see that her mother was frightened, though Svetlana tried bravely to hide her fear. "She still wasn't sure if she was going to be able to leave. Not until she actually got on the plane."

When she landed at Heathrow airport the next morning, Olga bypassed customs and was led through the diplomatic exit. She emerged to a sea of paparazzi and felt a sudden panic: she hadn't asked her mother what she was supposed to say! "That was my first whirlwind encounter with the paparazzi . . . cameras in my face. It was just huge. And it was on the news all night, and all the next day. Every news segment."[39]

A month shy of her fifteenth birthday, Olga was astonishingly poised and self-assured. It was clear to her that the press wanted her to demonize her experience. There had been sensationalized reports that the Soviets had been outraged when Olga refused to remove the cross she had worn in the USSR in defiance of "state atheist doctrine."[40] Sheer nonsense. When asked what it was like to be back, she told reporters she was looking forward to seeing her friends. Asked if she still considered herself American, she replied, "Of course." Did she regret her time in the Soviet Union? "No," she said. "It was really a great experience for anyone," adding, "The one thing I want to do is get straight back to school and do some studying."[41]

Her school friends had gotten wind of her return, but the press crush at the airport was so great, indeed frightening, and she was whisked away by the Russian officials so quickly, that they missed her. The Soviet Union still regarded Olga as a Soviet citizen going to a British boarding school. She spent the night at the Soviet Embassy and the next day was escorted to Saffron Walden. "We outran the paparazzi, as in a movie car chase. Luckily we weren't killed." That afternoon the headmaster came to her dorm and said, "Before you get back to your schoolwork, you have to give a press conference." The school assembly hall was packed with reporters and the curious. Olga remembered that, seeing them, she thought, *What a crazy, crazy aspect of my life.* "It was never so crazy before and has never been so crazy since."[42]

Svetlana was scheduled to fly out of Moscow on April 16. She made no effort to contact Joseph to say good-bye and asked her cousins not to accompany her to the airport. She believed she would never again see the "boys," now in their fifties and sixties, though they had been so kind to her; but the leave-taking would have been too emotional. Alexander Alliluyev said they acquiesced. "The situation was very tense. I am not a timid person," but if anything went wrong and the authorities refused to let her on the plane, he knew she had reached her limit. "I felt she could do something crazy."[43]

The morning of her departure, Svetlana surrendered her Soviet passport and her pension book to a representative from the Soviet Foreign Office waiting for her in the hotel lobby. He told her kindly that Olga had arrived in London safely. "Such a pleasant, smart girl," he said. A representative of the Georgian Mission drove her to the airport, where the cheerful young woman from the American Embassy escorted her directly to the Swissair plane on the tarmac because she had no exit visa in her new US passport. She was carrying Maka. When Olga insisted she take Maka, Svetlana was appalled. "Oh my God, I'm that woman. I'm traveling with a small dog!" But it turned out the Pekinese puppy was a comfort. Olga was amused to think of her mother on the plane with her little lapdog barking at everything. "Mom was the feisty lady with the feisty little dog!"[44]

The plane touched down briefly in Switzerland, so that Svetlana was now following the same route she had taken nineteen years before. But this was a very different journey. The US Embassy in Moscow had arranged her return as an American citizen, and she had chosen to go back to Wisconsin. There were no paparazzi to greet her at Chicago's O'Hare Airport. Her old friends Robert and Derry Graves drove her to Spring Green. Graves, who ran a restaurant, ski resort, and golf course next to Taliesin, had found her a small wooden farmhouse to rent. She told reporters who contacted her that she didn't want to talk about her personal life. "I will call you if I want to deny statements made about me. Otherwise, the public does not need to know where I am."[45] And she slipped again into anonymity.

Svetlana refused to harbor regrets, but she began to examine her last eighteen months in the USSR. Why had she gone? Why had her son been given permission to communicate with her that December 1982 after more than fifteen years of silence? His calls and letters were so loving; he was to meet her in Finland. Next he was in the hospital and calling for her to come. Had it all been orchestrated? After their first meeting, he'd been cold, and they hardly met again. Was it all a KGB plot to get her back?

All families are closed narratives, difficult to read from the outside. Depending on their view of Joseph, Svetlana's relatives had various opinions as to why she'd come back.

Her cousin Alexander Alliluyev didn't believe for a moment in a grand KGB plot. Joseph was a warm, very intelligent man whom he loved very much. Svetlana herself had made the impulsive decision to go to the Soviet Embassy in London in the fall of 1984 and request permission to return. And once she was under way there was no turning back.[46]

By contrast, Leonid Alliluyev and his wife, Galina, were not very fond of Joseph. Galina in particular found him a cold, cynical man, something of a snob; she remembered his many slights to her. But they too didn't believe he'd participated in any plot. In their opinion, the Soviets were as surprised as anybody when Svetlana showed up at the embassy, but of course, once she was back in Moscow, the government would have wanted to use her for propaganda purposes.[47]

But her nephew Alexander Burdonsky thought otherwise. He believed Svetlana's return had indeed been orchestrated. The plot had started quite far back when Kosygin was alive. It had been his idea. "To return her back, something in connection to Afghanistan. A distraction, perhaps, from the disastrous course of the war. I knew someone close to one of Andropov's relatives. That person told me this idea existed. As a form of a small political trick—Stalin has returned."[48] Svetlana would be Stalin resurrected at a time when the political foundations of the Soviet Union were shaky and it was necessary to rehabilitate the dictator's image to reestablish order and to bolster the credibility of the Communist Party.

Svetlana continued to assert that she had been lured back. Yes, she'd made an impulsive, disastrous decision when she'd visited the Soviet Embassy in London surreptitiously, but she'd done so because she believed her son needed her. All those letters. But he hadn't loved her at all. Once again, she'd been written into a script, lured into her role, and she'd fallen for the trick.

In an interview in 2005, Joseph himself dismissed the idea that he'd manipulated his mother. When they talked on the phone, he said, "I found myself in a tight spot. I could not simply tell her not to come. To just sit there and not rock the boat. If I'd told her that, I don't even know what would have happened. I did not, however, persuade her either. Just a couple of times I expressed the idea that people live somehow with their families and not across the ocean. Maybe this was taken as *luring*."[49]

One of the most outrageous theories came from Svetlana's old friend Andrei Sinyavsky and his wife Maria Rozanova, then living in exile in Paris. Sinyavsky told a journalist with London's *Daily Mail*, Nicholas Powell, that a Soviet agent named Oleg Bitov, working for the KGB, had engineered Svetlana's return. Rozanova maintained, "Extremely reliable sources in Germany talk about an affair between Bitov and Svetlana well before the couple re-defected." He had defected to Italy in September 1983, had sought asylum in Britain, and then, in mid-August 1984, had disappeared. The next time he was heard from, he was in Moscow.

The CIA believed the KGB had abducted him back to the USSR. To a Russian, it made more sense that he was part of a KGB plot, and the Sinyavskys were claiming that the point of the plot was to lure Svetlana Alliluyeva back to the USSR. Sinyavsky pointed out that as soon as Andropov came to power, Svetlana's son, Joseph, was allowed to phone her. And then Bitov made her his "mistress," luring her with romance. Asked if she was surprised when Svetlana redefected, Sinyavsky's wife was quoted as saying, "Princesses are always capricious. In every fairy tale."[50]

The connection between Bitov and Svetlana was entirely mythical. Years later it would be revealed that Bitov had defected but then, missing his family, had willingly returned to the Soviet Union.[51] He and Svetlana never met.

On the eve of perestroika (restructuring), with the ailing Gromyko still in power, it was easy to believe in conspiracies. George Kennan also seemed to credit the idea that there had been a KGB plot to lure Svetlana back to the USSR. In September 1987, Kennan wrote a letter to Frank C. Carlucci, assistant to the president for national security affairs, about Svetlana's current status, in which he made the offhand comment, "A few years ago, as you will recall, she returned to the Soviet Union, having been lured back there by her son, a doctor in Moscow, who, upon her arrival, at once washed his hands of her."[52] Perhaps he had picked this up from Svetlana herself or perhaps it came from his friend the journalist Patricia Blake, who continued to insist publicly that the invitation to return "was a KGB ploy, a long-term conspiracy to get her back to Russia."[53] Perhaps it was gossip, but Kennan made this remark to a very high-ranking White House official. Had he learned something from those conversations with Fritz Ermarth in 1984 when Svetlana had first returned to the Soviet Union? Ermarth was the CIA head of intelligence for the USSR and Eastern Europe and certainly had channels into the KGB. It is impossible to know.

What is clear is that nothing was ever clear in Soviet circles. But for Svetlana to actually believe, whether correctly or not, that her own son was capable of such duplicity was another excruciating betrayal.

It took her close friend Utya Djaparidze to get inside Svetlana's psyche. Djaparidze was still fearful for Svetlana. As a public figure, Svetlana was not seen as the woman she was, "a brave, utterly generous & honest woman." Instead she was "what any shabby, malicious fool of a journalist chooses to make of her." She was a shuttlecock in the Cold War game, forced by her famous name to play a political role. What people expected of her was "wholesale condemnation—in the East, of the West; in the West, of the East. It's a terrible situation."[54] Most terrible because it corrupted the one place a refugee and exile could call home: the world of family and private memory.

Chapter 33

American Reality

Svetlana and Olga together outside the Pleasant
Ridge hunting lodge in Wisconsin, 1994.

Svetlana settled into the farmhouse retreat that Robert and
Derry Graves had found for her in Spring Green. Though
everything around her spoke of Wesley Peters, who now ruled
at nearby Taliesin—Olgivanna Wright had died the previous
year—she found her isolation comforting. After the chaos of
the previous months, it was a solace to sit alone on her porch
stoop, watching the spring landscape awaken and the wild

cherry trees blanket the hillsides. She waited eagerly for the end of her daughter's school term, when Olga would be coming home for her summer holidays. Of course Svetlana was wary of how Americans would respond to her now that she was back. Expecting to be an object of recriminations, she wrote tentative letters to friends like Annelise and Joan Kennan, and Bob and Ramona Rayle, hoping she would be understood.

Raymond Anderson, a professor of journalism at the University of Wisconsin in nearby Madison, interviewed her in May 1986 for the *New York Times*. He asked the usual questions about why she had returned to the Soviet Union, and she responded bluntly that her son had been instructed to contact her. "It was really a dirty game, and quite possibly one played by the KGB." When Anderson asked her about life there, she was pleased, because she was rarely asked for her opinion about current politics. She replied that life there was hard. The country was in an economic deadlock, and even food and clothing were scarce. Mikhail Gorbachev might be sincere in his reforms, but he wasn't going deeply enough—the old dogma was still alive—and she doubted that his marshals and generals were in agreement with him. "Only time will show whether he and the others like him will overcome the monsters of bureaucracy, the army, and an outdated ideology."[1] Of course she was right in the long term. Resisting Gorbachev's efforts at perestroika, the Communist Party staged a military coup against him in August 1991. Though the coup lasted only two days, Gorbachev was forced to resign.

Svetlana insisted this would be her last interview. When Olga got home in July, she found a part-time job in a local Asian crafts shop. One morning a reporter came to the shop asking for Lana Peters. Olga and the shop owner hemmed and hawed and said yes, they knew her but no, she wasn't there. Suddenly from upstairs a figure descended with a kerchief tied around her head, carrying a mop and pail. As the washer-woman scurried through the shoppers, diligently mopping the floor, the journalist took no notice. Olga and the owner could hardly keep a straight face. It was Svetlana, offering her daughter an amusing lesson in how to avoid reporters.[2]

In the late summer of 1986, Svetlana bought a hunting lodge on a five-acre property deeper in the woods. It was about twelve miles outside Spring Green in an area known as Pleasant Ridge in Dodgeville Township. An architect had designed the lodge as a retreat with sliding glass doors opening out to the woods, isolated enough that deer came to the back door at sunset. It was a beautiful little house, the taxes were minimal, and Svetlana loved the idea that nobody could find her. Her finances were now very precarious. She had left money in an English bank for Olga, and the Hayakawas were helping so that Olga could return to the United States for vacations, but needing to earn money, Svetlana was busy reestablishing contacts with agents and publishers in an attempt to get *The Faraway Music* picked up in the United States. She also set out on a campaign to rehabilitate her reputation.

In February 1987, ten months after her return from the USSR, she sent out two form letters. The first one was addressed generally to "old friends and former Patrons." She complained about her portrayal in the US press as one who "hated America" (she was referring specifically to Patricia Blake's *Time* magazine article). "I NEVER said so. . . . Would you say a few words that . . . ON the 20th anniversary of my adopting this country as mine, . . . I do love this country BECAUSE I do LOVE my American daughter."[3]

In the second form letter, addressed simply to "Friends" and sent to about thirty people, she said she was trying to make her living as a writer, but "my books are in some kind of a vicious circle." She couldn't get her first two books reissued and no one wanted her third. She had only enough money for one more month and was asking for help in keeping her house in the woods. "It is hard for me to beg, but I must continue to write. This is my worst time I have ever met."[4]

Most of her friends were annoyed and even offended by her begging letter. In America you never asked people for money. You were meant to pull up your socks and make it on your own. But in writing her letter, Svetlana was acting on a basic Russian or Soviet assumption. Within one's circle of friends, if one was in need, it was typical to borrow money. The Russian word for *borrow* was "take," implying that the question of repayment was insignificant.[5] It was not embarrassing to ask for help.

Svetlana tried to see if she could revoke her Alliluyeva Charitable Trust, which still held $275,000 of her money. She'd spent $200,000 building the Brajesh Singh Hospital and had sustained it for twenty years. Financial reports had been sparse. Perhaps now that she was destitute, it was time for others to take over the project. But the Mercer County Superior Court determined that while she was legally permitted to reassign the beneficiaries, she could not claim any of the money for herself, because the trust was irrevocable in her lifetime. She redirected donations to the Medical Center at Princeton and the Stuart Country Day School.[6]

She looked for other sources of income. That May, she accepted an invitation to lecture on Gorbachev to history students at Mundelein College in Chicago. She summarized her assessment of Gorbachev in a letter to Philippa Hill.

He wants glasnost—openness, but <u>where are</u> the independent <u>open</u> newspapers <u>in which</u> people could vent out their opinions? There are still <u>none</u>. Unless they change and <u>undermine</u> their own one-party-regime and allow—legitimately—<u>other parties</u>—they can't have "openness."

It's all words, words, words still. But it will come, nevertheless, if not Gorbachev, the next fellow on the top will
have to call for reforms, anyway.[7]

However, despite the shrewdness of her assessment of Gorbachev, Svetlana found that the audience wanted to ask questions only about her father, which made her feel so helpless that
she thought she might have a nervous collapse. This was the
end of her lecturing career. She told Rosa Shand, "I am always
in the clouds of some or another illusion—a positive or a negative one. . . . I'll NEVER learn to live in the American reality.
It is beyond me."[8]

Svetlana didn't know it, but there was a scheme behind the
scenes to find money for her. She had purposefully not sent
George and Annelise Kennan her letter of desperation. She
could not beg from them, but friends forwarded her letter, and
Kennan decided to step in. He wrote to Frank Carlucci, assistant to the president for national security affairs, enclosing a
copy of the "circular letter" that "Svetlana (Djugashvili) Peters"
had sent to friends. Having given a précis of Svetlana's history,
Kennan remarked:

> Obviously she has brought her troubles upon herself and
> deserves little personal sympathy. . . . However, a number
> of her former friends, while fully realizing her responsi-
> bility for her own plight, would find it difficult to stand
> by and watch her becoming a bag woman; and I question
> whether it would be advisable, from the standpoint of our
> government to permit this to happen. . . . In view of the
> sensible and generous way in which she was treated by the
> Soviet authorities [when she returned in 1984], I think it
> would make a bad impression, invite invidious compari-
> sons, and not be in the interests of our government, if she

and her daughter (who is a nice girl and innocent of all complicity in her mother's follies) were to become public charges. At the least, such a turn of events would lend itself to adverse propagandistic exploitation.[9]

Kennan suggested that a small annuity of $300,000 be set aside, from which regular payments could be made to Svetlana—"necessarily clandestinely." Within a few weeks, Fritz Ermarth from the CIA phoned Kennan to say that he was confident the matter could be resolved, though it would take a bit of time.[10]

With Olgivanna Wright dead, Svetlana concluded that Taliesin was safe. Now she wanted only peace with Wesley Peters. Mostly she wanted Olga to have a relationship with her father and tried to persuade her to visit him. She'd tell Olga, "You know, he's a good man. You shouldn't hate him; you shouldn't say bad things about him." Olga would reply, "You know, Mommy, I won't talk to you about it. We'll just agree not to talk about it. I can't change what I've seen."[11]

However, on her Easter vacation that spring of 1987, Olga yielded to her mother's pressure and finally visited Wesley. People at Taliesin remembered the sixteen-year-old Olga, beautiful now, with her long hair spilling over her shoulders, sitting at the piano and singing Georgian songs in an ethereal voice,[12] but Olga herself found the communal life at Taliesin distressing and certainly felt no connection with her father. She told her mother she was grateful to her. "You gave me a great life. You took me out of there."[13] She was relieved when she got back to Friends' School.

Over the next winter in her hunting lodge, Svetlana worked on a new manuscript called "A Book for Granddaughters." It was to be an account of her and Olga's return to the USSR. She wrote her endless letters and did some translations. Knowing that her finances were precarious, her old friend Bob Rayle stepped in. "I tried to offer her CIA help, but she invariably refused."[14] Finally he managed to put her in touch with Ilya Levkov, a Russian émigré who ran a small press in New York called Liberty Publishing. That winter Levkov brought out *The Faraway Music* in Russian. The advance was minimal, but he also gave Svetlana the occasional book to translate into Russian, which brought in a bit of money. In January 1988, she flew to England, staying in Cambridge with Philippa Hill and spending time with Olga. There was some thought of her trying to settle there again, but it was only a brief illusion. After her flight back to Chicago, her bus to Wisconsin got caught in a winter blizzard. Her isolation in her hunting lodge in the backwoods began to seem daunting. She thought of relocating, but where?[15]

In June 1988, Svetlana wrote to Rosa Shand with surprising news. She had something to confess. She had fallen in love. The man's name was Tom Turner. "After years and years of 'frozen heart' I do love a man—and I cannot tell you what a great joy, regeneration and light this is to me. All is still in the stage of 'unfoldment.'"

A Texan by birth, Tom Turner was a fifty-two-year-old bachelor, ten years younger than Svetlana. He lived in Saint Louis. They had met two years previously in Illinois at the home of a friend and had kept up a friendship by correspondence, but recently they had begun to see each other. Svetlana told Rosa only a few friends knew their secret.

> It's just all developing beautifully BETWEEN us two. . . . I think it CAN develop into the most happy and wonderful relationship for us both. . . . I should NOT think ahead of time—this is NO GOOD. . . . Please, keep this secret. Sometimes I'm so happy—that I want to shout: "Tom is a wonderful man!" but I shouldn't.[16]

It was as if she were afraid to anticipate happiness, expecting that if she spoke, it would be whisked away. They would spend long hours on the telephone, and she would take the four-hundred-mile trip by bus to spend the weekend with him in Saint Louis, or he would come to visit her in Wisconsin.

Turner had an interesting background. He had apprenticed as an architect with Buckminster Fuller, but had then worked as a businessman. He was also a Dominican tertiary, or lay brother. Such individuals, married and single, worked in the community. He loved music and all things Russian. Completely indifferent to Svetlana's parentage, he delighted in taking her to meet his friends. Olga was still at school in England and never met Turner, but Svetlana wrote her long letters describing their lovely evenings cooking meals together—apparently Tom told her she was a great cook and would make a wonderful wife.[17] At one moment Olga thought they were getting married, something she secretly longed for. And then came the dreadful news. Several months into their friendship, Tom was diagnosed with terminal cancer.

It would seem that Svetlana's life was destined to turn in tragic circles. Once she had helped Brajesh Singh to die; now she would have to comfort a dying Tom Turner—which she did. Tom was not bedridden until the very end of his illness. Their loving relationship, with its terrible undertone, continued to the end.

Even as Tom Turner was dying, Svetlana suffered another collapse of her hopes. At the end of January 1989, three months shy of her eighteenth birthday, Olga shocked her mother by running away from school with a "sweet hippie boyfriend" named Hayden. One weekend when Olga was given leave from school to visit Hayden's family's estate—his father was a wealthy London banker—the two young lovers fled to Brighton. They were living in a Brighton bedsit: one room with a communal kitchen and bathroom. As soon as Svetlana found out her daughter had quit school, she commandeered friends to go to Brighton and knock on Olga and Hayden's door—they were too poor to have a phone—but no one seemed able to persuade Olga to return to Friends' School. Frustrated, Svetlana contacted Hayden's father and booked a flight to London on February 5. They would drive to Brighton together to bring their children home.

One morning Hayden looked out of the window of the bed-sit. "Oh my god! It's my dad." Olga looked out the window and said, "Oh my god! It's my mom." They invited their respective parents in for tea, and all four squatted on the floor, because apart from a mattress draped in Indian fabric, they had no furniture. When she looked back at that morning, Olga remembered her mother fondly.

> She had flown all that way to talk some sense into me and basically take me back to school. But when she saw how much we were in love, Mom—being such a romantic—just couldn't bring herself to separate us. We were such a beautiful pair and totally happy. She saw something from her past. Her father had done this to her when she was only sixteen, when she fell in love with Kapler. She wasn't going to do this to me. I guess she hoped that I would be able to sort this out for myself. Which I did. Hayden and I eventually went back to London and broke up. But my mother had to drive back to London that day with Hayden's angry father who was fuming: "Are you kidding me? You're not going to . . . no . . . that's not how we do this. . . ." But we were left there, yes.[18]

A disconsolate Svetlana flew back to Wisconsin. Of course she was angry. It would be Olga who didn't have the A-level marks to get into college. Her dreams for her daughter's education were dashed, while Hayden had his wealthy father behind him. In April, she put her hunting lodge up for sale and moved into an apartment in Madison.

Tom Turner died on June 3, 1989. When Svetlana attended his funeral in Saint Louis, she was moved to find how warmly his family accepted her. She wrote a bleak note to Philippa Hill in Cambridge. When her "dearest closest friend" died, although "both he and I knew it was coming, his death was a blow. NOT HAVING HIM around in the flesh IS very sad."[19] The note is poignant in its stoicism. Svetlana had been well trained in loss.

In August, two months after Tom Turner died, Svetlana was admitted to the emergency ward of a Madison hospital suffering an apparent heart attack.

She wrote to Philippa Hill that she felt she was sinking lower and lower from her "ideal." "Anger makes a sickly heart. . . . I am cracking on every seam." And then she went on a rant. She was angry at "stupid publishers, stupid newspapers, stupid politicians on my TV every night. Even stupid Gorbachev who BLEW such a GOOD CHANCE of BIG REFORMS in the USSR. . . . He missed his Supreme Hour." She ended her letter to Philippa, "Well, poor late Tom loved to talk about this, politics and all. Now I have nobody to talk with. Darn it. It's so sad."[20] Then she got the bill for her emergency stay in the hospital, which almost wiped out her savings.

How Svetlana survived financially was always mysterious, but it would seem that George Kennan's appeal to Fritz Ermarth to help her—"necessarily clandestinely"—had been answered. For some time, she had been receiving regular monthly payments for translation work from a Washington agency.[21] She claimed she did not know the name of her "benefactors." She told George and Annelise Kennan, "I do not know WHO decides my fate. I suppose people in Washington. . . . Nameless shadows. All top secret. I NEVER was asked."[22]

But she had begun to feel uneasy about the whole thing. While the checks arrived regularly, often no translation work followed. One of the checks had the name and address of a publishing house called Crocker located in Massachusetts. She wrote to inquire about her assignments but received no answer.

After Christmas, she wrote to Rosa Shand that she had made a new discovery. "The CIA people in Wash DC decided to pay me a 'pension' under a cover-up of a translation work. Can you imagine that stupidity? . . . [They] think that paying me money they are NOT humiliating me."[23] She told Rosa that she had contacted her employer and he (she did not identify who this was but implied it was a CIA officer) informed her that the firm did not exist. "We thought you understood."

Irate, she protested, "I felt like I was taken in. It was a cover-up." "I had never been anyone's spy and I couldn't live on a pension or assistance, whatever, from the CIA."[24]

Was her outrage sincere? Did she not suspect that her benefactors might be the CIA? It would seem that in her mind, as long as she was doing legitimate translation work, being unsure of the Washington source was not a problem. Many Soviet dissidents were supported in some way. The previous year, there had been Senate hearings, chaired by Senator Sam Nunn, to look into the general state of Soviet defectors in the United States; she'd been disappointed when she wasn't called to testify.[25] However, accepting a regular stipend directly from the CIA was another matter; it put her on a par with the KGB's Victor Louis. Bob Rayle insisted she invariably refused his offers of CIA support. Perhaps, being Russian, she could imagine that one day she would be asked to pay back the CIA's generosity.

Precipitately, Svetlana decided to bolt. It had been a desolate fall alone in her Madison apartment, without Tom, without Olga. She had reached another dead end. As the Soviet Union disintegrated and "Gorby-mania" pervaded America, she was certain her newly completed manuscript, "A Book for Granddaughters," would never be published in the United States. She had an open invitation to visit an old friend, Madame Helen Zamoyska, in Muret, France, and the Sinyavskys, with whom she had resumed correspondence, had implied that she might be able to find a French publisher. Underneath everything was, of course, her longing to be closer to Olga.

When Olga came home that December, Svetlana told her she was moving to France. The move, as usual, was hurried. Olga carried their old furniture off to secondhand stores, haggled over prices, and packed up the remainder of her mother's things, which were to be shipped to England. Svetlana had a last meal with Wesley Peters at their traditional restaurant, the Don Q Inn in nearby Dodgeville. He was sweet; the talk was good; they spoke of Olga's future education. And then she was gone.

She traveled first to the south of France, and then spent several weeks at a retreat at a Roman Catholic nunnery in Toulouse, about which she often spoke nostalgically. She visited the Sinyavskys in Paris, but it turned out they were not helpful in finding her a French publisher. She clearly hadn't heard the gossip they'd passed on to the London *Times* in 1984 about her having been lured back to the USSR by KGB agent Oleg Bitov. Had she known, she might have saved herself a frustrating trip.

Where could she go? She had decamped completely from Wisconsin. The only place her feet could take her now was England. Olga was working in a bank and renting digs in Muswell Hill with three friends. She invited her mother to join her. Svetlana stayed four months, but of course this arrangement couldn't last.

It was as if Svetlana had stepped into a void, but then a stone rose to give her a footing. Her former landlord in Cambridge, professor Robert Denman, put her in touch with Sir Richard Carr-Gomm, a philanthropist who had founded the Morpeth Society, a nonprofit charity that ran a number of privately funded housing complexes in London for distressed gentle-folk and indigent people.[26] Svetlana moved into 24 Delgarno Gardens in North Kensington, where she had a room and shared the communal kitchen and bathroom with five other residents—a strange echo of the old communal apartments in Moscow.

To friends in America, she extolled British benevolence. "English charity workers are quite special folks."[27] The city offered so many things free to seniors: city transport, concerts, libraries where she was able to study subjects she had always wanted to pursue. Her favorite excursion was to Regent's Park, where she sat to write her letters. She assured friends, "I don't mind to live on charity check. I don't mind to have furniture from a charity truck. I don't mind. It doesn't humiliate me at all. I didn't want to live on considerable pension, originating from CIA, because I don't think it's right. I had four books which could be published, and I could have money from my literary work."[28]

She was receiving about €60 a week from the Carr-Gomm Society, with which she paid her room and board and living expenses.[29] She spoke affectionately of fellow residents: "an American, a Chinese cook, a reformed alcoholic, a one-time housekeeper, a gay man of 24." The tedious part was sharing the bathroom, which nobody bothered to clean. Nevertheless, she would tell a British friend, "Fate always sends me unusual people who pull me out of the abyss."[30]

Svetlana started to march in London peace rallies to protest nuclear weapons. This was not a new obsession. A few

years back, she'd written to George Kennan, "OH, HOW I
WOULD LOVE to live under a government which does not
possess atom bombs and does not threaten anyone."[31] "George,
you are a great peacemaker. . . . PLEASE DO SOMETHING.
RIGHT NOW. SOMETHING REALLY BIG."[32] Svetlana
herself might have been able to muster considerable publicity
for the antinuclear cause, if it were known that Stalin's daughter was marching in London peace rallies, but she preferred to
remain anonymous, always afraid of enemies who would twist
her motives. When her friend Philippa Hill made the mistake
of calling her her "own worst enemy," she responded, surprisingly temperately:

> I do not think that I am my own worst enemy—simply
> because I do have so many Good & Terrible Enemies—so
> many as you, my dear, would never have. . . . My Enemies—
> are really not mine, but my Father's. But they use me as a
> substitute image. Every psychiatrist would explain this to
> you. I have to confront very real enmity, very real malice,
> and very real obstacles.[33]

Angela Lambert, a journalist for the *Independent*, managed
to track Svetlana down in March 1990 soon after her arrival in
London. Lambert must have touched something in Svetlana,
for she spoke with remarkable candor. She said she no longer
held the "pleasant illusion" that she could escape the *label* of
Stalin's daughter, and added, "It was partly my own fault":

> I lived my life the way I could—though I could have lived
> it better—within a certain limited framework called Fate.
> There is something fatal about my life. You can't regret
> your fate, though I do regret my mother didn't marry a
> carpenter. I was born into my parents' fate. I was born un-

der that name, that cross, and I never managed to jump out of it. I just passively followed the road of my pilgrimage.[34]

Passive was hardly the word that many would have applied to Svetlana, but it was the way she thought of herself.

Those who saw Svetlana as the Kremlin princess seemed to think she'd been brought up in fairy-tale indulgence. Instead, like all Soviet citizens, she had been trained to follow a strict code of obedience. Soviets were told where to live, where to work, where they couldn't travel. Svetlana looked to others—to the protectors, the mentors, the guides—for the direction she must take. This was what she meant by her passivity. But then she would rage: at herself, and at them for controlling her. "I could never emerge in my own capacity," she lamented. She didn't recognize that she had stood up to them all.

She told Lambert wistfully:

I want one thing: for my books to be published. I just dream that my story will finally reach readers. At least I would hope I can convince the readers of my book that I have had nothing to do with my father's philosophy and what he did. Then I shall feel I have done something. Without that, I see my life as totally useless.[35]

She smoothed with delicate hands the cloth covering the table they were sitting at and smiled at Lambert. "It's been a heavy life, my dear: heavy to listen to; heavy to live."

That November, she sent Rosa Shand a one-line Christmas card: "Dearest Rosa, I think—I'm <u>alive</u> after this dreadful year. It must be better now."[36] But her optimism had begun to sound a little phony. Even to her.

Chapter 34

"Never Wear a Tight Skirt If You Intend to Commit Suicide"

Svetlana and Olga together, c. 1994.

On May 3, 1991, Svetlana's friend Jerzy Kosinski committed suicide. He wrapped a plastic bag around his head and
suffocated to death, leaving a note: "I am going to put myself to
sleep now for a bit longer than usual. Call it Eternity."[1] When
she read about his death in the London newspapers, Svetlana

was profoundly shocked. Memories flooded in of the times she and Olga had visited him in New York—he'd taken them on a ride in a horse-drawn carriage through Central Park while his wife, Kiki, snapped photos. He'd signed her copy of his novel *The Painted Bird*, "For Svetlana who understands."[2] What did she understand? She must have known that Kosinski had lived since 1982 under accusations of plagiarism, of employing ghostwriters, and of having willfully distorted the facts of his experiences as a Holocaust survivor. Kosinski's defenders, like Zbigniew Brzezinski (national security adviser during the Carter administration), claimed that the Communist government of his native Poland had smeared him.[3] Was this what Svetlana, equally slandered by the Soviet Communists, understood? But she believed Kosinski had a good life: a beautiful wife, a lovely apartment, his books published. And now he was what she called a suicider.

The news of Kosinski's suicide sent her spiraling downward. She was living without money in gray, rainy London with no idea what cards fate was about to deal her. One day that May she walked to London Bridge and looked down into the muddy waters of the Thames. Hiking up her narrow skirt, she tried to climb the railing. A strong hand pulled her back to the pavement. Out of the corner of her eye, she saw a stocky figure with a red Irish face and gray hair in a dark raincoat walking quickly from the scene. Two young constables picked her up and packed her into a police car. As they drove her home, they chatted about the soccer match on the radio. When they arrived at her door, they told her sternly, "Never do that again!" In bed that night, she tried to put a plastic bag over her head. It didn't work. She fell asleep. The next morning she awoke and it all seemed a terrible nightmare.[4]

When Olga met her mother later that week for their ritual lunch in a pub, Svetlana told her about the attempted suicide. She spoke casually, as if she were talking about a walk in the park.[5] But something had changed. Svetlana now understood what suicide was about. It happened in a crazy moment and for crazy reasons. It was a dark day, it was raining, the wind blew your umbrella inside out, someone didn't keep an appointment for lunch, something triggered your despair. "You have to be very mad, mad like hell, with everybody or somebody or anybody or with everything."[6] Her father had shouted at her mother at a dinner party: "Hey you." If Nadya's suicide hadn't worked, she would have gotten up the next day and continued. Svetlana recalled her nanny saying that when the body was found, it looked as if her mother had been crawling toward the door, as if she regretted what she had done. Nadya might have been saved.[7]

At the pub, Svetlana even joked with Olga. "Never wear a tight skirt if you intend to commit suicide." Olga believed her mother now understood her own mother's despair. Suicide could simply be an impulsive accident, when no one was there to stop it. Olga felt Svetlana had finally forgiven her own mother for abandoning her.

That July Olga decided she would fly to Wisconsin on her holiday break from the bank. She wanted to try again with her father. She would surprise him. A week before she was due to fly out, she received word that Wes had suffered a stroke. When she arrived at Taliesin on the evening of July 16, her father was already unconscious, and he died during the night. She immediately phoned her mother to tell her. Svetlana didn't cry but kept repeating, "'Oh God, oh God, he was such a good man,' and then her voice trailed into silence, as if she'd left the phone on the counter and just walked off."[8]

Back in her charity digs in London, Svetlana wept for her ex-husband: "I didn't know how deeply he was still in me. He <u>was</u> a good man in many ways—it was the unfortunate surroundings (in Taliesin, etc.)—many envies & hatreds around us that destroyed <u>what</u> could be—in other circumstances—a good family life."[9] She believed that Olga felt the same way—her daughter discovered she loved her father after he died.

Olga had grown from being Svetlana's child to being her closest friend. When Svetlana came to live in London, Olga recalled, "By this time, the earth was really small for us. It didn't really matter where we lived. We would always see each other, we would always be together." With her daughter, Svetlana never held back. "We talked about so many painful things." Olga could look at her mother and father's marriage from a distance. When Svetlana met Wes, she didn't have the sense of calm she needed to make the right decision. "Blind to the many red flags at Taliesin, she had been swept off her feet." Olga felt her father could never have given her mother the love she needed. "Nor, his particular genius aside, could he meet her intellectually brow to brow."[10]

Olga saw her mother's pain. Sometimes Svetlana would fall into what Olga described as "the night terrors of a child alone and lost." "It would be like a cloud passing over. It was as if her brain started with a thought and ran with it to the point she no longer had any control over the thought or where it was going." Sometimes it happened when Svetlana was writing, but sometimes there seemed to be nothing that provoked it, or it would be a trivial moment, "the milk boiling over." "She would be inconsolable." "Something triggered a volcano of thoughts, memories, pain, anguish, fear about something coming up, surfacing to overwhelm her." Olga saw her mother, so deeply misunderstood, as a woman who needed unconditional love. "The people who have stuck by her the longest, who have remained friends, are the ones who saw that. They'd seen the volcano."[11]

Svetlana always seemed able to find friends. That July she met Nina Lobanov-Rostovsky, whose husband was a member of the aristocratic Lobanov-Rostovsky family. A few days before, Nina had set off for the supermarket when the porter at her block of flats in North Kensington stopped her to ask, "Madame, do you know who I saw walking by this morning? Stalin's daughter, Svetlana Stalin."

Nina replied, "Is that possible, David? What would she be doing in this neighborhood?" David said, "I think she was on her way to the Morpeth Society in the next block of flats. Shall I send her up to you if I see her again?" Certain he had made a mistake, Nina said, "Yes, you do that, David."[12]

On July 17—Nina remembered the date precisely—she was in her kitchen preparing for a dinner party when the doorbell rang. Assuming one of her guests had been kind enough to send flowers, she opened the door and there stood Svetlana, looking just like her photographs. Nina recalled the encounter as if it were a play.

SVETLANA: "Sorry to intrude, but your doorman said some Russians lived here and that I would be welcome."

ME: "Would you care for a cup of tea?"

SVETLANA (stepping across the threshold): "Have you ever known any Russian to turn down tea?"

We introduced ourselves formally. I explained that I was French and also preparing a ragout for a dinner party, and she followed me into the kitchen. I made a big teapot of strong tea, and Svetlana had several cups with five teaspoons of sugar in each cup. I also offered her some of the raspberries we were having for dessert. She sniffed them appreciatively and remarked, "English raspberries and other fruit smell almost as fragrant as those in Russia. I missed that in America. Fruit there has no fragrance. . . ." She talked a lot and I listened.[13]

That night Nina asked her husband if he minded that Stalin's daughter had visited. Stalin had imprisoned his entire family and executed his father, Dmitri Ivanovich Lobanov-Rostovsky, in 1948. He said he didn't mind as long as she made sure Svetlana never came when he was home.[14] Svetlana began to stop by regularly.

Nina soon discovered that friendship with Svetlana could be demanding. "She was highly intelligent, well educated, well read and could be warm, charming, and good company. She was a superb and poetic writer." But she was also mercurial. When some perceived hurt set her off, she would rage, send an angry letter, and then apologize. "Poor Svetlana. It was as though she had been flayed. She was super-sensitive and everything hurt."[15]

That summer of 1991, Svetlana suddenly had some wonderful news. She discovered that *A Book for Granddaughters* had been published in June in the Moscow magazine *Oktyabr.*[16] She'd sent the manuscript to her old friend Olga Rifkina, who had submitted it to the magazine without telling her. Because the Soviet Union had not signed the international copyright agreement, it wasn't unusual for a writer to find out, after the fact, that his or her work had been published without permission. But the way Svetlana found out was totally unexpected. She received a letter from her daughter Katya saying that she liked her book. *A Book for Granddaughters* ended with an appeal to Katya:

> And besides, only one look at the map shows you that not far from America's Alaskan shores, lie the shores of Soviet Kamchatka where my dear volcanologist, Katherine [Katya] lives and works and where my granddaughter Annie [Anya] will soon be going to school. I love geographical maps where huge spaces and distances are separated only by finger lengths. How close to each other are Kamchatka and Oregon: separated only by a big lake. . . . Someday my Katherine could be invited to cross the ocean to study Mt.

[Saint] Helen's volcano—for by then she will have become a leading specialist. And then—freed from the propaganda and brainwashing and artificial hatred—why not meet her American sister?[17]

Soon Svetlana received a phone call from Katya. It was shocking to hear her voice after twenty-five years of silence. She sounded like herself, like the sixteen-year–old adolescent Svetlana had abandoned in 1966. Katya's young daughter Anya even wrote her grandmother a note: "Do you love animals?" Svetlana was ecstatic. Knowing how poor she was, Nina gave her money to buy phone cards to call her daughter on public pay phones, because her residence had no phone.

That September, through Russian contacts, Svetlana sought out an American volcanologist, Thomas Miller, who made annual trips from his home base in Alaska to consult with volcanologists in Kamchatka. Miller had first gone to Russia in August 1991 in the middle of the unsuccessful coup d'état by the Communist Party hard-liners against Mikhail Gorbachev that eventually brought Boris Yeltsin to power. Miller found himself becoming an unofficial courier, carrying fifty to sixty letters out of Kamchatka to mail to various people around the world.[18] Svetlana asked him to carry a letter to her daughter, Mrs. Katherine Zhdanov, in Kluchi.

Soon Svetlana conceived the idea of bringing Katya and Anya to London for a brief visit. She even discussed with Tom Miller the possible plane route her daughter might take.[19] She asked Nina for £1,500 to pay for the plane tickets. Nina didn't have that kind of money, and furthermore knew her husband would be furious at Svetlana's presumption. Instead, she told Svetlana that the tenant upstairs was a respected Lebanese journalist who greatly admired her books and would certainly be willing to pay that amount to interview her. Svetlana went red and exploded. "Who did I think she was, willing to accept money to talk about herself? . . . She marched out and sent me several rough letters."[20] It took six months for their friendship to be repaired.

When Tom Miller wrote that he had met Katya profession-ally, Svetlana asked eagerly, "Does she speak a bit of English?" She knew so little about her daughter's life now—the idea of her tiny willful Katya monitoring erupting volcanoes amused her. "I'm sure they would erupt exactly when she presses some button on her desk."[21] She asked Miller to carry small trinkets to her granddaughter. Under Svetlana's pressure, Olga also sent a letter from America for Miller to deliver to her sister.

Miller, in fact, understood that Katya was an alcoholic, or a recovering alcoholic, and like her grandfather, rather author-itarian, although he didn't tell Svetlana this. But then, there was so little to tell. Katya had the reputation of being a recluse who came out of her cabin only to collect the newspaper or go to her workstation. Other Russians refused to speak about her. "Leave her alone," they said. "She's a widow. She's had enough."[22] Katya sent Svetlana the occasional note, though she said almost nothing about her life. Olga remembered her mother eagerly opening a letter from Katya that contained a photograph, only to discover it was a photograph of a volcano. The letter described the volcano in precise detail.[23]

Despite her disavowals, being indigent in London must have been humiliating for Svetlana—she couldn't afford to phone her daughter, buy her a plane ticket, or even put her up, though it is doubtful Katya would ever have come. Still, to most friends, Svetlana claimed to accept her poverty, and certainly few re-membered her complaining. She wrote to Rosa Shand:

> I prefer to live as I do. There is always some balance—
> Harmony—Equilibrium—in the General Plan of our lives,

designed, no doubt, by the Creator: and if I had my <u>first</u> 40 years living <u>on the top</u> of society (in USSR)—then I <u>must end up in total humility</u>, humbled to this simple frugality where <u>I am now</u>. All is right, all is correct; and the <u>Balance</u> is restored.[24]

There is certainly a willful pride in this declaration, but she was not entirely convincing.

Svetlana was in the hands of social workers who proved very kind. When she complained that the loud music of her young fellow residents kept her from sleeping, one social worker, a Nigerian student named Samson, immediately took on her case and, with her doctor's help, got her moved to a new room at the Ladbroke Grove residence belonging to the Carr-Gomm Charitable Society. As soon as she walked into her room at 280 Ladbroke Grove, she was taken aback by the aura of the place. "It was sunny. It was peaceful. It was perfect."[25]

Svetlana owned nothing, not a single stick of furniture, but at the charity depot, she was soon able to secure a secondhand table, a bed, a chair, and even a refrigerator, which she was allowed to keep in her room. She settled in. Looking back, she would say, "I was a perfect old pauper. In fact, I was very cheerful." Svetlana would say there was nothing terrible in wanting to own things. She had loved to buy and sell properties in the United States, but when "it is taken away from me, I don't cry about it. It doesn't affect me at all."[26] She and Samson were soon fond of each other and would fall into each other's arms when they met. He eventually discovered who she was, but she felt he was too young for "Stalin's daughter" to mean anything to him.

Now Svetlana was finally on her own. Olga had briefly married her best friend, a young Welshman, partly in order to be able to work in London. At their wedding, Svetlana wore a paper boater hat as a sign of protest, because one was supposed to marry for love. Olga, who'd inherited her mother's sarcastic streak, found this fantastically amusing.[27] But now she decided to move back to Wisconsin to work in the Tibetan craft shop in Spring Green where she'd had summer jobs. For the next several years, Olga visited her mother in London on stopovers during her expeditions to Nepal, Dharamsala, and other Asian destinations to purchase Tibetan art and textiles.

Nina Lobanov-Rostovsky could see that Svetlana was lonely without her daughter and began to invite her to the odd dinner party when her husband was away on business. At one such party, Svetlana met Hugh and Vanessa Thomas. He'd written a seminal book, which Svetlana deeply admired, on the Spanish Civil War, and soon she was a regular visitor to their home. Vanessa found her compelling.

> I remember Hugh and I thought she was like a little princess, living in this cell up the road. She was so simple, but she was awfully grand because she was very educated. She spoke French, and German, and very good English. She had very good manners, but humble—she was the daughter of the head of state of half the world! I don't mean she put on airs at all. She was grand in a way a princess would be if she were living in a cell. She never behaved as a pauper, never spoke about money. She was loftily above it in an essential way. She sort of gracefully fitted in. Of course we talked about our children. We were both besotted by our daughters.[28]

Vanessa's son Inigo Thomas worked for the *London Review of Books* and sent a request to Svetlana to write something for it. However, he made the mistake of addressing his letter to "Svetlana Alliluyeva." Svetlana rang up Vanessa almost apoplectic, saying she was not using that name and their son had exposed her. Vanessa apologized profusely, but she already took Svetlana's explosions as simply part of the landscape. "Svetlana longed for an explosion so that we could all pick it up again. I'm very English. I couldn't take all that Russian drama seriously."

Indeed, when Thomas also phoned to apologize, Svetlana invited him to tea. He remembered being shocked at finding Stalin's daughter in her charity digs: "broke, homeless, stateless, restless, pensionless."[29] She made him tea in the Formica kitchen with its worn floor and hard fluorescent lighting, ignoring her fellow resident, who was cooking an omelet on the communal stove. They drank their tea in her tidy bedroom, which held only a small bed folded into a sofa, a bookshelf, a chair, and a dressing table. There wasn't a single photograph or painting on the wall, but on the dresser stood a bust of Olga made by the sculptor Shenda Amery.

Svetlana's residence at 280 Ladbroke Grove, then owned by the Carr-Gomm Charitable Society, looks much the same in 2015 as it did when she lived there in the early 1990s.

And of course, the press tracked her down. An article appeared in the American magazine *People*. "Lana Peters, a solemn woman in a bulky jacket, keeps very much to herself on the bustling streets of London as she quietly browses in antique shops and the library. Who would suspect that she was once known as Svetlana, the only daughter of the infamous Soviet dictator Joseph Stalin?"[30] A photograph of a scowling Svetlana accompanied the piece. The house on Ladbroke Grove was described as "a group home for single people—many suffering from severe emotional problems." The article contained the usual dark commentary about her father, her mother's suicide, multiple divorces, lost children. There was nothing new in it, because her fellow residents had refused to talk to the reporter. Svetlana picked up and moved to a new residence on Nursery Lane around the corner.

But Svetlana's circle of friends was widening. Through Nina, she met the Mexican diplomat Raoul Ortiz. In his early sixties, he was elegant, a gifted writer, and a passionate reader of Proust. They would go to the cinema together, to embassy parties, to concerts, and to the occasional restaurant. Ortiz felt there were many Svetlanas. "She returned to a person whatever their expectations of her were. I was an exotic character. She loved photographs of trees in spring, spouting new flowers. Meeting me and establishing a friendship brought her a new spring."[31] They never once talked about politics in the Soviet Union. In fact, what made him unique was that he was outside the circle of those obsessed by the USSR.

But then Ortiz was posted to Paris. As he was preparing to leave, Svetlana suggested how wonderful it would be if she moved to Paris and they continued their friendship there. "Not that she would dream of shacking up together. But she was lonely, and I had a very free life and was afraid of sentimental attachments." He recognized that she saw him as a gateway to another life: "It is a mistake to think that Svetlana was running from something; rather she was always running towards something, a version of life that would be different, that would meet her expectations of what a contented life could be."[32] He didn't encourage her to move to Paris.

Svetlana met Laurence and Linda Kelly at a cocktail party at the Thomas home. When his father had served as British ambassador to the USSR in the late 1940s, Laurence Kelly spent six months at the British Embassy learning Russian. He knew firsthand the culture of paranoia that her father had instilled during the Anti-Cosmopolitan Campaign and the Doctors' Plot. When Kelly was introduced to Svetlana as the author of a biography of the famous nineteenth-century poet and novelist Mikhail Lermontov, she froze, and then explained that Lermontov was one of her favorite poets. Soon Kelly was showing her his specialized library on Lermontov. Together they delighted in the poem Lermontov wrote when exiled by the tsar to the Caucasus: "Farewell, Smelly Russia." Kelly was then working on research into Georgian history for his book *Diplomacy and Murder in Tehran* and promised to send Svetlana anything of interest he came across.

Svetlana would occasionally tell Kelly unexpected and entertaining anecdotes about her father, one of which was about Stalin "losing his cool" with his parrot.

> The English tobacco company Dunhill, a maker of pipes, had given Stalin a particularly fine pipe. In his flat in the Kremlin, his tame parrot used to imitate the awful noises of throat clearing and spit that pipe smokers make when they light up. One day Stalin was having a tough time signing many lists with Molotov and he came home in a terrible temper. The parrot began his routine. Stalin took out his Dunhill pipe and killed the parrot on the spot.[33]

Kelly found Svetlana immensely entertaining. "Poor Lana was a last stranded fish in a society that could not understand her."

The Kellys took to inviting Svetlana to stay at their cottage in Cumbria in the Lake District. The bucolic landscape with its undulating green hills, flocks of grazing sheep, and farm carts lumbering down the narrow roads spilling their hay was seductive; it seemed nothing had changed since the nineteenth century. One afternoon, the Kellys suggested a visit to Pamela Egremont, mistress of nearby Cockermouth Castle. She turned out to be an exquisitely beautiful woman in her sixties who had traveled all over Southeast Asia and China. Soon Svetlana was visiting her at her elegant London residence. Pamela Egremont's fondest memory of Svetlana was of her sitting on the living-room sofa talking about Stalin. She spoke of how her father had prevented her from studying literature at Moscow University because she would get involved with dreadful people like *poets.* "He looked very, very cross," she said.

> As Svetlana was telling me this, she stood up and stamped to the end of the room and stamped back again and suddenly her whole face looked almost like her father's (I'd seen pictures of him). She turned herself sort of into him, and then she plumped back on the sofa and said, "Don't talk to me again about my father."[34]

The people who most disgusted her, Svetlana told Pamela Egremont, were all the lackeys around her father in the Kremlin, always giving her little presents and trying to please her to get on her father's good side. "She saw through them. I thought she was an admirable woman, considering what she had gone through and all the parts she had to play." Only once did she experience Svetlana's vitriol. She had just read a new biography of Beria, and asked for Svetlana's opinion. Svetlana flared up. "Don't ever speak to me of that man. He killed eight of my relatives." While many American friends thought Svetlana was unstable, Pamela Egremont thought "she was amazingly normal, solid as a rock."

After her return from the USSR, Svetlana had resumed her friendship with Rosamond Richardson. Richardson was already well known for her books on gardening and cooking; she had a particular gift for writing about foods in their natural context. On one visit to Saffron Walden, as they were having tea, Svetlana suddenly turned to Rosamond and said, "We should do a book together."[35] Richardson remembered that it was as if the idea had flown in through the window. Svetlana was proposing a book based on Richardson's interviews with her. In her mind, she would at last be able to talk about the Alliluyevs and the succession of strong women in her family. She wanted it understood how the Revolution had destroyed them.[36] Only anger and black humor had saved her grandmother. In her last years, Nadya's mother, Olga, had lived alone in the Kremlin. Once she explained to Svetlana how she survived. "You know, I make lots of tea for myself. I put it on the table and I say, 'Bitte schön' [Have some] and then 'Danke schön' [Thank you], and then I drink."[37] Her grandmother couldn't do anything to stop Stalin, but her stoical self-discipline and black humor kept her going.

Listening to Svetlana's stories, Richardson commiserated. "How much you have suffered!" To which Svetlana replied that she had not suffered. It was the people returning from the camps who had suffered.[38] She often thought of her friend Irina Gogua, who had been very close to Nadya. Gogua had been arrested in the mid-1930s and spent seventeen years in prison and exile. She never spoke in detail of those years, but she did explain how she survived. Svetlana repeated Gogua's words as if they were scorched into her memory. "I built myself a theory. I had to accept what happened to me. It was totally unjust. I had done nothing, but I had to accept. Otherwise, I saw people who couldn't accept, who were bashing their heads on walls and protesting, and they were pretty soon dead, because they couldn't." And Svetlana added, "Oh yes, people get wise there. When it comes to the worst thing, you get wise."[39]

The project with Richardson soon solidified into a book about the Alliluyev family. Svetlana made several excited phone calls to Moscow to family members who rarely spoke publicly. She said to them, "Open the door to Rosamond. She's an authentic person."[40] With Svetlana's blessing, Richardson flew to Moscow with her translator and spent a week interviewing Svetlana's cousins and extended family. The family members spoke candidly to her, and their voices emerge as a tragic narrative of imprisonments, deaths, and disappearances under Stalin.

The trouble began when Richardson returned to London. Svetlana had expected to listen to and transcribe the tapes, but Richardson didn't offer them to her. She knew that Svetlana could be "tricky," as she put it, and some members of the family were not entirely flattering about her. Also, the family's conversations were about "what it was like to live under Stalin's shadow and clearly some nasty things were going to come out of the woodwork. I knew how fragile Lana was, emotionally, and I just didn't want to upset her about stuff she didn't need to see."[41]

Later Richardson would concede that she'd been wrong. Svetlana could take it all.

Instead Richardson gave her several of the chapters. Svetlana wrote to her cousin Kyra in Moscow that she was not impressed. Kyra recalled: "She said that Rosamond was too much into politics. But I think that everything they did to us, Alliluyevs, was politics. If it was not politics, what was it?"[42] But Svetlana was angry—Rosamond was writing another book about her father, not the Alliluyev family memoir she was hoping for. When it was published in 1993, Stalin's picture graced the front and back covers of the book. Sadly, it could not have been otherwise. It was Stalin, and the brutality that he and Beria (as the family insisted) had committed against the Alliluyevs, that sat at the core of family memories. Richardson received a very nasty letter from Svetlana. "I remember thinking if she'd been Stalin, I'd have been dead. I really felt the power of Stalin in that letter. The portcullis came down."[43] Richardson never heard from Svetlana again.

And Svetlana washed her hands of the book, though not without writing a letter to the *London Review of Books* in which she insisted that she and Richardson were supposed to be writing a book together about her mother's side of the Stalin family, until Richardson had cut her out. She added a nasty barb: "As an author of cookbooks, Ms. Richardson does not seem to be especially well qualified to write about Russian history."[44] She was right. The book's strength was not its historical account but its penetrating interviews.

When *The Long Shadow* was launched, Richardson invited Svetlana's cousin Kyra and Leonid's daughter Olga to come to London. Svetlana refused not only to attend the launch but also to see her relatives. Everyone thought this was extremely petty of her; she was behaving vindictively, just like her father. But ironically, anger over Richardson's book was not her motive.

When Kyra got back to Moscow, she learned the reason Svetlana had shut her out. Kyra's family reported that they'd had several irate calls from Svetlana while she was away. There was a new scandal. Before her departure for London, a British journalist had interviewed Kyra and reported that she was "looking for evidence that Stalin had murdered his wife Nadezhda Sergeevna Alliluyeva." Though Kyra was livid at the time—"I never said the things ascribed to me"—and her relatives called her nonstop advising her to publish a rebuttal, she did nothing: "The pie had already been cooked." Svetlana read the interview in the British press and could not forgive Kyra for such gossip. "I can only imagine her reaction to accusations that Stalin murdered her mother!" Kyra recalled, but in fact she knew Svetlana's reaction. The night before Kyra and her niece left London, they found an envelope slipped under the door of their hotel room. There was no note, only Kyra's photograph clipped from a London newspaper, from which the face had been cut out.[45]

In 1995, when the Kellys went to their cottage in the Lake District and Svetlana accompanied them, they asked their friend Mary Burkett if they could bring her to tea. Burkett lived in an extraordinary heritage home called Isel Hall just outside Penrith. Svetlana immediately fell in love with Isel Hall, and, by the end of the tea, asked if she could come and look after Mary, who was only two years older. She could be her cook.[46] Burkett, as outspoken and prickly as Svetlana, demurred. But one of Svetlana's most important friendships soon evolved.

Mary Burkett was an unusual woman. In 1962, when she was thirty-eight, she and her friend Genette Malet de Carteret, both amateur archaeologists, decided to drive their Land Rover from the Lake District to Persia in search of the legendary lost castle at Girdkuh. The trip was dangerous. Near Doğubeyazit in Turkey, the two women came under rifle fire when the local police mistook them for smugglers. The whole trip by car and ferry took seven and a half months. When Burkett returned to England, she turned herself into a world expert on the ancient craft of felt making.[47]

In their future correspondence, Burkett addressed Svetlana as "Dear Nomad." Though Svetlana did not travel far, she was always discarding her past. "Attachments create sorrow, the oldest Buddhist axiom," she told Mary.[48] Svetlana called Mary "Dear Warrior." She admired her as a fighter who had shaped her own life.

While Mary undertook her travels to conferences on felt

making or went hunting for new specimens in Switzerland, Poland, Syria, Yemen, or Georgia, Svetlana looked on longingly from afar. She told Mary she had so wanted to visit Morocco, Jordan, Saudi Arabia, Egypt—and India again. She sent Mary names of contacts and linguistic experts, spoke knowledgeably of Tibetan felt patterns, talked of the yurts of her childhood at Zubalovo, and noted the succession of rugs sent as gifts to the Kremlin that marked the politics shaping her young life: Caucasian rugs when her mother was alive; then Persian rugs during the war; and after 1949, Chinese rugs.

She occasionally took on political topics with Mary. "Machiavellian politicking everywhere," she wrote in one letter. From what she read and heard on the radio, things were totally out of control in Russia. Her volcanologist daughter was going unpaid, like all the scientists, and not responding to her letters. She was worried that the mixture of national humiliation, anger, inferiority complex, and cocky talk about the rest of the world would lead to some form of aggressive nationalism. The West must remember that Russia was an old culture with great dignity. Pride was an important but dangerous engine. "Being Russian means never saying sorry," she told Mary. "Even today, Russians are incapable of grief and atonement for Stalin's crimes. . . . That failure to face the bad bodes ill for the future. I see all things from the dark side. Please do forgive me for that."[49]

Svetlana was working with a new idea—to collect the four books she'd written into one volume, which she would call "Enchanted Pilgrimage." It would be the summary of her life's story. When a reporter asked her in 1996 if she was happy, she replied:

What is happiness? I am satisfied, and when you are 70 years old that is not bad. I have had very good times and very bad. I never consider myself as a martyr. Why should I complain? Complaining is the worst thing in the world. It does you no good. I may have a cross to bear but I am not suffering.[50]

Chapter 35

My Dear, They Haven't Changed a Bit

Svetlana and Olga celebrate New Year's Eve together in 1999.

In mid-September 1995, Svetlana decided to move to Cornwall, where she and her daughter Olga had spent several vacations in the early 1980s. She was discovering that the support she received from the Carr-Gomm Society was no longer enough to manage a reasonable life in London, but an affiliated charity called Abbeyfield ran several residences in Cornwall. She imagined the small village of Mullion on the east shore of Mount Bay would offer beautiful nature walks and silence. No crowds. The residence, called Melvin House, was shared among eight elderly women, with a housekeeper. Perched on a cliff, it felt more like a family-style boardinghouse than a charity home and even had a guest bedroom for friends of the residents who visited. Settling into her small room with her ten pots of geraniums, she wrote to Mary Burkett that she felt "very old, very old inside. I mean sometimes I feel all the things I carry within."[1] She wondered how Mary could live with all the ghosts roaming through Isel Hall. Her own ghosts never left her.

But then, at the beginning of 1996, she had an unexpected chance to exorcise at least some of her ghosts. In 1995, her cousin Vladimir Alliluyev wrote a memoir, *Chronicle of One Family*, and sent it to Svetlana, requesting that she translate it into English. Vladimir was the son of Nadya's sister Anna and Stanislav Redens. When she read his book, she was appalled. Vladimir was trumpeting a nostalgic return to Russia's Stalinist past and the rebirth of Soviet power in the guise "of a family album of Stalin's relatives! What a dark nightmare!"[2] She dragged out her Russian typewriter and wrote a long review of the book, which she sent to Olga Rifkina, who managed to get it broadcast on Russian radio.[3]

That her cousin was trying to whitewash the past was to her unbelievable. She wrote her review in eloquent Russian and then hurriedly translated it into English to send it to British and American friends, hoping it might be published in the West. (It wasn't.) She wrote as if in a state of shock. Could this really be Volodya?

Volodya, whose father had been arrested and perished in prison (rehabilitated posthumously)? Volodya, whose mother, a totally apolitical woman of weak health (she had TB) had to endure six years of solitary confinement? Is this Volodya who had himself enough of supervision from

NKVD, GPU, MGB and whatever else have been the names of those agencies, as had indeed our whole much-suffering family? Is this the same "Volodey" who was witty in his younger age . . . and was not afraid to laugh at this whole world of oppression, lies, and mortal danger . . . ?

She summarized Volodya's claims with disgust: "Let us also forgive Stalin for all the disregard of norms of democracy and laws" because he was supposedly "stern but just, something like Ivan the Terrible," and was "the great patriot of the motherland and the greatest war commander." She shuddered at the idea of a resurgence of the cult of her father.

She protested Volodya's efforts to whitewash the record of her brother Vasili—Vasili who had had the air force general Alexander Novikov thrown into prison simply for questioning him, who "despised the law" in his mistreatment of his first wife and children, and who'd gone on drunken binges. Now he was to be forgiven because "he is ours."

But the deepest blow to Svetlana was that Volodya said her mother's suicide was the result of "her sickness." She answered, "Enough, Volodya. It seems to me that I am in a dark, solitary hall of the Kremlin where, slowly, the accusers of my MOTHER appear with their verdict. SHE WAS, in truth, THE VICTIM of the system." Volodya had expunged her mother from history as merely "some sick woman."

Svetlana believed Volodya didn't write this *apologist* book alone, and in fact some members of the Alliluyev family would later concur that there were odd insertions, possibly as a condition of publication.[4] The book included "A Letter of Gratitude from Peasants to Redens," Volodya's father. What gratitude, Svetlana wanted to know, when the Chekists like Redens used brutal violence to force collectivization in the villages? The book suggested that the purges of the 1930s and of the war years, including the exile of entire ethnic groups, had been a "lawful defense of the rear"—and then blamed the KGB's Yezhov and Yagoda for any excesses, which had been "corrected by the justice of Lavrenty Beria." "How could Volodya write such things?" she asked. His own parents were victims of "our most dangerous relative of all—uncle Josef."

Her final damning comment was that Volodya emerged from his pages as a "convinced anti-Semite." Yulia Meltzer (wife of Yakov), Aleksei Kapler, and old Morozov (Svetlana's first husband's father)

> were all sent to prison by that same mighty relative of ours [Stalin]. Volodya has not a word of compassion for them. Has he totally forgotten those deeds? And what about all the ugly anti-Semitism of my brother Vasili who called my son a "zhidenok" [little Yid]. Grandfather and Grandmother Alliluyev had no such attitudes. These came later, introduced in the later years by the very same OGPU, VChK, MVD, KGB—by their cruel, middle-class, fascist trends. . . .
>
> Escape into the past is the worst sickness that can ever happen to us. . . . That wonderful past that suddenly sent out its deadly whiffs, like an opened grave. Why does our Volodya need that?[5]

She wrote to Philippa Hill that under her cousin's name, the Communist apparatchiks were trying to restore the "ancient regime." Millions of Russians were now longing for "the Glorious Past under that wise man, our unique incomparable leader (my father)." "What a lovely Superpower we've been. . . . One cannot blame them. They were duped and duped."[6]

The very next month, a disparaging article appeared in the London *Times*. Quoting the words of an Italian priest in the popular weekly *Chi*, the journalist Richard Beeston, stationed in Moscow, wrote, "Now at the age of 70, Svetlana Alliluyeva has reportedly decided to spend her remaining years as a nun, in her words, 'to atone for the sins of my father.'"[7] Apparently a Catholic nun in Chicago had revealed Svetlana's address in Cornwall. Svetlana wrote to Philippa Hill that these reports made her sound like a silly old fool. Why? The timing of the *Times* article was too coincidental. "I must assume this is the KGB's reply to <u>my kick to them</u>!"[8] Though many might call her paranoid, Svetlana could be forgiven for believing that, Victor Louis being dead, the KGB had found someone else to plant embarrassing anecdotes about her in the international press.

Within a week, she was outed in Cornwall. David Jones, a journalist for the *Daily Mail*, tracked her down.

> The teashop doorbell tinkles softly, and a squat, heavy-set old woman, with rheumy eyes and broken red veins ribboning her cheeks, peers suspiciously inside. It is a crisp winter morning in a remote West Country seaside village, and the place is deserted. Even so, she pulls down her black beret, raises the collar of her camel overcoat, and requests a table in the most conspiratorial corner. . . . Svetlana Peters (née Stalin)—her voice a strange mixture of drawing-room English and East European idioms—says, "Tell me please how did you find me here?"

This was the description of a bag lady. Svetlana had lost her possessions, her looks, her identity. Only her dignity and self-will were left. Jones quoted her disclaimer about her supposed retreat to an Italian convent. "I don't need a priest. I am fine on my own." She concluded the interview abruptly. "Enough now. . . . And listen to me—when we walk out of here, you go left and I go right."[9]

She wrote again to Philippa Hill: "We must never forget about the <u>continuity</u> of Russian police methods and <u>succession</u>

of <u>all</u> their leadership's violent cruelty when nothing else works. I've put <u>my foot</u> in the middle of the boiling pot of present-day passions and thus I cannot expect to be greeted there by the Old Order Supporters—<u>only by the liberal</u> side."[10] Two years later, in 1998, when the human rights activist Galina Starovoitova was gunned down in the entrance to her apartment building in Saint Petersburg, the murder only confirmed for Svetlana what she already believed. The FSB (as the new KGB was abbreviated) was a parallel power structure in Boris Yeltsin's "democratic" Russia and could act with impunity. Writing to Philippa about Starovoitova's assassination, she said, "My dear, they haven't changed a bit. Such a horror."[11]

Very shortly after her interview for the *Daily Mail*, Svetlana moved again. Abbeyfield had a vacancy in an old Victorian house in nearby Redruth, just when she needed it. She told Mary Burkett she was packing her yurt and locating to a new pasture—it was the gypsy wandering impulse she'd inherited from her grandfather Sergei. She moved to 52 Clinton Road, Redruth, and said she loved the small town with its narrow Victorian streets. And the sea was only thirty minutes away by bus.

The following year, Svetlana lived mostly through her correspondence, though the occasional friend visited. She managed to get back to the United States for a month's visit with Olga in Wisconsin and told Philippa Hill and Mary Burkett how loving and even overprotective her daughter had become. Olga was now phoning, sending presents, and writing regularly to ask what her mother needed. With no one to talk to, Svetlana walked over the hills and along seaside footpaths and took photographs of local landscapes. When she was a teenager, her brother Vasili had taught her how to develop photographs in his Kremlin darkroom. Philippa sent her a gift of a free pass to the Tate art gallery in Saint Ives. She also sent her money for walking shoes, for which Svetlana was exceedingly grateful.

In January 1997, the Abbeyfield Society found itself in a sudden financial crisis, and it seemed Svetlana would have to move to a new hostel. She refused. Olga had said that, in case of emergency, she should just come home. Svetlana could live with her. Svetlana moved briefly to a Carr-Gomm house at 7 Carack Street in Saint Ives and waited impatiently as Olga bought a house in Spring Green. She and Olga set the date of her return to America for November. She wrote to Mary Burkett, "Just eight months now . . . Oh to be with my Olga in her kitchen and to cook my own food. . . . What has become of my life, Mary? . . . I have a feeling that all will change as soon as I cross the Atlantic. I do not even care how, just change."[12]

Linda Kelly soon phoned Svetlana with the shocking news that Nina Lobanov-Rostovsky's sister in Paris had committed suicide. Svetlana knew what this meant and, dredging up painful thoughts of her mother, tried to console Nina.

> Linda Kelly said that your sister in Paris died tragically—
> and I know there will be a void in your life. . . . It's always so
> sad and frightening when one chooses that sort of death—
> it's certainly a case of some momentary madness, about
> which one (I'm sure) regrets at the second of conscious
> thinking. Those close <u>who are left</u>—are left in horror and
> disbelief—but it's too late—and <u>actually</u> their interference
> earlier wouldn't change what has been inwardly <u>decided</u>
> by those who perform a violent act. <u>Sixty-five years after</u>
> my mother did the same—I <u>still</u> cannot comprehend—
> accept—forgive—it. It bothers me that <u>she was</u> one of the
> <u>most dearly beloved</u> persons for me—and that I am, even
> now, unable to understand <u>her</u>. And—if <u>she</u> only knew the
> amount of terrible destruction she'd cause <u>to others around
> her</u>—she, most probably, would <u>stop</u> at the last moment. She
> made me study C. G. Jung for decades, <u>to find in his work</u>

an explanation—but I've found only an absolute division between the conscious <u>and</u> the unconscious, <u>the abyss between the two</u>, and too few hints about how to explain the latter in terms of the former. Enough of this! You have enough pain, without me.

She told Nina she was now returning to the United States. While she often felt "ostracized, humiliated, put down" by many, Nina had always been kind. "<u>You've been informal</u> with me, <u>un-prejudiced</u>, <u>willing to understand</u>, and <u>most generous</u>. <u>What else</u> can one demand? <u>Please do not remember me as a totally dreadful beast</u> and as an ungrateful woman—for I am neither."[13] One can imagine Svetlana's care in underlining those words as she wrote her letter so that they would carry the full weight of her gratitude.

Mary Burkett came to Cornwall for a last visit. "We sat on the island and the sun came out and the seagulls flew around us. We had a sort of closing time. She was going off to America, going into the unknown, and looking forward to it.[14]

On November 3, Svetlana was gone. The last few years had been hard—living, as she put it, "on the level of an English derelict."[15] It seemed the only regret she expressed at the time was that she couldn't find someone at the group home willing to take her ten potted geraniums, which were now blooming.

Chapter 36

Final Return

Svetlana in Spring Green, Wisconsin, in 2002
with her cat Black Nose.

Svetlana was happy to be back in Spring Green. She was now seventy-one, and it seemed to her that she had come full circle—she insisted this would be her last migration. It was characteristic that she said the years in England had been "a total waste of time,"[1] until she could reflect and become nostalgic, as if she had to shed the past completely before picking through it piecemeal to remember the good moments.

Olga had bought the house she had been renting and moved tenants into the upstairs apartment to help pay the mortgage.

She had filled the house with her Indian and Tibetan embroideries and statues. Mother, daughter, and two cats settled in for a lovely Thanksgiving and Christmas. Svetlana wrote to Mary Burkett that Olga had now become her "guardian, friend, and everything else." She was totally in her daughter's "young hands," but it was a weird feeling: "I love independence."[2] This was a familiar psychological ambivalence—to need to subsume herself totally in another and yet to be in charge. She tried to be careful not to criticize Olga. She sent friends photos of the Wisconsin River with its islands full of flowers and of her favorite spot, Orion Boat Landing, assuring them she loved Spring Green.

The arrangement worked for about fourteen months, until both Olga and Svetlana conceded that, as much as they tried to pretend otherwise, the generation gap between twenty-seven and seventy-two was too wide to bridge. Svetlana complained to her old friend Bob Rayle that Olga was a sociable creature, like her father, and loved company and loud music (the kind that set Svetlana's teeth on edge). The house was like a railway station with an open door.[3]

For Olga the months were hard. "She was my 'old' mother . . . she could age, but I couldn't. She got older and wiser, and I stayed young." As much as she loved her mother, it was clearly impossible for them to live together, but sometimes her compassion for her mother cracked her heart. "I think it was living that was the hard part for her. My mother never mastered that one . . . surviving but not living."[4]

By now, as an American senior citizen who had paid taxes and met the requirements, Svetlana was eligible for Social Security. By mutual agreement, she moved to a seniors residence in February 1999. Svetlana concluded, "I have to find ways to be happy where I am." She had her books, her radio, her daughter's visits, and her few good friends.

Elizabeth Coyne, who had helped her with the infant Olga at Taliesin all those years back and to whom she had given the Taliesin piano, had died tragically in a car accident, but Elizabeth's children, Michael Coyne and Kathy Rossing, remembered Svetlana warmly and attached her name to those exotic presents she'd given their mother. Wedding gifts for Svetlana and Wes had poured in from all over the world in 1970, and Svetlana sent some of them home to the children. Kathy still remembered a box of designer perfumes, all in little vials. "For a child, it was wonderful!" To them, Svetlana was simply Lana. "It was not important who her father was."

Kathy Rossing devoted much time to Svetlana because she was moved by the simplicity of Svetlana's relationship with Jennifer, her adult disabled daughter. "Our daughter has a kind of radar. I think she was born with it. She can tell who is sincere and who is not and Lana had the same radar." Lana loved to browse in the secondhand stores with Kathy and would buy little trinkets for her daughter, saying, 'Here. Take these for Jenny.'"[5]

At the beginning of 2001, Olga moved to the West Coast for work and to undertake a degree in accounting. Svetlana was desolate and wondered how she would survive without seeing Olga three or four times a week. Of course she was caustic; she was to be left behind to take care of Olga's two old cats.[6] Yet she was proud of Olga and would boast to friends that her daughter had initiative.[7] Olga would send her money whenever she could, and they talked regularly each weekend.

Still, for Svetlana money was always tight. She would have been the first to say the gift catalogs coming through the mail were her downfall. As Kathy Rossing remembered, "She loved those catalogs, the underlining and the circling. 'And what do you think about this?' she'd ask. 'Way overpriced,' I'd respond. And the post couldn't read her handwriting, and I would be the one to phone to track down the missing items."[8]

When Olga came for Christmas, there would be an exchange of presents. Svetlana loved to get gifts. "She was like a child in that respect. She'd just get giddy when you'd come with a bag, the anticipation of it. She didn't have a lot of people bringing her gifts, so when she got them, it was a fun time for her, as it was for us."

But then she loved to give gifts away. "You'd buy her something you thought she'd like, and as soon as she opened it, she might say, 'Oh, this would be wonderful for so-and-so.' She was so blatant about it. She wasn't trying to be offensive; it was just the way she was."[9] Often Svetlana could barely make her money last to the end of the month, yet she was always giving things away. Once Michael Coyne gave her a hundred dollars to buy something for herself, only to discover that she had turned the money over to some women who had bought a barn and were adopting stray cats.[10]

In her last years, Svetlana remained a nomad, but the geography she moved in was much reduced. She would move back and forth between two retirement homes, Ridgeview Commons and Richland Hill, and also back and forth within Spring Green. Partly it was because she loved to move, always thinking the next place would be better. But sometimes she would move because she thought journalists, or worse, had tracked her down.

Of course, no matter the residence, it was always the same small room. Kathy remembered that its main feature was the four-tiered narrow shelf on which Svetlana kept all her cherished photos: she had pictures of Olga; of Nanny Alexandra Andreevna; of her mother, Nadya; and of her grandmother

Olga. She had a photo of her beloved Black Sea and the wedding portrait of her and Wes.

Michael Coyne remembered those rooms. While many people still thought Svetlana had a lavish lifestyle, she actually "lived on hand-me-downs, in holey sweaters, wrapped up in blankets." She had an old VCR Olga had given her, and Coyne and Olga would search the Goodwill shops to find tapes of old movies for her. She still loved Elizabeth Taylor movies, since she remembered, when she was a child in the Kremlin, watching Taylor and those horses. Her little radio had an antenna, and she'd try to pick up the BBC. When one visited, one would find her reading, perhaps a biography of Georgia O'Keeffe or Anna Dostoyevsky's memoir of her husband. Or writing. If she could, she would try to persuade a friend to drive her to her favorite restaurant on her beloved Wisconsin River, where she would sit on the deck, eating a hamburger and drinking a glass of zinfandel, and watch the birds rise over the water as they had once done long ago at Zubalovo in her childhood.

Coyne had grown up in the Cold War era and had heard about Stalin in school, but only as he got older did he begin to recognize who this "Lana" was. "I started to realize her importance in history, her pedigree, and what she'd actually done and how this affected diplomatic relations, but she was just another part of the family actually." Of course he was curious about Stalin, but he didn't ask questions because he didn't want to destroy their friendship. He'd seen how this could happen. When the owner of an independent bookstore in Richland Center had grown curious about her past, she'd refused to set foot in the bookshop again. "My Mom, my sister Kathy, and I never pried. She was an individual. I never talked about her with friends. Few knew that I actually knew who she was. She was just Lana."[11]

By now Svetlana had developed severe scoliosis and had a terrible dowager's hump on her back, to a degree that she had to use a walker, which she called her "four-wheel drive."[12] She reassured Coyne that he shouldn't worry when she walked out "like Queen Victoria" with her cane. When she was young, her brother had taught her the right way to take a fall.[13]

She'd go to the secondhand store to buy her clothes. She would find an oversize man's shirt, rip out the seams, and resew it so that it fitted perfectly, almost disguising her deformity. She claimed to have learned this trick from her dressmakers in Moscow. Her closets were full of the Indian fabrics Olga sent, which she'd convert into pillows and clothes as gifts for friends. She also made herbal remedies and healing tinctures from Russian folk recipes she'd learned as a child from her nanny. Because he worked for the airlines, Coyne traveled a great deal, and whenever he returned from a trip, he always had small gifts for Lana: chocolates from Switzerland, tea from England. She'd listen to his stories about his travels as if living them vicariously. "She wasn't a happy person. She would laugh once in a while, but she was very serious." And she was still very opinionated. "If she didn't like something, she'd let you know."[14] She also had a willed optimism. She liked to quote Aleksei Kapler: "My old, long ago dead friend [Kapler died in 1979] in Moscow used to say: 'Life is like a zebra. You go through the black stripes, but you know that the white ones will follow.'"[15]

Svetlana always kept up-to-date with Russian politics. She confessed to Bob Rayle in 1997 that even she had not thought that the USSR would "utterly collapse" so soon. She'd expected changes within the Party, as happened in China, but "events went ahead of everybody's thinking." But with her usual sarcasm, she warned Bob that perhaps the changes weren't so profound. "Old drunk Yeltsin and all the 'apparatus' behind him are still the old 'bolshis,' only now masquerading to be something else."[16]

When her friend the volcanologist Thomas Miller told her he was planning a visit to Russia in January 2000, she told him to be very careful, especially if he intended to bring money to scientists, which could easily be construed as foreign interference. Miller believed that Svetlana's "sense of how power worked was impeccable."[17] On December 31, 1999, when Vladimir Putin became acting president after Boris Yeltsin unexpectedly resigned, she warned Miller:

> Russia is quickly (in <u>my</u> opinion) sliding back into the past—with that <u>awful</u> former KGB-SPY now as an acting president! I do hope and believe the people will <u>not</u> vote him into the Presidency—but, then of course elections always could be rigged. . . . The Tchetchen [Chechen] War—"the Glorious One"—was provoked by the old Russian method of provocation. The Tchetchens—feisty as they are—would <u>never</u> go outside their mountains <u>to bomb "cities</u> in Russia-proper"! That is just <u>not</u> the way of doing their Guerrilla-war—it was done by the KGB itself. And when Artem Borovik (investigative reporter) <u>wanted</u> to <u>see</u> more deeply into this business of Tchetchen War, and <u>how it was started</u>, he was quietly <u>disposed of</u> by the <u>same forces</u>.[*]
>
> I know all this—from the Times of Classic Communism & Cold War. The foreign leaders of these Democracies should <u>boycott</u> Putin—but, instead, they are waiting to

---

[*] On the eve of the 2000 presidential elections in Russia, Borovik died in a plane crash just before the publication of his investigation into an apartment bombing in Moscow and his article about Vladimir Putin's childhood.

embrace him, with good jugs of vodka. Ah, Thomas, be careful. The times of would-be-democracy are finished in Russia.[18]

She reserved most of her political invective for her letters to Bob Rayle. Surely he could understand what she was talking about when she railed against the current American administration's naïveté—or was it cynicism—as they misread what was going on in the new Russia. She wrote to say she was appalled when Vladimir Putin was elected in 2000.

Russia has changed the flag and some names, to be sure—yet it is still the <u>same USSR</u>, so far as I am concerned. And these days—when a shadowy KGB colonel <u>got on the top</u> (because he was wise enough to guarantee Boris Yeltsin to be spared from public <u>investigation</u>—and—most probably <u>prosecution</u>—in that field of corruption & money stealing—when the <u>New Man in Kremlin</u> is being pronounced by my local Public Radio as the "<u>sure hero of the Russians</u>," as their "sure choice" for the next president—I can only swear in Russian (which is a very heavy swear, but no one understands, thank God). . . .

Thinking about Russia (and how little it is understood here in these United States) ruins my sleep.[19]

She told Michael Coyne that Putin was reviving her father's cult of personality. Coyne recalled: "The things Putin was doing to instill the memory of Stalin, whether it would be statuary or different things, she did not agree with."[20] And, slowly, Svetlana began to believe that she, too, would become one of these symbols. She told Bob Rayle that she feared she might be deported back to Russia. Or after her death, perhaps a will might be fabricated stating that she wanted her remains to be buried in her homeland.[21]

For Rayle, of course, this was clearly paranoid. And it may have been. It was unlikely that President Putin was concerned with repatriating Stalin's daughter, alive or dead. But Svetlana was thinking like a Russian to whom symbols meant a great deal. Her paranoia had a logic: it was not she, Lana Peters, the Russians would be interested in; they would be interested in finishing the story of Stalin's greatness—the return of the prodigal daughter whom the West had stolen, but who had never really abandoned her father. It didn't seem to her inconceivable that her ashes would be part of the statuary to commemorate the resurrection of the great Stalin.

She wrote back to Rayle, who had obviously dismissed her concerns.

> I am pleased to know, though, that the idea of my "being sent home" upon requests of the communists or KGBists, strikes you as insane. I think—it is insane, too. But so is the whole business of Chechen war; and of the former red spy becoming new President of Russia. People know who I am—here and there—and is ENOUGH. . . . Nobody needs me there as Lana Peters; they need me as Svetlana Stalin.[22]

She told Rayle that, of course, everyone in Russia in her childhood had grown up paranoid and fearful. What did he expect? But if she were ever deported to Russia, she would arrive dead because she would kill herself on the way.

Svetlana perceived, again faster than many, what was happening to human rights in Russia under the surface. She saw the growing strength of the FSB (the former KGB), the restrictions on the media, the arrest of business oligarchs as a warning to stay out of politics, and later the passage of legislation that forced burdensome reporting requirements on Russian and foreign NCOs (noncommercial organizations), essentially charities and human rights organizations.[23] She lamented that the Russian people looked the other way; their standard of living had vastly improved as oil and gas sales boomed, but graft and corruption were rampant and, anyway, they were fed nationalist propaganda and the history of Russia's greatness "as if it were mother's milk."[24]

Perhaps for everyone in old age the world constricts and fear expands to fill the small circle of one's existence. Kathy Rossing was aware that Svetlana often lived in fear. She now believed that Russian intelligence agents might abduct her on the streets of Richland Center. When Kathy dismissed the idea, Svetlana replied, "You don't know what they could do. I saw people disappear. You don't understand. I saw people disappear all around me and they didn't come back." And Kathy thought, *You're right. I'm coming from a different background . . . .* "Lana could see a lot of things that had been present in her dad's government coming back. She thought Putin idolized her father and was fashioning himself after him. She always feared it would be her son Joseph's responsibility to come for her body."

Svetlana hired a lawyer in Spring Green to draw up a legal document that would prohibit Joseph from getting access to her body or her remains. Kathy and her brother helped pay her lawyer's fees in order to ease her mind. She gave Kathy a list of names at the State Department and other contacts. "If she came up missing, that's where she would be, and we needed to get the government involved to get her back here."[25]

Svetlana wrote to Bob Rayle that she was in physical pain. She was feeling old, she was feeling used, and she wanted the last word. "I want my reputation & character of a decent woman restored. I want my name as a writer, who writes her books without ghost-hired-persons, to be *restored*. I *want* my name

Svetlana not to sound as a *threat*."[26] Her deepest concern was
that people still believed she was a rich woman.[27] Some even
said she was masquerading as a welfare recipient. One of Olga's
boyfriends had asked her, "Do you have access to those funds,
stashed in Switzerland?" A Hungarian expatriate kept pester-
ing her: "Tell me, in secret, where do you keep those funds of
yours?"[28] That she herself had decided to stop in Switzerland
was a lie "worthy of the Kremlin." She complained to Bob, "It
hurts me and affects my life UNTIL this day."

In 2005, at age seventy-nine, Svetlana wrote Bob and Ramona Rayle a series of numbered letters. It was as if she hoped
to repeat the structure of her first book *Twenty Letters to a
Friend*. These letters were meant to correct the calumnies of
the past. Returning to old wounds, she retold the narrative of
her defection and arrival in America, raging at the lawyers, the
bankers, the diplomats, and the journalists who had swindled
and slandered her.

Svetlana's rage was intemperate and almost impressive.
Once started, she couldn't control her invective and would
give vent without restraint, leading many to compare her rages
to Stalin's. But one could also say that her anger was particularly Russian; it served as a purgative. She could never understand the American habit of diplomatic niceties. "Oh, how
I hate that American habit," she'd complain. "'How are you?'
'Fine!' 'Great!' You might be just widowed, but you HAVE to
say FINE!"[29] She nursed her hurt; she felt she had been used,
whatever the diplomatic expediencies. But her "Letters to Bob
and Ramona Rayle" petered out when her anger did, and she
dropped the idea.

Svetlana met Marie Anderson in the fall of 2005. A friend
had asked Marie if she could help move Svetlana to a new
residence—just a few boxes—because she had a car. Svetlana
had lost none of her persuasiveness. Marie took to driving her

when she needed to go somewhere. She vividly remembered the time they returned to Svetlana's apartment in Richland Center to find a stranger sitting in the foyer. In a heavily accented voice, he'd asked if they knew Lana Peters. He'd tried knocking on her door, but she hadn't answered. Marie responded, "No, not really," and Svetlana said, "Maybe she's gone for the weekend." After they returned to her room, Marie stayed with Svetlana, who was clearly frightened. It wasn't very long before there was a knock on the door. It was a local police officer, who knew who Svetlana was. Apparently the man, accompanied by a woman, was driving a rental car with New York plates. The woman had phoned the owner of the retirement home, and the owner, becoming suspicious, had called the police to check on Lana. The stranger claimed that all he wanted was to ask Svetlana to sign her book. The police escorted the couple out of town.[30]

On a trip through Spring Green in 2006, Bob and Ramona Rayle stopped to visit Svetlana one afternoon. She took them to visit the grave of Wesley Peters, and then they went to a restaurant where she and Bob reminisced about their time in India in 1967. How had she had the strength to make such a monumental decision? In a follow-up letter, she wrote: "Nowadays, weak and fearful, I often get amazed that I'd done that. I was afraid of nothing—then. I love to recall those days . . . such fun it was."[31] Her defection was her stamp on the world. She had "slapped the Soviet government in the face."[32] She had fooled them all.

In 2010, the journalist David Jones, who had interviewed her in remote Cornwall fourteen years before, tracked her down again to Richland Center, where, as he wrote, "Lana Peters, or Svetlana Stalin, as she was known before marriage removed the stain of her surname," was "hiding." Jones was shocked by the change in her appearance. Bent with scoliosis and wearing a gray tracksuit and pink blouse, she looked "every inch the American retiree." When he remarked on this, she asked, "Why not?" She'd been in America so long, she felt American. She liked hamburgers, American films, and speaking English. He wanted to know if she'd forgiven her father, a question that sparked "her legendary temper." "I don't forgive anything or anybody! If he could kill so many people, including my uncles and auntie, I will never forgive him. Never! . . . He broke my life. I want to explain to you, he broke my life!"[33] This would turn out to be her last interview.

Yet Olga believed that somehow, in the last two years of her life, her mother reached an unexpected peace. "She suddenly took things in stride. . . . When things happened that, before, would have knocked her for six, she would be able to laugh herself out of anger." Olga would say to herself, *Who are you and what have you done with my mother?* "We just got back our really joyous happy days. It was fun."[34]

Perhaps one of the things that consoled Svetlana was that a new friend, the author Nicholas Thompson, had been kind enough to contact the Washington copyright office regarding *Twenty Letters to a Friend*, and secured the copyright of her book under her own name. Priscilla Johnson McMillan also generously allowed her rights to the English translation to revert to Svetlana.[35] She could now leave her book to her daughter.

Svetlana seemed to have reached the kind of resolution she'd written about to her friend Linda Kelly: "I came to the conclusion that the <u>most important</u> thing in life is NOT 'Achievements,' but that humble, yet very difficult—ability to remain myself."[36]

In 2011 Svetlana was diagnosed with terminal cancer. She wrote to Mary Burkett that May: "I'm falling apart."[37] And to Philippa Hill she said, "I am slowly preparing to leave this world."[38] She often talked with Kathy Rossing about death.

To console her, Kathy told her about her own brother's dying. He'd been sent home from the hospital. She'd come into his room—it was just twenty-four hours before he died—and he had said to her, "Shush. Mother's here to get me." She told Svetlana, "You're going to see all those people who have passed before you, your nanny, your mom, and your grandma," but Svetlana just looked at her and said, "What about the people I don't want to see?" Kathy could tell from the look on her face whom she meant. "I didn't know how to answer her. . . . Certainly I think she was fearful of death for a while, but then, I don't know how, she resolved it within herself, and she seemed to be OK with going."

Svetlana wanted to be cremated and initially asked Kathy to ensure that her ashes were spread at Orion Boat Landing on the Wisconsin River. But then she said, "We can't do that because when people find out my ashes are in there, they'll think I polluted their river." No matter how much Kathy reassured her that this could be done in secret—"We have a canoe. No one needs to know"—Svetlana remained adamant. Someone would find out. She also prepared a legal document. Mr. Stafford at the funeral home had instructions to collect her body at the hospital, take it immediately to the crematorium, and get her ashes to Olga—"done and shipped before anyone had a chance to do anything else with them."[39]

She gave Kathy a photograph that she wanted displayed at her memorial service. Kathy found it absolutely hilarious. It was an image of a wide and empty sea under a full moon, broken only by a whale's tail breaching the surface and about to fall back down. Svetlana had written on the back: "Good-bye to you all from your Fish. (put the date: ___)."[40]

In November, Svetlana took a sudden turn for the worse and was transported to the Pine Valley hospital. She specifically instructed the hospital staff not to call Olga. She didn't want her daughter to see her dead body. She had seen her own mother's corpse and had backed away in terror on that long-ago morning in the GUM building in Moscow. Ever after, she carried that last image of her mother in her mind. Kathy believed Svetlana wanted to spare her daughter. "I don't think she realized the hurt it would cause her by shutting her out when she would have wanted to be the one there." The doctors finally persuaded Svetlana to call Olga. They said, "Your daughter deserves to know."

Her decline had been so sudden that Olga didn't know her mother was dying. She'd just spent the previous month with her, and they'd talked of Olga's coming back for Christmas. Olga immediately booked a flight. When she arrived too late, the doctors told her it wouldn't have mattered. They had instructions not to admit her to her mother's hospital room. Olga was angry with her mother and hurt—her mother was still protecting her after all these years. She'd missed her father's dying; she had wanted to be there for her mother.

Kathy Rossing was with Svetlana at the end. Svetlana couldn't speak but knew Kathy was there. She squeezed Kathy's hand and stared at her with a strange look in her eyes. Kathy wrapped Svetlana's hand around the scapular medal she always wore, yet it seemed "she wasn't ready to go." Kathy asked a nurse to call a local clergyman. When he came, he gave Svetlana words of peace to comfort her, and "it wasn't but a matter of minutes and then she was gone. I think it was more than a coincidence. Once he said some words over her, she passed peacefully."[41] Unlike her father to the end, she didn't struggle. "Her breathing just got shallower and shallower." How difficult it is to *perform* one's death. She did it gracefully.

Svetlana died on November 22, 2011, in the month of misery at the age of eighty-five, as she had predicted she would, and a little more than two weeks after the anniversary of her own mother's death seventy-nine years earlier.

She left her last words for her daughter in a typed letter. She spoke as if she were writing not before her death, but after it.

I am always with you, in loving ways. Remember that. We, who are now without bodily traits, only spirits, we love you on Earth nevertheless. Therefore, do not cry about us. Never, never cry about us. Because your cries only disturb us here. We cannot do anything about it. But we, the spirits now, always love you. We can feel sometimes. . . . *You* can feel sometimes . . . a warm wind or breath touching your skin. That is us. That *are* us. I know that, since I am now, too, only a spirit, only a soul . . . *only?* Oh, we can do a lot from here. We can protect you from a disaster, we can embrace you, there . . . like a warm cocoon. We can heal all your self-inflicted troubles because from here, high above Earth, we can see very well. And we can always help you out. But never, never cry about us, rather, think about us always with a smile. We love you forever and ever. I say *WE* . . . because we are many here, loving souls. Even my own so-perplexed mother; she finally got rid of those confusing earthly worries, and here she is a beautiful soul like she had been, indeed. We all love you. Do not cry about us. We love you. Your Mom. Sorry for bad typing, alas, I did not improve even here![42]

Olga collected her mother's ashes and scattered them in the Pacific Ocean. She had lost the person who loved her most deeply, and her mourning would be long.

Acknowledgments

Writing *Stalin's Daughter: The Extraordinary and Tumultuous Life of Svetlana Alliluyeva* presented challenges that were both exciting and daunting. I would like to thank those who helped me on a journey that took me from Toronto to Moscow, Saint Petersburg, Tbilisi, Gori, London, the Lake District, Washington, Princeton, New York, Portland, and elsewhere, during which I met remarkable people.

First and foremost I would like to thank Svetlana Alliluyeva's daughter Chrese Evans. Her remarkable openness in our long hours of conversation and correspondence and her permission to quote from her mother's unpublished works and letters have made it possible for Alliluyeva's voice to surface in this book. Sim Smiley was indispensable as I undertook research in the labyrinth of intelligence archives. My research assistant, Anastassia Kostrioukova, stayed with me throughout the project; her help in archival research, interviews, and much else was invaluable.

There are many people to thank: Olga Alliloueva, who introduced me to her Moscow family; Alexander Alliluyev, Leonid and Galina Alliluyev, and Alexander Burdonsky, whose shrewd readings of their relative Stalin and of his daughter are fascinating; Stepan Mikoyan for his courtesy and thoughtfulness; Alexander Ushakov for his candor; and Yelena Khanga for her esprit. Professor Marina Kaul of the

Russian State University of the Humanities helped me with visas and contacts. Jeff Parker encouraged me at the beginning of the project, and assisted me through the maze of Russia. I would like to thank Simon Sebag Montefiore for introducing me to the journalist Nestan Charkviani, whose Georgian warmth opened doors in Tbilisi; and Omari Tushurashvili at the Archive of the Georgian Ministry of Internal Affairs for his hospitality.

Of those in England, I want to thank Linda Kelly, who was so helpful in connecting me with Svetlana's British friends, and her husband, Laurence, for his amusing anecdotes about Stalin; Vanessa Thomas, who drove me through the sites of Svetlana's past and gave me access to invaluable documents; Philippa Hill, who offered me Svetlana's original letters; Nina Lobanov-Rostovsky for her insights; David and Clarissa Pryce-Jones, who made time for me; and the remarkable Mary Burkett, who hosted my stay in the Lake District. Rosamond Richardson was invariably generous with her time and her collection of Alliluyeva interview tapes and memorabilia.

Of those in the United States, I would like to single out Joan Kennan, who has been so generous in her replies to my endless queries; Robert and Ramona Rayle, who hosted my stay in Ashburn, Virginia, and helped shape my perspective of Svetlana; Kathy Rossing for her patience and for confirming my subject's sense of humor; Thomas Miller and Margaret Jameson, who generously offered me copies of letters; Rosa Shand, whose moving portrait of Svetlana Alliluyeva in her own writing is inspiring; Priscilla Johnson McMillan, so helpful in pursuing the mysteries of Svetlana's copyright; and Meryle Secrest, who generously offered me permission to quote from her fifty hours of taped interviews with Svetlana.

In writing this book I have had the help of specialists in Russian history. I would like particularly to thank Professor

Lynne Viola of the University of Toronto, who generously read my manuscript to correct any historical errors; Stephen Cohen, who provided me with contacts and whose work on Nikolai Bukharin and on the Gulag is an invaluable source; and Alan Barenberg, who allowed me to read the manuscript of his book *Gulag Town, Company Town: Forced Labor and Its Legacy in Vorkuta* before it was published, illuminating the mysteries of the Gulag administration.

I would like to thank my numerous research assistants and translators who helped me along the way, including Liza Kobrinsky, Andreas Vatiliotou, Andrei Osadchy, Nadia Ragbar, Oleksandr Melnyk, Andrey Gornostaev, and Liuba Turlova. I would also like to thank Elena Romanova and Brendan Sheehan.

Archivists are invaluable in the research process. I would like to thank Charlaine McCauley at the Lyndon Baines Johnson Library; Anne Marie Menta and Natalia Sciarini at the Beinecke Rare Book and Manuscript Library; Amanda Pike and Adriane Hanson at the Seeley G. Mudd Manuscript Library, Princeton; Jonathan Eaker at the Library of Congress; Jim Sam and Carol Leadenham at the Hoover Institution Library and Archives, Stanford University; Keith Call at the Wheaton College Archives and Special Collections; Anna Evgen'evna Tsar'kova at the Alliluev Apartment-Museum; Dasha Kondrashina at the Model School No. 25 museum; and Aliona Gennadi'evna Kozlova at the Archive of the Memorial Society International. I would also like to thank Henry Hardy of the Isaiah Berlin Literary Trust, Wolfson College, Oxford.

The Pierre Elliott Trudeau Foundation honored me with a three-year fellowship, which proved invaluable in the pursuit of my research.

Last, I must thank the most important person, my editor, Claire Wachtel at HarperCollins USA. It was in our conversations that the idea for this book first surfaced. To put it simply, she is brilliant, courageous, and infinitely supportive. I must also thank the remarkably inventive and efficient Hannah Wood, associate editor, Harper/Perennial, and Jane Beirn, senior director of publicity, for the care and enthusiasm she has shown my book. I want to thank my Canadian editor, the inspiring Iris Tupholme of HarperCollins Canada, who has supported me throughout my career; her assistant, Doug Richmond, who was always generous with his time and insights; Maria Golikova, who read the manuscript so sympathetically and carefully; Miranda Snyder, for her organizational skills and kindness; and my British editor, Clare Reihill of HarperCollins UK, for her hospitality and enthusiasm, as well as her assistant, Emmanuella Kwenortey, whose patience in photo documentation was invaluable. I would like to thank my agent, Jackie Kaiser, who offers her time, insight, and enthusiasm so generously and can always be counted on. Finally I owe deepest gratitude to my husband, Juan Opitz, who maintained his patience and support through the long research and writing process; he is always my most impassioned advocate.

Interviews

IN THE UNITED STATES

Chrese Evans (Olga Peters), Marie Anderson, Michael Coyne, Aris Georges, Millie Harford, Priscilla Johnson McMillan, Joan Kennan, Hella McVay, Thomas Miller, Walter Pozen, Robert and Ramona Rayle, Anne Reeves, Kathy Rossing, Alan Schwartz, Meryle Secrest, and Evgeniya Tucker.

IN RUSSIA

Alexander Pavlovich Alliluyev, Leonid Stanislavovich and Galina Ivanovna Alliluyev, Alexander Burdonsky, Marina

Rafailovna Kaul, Yelena Khanga, Diana Kondrashina, Stepan Anastasovich Mikoyan, and Alexander Mironovich Ushakov.

IN GEORGIA

Nestan Charkviani and Leila Sikmashvili.

IN ENGLAND

Mary Burkett, Pamela Egremont, Philippa Hill, Linda and Laurence Kelly, David and Clarissa Pryce-Jones, Jane Renfrew, Rosamond Richardson, and Vanessa Thomas.

IN CANADA

Olga Leonidovna Alliloueva and Frances Sedgwik.

IN MEXICO

Raoul Ortiz

List of Characters

In the USSR:

Vissarion "Beso" Djugashvili: Stalin's father; born in Georgia; a cobbler.

Ekaterina "Keke" Djugashvili: Stalin's mother, born in Georgia; seamstress and washerwoman; Stalin was her only surviving child.

Joseph "Soso" Vissarionovich Djugashvili: Svetlana's father; born in Gori, Georgia; revolutionary name Koba; adopted name Stalin ("steel") in 1913.

Nadezhda "Nadya" (Alliluyeva) Stalina: Stalin's second wife and Svetlana's mother; born in Baku, Azerbaijan.

Vasili "Vasya" Stalin: Svetlana's brother; born in Moscow, 1921; died of alcoholism.

Yakov "Yasha" Djugashvili: Svetlana's half brother; Stalin's eldest son by first wife; born in Tbilisi, Georgia; captured by Germans in 1941; died in POW camp in 1943; second wife, Yulia Meltzer, arrested 1941; released 1943.

Artyom Sergeev: adopted by Stalin when his father died in a train crash in 1921; lived with the Stalins until the late 1920s, when he returned to live with his mother.

Alexandra Andreevna Bychkova: served as Svetlana's nanny and as nanny to Svetlana's children; died in 1956.

Carolina Til: Latvian housekeeper who worked for the Stalins from 1927 to 1937, when she was dismissed during the "Great Terror."

Mikhail Klimov: Svetlana's bodyguard; reluctant witness to the love affair with Aleksei Kapler, 1942–43.

Valentina "Valechka" Istomina: Stalin's loyal housekeeper and rumored intimate companion; served at Stalin's Kuntsevo dacha from 1934 until Stalin's death.

SVETLANA'S RELATIVES:

The Alliluyevs:

Olga Alliluyeva: Svetlana's maternal grandmother; born in Georgia of German ancestry; mother of four children.

Sergei Alliluyev: Svetlana's maternal grandfather; railway worker and Bolshevik revolutionary; introduced Stalin into the Alliluyev family in 1900.

Pavel Alliluyev: Nadya's brother; died of a heart attack in 1938; his wife, Zhenya, was arrested in 1947; released 1954.

Anna Alliluyeva: Nadya's sister: arrested in 1948; released in 1954; husband, Stanislav Redens, the People's Commissar for Internal Affairs in Kazakhstan and former head of the OGPU in the Ukraine; executed in 1940.

Fyodor Alliluyev: Nadya's brother, born in 1898; had mental breakdown in 1918–19, during training exercises in the Russian Civil War.

Svetlana's Cousins and Childhood Companions:

Children of Pavel and Zhenya Alliluyev: Kyra arrested 1948; released 1953; Sergei; and Alexander.

Children of Anna and Stanislav Redens: Leonid; Vladimir.

Svetlana's Nephew:

Alexander Burdonsky: son of Svetlana's brother Vasili Stalin; rejected the name Stalin and assumed mother's name Burdonsky; well-known theater director.

Svanidzes:

Ekaterina "Kato" Svanidze: Stalin's first wife; Georgian; married 1906; died of typhus in 1907.

Alexander "Alyosha" Svanidze: brother of Stalin's first wife, Kato; worked for Soviet Bank for Foreign Trade until arrest and execution in 1941; wife, Maria Svanidze, former Georgian opera singer; diarist; executed in 1942. Only son "Johnik."

Mariko and Sashiko Svanidze: sisters of Stalin's first wife, Kato; Mariko was executed in 1942.

SVETLANA'S HUSBANDS IN THE USSR:

Grigori "Grisha" Morozov: Jewish friend of Vasili; married in 1944; divorced in 1947; went on to become a law professor.

Yuri Zhdanov: son of Supreme Soviet chairman Andrei Zhdanov; married 1949; divorced 1951; head of the Science Department of the Central Committee at age twenty-eight.

Johnreed "Johnik" (Ivan) Svanidze: sent to orphanage for children of the condemned; exiled to Kazakhstan to work in mines;

returned to Moscow in 1956; married Svetlana in church wedding, 1962; divorced after one year.

Brajesh Singh: son of the Rajah of Kalakankar in Uttar Pradesh; common-law husband; met Svetlana in 1963; died in 1966.

SVETLANA'S CHILDREN IN THE USSR:
Joseph Alliluyev: son of Grigori Morozov; born in 1945; neurologist; first wife, Elena; son Ilya; second wife, Lyuda; died in 2008.

Katya Zhdanov: daughter of Yuri Zhdanov; born in 1950; worked as a volcanologist in Kamchatka; daughter, Anya.

SVETLANA'S LOVERS IN THE USSR:
Aleksei Kapler: Jewish screenwriter; platonic love affair 1942–43; exiled by Stalin to Gulag for ten years.

Yuri Tomsky: son of Mikhail Tomsky, trade union leader who committed suicide in 1936; brought up in the Gulag as an orphan.

David Samoilov: born in 1920; Jewish; one of the most important Russian postwar poets; died 1990.

Andre Sinyavsky: dissident writer; arrested with Yuli Daniel in 1966; sentenced to seven years in the Gulag for anti-Soviet activity; released in 1971; emigrated to Paris with his wife, Maria Rozanova, in 1973; died 1997.

SVETLANA'S CIRCLE OF RUSSIAN FRIENDS:
Sergo Beria: childhood friend at Model School No. 25; son of Lavrenty Beria.

Ilya Ehrenburg: journalist; author of the novel *The Thaw* (1954), which gave its name to the post-Stalin period.

Lily Golden: researcher at the Institute of African Studies and the author of articles on African music and culture.

Kyra Golovko: actress; husband, Arsenii; chief of staff of the Navy of the USSR; friends at House on the Embankment.

Boris Gribanov: editor at Children's Literature Press; friend of David Samoilov.

Stepan Mikoyan: son of Stalin's minister Anastas Mikoyan; wife, Ella.

Marfa Peshkova: granddaughter of Maxim Gorky; married to Sergo Beria.

Olga Rifkina: fellow student at Model School No. 25; lifelong friend.

Fyodor Volkenstein: professor of chemistry in Moscow; inspired Svetlana to write *Twenty Letters to a Friend*.

STALIN'S MINISTERS AND OFFICIALS:

Lavrenty Beria: Mingrelian; chief of Stalin's secret police from 1938; Politburo member in charge of nuclear bomb; arrested after Stalin's death; executed 1953.

Nikita Khrushchev: Nadya's fellow student at Industrial Academy; first secretary of the Communist Party of the Soviet Union from 1953 to 1964; ousted 1964; "Secret Speech" in 1956 responsible for de-Stalinization policy; died in 1971.

Sergei Kirov: Secretary of the Leningrad Party; assassinated 1934; his assassination was prelude to the subsequent "Great Terror."

Anastas Mikoyan: deputy prime minister, 1937; chairman of Supreme Soviet of USSR, 1964; died in 1978.

Vyacheslav Molotov: first deputy premier from 1942 to 1957; dismissed by Khrushchev; retired in 1961; died in 1986.

Polina Molotov: wife of Vyacheslav; close friend of Nadya Stalin; Fisheries Commissar; arrested in 1948; released in 1953; died in 1970.

Andrei Zhdanov: chairman of the Supreme Soviet from 1938 to 1947; as head of Ideology, originated Zhdanov Doctrine; dismissed by Stalin 1947; died of a heart attack in 1948.

Abel Enukidze: Nadya's godfather, secretary of the Central Executive Committee; dismissed and arrested in 1935; executed in 1937.

General Nikolai Vlasik: chief of Stalin's security detail from 1931 to 1952; head of Guards Directorate; died in 1967.

Genrikh Yagoda: director of NKVD (Soviet Union's Security and Intelligence Agency) from 1934 to 1936; arrested in 1937; executed in 1938.

Nikolai Yezhov: director of the NKVD from 1936 to 1938; presided over "Great Terror"; arrested in 1939; executed in 1940.

VICTIMS OF ANTI-COSMOPOLITAN CAMPAIGN AND DOCTORS' PLOT:

Solomon Mikhoels: director of Moscow's Yiddish State Theater; head of the Jewish anti-Fascist Committee, killed in 1948, at the beginning of the Anti-Cosmopolitan Campaign.

Dr. Yakov Rapoport: Soviet pathologist; victim of the Doctors' Plot. Arrested in December 1952; released in March 1953.

In India:

I. A. Benediktov: Soviet ambassador to India; returned Svetlana's passport, enabling her defection in 1967.

Triloki Nath Kaul: Indian ambassador to the Soviet Union and a friend of Brajesh Singh; carried Svetlana's manuscript out of Moscow in 1966; daughter, Preeti.

Mrs. Kassirova: functionary in the Ministry of Foreign Affairs; Svetlana's minder on trip to India.

Dinesh Singh: nephew of Brajesh Singh; minister of State in government of Indira Gandhi from 1966 to 1967; daughter, Reva.

Suresh Singh: brother of Brajesh Singh; Svetlana's host during her stay in Kalakankar before her defection.

THE US EMBASSY IN INDIA:

Chester Bowles: US ambassador to India and Nepal in 1967; made the decision to give Svetlana a tourist visa to the United States; his term ended in 1968.

George Huey: consul at the US embassy in Delhi; the first officer to talk with Svetlana.

Robert Rayle: second secretary at the US embassy in Delhi, undercover CIA officer; accompanied Svetlana to Italy and Switzerland during her defection in 1967.

IN SWITZERLAND:

Antonino Janner: chief of the East European section of the Swiss Foreign Ministry; took charge of Svetlana.

United States:

Cass Canfield: publisher of Harper & Row; published Svetlana's first two books.

Fritz Ermarth: CIA national intelligence officer for the USSR and East Europe in 1984, when Svetlana returned to the USSR.

Edward Greenbaum: "the General"; partner in New York law firm Greenbaum Wolff & Ernst; handled Svetlana's visa and copyright; secured advance of $1.5 million.

Donald Jameson: CIA officer; instrumental in securing Svetlana's entry into the United States; assisted Svetlana during her early years in the United States.

George Kennan: ex-ambassador to the Soviet Union; faculty member at the Institute for Advanced Study in Princeton; wife, Annelise.

Foy Kohler: undersecretary of State in the Johnson administration in 1967; spearheaded refusal of asylum to Svetlana.

Alan Schwartz: lawyer; assistant to Edward Greenbaum.

Evan Thomas: executive vice president of Harper & Row.

Russian Government Officials (from 1967):

Yuri Andropov: appointed head of the KGB in 1967, shortly after Svetlana's defection; succeeded Brezhnev as general secretary of the Central Committee of the Communist Party (CPSU) in 1982; chairman of the Supreme Soviet (president) in June 1983; ill by August; died in 1984.

Leonid Brezhnev: replaced Khrushchev as general secretary of the CPSU from 1964 to 1982; reinitiated policies of repression; died 1982.

Mikhail Gorbachev: general secretary from 1985 to 1991; initiated failed policies of glasnost (openness) and perestroika (restructuring); granted Svetlana permission to leave the USSR in 1986.

Alexei Kosygin: premier in 1964 after ouster of Khrushchev; shared power with Brezhnev as part of collective leadership; died in 1980.

Mikhail Suslov: second secretary of the Communist Party of the Soviet Union; Party's chief ideologue; in 1966 refused Svetlana permission to marry Singh; died in 1982.

KGB AGENTS:

Vasiliy Fedorovich Sanko: kidnapped Evdokia Petrova, wife of KGB officer Vladimir Petrov, in 1954; reputed to have been sent to kidnap Svetlana in 1967.

Viktor Louis (Vitaly Yevgenyevich Lui): pirated Svetlana's *Twenty Letters to a Friend* and sold it to Flegon Press in London; sold family photos to *Stern* magazine.

George Kurpel: possible KGB agent; attempted to engineer defection of Svetlana's son, Joseph Alliluyev, in 1975.

Husband and Relatives in the United States:

Wesley Peters: head architect, the Frank Lloyd Wright Foundation: married to Svetlana from 1970 to 1972; died in 1991.

Senator Samuel Hayakawa: English professor; president of

San Francisco State University; US Senator for California from 1977 to 1983; died 1992; wife, Marge (Margedant), sister of Wesley Peters.

Olga Margedant Peters (Chrese Evans): Svetlana's daughter with Wesley Peters; born in San Rafael, California, in 1971.

TALIESIN FOUNDATION:

Olgivanna Wright: born Olga Ivanovna Lazovich in Montenegro in 1897; third wife of Frank Lloyd Wright (married in 1928); student of G. I. Gurdjieff; ran the Taliesin Fellowship from Wright's death in 1959 until her own death in 1985.

Iovanna Wright: only child of Frank Lloyd and Olgivanna Wright.

Svetlana (Hinzenberg) Wright: daughter of Olgivanna and first husband, Valdemar Hinzenberg; married Wesley Peters in 1934; died with her son, Daniel, in a car crash in 1946.

Brandoch Peters: born in 1941; son of Wesley and Svetlana Peters; survived a car crash at age five; cellist and failed cattle farmer.

LOVERS IN THE UNITED STATES:

Louis Fischer: journalist; author of ten books, including 1952 biography of Stalin; professor at Princeton, affiliated with the Woodrow Wilson School of Public and International Affairs when he met Svetlana in 1969.

Max Hayward: professor of Soviet literary politics at St. Antony's College, Oxford; translator of *Doctor Zhivago* and Svetlana's 1967 article "To Boris Leonidovich Pasternak."

Tom Turner: fifty-two-year-old businessman and Dominican tertiary (lay brother); died of cancer in 1989, a year after Svetlana and he began a relationship.

FRIENDS IN THE UNITED STATES:

Marie Anderson: friend in Spring Green, Wisconsin.

Arkady Belinkov: sentenced to death age twenty-three as anti-Soviet; reprieved: spent twelve years in the Gulag; fled with his wife, Natalia, to West Germany in 1968, and to the United States.

Douglas Bushnell: wealthy Princeton businessman who briefly played substitute father to Svetlana's daughter Olga in Princeton in 1977.

Paul Chavchavadze: Georgian prince from the Caucasus; fled to England and then to the United States in 1934; translated *Only One Year*; his wife, Nina, was the daughter of the tsar's uncle.

Michael Coyne: son of Elizabeth Coyne, Svetlana's close friend in Spring Green.

Joan Kennan: daughter of George Kennan; hosted Svetlana in the summer of 1967.

Priscilla Johnson McMillan: journalist specializing in Soviet affairs; translator of *Twenty Letters to a Friend*; Svetlana stayed at father's residence on her arrival in the United States.

Thomas Miller: American volcanologist, made annual trips to Kamchatka.

Walter Pozen: lawyer; second husband of Joan Kennan; helped sort Svetlana's finances.

Kathy Rossing: daughter of Elizabeth Coyne, Svetlana's close friend in Spring Green.

Rosa Shand: met Svetlana in Princeton; introduced her to Terry Waite and Quaker Friends' School.

Edmund Wilson: eminent critic of American literature; Russian expert.

In England:

Sir Isaiah Berlin: Russo-British philosopher, writer, translator; held professorships at Harvard and Oxford; facilitated Svetlana's move to England in 1982.

Mary Burkett: lived at Isel Hall in Cockermouth, England; world specialist on felt making.

Philippa Hill: widow of a well-known physicist; neighbor on Chaucer Road, Cambridge.

Linda and Laurence Kelly: neighbors in Cambridge: he wrote studies of Alexander Griboyedov and Mikhail Lermontov.

Nina Lobanov-Rostosky: neighbor in London; her husband's father was killed under Stalin.

Malcolm Muggeridge: British media personality, notorious for his conservative Christian propagandizing; hosted TV interview with Svetlana in 1981; wife, Kitty.

Lady (Jane) Renfrew: Cambridge professor and archaeologist; neighbor on Chaucer Road.

Rosamond Richardson: author, friend in Saffron Walden; wrote *The Long Shadow: Inside Stalin's Family*, in 1993, initially with Svetlana's cooperation.

Lady (Vanessa) Thomas: London friend; lived near Ladbroke Grove; husband, historian Sir Hugh Thomas.

Vera Suvchinskaya Traill: Russian émigrée; her grandfather was minister of war in Russia's Provisional government.

JOURNALISTS:

Patricia Blake: journalist; member of the Princeton circle of friends; Svetlana regarded her as a chief enemy for the *Time* magazine article on her return to the USSR.

George Krimsky: AP; attempted to help Joseph Alliluyev defect in 1975.

Tony Lucas: *New York Times*; exposed Robert Rayle as CIA officer in 1967 during flight from India.

Sources

Abbreviations of Names of Archives Cited

US GOVERNMENT ARCHIVES

NARA: National Archives and Records Administration, College Park, MD.

CIA DB: CIA Crest Database, NARA, College Park, MD.

LBJL, NSF: LBJ Presidential Library, National Security File, Intelligence File, Svetlana Alliluyeva.

RRL: Ronald Reagan Presidential Library, FG 002, Peters, Lana.

FBI: Federal Bureau of Investigation, Freedom of Information Act Request, Svetlana Alliluyeva née Svetlana Stalina, 1967–1985.

RUSSIAN ARCHIVES

GARF: Gosudarstvennyi arkhiv Rossiiskoi Federatsii (State Archive of the Russian Federation).

RGASPI: Rossiiskii gosudarstvennyi arkhiv sotsial'no-politicheskoi istorii (Russian State Archive of Socio-Political History).

MEM: Arkhiv mezhdunarodnogo obshchestva "Memorial" (Archive of the Memorial Society International).

BRITISH ARCHIVES

NAUK: National Archives, United Kingdom, Foreign Office, Defectors, Soviet Union, Svetlana Stalin.

GEORGIAN ARCHIVES

AMIG: Archive of the Ministry of Internal Affairs, Tbilisi, Georgia.

UNIVERSITY ARCHIVES

Katherina von Fraunhofer-Kosinski Collection of Jerzy Kosinski, Mark Weinbaum Papers, and Edmund Wilson Papers: Beinecke Rare Book and Manuscript Library (BRB), Yale University.

Letters of Isaiah Berlin, copyright © The Trustees of the Isaiah Berlin Literary Trust (IBLT) 2015, quoted with the permission of the Trustees.

Meryle Secrest Collection, Hoover Institution Archives (HIA).

George F. Kennan Papers (MC076), 1871–2005 (mostly 1950–2000), Public Policy Papers, Department of Rare Books and Special Collections, Princeton University Library (PUL).

Louis Fischer Papers (MC024), 1890–1977 (mostly 1935–1969), Public Policy Papers, Department of Rare Books and Special Collections, Princeton University Library (PUL).

Malcolm Muggeridge Papers, Special Collections, Wheaton College, Illinois (WCSC).

Museums

Muzei-kvartira Alliluyevykh (Apartment Museum of the Alliluyevs), Saint Petersburg.

Muzei "Dom na naberezhnoi" (House on the Embankment Museum), Moscow.

Moskovskaia obraztsovaia shkola 25 (Shkola 175) [Moscow Model School 25 (School 175)].

Istoriko-memorial'nyi muzei "Smol'nyi" (Smolny Historical and Memorial Museum), Saint Petersburg.

Joseph Stalin Museum, Gori, Georgia.

Private Collections

Letters from Alliluyeva in private collections (PC) of correspondents: Mary Burkett, Philippa Hill, Donald Jameson, Linda Kelly, Joan Kennan, Nina Lobanov-Rostovsky, Thomas Miller, Robert and Ramona Rayle, Rosa Shand, the Harper & Row Archive, and the HarperCollins Collection.

Notes

For abbreviations of archives, please refer to the list on page 630.

PREFACE
1. Letter to Mary Burkett, Apr. 7, 2009, private collection (PC), Mary Burkett.
2. Angela Lambert, *Independent*, Mar. 10, 1990: 29.
3. Robert Tucker, "Svetlana Inherited Her Tragic Flaw," *Washington Post*, Nov. 25, 1984, C1.
4. Svetlana Alliluyeva, *Only One Year*, trans. Paul Chavchavadze (New York: Harper & Row, 1969), 393.

PROLOGUE : THE DEFECTION
1. This account is a composite of details drawn from Alliluyeva, *Only One Year*; Robert Rayle, "Unpublished Autobiographical Essay," PC, Rayle; author's interview with Robert and Ramona Rayle, Ashburn, VA, July 18–19, 2013; Chester Bowles, "Memorandum for the Record; Subj: Defection of Svetlana Alliloueva [*sic*]," Mar. 15, 1967, NLJ/RAC 03-114, 26-B, LBJL; and Peter Earnest, "Peter Earnest in Conversation with Oleg Kalugin and Robert Rayle on Defection of Svetlana Alliluyeva," Dec. 4, 2006. International Spy Museum, Washington, DC. www.spymuseum .org/exhibition-experiences/agent-storm/listen-to-the-audio/episode/ the-litvinenko-murder-and-other-riddles-from-moscow.
2. Alliluyeva, *Only One Year*, 199.
3. Rayle, "Autobiographical Essay."
4. Bowles, "Memorandum."
5. Rayle, "Autobiographical Essay." See also Bowles, "Memorandum."
6. Alliluyeva, *Only One Year*, 200. See also Rayle, "Autobiographical Essay."
7. Rayle, "Autobiographical Essay."
8. Bowles, "Memorandum."
9. Time line provided by Robert Rayle on calendar, March 1967, PC, Rayle.
10. Bowles, "Memorandum."
11. Alliluyeva, *Only One Year*, 189.
12. Bowles, "Memorandum."
13. Alliluyeva, *Only One Year*, 206.

14. Author's interview with Robert and Ramona Rayle, Ashburn, VA, July 18–19, 2013.

15. Ibid.

16. Rayle, "Autobiographical Essay."

17. Ibid.

18. Ibid.

CHAPTER 1: THAT PLACE OF SUNSHINE

1. Svetlana Alliluyeva, *Twenty Letters to a Friend*, trans. Priscilla Johnson McMillan (New York: Harper & Row, 1967), 36.

2. Rosamond Richardson, *The Long Shadow: Inside Stalin's Family* (London: Little, Brown, 1993), 119.

3. Simon Sebag Montefiore, *Stalin: The Court of the Red Tsar* (New York: Knopf, 2004), 34.

4. Simon Sebag Montefiore, *Young Stalin* (London: Weidenfeld & Nicolson, 2007), 119. Tbilisi is the historical name of the city. The name Tiflis(i) became common after Georgia became part of the Russian Empire in 1783. Tiflis was officially changed back to Tbilisi in 1936. Letter to author from Nestan Charkviani, Jan. 5, 2015.

5. Montefiore, *Young Stalin*, 164–66.

6. Ibid., 135.

7. Ibid., 166.

8. Robert Service, *Stalin: A Biography* (London: Macmillan, 2004), 233.

9. Letter from Nadya Alliluyeva to Keke Djugashvili, Mar. 12, 1922, RGASPI, fond [stock] 558, opis [inventory] 11, doc. 1549, 40.

10. Boris Gribanov, "I pamiat'-sneg letit i past' ne mozhet: David Samoilov, kakim ia ego pomniu" ["And Memory as Snow Keeps Drifting: David Samoilov as I Remember Him"]. *Znamia: Yezhemesiachnyi literaturno-khudozhestvennyi i obshchestvenno-politicheskii zhurnal* [The Banner: A Monthly Literary, Artistic, and General Political Journal] 9 (2006): 160.

11. Montefiore, *Young Stalin*, 18. According to Montefiore, "In 1925 [Stalin] ordered his secretary Tovstukha to formalize the 1879 date." Montefiore speculates that Stalin had moved the date a year later to avoid conscription.

12. Alliluyeva, *Twenty Letters*, 95.

13. Ibid., 96.

14. Ibid.

15. Author's interview with Chrese Evans, Portland, OR, July 18, 2012.

16. Letter from N. S. Alliluyeva to M. O. Svanidze, Jan. 11, 1926, trans. Svetlana Alliluyeva, Meryle Secrest Collection, box 4, HIA.

17. *Kreml'-9* [Russian TV series] writers group, *Svetlana Stalina: Pobeg iz sem'i* [Svetlana Stalina: Escape from the Family], film, dir. Maksim Ivannikov, prod. Aleksei Pimanov, Oleg Vol'nov, and Sergei Medvedev (Tele-

kompaniya "Ostankino" and Federal'naia sluzhba okhrany Rossiiskoi Federatsii [Federal Service for the Protection of the Russian Federation], 2003); hereafter *Kreml'-9* writers, *Svetlana Stalina: Escape from the Family*.

18. Svetlana Alliluyeva, "Letter to Ehrenburg," Aug. 7, 1957, repr. Boris Frezinski, *Pisateli i Sovetskie vozhdi* [Writers and Soviet Leaders] (Moscow: Ellis Lak, 2008), 606.

19. Alliluyeva, *Twenty Letters*, 223.

20. Ibid., 29.

21. Author's interview with Stepan Mikoyan, Moscow, May 24, 2013.

22. Alliluyeva, *Twenty Letters*, 30.

23. Ibid., 110.

24. Meryle Secrest interview with Svetlana Alliluyeva, London, 1994, Secrest Collection, audio recording, group 2, tape 28, HIA.

25. Irina Kalistratovna Gogua, Transcription of Oral Stories, recorded by Irina Mikhailovna Chervakova, 1987–89, MEM, fond [stock] 1, opis [inventory] 3, delo [subject] 18, June 25, 1988, 63–64.

26. Alliluyeva, *Only One Year*, 379.

27. Alliluyeva, *Twenty Letters*, 32.

28. Stepan Mikoyan, *Memoirs of Military Test-Flying and Life with the Kremlin's Elite: An Autobiography* (London: Airlife Publishing, 1999), 35.

29. Alliluyeva, *Twenty Letters*, 28.

30. Ibid., 53.

31. Anna Alliluyeva and Sergei Alliluyev, *The Alliluyev Memoirs: Recollections of Svetlana Stalina's Maternal Aunt Anna Alliluyeva and Her Grandfather Sergei Alliluyev*, trans. David Tutaev (New York: Putnam's, 1967), 74. Hereafter: *Alliluyeva Memoirs*.

32. Ibid., 139.

33. Richardson, *Long Shadow*, 114.

34. Rosamond Richardson interview with Svetlana Alliluyeva, Saffron Walden, 1991, tape 3, PC, Richardson.

35. Alliluyeva, *Twenty Letters*, 43–44.

36. Ibid., 31.

37. Ibid., 140.

38. Ibid., 31.

39. Ibid., 36.

40. Ibid, 66.

CHAPTER 2: A MOTHERLESS CHILD

1. Alliluyeva, *Twenty Letters*, 107.

2. Larissa Vasilieva, *Kremlin Wives: The Secret Lives of the Women Behind the Kremlin Walls—from Lenin to Gorbachev* (New York: Arcade Publishing, 1994), 52.

3. Hiroaki Kuromiya, *Stalin: Profiles in Power* (London: Pearson Education, 2005), 95. During a show trial in November–December 1930, a group of so-called "industrial wreckers" and "bourgeois experts" were accused of "intentionally creating economic troubles," "political terrorism," and "conspiring with foreign powers, especially France." Their "alleged terrorist plans . . . prompted the Politburo resolution."

4. Montefiore, *Court of the Red Tsar*, 16.

5. Alliluyeva, *Twenty Letters*, 108–10. See also accounts by Service, *Stalin*, 292–93; Montefiore, *Court of the Red Tsar*, 3–22; and Edvard Radzinsky, *Stalin*, trans. H. T. Willetts (New York: Anchor, 1997), 287–89.

6. Alliluyeva, *Twenty Letters*, 110.

7. Montefiore, *Court of the Red Tsar*, 106. "There is a five-milimetre hole over the heart—an open hole. Conclusion—death was immediate from an open wound to the heart." Secret report of Dr. Kushner, GARF 7523c.149a.2-1-6.

8. This is nanny Alexandra Andreevna Bychkova's report of that morning. Alliluyeva, *Twenty Letters*, 109.

9. Montefiore, *Court of the Red Tsar*, 105; Alliluyeva, *Twenty Letters*, 112.

10. Maria Svanidze, "Diary of 1933–37," trans. Svetlana Alliluyeva, 19, Meryle Secrest Collection, box 3, HIA. In 1994, Svetlana Alliluyeva translated the diary of Maria Svanidze, released from the Archive of the Politburo, Communist Party of the Soviet Union, published in *Istochnik*, no. 1 (1993).

11. Montefiore, *Court of the Red Tsar*, 12. See also Service, *Stalin*, 289.

12. William Taubman, *Khrushchev: The Man and His Era* (New York: Norton, 2003), 85. She did however recommend Khrushchev to Stalin. "This was how I survived," Khrushchev said. "Nadya was 'my lottery ticket.'"

13. Author's interview with Alexander Alliluyev, Moscow, May 25, 2013. See also: "Mify o docheri Stalina," *Priamoi efir s Mikhailom Zelenskim* ["Myths About Stalin's Daughter," *Live with Mikhail Zelensky*], Rossia-1, Moscow, Dec. 19, 2011; hereafter: "Myths," *Live with Mikhail Zelensky*.

14. Kuromiya, *Stalin*, 40–42.

15. Letter to N. S. Alliluyeva, June 21, 1930, "To Nadezhda Sergeevna Alliluyeva Personally from Stalin: Correspondence 1928–31," 7, trans. Svetlana Alliluyeva, Meryle Secrest Collection, box 3, HIA. When the correspondence (1928–31) between Nadezhda Alliluyeva and Stalin from Stalin's personal archive was published by *Istochnik* in 1993, with commentary by Yu. Murin, Svetlana Alliluyeva personally translated the letters into English; she claimed copyright in 1994.

16. Letter to J. V. Stalin, Aug. 28, 1929, p. 2, Secrest Collection, HIA.

17. Alliluyeva, *Twenty Letters*, 104.

18. Enzo Biagi, *Svetlana: The Inside Story*, trans. Timothy Wilson (London: Hodder and Stoughton, 1967), 22.

19. Kuromiya, *Stalin*, 91.

20. Ibid., 97.

21. Ibid., 108.

22. Ibid.

23. Letter from N. S. Alliluyeva to J. V. Stalin, Sept. 16, 1929, 4–5, Secrest Collection, HIA.

24. Letter from J. V. Stalin to N. S. Alliluyeva, Sept. 23, 1929, 5, Secrest Collection, HIA.

25. Letter from J. V. Stalin to Ordzhonikidze, Sept. 23, 1929, 16, Secrest Collection, HIA.

26. Matthew Lenoe, *Closer to the Masses: Stalinist Culture, Social Revolution and Soviet Newspapers* (Cambridge, MA: Harvard University Press, 2004), 209.

27. N. S. Alliluyeva to J. V. Stalin, Sept. 27, 1929, 6, Secrest Collection, HIA.

28. Letter from N. S. Alliluyeva to J. V. Stalin, Sept. 19, 1930, 9, Secrest Collection, HIA.

29. Letter from J. V. Stalin to N. S. Alliluyeva, Sept. 24, 1930, 9, Secrest Collection, HIA.

30. Letter from N. S. Alliluyeva to J. V. Stalin, Oct. 6, 1930, 10, Secrest Collection, HIA.

31. Letter from J. V. Stalin to N. S. Alliluyeva, Oct. 8, 1930, 11, Secrest Collection, HIA.

32. Letter from N. S. Alliluyeva to J. V. Stalin, Sept. 12, 1930, 8, Secrest Collection, HIA.

33. Gogua, Transcription of Oral Stories, MEM.

34. "Myths," *Live with Mikhail Zelensky*. Alexander Alliluyev remarks that he has never spoken of this before. Confirmed in author's interview with Alexander Alliluyev, Moscow, May 25, 2013.

35. Alliluyeva, *Twenty Letters*, 106.

36. Gogua, Transcription of Oral Stories, MEM.

37. Alliluyeva, *Twenty Letters*, 112.

38. Vyacheslav Molotov, *Molotov Remembers: Inside Kremlin Politics— Conversations with Felix Chuev*, ed. Albert Resis (Chicago: Ivan R. Dee, 1993), 174.

39. Richardson, *Long Shadow*, 126.

40. Alliluyeva, *Twenty Letters*, 113. See *Alliluyev Memoirs*, xviii.

41. Montefiore, *Young Stalin*, 315.

42. *Kreml'-9* writers, *Svetlana Stalina: Escape from the Family*, comments of Artyom Sergeev.

43. Ibid., comments of Marfa Peshkova.

CHAPTER 3: THE HOSTESS AND THE PEASANT

1. Alliluyeva, *Twenty Letters*, 122.

2. Ibid., 43.

3. Merzhanov was arrested in 1942 and sentenced to ten years in a forced-labor camp.

4. Yuri Druzhnikov, "Visiting Stalin's, Uninvited," trans. Thomas Moore, from *Contemporary Russian Myths*, www.druzhnikov.com/english/text/vizit1.html.

5. Molotov, *Molotov Remembers*, 208.

6. Alliluyeva, *Twenty Letters*, 132.

7. Letter from S. Alliluyeva to Stalin, Aug. 5, 1933, RGASPI, KPSS fond 558, opis 11, D 1552, doc. 14, 19.

8. Candide Charkviani, *Napikri da naazrevi* [My Life and Reflections], trans. Nestan Charkviani (Tbilisi: Merani Publishing House, 2004), 503. Charkviani was a Georgian writer and thinker who became first secretary of the Central Committee of Georgia in 1938. He was demoted in 1952, probably for failing to repress a nationalist counterrevolutionary "ring" in the Georgian Communist Party. Charkviani secretly wrote his memoirs in 1954.

9. Alliluyeva, *Twenty Letters*, 97.

10. Ibid. Svetlana corrected Pamela Johnson McMillan's translation of "Housekeeper" to "Hostess," and her father's pet name for her to "Svetanka."

11. Alliluyeva, *Twenty Letters*, 151.

12. Letter from S. Alliluyeva to Stalin, Sept. 15, 1933. RGASPI, KPSS fond 558, opis 11, D 1552, doc. 14, 20.

13. Alliluyeva, *Twenty Letters*, 150.

14. Nikita Khrushchev, *Khrushchev Remembers*, trans. Strobe Talbot (New York: Bantam, 1971), 310–11.

15. James A. Hudson, *Svetlana Alliluyeva: Flight to Freedom* (New York: Tower Books, 1967), 30.

16. Alliluyeva, *Twenty Letters*, 144.

17. Alliluyeva, *Only One Year*, 389.

18. Alliluyeva, *Twenty Letters*, 143.

19. Ibid., 121.

20. Author's interview with Alexander Alliluyev, Moscow, May 25, 2013.

21. Alliluyeva, *Twenty Letters*, 154.

22. Larry E. Holmes, *Stalin's School: Model School No. 25, 1931–1937* (Pittsburgh, PA: University of Pittsburgh Press, 1999), 71.

23. Svanidze, "Diary of 1933–37," 18, Secrest Collection, box 3, HIA.

24. Rosamond Richardson interview with Svetlana Alliluyeva, Saffron Walden, 1991, tape 1. PC, Richardson.

25. Holmes, *Stalin's School*, 22.

26. Ibid., 37.

27. Ibid., 36.

28. The school's mandate was equality among the classes. In 1932, the school accommodated 1,150 pupils, 61 percent of whom were children of workers, but ironically, this percentage steadily declined. Soon "the proletarian element dropped further to 34% in 1934." "One former pupil, Lusia Davydova, recalled that her 1937 graduating class contained only one representative of the working class whom his classmates called 'the working class stratum.'" Holmes, *Stalin's School*, 32.

29. Holmes, *Stalin's School*, 39-41.

30. Ibid., 10, 18.

31. Ibid., 37.

32. Alliluyeva, *Only One Year*, 142.

33. Author's interview with Diana Kondrashina of School 175 (formerly Model School No. 25), Moscow, June 5, 2013.

34. Holmes, *Stalin's School*, 165–68.

35. Author's interview with Diana Kondrashina of School 175, Moscow, June 5, 2013.

36. Holmes, *Stalin's School*, 166. Joining the Komsomol happened at the age of fourteen, until, at the age of twenty-eight, one became eligible to apply for Communist Party membership. Along with a pin, as a member of the Komsomol, one got a membership book with dates when dues were paid.

37. Svanidze, "Diary of 1933–37," 22, Secrest Collection, HIA.

38. Letter from Vasili Djugashvili to Stalin, 5 August 1933, RGASPI, KPSS fond 558, opis 11, D 1552, doc. 3, 3.

39. Letter from Vasili Djugashvili to Stalin, Sept. 26 (no year). RGASPI, KPSS fond 558, opis 11, D 1552, doc. 8, 10.

40. Author's interview with Chrese Evans, Portland, OR, July 19, 2012.

41. Meryle Secrest interview with Svetlana Alliluyeva, audio recording, group 1, tape 21, HIA.

42. Holmes, *Stalin's School*, 167–68.

43. Ibid., 168.

44. Ibid., 123.

CHAPTER 4: THE TERROR

1. Svanidze, "Diary of 1933–37," 9, Secrest Collection, HIA.

2. Rosamond Richardson interview with Svetlana Alliluyeva, Saffron Walden, 1991, tape 1, PC, Richardson.

3. Montefiore, *Court of the Red Tsar*, 162.

4. Svanidze, "Diary of 1933–37," 11–12, Secrest Collection, HIA.

5. Matthew E. Lenoe, *The Kirov Murder and Soviet History* (New Haven, CT: Yale University Press, 2010), 252.

6. Lenoe claims that Stalin was probably not behind the murder.

7. Stephen Cohen, *The Victims Return: Survivors of the Gulag After Stalin* (New York: I. B. Tauris, 2012), 2.

8. Kuromiya, *Stalin*, 134.

9. What could motivate such a slaughter? Was this simply the psychotic murderousness of a brutal dictator, or was there a more complex and sinister rationale behind it? The historian Hiroaki Kuromiya suggests that Stalin was watching Hitler closely. The Great Terror was a "pre-emptive strike" to cleanse the country of all disloyal factions in the face of the world war between Fascism and Communism that he was certain was imminent. In the chaos of war, internal opponents of his rule would take advantage of the disaster and mount a rebellion from within, as the Bolsheviks had done during World War I. Fascist enemies inside the country were even more dangerous than those outside and had to be purged. Kuromiya, *Stalin*, 128.

10. A large part of the terror consisted of various "national" operations, in which nationalities like Poles and Germans were targeted, which might explain Til's dismissal.

11. Alliluyeva, *Twenty Letters*, 130–31.

12. Ibid., 133.

13. Alliluyeva, *Only One Year*, 5.

14. Service, *Stalin*, 339.

15. Svanidze, "Diary of 1933–37," 27–28, Secrest Collection, HIA.

16. Montefiore, *Court of the Red Tsar*, 269.

17. Alliluyeva, *Only One Year*, 148.

18. Alliluyeva, *Twenty Letters*, 148.

19. Author's interview with Alexander Alliluyev, Moscow, May 25, 2013.

20. Alliluyeva, *Twenty Letters*, 55.

21. Author's interview with Alexander Alliluyev, Moscow, May 27, 2013.

22. Alliluyeva, *Twenty Letters*, 55.

23. Author's interview with Alexander Alliluyev, Moscow, May 27, 2013.

24. Ibid.

25. Montefiore, *Court of the Red Tsar*, 269.

26. Ibid.

27. Service, *Stalin*, 352–53.

28. After November 1938, Stalin slowed down the Terror, though he did not end it. He blamed the Terror on "mistakes" committed by NKVD men under the sway of Nikolai Yezhov. Yezhov, head of the NKVD, was executed in 1940.

29. Orlando Figes, *The Whisperers: Private Life in Stalin's Russia* (New York: Picador, 2008), 283–84.

30. Montefiore, *Court of the Red Tsar*, 325.

31. Alliluyeva, *Twenty Letters*, 124.

32. Biagi, *Svetlana: The Inside Story*, 70.

33. Alliluyeva, *Only One Year*, 151.

34. Holmes, *Stalin's School*, 98—recalled by student Yuliia Kapusto.

35. Meryle Secrest interview with Svetlana Alliluyeva, audio recording, group 2, tape 1, HIA.

36. Alliluyeva, *Only One Year*, 151.

37. Ibid., 148.

38. Alliluyeva, *Twenty Letters*, 141.

39. Svanidze, "Diary of 1933–37," 2–3, Secrest Collection, HIA.

40. Ibid.

CHAPTER 5: THE CIRCLE OF SECRETS AND LIES

1. Alliluyeva, *Twenty Letters*, 140.

2. Rosamond Richardson interview with Svetlana Alliluyeva, Saffron Walden, 1991, tape 2, PC, Richardson.

3. Author's interview with Leonid and Galina Alliluyev, Moscow, May 17, 2013.

4. Letter from S. Alliluyeva to Stalin, Aug. 5, 1940, RGASPI, KPSS fond 558, opis 11, D 1552, doc. 29, 40.

5. Letter from S. Alliluyeva to Stalin, Aug. 22, 1940, RGASPI, KPSS fond 558, opis 11, D 1552, doc. 30, 41.

6. Alliluyeva, *Only One Year*, 381.

7. Letter to Mary Burkett, Sept. 2, 1995, PC, Burkett.

8. Kuromiya, *Stalin*, 150. This number is taken from Nikita Khrushchev, *The Crimes of the Stalin Era: Special Report to the 20th Congress of the Communist Party of the Soviet Union* [Secret Speech], annot. Boris I. Nicolaevsky (New York: New Leader, 1962), 37.

9. Mikoyan, *Memoirs of Military Test-Flying*, 102.

10. Kuromiya, *Stalin*, 151. There are several versions of Stalin's expletive.

11. Richard Overy, *Russia's War: A History of the Soviet War Effort, 1941–1945* (New York: Penguin, 1998), 78.

12. Montefiore, *Court of the Red Tsar*, 375.

13. Ibid., 378.

14. Alliluyeva, *Only One Year*, 392.

15. Montefiore, *Court of the Red Tsar*, 372.

16. Sergeev quoted in Molotov, *Molotov Remembers*, 211.

17. *Kreml'-9* writers, *Svetlana Stalina: Escape from the Family*, comments of Marfa Peshkova.

18. Alliluyeva, *Twenty Letters*, 160.

19. Letter from J. Stalin to Nadya Alliluyeva, Apr. 9, 1928, 2, Secrest Collection, HIA.

20. Alliluyeva, *Twenty Letters*, 101.

21. Ibid., 159.

22. Ibid.

23. Author's interview with Leonid and Galina Alliluyev, Moscow, May 17, 2013.

24. Alliluyeva, *Twenty Letters*, 161.

25. Overy, *Russia's War*, 80–81.

26. Biagi, *Svetlana: The Inside Story*, 47–48. Biagi's interview with Yulia's daughter Gulia.

27. Radzinsky, *Stalin*, 476. See also Montefiore, *Court of the Red Tsar*, 378–79.

28. Radzinsky, *Stalin*, 474. Yakov's capture is briefly dramatized in the film *Europa Europa*.

29. Letter from S. Alliluyeva to Stalin, Sept. 19, 1941, RGASPI, KPSS fond 558, opis 11, D 1552, doc. 30, 43–44.

30. Alliluyeva, *Twenty Letters*, 168. A thorough search of the magazines Alliluyeva indicated she was reading turned up no such article. Leon Trotsky wrote about rumors of Nadya's suicide in his article "Joseph Stalin: Hitler's New Friend Is Sized Up by an Old Foe," *Life*, Oct. 2, 1939, 72, which suggests that this was a common rumor, but it is unlikely this article was Svetlana's source. An article by Trotsky would never have been left lying around. Its discovery would have meant someone's death.

31. *Kreml'-9* writers, *Svetlana Stalina: Escape from the Family*, comments of Marfa Peshkova.

32. Alliluyeva, *Twenty Letters*, 169.

CHAPTER 6: LOVE STORY

1. Alliluyeva, *Twenty Letters*, 171.

2. *Kreml'-9* writers, *Svetlana Stalina: Escape from the Family*, comments of Marfa Peshkova. See also Alliluyeva, *Twenty Letters*, 155.

3. Olga Rifkina, *Puti neispovedimye* [Inscrutable Paths] (Moscow: Progress-Traditsia, 2003), 72; henceforth, Rifkina, *Inscrutable Paths*.

4. Ibid., 71–72.

5. "Myths," *Live with Mikhail Zelensky*, comments of Olga Rifkina.

6. Rifkina, *Inscrutable Paths*, 74.

7. Ibid., 87.

8. Ibid., 88.

9. Ibid., 90.

10. Ibid., 72–73.

11. Ibid., 74.

12. Author's interview with Stepan Mikoyan, Moscow, May 24, 2013.

13. Biagi, *Svetlana: The Inside Story*, 19.

14. Mikoyan, *Memoirs of Military Test-Flying*, 84.

15. *Kreml'9* writers, *Svetlana Stalina: Escape from the Family*, comments of Marfa Peshkova.

16. Biagi, *Svetlana: The Inside Story*, 20–21.

17. In an interview with Meryle Secrest, Alliluyeva made it clear that before she met Kapler she already knew that her mother had committed suicide. Secrest Collection, Mar. 1994, audio recording, group 2, tape 2, HIA.

18. Biagi, *Svetlana: The Inside Story*, 22.

19. Alliluyeva, *Twenty Letters*, 174.

20. Ibid., 176.

21. Ibid., 175–76.

22. Ibid., 175.

23. Ibid., 176.

24. Biagi, *Svetlana: The Inside Story*, 21, 26.

25. Vladimir Alliluyev, *Khronika odnoi sem'i: Alliluyevy—Stalin*. [Chronicle of One Family: Alliluyevs—Stalin] (Moscow: Molodaia Gvardiia, 1995, 2002), 177.

26. A. Kapler, "Letter of Lieutenant L. from Stalingrad," trans. Anastassia Kostrioukova, *Pravda*, Dec. 14, 1942.

27. Alliluyeva, *Twenty Letters*, 177.

28. *Kreml'-9* writers, *Svetlana Stalina: Escape from the Family*, comments of Marfa Peshkova.

29. Meryle Secrest interview with Svetlana Alliluyeva, audio recording, group 2, tape 3, HIA.

30. Alliluyeva, *Twenty Letters*, 178. This is Svetlana Alliluyeva's account. The conversation is dramatized in *Kreml'-9* writers, *Svetlana Stalina: Escape from the Family*. The document quoted, Top Secret, Copy no. 1, is difficult to authenticate.

31. Biagi, *Svetlana: The Inside Story*, 27.

32. Ibid.

33. Gribanov, "And Memory as Snow Keeps Drifting," 159.

34. Biagi, *Svetlana: The Inside Story*, 25.

35. Author's interview with Alexander Burdonsky, Moscow, June 1, 2013.

36. Alliluyeva, *Twenty Letters*, 180–81.

37. Ibid., 181.

38. Letter to Malcolm Muggeridge, Apr. 21, 1981, Malcolm Muggeridge Papers (SC-4), WCSC.

39. Alan Barenberg, *Gulag Town, Company Town: Forced Labor and Its Legacy in Vorkuta* (New Haven, CT: Yale University Press, 2014), 70.

40. *Kreml'-9* writers, *Svetlana Stalina: Escape from the Family*, comments of Vladimir Alliluev. See also Alliluyeva, *Twenty Letters*, 185.

41. Alliluyeva, *Only One Year*, 150.

42. Letter to Malcolm Muggeridge, Apr. 21, 1981, WCSC.

CHAPTER 7: A JEWISH WEDDING

1. Kuromiya, *Stalin*, 158.

2. Molotov, *Molotov Remembers*, 209.

3. Alliluyeva, *Twenty Letters*, 163.

4. Author's interview with Leonid and Galina Alliluyev, Moscow, May 17, 2013. Svetlana's cousin, Leonid Alliluyev, claimed that if either Vasili

or Svetlana knew of the proposed exchange, neither told anyone else in the family, and it was not publicly known: "If such an attempt had taken place, no 'Public Communications' could have been possible. In our country, it was out of the question."

5. Meryle Secrest interview with Svetlana Alliluyeva, audio recording, group 2, tape 3. HIA.

6. Radzinsky, *Stalin*, 478–89. See also Montefiore, *Court of the Red Tsar*, 445–46.

7. Letter to author from Stepan Mikoyan, Aug. 10, 2013.

8. Letter to the author from Professor Lynne Viola, July 20, 2014.

9. Alliluyeva, *Twenty Letters*, 162.

10. Overy, *Russia's War*, 158–60.

11. Letter to author from Stepan Mikoyan, Aug. 10, 2013.

12. Alliluyeva, *Twenty Letters*, 184.

13. Letter no. 2 to Robert Rayle, Aug. 23, 2005, PC, Rayle.

14. Rifkina, *Inscrutable Paths*, 92–93.

15. Alliluyeva, *Only One Year*, 150.

16. Ibid., 410.

17. Alliluyeva, *Twenty Letters*, 134.

18. Rifkina, *Inscrutable Paths*, 93–94.

19. Biagi, *Svetlana: The Inside Story*, 116.

20. Meryle Secrest interview with Svetlana Alliluyeva, audio recording, group 2, tape 6, HIA.

21. Ibid.

22. Alliluyeva, *Only One Year*, 152.

23. Alliluyeva, *Twenty Letters*, 187.

24. Meryle Secrest interview with Svetlana Alliluyeva, audio recording, group 2, tape 6, HIA.

25. Radzinsky, *Stalin*, 317.

26. *Kreml'-9* writers, *Svetlana Stalina: Escape from the Family*, comments of Marfa Peshkova.

27. John Lewis Gaddis, *George F. Kennan: An American Life* (New York: Penguin Press, 2011), 194.

28. Meryle Secrest interview with Svetlana Alliluyeva, audio recording, group 2, tape 6. HIA.

29. Overy, *Russia's War*, 287–89. See also Harrison Salisbury, "Fifty Years That Shook the World," in *The Soviet Union: The Fifty Years*, ed. Harrison E. Salisbury (New York: Harcourt, Brace & World), 1967), 25.

30. Meryle Secrest interview with Svetlana Alliluyeva, London, audio recording, group 2, tape 6. HIA.

31. Author's interview with Leonid and Galina Alliluyev, Moscow, May 17, 2013.

32. Svetlana Alliluyeva, *The Faraway Music* (New Delhi: Lancer International, 1984), 78.

33. Author's interview with Chrese Evans, Portland, OR, Feb. 25, 2013.

34. Letter from S. Alliluyeva to Stalin, Dec. 1, 1945, RGASPI, KPSS fond 558, opis 11, D 1552, doc. 33, 50.

35. *Kreml'-9* writers, *Svetlana Stalina: Escape from the Family*, comments of Marfa Peshkova.

36. Alliluyev, *Chronicle of One Family*, 189.

37. *Svetlana*, television documentary, dir. Irina Gedrovich, Fabryka Kino (distributor), 2008, comment by Svetlana Alliluyeva. See also Rosamond Richardson interview with Svetlana Alliluyeva, Saffron Walden, 1991, tape 4, PC, Richardson.

38. The 1936 decree was called "On the Protection of Motherhood and Infancy." Catriona Kelly, *Children's World: Growing Up in Russia, 1890–1991* (New Haven, CT: Yale University Press, 2007), 103.

39. Letter to Rosa Shand, May 22, 1978, PC, Shand.

40. Letter to Joan Kennan, Jan. 15, 1970, PC, J. Kennan.

41. Alliluyeva, *Only One Year*, 384–86.

42. Alliluyeva, *Twenty Letters*, 191; *Only One Year*, 384. For confirmation of Svetlana's description of Stalin's dinner parties, see Milovan Djilas, *Conversations with Stalin* (New York: Harcourt, Brace & World, 1962), 76–77.

43. Rosamond Richardson interview with Svetlana Alliluyeva, Saffron Walden, 1991, tape 4, PC, Richardson.

44. Sergo Beria, *Beria, My Father: Inside Stalin's Kremlin*, trans. Brian Pearce (London: Duckworth, 2001), 152.

45. Ibid., 192.

CHAPTER 8: THE ANTI-COSMOPOLITAN CAMPAIGN

1. Montefiore, *Court of the Red Tsar*, 6.

2. Nicholas Thompson, *The Hawk and the Dove: Paul Nitze, George Kennan, and the History of the Cold War* (New York: Holt, 2009), 61.

3. It is now claimed that the Soviets would have made the scientific breakthrough on their own. It is estimated that the information gathered through espionage probably accelerated the Soviet nuclear program by two years. See Malcolm Gladwell, "Trust No One: Kim Philby and the Hazards of Mistrust," *New Yorker*, July 28, 2014.

4. Thompson, *Hawk and the Dove*, 83.

5. Author's interview with Alexander Alliluyev, Moscow, May 25, 2013.

6. Richardson, *Long Shadow*, 215.

7. Ibid., 221–23.

8. Ibid., 224.

9. Ibid., 216.

10. Ibid., 217.

11. Ibid., 216.

12. Ibid., 223.

13. Ibid., 222.

14. Ibid., 230.

15. Ibid., 232.

16. Alliluyev, *Chronicle of One Family,* 261–62. In his examination of the files, Vladimir Alliluyev noted that there was no proof of Anna's guilt. Her arrest was built on unlawful testimony by her relatives arrested shortly before—E. A. Alliluyeva (Zhenya), her husband N. V. Molochnikov, and their daughter Kyra (Protocol no. 22 of Special Committee of Ministry of State Security of USSR).

17. Richardson, *Long Shadow,* 231.

18. Alliluyeva, *Twenty Letters,* 196–97, and *Only One Year,* 155.

19. Author's interview with Alexander Alliluyev, Moscow, May 25, 2013.

20. Richardson, *Long Shadow,* 227.

21. Supposedly Beria had carried out traitorous acts against the Bolsheviks during the Civil War of 1917–20 and had barely escaped execution. In fact, this was a common rumor; Beria claimed to have been working undercover for the Bolsheviks. However, Beria did seem to target Redens. Redens had been his boss in the Transcaucasian GPU (secret police) until Beria engineered his ouster.

22. Richardson, *Long Shadow,* 242–43.

23. Ibid., 245.

24. The JAC was reviving an old suggestion of creating a Jewish republic in Crimea.

25. Alliluyeva, *Only One Year,* 153–54. Not everyone believed Svetlana could actually have witnessed this. Her cousin Leonid Alliluyev remained skeptical. Author's interview with Leonid and Galina Alliluyev, Moscow, May 17, 2013.

26. Joshua Rubenstein and Vladimir P. Naumov, *Stalin's Secret Pogrom: The Postwar Inquisition of the Jewish Anti-Fascist Committee* (New Haven, CT: Yale University Press, 2005), 2–3.

27. Kuromiya, *Stalin,* 193.

28. Yakov Rapoport, *The Doctors' Plot: A Survivor's Memoir of Stalin's Last Act of Terror Against Jews and Science* (Cambridge, MA: Harvard University Press, 1991), 33.

29. Rubenstein and Naumov, *Stalin's Secret Pogrom,* 39–40. The authors claim Mikhoels's death was not an accident. He was "lured" from his hotel and driven to the country house of the head of the Belarus security forces, where he was murdered on Stalin's direct orders. The executioners phoned Stalin for advice on how to camouflage the murder. "Well, it's an automobile accident," he said.

30. Alliluyeva, *Twenty Letters,* 196.

31. Letter from S. Alliluyeva to Stalin, Dec. 1, 1945, RGASPI, KPSS fond 558, opis 11, D 1552, doc. 33, 49–50.

32. Alliluyeva, *Only One Year,* 373–74.

33. Alliluyeva, *Twenty Letters*, 56.
34. *Alliluyev Memoirs*, xii.
35. P. Fedoseyev, "Irresponsible Thinking," *Pravda* 119, no. 10510 (May 14, 1947): 3.
36. Alliluyeva, *Twenty Letters*, 61.
37. Alliluyeva, *Only One Year*, 169.
38. Alliluyeva, *Twenty Letters*, 193.
39. Ibid., 113.
40. Michael Arlen, *The Green Hat* (New York: George H. Doran Co., 1924); mentioned in Alliluyeva, *Twenty Letters*, 113, 193.
41. Alliluyeva, *Twenty Letters*, 195.
42. Alliluyeva, *Only One Year*, 155.

CHAPTER 9: EVERYTHING SILENT, AS BEFORE A STORM

1. Alliluyeva, *Only One Year*, 388.
2. Alliluyeva, *Twenty Letters*, 68–69.
3. Alliluyev, *Chronicle of One Family*, 68.
4. Author's interview with Stepan Mikoyan, May 24, 2013.
5. Charkviani, *My Life and Reflections*, 503.
6. Ibid., 505.
7. Alliluyeva, *Twenty Letters*, 192–93.
8. Author's interview with Stepan Mikoyan, Moscow, May 24, 2013.
9. Montefiore, *Court of the Red Tsar*, 137.
10. Meryle Secrest Interview with Svetlana Alliluyeva, audio recordings, group 2, tape 8. HIA.
11. Service, *Stalin*, 307. See also Jonathan Brent and Vladimir P. Naumov, *Stalin's Last Crime: The Plot Against the Jewish Doctors, 1948–1953* (New York: HarperCollins, 2003), 71–77; and Pavel Sudoplatov and Anatoli Sudoplatov with Jerrold L. Schecter and Leona P. Schecter, *Special Tasks: The Memoirs of an Unwanted Witness* (New York: Little, Brown, 1995), 317–18.
12. Brent and Naumov, *Stalin's Last Crime*, 78.
13. For the full text of the letter, see Brent and Naumov, *Stalin's Last Crime*, 81.
14. Alliluyeva, *Only One Year*, 380.
15. Beria, *Beria, My Father*, 152–53.
16. *Kreml'-9* writers, *Svetlana Stalina: Escape from the Family*, comments of Stepan Mikoyan.
17. Kyra Golovko, "Svetlana Alliluyeva: odinochestvo i nasledstvo" ["Svetlana Alliluyeva: Solitude and Inheritance"], *Izvestia*, no. 95 (Oct. 17, 2008): 10.
18. Ibid.

19. Ibid.

20. Figes, *Whisperers*, 487–92

21. Alliluyeva, *Only One Year*, 391.

22. Alliluyeva, *Twenty Letters*, 197–98.

23. Kelly, *Children's World: Growing Up in Russia*, 645, n. 203.

24. Letter to S. Alliluyeva from Stalin, May 10, 1950, Alliluyeva, *Twenty Letters*, 199.

25. Ibid., 198.

26. Author's interview with Chrese Evans, Portland, OR, July 16, 2012.

27. Letter to author from Professor Lynne Viola, July 20, 2014.

28. Golovko, "Svetlana Alliluyeva: Solitude and Inheritance," 10.

29. Letter from S. Alliluyeva to Stalin, RGASPI, KPSS fond 558, opis 11, D 1552, doc. 37, 55–56.

30. Charkviani, *My Life and Reflections*, 507.

31. Meryle Secrest Interview with Svetlana Alliluyeva, audio recording, group 1, tape 9, HIA.

32. Biagi, *Svetlana: The Inside Story*, 135.

33. Alliluyeva, *Twenty Letters*, 211.

34. Ibid., 209.

35. *Svetlana About Svetlana*, film, directed by Lana Parshina, 2008.

36. Letter from S. Alliluyeva to Stalin, RGASPI, KPSS fond 558 opis 11, D 1552, doc. 36, 54.

37. Alliluyeva, *Twenty Letters*, 71.

38. Konstantin Simonov, "Through the Eyes of My Generation: Meditations on Stalin," *Soviet Literature*, Moscow, no. 5 (494) (1989): 79.

39. Khrushchev, *Khrushchev Remembers*, 321; also Taubman, *Khrushchev*, 214.

40. Khrushchev, *Khrushchev Remembers*, 309–10. Khrushchev suggests that it was New Year's Day. Alliluyeva says the last time she saw her father was his birthday.

41. Rapoport, *Doctors' Plot*, 74–75.

42. Ibid., 71.

43. Ibid., 221.

44. Konstantin Simonov, "Through the Eyes of My Generation," 87–88.

45. Alliluyeva, *Only One Year*, 155.

46. Alliluyeva, *Twenty Letters*, 197.

47. Rapoport, *Doctors' Plot*, 243.

48. Alliluyeva, *Twenty Letters*, 207. There is some evidence, however, that Stalin had begun to "phase down his propaganda campaign around the Doctors' Plot." His health was too seriously impaired for him to carry out another Great Terror. Gennadi Kostyrchenko, "The Genesis of Establishment Anti-Semitism in the USSR: The Black Years, 1948–53," in *Revolution, Repression, and Revival: The Soviet Jewish Experience*, ed. Zvi

Gitelman and Yaacov Ro'i (Lanham, MD: Rowman & Littlefield, 2007), 189–90.

49. Alliluyeva, *Only One Year*, 155.

50. Ibid., 155.

CHAPTER 10: THE DEATH OF THE *VOZHD*

1. Meryle Secrest interview with Svetlana Alliluyeva, audio recording, group 1, tape 17, HIA.

2. Ibid. See also Richardson, *Long Shadow*, 250.

3. Montefiore, *Court of the Red Tsar*, 636–37.

4. Khrushchev, *Khrushchev Remembers*, 340.

5. Amy Knight, *Beria: Stalin's First Lieutenant* (Princeton, NJ: Princeton University Press, 1993), 176–78. See also Service, *Stalin*, 582–86; and Radzinsky, *Stalin*, 571–72. Radzinsky claimed to have interviewed Lozgachev.

6. Montefiore, *Court of the Red Tsar*, 639.

7. Taubman, *Khrushchev*, 237.

8. Brent and Naumov, *Stalin's Last Crime*, 212. Vinogradov had treated Zhdanov.

9. Montefiore, *Court of the Red Tsar*, 643.

10. Alliluyeva, *Twenty Letters*, 6–7.

11. Rapoport, *Doctors' Plot*, 151–52.

12. Khrushchev, *Khrushchev Remembers*, 342.

13. Alliluyeva, *Twenty Letters*, 215.

14. Ibid., 9.

15. Ibid.

16. Ibid., 8.

17. Service, *Stalin*, 576.

18. Alliluyeva, *Twenty Letters*, 10.

19. Khrushchev, *Khrushchev Remembers*, 347.

20. Biagi, *Svetlana: The Inside Story*, 86.

21. Alliluyeva, *Twenty Letters*, 14

22. Ibid., 222.

23. Decades later she would develop a conspiracy theory. According to Stalin's maid, he had been found on the floor between the table with the telephone and his couch. He had obviously taken a phone call. Her father had very high blood pressure, which was why he refused to fly on planes. Svetlana became suspicious of the details surrounding his death—the delay in calling the doctors, the emptying of his dacha. Once in the United States, she consulted an American specialist, who told her that a very strong impulse or sound could be sent through the telephone to the unprotected ear and cause a stroke. It was an efficient way to kill someone with high blood pressure, and her father's was 200/80. Why did "Beria's people" empty the

furniture at his dacha the day after his death, if not to conceal something? Beria was a technological wizard. Meryle Secrest interview with Svetlana Alliluyeva, London, March 1994, Secrest Collection, audio recordings, group 1, tape 9, HIA.

24. Molotov, *Molotov Remembers*, 210.

25. Richardson, *Long Shadow*, 254.

26. Rapoport, *Doctors' Plot*, 20.

27. Simonov, "Through the Eyes of My Generation," 96.

28. Ibid., 96–97.

29. Oleg Kalugin, *Spymaster: My Thirty-Two Years in Intelligence and Espionage Against the West* (New York: Basic Books, 2009), 10–11.

CHAPTER 11: THE GHOSTS RETURN

1. Alliluyeva, *Twenty Letters*, 222.

2. Cohen, *Victims Return*, 33–35.

3. Ibid.

4. Figes, *Whisperers*, 538; also Adam Hochschild, *The Unquiet Ghost: Russians Remember Stalin* (London: Penguin, 1994), 223.

5. Rapoport, *Doctors' Plot*, 187–88.

6. Ibid., 182–83.

7. Ibid., 184–85.

8. Richardson, *Long Shadow*, 232.

9. Ibid. Leonid Alliluyev believed his mother was suffering from the "schizophrenia" that plagued her family. The family believed it had destroyed Anna's brother Fyodor. But when, in 1993, Leonid searched down Anna's rehabilitation files, Case P-212 (many families of prisoners made such searches in the glasnost years), the files did "not contain any hints that Anna was mentally ill." What they did make clear was that, on December 27, 1952, the sentence of Prisoner no. 23, now in Vladimirskaia prison, was prolonged for five more years by S. A. Golidze, an associate of Beria. Only Stalin's death saved her. On April 2, 1954, Anna was moved to Moscow, rehabilitated, and released to her family. Alliluyev, *Chronicle of One Family*, 271–72.

10. Richardson, *Long Shadow*, 233.

11. Ibid., 244.

12. Ibid., 234.

13. Ibid., 223.

14. Ibid.

15. Ibid., 225.

16. Ibid., 239.

17. See Eugenia Aleksandrovna (Zhenya) Alliluyeva Correspondence, GARF, fond 9542, opis 1, no. 85, 9–20

18. Richardson, *Long Shadow*, 241–42.

19. Ibid., 234.

20. *Pravda*, Dec. 17, 1953.

21. Many, including Svetlana, claimed that Beria was executed a few days after his arrest in July. Alliluyeva, *Only One Year*, 375–76. His trial, which was announced on December 17 and lasted from December 18 to 23, may have been staged long after his death. Knight, *Beria*, 220-22.

22. Richardson, *Long Shadow*, 256.

23. Alliluyeva, *Twenty Letters*, 218–19.

24. Ibid., 16.

25. Biagi, *Svetlana: The Inside Story*, 139 (interview with Joseph Alliluyev).

26. Gribanov, "And Memory as Snow Keeps Drifting," 161.

27. *Kreml'-9* writers, *Svetlana Stalina: Escape from the Family*, comments of Artyom Sergeev.

28. Author's interview with Leonid and Galina Alliluyev, Moscow, May 17, 2013.

29. Author's interview with Alexander Burdonsky, Moscow, June 1, 2013.

30. Author's interview with Leonid and Galina Alliluyev, Moscow, May 17, 2013.

31. A degree that is midway between a Western master's degree and a PhD.

32. Alliluyeva, *Twenty Letters*, 17.

33. Joshua Rubenstein, *Tangled Loyalties: The Life and Times of Ilya Ehrenburg* (Tucaloosa: University of Alabama Press, 1999), 281. When members of the editorial board of *Znamya* got the book, they balked at the title. "It gives the impression that everything has been a mistake until now: Let it be called *Nov* (Renewal) or *Novaya Stupen* (A New Stage)."

34. Alliluyeva, *Only One Year*, 177.

35. Alliluyeva, "Letter to Ehrenburg," 607.

36. Rubenstein, *Tangled Loyalties*, 212–17, 307.

37. Biagi, *Svetlana: The Inside Story*, 33.

38. Ibid., 33.

39. *Svetlana* (film), 2008, interview with Svetlana Alliluyeva.

40. Alliluyeva, "Letter to Ehrenburg," 607.

41. Meryle Secrest interview with Svetlana Alliluyeva, audio recording, group 2, tape 5, HIA.

42. Biagi, *Svetlana: The Inside Story*, 34–35.

43. Ibid., 35.

44. Leningrad would revert to its traditional name, Saint Petersburg, in 1991.

45. Author's visit to Alliluyev Apartment Museum, Saint Petersburg, May 20, 2013.

46. Alliluyeva, *Twenty Letters*, 89.

47. Ibid., 223.

CHAPTER 12: THE GENERALISSIMO'S DAUGHTER

1. Alliluyeva, *Only One Year*, 161.
2. Khrushchev, *The Crimes of the Stalin Era*, 3–67.
3. Alliluyeva, *Only One Year*, 162, 166.
4. Author's interview with Stepan Mikoyan, Moscow, May 24, 2013.
5. Biagi, *Svetlana: The Inside Story*, 95.
6. Simonov, "Through the Eyes of My Generation," 43.
7. Ibid., 48.
8. Biagi, *Svetlana: The Inside Story*, 36.
9. Golovko, "Svetlana Alliluyeva: Solitude and Inheritance," 10.
10. Author's interview with Alexander Ushakov, Gorky Institute, Moscow, June 4, 2013.
11. Ibid.
12. Ironically, the source of this anecdote is the FBI. "Anecdote about Svetlana and Synyavsky at Gorky Inst. In bio of Sinyavsky by Alfreda Aucouturier," FBI file 105-163639-A.
13. Meryle Secrest Interview with Svetlana Alliluyeva, audio recordng, group 1, tape 13. HIA.
14. Sheila Fitzpatrick, *A Spy in the Archives: A Memoir of Cold War Russia* (London: I. B. Tauris, 2013), 39–40.
15. Galina Belaya,"Ia rodom iz shestidesiatykh" ["I Am from the Sixties"], *Novoe literaturnoe obozrenie* 70 (June 2004): 216.
16. Alliluyeva, *Only One Year*, 166.
17. Boris Runin, *"Moie okruzhenie," Zapiski sluchaino utselevshego* ["My Milieu," Notes by the One Who Accidentally Survived] (Moscow: Vozvrashchenie, 2010), 224–25. See also Miklós Kun, *Stalin: An Unknown Portrait* (Budapest: CEU Press, 2003), 417.
18. Gribanov, "And Memory as Snow Keeps Drifting," 161.
19. Alliluyev, *Chronicle of One Family*, 68–69.
20. Richardson, *Long Shadow*, 259.
21. Mikoyan, *Memoirs of Military Test-Flying*, 146.
22. Gribanov, "And Memory as Snow Keeps Drifting," 157.
23. Author's interview with Stepan Mikoyan, Moscow, May 24, 2013.
24. Gribanov, "And Memory as Snow Keeps Drifting," 157–58.
25. Vladislav Zubok, *Zhivago's Children: The Last Russian Intelligentsia* (Cambridge, MA: Belknap Press of Harvard University, 2009), 327.
26. Gribanov, "And Memory as Snow Keeps Drifting," 159.
27. Ibid., 160.
28. Ibid., 161.
29. Ibid., 158.
30. David Samoilov, *Podennye zapisi* (Daily Notes), 2 vols. (Moscow: Vremia, 2002), vol. 1, 300, entry for Nov. 17, 1960.

31. Ibid., vol. 2, p. 30, entry for Mar. 24, 1967.

CHAPTER 13: POST-THAW

 1. Ronald Hingley, *Pasternak: A Biography* (New York: Knopf, 1983), 237, 241.

 2. Alliluyeva, *Only One Year*, 293.

 3. Ibid., 295.

 4. Author's interview with Alexander Ushakov, Moscow, June 4, 2013.

 5. Maria Rozanova, "Vdova znamenitogo pisatelia i dissidenta Sinyavskogo Mariia Rozanova: 'Alliluyeva mne skazala, "Masha, vy uveli Andreiia u zheny, a seichas ia uvozhu ego ot vas"'" ("The Widow of the Famous Writer and Dissident Andrei Sinyavsky, Maria Rozanova: 'Alliluyeva told me, "Masha, you took Andrei from his wife. Now I take him away from you."'"), *Bul'var Gordona*, no. 40 (232) (Oct. 6, 2009): 12–14. This story became common currency at the Gorky Institute. Interview with Alexander Ushakov, Moscow, June 4, 2013.

 6. Interview with Chrese Evans, Portland, OR, Feb. 27, 2013.

 7. Letter to Malcolm Muggeridge, Mar. 9, 1970, Muggeridge Papers, Special Collections, Wheaton College, Illinois WCSC.

 8. Alliluyeva, *Twenty Letters*, 219–21.

 9. Ibid., 80. See also Kun, *Stalin: An Unknown Portrait*, 416–17.

10. Meryle Secrest interview with Svetlana Alliluyeva, audio recording, group 1, tape 14, HIA.

11. Biagi, *Svetlana: The Inside Story*, 122.

12. Though Svetlana never referred to this marriage, her cousin Leonid remembers that it took place in a church in 1962. Interview with Leonid Alliluyev, Moscow, May 17, 2013. Boris Gribanov remembered Svetlana introducing him to her new husband at the funeral of Ashkhen Lazarevna Mikoyan, on November 5, 1962. Gribanov, "And Memory as Snow Keeps Drifting," 161. A divorce announcement eventually appeared in *Vechernaya Moskva*. "Svanidze, Ivan Aleksandrovich [Dobrolyubov Street 35, apartment 11] filed for divorce against Alliluyeva, Svetlana Josifovna [Serafimovich Street 2, Apartment 179]. The case will be considered by the Timiryazev District People's Court." See Kun, *Stalin: An Unknown Portrait*, 417.

13. His sentence was commuted in 1965 after international protests, and he was permitted to emigrate from the country.

14. Lily Golden, *My Long Journey Home* (Chicago: Third World Press, 2002), 149.

15. Yelena Khanga, with Susan Jacoby, *Soul to Soul: The Story of a Black Russian American Family 1865–1992* (New York: Norton, 1992), 49.

16. Golden, *Long Journey Home*, 149.

17. Ibid., 149–50.

18. Khanga, *Soul to Soul*, 138.

19. Golden, *Long Journey Home*, 150.

20. Khanga, *Soul to Soul*, 138.

21. Golden, *Long Journey Home*, 151.

22. Alliluyeva, *Only One Year*, 238.

23. Ibid., 101.

24. "Myths," *Live with Mikhail Zelensky* (television), comments of Olga Rifkina.

25. Meryle Secrest interview with Svetlana Alliluyeva, audio recording, group 1, tape 12. HIA.

26. Alliluyeva, *Twenty Letters*, 92–94.

27. Ibid., 235.

28. Ibid., 119–20.

CHAPTER 14: THE GENTLE BRAHMAN

 1. Terry Morris, "Svetlana: A Love Story," *McCall's*, July 1967, 143.

 2. Alliluyeva, *Only One Year*, 21.

 3. Comment by Frances Sedgwik, a Canadian foreign exchange student at the International School who ended up in the Kuntsevo hospital in 1963 at the same time as Svetlana. Author's interview with Frances Sedgwik, Toronto, Nov. 13, 2013.

 4. Alliluyeva, *Only One Year*, 27.

 5. Ibid., 31.

 6. Biagi, *Svetlana: The Inside Story*, 110.

 7. Morris, "Svetlana: A Love Story," 143.

 8. Alliluyev, *Chronicle of One Family*, 69.

 9. Alliluyeva, *Only One Year*, 180.

10. Ibid., 37.

11. Mikoyan, *Memoirs of Military Test-Flying*, 146.

12. Alliluyeva, *Only One Year*, 41–42.

13. Vladimir V. Kara-Murza, writer and producer, *They Chose Freedom: Dissident Movement from 1950s to 1991*, documentary film, 2013, comments of Alexander Yesenin-Volpin.

14. Max Hayward, ed., *On Trial: The Soviet State Versus "Abram Tertz" and "Nikolai Arzhak"* (New York: Harper & Row, 1966), 41–42. Though his supporters thought he would be given amnesty, Sinyavsky served almost his full sentence and was released in 1971; he was allowed to immigrate to Paris in 1973.

15. Alliluyeva, *Only One Year*, 39–40.

16. Author's interview with Alexander Ushakov, Moscow, June 4, 2013.

17. Alliluyeva, *Only One Year*, 177–78. Galina Belaya, in her article "I Am from the Sixties" (*Novoe literaturnoe obozrenie*, 70), confirms that staff members at the Gorky Institute were forced to sign an open letter denouncing Sinyavsky. She claims to have refused to sign the letter.

18. Martin Ebon, *Svetlana: The Incredible Story of Stalin's Daughter* (New York: Signet, 1967), 138.

19. The United Arab Republic was a short-lived merger between Syria and Egypt that lasted from 1958 to 1961, though Egypt continued to be officially known as the "United Arab Republic" until 1971.

20. Alliluyeva, *Only One Year*, 43.

21. Ibid., 48.

22. Meryle Secrest interview with Svetlana Alliluyeva, audio recording, group 2, tape 17, HIA.

23. Mikoyan, *Memoirs of Military Test-Flying*, 147.

24. Svetlana Alliluyeva letter to Suresh Singh, reprinted in Morris, "Svetlana: A Love Story," 74.

25. Alliluyeva, *Only One Year*, 54.

26. Biagi, *Svetlana: The Inside Story*, 114.

27. Ibid., 114.

CHAPTER 15: ON THE BANKS OF THE GANGES

1. Morris, "Svetlana: A Love Story," 143.

2. Ebon, *Svetlana: The Incredible Story*, 12; Hudson, *Svetlana Alliluyeva: Flight to Freedom*, 78; and Alliluyeva, *Only One Year*, 62.

3. Alliluyeva, *Only One Year*, 72.

4. Ibid., 81.

5. Morris, "Svetlana: A Love Story," 143.

6. Alliluyeva, *Only One Year*, 99.

7. Chester Bowles, *Ambassador's Report* (New York: Harper & Bros., 1954), 74.

8. Alliluyeva, *Only One Year*, 111.

9. Ibid., 119.

10. Ibid.

11. Ibid., 140.

12. Morris, "Svetlana: A Love Story," 146; and Alliluyeva, *Only One Year*, 189.

13. Morris, "Svetlana: A Love Story," 146.

14. Marilyn Silverstone, "The Suburbanization of Svetlana," *Look*, Sept. 9, 1969, 56.

15. Alliluyeva, *Only One Year*, 191.

CHAPTER 16: ITALIAN COMIC OPERA

1. Telegram from Secretary of State Rusk to L. Thompson, American ambassador to the Soviet Union, Secret, Flash, Mar. 6, 1967, LBJL, NSF, Intelligence, Svetlana Alliluyeva, NLJ/RAC 12-91.

2. LBJL, Recordings and Transcripts, tape F67.08, side B, PNO 3.

3. Telegram from L. Thompson to Rusk, Mar. 7, 1967, LBJL, NSF, Intelligence, Svetlana Alliluyeva, NLJ/RAC 03-113.

4. CIA DB, NARA, Congressional Record, March 15, 1967, S3867–68.

5. CIA DB, NARA, AMB file, Foreign Report, Jan. 5, 1967, CIA-RDP70B00338R00030009013-1.

6. Peter Earnest, International Spy Museum, Washington, DC, podcast, Peter Earnest in Conversation with Oleg Kalugin and Robert Rayle on Defection of Svetlana Alliluyeva, Dec. 4, 2006, www.spymuseum.org/exhibition-experiences/agent-storm/listen-to-the-audio/episode/the-litvinenko-murder-and-other-riddles-from-moscow.

7. Rayle, "Unpublished Autobiographical Essay," PC, Rayle.

8. Earnest, International Spy Museum podcast.

9. W. Rostow to President, Friday, Mar. 10, 1967, 8:45 AM, LBJL, NSF, Intelligence, Svetlana Alliluyeva, NLJ/ RAC 03-115 E.O. 12958, Sec. 3.5.

10. Rayle, "Unpublished Autobiographical Essay," PC, Rayle.

11. Herewith Verbatim Copy: Letter from Svetlana Alliluyeva to Children, Mar. 9, 1967, LBJL, NSF, Intelligence, Svetlana Alliluyeva, NLJ/ RAC 03-113.

12. Rayle, "Unpublished Autobiographical Essay," PC, Rayle.

13. Alliluyeva, *Faraway Music*, 144.

14. Secret: From New Delhi, Mar. 15, 17, 1967, NARA: E.O. 13292, Sec. 3.5. NLJ 03-145.

15. Alliluyeva, *Faraway Music*, 146.

16. Rayle, "Unpublished Autobiographical Essay," PC, Rayle.

17. Alliluyeva, *Faraway Music*, 147.

18. Secret: From New Delhi, Mar. 15, 17, 1967, NARA: E.O. 13292, Sec. 3.5. NLJ 03-145.

19. "Stalin's Daughter Said to Quit Soviet Union and May Have Approached US Aides," *New York Times*, Mar. 10, 1967.

20. Rayle, "Unpublished Autobiographical Essay," PC, Rayle.

21. Secret: From New Delhi, Mar. 15, 17, 1967, NARA, E.O. 13292, Sec. 3.5. NLJ 03-145.

22. Alliluyeva, *Only One Year*, 207.

CHAPTER 17: DIPLOMATIC FURY

1. Morris, "Svetlana: A Love Story," 146.

2. Text of Indian protest note, C. S. Jha to Chester Bowles, Mar. 9, 1967, LBJL, NSF, Intelligence, Svetlana Alliluyeva, NLJ/RAC 03-113 E.O. 13292 Sec. 3.5.

3. Letter to Mr. C. S. Jha, Foreign Secretary, Ministry of External Affairs, Government of India, from Chester Bowles, March 10, 1967, LBJL, NSF, Intelligence, Svetlana Alliluyeva, NLJ/RAC 03-113 E.O. 13292 Sec. 3.5.

4. From Moscow, Mar. 13, 1967, attached to text of Indian protest note, Mar. 9, 1967.

5. Gene Sosin, *Sparks of Liberty: An Insider's Memoir of Radio Liberty* [Radio Free Europe] (University Park: Pennsylvania State University Press, 1999), 118.

6. NARA RG 59 Central Foreign Policy Files 1967–1969, Pol 30 USSR box 2684, folder POL 30 USSR: 012608, Mar. 13, 1967.

7. Author's interview with Leonid and Galina Alliluyev, Moscow, May 17, 2013.

8. Soviet statement on Alliluyeva's defection, NARA RG 59 Central Foreign Policy Files 1967–1969, Pol 30 USSR box 2684, folder POL 30 USSR: 008007, May 9, 1967.

9. Author's telephone conversation with Marvin Kalb, Apr. 9, 2012. There was indeed some eliding of the truth. The US Embassy in Bern determined the "line" to be taken: Mrs. Allilueva (*sic*) "asked the American authorities to get in touch with the Swiss authorities . . . Mrs. Allilueva wishes to rest for a few weeks in Switzerland. Towards the Swiss authorities she expressed her special wish not to issue any statements to the press and the public." NARA RG 59 Central Foreign Policy Files 1967–1969, Pol 30 USSR box 2684, folder POL 30 USSR: 012407, Fr AMEM BASSY BERN to SECSTATE WASHDC, Mar. 13, 1967.

10. Alliluyeva, *Only One Year*, 213.

11. Letter to author from Ramona Rayle, Oct. 12, 2014.

12. Alliluyeva, *Only One Year*, 210.

13. Rosamond Richardson interview with Svetlana Alliluyeva (Lana Peters), Saffron Walden, 1991, tape 4, PC, Richardson.

14. Alliluyeva, *Only One Year*, 216.

15. Gaddis, *Hawk and the Dove*, 599–60.

16. Letter from Ambassador Chester Bowles to Secretary Rusk, from New Delhi, Mar. 15, 1967, NARA, RAC NLJ 010-003-6-7.

17. Gaddis, *Hawk and the Dove*, 318.

18. John Gaddis, interview with George and Annelise Kennan, George F. Kennan Papers, MC 256, box 6, folder 1, PUL.

19. Letter from Chester Bowles to Walt Rostow, Eyes Only, Mar. 18, 1967, LBJL, NSF, Intelligence, Svetlana Alliluyeva, State Dept. Guidelines, EO 12958. Sec. 3.5.

20. Greenbaum had just represented Harper & Row in its dispute with Jacqueline Kennedy over the publication of William Manchester's *The Death of a President*.

21. Author's interview with Walter Pozen, son-in-law of George Kennan, New York, Feb. 12, 2013.

22. George F. Kennan Papers, MC 076, box 22, folder 5: Jameson, Donald, PUL.

23. Alliluyeva, *Only One Year*, 214.

24. Ibid., 215.

25. Ibid., 218.

26. Ibid.

27. Author's interview with Walter Pozen, New York, Feb. 12, 2013.

28. "Stalin's Daughter in the US to 'Seek Self-Expression': 2 Americans Had Role in Decision," *New York Times*, Apr. 22, 1967.

29. Ibid.

30. Ibid.

31. To New Delhi, Apr. 6, 1967, "Foll is summary of status and recent non-Indian developments in Svetlana case: Pls pass to Ambassador Bowles," LBJL, NSF, Intelligence, Svetlana Alliluyeva, NLJ/RAC 03-113 E.O. 13292 Sec. 3.5.

32. Andrei Sedykh, "Milliony Svetlany" [Svetlana's Millions], *Novoye Russkoye Slovo*, Apr. 15, 1973.

CHAPTER 18: ATTORNEYS AT WORK

1. Author's interview with Alan Schwartz, Los Angeles, Dec. 5, 2013.

2. "Stalin's Daughter in the US to Seek 'Self-Expression,'" *New York Times*, Apr. 22, 1967.

3. Author's interview with Alan Schwartz, Los Angeles, Dec. 5, 2013.

4. Letter from Greenbaum to Evan Thomas, May 26, 1967, outlining his account of events, PC, HarperCollins Collection.

5. "Publishing," *Time*, May 26, 1967, 38.

6. Other translators on the list were Patricia Blake, Robert Tucker, and Max Hayward.

7. Author's interview with Priscilla Johnson McMillan, Jan. 21, 2013.

8. Ibid.

9. Alliluyeva, *Only One Year*, 226.

10. Ibid., 228.

11. Golden, *My Long Journey Home*, 154–55.

12. Author's interview with Golden's daughter Yelena Khanga, Moscow, Jan. 28, 2014.

13. Author's interview with Leonid and Galina Alliluyev, Moscow, May 17, 2013.

14. Ana Petrovna and Mikhail Leshynsky, *Poslednee interview* [The Last Interview] (Moscow: Algoritm, 2013), 71–72, hereafter Petrova and Leshynsky, *Last Interview*.

15. Ibid., 73.

16. "Myths," *Live with Mikhail Zelensky*, comments of Olga Fedorovna Redlova.

17. Svetlana Alliluyeva,"To Boris Leonidovich Pasternak," trans. Max Hayward, *Atlantic* 219, no. 6 (June 1967): 133–40.

18. Ibid., 135.

19. Ibid., 140.

20. Author's interview with Alan Schwartz, Los Angeles, Dec. 5, 2013.

21. Alliluyeva, *Faraway Music*, appendix, p. 181.

22. Author's interview with Alan Schwartz, Los Angeles, Dec. 5, 2013.

23. Meryle Secrest interview with Svetlana Alliluyeva, audio recordings, group 1, tape 7, HIA.

24. Author's interview with Alan Schwartz, Los Angeles, Dec. 5, 2013.

25. Sedykh, "Svetlana's Millions."

26. *Journal*, Offices of the Legislative Council [of the USSR], Tuesday, May 23, 1967; Nikodia Tsonev, CIA DB, Svetlana Alliluyeva, Press Items.

27. Alexander Kolesnik, *Mify i pravdy o sem'e Stalina* [Myths and Truths About Stalin's Family] (Moscow: Technivest, 1991), 46. "In May of 1943 [other sources said 1941], Germans in the area of Zimni station (Moscow-Riga railway line) threw leaflets in the location of our troops that stated that I. V. Stalin, during the critical period for our country in 1941, transferred, on the chance of defeat, 2 million rubles into a Swiss bank. The leaflets were gathered and burned. At the time, no one believed it."

28. "$300 Million Gold for Svetlana," *Washington Observer Newsletter*, June 15, 1967, CIA DB, NARA, AMB file CIA-RDP73B. The *Newsletter* was a right-wing gossip sheet, but important enough that the CIA kept a copy in its files.

29. Memorandum for the President, Mar. 30, 1967, LBJL, NSF, Intelligence, Svetlana Alliluyeva, NARA, NLJ/RAC 010.003005/18.

30. From USUN NEW YORK to RUEHC/SECSTATE, WASHDC, Apr. 24, 1969, NARA, RG 59, Central Foreign Policy Files 1967–1969, Pol 30 USSR box 2684.

31. Author's interview with Alan Schwartz, Los Angeles, Dec. 5, 2013.

32. Letter to Eddie Greenbaum from George Kennan, Apr. 15, 1967, PC, HarperCollins Collection.

33. Sir Paul Gore-Booth, NAUK, Foreign Office, FCO 95/14, File No. IR 1/5/4, Confidential Defectors: Soviet Union: Svetlana Stalin, May 1, 1967.

34. The Soviets were certain the CIA had "prepared, arranged, and financed" the whole thing. The Soviets were convinced the Johnson administration's decision to delay Svetlana's entry into the United States was merely "part of the overall plot." FBI files UPI-68 and 105-163639-A.

35. Greenbaum, Wolff & Ernst, transcript of press conference interview, Aug. 15 1967, PC, HarperCollins Collection.

CHAPTER 19: THE ARRIVAL

1. FBI file 105-163639/53673, Confidential: From John Edgar Hoover to Director of Intelligence, Dept. of State, Apr. 25, 1967. Hoover warned that "unauthorized disclosure would reveal Bureau investigative interest in diplomatic personnel which could be prejudicial to the defense interests of the Nation."

2. Ebon, *Svetlana: The Incredible Story*, 153; and Biagi, *Svetlana: The Inside Story*, 150. Nicholas Thompson repeats this in *Hawk and the Dove*, 228.

3. Garry Wills and Ovid Demaris, "The Svetlana Papers," *Esquire*, November 1967, 176.

4. "Stalin's Daughter in the US to Seek 'Self-Expression,'" *New York Times*, Apr. 22, 1967.

5. Ibid.

6. Alliluyeva, *Only One Year*, 319. See also Zubok, *Zhivago's Children*, 213–17, for an account of Khrushchev's famous attack on Voznesensky at the House of the Unions in 1963, which caused Voznesensky to have a nervous breakdown.

7. Ron Popeski, "Ex-KGB Head Semichastny Dies at 77," *St. Petersburg Times*, no. 636, Jan. 16, 2001. See also Ebon, *Svetlana: The Incredible Story*, 152.

8. Author's interview with Priscilla Johnson McMillan, Jan. 21, 2013.

9. "Stalin's Daughter in the US to Seek 'Self-Expression.'"

10. Ibid.

11. Wills and Demaris, "Svetlana Papers," 176–77.

12. Memorandum for the Record, Apr. 1, 1967, Subject: Telephone Conversation with George Kennan, Mar. 31, 1967, Sanitized, NARA, NLJ 03-145, E.O. 13292, Sec. 3.5.

13. From AMEMBASSY TEHRAN TO RUEHC/SECSTATE AMEMBASSY MOSCOW, Subj: Svetlana, May 9, 1967, NARA, RG 59, Central Foreign Policy Files 1967–69, Pol 30 USSR box 2684, Confidential.

14. "Transcript of Mrs. Alliluyeva's Statement and Her Replies at News Conference," *New York Times*, Apr. 27, 1967.

15. Wills and Demaris, "Svetlana Papers," 178.

16. Alliluyeva, *Only One Year*, 317.

17. Ibid., 314.

18. Wills and Demaris, "Svetlana Papers," 178.

19. "Mrs. Alliluyeva Goes Shopping on the Miracle Mile," *New York Times*, Apr. 29, 1967.

20. Author's interview with Priscilla Johnson McMillan, Jan. 21, 2013.

21. Ibid.

22. Ibid.

23. Letter to author from Priscilla McMillan, July 7, 2014.

24. Meryle Secrest interview with Svetlana Alliluyeva, audio recording, group 2, tape 4, HIA.

CHAPTER 20: A MYSTERIOUS FIGURE

1. Alliluyeva, *Only One Year*, 318.

2. "Johnson, Kosygin Talk 5 Hours," *New York Times*, June 24, 1967. Ko-

sygin is identified as premier even though his title was chairman of the Council of Ministers.

3. Alliluyeva, *Only One Year*, 335.

4. Thompson, *Hawk and the Dove*, 228.

5. NAUK, Foreign Office, Defectors, Soviet Union, Svetlana Stalin, FCO 95/14 C507421, Monday, July 3, 1967: Metropolitan Pimen's interview, *Izvestia*, July 1, 1967, in full.

6. NAUK, Foreign Office, Defectors, Soviet Union, Svetlana Stalin, FCO 95/14 C507421, June 28, 1967.

7. Author's interview with Priscilla Johnson McMillan, Jan. 21, 2013.

8. John Barron, *KGB: The Secret Work of Soviet Secret Agents* (New York: Bantam, 1974), 239. The British author Laurence Kelly met Victor Louis, who had long worked for the *Evening Standard*, when Louis was dying of cancer. "He was a Colonel in the KGB and died with full KGB honors," Kelly asserted. Author's interview with Linda and Laurence Kelly, London, June 24, 2013.

9. Arkady Belinkov and Natalia Belinkova, "O Viktore Loui: Interview v amerikanskoi bol'nichnoi palate" ["About Viktor Lui: Interview from an American Hospital Room"], *Raspria s vekom v dva golosa* [Two Voices in Clash with the Century] (Moscow: Novoe literaturnoe obozrenie, 2008), 422–28. Arkady Belinkov first met Victor Louis in Northern Kazakhstan in 1954 in the Ninth Spasski Ward of the Administration of Corrective and Labor Camp.

10. Nikita Khrushchev, *Memoirs of Nikita Khrushchev*, vol. 1, *Commissar 1918– 1945*, ed. Sergei Khrushchev, trans. George Shriver (University Park: Pennsylvania State University Press, 2004), appendix, 737.

11. "The Svetlana Memoirs," *Bookseller*, Aug. 12, 1967, p. 1328.

12. "Svetlana Copyright Hearing," *Bookseller*, Aug. 26, 1967, p. 1472.

13. Edmund Wilson, *The Sixties: The Last Journal, 1960–72*, ed. Lewis Dabney (New York: Farrar, Straus & Giroux, 1993), 670.

14. Letter from Evan Thomas to Greenbaum, June 2, 1967, PC, Harper-Collins Collection.

15. "Svetlana Stalin: My Father Was a Good Person," *Stern*, no. 33 (Aug. 13, 1967): 11–21. Articles were published on Aug. 13, 20, 27, and Sept. 3.

16. "Mother Is a Little Bit Screwed Up," *Stern*, no. 35 (Aug. 27, 1967): 33–40.

17. Biagi, *Svetlana: The Inside Story*, 69, 143–44.

18. Ibid., 37–38.

19. Ibid., 141.

20. Alliluyeva, *Only One Year*, 336–39.

21. Ibid., 340.

22. Alliluyeva, "To Boris Leonidovich Pasternak," 133.

23. Author's interview with Joan Kennan, Washington, Dec. 5, 2012.

24. Fitzpatrick, *A Spy in the Archives*, 10.

25. Ibid., 338.
26. Author's interview with Joan Kennan, Washington, Dec. 5, 2012.
27. Author's interview with Priscilla Johnson McMillan, Jan. 21, 2013.
28. Letter to Joan Kennan, Oct. 26, 1967, PC, J. Kennan.
29. Ibid.
30. Ibid.
31. Alliluyeva, *Only One Year*, 339.

CHAPTER 21: LETTERS TO A FRIEND
1. Alliluyeva, *Only One Year*, 344.
2. Ibid., 343.
3. Ibid., 347.
4. Letter to Evan Thomas, Sept. 14, 1967, PC, HarperCollins Collection.
5. Alliluyeva, *Only One Year*, 399.
6. Letter from Donald Jameson to George Kennan, Oct. 12, 1967, PUL, G. Kennan Papers, MC 076, box 22, folder 5, Jameson, Donald.
7. Bertram Wolfe, "Svetlana's Life: A Soul Laid Bare," *Chicago Daily News*, Sept. 23, 1967.
8. Arthur Schlesinger, "Twenty Letters to a Father," *Atlantic*, November 1967.
9. Olga Carlisle, "Dictator's Daughter," *New York Times Book Review* 72, no. 39 (Sept. 24, 1967).
10. Arthur Koestler, "Stalin's Svetlana Writes Book of Homely Reflections," *London Times Sunday Magazine*, Oct. 15, 1967.
11. Alexander Werth, "Svetlana: Who Needs Her?" *Nation*, Nov. 6, 1967.
12. Elizabeth Hardwick, "The Crown Jewels," *New York Review of Books*, Oct. 12, 1967.
13. "Mrs. Alliluyeva Donates $340,000," *New York Times,* Oct. 26, 1967.
14. Ibid.
15. Silverstone, "Suburbanization of Svetlana," 59.
16. Letter to Joan Kennan, Oct. 26, 1967, PC, J. Kennan.
17. Edmund Wilson, "Books: Two Soviet Households," *New Yorker*, Dec. 9, 1967.
18. Alliluyeva, *Twenty Letters*, 255.

CHAPTER 22: A CRUEL REBUFF
1. Meryle Secrest interview with Svetlana Alliluyeva, audio recording, group 1, tape 12, HIA.
2. NARA, RG 59, Central Foreign Policy Files 1967–69, Political and Defense Pol 29 USSR, To Pol 30 USSR, Memorandum of Conversation: General Edward Greenbaum to Foy Kohler, Dec. 4, 1967.
3. Alliluyeva, *Only One Year*, 441.

4. Silverstone, "Suburbanization of Svetlana," 56.

5. Meryle Secrest interview with Svetlana Alliluyeva, audio recording, group 2, tape 1, HIA. Alliluyeva claimed it was a joke.

6. Reported by Evgeniya Tucker, telephone interview with author, Mar. 14, 2013.

7. Paul Preston, *We Saw Spain Die: Foreign Correspondents in the Spanish Civil War* (London: Constable & Robinson, 2008), 216.

8. Ibid., 257.

9. Louis Fischer, *Men and Politics: An Autobiography* (New York: Duell, Sloan & Pearce, 1941), 90–91.

10. Milovan Djilas, *Conversations with Stalin*, trans. Michael B. Petrovich (New York: Harcourt, Brace & World, 1962), 70.

11. Letter to Louis Fischer, Apr. 5, 1968, Louis Fischer Papers, MC 204, box 1, folder 7, 1968–69, PUL.

12. Letter to Louis Fischer, Apr. 8, 1968, PUL.

13. Letter to Louis Fischer, Apr. 5, 1968, PUL.

14. Letter to Louis Fischer, June 6, 1968, PUL.

15. Letter to Louis Fischer, June 8, 1968, PUL.

16. Letter to Louis Fischer, Apr. 5, 1968, PUL.

17. Letter to author from Robert Rayle, Sept. 24, 2013.

18. Author's interview with Robert and Ramona Rayle, Ashburn, VA, July 18–19, 2013.

19. Letter to Louis Fischer, Aug. 27, 1968, PUL.

20. United States Immigration and Naturalization Service.

21. Letter to Louis Fischer, June 27, 1968, PUL.

22. Ibid.

23. Alliluyeva, *Faraway Music*, 31.

24. Ibid., 34.

25. Letter from Ark. Belinkov to Svetlana Alliluyeva, Aug. 18, 1968, Louis Fischer Papers, MC 24, box 1, folder 7, Allilueva, Svetlana Stalina, 1968–69, PUL.

26. Ibid.

27. Belinkov and Belinkova, *Two Voices in Clash with the Century*, 399.

28. Letter to Edmund Wilson, Aug. 13, 1968, translated from Russian, Edmund Wilson Papers, folder 32, Allilueva, Svetlana, 1968–79, PUL.

29. Belinkov and Belinkova, *Two Voices in Clash with the Century*, 400.

30. Letter to Louis Fischer, Aug. 29, 1968, PUL.

31. Letter to Louis Fischer, Sept. 3, 1968, PUL.

32. Letter to Louis Fischer, Aug. 19, 1968, PUL.

33. Letter to Louis Fischer, Sept. 8, 1968, PUL.

34. Letter to Louis Fischer, Sept. 17, 1968, PUL.

35. Preston, *We Saw Spain Die*, 261–62; and 'Dede' to Fischer (undated), box 10, folder 1, Fischer Papers, PUL.

36. Letters to Louis Fischer, Oct. 26, 30, 1968, PUL.

37. Letter to Joan Kennan, Oct. 29, 1968, PC, J. Kennan.

38. Letter to Fischer, Nov. 13, 1968, PUL.

39. Letter from Fischer to Alliluleyva, Nov. 24, 1968, PUL.

40. Patricia Blake, "The Saga of Stalin's 'Little Sparrow,'" *Time*, Jan. 28, 1985, 49.

41. Preston, *We Saw Spain Die*, 261; and undated letter (1957), box 10, folder 1, Fischer Papers, PUL.

42. Preston, *We Saw Spain Die*, 262

43. Author's interview with Priscilla Johnson McMillan, Jan. 21, 2013.

44. Author's interview with Joan Kennan, Washington, Dec. 5, 2012.

CHAPTER 23: ONLY ONE YEAR

1. Letter to Louis Fischer, Dec. 26, 1968, PUL.

2. Wilson, *The Sixties*, 754–55.

3. Ibid., 758.

4. Ibid.

5. Author's interview with David and Clarissa Pryce-Jones, London, June 25, 2013.

6. Letter to Louis Fischer, Feb. 3, 1969, PUL.

7. Letter to Louis Fischer, Mar. 5, 1969, PUL.

8. Letter to Louis Fischer, Mar. 28, 1969, PUL.

9. Letter to Louis Fischer, May 12, 1969, PUL.

10. Letter to Annelise Kennan, Apr. 24, 1969, George F. Kennan Papers, MC 076, box 38, folder 6, PUL.

11. Letter to Louis Fischer, June 13, 1969, PUL.

12. Letter to Louis Fischer, Aug. 7, 1969, PUL.

13. Letter from Cass Canfield to W. A. R. Collins, Nov. 27, 1968, PC, HarperCollins Collection.

14. Letter from Cass Canfield to P. Chavchavadze, Dec. 3, 1968, PC, Harper-Collins Collection.

15. Harrison Salisbury wrote to George Kennan that he thought Svetlana was right about Beria and that reviewers should not have been so contemptuous of her insistence that Beria had a sinister influence over her father. Letter, June 8, 1967, George Kennan Papers, MC 076, Salisbury, Harrison, box 43, folder 2, PUL.

16. Alliluyeva, *Only One Year*, 141–43.

17. Ibid., 181–82, 358.

18. Ibid., 362.

19. Ibid., 393.

20. Ibid., 169.

21. Ibid., 181.

22. Ibid., 175.

23. Ibid., 182.

24. Edmund Wilson, *Letters on Literature and Politics 1912–1972*, ed. Elena Wilson (New York: Farrar, Straus & Giroux, 1977), 702, letter dated July 1, 1969.

25. Wilson, *The Sixties*, 809.

26. Silverstone, "Suburbanization of Svetlana," 55.

27. "Andropov: KGB Meeting November 5, 1969," Meryle Secrest Collection, Svetlana Peters: General File, HIA.

28. Author's interview with Olga Alliluyeva, Toronto, May 5, 2012.

29. Belinkov and Belinkova, *Two Voices in Clash with the Century*, 400–401.

30. Letter to Louis Fischer, Sept. 8, 1968, PUL.

31. Letter to Louis Fischer, Mar. 5, 1969, PUL.

32. Robert Tucker, "Svetlana Inherited Her Tragic Flaw," *Washington Post*, Nov. 25, 1984.

33. Meryle Secrest interview with Svetlana Alliluyeva, audio recording, group 1, tape 18, HIA.

34. Letter to Robert and Ramona Rayle, Dec. 9, 2008, PC, Rayle.

35. Louis Fischer, *Russia's Road from Peace to War: Soviet Foreign Relations 1917–1941* (New York: Harper & Row, 1969), 301.

36. Letter to Robert Rayle, Aug. 23, 2005, letter no. 3, PC, Rayle.

37. "Moscow Ends Svetlana Alliluyeva's Soviet Citizenship," *New York Times*, Jan. 22, 1970, p. 3.

38. Alliluyeva, *Faraway Music*, 48.

39. Edmund Wilson, review of *Only One Year*, *New Yorker* 45, no. 32 (Sept. 27, 1967): 153.

40. Margaret Parton, "Only One Year," *Saturday Review* 52, no. 40 (Oct. 4, 1969): 44.

41. "Svetlana Faces Life," Book Review, *Life*, Oct. 3, 1969, 12.

42. Philip Rahv, "The Princess," *Commentary* 49, no. 3 (March 1970): 71.

43. Bernard D. Nossiter, "Svetlana Charges Distortions," *Washington Post*, Feb. 26, 1970, p. 11.

44. Letter to Louis Fischer, Sept. 3, 1968, PUL.

45. Author's interview with Yelena Khanga, Moscow, Jan. 28, 2014.

46. Author's interview with Leonid and Galina Alliluyev, Moscow, May 17, 2013.

47. Golden, *Long Journey Home*, 155–56.

CHAPTER 24: THE TALIESIN FIASCO

1. Alliluyeva, *Faraway Music*, 56.

2. Roger Friedland and Harold Zellman, *The Fellowship: The Untold Story of Frank Lloyd Wright and the Taliesin Fellowship* (New York: HarperCollins, 2006), 50.

3. Meryle Secrest, *Frank Lloyd Wright: A Biography* (New York: Harper-Collins, 1992), 510.

4. Ibid.

5. Ibid., 512.

6. Ibid., 513–14.

7. Kamal Amin, *Reflections from the Shining Brow: My Years with Frank Lloyd Wright and Olgivanna Lazarovich* (McKinleyville, CA: Fithian Press, 2004), 216.

8. Author's interview with Aris Georges, Spring Green, WI, Aug. 27, 2012.

9. Alliluyeva, *Faraway Music*, 57.

10. Meryle Secrest interview with Svetlana Alliluyeva, audio recording, group 1, tape 3, HIA.

11. Alliluyeva, *Faraway Music*, 60.

12. Ibid.

13. Meryle Secrest interview with Svetlana Alliluyeva, audio recording, group 1, tape 3, HIA.

14. Alliluyeva, *Faraway Music*, 62.

15. Amin, *Reflections*, 216–18.

16. Ibid.

17. Meryle Secrest interview with Svetlana Alliluyeva, audio recording, group 1, tape 5, HIA.

18. Alliluyeva, *Faraway Music*, 62.

19. Amin, *Reflections*, 219.

20. Author's interview with Alan Schwartz, Los Angeles, Dec. 5, 2013.

21. Alliluyeva, *Faraway Music*, 63.

22. Author's interview with Alan Schwartz, Los Angeles, Dec. 5, 2013.

23. Ibid.

24. Amin, *Reflections*, 219.

25. Friedland and Zellman, *The Fellowship*, 568. Quitclaim deed filed Apr. 4, 1970, Iowa County land records.

26. Friedland and Zellman, *The Fellowship*, 568. Comment attributed to O. P. Reed, Nov. 8, 1999.

27. Meryle Secrest interview with Svetlana Alliluyeva, audio recording, group 1, tape 6, HIA.

28. Amin, *Reflections*, 223.

29. Alliluyeva, *Faraway Music*, 65.

30. Letter to George Kennan, July 3, 1970, Kennan Papers, box 38, folder 6, PUL.

31. Friedland and Zellman, *The Fellowship*, 568.

32. Alliluyeva, *Faraway Music*, 68.
33. Author's interview with Walter Pozen, New York, Feb. 12, 2013.
34. Friedland and Zellman, *The Fellowship*, 568.
35. Letter to Donald Jameson, June 2, 1970, PC, Margaret Jameson.
36. Ibid.
37. Ibid.
38. Amin, *Reflections*, 217.

CHAPTER 25: THE MONTENEGRIN'S COURTIER
1. Friedland and Zellman, *The Fellowship*, 569, interview with Lana Peters, June 14, 2000.
2. Alliluyeva, *Faraway Music*, 67.
3. Friedland and Zellman, *The Fellowship*, 569.
4. Ibid., 573.
5. Amin, *Reflections*, 226.
6. Alliluyeva, *Faraway Music*, 76.
7. Friedland and Zellman, *The Fellowship*, 577.
8. Alliluyeva, *Faraway Music*, 77.
9. Friedland and Zellman, *The Fellowship*, 574.
10. Letter to George Kennan, Mar. 26, 1971, Kennan Papers, box 38, folder 6, PUL.
11. Letter to Joan Kennan, June 26, 1971, PC, J. Kennan.
12. Alliluyeva, *Faraway Music*, 80.
13. Ibid., 81.
14. Ibid., 63.
15. Financial report of law firm Strook & Strook & Lavan, May 31, 1972, "Valuation of Details of Aldebaran Enterprise," PC, J. Kennan.
16. Svetlana Alliluyeva, "Book for Granddaughters," unpublished typescript in English, Svetlana Peters II: General File, HIA, published as *Kniga dlia vnuchek: puteshestvie na rodinu* [A Book for Granddaughters: Journey to the Motherland] (New York: Liberty Publishing House, 1991), 186. Svetlana wrote on the typed title page: "Authorized version in English prepared from the Russian original by the author. 1988–89." It was published in Russian by Liberty in 1991, but never in English.
17. Letter to Annelise Kennan, Oct. 6, 1971, Kennan Papers, box 38, folder 6, PUL.
18. Author's interview with Aris Georges, Spring Green, WI, Aug. 27, 2012.
19. Alliluyeva, *Faraway Music*, 69.
20. Amin, *Reflections*, 223.
21. Alliluyeva, *Faraway Music*, 87–88.
22. Ibid., 57.

23. Ibid., 61.

24. Letter to George Kennan, June 15, 1970, Kennan Papers, box 38, folder 6, PUL.

25. Amin, *Reflections*, 223.

26. Friedland and Zellman, *The Fellowship*, 576, interview with Don and Virginia Lovness, Apr. 15, 1996.

27. Amin, *Reflections*, 225.

28. Friedland and Zellman, *The Fellowship*, 576.

29. Financial report of law firm Strook & Strook & Lavan, May 31, 1972, "Valuation of Details of Aldebaran Enterprise," PC, J. Kennan.

30. Author's interview with Joan Kennan, Washington, Dec. 5, 2012.

31. Author's interview with Walter Pozen, New York, Feb. 12, 2013.

32. Author's interview with Michael Coyne, Dec. 17, 2013.

33. Alliluyeva, *Faraway Music*, 94.

34. Ibid., 96.

35. "Stalin's Daughter Leaves Her Husband," *New York Times*, Feb. 23, 1972.

36. "Joseph Stalin's Daughter Leaves Her Husband," *Danville Register and Bee*, Feb. 23, 1972.

37. Ibid.

38. "Stalin's Daughter Disputes Husband on Separation," *New York Times*, Feb. 24, 1972.

39. Ibid.

40. Friedland and Zellman, *The Fellowship*, 577, interview with Iovanna Wright, July 24, 2000.

41. Letter to Joan Kennan, Apr. 3, 1972, PC, J. Kennan.

42. Author's interview with Walter Pozen, New York, Feb. 12, 2013; and financial report of law firm Strook & Strook & Lavan, May 31, 1972, "Valuation of Details of Aldebaran Enterprise," PC, J. Kennan.

43. Wilson, *The Sixties*, 877.

44. Author's interview with Joan Kennan, Washington, Dec. 5, 2012.

45. Author's interview with Walter Pozen, New York, Feb. 12, 2013.

46. Letter to Joan Kennan, May 23, 1972, PC, J. Kennan.

47. Letter to Joan Kennan, June 3, 1972, PC, J. Kennan.

CHAPTER 26: STALIN'S DAUGHTER CUTTING THE GRASS

1. Letter to Annelise Kennan, Aug. 7, 1972, Kennan Papers, box 38, folder 6, PUL.

2. Ibid.

3. Letter to George Kennan, June 1, 1973, Kennan Papers, box 38, folder 6, PUL.

4. Ibid.

5. Author's interview with Hella McVay, Princeton, Dec. 3, 2012.

6. Letter to Jerzy Kosinski, undated, Katherina von Fraunhofer-Kosinski Collection of Jerzy Kosinski, Gen. Mss. 742, box 24, Misc. Correspondence, BRB.

7. Jerzy Kosinski, *Blind Date* (Boston: Houghton Mifflin, 1977), 78–79.

8. Author's interview with Evgeniya Tucker, Feb. 14, 2013.

9. Rosa Shand, "Wheel of Fire," *Southwest Review* 87, no. 1 (January 2002): 90.

10. Ibid., 92.

11. Ibid., 93–94

12. Ibid., 95.

13. Anna Akhmatova, *Requiem* and *Poem Without a Hero*, trans. D. M. Thomas. The poem was banned in the USSR and was first published in Munich in 1963.

14. Shand, "Wheel of Fire," 95.

15. Alliluyeva, *Faraway Music*, 127.

16. Author's interview with Millie Harford, Princeton, Dec. 3, 2012.

17. Ibid.

18. Ibid.

19. Letter to Rosa Shand, Nov. 5, 1974, PC, Shand.

20. Letter to Annelise Kennan, July 28, 1975, Kennan Papers, box 38, folder 6, PUL.

21. Letter to Donald Jameson, Nov. 6, 1973, PC, Margaret Jameson.

22. Alliluyeva, *Faraway Music*, 116.

23. Letter to Annelise Kennan, July 28, 1975, Kennan Papers, box 38, folder 6, PUL.

24. Letter to Annelise Kennan, July 22, 1974, Kennan Papers, box 38, folder 6, PUL.

25. Ibid.

26. Letter to Rosa Shand, Mar. 25, 1975, PC, Shand.

27. Letter to author from George Krimsky, Aug. 27, 2014.

28. Letter from "A Friend" to George Kennan, Aug. 5, 1975, Kennan Papers, box 38 folder 5, PUL.

29. Thompson, *Hawk and the Dove*, 248; and letter from Mark Garrison, Department of State, to George Kennan, Aug. 14, 1975, Kennan Papers, box 38, folder 5, PUL.

30. Nicholas Thompson interview with George Krimsky, June 22, 2008. See Thompson, *Hawk and the Dove*, 248–50.

31. Letter to George Kennan, Oct. 15, 1975, Kennan Papers, box 38, folder 5, PUL.

32. Thompson, *Hawk and the Dove*, 249.

33. Sharon Schlegel, "I Don't Want to Be Svetlana Any More," *Washington Post*, July 29, 1979, 7.

CHAPTER 27: A KGB STOOL PIGEON

1. Letter to George Kennan, Aug. 1, 1977, Kennan Papers, box 38, file 4, PUL.

2. Author's interview with Chrese Evans, Portland, OR, Feb. 23, 2013.

3. Letter to George Kennan, Aug. 1, 1977, Kennan Papers, box 38, file 4, PUL.

4. Letter to Joan Kennan, July 14, 1976, PC, J. Kennan.

5. "DIA Cites Soviet Microwave Research," *Christian Science Monitor*, Nov. 22, 1976.

6. Letter to Donald Jameson, Nov. 20, 1976, PC, Margaret Jameson.

7. Letter to George Kennan, Feb. 2, 1977, Kennan Papers, box 38, folder 4, PUL.

8. Letter to George Kennan, Apr. 23, 1977, Kennan Papers, box 38, folder 4, PUL.

9. Letter to Joan Kennan, June 6, 1977, PC, J. Kennan.

10. Letters to Joan Kennan, June 6, 1977, and Oct. 25, 1978, PC, J. Kennan.

11. "A Letter from the Publisher," *Time*, Feb. 21, 1977.

12. Letter from Alexander Kurpel, Mar. 17, 1977, Kennan Papers, box 38, folder 4, PUL.

13. Letter from George Krimsky to Svetlana (Mrs. Peters), May 2, 1977, Kennan Papers, box 38, folder 4, PUL.

14. Letter from Gregory Morozov, June 29, 1977, trans. Svetlana Alliluyeva, Kennan Papers, box 38, folder 4, PUL.

15. Letter from George Kennan to Svetlana, May 14, 1977, Kennan Papers, box 38, folder 4, PUL.

16. Petrovna and Leshynsky, *Last Interview*, 72–73.

17. Ibid., 73–74.

18. Letter from George Kennan to Svetlana, Sept. 23, 1977, Kennan Papers, box 38, folder 4, PUL.

CHAPTER 28: LANA PETERS, AMERICAN CITIZEN

1. Letter to George Kennan, July 9, 1978, Kennan Papers, box 38, folder 4, PUL.

2. Letter of reference from George Kennan to "Immigration and Natural-ization Service," Sept. 14, 1978, Kennan Papers, box 38, folder 4, PUL.

3. Author's interview with Millie Harford, Princeton, Dec. 3, 2012.

4. Alliluyeva, *Faraway Music*, 156.

5. Author's interview with Millie Harford, Princeton, Dec. 3, 2012.

6. George Bailey, "Svetlana's Flight Back Where Her Troubles Began," *Washington Post*, Nov. 8, 1984.

7. Letter to Joan Kennan, Dec. 22, 1979, PC, J. Kennan.

8. Author's interview with Chrese Evans, Portland, OR, July 17, 2012.

9. Alliluyeva, *Faraway Music*, 141.

10. Ibid., 142–44.

11. Ibid., 144.

12. Letter to Joan Kennan, July 30, 1986, PC, J. Kennan.

13. Ibid.

14. Letter to George Kennan, Nov. 13, 1978, Kennan Papers, box 38, folder 4, PUL.

15. Letter to Robert Rayle, undated, PC, Rayle.

16. Sharon Schlegel, "I Don't Want to Be Svetlana Any More," *Washington Post*, July 29, 1979.

17. Ibid.

18. Letter to George Kennan, Aug. 4, 1979, Kennan Papers, box 38, folder 4, PUL.

19. Letter to George Kennan, Nov. 13, 1978, Kennan Papers, box 38, folder 4, PUL.

20. Letter to Joan Kennan, Dec. 22, 1979, PC, J. Kennan.

21. Letter from George Kennan to D. Jameson, June 15, 1984, Kennan Papers, box 22, folder 5, Jameson, Donald, PUL.

22. Author's interview with Alan Schwartz, Los Angeles, Dec. 5, 2013.

23. Author's interview with Chrese Evans, Portland, OR, Feb. 27, 2013.

24. Alliluyeva, *Faraway Music*, 137.

25. Letter to Rosa Shand, Feb. 15, 1980, PC, Shand.

26. Author's interview with Chrese Evans, Portland, OR, Feb. 27, 2013.

CHAPTER 29: THE MODERN JUNGLE OF FREEDOM

1. Rosa Shand, "The Will to Be," unpublished correspondence between Rosa Shand and Svetlana Alliluyeva, with Shand's journal entries, p. 26, PC, Shand. Shand noted Svetlana was "careful about asking for a 'light' drink, and certainly did not drink too much."

2. Shand, "Wheel of Fire," 97.

3. Shand, "Will to Be," 66.

4. Shand, "Wheel of Fire," 98.

5. Shand, "Will to Be," 24.

6. Shand, "Wheel of Fire," 100.

7. Letter to Malcolm Muggeridge, Mar. 9, 1970, SC-4, WCSC.

8. Shand, "Will to Be," 29–30.

9. Ibid, 31.

10. Letter to Rosa Shand, Sept. 21, 1981, PC, Shand.

11. Letter from Malcolm Muggeridge, Feb. 2, 1981, WCSC.

12. Letter to Malcolm Muggeridge, Feb. 17, 1981, WCSC.

13. Letter to Malcolm Muggeridge, Apr. 4, 1981, WCSC.

14. Author's interview with Chrese Evans, Portland, OR, Feb. 25, 2013.

15. Shand, "Will to Be," 68.

16. Letter to Malcolm and Kitty Muggeridge, Nov. 30, 1981, WCSC.

17. Letter to Kitty Muggeridge, Sept. 15, 1981, WCSC.

18. Letter to Kitty Muggeridge, Aug. 24, 1981, WCSC.

19. Letter to Kitty Muggeridge, Sept. 15, 1981, WCSC.

20. Ibid.

21. Letter to Rosa Shand, Sept. 15, 1981, PC, Shand.

22. Letter to Rosa Shand, Sept. 21, 1981, PC, Shand.

23. Fitzpatrick, *Spy in the Archives*, 336.

24. Letter to Rosa Shand, Sept. 21, 1981, PC, Shand.

25. Letter to Mrs. Ronald Reagan, Jan. 27, 1982, Ronald Reagan Presidential Library, FG 002, Peters, Lana.

26. Shand, "Will to Be," 65.

27. Undated letter to Isaiah Berlin, 1982, Isaiah Berlin Literary Trust.

28. Shand, "Will to Be," 71–72.

29. Letter to Lana Peters from Isaiah Berlin, Jan. 13, 1982, the Trustees of the Isaiah Berlin Literary Trust 2015, quoted with the permission of the Trustees.

30. Letter "To Whom It May Concern," from Hugo Brunner, Apr. 8, 1982, Isaiah Berlin Literary Trust.

31. Letter to Lady Berlin, Apr. 13, 1982, Isaiah Berlin Literary Trust.

32. Letter to Sir Isaiah Berlin, Mar. 20, 1982, Isaiah Berlin Literary Trust.

33. Letter from Isaiah Berlin to Francis Graham-Harrison, May 13, 1982, the Trustees of the Isaiah Berlin Literary Trust 2015, quoted with the permission of the Trustees.

CHAPTER 30: CHAUCER ROAD

1. Letter to Rosa Shand, Oct. 18, 1982, PC, Shand.

2. Letter to Isaiah Berlin, Oct. 8, 1982, Isaiah Berlin Literary Trust (IBLT).

3. Author's interview with Chrese Evans, Portland, OR, July 17, 2012.

4. Letter to Isaiah Berlin, Aug. 29, 1982, translated from Russian, Isaiah Berlin Literary Trust.

5. Letter from Isaiah Berlin to Francis Graham-Harrison, May 12, 1982, the Trustees of the Isaiah Berlin Literary Trust 2015, quoted with the permission of the Trustees.

6. Letter to Isaiah Berlin, Nov. 17, 1982, Isaiah Berlin Literary Trust.

7. Author's interview with Chrese Evans, Portland, OR, July 17, 2012.

8. Ibid.

9. Letter to Rosa Shand, July 13, 1983, PC, Shand.

10. Author's interview with Jane Renfrew, Cambridge, UK, June 23, 2013.

11. Letter to author from Philippa Hill, Aug. 1, 2013.

12. Author's interview with Philippa Hill, Cambridge, UK, June 23, 2013.
13. Author's interview with Rosamond Richardson, Saffron Walden, June 22, 2013.
14. Ibid.
15. Author's interview with Jane Renfrew, Cambridge, UK, June 23, 2013.
16. Author's interview with Chrese Evans, Portland, OR, Feb. 26, 2013.
17. Author's interview with Jane Renfrew, Cambridge, UK, June 23, 2013.
18. R. W. Apple Jr., "Stalin's Daughter Living in British University Town," *New York Times*, May 22, 1983.
19. Letter to Malcolm Muggeridge, Apr. 20, 1983, WCSC.
20. Letter to Aline Berlin, Apr. 15, 1983, Isaiah Berlin Literary Trust.
21. Letter from Hugo Brunner, Sept. 14, 1983, Isaiah Berlin Literary Trust.
22. Author's interview with Jane Renfrew, Cambridge, UK, June 23, 2013.
23. Alliluyeva, *Faraway Music*, 167.
24. Edwin McDowell, "Hints of Loneliness and Dashed Hopes," *New York Times*, Nov. 3, 1984.
25. Letter to Isaiah Berlin, Jan. 3, 1984, Isaiah Berlin Literary Trust.
26. Letter to Isaiah Berlin, Oct. 18, 1983, Isaiah Berlin Literary Trust.
27. Letter from Isaiah Berlin, Jan. 6, 1984, the Trustees of the Isaiah Berlin Literary Trust 2015, quoted with the permission of the Trustees.
28. Letter to Isaiah Berlin, Jan. 11, 1984, Isaiah Berlin Literary Trust.
29. Letter to Isaiah Berlin, Sept. 9, 1984, Isaiah Berlin Literary Trust.
30. Letter from Vera Traill to Isaiah Berlin, Mar. 2, 1984, Isaiah Berlin Literary Trust.
31. Ibid.
32. Letter to Rosa Shand, July 30, 1984, PC, Shand.
33. Author's interview with Jane Renfrew, Cambridge, UK, June 23, 2013.
34. Author's interview with Philippa Hill, Cambridge, UK, June 23, 2013.
35. Edwin McDowell, "Hints of Loneliness and Dashed Hopes," *New York Times*, Nov. 3, 1984.
36. Patricia Blake, "Svetlana Returns to Her 'Prison,'" *Time*, Nov. 12, 1984.
37. Robert D. McFadden, "Some Say Stalin's Daughter Grew Unhappy in the West," *New York Times*, Nov. 3, 1984.
38. Svetlana Alliluyeva, "Book for Granddaughters," unpublished typescript in English, 13–15, Meryle Secrest Collection, General File, HIA.
39. Author's interview with Chrese Evans, Portland, OR, July 17, 2012.
40. Ibid.

CHAPTER 31: BACK IN THE USSR
1. Author's interview with Chrese Evans, Portland, OR, Feb. 26, 2013.
2. Ibid.
3. Alliluyeva, "Book for Granddaughters," 62.

4. Author's interview with Chrese Evans, Portland, OR, Feb. 26, 2013.

5. Ibid.

6. Alliluyeva, "Book for Granddaughters," 51.

7. Ibid., 19.

8. Author's interview with Chrese Evans, Portland, OR, Feb. 26, 2013.

9. Serge Schmemann, "Stalin's Daughter Back in Soviet After 17 Years," *New York Times*, Nov. 3, 1984.

10. Ibid.

11. Alliluyeva, "Book for Granddaughters," 61.

12. Dusko Doder, "Stalin's Daughter Explains Decision: Alliluyeva Says She Was Manipulated by the CIA, Became Homesick for Family," *Washington Post*, Nov. 17, 1984.

13. "Stalin's Daughter Vows: I Will Never Go Back," *New York Times*, Apr. 19, 1986.

14. Doder, "Stalin's Daughter Explains Decision."

15. The actual title of the equivalent of president under the Constitution of the USSR was general secretary of the Central Committee of the Communist Party.

16. Dusko Doder, "Soviets Polishing Stalin's Image," *Washington Post*, Nov. 26, 1984.

17. Schmemann, "Stalin's Daughter Back in Soviet After 17 Years."

18. George Bailey, "Svetlana's Flight: Back Where Her Troubles Began," *Washington Post*, Nov. 8, 1984.

19. Robert Tucker, "Svetlana Inherited Her Tragic Flaw," *Washington Post*, Nov. 25, 1984.

20. Fitzpatrick, *Spy in the Archives*, 238.

21. Author's interview with Jane Renfrew, Cambridge, UK, June 23, 2013.

22. Blake, "The Saga of 'Stalin's Little Sparrow.'"

23. Ibid., 56.

24. McFadden, "Some Say Stalin's Daughter Grew Unhappy in the West."

25. Author's interview with Chrese Evans, Portland, OR, Feb. 26, 2013.

26. Memo from Liz to George Kennan, Nov. 2, 1984, Kennan Papers, box 38, folder 5, PUL.

27. Secretary's memorandum, Nov. 2, 1984, Kennan Papers, box 38, folder 5, PUL.

28. Alliluyeva, "Book for Granddaughters," 60.

29. Author's interview with Chrese Evans, Portland, OR, Feb. 26, 2013.

30. Alliluyeva, "Book for Granddaughters," 65.

31. Author's interview with Chrese Evans, Portland, OR, Feb. 26, 2013.

32. Author's interview with Yelena Khanga, Moscow, Jan. 21, 2014.

33. Author's interview with Chrese Evans, Portland, OR, Mar. 27, 2014.

34. Author's interview with Chrese Evans, Portland, OR, Feb. 26, 2013.

35. Author's interview with Alexander Burdonsky, Moscow, June 1, 2013.

36. A famous ballerina of the Mariinsky Theater.

37. Author's interview with Alexander Burdonsky, Moscow, June 1, 2013.

38. Ibid.

39. Meryle Secrest interview with Svetlana Alliluyeva, audio recording, group 2, tape 14, HIA.

CHAPTER 32: TBILISI INTERLUDE

1. Author's interview with Chrese Evans, Portland, OR, Feb. 26, 2013.

2. Ibid.

3. Anyone traveling internationally would have been vetted by the Georgian KGB.

4. Author's interview with Alexander Alliluyev, Moscow, May 25, 2013.

5. Letter to author from Tamara Dovgan, Saint Petersburg, Aug. 28, 2013.

6. Alliluyeva, "Book for Granddaughters," 100.

7. Ibid., 146.

8. Richard Owen, "Svetlana to Make Home in Tbilisi," *New York Times*, Dec. 17, 1984.

9. Alliluyeva, "Book for Granddaughters," 137.

10. Ibid., 146. Svetlana also quoted her daughter's words in a letter to Joan Kennan, May 5, 1986, PC, J. Kennan.

11. Author's interview with Chrese Evans, Portland, OR, Feb. 26, 2013.

12. Mikoyan, *Memoirs of Military Test-Flying*, 149.

13. Petrova and Leshynsky, *Last Interview*, 16.

14. Ibid.

15. Ibid., 99.

16. Letter from Vera Traill to Isaiah Berlin, July 9, 1985, the Isaiah Berlin Literary Trust.

17. Letter to Joan Kennan, Dec. [undated], 1985, PC, J. Kennan.

18. Letter to Rosa Shand, Jan. 20, 1986, PC, Shand.

19. Letter from Rosa Shand, Feb. [no date], 1986, PC, Rosa Shand.

20. Letter to Rosa Shand from Utya Djaparidze, Palm Sunday 1986, PC, Shand.

21. Author's interview with Leonid and Galina Alliluyev, Moscow, May 17, 2013.

22. Alliluyeva, "Book for Granddaughters," 145.

23. Ibid., 156.

24. Ibid., 155.

25. Ibid., 159–60.

26. Top Secret Minutes of Meeting of the Politburo of the Central Committee of the Communist Party of the Soviet Union, Mar. 20, 1986, Meryle Secrest Collection, Svetlana Peters General File, HIA.

27. Alliluyeva, "Book for Granddaughters," 160.

28. Author's interview with Leonid and Galina Alliluyev, Moscow, May 17, 2013.

29. Alliluyeva, "Book for Granddaughters," 164.

30. Author's interview with Leila Sikmashvili, Tbilisi, Georgia, June 15, 2013.

31. Author's interview with Chrese Evans, Portland, OR, Feb. 26, 2013.

32. Author's interview with Alexander Burdonsky, Moscow, June 1, 1913.

33. "Stalin Kin Likely to Be Rebuffed," *Philadelphia Inquirer*, Apr. 1, 1986.

34. Author's interview with Chrese Evans, Portland, OR, Feb. 26, 2013.

35. Letter Series to Robert and Ramona Rayle, July–September 2005, PC, Rayle.

36. Raymond H. Anderson, "Talk with Stalin's Daughter: Why She Left Soviet Again," *New York Times*, May 18, 1986.

37. Alliluyeva, "Book for Granddaughters," 170.

38. Sarah Booth Conroy, "The Odyssey of Stalin's Granddaughter," *Washington Post*, Apr. 15, 1986.

39. Author's interview with Chrese Evans, Portland, OR, Feb. 26, 2013.

40. "Stalin's Grandchild Is in England," *USA Today*, Apr. 16, 1986.

41. "Svetlana's Girl Flies Back," (London) *Times*, Apr. 6, 1986.

42. Author's interview with Chrese Evans, Portland, OR, Feb. 26, 2013.

43. Author's interview with Alexander Alliluyev, Moscow, May 25, 2013.

44. Author's interview with Chrese Evans, Portland, OR, Feb. 26, 2013.

45. "The People Who Care for Me Are in America," *Washington Post*, Apr. 18, 1986.

46. Author's interview with Alexander Alliluyev, Moscow, May 25, 2013.

47. Author's interview with Leonid and Galina Alliluyev, Moscow, May 17, 2013.

48. Author's interview with Alexander Burdonsky, Moscow, June 1, 2013.

49. Petrovna and Leshynsky, *Last Interview*, 94–95.

50. Nicholas Powell, "Svetlana Lured by KGB Man," (London) *Sunday Mail*, Nov. 11, 1984. The article included five letters from Alliluyeva to the Sinyavskys, in one of which she complains that, while a beauty, Olga follows the rebellious tide of British youth; this leads A. Sinyavsky to conclude that "her letters to us show how estranged she felt from Olga."

51. Duff Hart-Davis (London), *Independent*, Aug. 17, 1994.

52. Letter from George Kennan to Frank Carlucci, Sept. 10, 1987, Kennan Papers, box 38 folder 3, PUL.

53. Blake reported this to Melissa Akin, "Stalin's Daughter Shuns Public Attention," *Las Vegas Sun*, June 13, 1996.

54. Letter from Utya Djaparidze to Rosa Shand, Sept. 30, 1986, PC, Shand.

CHAPTER 33: AMERICAN REALITY

1. Anderson, "Talk with Stalin's Daughter: Why She Left Soviet Again."

2. Author's interview with Chrese Evans, Portland, OR, Mar. 27, 2014.

3. From Svetlana Alliluyeva to "Dear old friends and former Patrons," Feb. 25, 1987, Kennan Papers, box 38, folder 3, PUL.

4. Round-robin letter from Lana Peters to "Dear friend," Feb. [undated], 1987, Kennan Papers, box 38, folder 3, PUL.

5. Fitzpatrick, *Spy in the Archives*, 278.

6. Virginia Mills, "Judge Restores Peters as Trustee of Charity Group," *Trenton Times*, Jan. 2, 1987.

7. Letter to Philippa Hill, June 22, 1987, PC, Hill.

8. Letter to Rosa Shand, July 29, 1987, PC, Shand.

9. George Kennan letter to F. Carlucci, Sept. 10, 1987, Kennan Papers, box 38, folder 3, PUL.

10. Memo to file: from George Kennan, Oct. 7, 1987, Kennan Papers, box 38, folder 3, PUL.

11. Author's interview with Chrese Evans, Portland, OR, Feb. 25, 2013.

12. Author's interview with Aris Georges, Spring Green, WI, Aug. 27, 2012.

13. Author's interview with Chrese Evans, Portland, OR, July 17, 2012.

14. Letter to author from Robert Rayle, Nov. 5, 2013.

15. Letter to Philippa Hill, Feb. 13, 1988, PC, Hill.

16. Letter to Rosa Shand, June 6, 1988, PC, Shand.

17. Letter to author from Chrese Evans, July 10, 2014.

18. Author's interview with Chrese Evans, Portland, OR, July 17, 2012.

19. Letter to Philippa Hill, undated, PC, Hill.

20. Letter to Philippa Hill, undated, PC, Hill.

21. When she visited in the late 1980s, Olga remembered her mother's long telephone conversation about these translations and how annoyed Svetlana had seemed about the whole thing. Author's interview with Chrese Evans, Portland, OR, July 17, 2012.

22. Letter to George and Annelise Kennan, Sept. 25, 1988, PC, Joan Kennan.

23. Letter to Rosa Shand, Jan. 2, 1990, from France, PC, Shand.

24. Meryle Secrest interview with Svetlana Alliluyeva, audio recording, group 2, tape 26, HIA.

25. Letter to George and Annelise Kennan, Sept. 25, 1988, PC, J. Kennan.

26. Richard Culling Carr-Gomm, OBE, was the founder of the Abbeyfield Society, the Morpeth Society, and the Carr-Gomm Society, UK non-profit national charities providing care and housing for disadvantaged and lonely people.

27. Letter to Rosa Shand, Aug. 20, 1991, PC, Shand.

28. Meryle Secrest interview with Svetlana Alliluyeva, audio recording, group 2, tape 26, HIA.

29. Letter to Robert Rayle, Dec. 21, 1994, PC, Rayle.

30. Letter to Mary Burkett, Mar. 30, 1996, PC, Burkett.

31. Letter to George Kennan, July 27, 1983, Kennan Papers, box 38, folder 3, PUL.

32. Letter to George Kennan, Nov. 23, 1983, Kennan Papers, box 38, folder 3, PUL.

33. Letter to Philippa Hill, Oct. 22, 1989, PC, Hill.

34. Angela Lambert, "Stalin's Prisoner to the End," (London) *Independent*, Mar. 10, 1990.

35. Ibid.

36. Christmas card to Rosa Shand, Nov. 11, 1990, PC, Shand.

CHAPTER 34: "NEVER WEAR A TIGHT SKIRT IF YOU INTEND TO COMMIT SUICIDE"

1. *Newsweek*, May 13, 1991.

2. Svetlana Peters, "Dear Vanessa: Some Last Thoughts of an Ordinary Woman," unpublished manuscript, 49 pages, November 2005, Wisconsin, 20, PC, V. Thomas.

3. John Taylor, "The Haunted Bird: The Death and Life of Jerzy Kosinski," *New York* 24, no. 27 (July 15, 1991): 30.

4. Peters, "Dear Vanessa," 20.

5. Author's interview with Chrese Evans, Portland, OR, Feb. 26, 2013.

6. Meryle Secrest interview with Svetlana Alliluyeva, audio recording, group 1, tape 1, HIA.

7. Author's interview with Chrese Evans, Portland, OR, Feb. 26, 2013.

8. Ibid.

9. Letter to Rosa Shand, Aug. 20, 1991, PC, Shand.

10. Author's interview with Chrese Evans, Portland, OR, Feb. 26, 2013.

11. Ibid.

12. Letter to author from Nina Lobanov-Rostovsky, Apr. 17, 2013.

13. Ibid.

14. Nina's husband was the son of Dmitri Ivanovich Lobanov-Rostovsky (1907–1948).

15. Letter to author from Nina Lobanov-Rostovsky, Apr. 17, 2013.

16. *Oktyabr*, no. 6 (1991): 13–86.

17. Alliluyeva, "Book for Granddaughters," 193.

18. Author's interview with Thomas Miller, Anchorage, AK, Sept. 28, 2013.

19. Letter to Thomas Miller, Jan. 21, 1993, PC, Miller.

20. Letter to author from Nina Lobanov-Rostovsky, Apr. 17, 2013.

21. Letter to Thomas Miller, Sept. 13, 1993, PC, Miller.

22. Author's interview with Thomas Miller, Anchorage, AK, Sept. 28, 2013.

23. Author's interview with Chrese Evans, Portland, OR, July 17, 2012.

24. Letter to Rosa Shand, Aug. 8, 1992, PC, Shand.

25. Meryle Secrest interview with Svetlana Alliluyeva, audio recording, group 1, tape 5, HIA.

26. Ibid.

27. Author's interview with Chrese Evans, Portland, OR, July 18, 2012.

28. Author's interview with Vanessa Thomas, London, June 25, 2013.

29. Inigo Thomas, "Tea with Stalin's Daughter," *LRB* blog, Dec. 1, 2011, www .lrb.co.uk/blog/2011/12/01/inigo-thomas/tea-with-stalin%E2%80%99s -daughter/.

30. Alex Prud'Homme and Liz Corcoran, *People*, Dec. 10, 1992.

31. Author's interview with Raoul Ortiz, Mexico City, Dec. 9, 2013.

32. Ibid.

33. Author's interview with Laurence and Linda Kelly, London, June 24, 2013.

34. Author's interview with Pamela Egremont, London, June 25, 2013.

35. Author's interview with Rosamond Richardson, Saffron Walden, June 22, 2013.

36. Meryle Secrest interview with Svetlana Alliluyeva, audio recording, group 1, tape 18, and group 2, tape 21, HIA.

37. Meryle Secrest interview with Svetlana Alliluyeva, audio recording, group 1, tape 18, HIA.

38. Rosamond Richardson interview with Svetlana Alliluyeva, Saffron Walden, 1991, tape 4, PC, Richardson.

39. Meryle Secrest interview with Svetlana Alliluyeva, audio recording, group 2, tape 22, HIA.

40. Author's interview with Rosamond Richardson, Saffron Walden, June 22, 2013.

41. Ibid.

42. Kyra Alliluyeva, *Plemiannitsa Stalina* [Stalin's Niece] (Moscow: Vagrius, 2006), 345–51.

43. Author's interview with Rosamond Richardson, Saffron Walden, June 22, 2013.

44. Letters: "Inside Stalin's Family," *London Review of Books*, Mar. 25, 1993.

45. Alliluyeva, *Stalin's Niece*, 344.

46. Author's interview with Mary Burkett, Penrith, UK, June 20–21, 2013.

47. Ben Verinder, *I Felt Like an Adventure: A Life of Mary Burkett* (Langley Park, Durham, UK: Memoir Club, 2008).

48. Letter to Mary Burkett, Feb. 10, 1997, PC, Burkett.

49. Letter to Mary Burkett, Mar. 4, 1996, PC, Burkett.

50. David Jones, "Revealed," (London) *Daily Mail*, Feb. 15, 1996.

CHAPTER 35: MY DEAR, THEY HAVEN'T CHANGED A BIT

1. Letter to Mary Burkett, Sept. 9, 1995, PC, Burkett.

2. Melissa Akin, "Stalin's Daughter Shuns Public Attention," *Las Vegas Sun*, June 13, 1996.

3. Svetlana Alliluyeva, "Sorry, Dear Relative," 1996, review of Vladimir Fedorovitch Alliluyev, *Chronicle of a Family*, Kennan Papers, box 2, file 3, PUL.

4. Galina Alliluyeva, wife of Leonid, also believed that someone else inserted material into Vladimir's memoir, possibly as a condition of publication. Author's interview with Leonid and Galina Alliluyeva, Moscow, May 17, 2013.

5. Alliluyeva, "Sorry, Dear Relative."

6. Letter to Philippa Hill, Feb. 18, 1996, PC, Hill.

7. Richard Beeston, "Stalin's Daughter Seeks Sanctuary by Taking the Veil," (London) *Times*, Feb. 8, 1996.

8. Letter to Philippa Hill, Mar. 2, 1996, PC, Hill.

9. David Jones, "Revealed: Why Stalin's Daughter Has Chosen to Lead a Life of Poverty in a Remote English Village," (London) *Daily Mail*, Feb. 15, 1996.

10. Letter to Philippa Hill, Mar. 2, 1996, PC, Hill.

11. Undated letter [1998] to Philippa Hill, PC, Hill. Some believed that Russia's state security services, the FSB, murdered Starovoitova because she was using her influence with Boris Yeltsin to oppose the appointment of Yevgeny Primakov, a former KGB general, as prime minister.

12. Letter to Mary Burkett, Mar. 6, 1997, PC, Burkett.

13. Letter to Nina Lobanov-Rostovsky, Aug. 2, 1997, PC, Nina Lobanov-Rostovsky.

14. Author's interview with Mary Burkett, Penrith, UK, June 21, 2013.

15. Letter to Nina Lobanov-Rostovsky, Aug. 2, 1997, PC, Nina Lobanov-Rostovsky.

CHAPTER 36: FINAL RETURN

1. Letter to Robert Rayle, Nov. 21, 1997, PC, Rayle.

2. Letter to Mary Burkett, Nov. 17, 1997, PC, Burkett.

3. Letter to Robert Rayle, Nov. 24, 1999, PC, Rayle.

4. Author's interview with Chrese Evans, Portland, OR, July 17, 2012.

5. Author's interview with Kathy Rossing, Lone Rock, WI, Nov. 27, 2013.

6. Letter to Thomas Miller, Nov. 18, 2000, PC, Miller.

7. Letter to Thomas Miller, Sept. 6, 2003, PC, Miller.

8. Author's interview with Kathy Rossing, Lone Rock, WI, Nov. 27, 2013.

9. Ibid.

10. Author's interview with Michael Coyne, Washington, DC, Dec. 17, 2013.

11. Ibid.

12. Letter to Ramona Rayle, Oct. 13, 2006, PC, Rayle.

13. Author's interview with Michael Coyne, Washington, DC, Dec. 17, 2013.

14. Ibid.

15. Letter to Mary Burkett, Aug. 12, 2005, PC, Burkett.

16. Letter to Robert Rayle, June 23, 1997, PC, Rayle.

17. Author's interview with Thomas Miller, Anchorage, AK, Sept. 28, 2013.

18. Letter to Thomas Miller, Mar. 14, 2000, PC, Miller.

19. Letter to Robert Rayle, Jan. 24, 2000, PC, Rayle.

20. Author's interview with Michael Coyne, Washington, DC, Dec. 17, 2013.

21. Letter to Robert Rayle, Sept. 30, 2000, PC, Rayle.

22. Letter to Robert Rayle, Jan. 24, 2000, PC, Rayle.

23. Russian Federation Law on Introducing Amendments to Certain Legislative Acts of the Russian Federation (the 2006 Russian NCO Law) imposed burdensome reporting requirements on Russian NCOs (NGOs) with severe penalties for noncompliance, as well as on foreign NCOs operating in Russia.

24. Letter to Robert Rayle, Jan. 24, 2000, PC, Rayle.

25. Author's interview with Kathy Rossing, Lone Rock, WI, Nov. 27, 2013.

26. Letter to Robert Rayle, Feb. 11, 2000, PC, Rayle.

27. Michael Coyne noted that the blog posts at the time of Svetlana's death still referred to her wealth. Author's interview with Michael Coyne, Washington, DC, Dec. 17, 2013.

28. Letter to Robert Rayle, Jan. 25, 2000, PC, Rayle.

29. Letter to Annelise Kennan, Sept. 13, 1986, Kennan Papers, box 38, folder 6, PUL.

30. Author's interview with Marie Anderson, Spring Green, WI, Aug. 28, 2012.

31. Letter to Robert and Ramona Rayle, June 19, 2006, PC, Rayle.

32. Alliluyeva, *Faraway Music*, 142.

33. David Jones, "Still Running from Stalin," (London) *Daily Mail* Online, Apr. 23, 2010, www.dailymail.co.uk/news/article-1268374/Still-running -Stalin-Tyrants-daughter-84-tells-tragic-life-escaping-legacy-new-home -sleepy-U-S-farming-town.html.

34. Author's interview with Chrese Evans, Portland, OR, Feb. 28, 2013.

35. Certification of Recordation, Feb. 23, 2010, Washington Copyright Office; and correspondence to author from Nicholas Thompson, June 8, 2014.

36. Letter to Linda Kelly, Dec. 14, 2003, PC, Kelly.

37. Letter to Mary Burkett, May 19, 2011, PC, Burkett.

38. Letter to Philippa Hill, May 6, 2011, PC, Hill.
39. Author's interview with Kathy Rossing, Lone Rock, WI, Nov. 27, 2013.
40. Ibid.
41. Ibid.
42. Letter to Chrese Evans, undated 2011. A few months earlier, Svetlana Alliluyeva gave this letter to her lawyer with instructions to give it to her daughter after her death. Letter to author from Chrese Evans, Jan. 1, 2015, PC, Chrese Evans.

Bibliography

Alliluyev, Vladimir. *Khronika odnoi sem'i: Alliluyevy—Stalin* [Chronicle of One Family: Alliluyevs—Stalin] Moscow: Molodaia Gvardiia, 1995, 2002.

Alliluyeva, Anna, and Sergei Alliluyev. *The Alliluyev Memoirs: Recollections of Svetlana Stalina's Maternal Aunt Anna Alliluyeva and Her Grandfather Sergei Alliluyev*, trans. David Tutaev. New York: Putnam's, 1967.

Alliluyeva, Kyra. *Plemiannitsa Stalina* [Stalin's Niece]. Moscow: Vagrius, 2006.

Alliluyeva, Svetlana. "Book for Granddaughters," unpublished typescript in English. Svetlana Peters II: General File, Hoover Institution Archives. *Kniga dlia vnuchek: puteshestvie na rodinu* [A Book for Granddaughters: Journey to the Motherland]. New York: Liberty Publishing House, 1991.

———. *The Faraway Music*. New Delhi: Lancer International, 1984. *Dalekaia muzyka*. New York: Liberty Publishing House, 1988.

———. "Letter to Ehrenburg, 7 August 1957," reprinted in Boris Frezinski, *Pisateli i Sovetskie vozhdi* [Writers and Soviet Leaders]. Moscow: Ellis Lak, 2008.

———. *Only One Year*, trans. Paul Chavchavadze. New York: Harper & Row, 1969. *Tol'ko odin god*. New York: Harper Colophon Books, 1969.

———. "To Boris Leonidovich Pasternak," trans. Max Hayward. *Atlantic* 219, no. 6 (June 1967): 133–40.

———. *Twenty Letters to a Friend*, trans. Priscilla Johnson McMillan. New York: Harper & Row, 1967. *Dvadtsat' pisem k drugu*. London: Hutchinson, 1967.

Amin, Kamal. *Reflections from the Shining Brow: My Years with Frank Lloyd Wright and Olgivanna Lazarovich*. McKinleyville, CA: Fithian Press, 2004.

Applebaum, Anne. *Gulag: A History*. London: Penguin Books, 2004.

Arlen, Michael. *The Green Hat*. New York: George H. Doran Co., 1924.

Barbusse, Henri. *Stalin: A New World Seen Through One Man*. Trans. Vyvyan Holland. New York: Macmillan, 1935.

Barenberg, Alan. *Gulag Town, Company Town: Forced Labor and Its Legacy in Vorkuta*. New Haven, CT: Yale University Press, 2014.

Barnes, Steven A. *Death and Redemption: The Gulag and the Shaping of Soviet History*. Princeton, NJ: Princeton University Press, 2011.

Barron, John. *KGB: The Secret Work of Soviet Secret Agents*. New York: Bantam Books, 1974.

Belaya, Galina. "Ia rodom iz shestidesiatykh" ["I Am from the Sixties"]. *Novoe literaturnoe obozrenie* [New Literary Review] 70 (June 2006): 210–28.

Belinkov, Arkady, and Natalia Belinkova. *Raspria s vekom v dva golosa* [Two Voices in Clash with the Century]. Moscow: Novoe literaturnoe obozrenie, 2008.

Beria, Sergo. *Beria, My Father: Inside Stalin's Kremlin*. Trans. Brian Pearce. London: Duckworth, 2001.

Biagi, Enzo. *Svetlana: The Inside Story*. Trans. Timothy Wilson. London: Hodder & Stoughton, 1967.

Blake, Patricia. "The Saga of Stalin's 'Little Sparrow.'" *Time*, Jan. 28, 1985.

Bowles, Chester. *Ambassador's Report*. New York: Harper & Bros., 1954.

Brent, Jonathan, and Vladimir P. Naumov, *Stalin's Last Crime: The Plot Against the Jewish Doctors, 1948–1953*. New York: HarperCollins, 2003.

Charkviani, Candide. *Napikri da naazrevi* [My Life and Reflections]. Trans. Nestan Charkviani. Tbilisi: Merani Publishing House, 2004.

Chigirin, I. *Svetlana*. Moscow: Velikolukskaia tipografiia, 2013.

Cohen, Stephen F. *The Victims Return: Survivors of the Gulag After Stalin*. New York: I. B. Tauris, 2012.

Conquest, Robert. *The Great Terror: A Reassessment*. Oxford: Oxford University Press, 1990.

Deviatov, S., A. Shefov, and Iu. Iur'ev. *Blizhniaia dacha Stalina: Opyt istoricheskogo putivoditelia* [Stalin's Blizhniaia Dacha: An Experiment in a Historical Guidebook]. Moscow: Kremlin Multimedia, 2011.

Djilas, Milovan. *Conversations with Stalin*. Trans. Michael B. Petrovich. New York: Harcourt, Brace & World, 1962.

Dostoyevsky, Fyodor. *Demons*. Trans. Robert A. Maguire. London: Penguin Classics, 2008.

———. *The Gambler*. Trans. Constance Garnett. New York: Modern Library, 2003.

Druzhnikov, Yuri. "Visiting Stalin's, Uninvited," trans. Thomas Moore, from *Contemporary Russian Myths*, www.druzhnikov.com/english/text/vizit1.html.

Eaton, Katherine B. *Daily Life in the Soviet Union*. Westport, CT: Greenwood Press, 2004.

Ebon, Martin. *Svetlana: The Incredible Story of Stalin's Daughter*. New York: Signet Books, 1967.

Ehrenburg, Ilya. *The Thaw*. Trans. Manya Harari. London: Harvill, 1955.

Figes, Orlando. *The Whisperers: Private Life in Stalin's Russia*. New York: Picador, 2008.

Fischer, Louis. *The Life and Death of Stalin*. New York: Harper & Bros., 1952.

———. *Men and Politics: An Autobiography*. New York: Duell, Sloan & Pearce, 1941.

————. *Russia's Road from Peace to War: Soviet Foreign Relations 1917–1941.* New York: Harper & Row, 1969.

Fitzpatrick, Sheila. *Everyday Stalinism: Ordinary Life in Extraordinary Times— Soviet Russia in the 1930s.* New York: Oxford University Press, 1999.

————. *The Russian Revolution.* Oxford: Oxford University Press, 1994.

————. *A Spy in the Archives: A Memoir of Cold War Russia.* London: I. B. Tauris, 2013.

Friedland, Roger, and Harold Zellman. *The Fellowship: The Untold Story of Frank Lloyd Wright and the Taliesin Fellowship.* New York: HarperCollins, 2006.

Gaddis, John Lewis. *George F. Kennan: An American Life.* New York: Penguin Press, 2011.

Ginzburg, Eugenia Semyonovna. *Journey into the Whirlwind.* Trans. Paul Stevenson and Max Hayward. Harcourt Brace, 1967.

Gitelman, Zvi. *Anti-Semitism in the USSR: Sources, Types, Consequences.* New York: Synagogue Council of America, 1974.

Gitelman, Zvi, and Yaacov Ro'i, eds. *Revolution, Repression and Revival: The Soviet Jewish Experience.* Lanham, MD: Rowman & Littlefield, 2007.

Gogua, Irina Kalistratovna. Transcription of Oral Stories, Recorded by Irina Mikhailovna Chervakova, 1987–89. Memorial Archive (MEM), Fond 1, opis 3, delo 18, June 25, 1988.

Golden, Lily. *My Long Journey Home.* Chicago: Third World Press, 2002.

Golovko, Kyra. "Svetlana Alliluyeva: odinochestvo i nasledstvo" ["Svetlana Alliluyeva: Solitude and Inheritance"]. *Izvestia,* no. 95 (Oct. 17, 2008): 10.

Gribanov, Boris. "I pamiat'-sneg letit i past' ne mozhet: David Samoilov, kakim ia ego pomniu" ["And Memory as Snow Keeps Drifting: David Samoilov as I Remember Him"]. *Znamia: yezhemesiachnyi literaturno-khudozhestvennyi i obshchestvenno-politicheskii zhurnal* 9 (2006): 132–68.

Grugman, Rafael. *Svtelana Alliluyeva: Piat' zhiznei.* [Svetlana Alliluyeva: Five Lives]. Rostov-on-Don: Feniks, 2012.

Hayward, Max, ed. *On Trial: The Soviet State Versus "Abram Tertz" and "Nikolai Arzhak."* New York: Harper & Row, 1966.

Hingley, Ronald. *Pasternak: A Biography.* New York: Knopf, 1983.

Hochschild, Adam. *The Unquiet Ghost: Russians Remember Stalin.* London: Penguin Books, 1994.

Hudson, James A. *Svetlana Alliluyeva: Flight to Freedom.* New York: Tower, 1967.

Kalugin, Oleg. *Spymaster: My Thirty-Two Years in Intelligence and Espionage Against the West.* New York: Basic Books, 2009.

Kelly, Catriona. *Children's World: Growing Up in Russia, 1890–1991.* New Haven, CT: Yale University Press, 2007.

Khanga, Yelena, with Susan Jacoby. *Soul to Soul: The Story of a Black Russian American Family 1865–1992.* New York: Norton, 1992.

Khrushchev, Nikita. *The Crimes of the Stalin Era: Special Report to the 20th Congress of the Communist Party of the Soviet Union* [Secret Speech], annotated by Boris I. Nicolaevsky. New York: The New Leader, 1962. (Translation of: Rech'na zakrytom zasedanii XX s"ezda KPSS.)

———. *Khrushchev Remembers*, trans. Strobe Talbot. New York: Bantam Books, 1971.

———. *Memoirs of Nikita Khrushchev*, vol. 1, *Commissar 1918–1945*, ed. Sergei Khrushchev, trans. George Shriver. University Park: Pennslyvania State University Press, 2004.

Knight, Amy. *Beria: Stalin's First Lieutenant.* Princeton, NJ: Princeton University Press, 1993.

Kochan, Lionel, ed. *The Jews in Soviet Russia Since 1917.* London: Oxford University Press, 1972.

Kolesnik, Alexander. *Mify i pravdy o sem'e Stalina* [Myths and Truths About Stalin's Family]. Moscow: Technivest, 1991.

Kosinski, Jerzy. *Blind Date.* Boston: Houghton Mifflin, 1977.

Kun, Miklós. *Stalin: An Unknown Portrait.* Budapest: CEU Press, 2003.

Kuromiya, Hiroaki. *Stalin: Profiles in Power.* London: Pearson Education, 2005.

Lenoe, Matthew E. *Closer to the Masses: Stalinist Culture, Social Revolution and Soviet Newspapers.* Cambridge, MA: Harvard University Press, 2004.

———. *The Kirov Murder and Soviet History.* New Haven, CT: Yale University Press, 2010.

Levin, Nora. *The Jews in the Soviet Union Since 1917: Paradox of Survival.* New York: New York University Press, 1988.

Medvedev, Roy, and Zhores Medvedev. *The Unknown Stalin: His Life, Death, and Legacy*, trans. Ellen Dahrendorf. New York: Overlook Press, 2004.

Meyers, Jeffrey. *Edmund Wilson: A Biography.* New York: Houghton Mifflin, 1995.

Mikoyan, Stepan Anastasovich. *Memoirs of Military Test-Flying and Life with the Kremlin's Elite: An Autobiography*, trans. Aschen Mikoyan. London: Airlife Publishing, 1999.

Molotov, Vyacheslav. *Molotov Remembers: Inside Kremlin Politics—Conversations with Felix Chuev*, ed. Albert Resis. Chicago: Ivan R. Dee, 1993.

Montefiore, Simon Sebag. *Stalin: The Court of the Red Tsar.* New York: Knopf, 2004.

———. *Young Stalin.* London: Weidenfeld & Nicolson, 2007.

Morris, Terry. "Svetlana: A Love Story." *McCall's*, July 1967.

Overy, Richard. *Russia's War: A History of the Soviet War Effort, 1941–1945.* London: Penguin, 1998.

Pasternak, Boris. *Doctor Zhivago*, trans. Max Hayward and Manya Harari. New York: Pantheon, 1991.

Petrova, Ana, and Mikhail Leshynsky. *Poslednee interview* [Last Interview]. Moscow: Algoritm, 2013.

Pimanov, Aleksei. *Stalin: semeinaia tragediia vozhdia narodov* [Stalin: The Family Tragedy of the Supreme Leader]. Moscow: Eksmo algoritm, 2012.

Preston, Paul. *We Saw Spain Die: Foreign Correspondents in the Spanish Civil War.* London: Constable, & Robinson, 2008.

Radzinsky, Edvard. *Stalin.* New York: Anchor, 1997.

Rapoport, Yakov. *The Doctors' Plot: A Survivor's Memoir of Stalin's Last Act of Terror Against Jews and Science.* Cambridge, MA: Harvard University Press, 1991.

Rayle, Robert. "Unpublished Autobiographical Essay." Private Collection (PC) of Robert Rayle.

Richardson, Rosamond. *The Long Shadow: Inside Stalin's Family.* London: Little, Brown, 1993.

Rifkina, Olga. *Puti neispovedimye* [Inscrutable Paths]. Moscow: Progress-Traditsia, 2003.

Rozanova, Maria, "Vdova znamenitogo pisatelia i dissidenta Sinyavskogo Mariia Rozanova: 'Alliluyeva mne skazala: "Masha, vy uveli Andreiia u zheny, a seichas ia uvozhu ego ot vas"'" ("The Widow of the Famous Writer and Dissident Andrei Sinyavsky, Maria Rozanova: 'Alliluyeva told me: "Masha, you took Andrei from his wife. Now I take him away from you."'"). *Bul'var Gordona*, no. 40 (232) (Oct. 6, 2009).

Rubenstein, Joshua. *Tangled Loyalties: The Life and Times of Ilya Ehrenburg.* Tuscaloosa: University of Alabama Press, 1999.

Rubenstein, Joshua, and Vladimir P. Naumov. *Stalin's Secret Pogrom: The Postwar Inquisition of the Jewish Anti-Fascist Committee.* New Haven, CT: Yale University Press, 2005.

Runin, Boris. *"Moie okruzhenie," Zapiski sluchaino utselevshego* ["My Milieu," Notes by the One Who Accidentally Survived]. Moscow: Vozvrashchenie, 2010.

Salisbury, Harrison, ed. *The Soviet Union: The Fifty Years.* New York: Harcourt, Brace & World, 1967.

Samoilov, David. *Podennye zapisi* [Daily Notes], 2 vols. Moscow: Vremia, 2002.

Secrest, Meryle. *Frank Lloyd Wright: A Biography.* New York: HarperCollins, 1992.

Sedykh, Andrei. "Milliony Svetlany" ["Svetlana's Millions"]. *Novoye Russkoye Slovo*, Apr. 15, 1973.

Service, Robert. *Stalin: A Biography.* London: Macmillan, 2004.

Shand, Rosa. "Wheel of Fire," *Southwest Review* 18, no. 1 (January 2002): 87.

———. "The Will to Be: Letters of Svetlana Alliluyeva to Rosa Shand." Unpublished manuscript (166 pages) of Alliluyeva's letters to Shand with Shand's journal entries. PC, Shand.

Silverstone, Marilyn. "The Suburbanization of Svetlana." *Look*, Sept. 9, 1969.

Simonov, Konstantin. "Through the Eyes of My Generation: Meditations on Stalin." *Soviet Literature* (Moscow), no. 4 (493) and no. 5 (494), 1989.

Sinyavsky, Andrei. *Soviet Civilization: A Cultural History*, trans. Joanne Turnbull. New York: Little, Brown, 1988.

Smith, Douglas. *Former People: The Final Days of the Russian Aristocracy*. New York: Farrar, Straus & Giroux, 2012.

Snyder, Timothy. *Bloodlands: Europe Between Hitler and Stalin*. London: Vintage Books, 2011.

Sosin, Gene. *Sparks of Liberty: An Insider's Memoir of Radio Liberty* [Radio Free Europe]. University Park: Pennsylvania State University Press, 1999.

Sudoplatov, Pavel, and Anatoli Sudoplatov, with Jerrold L. Schecter and Leona P. Schecter. *Special Tasks: The Memoirs of an Unwanted Witness*. New York: Little, Brown, 1995.

Svanidze, Maria. "Diary of 1933–37," trans. Svetlana Alliluyeva. Meryle Secrest Papers, Hoover Institution Archives.

Taubman, William. *Khrushchev: The Man and His Era*. New York: Norton, 2003.

Thompson, Nicholas. *The Hawk and the Dove: Paul Nitze, George Kennan, and the History of the Cold War*. New York: Henry Holt, 2009.

Tucker, Robert C. *Stalin in Power: The Revolution from Above, 1928–1941*. New York: Norton, 1990.

Vasilieva, Larisa. *Deti Kremlia: Fakty, vospominaniia, dokumenty, slukhi, legendy i vzgliad avtora* [Kremlin's Children: Facts, Memories, Documents, Rumors, Legends, and the Author's Perspective]. Moscow: Vagrius, 2008.

———. *Kremlin Wives*. Trans. Cathy Porter. New York: Arcade Publishing, 1994.

Verinder, Ben. *I Felt Like an Adventure: A Life of Mary Burkett*. Langley Park, Durham, UK: Memoir Club, 2008.

Volodarskii, Eduard. *Vasili Stalin: syn vozhdia*. [Vasili Stalin: The Supreme Leader's Son]. Moscow: Prozaik, 2012.

Wilson, Edmund. *Letters on Literature and Politics 1912-1972*, ed. Elena Wilson. New York: Farrar, Straus & Giroux, 1977.

———. *The Sixties: The Last Journal, 1960–72*, ed. Lewis Dabney. New York: Farrar, Straus & Giroux, 1993.

Zubok, Vladislav. *Zhivago's Children: The Last Russian Intelligentsia*. Cambridge, MA: Belknap Press of Harvard University, 2009.

Film and Television

Earnest, Peter. "Peter Earnest in Conversation with Oleg Kalugin and Robert Rayle on Defection of Svetlana Alliluyeva," Dec. 4, 2006. International Spy Museum, Washington, DC, www.spymuseum.org/exhibition-experiences/

agent-storm/listen-to-the-audio/episode/the-litvinenko-murder-and-other
-riddles-from-moscow.

Kreml'-9 [Russian TV series] writers group. *Svetlana Stalina: Pobeg iz sem'i* [Svetlana Stalina: Escape from the Family], film, dir. Maksim Ivannikov, prod. Aleksei Pimanov, Oleg Vol'nov, and Sergei Medvedev. Telekompaniia "Ostankino" and Federal'naia sluzhba okhrany Rossiiskoi Federatsii [Federal Service for the Protection of the Russian Federation], 2003.

"Mify o docheri Stalina" [Myths About Stalin's Daughter]. *Priamoi efir s Mikhailom Zelenskim* [Live with Mikhail Zelensky]. Rossia-1, Moscow, Dec. 19, 2011.

Svetlana, television documentary, dir. Irina Gedrovich. Fabryka Kino (distributor), 2008.

Svetlana About Svetlana, film, writer, dir. Lana Parshina, 2008. Distributed by Icarus Films, 2009.

Unpublished Interviews

Meryle Secrest interviews with Svetlana Alliluyeva, London, Mar. 4–17, 1994. Meryle Secrest Collection, Audio recordings: Group 1, Tapes 1–21; Group 2, Tapes 1–28, Hoover Institution Archives.

Rosamond Richardson interviews with Svetlana Alliluyeva, Saffron Walden, 1991. Audio recordings, Tapes 1-6. Private Collection of Rosamond Richardson.

Illustration Credits

Page v: Svetlana Alliluyeva private collection; courtesy of Chrese Evans.

Page xii: Illustrator.

Page 13:   Svetlana Alliluyeva private collection; courtesy of Chrese Evans.

Page 17:   Svetlana Alliluyeva private collection; courtesy of Chrese Evans.

Page 19:   Svetlana Alliluyeva private collection; courtesy of Chrese Evans.

Page 21:   Svetlana Alliluyeva private collection; courtesy of Chrese Evans.

Page 25:   Svetlana Alliluyeva private collection; courtesy of Chrese Evans.

Page 34:   Svetlana Alliluyeva private collection; courtesy of Chrese Evans.

Page 38:   Svetlana Alliluyeva private collection; courtesy of Chrese Evans.

Page 43:   Svetlana Alliluyeva private collection; courtesy of Chrese Evans.

Page 53:   Meryle Secrest Collection, Hoover Institution Archives, Stanford University.

Page 55:   Svetlana Alliluyeva private collection; courtesy of Chrese Evans.

Page 57:   Svetlana Alliluyeva private collection; courtesy of Chrese Evans.

Page 65:   Svetlana Alliluyeva private collection; courtesy of Chrese Evans.

Page 67:   Meryle Secrest Collection, Hoover Institution Archives, Stanford University. Courtesy of Chrese Evans.

Page 75:   Courtesy of RGASPI (Russian State Archive of Social and Political History), Fund 558, Inventory 11, Doc 1653, p. 23.

Page 83:   Svetlana Alliluyeva private collection; courtesy of Chrese Evans.

Page 86:   Photograph by: Sovfoto/UIG via Getty Images

Page 89:   Svetlana Alliluyeva private collection; courtesy of Chrese Evans.

Page 97:   Svetlana Alliluyeva private collection; courtesy of Chrese Evans.

Page 99:   Meryle Secrest Collection, Hoover Institution Archives, Stanford University.

Page 105:   Meryle Secrest Collection, Hoover Institution Archives, Stanford University. Courtesy of Chrese Evans.

Page 110:   Svetlana Alliluyeva private collection; courtesy of Chrese Evans.

Page 112:   Stepan Mikoyan private collection; courtesy of Stepan Mikoyan.

Page 113:   Public domain.

Page 119:   Courtesy of the author.

Page 124:   Courtesy of the author.

Page 139:   Courtesy of RGASPI (Russian State Archive of Social and Political History), Fund 558, Inventory 11, Doc 1653, p. 23.

Page 145:   Svetlana Alliluyeva private collection; courtesy of Chrese Evans.

Page 157:   Svetlana Alliluyeva private collection; courtesy of Chrese Evans.

Page 179:   Stepan Mikoyan private collection; courtesy of Stepan Mikoyan.

Page 193:   Public domain.

Page 207:   Svetlana Alliluyeva private collection; courtesy of Chrese Evans.

Page 211:   Courtesy of Sergei Khrushchev.

Page 225:   Courtesy of the author.

Page 241:   Public domain.

Page 260:   New York World-Telegram and the Sun Newspaper Photograph Collection (Library of Congress).

Page 275:   Courtesy of Robert and Ramona Rayle.

Page 286:   Courtesy of Library of Congress, LC-U9–15312, #22A.

Page 298:   UPI.

Page 313:   AP Photo.

Page 324:   Copyright © Marilyn Silverstone/Magnum Photos.

Page 338:   Copyright © Marilyn Silverstone/Magnum Photos.

Page 349:   Copyright © Marilyn Silverstone/Magnum Photos.

Page 368:   Copyright © Marilyn Silverstone/Magnum Photos.

Page 388:   Courtesy of John Amarantides.

Page 391:   Courtesy of Ann Zane Shanks.

Page 396:   Alfred Eisenstaedt/LIFE Picture Collection/Getty Images.

Page 408:   Courtesy of John Amarantides.

Page 413:   Courtesy of Ann Zane Shanks.

Page 428:   Copyright © George Krimsky. Rare Books and Special Collections, Princeton University Library, George F. Kennan Papers (MC076).

Page 439:   Svetlana Alliluyeva private collection; courtesy of Chrese Evans.

Page 446:   Courtesy of Rosa Shand.

Page 465:   Keystone/Stringer

Page 483:   Courtesy of the Trustees of the Isaiah Berlin Literary Trust and reproduced with their permission.

Page 501:   Courtesy of Rosa Shand.

Page 520:   AP Photo.

Page 541:   AP Photo/Boris Yurchenko.

Page 565:   Courtesy of Rosa Shand.

Page 580:   Meryle Secrest Collection, Hoover Institution Archives, Stanford University. Courtesy of Chrese Evans.

Page 590:   Courtesy of the author.

Page 600:   Meryle Secrest Collection, Hoover Institution Archives, Stanford University. Courtesy of Rebecca Sadler.

Page 608:   Courtesy of John Amarantides.

Index

Page numbers of photographs appear in italics.

About the Author

ROSEMARY SULLIVAN has written poetry, short fiction, biography, literary criticism, reviews, and articles. Her recent books include the critically acclaimed *Villa Air-Bel* and *Labyrinth of Desire*. She is a professor emeritus at the University of Toronto and has been awarded Guggenheim, Camargo, and Trudeau Fellowships. She is a recipient of the Lorne Pierce Medal awarded by the Royal Society of Canada for her contribution to literature and culture, and is an Officer of the Order of Canada.